I0819986

Books by Quintus Curtius

Translations:

Lives of the Great Commanders
On Moral Ends
On Duties
Sallust: Conspiracy of Catiline and War of Jugurtha
Stoic Paradoxes

Essay Collections:

Thirty-Seven
Pantheon
Pathways

Contributing Author:

The Plutocratic Insurgency Reader

About The Translator

Quintus Curtius is the pen name of writer and translator George Thomas. He graduated from MIT in 1990 and served on active duty for a number of years as a US Marine Corps officer, with deployed service worldwide. After leaving active duty, he enrolled in law school and began to practice law after graduating in 1998. He resides in Kansas City and travels frequently. He can be found at www.qcurtius.com.

DIGEST

A Collection of Essays

By
QUINTUS CURTIUS

Digest

Cover art by James Seehafer

Printed in Charleston, South Carolina, USA

Published by

Fortress of the Mind Publications

www.qcurtius.com

ISBN: 978-0-578-64587-2

Hoc tamen expositum cunctis nullique negatum
Numen ab humani solum se labe furoris vindicat.

Yet only this divine power—open to all and forbidden to no one—
Preserves itself from the stain of human infamy.

Lucan V.102

Be substantially great in thyself, and more than thou appearest unto others; and let the World be deceived in thee, as they are in the Lights of Heaven. Hang early Plummets upon the Heels of Pride, and let Ambition have but an Epicycle or narrow Circuit in thee. Measure not thyself by thy Morning shadow, but by the Extent of thy Grave; and reckon thyself above the Earth by the Line thou must be contented with under it.

—Sir Thomas Browne

TABLE OF CONTENTS

AUTHOR TO READER

Auctor Ad Lectorem Benevolum

The essays in this book were originally published at my website *Fortress of the Mind* (qcurtius.com) between 2016 and January 2020. Some of them have been expanded. I have here divided them into four general categories:

Part I: Moral and Ethical Thought
Part II: Wisdom of the Near East
Part III: Travel and Exploration
Part IV: History, Language, and Literature

No branch of knowledge is tangential to the curve of wisdom. While the range of subjects is large, the length of each essay is mercifully short, allowing the reader to peruse these pages as opportunity and interest may permit. As a vehicle for the transmission of ideas, the essay is a laudable invention; its length stimulates the mind without overwhelming the patience, ensuring that topical points are retained in the memory long after a book's cover has been closed. As every numbered essay stands alone as a separate writing, the reader may open the book and begin at any page.

The largest number of entries is found in Part I. "To speak generally," said Plutarch, "what we are wont to say about the arts and sciences is also true of moral excellence, for to its perfect development three things must meet together, natural ability, theory, and practice...If any of these elements be wanting, excellence must be so far deficient."[1] We agree with him. He understood that those who

---

[1] *Plutarch's Morals*, London: George Bell & Sons (1898), p. 2 (*On Education* IV).

wished to make progress in moral development needed not only to study theory, but also to apply this theory in grappling with worldly problems. It is my hope that readers find in these essays some principles that may be deployed in the rigorous *palaestra* of life. Our age hungers for answers to the immemorial questions, and senses, in its heart of hearts, that it has been systematically deprived of the wisdom and guidance of the past by a modern culture obsessed with grotesque novelty, smug superficiality, and transient stimulations.

The essays in Part II feature moral wisdom found in selected anecdotes from the literary traditions of the Near East. Part II also contains its own brief introduction. The content of Parts III and IV is self-explanatory. Of what has transpired before us, there are always new tales to tell. The currents of the past flow constantly around us, and we must at times allow ourselves to be carried along by their surges.

No written effort is completed without the assistance of many hands. Thanks are owed to the patient friends whose encouragement, suggestions, and senses of humor I have valued over the years, especially Zeljko Ivic, James Seehafer, and Dr. Michael Fontaine of Cornell University, to whom this book is respectfully dedicated. Special thanks are also owed to my parents for a lifetime of unremitting support.

And as this volume has already burst its seams, we need not linger here with additional commentary. The art of leaving people alone, is an art that is not well-known. Diogenes Laertius tells us that the philosopher Zeno was once faced with a man who continued to speak beyond the point of utility, and who would not listen to cues to stop. The old Stoic told him: "Your ears have slid down and merged with your tongue."[2]

Quintus Curtius
Overland Park, Kansas
January 2020

[2] Diogenes Laertius VII.21.

QUINTI CURTII
SCRIPTA SELECTA

ANNIS MMXVI—MMXIX

In Quibus Continentur
Quaestiones Et Tractationes Selectae
De Variis Argumentis Moralibus,
Philosophicis Et Historicis.
Additus Etiam In Fine Nominum Ac Rerum Index.

CAROLOPOLI:
ANNO MMXX

Excudebat *Castellum Mentis* Typographus.

VIRO NOBILISSIMO AC GENEROSISSIMO
DOCTORI MICHAELI FONTANO

HOC MUNUSCULUM
IN PERENNE GRATI ANIMI MONUMENTUM

D.D.D.

QUINTUS CURTIUS
AUCTOR

Ad rem iudicandam animis mentibusque nostris ducimur.

PART I: THOUGHT

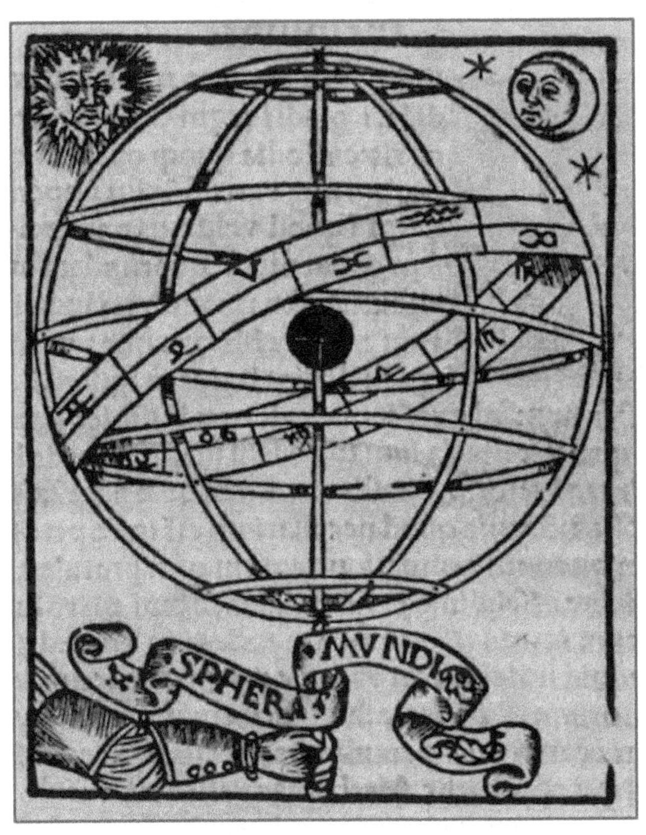

1. Preserving Something For Time To Make Better

Before I explore the main subject of this essay, I wanted to relate a tale about Alexander the Great's leadership acumen. The historian Arrian relates an event he believes best distills Alexander's genius for command. It can be found in VI.26 of his *History of Alexander.* When Alexander and his army were passing through the Gedrosian desert (a part of what is now Baluchistan), they ran low on water and began to be tormented by extreme thirst. Water was almost nowhere to be found, and it would be some time before they could reach a reliable aquifer.

As he always did, Alexander was leading from the front, marching with his men on foot; all could see that he was sharing their burdens and trials. He knew that a soldier can better handle hardship if he sees his leader by his side. A small party of his men had gone off to scout the area and see if they could locate water. This they did; they filled up a bladder from a miserable, fetid pool in some gully. As the scouting party returned to the column, it poured some water into a helmet and gave it to their leader. Alexander thanked them for it, then poured the water out onto the ground. He was no better than his men, he meant to say; and if the rest of them could not drink, then neither would he. "I cannot praise this act too highly," says Arrian, "for it was proof, if anything was, not only of his power of endurance, but also of his genius for leadership." This is an accurate assessment. Compare this ethic with the ethic we see all too often on display in our own experience. Our own "leaders" seem to adhere to the rule of "Do as I say, not as I do." What concerns them is what is good for the elites, not what is good for society as a whole.

Among the many other good anecdotes about Alexander, I like best the following. As the Macedonian conqueror was moving through northern India, he came into contact with a civilization even older and deeper than his own. He would be reminded of this on occasion. One day, as Arrian tells us (VII.1), Alexander encountered a small group of Indian wise men; they must have been adherents of a local faith. Upon Alexander's approach, the Indian sages showed not the slightest interest. This startled the king, who was used to being treated with great deference. As he got closer, the Indian philosophers rose and stamped their feet. Through an interpreter, he asked them the meaning of this odd behavior. This was their response:

> O King, every man can only possess as much of this earth that lies under our feet here. You are a man just like us; but you are always occupied with some project, and are usually up to no good. You have journeyed a long distance from your home, and have become a nuisance to yourself and others. But you will eventually die, and then will only own as much of this earth as it takes to bury you.

Arrian says that Alexander expressed his "approval" of these words, and perhaps this is true. But I am not so sure. More likely is that he was taken aback at these blunt words of the Indian philosophers. Yet what possible response could he make to such a pronouncement? We spend so much of our time running around in pursuit of inane goals that we fail to consider what it all leads to. As in most things, of course, there is a balance. We cannot simply throw up our hands and withdraw from the responsibilities of life, but at the same time, we should have our eyes on the sun-dial of life. Its shadow lengthens and contracts; and with each of these iterations, our time on this earth passes away ever so steadily. We can lust after land, goods, possessions, and everything else; but in the final analysis it will not be these possessions that confer immortality. What will remain are our achievements, the record of our deeds, and our contributions to the advancement of knowledge, morals, and ethics; what will also remain are our progeny, the children we raise and bequeath to the world, as they merge into humanity's faceless mists. These are the things that will live forever.

But to appreciate these things takes time. The mind has to mature into them; they cannot be learned except through experience and time. And this reminds me of another anecdote I read in Aulus Gellius's *Attic Nights* (XIII.2). Two Roman poets and tragedians, Marcus Pacuvius and Lucius Accius, once had a chance meeting. Accius was traveling to the city of Tarentum, and he stopped to visit Pacuvius, who was then an elderly man living in that city. The two of them discussed one of Accius's plays, *Atreus*. Pacuvius said he liked the play, but that it seemed to him to be a little rough around the edges. Accius admitted that this was so; but he also said it was a good thing. He explained himself: "I am glad that what I wrote was a bit unpolished. They say that a man's mind can be compared with a ripening fruit: the fruits that are bitter and tough eventually mellow into something juicy and sweet. But the fruits that start out ripe and juicy quickly end up rotten and spoiled. He concluded by saying:

> Relinquendum igitur visum est in ingenio quod dies atque aetas mitificet.

And this means, "Thus it seems to me that something should be left in the mind that time and age might improve." So while we should seek to improve, we should not rush the process with exaggerated haste. Things will ripen as they ripen; we should not become unduly worried if we are still rough and unpolished. Better to ripen gradually, than to ferment and spoil too soon.

2. Between Mouth And Morsel

The Roman writer Aulus Gellius relates an anecdote about his discovery of the meaning of an old proverb. He tells us that he read the following line in one of the speeches of Marcus Cato Censorius:

> Saepe audivi inter os atque offam multa intervenire posse. [XIII.18]

This sentence says, "I have often heard that many things can come between the mouth and a morsel of food." It is an unusual expression, and Gellius was not alone in being mystified by it. The word *offa* is defined as a lump or pellet of flour, or as a "bite of food" in general; the best translation in this context would be "morsel." But what is the expression supposed to signify? What could be the meaning of something coming between a mouth and a hovering bite of food? The expression was turned over to a learned man familiar with old literature, and he was able to shed light on its meaning. He quoted a related Greek expression, which made it clear that the phrase is used to express the idea that Fate can often intervene to deny us what we want. In other words, we should not consider a morsel of food to be "in the mouth" until it is actually there, and is being chewed.

When I first heard this expression, I thought it was both memorable and useful. For it seems to me that we are constantly in the habit of "counting our chickens before they are hatched." We do this in ways that are both overt and subtle; but it is the subtle way that is the most corrosive to our lives. We think that just because we "possess" something, or have it on our fork, then it is as good as already in the gullet. And this is not true. Even when we do have something, my experience is that it is not easy to hold on to it. So many intervening events or circumstances can deprive us of what we want. Consider the man who has a large income. His money rolls in, and he feels satisfied with the numbers that appear on his paystubs, his W-2 forms, and his tax returns. He can now sleep at night because, at long last, his money troubles are finally over.

Or are they? As his income grows, so do his wants and needs. Ever so imperceptibly, his expenses creep up, higher and higher. Those things that he once scoffed at as frivolous luxuries, he now eyes with longing and envy. His girlfriend or wife, aware of his prosperity, does nothing to dissuade him from spending; indeed, she demands more and more herself. The numbers are there; the times are good, and he believes that they will stay good. Until they are not, of course. Suddenly things slow down at work. The volume of customers and clients, once so high, now slowly declines. And when this happens, the man begins to panic; the car payments, the boat payments, the house payments, and the furniture payments do not stop. He now feels like all he does is pay bills. How he longs for his old life! But there is no way back; for he does not have the fortitude to confront his wife and tell her that they need to make lifestyle changes.

And this is how these things happen. *It is not what you earn, but what you retain, that matters*. There are people making colossal salaries, yet who hardly have enough in their pockets for a decent meal at a slop-house. And this is often because they are unable to control their habits and desires. *Between their mouths and their desired morsels, something bad has intervened, as old Cato would have said.* Granted that this is true: but what does it mean for us? It seems to me that we spend far too much time focusing on how to get things, *and not enough time on how to keep them.*

Everyone wants to be successful and prosperous; and to this end they learn a trade, work hard, and devote themselves to their professions. But they give hardly any thought on how to acquire the discipline and character that will help them to retain their riches. Do you think that it is easy to hold on to what you have? Do you think it makes sense to spend years learning how to acquire something, and yet have no idea how to keep it? Well? What is your answer? It is of no use to learn how to fish, if we are unable to transport the fish from the river to our kitchen for eating. Training in discipline, character, and virtue is the way we learn how to keep our riches. In life one must study all things; one must seek to learn positives, negatives, and neutrals. The physician Galen says, in his *Art of Medicine*, that the study of medicine consisted of three components:

> Medicine is the knowledge of those things that are healthy, those that are unhealthy, and those that are neither. [*Art of Med.* I.307]

So we have to consider matters from various perspectives. Yet so few people think about this. They are so fixated on gratifying their desires, that they are oblivious to the fact that they will lose everything unless they learn the skills to handle their desires. They are blind to the fact that *preservation* is an entirely different skill from *acquisition.* You do not put a welding machine in the hands of a child; and so you do not hand over a pile of riches to an undisciplined man with no understanding of what is good, and what is bad. He is blind to the concept of good and evil without some training in wisdom. It is essential for us to polish our characters, and to make the study of wisdom a lifetime pursuit. It is not optional; it is the only way to prevent disaster from overtaking us in life. For Fortune, that implacable mistress, has a thousand devious ways of coming between mouth and morsel.

3. A Man Is Often The Cause Of His Own Misfortunes

A reasonable amount of experience in life teaches us that we are often the source of the wrongs that fall upon our shoulders. This is not always true, of course; but even a short period of honest reflection will reveal to us, if we examine the details of things, that we might have handled some situations better than we in fact did. Learning does not take place without honest examination; and the first person who is in need of this honesty is ourselves.

The anecdote that follows illustrates this point with particular clarity. It is adapted from Ibn Muqaffa's book of wisdom, *Kalila and Dimna*, a work I will refer to again in these pages. Much like the collection of tales now known as the *Thousand and One Nights*, it has unfortunately been sanitized and marketed as a children's book; but as the reader will quickly discover in the lines that follow, these stories are not for children's ears at all. The reader may be assured that the original versions of these works of literature are, by modern standards, frequently graphic and unsettling. Wisdom was not sugar-coated in the old days to spare out sensibilities. But let us now turn to Ibn Muqaffa's anecdote.

There was once a monk who had become the favorite of some sovereign. He received from his king a gift of a robe, which was of a very fine and lush material. One day a thief saw the monk with this robe, and determined to have it for himself. He approached the monk, flattered him as a man of learning, and said he wanted to be instructed in arts of wisdom. The monk accepted this story, let the thief into his house, and thought no more of it. The thief, now able to carry out his theft, made off with the robe, much to the monk's chagrin. So the monk decided to take to the road, and see if he could not find his robe in the surrounding area.

And as he was traveling along the road by horseback, he observed a curious incident. Two angry goats were fighting with each other, and each had wounded the bodies of the other. As this was happening, a fox was following behind the two of them, licking up the small quantities of blood on the ground that flowed from their wounds. When the two fighting goats became aware of this, they became incensed; they both attacked the fox with such ferocity that they killed him. The monk continued on his journey and eventually reached a small town. He could not find any inn to take him, but was able to secure lodging at the house of an older woman with a beautiful daughter. This old woman had a very beautiful young maid who worked for her; and, knowing the desires that resided in the hearts of men, she was willing to traffic in this young girl's beauty for a price. The maid had recently fallen in love with a local man, however, and this man was determined to marry her. The old woman knew that this relationship would endanger her money-making enterprise, and so resolved to murder the young man.

The old woman's plan was to kill him when he visited the maid. He came by the house to see the maid, and she plied him with intoxicating liquors; she then took a thin, hollow reed, and dipped it in poison powder, with the plan of blowing the powder into his ears as he slept. Unfortunately for her, she accidentally caught her breath, and inhaled suddenly; this reflex caused the poison to enter her mouth and go down her throat, killing her within minutes. The monk, who was staying at the house, learned of these happenings, and left the scene quickly.

The monk continued to travel. He then sought lodging with a shoemaker and his wife. Now it happened that the wife of this shoemaker had a secret affair going on, and she had confided her little secret to her friend, the wife of a surgeon. She told the surgeon's wife to ask her lover to come to her house, since the shoemaker would be preoccupied with trying to accommodate the monk and render him hospitality. The lover arrived unwittingly at the house of the shoemaker, thinking he would be able to see his wife. But the cobbler came home unexpectedly, and was drunk; he guessed the reason for the man's presence at his doorstep. The cobbler grew infuriated, found his wife, and tied her to a pillar in the residence. He then went to sleep, to allow the effects of his drunkenness to wear off.

The surgeon's wife eventually showed up at the house, and found her friend, the shoemaker's wife, tied up inside. The shoemaker's wife begged her friend, the surgeon's wife, to untie her and take her place, so that she could see her lover. If she would do this, she promised the surgeon's wife she would return as quickly as possible; and the surgeon's wife foolishly agreed to this scheme. Unfortunately, the shoemaker by now had awakened, and called out to the person he thought was his wife. When she did not answer him–for fear of revealing her identity–the cobbler grew enraged, seized a knife, and cut off her nose. Just about this time, the surgeon's wife came back home, and found to her horror what violence had taken place. She did was she could for the surgeon's wife, untying her and sending her home with a bandaged face.

She furiously condemned the shoemaker for his barbarous violence, but there was not much that could be done at this point. The maimed wife of the surgeon went back to her own residence, trying to think of some way to explain how this shocking misfortune had happened to her. When she made her injury clear to the household, everyone in the family blamed the surgeon, believing that he had cut off his wife's nose in some fit of insane violence. The police arrived and hauled the innocent surgeon in front of a *qadi* (a judge), who interrogated him at great length. The *qadi* did not believe the surgeon's protestations of innocence; in fact, he took a strong disliking to him. The surgeon's wife tried to intervene, but the judge ordered that the surgeon, whom he believed to be guilty of domestic violence, *should himself have his nose amputated.*

Now this horrible injustice was on the verge of being performed, when our friend the monk suddenly arrived in court to explain the truth of what had happened. He spoke words to this effect: "O *qadi*, I have learned much in the past few days. I have seen how we are often the source of our own misfortunes. By God, let me tell you how I know this. I myself was robbed of my cloak, a valuable item that was given to me by the king. But it was my fault that this happened, for I let into my house a man of bad character and a thief. Later I witnessed the death of a fox. But it was the fox's fault that he was killed; he should never have interfered in the fights of other parties. For this stupidity, he paid the price. Later I learned that an evil woman was killed by the murderous plan that she created for an innocent party. And finally, by God, let me say that it was not the surgeon who was responsible for the loss of his wife's nose, but her own foolishness in changing places with a friend who did not deserve such a gesture. In such ways do we see how we are the authors of our own misfortune."

This is the substance of the tale as related by Ibn Muqaffa. We probably know many people who are constantly looking to shift the blame for their bad luck on to the shoulders of others. A little bit of probing, however, will often reveal that they themselves created or nurtured the problem that now afflicts them. The correct way to handle misfortune, Ibn Muqaffa tells us, is *first* to reflect on our previously happy state, and try to find a way back to that state; *second*, we should try to find ways of making the most of our present circumstances that we enjoy now; and *third*, we must regulate our conduct carefully in the future, so that we do not miss any coming opportunities for improving ourselves.

This is what a responsible person does, of course. But we live in a world of deeply irresponsible people who are always looking to shift the blame for their circumstances on to the shoulders of others. Many of these people are so-called "leaders." Ibn Muqaffa says this with regard to weak, foolish rulers who try to blame others for their incompetence:

> The weakest king is he who occupies himself with trifles, without paying any regard to future events, and who like the furious elephant, giving himself up blindly to the guidance of his passions, never fails, if affairs through his own mismanagement or idle indifference go wrong, either to charge his people with treason, or his ministers with incapacity.

Of the truth of this statement, there can be no doubt.

4. The Man In The Well, And The Path Of Wisdom

In his allegorical work *Kalila and Dimna*, writer Ibn Muqaffa describes the journey to wisdom of one of his characters, a man named Barzouyeh. Barzouyeh was the man sent by the king of Persia to India for the purpose of acquiring the precious text of *Kalila and Dimna,* which was reputed to contain a treasure-trove of worldly wisdom. Ibn Muqaffa spends a good deal of time discussing Barzouyeh's education and path to wisdom, and it will be instructive for us to relate it here. When he was still a young man in Persia, and once he had completed the rudiments of his medical education, Barzouyeh realized that he had four choices in life. He explains further:

> I had to choose, as it appeared to me, between four things, which in general occupy the attention and engage the affections of men: *the acquiring of riches, the procuring of a good name, the means of temporal enjoyment, and the provision for a future state.* And discovering from the writings of the physicians, that the last was the aim which they constantly had in view, I determined to persevere in the profession which I had chosen, lest I should be like the merchant who sold a precious ruby for a pearl that was of no value.[3]

[3] Knatchbull, Wyndham, *Kalila and Dimna*, London: W. Baxter (1819). The quotes have been edited slightly.

In other words, he realized that it was important to be practical, and to seek to earn a living in the profession that he had chosen. He could also see that life itself was fleeting and impermanent, and that it was better to focus oneself on the acquisition of wisdom than to waste time on fooleries and distractions:

> With these reflections I endeavored to fortify my resolution of *preferring only what was substantially good*, knowing that our body from its very constitution is subject to corruption, and that life, which is transitory, may be compared to a statue, whose detached members are kept together by a single nail, which being removed, the several joints give way, and the parts fall asunder; and of what solid or lasting advantage is the society of friends or lovers, whose pleasures are often purchased at great expense, and put an end to by a trifling interruption, as a wooden dish, which has been used for the table, when it is broken, is good for nothing but to become fuel for the fire.

He realized more and more that if he made worthless and impermanent things the focus of his attentions, he would be repaid with misery and emotional turmoil. His curiosity eventually led him to examine the various religions, and to see what the doctrines of each of them happened to be. Yet the conversations he had with various people on the subject turned out to be unfulfilling: every person had his own opinion, and was convinced that his own creed was the best. It was best, he thought, simply to adhere to the "persuasion of my forefathers." His own mortality was a fact that he was increasingly aware of:

> I could not, however, forget that the term of my existence was fast approaching, and the end of all worldly things was near at hand, and that the thread of life is often cut asunder in the very moment that health and happiness promise to secure and enliven the continuance of our being...I began to see clearly the inconvenience and danger of an unsettled state of mind, without any determinate rule of conduct or

> opinion, and resolved, by listening to that warning voice which never fails to make itself distinctly heard within us...

Our physical gratifications are pleasing for the moment, but temporary and illusory, vanishing like the early morning mist. Man is like the dog who gnaws at an old bone, convinced that its faint scent of meat may yet retain some nourishment, but does not. And the longer we gnaw the bone, the more it chafes our gums and causes us to bleed. Another analogy he uses about the physical pleasures is that they are like a bag of honey with a pool of poison at the bottom of it: the taste of the honey is sweet as we consume it, but the poison at the bottom of the bag gets ever closer to our fingers. The only way forward, Barzouyeh realized, was to adopt the path of wisdom, no matter how difficult it might be. There was really no other practical choice. For he could clearly see that his society was in a state of decay, and that the only way to shield himself from evil was to adopt wisdom as his external armor. He noted, using language that evokes Sallust, that in his era:

> Honest men grew indifferent, and the bad found their account in wickedness; understanding was set at nought, and vanity had taken its place; the oppressor walked boldly in open day, and lust and covetousness had laid aside all restraint and shame, because contentment was looked upon as weakness. Reputation was no longer an object of anxiety, because worthlessness had come into honor and power, and men of character were obliged to retire before the pretensions of aspiring and successful criminality; and it was painful to behold amidst this triumph of evil over everything that was good, how men possessed of reason could so far forget the dignity of their nature, and the proud eminence on which they stood, as to lose sight in sensual gratifications of the high destiny of their soul.

Eventually Barzouyeh is able to convey an analogy that expresses his view of man's condition. A man, he tells us, is like a rider who is thrown from an elephant and tumbles into a well. But as he falls into the well, he is able to grasp the projecting branches near the surface of the well, and save himself at first from a precipitous plunge into the interior. He finds something to hold on to: his hands grasp two branches, and his feet find two apparent stones along the wall of the well to rest on. Yet as he looks more closely at his feet, he realizes that these "stones" are really the heads of four snakes that have come out of their holes. To make matters worse, he can just barely see that at the bottom of the well is an open-mouthed dragon, ready to consume him if he should fall from his treacherous perch.

And as he looks upward to the two branches he clings to, he can see that there are two rats (one white and one black) that are slowly nibbling at the branches. Finally, there is a beehive close to him: and as he tastes it, he is so enraptured by its sweetness that he forgets all the perils that hover over him at that moment. He forgets about the dragon below him; he forgets about the rats slowly gnawing at the branches holding him in place; and he forgets about the four snake heads on which he stands. But this terrible predicament had an allegorical meaning for Barzouyeh. The well represented "the world with its train of ills which belong to it." The snakes are the four humors of the human body, which can become toxic and lethal of they are disturbed; the two rats represent night and day, which are lead us inevitably to old age and death; the dragon is mortality itself, which is waiting for all of us; they honey represents voluptuary desires, which serve to distract us from our responsibilities. This was the meaning of Barzouyeh's analogy of the man perilously clinging to life inside a well. This was, to him, how each person finds himself in the world. He drew the requisite conclusions from this:

> I therefore finally determined to remain in my present state, watching over my actions, with the steady purpose of carrying them to the highest degree of perfection of which I should be capable, in the hope that I should one day find a guide for my conduct, a controlling power for the affections of my soul, and a faithful administrator of my worldly affairs.

By this he meant that he would continue with his professional responsibilities, and devote himself more and more to the study of wisdom which, he knows, alone had the power to save a man from misery or an early demise. This is what gives life meaning, and can enable us to transcend the precarious nature of our physical state.

5. Augustine's *Misericorditer*: Benevolent Severity Towards Enemies

I have recently learned of an interesting doctrine articulated by St. Augustine in one of his letters. The letter in question is Epistula 138, and I should describe briefly its context. One of Augustine's friends was a pagan senator in Rome named Volusian; his mother happened to be a Christian, but he himself was not. The sack of Rome by Alaric in 410 A.D. had been a deeply shocking event for everyone in the Roman world, no matter what their religion was. There very much existed an atmosphere of despair. People wondered how such a thing could have happened to what was supposedly the strongest military state in the world.

I rarely wade into theological waters, but it seems to me that this doctrine of Augustine's has some relevance and applicability to our present social conditions. The question that Volusian put to Augustine was this: could it be true that Christianity's alleged ethic of "turn thy cheek" was harmful to the fighting spirit of the Roman state? Was it not true that the Christian writings counseled a timid ethic of love and forbearance? Augustine skillfully argued that there was nothing in Christian doctrine that prevented an individual or a state from engaging in conflict to take corrective action against enemies. He used the Latin word *misericorditer* as part of his explanation; the word means "with pity," or "with compassion." This subtle theologian proposed that it was actually in the interests of our enemies that their behavior be corrected. Those who were mired in evil and corruption often could not see it; they needed to be shown the correct way if their behavior was crossing all acceptable human conduct. In other words, he seemed to be saying, there was such a thing as a just conflict, and a good fight.

He first reminds us that a righteous man should be prepared to tolerate, up to a point, injury from others:

> Wherefore a righteous and pious man ought to be prepared to endure with patience injury from those whom he desires to make good, so that the number

> of good men may be increased, instead of himself being added, by retaliation of injury, to the number of wicked men. [II.12]

But at the same time, there were limits to how much injury or offense one can take. At some point, stern, corrective action needed to be taken. The phrase he uses (or the translator here uses) is "benevolent severity." A stern father must on occasion use such benevolent severity when all other methods of reasonable persuasion have failed:

> These precepts concerning patience ought to be always retained in the habitual discipline of the heart, and the benevolence which prevents the recompensing of evil for evil must be always fully cherished in the disposition. At the same time, many things must be done in correcting with a certain *benevolent severity*, even against their own wishes, men whose welfare rather than their wishes it is our duty to consult and the Christian Scriptures have most unambiguously commended this virtue in a magistrate. For in the correction of a son, even with some sternness, there is assuredly no diminution of a father's love; yet, in the correction, that is done which is received with reluctance and pain by one whom it seems necessary to heal by pain.

Finally Augustine comes to the heart of the matter, and to the implications of his doctrine for society. When someone has transgressed all reasonable boundaries, and has surrendered himself to evil and moral corruption, then decisive action needs to be taken to correct the problem. Freedom should not be confused with license; and he who abuses the freedoms his society gives him must be firmly shown the error of his ways. The "foundations of virtue" cannot be allowed to become weakened in a healthy society. This long quote summarizes what he means:

> But the perverse and froward hearts of men think human affairs are prosperous when men are concerned about magnificent mansions, and indifferent

> to the ruin of souls; when mighty theatres are built up, and the foundations of virtue are undermined; when the madness of extravagance is highly esteemed, and works of mercy are scorned; when, out of the wealth and affluence of rich men, luxurious provision is made for actors, and the poor are grudged the necessaries of life; when that God who, by the public declarations of His doctrine, protests against public vice, is blasphemed by impious communities, which demand gods of such character that even those theatrical representations which bring disgrace to both body and soul are fitly performed in honour of them. If God permit these things to prevail, He is in that permission showing more grievous displeasure: if He leave these crimes unpunished, such impunity is a more terrible judgment. When, on the other hand, He overthrows the props of vice, and reduces to poverty those lusts which were nursed by plenty, He afflicts in mercy. And in mercy, also, if such a thing were possible, *even wars might be waged by the good, in order that, by bringing under the yoke the unbridled lusts of men, those vices might be abolished which ought, under a just government, to be either extirpated or suppressed.*[4]

The meaning of these words, of course, may be open to varying interpretations; but Augustine is reminding us that moral corruption and decay can have severe consequences. Clearly he saw the military weakness of the Roman state more a result of moral corruption, than a result of the alleged subversiveness of Christian doctrine. The excerpts from Augustine's letter quoted here are not my own translations, but I am confident of their reliability.

What is appealing about Augustine's doctrine is that it offers a prescription for action. Evil can and should be resisted. We must not hide under rocks or behind trees and pretend that what we are seeing is something different from what we are seeing. Other Churchmen of his era were not as optimistic; they had surrendered

[4] These quotes from Augustine are from http://www.newadvent.org/fathers/1102138.htm.

themselves to what looks very much like despair. One of the best examples of this mentality is Salvian, who was born around 400 A.D. His chief work is *De Gubernatione Dei*, or *On the Government of God*. The picture he paints in his book is an unrelentingly gloomy one. As Salvian saw things, Rome was already too far gone to rehabilitate. He puts the blame for Rome's military defeats squarely on the shoulders of the degenerate Romans: as he saw it, their disasters were caused by their own debilitating political and moral corruption. We must concede that there is some truth in this harsh indictment.

Salvian contrasts the supposed barbaric "virtue" of the Germans, Alans, and Huns, with the Romans' effete taste for luxury and physical pleasure. Rome's barbarian enemies, he says, may have been uncouth brutes, but at least the Germans and Huns did not oppress their poor or live in luxurious sin. The barbarians were fit, thin, and brave, while the Romans had become fat, weak, and corrupt. The Saxons and Vandals may have been treacherous, but their people were chaste in comparison with the wealthy denizens of Rome's urban centers. This, at any rate, is how Salvian saw things. Was he correct?

We must always take the sermons of theologians with a grain of salt; they are looking at the world from a certain perspective, and everything they see tends to confirm that perspective. There was much corruption in his age, but one could equally say that there was a patient, silent majority that went about its business, and took care of its responsibilities, as best it could. He undoubtedly exaggerates the alleged moral virtues of the barbarians; the student of history knows that at all times and in every place, man tends to sin within his available means and abilities. If the barbarians were "chaste," it was only because they were not yet rich enough to experiment with corruption. Yet Salvian's picture offers us a window on the mood of his era. His despair and anguish were real, even if he interpreted events through the lens of his own education and training.

6. The Tale Of Firuz, King Of Persia

The following story is told by the political theorist Ibn Zafar (1104–1172?) in his treatise on the art of government. We will encounter him again in these pages, and will discuss many of his ideas on leadership, governance, and the conduct of foreign affairs. There are times when anecdotes can bring certain principles into sharp focus, and we will share one now.

There was once a Persian king named Firuz, the son of Yezdejird. He was engaged in struggles with the Hephthalites, a people of central Asia who flourished in the fifth and six centuries A.D. Firuz was once taken prisoner by a Hephthalite ruler named Khush-nawaz, who soon released him after Firuz agreed to a peace treaty. One of the terms of the treaty was that Firuz promised not to cross a certain stone boundary marker that Khush-nawaz placed on the border between his land and Firuz's domains.

Here we should say a few words about the personality and character of Firuz. He was an arrogant, boastful, hollow man. He liked to posture as if he were a strong leader, but his braggadocio on close inspection turned out to be the empty utterances of an egotistical con-artist. Many people were seduced by his false demagoguery. He did not have a belief system outside of himself and his own aggrandizement. Morally corrupt, greedy, and vindictive, he cared only about promoting himself, and would do or say anything to that end. For this reason, he was easily manipulated by powerful men in his kingdom; and he was also willing to put himself at the service of foreign governments who used him for their own benefits.

So Firuz signed the treaty with his rival and was released from captivity. But upon returning home, his scheming mind would not rest until he had found a way to get out of his agreement. He decided to wage war again with Khush-nawaz. Firuz's ministers were frantic, and warned him not to do this. They knew such a course of action was foolish, and would bring ruin on himself and his government. But he thought he knew better. He told his ministers: "I agreed never to cross that stone marker. So I will pull up the marker and place it on the back of one of my war-elephants that moves at the head of my army. This way, I will never have broken my word!" These are the kinds of word games that Firuz liked to indulge in. Dishonest, unjust, and morally bankrupt, he thought he could evade the spirit of his agreements by parsing out their words in rigid detail. But his little games fooled no one. And here Ibn Zafar reminds us, in so many words:

> The ruler who too much likes the sound of his own voice is headed for disaster. He who arrogantly elevates himself over others will eventually be cut

> down to size. Greed blinds rulers to the truth and clouds their decision-making. Passion has a stronger hold over the human mind than does reasoned understanding. When greed or anger cloud a ruler's judgment, terrible outcomes may result.[5]

So Firuz prepared for war. He would not listen to those voices telling him that wars are easy to enter, but very difficult to depart from. His ministers also warned him not to exceed his authority; even though he was king, there were limits on his power. It violated the laws of nations to break treaties that he had signed with foreign rulers, and there would be consequences for such actions. One of Firuz's ministers told him the following:

> There are five things that can bring about the fall of a king.
>
> **The first** is when a king believes propaganda and refuses to consider the consequences of his actions.
>
> **The second** is when he turns against his people by pursuing policies that hurt them.
>
> **The third** is when he is unable to collect enough revenue to fund his operations.
>
> **The fourth** is when he favors one clique and disregards others, and forgets that his job is to serve all the people, not just some of them.
>
> **The fifth** is when he rejects the advice of experienced and learned advisors. The man who will not listen to sound advice is no better than an insensate beast. He is like an animal, and deserves to be thought of as one.

Firuz proceeded to the stone boundary marker and gave it to his war-elephant, as he explained he would do. His army marched forward. As they did so, he learned that one of his knights had callously killed a poor local man. The slain man's brother soon appeared in front of Firuz, asking him for justice. The brother said he

---

[5] The quotes of Ibn Zafar in this volume are from the translation of Kechichian, J.A. & Dekmejian, R.H. (*trans.*), *The Just Prince: A Manual of Leadership*, London: Saqi Books (2003).

wanted to avenge himself against the knight who had murdered his brother. But Firuz did not care about this injustice. He cared only about himself and his thirst for glory in battle. He dismissed the brother, who, upon leaving the court, drew his dagger (*khanjar*) and rushed at the offending knight. The guilty knight ran away. But the brother failed to kill him, and was thrown out of court.

One of Firuz's ministers heard about this incident and appealed to the king to do justice for the brother of the murdered man. He said that the brother should be entitled to financial compensation, or he should be entitled to fight the knight in a duel. "The knight is guilty of murder," the minister told him. "Why else would he have run away when this poor peasant rushed at him with a dagger?" Eventually, Firuz was persuaded to arrange a duel between the brother and the knight. The poor brother was advised by his friends and family not to fight the armed knight. They told him that the knight was a military man of experience, and that he would easily be able to defeat him. The poor man waved aside these concerns, saying:

> I will deal with him. He killed my brother, and I must avenge this act. The knight is mounted, yes, but he is mounted on the horse of arrogance, vanity, and lies. I have justice and truth on my side. His armor is the armor of injustice and oppression. For these reasons I will triumph.

When Firuz's ministers heard of the poor man's words, they were deeply impressed. They knew that this man would rather die than see his brother's murder go unpunished. Such men, they knew, are nearly unstoppable when aroused. So they took the king aside again and said, "Sire, you should reconsider this duel. This poor man is burning with ferocity, and your knight knows, deep in his heart, that he is guilty of a wrong. Your knight is going to be killed. Better to pay this poor man some compensation and send him on his way. Either that, or try the knight and punish him under the law." Once again, Firuz refused to listen to advice. He, of course, always knew best. So the duel took place. The poor man was able to dodge the blows of the mounted knight; he then lunged at his opponent, toppled him off his horse, and drove a sword through his neck. The blood of the knight flowed out into the dirt. Ibn Zafar at this point reminds us that

> Passion easily begins fights, but ends them terribly. Passion is like a fire than cannot be put out; it is like the waters of a river that have burst their embankments. He who is in the grip of passion acts like a renegade, unable to control his actions. Such a man is a prisoner of emotion, and will soon be led to ruin.

One might have thought that Firuz would reflect on the fate of his knight. He might have observed that those who commit crimes, and act in the service of oppression and arrogance, are no match for those whose cause is just. Those who are fighting a righteous cause will be filled with ardor; their spirits will not be deterred, even if they are facing a more well-equipped enemy. These were the considerations that Firuz should have pondered; but he did not. He set his army in motion once more, and proceeded with his military attack against the Hephthalites. But Khush-nawaz was ready for him. He brought out his own forces to meet the invasion, and defeated Firuz and his army, killing many of them and putting the rest to rout. Firuz was captured and slain, and Khush-nawaz enjoyed an unqualified triumph.

7. The Tale Of The Two Foxes

Ibn Zafar's well of wisdom provides us with another fable to ponder. How the reader relates it to his or her own life experience, or to the world's current events, will be up to him or her to decide. While the narrative below is my own, I have also included some of Ibn Zafar's quotes (as translated by J. Kechichian and R. Dekmejian, with minor editing by me, in their excellent edition of the *Sulwan Al-Muta'*) as they appear at relevant points in the story.

There was once a fox named Dhalim (ظالم, or "oppressor") who lived in a very capacious and comfortable den he had excavated from the earth. It was situated in a good location, with access to good hunting areas in all directions. One day, after returning from the hunt, he was dismayed to find his den had been occupied by a snake. The snake would not leave; and despite Dhalim's ever more urgent pleadings, the snake was adamant in its refusal to move. It was clear that he had stolen it as his own, and would not relinquish it. In the face of this situation there was little that Dhalim could do.

So Dhalim left to find another den. After much trekking over the countryside, he came upon a den that seemed ideal for his situation. He asked various other animals if they knew to whom the den belonged. Dhalim was told that the hole was the property of a fox named Mufawwad (مفوض, or "trusting"), who had inherited it from his father. Mufawwad invited Dhalim into his den–courteous as he was–to find out what it was that he wanted. Dhalim related, in agonized detail, how he had lost his home as a result of the snake's thievery. Mufawwad told his visitor that he should try to avenge himself on the snake, kill him, and reclaim his home.

> Thus it is said: He who suspects his enemy is almost as far advanced as he who leads forth an army against him. Cunning often ensures victory over a powerful tribe. It is better to die in a fire than to live in dishonor. But if you would use force against an enemy, do not attack him unless you know him to be weaker than yourself; and if you would rely on ruse, never estimate him too highly, whatever may be his power.

So the two foxes set out back to Dhalim's former den to see what they could do together. Mufawwad had essentially offered to help his friend reclaim his home. They wanted to make a realistic appraisal of the situation, and devise some suitable stratagem to accomplish their goal.

> It is said: All enterprises may be ruined by three causes. First, a plan fails if it is imparted to several individuals before it is fully divulged. Second, everything is spoiled if those in the secret are rivals, or envious of one another, because love or hatred entered their calculation. Third, if the direction of an enterprise is assumed by one who has not been on the spot from the beginning, but rather by someone who came in at a later time. Then the old leader will be jealous and envious of the new one.

The two foxes eventually came to Dhalim's old den. The two friends knew that the best kind of plan is that one which has been reached after mature deliberation. A hasty plan, in their minds, was a reckless plan. They both resolved to sleep on the problem, and to come up with a decent plan the next day. Dhalim agreed to spend the night at Mufawwad's den. As he did so, he began to take a more careful look around his friend's house. He could see that it was large, comfortable, and ideally situated. Although he could not help himself, he began to feel those first gnawing pangs of jealousy. He slowly began to be possessed with a desire to take Mufawwad's den for his own. This thought grew stronger hour by hour, and he soon even forgot to come up with a plan for reclaiming his own old house. Even if things came to a fight, he thought he was bigger than Mufawwad and would be able to impose his will on him.

> Verily, said Ibn Zafar, the wicked man is like a fire. If you feed him, he blazes up. He is also like wine, which makes a prey of him who loves it; and a slave of him who pursues it. Thus, a natural malignity cannot be conquered by sheer profits. *He is a wise man who places trial before intimacy, examination before choice, and confidence before love.*

What Ibn Zafar means in this last sentence is that comradeship, friendship, or love must be earned. It should not be bestowed too easily on others, since many will not deserve it. Worse still, they will begin to act with malice towards you. But to return to our story.

The next morning, Mufawwad told Dhalim that he had thought things over, and that he would help Dhalim dig a new den in a place close to his old den. He urged Dhalim to abandon his old den, and take solace in digging a new one. Sometimes it is better, he said, just to move on, especially when the risks outweighed the rewards. But Dhalim was adamant. He would not consider this option. He said he might die of grief and repressed rage were he ever to give up his home to an occupying snake. Relocating was out of the question, he said. Mufawwad could see that he would not be able to dissuade his friend. So, taking everything under consideration, he agreed to help Dhalim seek his revenge on the snake. He told Dhalim: "I have an idea. We need to find some long sticks that are suitable for setting on fire. We can light one or more of them on fire, and shove them into your old den, thereby killing the snake living there. If the snake leaves, the fire will roast him; and if he remains inside, he will be suffocated."

So the two of them set about looking for kindling and tinder. It was now night. Each fox went his separate ways to find sticks. Mufawwad did his job, but Dhalim was still fixated on stealing Mufawwad's own den for himself. He was still consumed by jealousy and covetousness. Once he had gathered all his material, he made his way to Mufawwad's den and sealed himself up inside, using the wood, sticks, and leaves as a barrier.

> It is said: Many have perished in attacks and ambushes planned by themselves; many have fallen into their own traps, or have wounded themselves with their own weapons.

Mufawwad had finished gathering his sticks, and had some flaming embers also, but he could not find Dhalim. He imagined that his friend had lost interest in getting rid of the snake, and had wandered off. So he went back to his own den, and found the entrance blocked. Mufawwad could not figure out what was going on. As he was examining the situation, he dropped his sticks and embers. To make sure that a forest fire would not start, he placed his embers near the front of his den while he walked around the immediate vicinity. Of course, the smoke from the burning embers at the front of den's entrance filled Mufawwad's den, where Dhalim had secured himself. The fumes began to choke him, and he died soon after. So was Dhalim killed by the same stratagem that he and Mufawwad had planned to use on the snake that had stolen Dhalim's den. After discovering what had happened, Mufawwad said to himself, "Injustice is a weapon that hurts those who try to wield it. The unjust man is killed by his own knife, and is brought to the brink of disaster by his own feet."

> It is said: Sovereignty and injustice cannot share a throne...Every sinner will find one to pardon him, except the unjust, in whose fall all rejoice with one accord. *As much as injustice gives you, so much does it take away from you.*

Mufawwad then entered his home and removed the smoking carcass of his so-called "friend" Dhalim, the unjust. From this point on, he was always watchful for the schemes and plans of those who postured as good men, but who really were not. He became aware that unjust liars, con artists, frauds, and demagogues are often found in government and politics, as well as in normal life. Those who try to make a career of lying, deception, and con artistry will eventually be called to account for their lives of wickedness. This reckoning may be postponed for a time, for the unjust are good at covering their tracks. But sooner or later, the price will be paid. Corrupt leaders who attempt to set traps for others in order to distract attention from their own evils, are often brought down by the weight of their intrinsic malice.

8. The Meaning Of Self-Denial

One of the primary virtues that Ibn Zafar believes a good leader should possess is the virtue of self-denial. In Arabic this word is زهد, or "renunciation" of worldly things. What he means by this is that no leader–or any other person, for that matter–can ever become truly great until he learns how to subordinate his desires in the face of higher purposes. The following tale appears near the end of his treatise of political philosophy, the *Sulwan al-Muta'*, a book we have discussed in several previous essays.

There was once a diligent herdsman who kept scrupulous care of a large number of cattle. The cattle were owned by various townspeople, but he was hired to take care of them. He was very much praised by the local villagers for his good work. Sometimes the herdsman liked to spend time relaxing in the lush fields near a monastery, once his work was done. Every so often, a monk from the monastery would come out, and the two would talk; and the herdsman never talked about anything but how hard his life was.

The monk eventually asked him why he did nothing but complain. The herdsman responded by saying that no one else was willing to do his difficult job, that he was trying to make his family and others happy, and that he did take some pride in doing a difficult job well. But the monk was not convinced. He asked the herdsman again why he continued to look after the welfare of others, rather than his own happiness. The monk demanded to know the purpose behind the herdsman's diligence and application.

Finally, the herdsman told the monk this: "Yes, I put myself through a lot of trouble. But in return I can do what I want, I can go where I want, and I can make use of the meat and milk of my herd. I feel like I am managing my own property. This was what the herdsman said. The monk weighed these comments carefully, and rejoined, "This sounds like exactly the same thing that a monk once said, before he realized the error of his ways." The herdsman replied, "Tell me, brother, the story behind what you are saying." And so the monk related the following tale.

There was once a monk who was on a pilgrimage; he encountered a decrepit monastery in a beautiful location and decided to remain there. There were some monks already on the grounds, but all in all, the place was quite shabby. So the new pilgrim set about to help restore the monastery: he repaired the walls, cleaned out the garden and farmhouse, and dredged some of the canals that had become silted in and were needed for irrigation. As a result of all this work, things began to look better, and the revenues of the monastery improved markedly. The monastery attracted new men, and almond trees, vineyards, olive trees, and other crops were planted. Eventually the monk began to collect a sizeable amount of money; but he was also neglecting his duties in tending to the needs of the community.

> It is said that wealth is like water. He who does not open a gate to carry off its overflow, drowns in it. The assistance we provide others through our wealth and influence is the amulet that preserves them both.

Other problems also arose. The other monks began to feel that the new pilgrim-monk was hoarding too much wealth in his own hands, and not sharing it as he should. Eventually, feelings ran high against him. The other monks told the pilgrim-monk to share his wealth; but he would not listen. "Why should I share with you what I have earned through my own diligence and effort?" The other monks responded by saying, "That is irrelevant. These riches belong to God, who permitted you to gain them in the first place. It is your duty to distribute some of this wealth in shares."

But the pilgrim-monk, individualist that he was, was unmoved. "We will see whose wealth this is," was his angry retort. So that night he ordered his servants to cut down the olive trees, almond groves, and vineyards. The other monks were horrified at discovering this. But the pilgrim-monk responded by saying that those things were his to do as he wished with them. The other monks beat him up and threw him out of the monastery, leaving him just as poor and alone as he had been when he first arrived there on pilgrimage.

And as the expelled monk walked away from the grounds of the monastery, he saw the devastation around him. He reflected on how he had wasted so much of his effort and his life. He began to realize how his evil behaviors had brought him to ruin. He said to himself: "Everything in this world is temporary. We do not really own things; we merely lease them, and our enjoyment of them is in some ways dependent on our links to others in our community. The world is like a bridge that can lead us to a good place, as long as we are careful when we cross it. But he who wastes his time in selfish frivolities, and does not cross the bridge properly, will fall off it. And once that happens, he is doomed. What you enjoy today, may corrupt you tomorrow. You think they belong to you, but they can be taken away more easily than you can imagine. Fortune likes to play games with us, and likes to remind us that She controls all things. The wise man will prepare himself to lose everything, so that he is not devastated if it happens. If one's eyes are too focused on the material things of the world, he will be unable to leave them. This is done by practicing self-denial." And these were truly spoken words. Ibn Zafar said:

> He who is accustomed to luxury will miss its loss more bitterly than he who does not cherish it. If luxury is suddenly yanked away from such an individual, he will be filled with sorrow. Let him who seeks to accumulate wealth cultivate such virtues as may serve him for an escort as he prepares to meet his Creator. Vulgarity destroys peace and ushers in sorrows.

This was the tale told to the herdsman. He recognized the truth and wisdom of what the monk had told him. So he then asked the monk what he thought he, the herdsman, should do with his cattle. The monk said, "I have removed the veil of ignorance that was covering your eyes, and preventing you from seeing the folly of your attitude. As I see it, you should return the cattle to their owners, and think of your own happiness. You should unburden yourself from these fixations; they are no more than parasites that prevent you from achieving fulfillment and joy." Ibn Zafar here concludes his tale. In the same theme of the tale, he writes the following lines:

> You who speak evil of Fate, are you exempt from all blame, are you free from the weaknesses of human nature?
>
> Do you possess an agreement that specifies your days, or are you not a fool deceived by the vanities of the world?
>
> Awaken and remain forever in the world, you who have seen death, or tell me whether man has any power to defraud the sepulchre of its prey.
>
> Where is Chosroes Anushirvan, the greatest among monarchs, gone?
>
> Where did Sapor go before him, and those of the fair-skinned race, the gallant kings of the Romans?
>
> Why are there no memorials for any one of them?...
>
> Favorites of Fortune, kings, and lawgivers, are all buried within the tomb.
>
> And their ashes are just as the withered leaf that is whirled about in the air by the wind.

Many leaders today have forgotten these lessons. They deny themselves nothing while demanding greater and greater sacrifices from others. Convinced of their own omnipotence, they arrogantly hoard more and more, while at the same time refusing to render justice to the people they are supposed to be serving. Unaware or unconcerned with the lessons of history or the rules of social conduct, they believe that no rules apply to them. These men, and the people who cheer them on, will learn in due course where such behavior leads.

9. A Jaguar Hunt On The Taquary, And The Precepts Of Pythagoras

Every man is a jumble of paradoxes. The same man can harbor sentiments of the most noble, generous, and elevated type; and at the same time, he can retain the capability to deliver lethal blows for necessity or sport. It is almost as if the altruist or artist needs a bit of tempering with a dash of Tamerlane. Consider Theodore Roosevelt, the president generally considered the primary voice of conservationism in the twentieth century. From an early age, he showed a great sensitivity to the natural world and biology–so much so that he seriously considered becoming a scientist. One of his first books was on the bird species that resided near his home in the state of New York. During his life he always remained an astute observer of animal behavior. Consider this passage, taken from his *Through the Brazilian Wilderness*, his account of the famed exploration of the Rio da Duvida:

> These common Argentine birds, most of them of the open country, and all of them with a strikingly advertising coloration, are interesting because of their beauty and their habits. They are also interesting because they offer such illuminating examples of the truth that many of the most common and successful birds not merely lack a concealing coloration, but possess a coloration which is in the highest degree revealing...Evidently in their cases neither the coloration nor any habit of concealment based on the coloration is a survival factor, and this although they live in a land teeming with beard-eating hawks.

How do we account for the fact that the author of this passage, which reveals such a sympathetic appreciation of nature's mysterious ways, was the same man who wrote this:

> Caymans were becoming more plentiful...They are often dangerous to domestic animals, and are always destructive to fish, and it is good to shoot them. I killed half a dozen, and missed nearly as many more–a throbbing boat does not improve one's aim.

The answer is quite simple, really. Man is a complicated being, full of paradoxes. He is not so elevated from nature, or his primeval ancestors, as to be exempt from the same laws that governed them. He needs to satisfy his blood-lust every now and then. He craves the thrill of the pursuit, the closing in on the prey, and the feel of delivering that final blow. You cannot fault him for this; and you cannot condemn him for it, either. For no man is a pure altruist; even the most angelic harbor, in the recesses of their hearts, carefully concealed impulses of aggression. They are simply sublimated into socially accepted forms, or re-directed into softer manifestations.

This is why America's greatest conservation president saw nothing paradoxical about titling one of the chapters of his book "A Jaguar Hunt on the Taquary." He had no problem with this at all, because Theodore was a killer, in his heart of hearts. He was a refined, erudite, brave, and civilized man, of course, a man I admire deeply; but he also had a streak of the barbarian in him. Presumably he would have been pleased at hearing this observation. He had no problem gunning down one of the most beautiful animals of South America, the jaguar, and writing about the deed with relish:

> At last, on the edge of a patch of jungle, in wet ground, we came on fresh jaguar tracks. Both the jaguar hounds challenged the sign…The dogs had entered a patch of tall tree jungle, and as we cantered up through the marsh we saw the jaguar high among the forked limbs of a taruman tree. It was a beautiful picture–the spotted coat of the big, lithe, formidable cat fairly shone as it snarled defiance at the pack below. I did not trust the pack; the dogs were not stanch, and if the jaguar came down and started I feared we might lose it. So I fired at once, from a distance of seventy yards. I was using my favorite rifle, the little Springfield with which I have killed most kinds of African game, from the lion and elephant down…At the shot the jaguar fell like a sack of sand through the branches, and although it staggered to its feet it went but a score of yards before it sank down…

It is remarkable, really, when you think about it: that is, how these two contradictory impulses–preservation and destruction–can co-exist in a great man at the same time. Or maybe we are wrong to say "contradictory impulses." Perhaps the truth is that the two impulses spring from the *same impulse* in man's heart: the reverence and awe that he feels for the natural world. He wants at the same time to preserve nature, and to slay it, in order to keep it for himself. He *covets*, and has this need *to possess*. This is how we should reconcile these apparently conflicting impulses. We cannot take the good Theodore without the "bad" Theodore: they are part and parcel of the same man. He would never have been able to achieve what he achieved without his tincture of barbarism.

The wisest sages of old were aware of this. They saw that one of their primary duties would be to train men to keep these barbarous impulses under the surface. They did not wish to slay the beast within, only to keep it well-restrained. Pythagoras (c. 582 B.C.–500 B.C.) was one of the first, and most influential, of the early Greek philosophers. The school he founded in southern Italy (a Greek colony called then *Magna Graecia*) bore many similarities to an organized religion.

According to the biographer Diogenes Laertius (*Lives of the Philosophers* VIII.10), Pythagoras divided a man's life into four "quarters" as follows: twenty years a boy; twenty years a youth; twenty years a young man; and twenty years an old man. He said these four quarters corresponded with the four seasons of nature (spring, summer, fall, and winter). Youth, he knew, burned bright and hot; but old age brought on a calming, cooling effect, an inevitable slowing-down of the bodily machine. Pythagoras also supposedly advanced the following guidelines for men. Diogenes (VIII.17) calls them "watchwords" or "precepts":

Don't stir the fire with a knife.
Don't step over the beam of a balance.
Don't sit down on your bushel.
Don't eat your heart.
Don't help a man off with a load, but help him on.
Always roll your bed-clothes up.
Don't put God's image on the circle of a ring.
Don't leave the pan's imprint on the ashes.
Don't wipe up a mess with a torch.
Don't commit a nuisance towards the sun.
Don't walk the highway.
Don't shake hands too eagerly.
Don't have swallows under your own roof.

Don't keep birds with hooked claws.
Don't urinate on or stand on your own hair or nail clippings.
Turn the sharp blade away.
When you go abroad, don't turn around at the frontier.

Some of these maxims are obscure; but wisdom should require a little effort to appreciate, and Pythagoras knew this very well. But Diogenes Laertius does venture to explain some of these admonitions. "Don't stir the fire with a knife" meant, do not antagonize the powerful against you. "Don't step over the beam of a balance" meant not to overstep the rules of fairness, equity, or justice. "Don't sit down on your bushel" meant to take care of your future needs (a bushel symbolized a grain ration). "Don't eat your heart" meant not to spend your life fretting about things you cannot control. "Don't turn around at the frontier when you go abroad" meant not to become too attached to the things of this life, as death may claim you at any time.

Frustratingly, Diogenes does not explain all of Pythagoras's precepts. He says only, "The explanations of the rest are similar, and would take too long to go through." We may, then, venture our own explanations for the remainder. "Don't put God's image in the circle of a ring" perhaps meant not to profane sacred things; "Don't commit a nuisance toward the sun" may have meant the same thing, since the Pythagoreans held the sun to be sacred; "Don't urinate on or stand on your own hair and nail clippings" may have been an earthy admonition not to bring messes or problems into one's life. The remainder are a bit more straightforward.

Physical and mental equilibrium was important to Pythagoras. This should come as no surprise, seeing how obsessed he was about numbers and ratios. The only way a man could retain his internal balance–that is, to reconcile those conflicting, warring impulses within himself–was to try to live a disciplined, ordered, unadorned life. Man possessed intelligence, reason, and passion, he taught. Passion resided in the heart, while the other two were contained in the brain. The proper balancing of these elements was what kept a man on a straight path. For Pythagoras, passion was not something to be ashamed of; it was a natural condition of the human animal, and should be channeled to positive uses. Sensitive altruism and savagery were, he knew, two sides of the same coin.

Pythagoras understood the need for rules, guidelines, and admonitions. Read his precepts again: they are all suggestions about behavior. He knew very well what lurked underneath man's placid exterior, and spent his life trying to discipline and tame these primeval impulses. But he accepted man *as he was*, and never tried to pile guilt or shame on him for being the amiable barbarian *that he was*. He knew that those base impulses in man could be the source of just as much good as evil. Those impulses should never be abolished or amputated, only controlled, harnessed, and restrained for our productive use. Masculine virtue, Pythagoras knew, needs a bit of blood-lust, a dash of savagery, to give it potency and life. I think he would have had no problem understanding a man like Theodore Roosevelt.

10. Rejecting Cynicism And Nihilism, And Embracing An Ennobling Vision

It is the responsibility of every man to keep himself out of the abyss. Yet he cannot do this job alone; a set of guiding principles must light the way along the dark and confusing pathways of the forest. In some cases, he must be hectored, badgered, cajoled, and—in some instances—forced to keep himself along the path; in other cases, he need only be guided by gentle instruction in the illuminating lights of philosophical inquiry. Every situation is different, and calls for different remedies. And yet man is a slippery animal. Often he does not say what he means; he likes to cloak his true desires and motivations in garments of varying cut and color. Rare is the man who is honest with others; even rarer is he who is honest with himself. As Leonardo Bruni reminds us,

> The motivations of man are dark; very often his words and face will deceive.[6]

Before the decline of institutions and religions, a man could be assured that an elaborate system of social rules and obligations would point the direction of his life. His fears, desires, weaknesses, and foibles would be checked and banked on every side by religion,

---

[6] Bruni, *History of the Florentine People*, III.36.

family, clan, and the obligations to the state. So while his degree of "freedom" may not have enjoyed the latitude of modern man, his soul in many ways was assured of a certain level of peace from the constant distractions of desire and uncertainty that torment us today. We should not be too certain that we are superior to our ancestors. The rudder of stability is desperately needed in the face of Fortune's constant attempts to overturn our raft:

> Time brings us many challenges, and countless vicissitudes slither across our paths.[7]

So we cannot count on the guides that once served us: they are gone. The traditional social structures of the past have declined or vanished, and man is left to face the world alone, with nothing but his hands, his brain, and his sword. But these, it turns out, are enough. For the man animated by the right spirit, the soul imbued with the right excellences, can move mountains, master himself, and cope with the cruelties of Fortune.

He must first free himself from the enervating nihilism and cynicism that is so much a feature of modern life. One does not fully appreciate the toxicity of this brew until one travels extensively, or until one hears about the sad fates of celebrities who, despite enjoying the lives of kings and queens, still are unable to find ways to calm the tumescence generated by their unguided souls. Some people believe that cynicism and nihilism provide a refuge from the world's unpleasant truths; they scorn the traditions and rules of the past, and believe themselves to be above such things. Of course this is nothing but ignorance and arrogance on their part; they forget that institutions develop over millennia to serve very practical purposes:

> Even if man cannot do so, time and experience—the ultimate controllers of events—reject what is bad, and do not permit them to survive for long.[8]

And so they cut their ties to the few things that might save them, becoming rudderless and adrift, floating on the empty ocean. When

---

[7] Bruni, III.38.
[8] III.59.

this happens, they are at the mercy of all sorts of predators that appear in various guises: lust, greed, the need for acceptance, vanity, and similar evils of these types. And it is a man's own fault, in many ways, for he has failed to develop a personal creed that would have protected him from the storms of Fate. Of course suicide is no solution; there is a good reason why the world's major religions condemn it, and believe it to be a sin. Your life is not yours to traffic as you please; you are not permitted simply to vanish when you wish, to leave others to deal with your problems. This is unmanly, and cannot be called anything other than craven. There are some rare exceptions to this rule, as the ancient sages tell us, such that taking one's life may be permitted or even desirable. But these exceptions are rare: soldiers in hopeless situations, or those suffering from terminal illnesses, may be seen as qualifying exceptions. In a battle in 1289 between the Florentines and the Aretines, one Bishop Guglielmino of Arezzo, when told by an attendant that his infantry forces could not be saved from destruction, said:

> Then death will be the common fate of myself and my soldiers. I will never abandon the men I have led into danger.[9]

He thereupon re-entered the battle with the fury of a doomed man, and fought bravely until he was cut down. He is remembered today as a model of bravery, while generals like Arthur Percival, who led British forces in Singapore in 1942, are rightfully seen as disgraces to their profession. No commander should ever abandon his men on the field, as Douglas MacArthur did in the Philippines in 1941 when he escaped to Australia in a motorboat while his men suffered and died in captivity. It does not matter that he was "ordered" to evacuate by his president; these were orders that he should have disobeyed. He proved more than willing to disobey orders when it was expedient for him to do so, but could not muster the determination to stand his ground and fight the invading Japanese to the death, thereby guaranteeing his immortality as a commander of unquestioned bravery. On this matter, of course, every reader will have to decide for himself. But let us return to our topic. When we speak of embracing an ethic that gives our life a

[9] IV.10.

transcendent meaning, I am talking about an ethic that ennobles man, and dignifies his mortal struggle. As Cicero tells us in *On Moral Ends*:

> Who really thinks that the wise man, when he has decided that his life must end, will not be emotionally moved by saying goodbye to his family, and by leaving behind the flame of life? The power of our nature is quite clearly apparent in this predictable result, since many men will tolerate destitute beggary in order to continue living; some men advanced in age are distressed by the realization of their impending death, and suffer what we witness Philoctetes suffering in Accius's play. Despite being tormented by physical agonies that could not be alleviated, he prolonged his life by taking up the sport of bird-catching:
>
> *He was slow, but brought down the speedy with arrows;*
> *And standing, he brought down the swift in flight.*
>
> Accius also tells us that by weaving together feathers, Philoctetes constructed a functional article of clothing…From all this it can be seen that, because we love ourselves and want everything in our minds and bodies to be perfect, these attributes are precious to us for their own sakes, and are of the utmost significance in leading a happy life. If a man's objective is to preserve himself, he will certainly hold his constituent parts to be most dear. The more perfect they are, and the more praiseworthy they become in their own category, the more dear they will be held. We seek a life that should be permeated with the virtues of body and mind: *and this life must constitute the Supreme Good, since it exists as the Ultimate End of all desirable things*. Once this is clearly understood, we cannot doubt that, since men cherish themselves for their own sakes and of their own free will, the parts of the body and mind and the respective capabilities of each that are in motion or

> at rest are cultivated for their own special value, and desired for their own sakes.
>
> We may conclude from these observations that the capabilities most desired by us are those that display the greatest excellence; *so that the virtue we should most seek, the virtue that is desirable for its own sake, is the virtue derived from the best part of our being*. It is thus inevitable that the mind's virtue will come before the body's virtue, and the mind's voluntary virtues will be superior to the involuntary ones. The voluntary virtues are indeed preeminent and truly deserving of the name, because they arise from reason, the quality in man that is the most divinely inspired. The Supreme Good for all insentient or nearly insentient organisms created and guided by nature resides in their physical bodies; along these lines, I believe it has been accurately said about the pig that its mind was given to it by nature to act as salt, so that its body would not spoil. [V.11, V.13]

Very few situations are so hopeless that one would need recourse to suicide. Such a decision must be counted as unmanly, and unworthy of the purpose for which man was placed on this earth. Man is not an inanimate beast, fit only for eating, drinking, sleeping, and wandering around; he is a divine being endowed by Nature with the ability to comprehend, in some way, her secrets. To embrace nihilism and cynicism is nothing less than an offense against Nature herself: it is the action of an ingrate.

A man must start from an early age to prepare his mind for this ethic. He must protect himself from negative, destructive ideologies that seek to turn him into a coward or a slave. He must walk erect, with proper bearing, so as to communicate pride in himself and in his life's mission. Other people will notice this. The slide into moral corruption and degradation begins with bad posture and a slovenly attitude toward one's person. As Cicero says, again in *On Moral Ends*:

> In form, appearance, and disposition, the various parts of our body are clearly well-suited to our nature. Neither is there any doubt that the utility to man of the face, eyes, ears, and other bodily parts can be

> readily comprehended. But it is certainly a requirement that these bodily parts be healthy, well-conditioned, and capable of their natural movements and functions, to the extent that no vital component should be missing, unsound or incapacitated. Nature indeed wishes it to be so. There is, moreover, an expected kind of activity which holds the motions and physical positions of the body in congruence with nature. If a man were to violate these requirements through some distortion, deviation, or deformity of movement or physical bearing—for example, if he were to walk on his hands, or walk backwards instead of forwards—then he would look as if he were running away from himself, discarding his humanity, and despising his own nature. For this reason certain ways of sitting, various hunched-over postures, and physically weak movements (of the type habitually done by the impudent or the unmanly) are contrary to nature; and although such behavior arises from a mental deficiency, it nevertheless appears as if man's nature is being bodily degraded. [V.12]

Any action that a man takes to degrade or defile his nature is a step along the road to ruin. Of course there will be missteps along the way; no one is perfect, and life's detours and byways are an essential part of the learning process. Yet there must always be a concern for what is our Ultimate Good in this life, that is, what gives our struggle meaning and purpose. It is this knowledge that will keep us out of the abyss.

And should we ever lose heart, should we ever begin to despair, let us stand beneath the *oculus* of the Pantheon in Rome; let us muse among the colossal ruins of Angkor Wat in Cambodia, or the sand-blasted stones of Karnak and Luxor; let us gaze in wonder on *Il Toro Farnese* in Naples, or the dome of St. Paul's Cathedral in London, or the haunting spires of La Sagrada Familia in Barcelona; let us, too, walk in solemn reverence through the halls of Versailles, or the gilded rooms of the old czars in St. Petersburg. Stand there, my brother, and hold your breath as you gaze upward. Say to yourself, *I came from this, and I am yet a part of this. Never will I abandon hope*.

11. The Journey Through Life, And Out Of Life

When one examines the characters of different civilizations, one begins to notice commonalities of concern: that is, recurring cultural patterns. This is especially true in the most ancient of civilizations. There is this obsession with capturing the Spirit of Life, mastering its principles, and using that Mastery as a sort of pole-vault, if you will, to leap over the Wall of Life into the realm of the After-Life. Look at those old Assyrian stone reliefs, showing the bearded kings pollinating their date-plants, which were the staff of life in the ancient Near East. Look at the pharaoh smiting his enemies with a mace, and enjoying every minute of it. Mastering life in order to master death, in other words. You just feel it in these ancient places: for our ancestors had an instinctive grasp of this need to capture the Ideal of Life in order to master death, when it eventually came knocking. These concerns were focused on mastering:

1. The capabilities of the senses
2. The potential of the intellect
3. The balance between procreation and destruction

And if man could master these things, he would be able to exert some control over himself and his environment. This control would mean he could prepare himself for the after-life. He would be able to appease those froth-mouthed gods who tormented him in his sleep, and occupied his thoughts during sunrise. D.H. Lawrence, when he visited some old Etruscan tombs in the 1920s, was able to see this:

> But one radical thing the Etruscan people never forgot, because it was in their blood as well as in the blood of their masters [the Romans]: and that was the mystery of the journey out of life, and into death; the death-journey, and the sojourn in the after-life. The wonder of their soul continued to play round the mystery of this journey and this sojourn. In the tombs we see it: throes of wonder and vivid feeling throbbing over death. Man moves naked and glowing through the universe. Then comes death: he dives

> into the sea, he departs into the underworld. The sea is that vast primordial creature that has a soul also, whose inwardness is womb of all things, out of which all things emerged, and into which they are devoured back. Balancing the sea is the earth of inner fire, of after-life and before-life.

Maybe it is so. We instinctively feel it, in these old places. Around every reminder of life—every erect phallic symbol in stone announcing the presence of life—is an equally counterbalancing symbol of death. I saw it in Tusculum, too, in the Alban Hills outside Rome, as an erect column of stone balanced out a crushed skull being slowly excavated from the earth. It is a dichotomy, a duality. We can ignore it, or say it is nothing. But perhaps there is something to it. This journey out of life begins with an understanding of the capabilities of the senses. But what does this mean? How can anyone know the capabilities of the senses? We have to feel our way along, as if we were crossing a roaring stream stone by stone: step our way gradually along, lest we plunge into the boiling rapids. As Cicero says in *On Moral Ends* (V.15):

> Man's powers are so created by nature that they seem to have been made for him to acquire every virtue. So children are moved by the likenesses of the virtues without needing to be taught, since they carry the seeds of virtue within themselves; these are the primary elements of human nature that, once they have germinated, will grow into fully-developed virtue. For we have been designed from birth to hold within ourselves the principles of creative action, love, kindness, and gratitude; we also possess intellects well-adapted for knowledge, prudence, and courage. The opposites of these qualities are alien to us. It makes perfect sense that we detect in children those sparks of virtue I have just noted; the flame of the philosopher's reason should be kindled from these divine sparks, so that a mature man, following reason as a divine light, may attain nature's ultimate purpose. As I have often said, the capabilities of our nature are understood through a

> fog of uncertainty in our early years, since our minds remain feeble; yet with the progress of years, the intellect is fortified, and apprehends the power of human nature. It learns that this nature can make further progress: by itself, its power remains inchoate.

We know our senses, because we love ourselves and know ourselves. I do not subscribe to the view, so common among us moderns, that we need to "get in touch" with ourselves, that we need to somehow "realize" ourselves. No. There is no "getting in touch." We *already know* ourselves, in our deepest bones. That is not the issue, and that is not the point. *The problem is not knowing, the problem is what to do with what we know.* The real question is: what are we going to do with this knowledge? Are we going to launch ourselves out into the world and conquer our share, or are we going to slink into an obsequious subservience to the slave-master? Every man makes this decision at some point in his life, whether he cares to admit it or not. Old Cicero knew this precisely. He was not impressed with man's squealing about "not knowing myself." He was a man of worldly affairs, and had no illusions about the nature of man. He knew that man loved himself, and craved the elevation of his person. Again in *On Moral Ends* (V.17) he says:

> Let me begin with the body. Do you notice that people will conceal a limb that is deformed, dysfunctional, or impaired, and that they make great efforts to hide, if possible, this physical impairment, or at least minimize its visibility? They will endure much pain to rehabilitate their bodies, even if the condition of their limbs will not only *not* improve, but will even get worse. All men inherently believe themselves to be desirable as a whole—not because of some external reason, but because of themselves.

So we have this self-love, this awareness of the senses, that primes the intellect. The activation of the senses leads to this: the necessity for self-preservation and reproduction. This sensory-awareness is what gives each of us his spark. You can see it in people, if you look attentively enough. Some people just have that spark. Some do not. It starts in the base of the spine, and works its way inexorably upward, to animate a man's entire frame, conferring the Flame of Life on him. This is what makes a good soldier walk upright, with pride and strength; and the lack of this divine spark is what makes the hunched-over cur such a useless, detestable animal. He really is a reprehensible thing, an animal unfit for the journey.

And the essence of the intellect is to know this, to appreciate it in one's bones. Every sense must be actuated with this power of reason: this *vis rationis*. As Theodore Roosevelt was stumbling down the River of Doubt in the Amazon in 1914, he was surprised to see that most of the creatures of the jungle remained hidden. He expected to find game for the taking, yet he could find nothing. This was not like the savannahs of East Africa, those hunting grounds where game proliferated. No: this was something very, very different. The competition for life and resources occupied every calorie of energy, every square centimeter of space, for every organism. It did not matter whether the organism was a plant or an animal. It was pure, elemental struggle: competition refined to its must pure capacity. This is the jungle. You can try to sugar-coat it all you want. But you cannot escape that elemental truth.

This balance between procreation and destruction is the essence of life, and the elemental force that every civilization in history has sought to understand and to master. The will to survive is an activation of all the senses, all directed to one purpose. We cannot shrink from this knowledge, or evade it with pleasantries and artful misdirection: we can try, of course. Modern man is expert in nothing so much as lying to himself, in averting his eyes from the truth. Is it so bad to say that the jungle cat is one of Nature's great creations, in its perfect balance of destructive power and the Will to Life? Is it so bad to say that there is nothing more life-affirming, nothing so inspiring, than to see a warrior walk erect, his spine as solid as an oak, confident in his powers and in the refined activity of his senses? In some ways I suspect that modern man's queasiness with this truth is the source of many of his complexes. He would be better off if he spent some time in Nature's cathedrals, or among the ancient places.

12. The Oppressive Burdens Of The Powerful

Many men are in the habit of seeing only the privileges of the powerful, while failing to take note of the crushing burdens that such men must carry. Nothing in this world is gifted to us for free; there is a price to be paid for every acquisition, every privilege, and every benefit. This cost may not be apparent at first; but over time, it will make itself known. Those who occupy positions of power are servants of that power. The office itself issues forth its own slithery tentacles that wrap themselves around the limbs of the office-holder, restraining him and binding him in a hundred different ways. He thinks at first that he is free to do as he wishes; but circumstances and experience teach him otherwise. This reality was what the Roman writer and diplomat Sidonius Apollinaris (430–489 A.D.) had in mind when he wrote these words to his friend and confidant Serranus:

> But I will never endorse the idea that people who stand on the steep and slippery mountain-tops of our country are fortunate. [*Sed sententiae tali numquam ego assentior, ut fortunatos putem qui rei publicae praecipitibus ac lubricis culminibus insistunt.*] For one can barely convey the miseries which come every hour in the lives of these supposedly happy men, if even they should be called "happy" when they adopt this name just as Sulla did. These are men who have violated both human and divine law, and who think the greatest happiness is equivalent to the greatest power. They are miserable on account of this, because they do not fully comprehend that they are dominated by a most unrelenting slave-driver. [*Epistulae* II.13]

Sidonius's quote above mentions Sulla, who was an especially vindictive dictator just before Cicero's time. He gave himself–or his terrified followers gave him–the nickname "Felix," which in Latin means "happy." Sulla the Happy! When he had secured power for himself, he made a point of hunting down and massacring all those who had previously opposed him. Yet I wonder how happy he could really have been; for as the ancient writers tell us, he felt compelled to have the following words inscribed on his funeral monument:

> There was neither a single friend, nor a single enemy, whom I did not repay in full.

Those who have never been in a position of great power or responsibility usually shake their heads, or roll their eyes, at such words, believing them to be exaggerations or distortions. "It wouldn't happen to me!" they say. "I would be able to handle it, because it is all about maintaining one's balance." The bad things of this world always happen to others, never to them. Of course there is merit to this view. Some men were born to lead, and enjoy occupying the limelights of notoriety and authority. And I would never say that wealth is an unmitigated evil: I prefer to think of it as a dense, massive object that has, so to speak, *its own gravitational field.*

We must learn how to navigate its force-field; we must acquire the wisdom to learn how wealth and power "warp space-time" simply by virtue of their existence. Anyone or anything within the range of their gravitational field will be affected by it. We must arm and equip ourselves to live with the forces they exert on us, and on others. Above all, we must remember that all comes with a price, and that price will be paid in health, tranquility, peace of mind, and freedom. It cannot be otherwise.

Nothing comes without a price in this world except the attributes we have been gifted from Nature. This was the purpose behind the old fable of the Sword of Damocles. Many have heard this phrase, but the details of the story are not widely known. Damocles was a Sicilian from Syracuse, and a friend of the dictator Dionysius. Damocles would express his admiration for the dictator's apparently perfect life of power and privilege. During one meal, Dionysius grew tired of such talk and offered his friend an opportunity to switch places with him just for the duration of the meal. Damocles accepted the offer, removed his purple robes, and draped them over the back of his overjoyed friend; he then sat him down on a luxurious couch covered with precious objects and beautiful cushions.

Sumptuous foods and wines were brought in, one after the other, to satiate the palate of the overjoyed Syracusan. There were exotic meats, Falernian wines, perfumes, flower-petals, and all of the other things that one would associate with royalty. But as Damocles reclined on the couch, he looked up and saw a large sword hanging from the carved and painted ceiling; it was not only hanging, but shaking, and appeared about to fall at any moment and impale him bodily. The sword was attached to the ceiling by only one horsehair, and it swayed back and forth as gentle drafts moved through the palace. In these circumstances, it became impossible for Damocles to enjoy his meal, as he could not get the image of the sword out of his mind. With every bite he took, and with every sip of wine he drank, its image maintained itself in his mind.

He could not finish his meal quickly enough. When he had choked down the last morsel of food, he moved away from the couch, took off Dionysius's robe, and bolted from the palace. As he was leaving, he looked with fondness and relief on his relatively low position and economic station. He now understood–not in an abstract way, but in a very real, tangible way–that the trappings of power and privilege are nothing more than a cage. One may hold on to riches, he now knew, and at the same time be gripped by another, outside force. This was the realization that came to Damocles after only sitting in Dionysius's seat for a few short moments. As Sidonius says at the close of his letter to Serranus,

> I do not know, my lordly brother, whether those who occupy such positions of power are happy; yet there is no question that those who reach them are miserable.

13. The Pursuit Of Work, And The Quest For Ideals

In 1893 Leo Tolstoy published an essay whose title was rather clumsily translated into English as "Non-Acting." In it the great novelist compared the relative merits of two positions, one held by Emile Zola, and the other held by Alexandre Dumas. Both Zola and Dumas had been asked to state their opinions on what they believed to be the basic forces that move, or should move, humanity. Tolstoy, mystic that he was, saw these rival opinions in terms of a cosmic competition between "the force of routine, tending to keep humanity in its accustomed path," and "the force of reason and love, drawing humanity towards the light." Tolstoy's conclusions may not be to everyone's taste, but his observations–as always–reveal profound moral truths. As in so many philosophical discussions, it is not so much the final conclusion that matters (if such a thing is even possible), but the observations made along the way, that are important. Let us first hear what Zola and Dumas have to say; we may then indulge some of our own thoughts on these matters. Zola presents himself as the apostle of work. His views were given during a speech to a group of young people, the relevant parts of which I have extracted below.

> I have reached an age at which we begin to regret our departed youth, and to pay attention to the efforts of the rising generation that is climbing up behind us. It is they who will both judge us and carry on our work. In them I feel the future coming to birth, and at times I ask myself, not without some anxiety, what of all our efforts will they reject and what they will retain?...For it cannot last except through them, and it will disappear unless they accept it, to enlarge it and bring it to completion...
>
> I am therefore also going to finish by proposing to you a faith, and by beseeching you to have faith in work. Work, young people! I well know how trivial such advice appears; no speech-day passes at which it is not repeated amid the general indifference of the scholars. But I ask you to reflect on it, and I–who have been nothing but a worker–will permit myself to speak of all the benefit I have derived from the long task that has filled my life. I had no easy start in life; I have known want and despair. Later on I lived in strife and I live in it still–discussed, denied, covered with abuse. Well, I have had but one faith, one strength–work! What has sustained me was the enormous labor I set myself...
>
> Work! Remember, gentlemen, that it is the sole law of the world, the regulator bringing organic matter to its unknown goal! Life has no other meaning, no other *raison d'etre*; we each of us appear but to

> perform our allotted task and to disappear. One cannot define life otherwise than by the movement it receives and bequeaths, and which is in reality nothing but work, work at the final achievement accomplished by all the ages... Nothing is less wholesome for men and nations than illusion; it stifles effort, it blinds, it is the vanity of the weak... The only strong people are those work, and it is only work that gives courage and faith. To conquer it is necessary that the arsenals should be full, that one should have the strongest and most perfect armament, that the army should be trained, and should have confidence in its chiefs and in itself...A man who works is always kind. So I am convinced that the only faith that can save us is a belief in the efficacy of accomplished toil. Certainly it is pleasant to dream of eternity. But for an honest man it is enough to have lived his life doing his work.

So Zola sets himself up as the apostle of work, or unrelenting labor. There is much merit in this view. I know from my own experience that what has sustained me in life has been the single-minded focus on goals and achievement. One cannot philosophize unless one has earned the right to do so. There will be many times in our lives when we do not know the answers to complex problems; but, if we keep our heads down and continue to put one foot in front of the other, solutions eventually present themselves. Work distracts our minds from troubling questions for which life has no answer. Work gives us meaning, purpose, and that forward momentum which is such an essential psychological ingredient in success.

And yet Zola very much overstates his case. He could not help himself; he was an impassioned activist, a man burning with a sense of injustice who had no patience for slow deliberations. But is it really true that work is the only thing there is? Is the search for transcendent ideals useless, or, as he characterizes it, unwholesome vanity? No. Work is what we must do to live, prosper, and achieve our dreams; but the search for a higher meaning is not only the sole thing that can truly satisfy a man's soul, it is the sole thing that can be called a Supreme Good. The only soul that is permanently satisfied with work is the soul of the beast: the ox, the donkey, or the squirrel foraging for its nuts and seeds. Tolstoy had this to say in response to Zola's glorification of labor:

> The most cruel of men–the Neros, the Peter the Greats–were constantly occupied, never remaining for a moment at their own disposal without activity or amusement. If work be not actually a vice, it can from no point of view be considered a virtue. It can no more be considered a virtue than nutrition. Work is a necessity, to be deprived of which involves suffering, and to raise it to the rank of a merit is as monstrous as it would be to do the same for nutrition. The strange value our society attaches to work can only be explained as a reaction from the view held by our ancestors, who thought idleness an attribute of nobility and almost a merit, as indeed it is still regarded by some rich and uneducated people today…In my opinion not only is work not a virtue, but in our ill-organized society it is often a moral anaesthetic, like tobacco, wine, and other means of stupefying and blinding oneself to the disorder and emptiness of our lives. And it is just as such that M. Zola recommends it to young people.

It is a pity that these two great minds–Zola and Tolstoy–were drawn to such opposite extremes on an issue like work. It apparently never occurred to either of them that the ancient Greek admonition for moderation would have provided the right balance they both seemed to be looking for. That is: work *in excess* becomes stultifying blindness, but work *in moderation* is a positive virtue and indeed a necessity for the healthy man. The wise man needs *both* action *and* philosophical speculation; each complements the other, and each gives meaning to the other. But neither Zola nor Tolstoy were able to make this nuanced observation, because neither of them was as well-rounded as he should have been. We will now consider Alexandre Dumas's comments:

> Each new generation indeed comes with ideas and passions old as life itself, which it believes no one has ever had before, for it finds itself subject to

> their influence for the first time and is convinced it is about to change the aspect of everything…[Man] sees around him a universe which existed before he did and will hast after his is gone; he feels and knows it to be eternal and he would like to share in its duration. From the moment he was called to life he demanded his share of the permanent life that surrounds him, raises him, mocks him and destroys him. Now that he has begun he does not wish to end. He now loudly demands, now in low tones pleads for, a certainty which ever evades him–fortunately, since certain knowledge would mean for him immobility and death, for the most powerful motor of human energy is uncertainty…
>
> Who is in the right in this dispute? All are right while they seek; none are right when they begin to threaten. Between truth which is the aim, and free inquiry to which all have a right, force is quite out-of-place notwithstanding celebrated examples to the contrary. Force merely drives further back that at which we aim. It is not merely cruel, it is also useless, and that is the worst of faults in all that concerns civilization. No blows, however forcibly delivered, will ever prove the existence or non-existence of God. Zola recently, in a remarkable address to students, recommended to them work as a remedy and even as a panacea for all the ills of life. *Labor improbus omnia vincit.*

Dumas recognizes that man cannot be satisfied by work alone. The soul is an essential component of our existence, and it will try to seek out the Ultimate Good despite our attempts to prevent it. A rational man will philosophically accept that he needs, on the level of the corporeal body, a daily routine of work to calm the tumescence of his roaming soul; but he will also, during his free and quiet moments, recognize that philosophical speculation is just as essential for his health. He will instinctively feel that his search for the Ultimate Good–that which confers the happy life–is far more important and vital than punching the employer's time-clock, stuffing his face with expensive foods, or studying the numeric results of compound interest in his brokerage statements. As Cicero says in *On Moral Ends* (V.72):

> At the same time [the true philosopher] will appreciate that virtue has such power, and moral goodness has such authority, that by comparison the other goods, while not rendered entirely worthless, are so deficient in value as to appear to be worthless.

Work is vital because it keeps us mentally healthy, assists us in focusing our thoughts, teaches us about our fellows, and provides us the resources needed to pursue the great mysteries of our existence. We must find a way to balance out these two extremes, represented on one end by Zola, the apostle of labor, and Tolstoy and Dumas on the other end, the apostles of other-worldliness. Each becomes an unmitigated evil in the absence of the other: work without thought is slavery, and thought without work is dissolute vanity.

14. On The Acceptance Of Disappointments

There is no man who can boast of having enjoyed an unbroken string of successes. The variability of Fortune, a pervasive theme in these pages, is a force of nature that ensures success will be liberally interspersed by failure. So it seems to me that we ought to spend just as much time–perhaps even more time–in equipping ourselves with the tools needed to deal with defeats and disappointments, than we do in preparing ourselves for short-lived victory parades. The seasoned, mature mind will wave to the crowd, and enjoy his moment of reflected glory, remembering all the while that dejection is waiting for him just around the next corner. I believe it was Theodore Roosevelt who said that, nearly as soon as man passes through the triumphal arches of his victory parade, the crowd will be ready to pelt him in the back with bricks. And this is undoubtedly true.

Most of the problem lies in the fact that we are creatures of expectancy. Anticipation of glory tricks our minds into believing that glory has already arrived. The riches that might require years of sustained effort to acquire will often seem closer than they really are, tantalizing our minds and oppressing our focus on what matters at the present moment. That which we desire, we believe we are owed. Herodotus (I.187-190) tells us of a Babylonian queen named Nitocris who sought to make this very point as her final statement to the living. He says that the queen constructed a tomb for herself over one of the main gateways leading into Babylon, so that it towered over the entrance that people walked through. On the outside of the tomb she had inscribed the following words:

> If any king of Babylon is in need of funds, let him open my sarcophagus and take as much as he needs. This should only be done in case of dire need. Anyone who disturbs my tomb for any other reason will regret it.

The tomb of Queen Nitocris apparently lay undisturbed for many years until the advent of Darius I of Persia, who lived from 550 to 486 B.C. Darius resented the location of the tomb, for to him it was bad luck to have to pass under a corpse; more importantly, perhaps, he resented knowing that there was a treasure-chest of gold that could be put to better use than accompanying an expired queen. He thus ordered his retainers to open Nitocris's tomb. Inside he found it contained only the preserved body of the great queen, along with this message:

> If you, friend, had not been so greedy and eager to lay your hands on the property of others by dishonorable means, you would never have disturbed the tomb of the dead.

In this way did the queen have the last laugh at the follies of the living. We are not told what Darius's response to this disappointment was; but royalty is not inclined to be philosophical where matters of state finances are concerned. Better was the way in which that great scholar and man of letters, Dr. Samuel Johnson, handled a bitter literary disappointment. According to James Boswell, whose life of Johnson remains one of the great biographies in the English language, Johnson had worked extremely hard to write and produce his play *Irene*. It was performed in London at the Drury Lane Theatre on February 6, 1749, and ran for nine nights; but it was not a success. The public greeted it with apathy. Only another writer, who has himself invested heart and soul in an artistic creation, can know the sting of disappointment that accompanies such an event; and for a man of Johnson's pride, the incident must have been deeply wounding. But he did not retreat into self-pity. Boswell elaborates:

> When asked how he felt about the ill success of his tragedy [*Irene*], he replied, "Like the Monument." Meaning that he continued firm and unmoved as that column. And let it be remembered, as an admonition to the *genus irratibile* of dramatick writers, that this great man, instead of peevishly complaining of the bad taste of the town, submitted to its decision without a murmur. He had, indeed, on all occasions, a great deference to the general opinion: "A man (said he) who writes a book, thinks himself wiser or wittier than the rest of mankind; he supposes that he can instruct or amuse them, and the publick to whom he appeals, must, after all, be the judges of his pretensions."

This was the wise way in which Johnson philosophically accepted his disappointment. He continued to write, of course, and is now remembered as one of the key figures of eighteenth-century English literature. Even a great writer cannot expect every product of his pen to be golden. What matters is that he should continue, and never lose faith in himself. As I see things, a man should do the following practical things to shield himself from the sting of disappointment. He should first recognize that not all disappointments are equal. Some are trifling or superficial, such as those that relate to lost opportunities or missed chances. Others are more profound, and cut to the core of our being, leaving us with an anguished sense of vacuity. Superficial disappointments should be glossed over with a minimum of fuss. The more serious disappointments require specific treatment. *I have found from experience that it is a good idea to rehearse with oneself a way of explaining the disappointment to others.* Internal feelings are one thing; shame is another.

People have a way of knowing when something bad happens. Human nature has more than a touch of cruelty; and nothing so amuses the crowd as to see its hero stub his toe. If you suffer some embarrassment, expect others to bring it to your attention in one way or another. Their purpose in bringing up an unpleasant topic is to see how you react. *Will he squirm? Will he try to deny it?* These are the questions that people would truly like to ask. One must have some intelligent way of responding. The ideal response should (1) not seek to blame others for the incident; (2) not be too lengthy; (3) not be bitter or negative; (4) be relatively light-hearted; and (5) should convey a sense of philosophical acceptance of the bad fortune. What matters is not bad fortune, since this affects everyone; what matters is how we handle it. This does not mean that we go around begging for sympathy from others; what I mean is that we need to find ways of tactfully acknowledging reality–for failure cannot be concealed–while not dwelling on it. Disappointment can never be avoided; and what we cannot avoid, we should welcome:

> Cupias, quodcumque necesse est. [Lucan IV.487]

Meaning "what is inevitable, you should look forward to." As for how we should internally accept disappointments, the answer is provided by philosophy. We must know, and truly believe, that virtue is its own reward, and remains the only true wealth. All other wealth is fleeting and impermanent. We must know, and truly believe, that no material setback or tragedy can strip us of this true wealth. Virtue is within the grasp of nearly all, provided he works hard enough and has the necessary tenacity. When hungry, call on thirst for help; when thirsty, call on hunger. Masculine virtue is the sword that protects us from disappointment, as well as most other ills of the mind:

> Ignorantque datos, ne quisquam serviat, enses. [Lucan IV.579]

That is, "And they do not realize that swords have been provided so that no man may ever be enslaved." With this sword, let us then try to emulate Samuel Johnson in the face of grief and defeat, when he said that he remained "Like the Monument," and moved forward in perseverance and steadfastness.

15. The Architect Of The Imagination

Man was born for action. Even if he does not know this–especially if he does not know this–his physical being revolts from long intermissions of supine inertia, and craves the physical release of the violent contest. This is part of his blood-spirit, his irreconcilable inner Being. He can try to deny this, and he can try to avoid the consequences of this reality; but in the end the same simple truth returns to stare him in the face. Even the corpulent sloth will light up like a pinball machine when asked to discuss topics that are of intense interest to him; he will leap out his chair, gesticulate wildly, and hold forth on that topic to which all his energies are directed. Within him is that fundamental desire for action, and this no amount of subcutaneous body fat can suppress. As Cicero reminds us in *On Moral Ends*:

> Thus he who is most endowed with natural aptitude and accomplishments would never want to live a life in which he was stripped of his ability to act, even if he were able to indulge in the most seductive pleasures. Such men prefer to focus on their personal affairs; if they happen to have a more elevated spirit, they may seize the opportunity for a position of civil or military command; or, instead, they may dedicate their energies to intellectual study. Physical pleasure is so far from being their goal that they will accept stress, burdens, and sleeplessness in the service of the best part of man's nature, which in us must be considered divine. They delight in the acuteness of their minds and characters, requiring neither physical pleasure nor respite from their labors. [V.20]

And this is most certainly true. Yet it seems to me that there is no greater stimulus to the spirit of action than the human imagination. It is that divine spark that sets in motion the other sensations and corporeal causes; and from this spark are generated the flames that sear the soul. Action may be possible in the absence of imagination, but no truly great action was ever undertaken without it. No more worthy boot ever collided with the hesitant man's backside. We must, then, turn our attention to what cultivates and supports the imagination. No one doubts that imagination is an innate ability, a talent much like the ability to play a musical instrument, to play a sport, to speak, write, or any other thing of this sort. But this does not mean that anyone can cultivate his imagination, or develop whatever talents that Nature has conferred on him. Some will have more, and others will have less: this is the way of Nature, and one must be realistic about what can and cannot be done. Despite this, you will find that with work, practice, and a certain amount of humility, amazing progress can be made in the development of the imagination. We will now try to describe some general principles on how this may be accomplished.

Care of the Physical Health. No mental activity of any worth takes place within a degraded and corrupted body. Sloth, lassitude, and inertia combine to slow down the reflexes, drain away masculine virtue, and ossify the mind. Mind and body are not separate, but essentially one. And if we accept that the workings of the imagination are a mental activity–which they undoubtedly are–then it must follow that a healthy body is an essential prerequisite for a productive imagination. Note that I am not speaking here of those unfortunate souls who, through no fault of their own, have lost the use of limbs or organs, and become debilitated in some way; instead, I am speaking of those who neglect their physical condition, allowing their bodies to become the cesspools of Hades rather than temples of Athena. Poor diet, inadequate nutrition, lack of exercise, and pernicious bodily habits are the real culprits here. So before our *Argo* can set sail on its voyage to seek the Golden Fleece, then, we must restore our physical condition to its proper state, the state in which it was intended to be by Nature.

The Experience of Travel. Knowledge begins with the senses. Is there anyone who will doubt this? A muscle will atrophy if it is not used. The senses are the same way. Sense-perception must be bombarded with stimuli, in the same way that physicist Ernest Rutherford showered his laboratory test-screens with particles to prove one physical principle or another. A thorough deluge of stimuli works wonders in this regard. There are few ways of accomplishing this better than the experience of travel to foreign places. We must explore, poke, penetrate, and dive into the world of the Unknown, and permit our hesitant sensibilities to be confronted with the strange, the unfamiliar, and the dangerous.

This will have the result of opening up our perceptions to things previously thought impossible, and to ideas that were previously unthinkable. All travel is exploration in one way or another; the two concepts are interchangeable. The man of action must literally throw himself into unfamiliar arenas, and see how he responds. And when I say "arena," I mean precisely this: *the world is a battleground of sensation and understanding, where we must fight to master, and make our own, that which has until now been beyond our comprehension.* Knowledge is not for the timid.

The Experience of Other Physical Activities. Travel and exploration are not the only activities that unfreeze the mind. Games, sports, social interactions and relations, and all activities associated with these things do much the same thing, and should never be neglected. Here again, it is the bombardment of the senses that is what we are seeking. The activities must be positive; I do not subscribe to the idea that the powers of imagination can be accessed in any sustained, meaningful way through the use of chemical substances or alcohol. It seems to me that those who advocate this commit the error of confusing the giddiness of the mind for the expansion of the spirit: intoxication is not enlightenment, but undisciplined stimulation. Discipline and self-control must act as the ballast for any voyage of exploration, as their absence causes the ship of the mind to float aimlessly upon the water.

The Experience of Reading and Study. To see the world through the eyes of another is a good thing. This is one of the chief experiences of reading and study. We enter the mind of another and learn how he interprets the world; it is, in a way, another form of stimulation. But it is a more refined sort of stimulation than that which comes from travel, games, sport, or play. Ideas can be described in all their nuances. Fine points of differentiation can be laid out, discussed, and pondered; and, by so doing, our traveler of the senses gains new perspectives and vistas. He cannot help but be enriched and broadened by this experience. The eyes read the words, and the imagination supplies the rest. Some of the old Romans took a dim view of speculative fiction, those *fictae fabulae* ("invented tales," as they called such literary endeavors) that they thought added little to a man's education. In this they were mistaken, and should have known better. Consider this short passage from Robert Louis Stevenson's adventure classic *Kidnapped,* a veritable triumph of imaginative writing, in which young David Balfour almost meets his death in the House of Shaws at the treacherous hands of his uncle:

> Well, I had come close to one of these turns, when, feeling forward as usual, my hand slipped upon an edge and found nothing but emptiness beyond it. The stair had been carried no higher: to set a stranger mounting it in the darkness was to send him straight to his death; and (although, thanks to the lightning and my own precautions, I was safe enough) the mere thought of the peril in which I might have stood, and the dreadful height I might have fallen from, brought out the sweat upon my body and relaxed my joints.

We can almost feel the waves of rage and horror course through Balfour's frame. We need only read the description of events, and our imaginations supply the requisite emotion. How many of us have not, deep in our hearts, suspected our relatives of plotting to do us evil? How many of us have rightly thirsted for revenge upon those who would do us physical harm? And so the power of the imagination works this purpose: *to satisfy our deepest cravings, and to make real that which was previously only disincarnate.*

Discipline and Courage. There is a common misunderstanding that the activation of the imagination involves–even necessitates–some kind of free-wheeling, outlaw spirit that "makes its own rules" and finds "creative insight" in substance-induced hazes or ego-tripping frivolities that lead nowhere. This is not illumination, but concealment. It is a convenient way to avoid coming into contact with necessary truths. I am not a teetotaler; I enjoy alcoholic drinks, but do not use any other type of drug. Leo Tolstoy, in his essay *Why Do Men Stupefy Themselves?*, proposed a reason why men sought out intoxication. He begins by noting:

> All human life, we may say, consists solely of these two activities: (1) bringing one's activities into harmony with conscience, or (2) hiding from oneself the indications of conscience in order to be able to continue to live as before.

Men use drugs, he reasoned, *in order to stifle the voice of their own consciences*. It is a way of avoiding a confrontation with the honest inner voice. This was Tolstoy's unique explanation. He was a mystic, but he was offering a profound truth. We may agree or disagree with Tolstoy, but the fact remains that the architect of the imagination cannot be an undisciplined, free-floating spirit, dodging the responsibilities of life by taking refuge in intoxication and excessive indulgence in voluptuary pleasures. This is vanity, corruption and dissolution, and unworthy of a man. No: the architect must be a man of discipline and order, a man firm in his convictions, and a man who understands the necessity of masculine virtue in guiding and directing the affairs of the mind. *The cultivation of the imagination is not some escape into fantasy, but an intense concentration on the production of some art or science.*

Courage and Conviction. These are the architect's final ingredients. All the creative, imaginative effort in the world is of little use if the architect does not have the courage to deliver his results to the public. Many are unwilling to do so, fearful of the verdict that may result. But one must submit to the workings of Fate in these matters. When Dr. Samuel Johnson learned that one of his plays had flopped in London, he was calmly philosophical about it. Boswell tells us:

> When asked how he felt upon the ill success of his tragedy, he replied, "Like the Monument"; meaning that he continued firm and unmoved as that column. And let it be remembered, as an admonition to the *genus irritabile* [irritable species] of dramatick writers, that this great man, instead of peevishly complaining of the bad taste of the town, submitted to its decision without a murmur.

If only we had the attitude of Dr. Johnson! But at the same time, a man must take pride in his work, and believe with the firmest conviction that what he is doing is important and for all time. Without this passionate devotion, he will never be able to give his work that necessary tang needed to capture the imaginations of others. In this connection, I very much like the attitude taken by Arrian in his *History of Alexander the Great*, when he tells us proudly,

> And that is the reason why I have embarked upon the project of writing this history, in the belief that I am not unworthy to set clear before men's eyes the

> story of Alexander's life. No matter who I am that make this claim, I need not declare my name–though it is by no means unheard of in the world; I need not specify my country and family, or any official position I may have held. Rather let me say this: that this book of mine is, and has been from my youth, more precious than country and kin and public advancement–indeed, for me *it is* these things. And that is why I venture to enter into the company of the great masters of Greek literature, as Alexander, of whom I write, was the great master of the profession of arms. [I.12; *Trans. by A. de Selincourt*]

This is the kind of bold attitude needed to confront and master a great enterprise. He did not shy away from what he knew and intended to do. From his youth, the great deeds of Alexander had captured his spirit and arrested his attentions; moved by them, he set about preparing to write his history; then he donned his armor, entered the arena, and produced. All worthy dreams come with a cost, and the price is always high; only nightmares are free. The architect of the imagination designed his structure and built it without fussing about the opinion or reactions of this or that person. The edifice still stands, to this day.

16. Do Not Be Too Proud Of Your Generosity

I have always counted myself fortunate when receiving the generosity of another. I have never paused to ask questions about the circumstances of the giver, or to weigh the relative merits of a gift. To be graced with the kindness of another is enough. Perhaps what matters more is the sincerity of the giver; for a gift wrapped in cold anonymity is valued less than a benefaction derived from proximate familiarity. We appreciate any generosity, but are more likely to cherish that which carries this aura. There is an old story that illustrates this point. There was an eighth century Arab general named Ma'an Ibn Za'ida Al-Shaybani. He originally served the Umayyad caliphs; and having been spared execution when the Abbasids took power, he was able to secure a pardon from the caliph Al-Mansur.

Around 759 A.D. he was appointed governor of Yemen, and energetically brought the region under Abbasid control. His biographer Ibn Khallikan[10] describes him as an effective commander known for his unsolicited acts of generosity. He relates a particular anecdote that I will now retell.

Ma'an eventually fell out of favor of the caliph Al-Mansur, and the caliph ordered a search to be made for him, presumably to put him in prison. One day, as Ma'an was leaving one of the gates of Baghdad named Bab Harb, which in English means "Gate of War," he was stopped by a common soldier who recognized him and knew he was a wanted man.

"You are Ma'an, son of Zaida, the person whom the caliph is looking for," he declared.

"What! How can you say this?" said Ma'an. "Where is the similarity between me and Ma'an?"

"By God! Do not try to deny it, sir, for I know you better than you know yourself!" replied the soldier. Seeing that the soldier was serious, Ma'an relented. He produced a jewel from his pocket and gave it to the soldier.

"I want you to have this," he said. "It is worth many times what the caliph is offering as a reward for my capture." The soldier took it, and examined it closely. Then he said, "You speak the truth, general, as to its value. But I cannot accept it without first asking you a question."

"Ask me your question, brother," said Ma'an.

"It is said by all that you are known for your generosity. But let me ask you this: was there ever a time that you gave away all of your fortune?"

"No, never," said Ma'an.

"One half, or one-third?" was the next question.

"No, I must say not," replied Ma'an.

"And how about one tenth?" the soldier pressed him.

"Yes, I think I may have done so," was Ma'an's answer.

"Well then, by God, this was no great burden for you. But I, a simple soldier in the employ of the caliph Abu Jafaar Al-Mansur, live on only twenty dirhams per month. This jewel you just gave me is worth many thousands of dinars. And now I wish to give it back to you. I give it to you as a token of appreciation for you acts

---

[10] Vol. III, p. 400 in M. de Slane's edition (See the introduction to Part II, below).

of generosity, and for the good you have done. But I also want you to know now that there is a man in the world more generous than you, sir. So from now, be not too proud of your acts of generosity." As the soldier said this, he returned the jewel to Ma'an, and allowed him to proceed, thereby letting him go free.

This was almost more than Ma'an could bear. For in the traditional ways of the Arabs, to be bested in an act of generosity could be seen as a serious loss of face. Ma'an said to him, "By God! You have disgraced me! I would suffer less from the loss of my life's blood than from what you have just done. Please take back what I have given you, for I can make do without it."

At this the soldier laughed and said, "O General, I can see you would like to cancel my words. By God, I will never take a reward for doing a good action. For me, that is its own reward." And with this, he turned away and left. Ma'an later tried to find this soldier, and hired many assistants to try to find him and repay him. But he was never located, and Ma'an never could discover who he was. To me this story wonderfully illustrates the point that we should never be too proud of our own generosity. What matters, as we said earlier, is the sincerity of the giver and his emotional connection to the recipient. In the contest of magnanimity between the soldier and Ma'an, it was the soldier who more perfectly exemplified what Cicero would have called *magnitudo animi,* or greatness of soul.

We may contrast this tale with story related by the Renaissance humanist Petrarch, a man who was so revelatory in his letters and essays that I almost feel as if I know him personally. Around 1359 he wrote a letter (*Familiares* XXI.11) to one of his friends, a man named Neri Morando. He says that there was a certain goldsmith who lived in the city of Bergamo who earnestly wished to meet him. Petrarch was a famous man, and this goldsmith had collected all of his writings. He was an old man and, as Petrarch says, he was "seized with a most ardent desire to win my friendship." The man invited Petrarch to his house, and won over the scholar with his sincerity and good nature:

> No one surely would have been so rude and surly as to refuse to see him...How could I have done otherwise? I was completely vanquished by the man's attractive countenance and his sincere and persistent

> attentions, and received him with hearty and unreserved good-will...He seemed to have reached the very summit of his fondest hopes and to be metamorphosed by his joy...Certainly no one ever enjoyed the hospitality of so delighted a host. In fact his delight was so great that his friends began to fear for his sanity, or lest, as has happened to not a few, he should actually die of joy. [*Trans. by J.H. Robinson*]

Petrarch was deeply impressed by the simple sincerity of the goldsmith; he thought the incident important enough to make it the subject of one of his letters (which, in those days, were really essays meant for posterity). The goldsmith was not proud of his generosity; it came naturally to him, and sprang from the deepest well of his soul. He had no desire or need to make a display of it. The gratitude that the goldsmith felt towards Petrarch was, I think, a result of the inspiration and solace he derived from reading the humanist's works. When one has inspired us to see life in a new way, or to take a new path in life, we are willing to do almost anything to show our appreciation. As I see it, Petrarch correctly identifies the quality that gave the goldsmith his greatness of soul. He says that the goldsmith had the "*best gift that nature can bestow, for he is an admirer and lover of all that is good and beautiful.*"

17. Why We Should Forgive The Faults Of Our Heroes

There comes a time in the life of every son or daughter when they begin to see their parents as flawed mortals. Before this, they are still under the spell of their upbringing; they perceive their parents more as imposing authority figures than as anything else. I am not sure exactly when, or how, this transition takes place; for some it may be one event, for others it may be a series of events, or an incremental process. But it does happen, and the son begins to see the father as the human being he is, in all his definitive defects and foibles.

It is the same, or should be the same, for our historical heroes. We admire our heroes for their superlative qualities of personality; but we should love them for their flaws and defects. The former qualities are instructive, but the latter are what make us love them.

I do not see this as something to be regretted; I see it as a necessary and vital extension of the rhythm of life. Who would want to be perfect? Who can expect to enjoy a life so charmed that it becomes nothing more than a string of successes? The wise man will shun such a life; he knows that Fortune has a way of averaging things out, of balancing good with bad, so that dizzying success will be followed by catastrophic failure. This is how it turned out to be for Polycrates of Samos, whom Cicero says (*On Moral Ends* V.92) had the nickname "*Felix*," which in Latin means "The Fortunate."

Herodotus tells us (III.40) that Polycrates enjoyed so much success that he began to be afraid that he might unwittingly be offending the gods. He knew that pride was the greatest of all sins; and, in his consternation, he wrote to his friend Amasis, the King of Egypt, to ask for guidance. Amasis wrote back to him and said that he was alarmed at Polycrates's constant good fortune: "For I have never yet heard of a man who after an unbroken run of luck was not finally brought to complete ruin." Amasis's suggestion was for Polycrates to throw away something precious; in this way, he might interrupt his good fortune with a countervailing incidence of misfortune.

And so Polycrates did exactly this; he took his favorite signet ring, a ring of great value, and threw it into the sea. About five days later, a fisherman of Samos happened to catch a large fish, and thought it would make a good present for Polycrates; he gave it to him, and when his attendants cut it open in preparation for consumption, they found the signet ring in its belly. When Amasis heard about this, he knew that Polycrates was doomed; for he believed the story was an ominous sign that some men could not escape their destiny. So it turned out to be: for he was later deposed and executed by one of the satraps of the Persian king Darius.

But we have strayed a bit from our subject. We must love our heroes for their flaws and their faults; their weaknesses remind us of our own, and inspire us with the knowledge that even flawed men can rise to greatness. I never quite understood the position of those who think their heroes should be perfect. Perhaps they themselves lack confidence in themselves, and feel that the flaws of their heroes somehow reflect on them. Or perhaps they prefer the superficial nature of things, and are unwilling to learn the real nature of men's characters. There were few men who have loved Cicero more than Petrarch; one could say that the father of humanism owed more to Cicero than any other author. Petrarch personally sought out and discovered hundreds of the old consul's letters that were buried in forgotten libraries. Yet even he was irritated by the unbalanced adulation of the old consul by one of his friends. Of course Cicero was a great man; I can say this as one of his devoted students, as a man who has labored for years to translate his works for a modern audience.

Yet even the old consul had his flaws; and no honest translator or biographer can overlook them. In a letter to one Pulice di Vicenza (*Familares* XXIV.2), Petrarch expands on his views, which he expressed at a meeting with some friends:

> Still, there is nothing in this world that is absolutely perfect; never has the man existed in whom the critic, were he ever so lenient, would see nothing at all to reprehend. So it chanced that while I expressed admiration for Cicero, almost without reservation, as a man whom I loved and honored above all others, and amazement too at his golden eloquence and heavenly genius, I found at the same time a little fault with his fickleness and inconsistency, traits that are revealed everywhere in his life and works. At once I saw that all who were present were astonished at so unusual an opinion, and one among them especially so. [*Trans. by J.H. Robinson*]

No one knew Cicero better than Petrarch, and I consider his views to have far more credibility than the man who showed nothing but uncritical adulation. Anyone can worship; but it takes a penetrating and independent mind to make an honest appraisal of strengths and weaknesses. Petrarch further relates how this old man was offended by Petrarch's noting of Cicero's faults:

> But the old man stood his ground, more stubbornly even than before. He was so blinded by love of his hero and by the brightness of his name that he preferred to praise him even when he was in the wrong...He would not be thought to condemn anything at all in so great a man. And when we asked him if he found it impossible to believe that Cicero

> had made mistakes, he would close his eyes and turn his face away and exclaim with a groan, as if he had been smitten, "Alas! Alas! Is my beloved Cicero accused of doing wrong?"

As I see it, this kind of attitude shows more superficiality than it does insight. Why would anyone feel discomfort at being reminded of the faults of his heroes? For me, knowing my heroes have warts is far more inspiring than imagining them as demigods. No one would ever be able to measure up to such a standard; such an attitude transforms our heroes into cartoon characters. Petrarch's final thoughts strike just the right balance:

> What could I say, I who am myself so great an admirer of Cicero's genius?...I have dealt familiarly with these great geniuses, and perhaps boldly, but lovingly, but sorrowfully, but truthfully, I think... The fact is that I still grieve over the fate of these great men; but I do not lament their faults any the less because of that.

This is a mature, balanced understanding, born of exhaustive study and intimate acquaintance with the great man's writings. I have to say that I can relate to Petrarch's feelings of regret and grief. I have lived with Cicero's *Stoic Paradoxes, On Duties*, and *On Moral Ends* for many years; I feel as if I am a pupil of the old consul himself. In a way, I am. I am staggered by his profound knowledge of philosophical subjects, his worldly wisdom, his soaring eloquence, and his tender solicitude towards others. Yet, like Petrarch, I am sometimes dismayed by Cicero's inability to see how the republic had evolved in his final years, and by his apparently pointless political quarrels with men more powerful than he. As I stood at Tusculum recently, I could not but help feel sorrow that the old man did not live out his final years there in peace and quiet, as he should have. Instead, he chose to enter political fights that led directly to his death. I do not condemn him, for every man is driven by his own personal demons; I only feel sorrow at his fate, which seems undeserved for so great a man. It reminds me of something said beautifully by the historian Velleius Paterculus:

> Adeo natura a rectis in prava, a pravis in vitia, a vitiis in praecipitia pevenitur. [II.10]

This means, "Thus does nature evolve from the morally good to the corrupt, from the corrupt to vice, and from there to the pit of vices."

18. On The Solitary Life

The scholar Petrarch once secured an audience with the Holy Roman Emperor Charles IV, who lived from 1316 to 1378. His meeting with the emperor at Lombardy in 1354 is described in one of Petrarch's luminous letters (*Familiares* XIX.3). It was a charming custom of those days that kings and popes would occasionally seek out men of letters for the purpose of philosophical inquiry. Perhaps kings preferred to talk with scholars because they were removed from the concerns of power, and could speak with a frankness that was lacking with the royal ministers and advisors.

Charles first asked Petrarch about the progress of one of his books, a tome entitled *De Viris Illustribus* (*Lives of Famous Men*). Petrarch informed him that it was still a work in progress, but that he would send the emperor a copy once it was finished. "I promise that you will have it, Caesar, if your valor approves itself, and my life is spared" Petrarch somewhat insolently told him. By this I suppose he meant that the emperor would have to deserve the book by virtue of his good deeds; and that it would be sent provided Petrarch's advancing years did not degrade his writing faculties. He then went on say, in words that could have been spoken by Cicero, these words:

> As for you, Caesar, you will know yourself to be worthy of this gift, and of a book bearing such a title, when you shall be distinguished not in name only, and by the possessions of a diadem, insignificant in itself, but also by your deeds; and when, by the greatness of your character, you shall have placed yourself upon a level with the illustrious men of the past. You must so live that posterity shall read of your great deeds as you read of those of the ancients.

How I wish our modern leaders might hear and implement these words! But that is a subject for a different place. It might be expected that such impertinent talk to an emperor would be met with hostility or dismissal; but Charles readily accepted Petrarch's counsel, and took it in stride. The scholar then presented the emperor with some ancient Roman gold and silver coins. He told the emperor that he must not only learn about the deeds and attitudes of the great man stamped on the precious metals; he must strive to *emulate their example* in his own life. As he presented the coins to Charles, he gave a brief summary of the lives of the figures on each coin. Petrarch reports that Charles was delighted with this dialogue, and pressed the Italian scholar for more information. He asked to hear of Petrarch's life history, his favorite anecdotes, and of his future plans. When it came to the future, Petrarch confessed his momentary uncertainty.

He told the emperor that, despite his best intentions, he had been "unable to bring his work to the state of perfection" that he would have liked. He was finding it difficult, he candidly admitted, to break free from the bad habits of the past. Charles tried to be more specific. "What I would like to know, sir, is what type of life pleases you best." On this subject Petrarch was well-equipped to answer. He told the emperor that it was the life of solitude that pleased him most. For him such a life was superior to any that could result from a life of public attention. The forests and mountains called him, as did his literary work; and this was what mattered to him most. But here the emperor smiled, and said:

> All this I well know, and have intentionally led you step by step, by my questions, to this confession. While I agree with many of your opinions, I must deprecate this notion of yours.

So here a stimulating debate arose between these two great men: one a man of letters, the other a man of temporal power. Petrarch warned Charles not to attempt to debate him on this subject, for he believed he would easily be able to demolish the monarch's pretensions. Nevertheless Charles decided to engage, and the two of them sparred. Petrarch pronounced him a worthy adversary; and each of them left the playing field believing himself the victor. This is always a good sign of a successful debate, and the two of them parted on amicable terms.

No doubt Petrarch detailed the merits of a life of peace and solitude. These were subjects he touched on in his memoir *My Secret Book*. What is the use of having a family solely for the purpose of procreation? If it is for the vain hope of "being remembered," we should think again, because we may be disappointed. Do any of us remember the names and deeds of our own great-grandfathers, or great-great-grandfathers? No. Why, then, should we think our remote descendants will remember us? Is it not true that *what live forever are great deeds and virtue*, rather than human beings, who may or may not be worthy of remembrance? Should not posterity judge us by our accomplishments? The world is a hurricane of anxieties, torments, and disappointments, Petrarch might have added. Our vanity will not save us, either; for the body withers and declines in time. He quotes Juvenal (X.172), who reminds us with his usual brutality,

Mors sola fatetur quantula sint hominum corpuscula,

And this means, "Only death discloses how pathetic are the bodies of men." Celebrate your body now, my friend; but know that those who see you in death will have a very different impression of your glorious musculature. Chasing after spoils and honors is ultimately futile; the only lasting satisfaction, Petrarch would have said, is to be found in the life of moral rectitude. He was a disciple of Cicero in the marrow of his bones.

Petrarch tells us that he accompanied the emperor as he left Milan and proceeded to Piacenza. At this point, a Tuscan soldier recognized Petrarch and took him by the hand. The soldier then turned to the emperor and said, "Sire, this is the man whom I have often told you about. If you accomplish great deeds, he will not allow your name to be forgotten; otherwise, he will know when to speak and when to keep silent." Assuming this anecdote is true–and I have no reason to doubt it–it is meant as a sly reminder from Petrarch that historians and scholars will have the last word with regard to whether a ruler is remembered favorably or unfavorably by posterity.

But is it true that the life of solitude the best life? I tend to think that we must first ask what we mean by "solitude." If solitude be a stubborn withdrawal from the affairs of society, and a timid retreat into an isolated hermitage, then I must confess I am no proponent of the "solitary life." To me such a life seems to be no life at all. It is nothing less than a negation of life. Cicero never advocated such a reticent course; he was a patriot and a man of public affairs. He was constantly interested in the hustle and flow of events, and could not help involving himself in them as he saw it. I will not condemn those who see this differently; for every man must find his own path, and what is right for me cannot be imposed on another without offending Nature.

It is only that I think a man of ability has some responsibility to contribute to his society's collective betterment. The man of ability should strive to do what he can to right the wrongs he sees, within the scope of the powers given to him by Fortune. He should relish the solitude and peace that comes as a reward for a job well done; but *the satisfaction of solitude should be earned through the accomplishment of good works*. This seems to me the better way of evaluating the question. In this regard I find a certain anecdote by Boccaccio to be relevant. In his *Lives of Famous Women*, he tells us about a woman named Busa, who was from the town of Canosa. She seems to have lived a solitary life. When the Roman army was catastrophically defeated at Cannae by Hannibal, a panic took hold in the army. Defeated remnants of the army were in confusion and despair. Boccaccio says that Busa took it upon herself to act as an angel of mercy to many of the despairing soldiers. She comforted them; dressed their wounds; opened her house and estate to them for recuperation; and showed them tender mercies in their hour of need. No one commanded her to do this. No one forced her to do this. She took it upon herself to perform this singular act of mercy. She even gave some of them money when they left her estate.

In evaluating her actions, Boccaccio reckons them as greater than the feats of largesse performed by Alexander the Great. For him it was nothing to give away what he could not use himself. But Busa gave away what was hers and what she herself needed. Alexander gave to acquire and secure his reputation; but she gave because it was in her nature. Busa, he says, deserved more glory for her selfless acts than Alexander. And this is how it seems to me also. The solitary life can redeem itself only if it permits those who practice it to contribute honorably to their fellows. If it cannot do this, of what use is it?

Were we born to live our lives in seclusion, behind bolted doors and snarling suspicions? Or were we created for the purpose of achieving great deeds, and overcoming insurmountable obstacles? Our bodies are transitory and ephemeral, and will be nothing but desiccated husks in due course; but our actions will live forever, and will in time be weighed by Fortune's scales. And this is what Sallust meant when he said, in the opening paragraph of his monograph *Catiline*, that "masculine virtue is pure, and eternal."

A point that is perhaps related to our theme is this: we should not be too quick to judge our heroes by the standards of our own time. Our exemplars need to be studied in the context of their age, location, culture, and background. We do a great injustice to historical figures if we judge them by contemporary standards. Will any great man survive such scrutiny? What will our own descendants say about us? I can only hope that they will make allowances for our limitations of culture and perspective. I am about to read a new biography of the baseball player Ty Cobb, and hope that the author will judge him more by the standards of his own era, than by ours. As I see it, it is better to judge of a man's character *by looking at how his opinions evolved over time*. A random sample of opinion will not do; we must look at evolutions of thought, spread out over time. Some men grow into greatness; some are able to rise to certain occasions, and become greater as a result. For it is a common pitfall among men to judge others harshly while overlooking the extensive list of their own flaws. As Velleius Paterculus again warns:

> Adeo familiare est hominibus omnia sibi ignoscere,
> nihil aliis remittere, et invidiam rerum non ad causam,
> sed ad voluntatem personasque dirigere. [II.30]

This means, "All men are in the habit of being unmindful of their own foibles, and allowing for none in others; they spew their anger not at the real causes of things, but at people and perceived intentions." This is a statement I am very much inclined to agree with. I try not to be too quick to judge others, especially historical figures; for they are products of conditions and circumstances that I, far remote from their era, can only dimly perceive. I love them, warts and all, and hope I will have the wisdom to know when to hold my tongue in judgment.

19. Surge And Consolidate, Surge And Recuperate

There is a line in one of Seneca's letters (107.11) that reads:

Ducunt volentem fata, nolentem trahunt.

Seneca is quoting a line by the philosopher Cleanthes, which means, "The fates lead along the willing, and carry along the unwilling." It does not matter whether we want, or do not want, to move in some direction; we will be brought there by the operation of Fate. Of course there are many who will say that this is nothing but a crude fatalism that promotes resignation and apathy. Carried to excess, the idea does lend itself to these sentiments. On the other hand, I am sure that there are many who can confirm that, in some cases, doing nothing is better than constantly straining to force a certain outcome.

The harder you try, the more your goal recedes into the distance; ignore it for a bit and go about your business, and watch it move closer to you. There is something in this ethic. I am not sure how far it can be taken, or what its precise parameters are; but I know there is some truth to it. Or perhaps it is just the voice of exhaustion whispering in my ears. The man of action is accustomed to trying to control events; he wants to seize the bulls of Knossos by the horns, and leap over them while Minos watches in delight. He wants to perform, to accomplish, and finds it difficult to accept the role of the spectator. Yet Nature grinds him down, too. With the passage of years, the sinews become less supple, the muscles less resilient; and the irritations and inanities of the world begin to oppress his spirit. How tempting it is to renounce control for once, brother, and surrender to some higher force that places no demands on us!

Herodotus says (III.128) that the Persian King Darius once seriously injured his foot. He was out hunting, overreached himself, and dislocated his ankle. The pain from the injury was severe; Darius tried to remedy it himself, to no avail. So he called upon his Egyptian doctors, who had a reputation for healing with minimally invasive procedures. But here they did him no good; in fact, the poor king was left in worse shape than when they began their treatments. For seven days and nights he could not sleep. Finally, unable to stand the situation any longer, one of his attendants told him about the reputation of the Greek doctor Democedes of Crotona. He was supposed to have worked medical wonders in Sardis, so Darius sent for him without delay.

But Democedes arrived at Darius's court in a wretched state. He had fallen on hard times and been enslaved. He was dressed in rags and was in shackles. Darius asked Democedes if he was a capable doctor, and if he could heal the king's foot. The unfortunate Greek was afraid of answering in the affirmative, aware that he might be forced to stay at the court of the Persian king for the rest of his life. Darius detected the wily Greek's deception, and had his own way of resolving the issue. He ordered an attendant to fetch a whip and some iron spikes; the sight of these instruments of torture would be enough, he knew, to reduce matters to their essentials. Democedes still tried to equivocate; he said he did have some medical training, but was not an expert. This was good enough for Darius, who ordered him to examine the royal ankle. As Greek medical techniques were superior to those of the king's other doctors, Darius was healed in short order.

The king was most grateful, as he had never expected such a result. To reward Democedes, he presented him with a set of gold chains. Half in jest, the Greek asked the king if he intended to double his sufferings by adding a set of gold chains to the iron ones that already fettered him. Laughing, Darius told him that this was not the case; and to prove it, he sent Democedes to spend some time with his many wives. He was announced by the eunuchs there as the man who had cured the king; and on hearing this, his wives presented him with cup after cup of gold coins. From that point, Democedes was able to live in a large house in Susa, and enjoyed every privilege of being a royal intimate. The only thing he could not do was return home to Greece. He had made great advances from his previous condition, but now he needed time to consolidate and evaluate his current situation.

The more he tried to cause a certain outcome to take place, the more it slipped away from his grasp. He desperately wanted to get back home, but he was not permitted to leave. At some point, he gave up all hope of ever returning home. But one day, something happened to change his luck. Darius's wife, the Queen Atossa, became ill with breast cancer; an ulcer appeared on her breast, and she raised the matter with Democedes. He removed the cyst with surgery, and asked of her in return that she do him a favor. The favor, he said, was to talk to Darius and convince him to send Democedes back to Greece as an advisor and scout for the king's planned invasion of that country. When the opportunity was right, he gave the Persians the slip and escaped into the Greek countryside, and eventually made his way back to Crotona. He even married. He had bided his time, and the fates had smiled on him.

Stories like this cause me to believe that sometimes we should stay alert, observe events, and wait for the right opportunities to come along. I am not sure of the right balance between action and inaction. Perhaps no one is. To me it seems more a matter of instinct than anything else. Bursts of action should perhaps be followed by recuperative bouts of inaction. *We should surge and then consolidate, surge and then recuperate.* Or perhaps it is fate, which carries us along whether we are willing or unwilling.

20. Observations On Classic Greek Art

I have spent the past two days in Athens seeking out some of the monuments of classic Greek art. I have tried to see as many works of art and architecture as was reasonably possible, and thought I would here provide the impressions gained from these observations.

There will always be a clear difference between what is beautiful, and what is ugly. One would think this kind of statement would be unnecessary: that it is a statement of the obvious. Alas, in today's world, this is not so. We are constantly bombarded with images of corruption, moral degeneracy, and ugliness; modern consumer culture is an assault on the senses, an offence to decency, a deliberate attempt to degrade the humanistic ethic. Our mass media is engaged in a coordinated campaign to convince us that depravity and ugliness is "good"; that beauty is "relative" and therefore meaningless; and that every person can "make up his own rules" as he sees fit. Images of ugliness and corruption are placed on magazines, and thrown in our face in films and television. This is nothing less than an affront to decency, and an attack on truth.

This was not always so. In art, the ancient Greek culture held out perfection of form and proportion as an ideal; beauty was worshipped, and this had the advantage of giving people something positive to aspire to. As I see it, there is no clearer sign of our social decay than the media's constant debasement of beauty and goodness, and its attempt to foist on us its own degenerate conception of humanity. It is almost as if our culture wants to *redefine* what it means to be human. But once you have laid eyes on true beauty and perfection of form, it is almost as if you become immunized to ugliness and corruption; you instinctively seek out that which is good, and reject with disgust that which is ugly. This actually happens. *In every way, whenever possible, we must celebrate and restore an ethic that ennobles humanity, rather than drags it down.*

I am not saying that ancient Greek society was perfect, as no doubt a malicious interpretation of the above paragraphs will argue. It had just as many evils, injustices, and flaws as our own. They have been cataloged before, and need not be repeated here. My point is confined to an artistic and educational ideal only. Beauty is beauty, and ugly is ugly, and never the twain will meet. My point is that man needs an ideal: and it is far better for him to cast his eyes skyward, than down into the cesspool. I am not saying every person needs to be a paragon of beauty; beauty is just as much about proportion and balance as it is about allure. We can all, at least, acknowledge an ideal, and accept its truth, and aim for it as much as reasonably possible. The more one walks through the corridors of the National Archaeological Museum, the more one becomes outraged at the modern media's concerted efforts to denigrate and degrade beauty. More than ever, I am convinced that the Western media's attempts to normalize ugliness, evil, and corruption is fundamentally antisocial and destructive. It should be swept away, and replaced with an entirely different ethic.

Education must address both the mental and the physical. Despite all the lip service paid to physical fitness and conditioning, our people sink further and further into a morass of obesity and inactivity. No mental activity can be useful without an accompanying physical regimen. It was significant, I think, that the only identifiable areas preserved at Aristotle's Lyceum and at Plato's Academy were the gymnasia. Wrestling and other forms of physical activity were considered and essential part of a man's education. Can anything more be said? Meanwhile, the modern "educated man" flounces around with no strength of limb or body, unable to will his frame to great things; physical weakness goes hand-in-hand with moral and mental weakness, and they cycle of decay continues. I have known this for a long time, but my observations in Greece–

especially seeing the Lyceum and the Academy–have reinforced this lesson powerfully. Men of character and good judgment can never be created in a society that has embraced a flawed conception of education. Today, discipline and behavior have degraded; every man sees himself as his own little emperor, and cares nothing about the common good. Physical education, submission to authority, and iron discipline can cure these destructive conceits that plague us today.

I am of course not saying that every person needs to be an Olympic athlete. What I am saying is that physical fitness and conditioning should be restored as a central part of the education of the youth. We need far, far less obsessing over the "internet" and push-button convenience, and far more emphasis on getting ourselves into the sand of the palaestra, and grappling with an opponent. Unless this happens, current and future generations will not be prepared to deal with the moral, physical, and military challenges that will certainly confront them. They will collapse like a house of cards, as did all nations who neglected the health of the youth.

Greek art was much more sophisticated and subtle than I had previously appreciated. When museum pieces are seen in foreign countries, divorced from their original locus, we don't get the chance to appreciate all of their merits. But seeing all the pieces housed in the National Archaeological Museum in Athens has given me a better ability to place all these pieces in context. The weapons of the Archaic period were far more sophisticated than I had realized; the warriors of Homer's day and earlier went into battle with spear points that were much more finely engineered than I had believed possible. The metallurgical processes and the final execution of the designs were very impressive. I was also struck by the tenderness and emotional quality of the funeral stele. These, I think, are very underappreciated. On these large grave markers are placed images showing the departed shaking hands and saying goodbye to their friends and family; we see scenes of anguish, hope, and grief that show us just how much family meant to the ancients. Art was meant to enhance human life, to provide solace for the needy, and to provide an ideal to the aspirant. It was not, as now, intended to be an outlet for someone's socially destructive impulses or psychoses.

21. Xenophon's Dream, And The Power Of Character

When a man is under the duress of extreme events, he sometimes finds himself wracked by indecision. He will mull over various courses of action in his head; he will script out different scenarios in his imagination; and he will ponder his predicament from multiple perspectives. And yet, when he has finished with these troublesome cogitations, he may find a course of action still eludes him; but at some point, a moment of inspiration will arrive to pierce the gloom, and confer on him the guidance he has desperately been seeking. When this happens, he must unhesitatingly seize the present hour for action, and proceed with his rendezvous with Fate.

As a young man, the Greek professional soldier and philosopher Xenophon volunteered to participate in a military expedition raised by the Persian prince Cyrus the Younger around 401 B.C. Greek mercenaries were highly valued in those days, as they came from a respected military tradition. They were disciplined, hardy, and knew how to fight as a group. Cyrus's purpose was to seize the Persian throne, which he believed was rightfully his, from his brother Artaxerxes II. Xenophon (c. 430 B.C.–c. 354 B.C.) was an idealistic, pious young man looking for an adventure and a liege lord to serve; he had been a student and follower of the philosopher Socrates, but had latent abilities as a military commander as well. His account of the expedition to Persia, called the *Anabasis*, is one of the great works of ancient Greek literature. Xenophon speaks of himself in the third-person, but always in a modest way; his honest and intense personality shine through on nearly every page. He tells us that he did not originally plan to join the expedition:

> There was a man in the army named Xenophon, an Athenian, who was neither general nor captain nor private, but had accompanied the expedition because Proxenus, an old friend of his, had sent him at his home an invitation to go with him. Proxenus had also promised him that, if he would go, he would make him a friend of Cyrus, whom he himself regarded, so he said, as worth more to him than was his native state. [III.1.4; *Trans. by C. Brownson*]

Cyrus gathered his mercenary army, called the "Ten Thousand," and proceeded to march inland in an attempt to confront Artaxerxes. In 401 B.C. the rival armies clashed in Babylon at the Battle of Cunaxa; and although the Ten Thousand could claim victory, their leader Cyrus was slain in the melee. This reversal now rendered the purpose of their expedition moot, and the Greeks were faced with a terrible situation. They were cut off, isolated, and without adequate supplies deep in hostile territory. Artaxerxes would have preferred to have them all killed, but decided to make use of treachery. A Persian satrap named Tissaphernes lured the Greek military leadership to what was supposed to be truce talks. He then had his opponents killed or arrested, among them the Spartan general Clearchus:

> When they reached Tissaphernes's doors, the generals were invited in–Proxenus the Beootian, Menon the Thessalian, Agias the Arcadian, Clearchus the Laconian, and Socrates the Achaean–while the captains waited at the doors. Not long afterward, at the same signal, those within were seized and those outside were cut down. After this some of the barbarian horsemen rode about over the plain and killed every Greek they met, whether slave or freeman. [II.5]

When news of this secondary disaster spread among the Ten Thousand, morale hit rock bottom. The men were disconsolate; they were friendless, trapped in the middle of Asia, and had very little in the way of supplies. It is difficult for us to imagine, in this era of air power and easy access to resupply, just how isolated an army in this situation could truly be. Xenophon tells us that he, like everyone else, was unable to sleep. He pondered his current predicament over and over again. He did not know what the right course of action was. He was a young man, but was possessed of a very strong character and good judgment; Socrates's philosophical training had fortified him well for hardship. One night, in the depths of despair, he was visited by a dream. He tells us (III.1) that in his dream he saw a bolt of lightning hit his father's house and set it on fire. He then awoke suddenly; he believed he had been visited by some kind of sign from Zeus. He was not sure if the dream should be interpreted positively or negatively, but he knew something significant had happened. He describes his thoughts:

> Now what it really means to have such a dream one may learn from the events which followed the dream–and they were these: firstly, on the moment of his awakening the thought occurred to him: "Why do I lie here? The night is wearing on, and at daybreak it is likely the enemy will be upon us. And if we fall into the King's hands, what is there to prevent our living to behold all the grievous sights and to experience all the most dreadful sufferings, and then being put to death with insult?..." [III.1]

But he knew now what he must do. Xenophon called together some of the Greek captains and gave them his opinion. He told them that no one was making adequate preparations for their defense, and that the Persians would soon be attacking them. We must act now, he said, and act quickly, so that we do not become victims like the captains and generals who tried to parley with Tissaphernes. We are better men than they, he said, and the gods would be on our side:

> Besides, we have bodies more capable than theirs of bearing cold and heat and toil, and we likewise, by the blessing of the gods, have better souls; and these men are more liable than we to be wounded and killed, if the gods again, as on that former day, grant us victory...let us take the lead ourselves and arouse the rest to valor. Show yourselves the best of the captains, and more worthy to be generals than the generals themselves. As for me, if you choose to set out upon this course, I am ready to follow you; but if you assign me the leadership, I do not plead my youth as an excuse; rather, I believe I am in the very prime of my power to ward off dangers from my own head. [III.1]

What military commander today would make a point of claiming his men had "better souls" than the enemy? And yet this invocation bespoke of the power of philosophical training in forging a strong man's character; Xenophon had a great spirit, and the Socratic training of his morals and character had made it even better. Would that we had such leaders today, men imbued with idealism and piety, ready to undertake struggle and sacrifice for something greater than themselves! Xenophon tells us that all present except one were persuaded by his words. This man, named Apollonides, was a negative defeatist. He went on and on about how their situation was hopeless, and that they should try to make more efforts to talk to Artaxerxes and negotiate some kind of surrender. Xenophon cut him off sharply. He chided Apollonides, telling him that the dead Greek captains and generals had already tried that course, and it had gained nothing except their ignominious deaths. And the Greeks who had been taken alive, he said, were they not at this precise moment being tortured and degraded by Tissaphernes's men? Xenophon mocked his opponent, calling him unfit for command, as well as an effeminate disgrace; Apollonides eventually scuttled away in shame.

This was how Xenophon managed to assume a leadership position in the army of the Ten Thousand. The army went on to endure an incredible number of trials, escapes, adventures, and fighting retreats as it made its way back to friendly territory. As we have already noted, Xenophon was not originally a professional military man; before joining the expedition he seems to have had little or no practical military experience. As Sir Francis Bacon says, in his essay *Of The True Greatness of Kingdoms and Estates:*

> Walled towns, stored arsenals and armouries, goodly races of horse, chariots of war, elephants, ordnance, artillery, and the like: all this is but a sheep in lion's skin, except the breed and disposition of the people be stout and warlike...Neither is money the sinews of war (as it is trivially said), where the sinews of men's arms, in base and effeminate people, are failing.

That is, weapons and provisions are illusions, and do not make a man or a people strong: only strong character can do this. Yet hardship has a way of raising up men of good character to leadership positions. During times of peace and quiescence, men of great character and leadership ability are often passed over or hidden away. Their talents and abilities are rarely appreciated by those who know only comfort and security. When we neglect men of talent, character, and masculine virtue, and exalt the incapable, the corrupt, the venal, and the incompetent, we put our very security at risk. But in times of crisis, everything can change. The situation selects the man; and the man masters the situation through force of will.

22. On Idle Or Trifling Speech

There are some who say that idle talk has no purpose, and should be avoided. Yet in many cases it serves valuable purposes: it enables us to test ideas or plans on our friends, and solicit their opinions; it enables us to relieve stress; and it enables us to pass the time in conversational pleasantry. Not every dialogue needs to have a definite purpose; sometimes the exchange of words themselves becomes a form of relaxation. The exchange below is taken verbatim from James Boswell's famous *Life of Samuel Johnson*. In the short dialogue between himself and his biographer, Johnson, that great man of English letters, makes the point that it may be well to make idle speech, as long as one does not unduly subscribe to its banalities:

> Boswell. "I wish much to be in Parliament, sir."
>
> Johnson. "Why, sir, unless you come resolved to support any administration, you would be in the worse for being in Parliament, because you would be obliged to live more expensively."
>
> Boswell. "Perhaps, sir, I should be the less happy for being in Parliament. I never would sell my vote, and I should be vexed if things went wrong."
>
> Johnson. "That's cant, sir. It would not vex you more in the house than in the gallery: public affairs vex no man."
>
> Boswell. "Have not they vexed yourself a little, sir? Have not you been vexed by all the turbulence of this reign, and by that absurd vote of the House of Commons, 'That the influence of the Crown has

> increased, is increasing, and ought to be diminished?'"
>
> Johnson. "Sir, I have never slept an hour less, nor eat an ounce less meat. I would have knocked the factious dogs on the head, to be sure; but I was not vexed."
>
> Boswell. "I declare, sir, upon my honor, I did imagine I was vexed, and took a pride in it; but it was, perhaps, cant; for I own I neither ate less, nor slept less."
>
> Johnson. "My dear friend, clear your mind of cant. You may talk as other people do; you may say to a man, 'Sir, I am your most humble servant.' You are not his most humble servant. You may say, 'These are bad times; it is a melancholy thing to be reserved to such times.' You don't mind the times. You tell a man, 'I am sorry you had such bad weather the last day of your journey, and were so much wet.' You don't care sixpence whether his is wet or dry. You may talk in this matter; it is a mode of talking in society: but don't think foolishly."

The point, of course, is that social pleasantries must be kept in their place, and not allowed to contaminate the lucidity of judgment. And yet is important to master the art of small talk; one cannot aspire to large talk unless one has first mastered its lesser cousin. An excess of either type of talk unbalances a man: too much idle talk, and he becomes an irritant; too much grand talk, and he takes on the aspect of an eccentric social outcast. Along these same lines, there is a charming anecdote Boswell tells of a chance meeting between Dr. Johnson and one of his old school classmates. The two men had not seen each other in about forty years. Boswell relates the tale, and reflects on its poignant conclusion:

> And now [April 17th, 1778] I am to give a pretty full account of one of the most curious incidents in Johnson's life, of which he himself has made the following minute on this day. 'In my return from church, I was accosted by Edwards, an old fellow-collegian, who had not seen me since 1729. He knew

me, and asked if I remembered one Edwards; I did not at first recollect the name, but gradually as we walked along, recovered it, and told him a conversation that had passed at an ale-house between us. My purpose is to continue our acquaintance…'

Edwards. "Ah, sir! We are old men now."

Johnson (who never liked to think of being old). "Don't let us discourage one another."

Edwards. "Why, Doctor, you look stout and hearty, I am happy to see you so; for the newspapers told us you were very ill."

Johnson. "Aye, sir, they are always telling lies of us *old fellows*."

Wishing to be present at more of so singular a conversation as that between two fellow-collegians, who had lived forty years in London without ever having chanced to meet, I whispered to Mr. Edwards that Dr. Johnson was going home, and that he had better accompany him now. So Edwards walked along with us, I eagerly assisting to keep up the conversation…When we got to Dr. Johnson's house, and were seated in his library, the dialogue went on admirably.

Edwards. "Sir, I remember you would not let us say *prodigious* at College. For even then, sir, (turning to me), he was delicate in language, and we all feared him."

Johnson (to Edwards). "From your having practiced the law so long, sir, I presume you must be rich."

Edwards. "No, sir, I got a good deal of money; but I had a number of poor relations to whom I gave a great part of it."

Johnson. "Sir, you have then been rich in the most valuable sense of the word."

Edwards. "But I shall not die rich."

Johnson. "Nay, sure, sir, it is better to *live* rich than to *die* rich."

Edwards. "You are a philosopher, Dr. Johnson. I have tried too in my time to be a philosopher; but,

> I don't know how, cheerfulness was always breaking in."
>
> This interview confirmed my opinion of Johnson's most humane and benevolent heart. His cordial and placid behavior to an old fellow-collegian, a man so different from himself; and his telling him that he would go down on his farm and visit him, showed a kindness of disposition very rare at an advanced age…
>
> Edwards walked off, seemingly highly pleased with the honor of having been thus noticed by Dr. Johnson. When he was gone, I said to Johnson, I thought him but a weak man. [Johnson replied] "Why yes, sir. Here is a man who has passed through life without experience: yet I would rather have him with me than a more sensible man who will not talk readily. This man is always willing to say what he has to say."

It is not necessary always to speak of weighty matters. Sometimes there is more value to be had in a conversation that centers on pointless trivia. It seems to me, from reflecting on these anecdotes about Dr. Johnson, that it is better for our well-being to seek out associates who have something pleasant and constructive to say for themselves, rather than spend our time with those who are branded with perpetual scowls. There is no need to pass judgment on all things, or pronounce a verdict on every question. There is wisdom in levity, and longevity in lightheartedness. Cant has its uses; so let us use it in good health.

23. The Liberation Of The Mind

From birth we are surrounded by the inherited and imposed belief systems of our environment. Such systems exert a silent force on our thinking; they channel our behaviors within defined limits, and demarcate the boundaries of conventional thought. They can become so pervasive that they escape even our own notice. We should not necessarily see this as an evil, for custom and tradition provide, on balance, a certain predictability and stability that makes for civilized leisure and artistic creation; and society must have some immovable foundation upon which to direct its spires skyward.

And yet this same predictability and permanence can easily stifle the creative individual. He who wishes to explore, create, and seek the answers to important questions will find that he needs to activate his mind in unconventional ways. For him the inherited wisdom is an intellectual prison; he must burst through the barriers imposed by orthodoxy, and hack his way through the jungles of the Unknown. He craves a mission, a purpose, and some kind of divine spark to energize his quest. He must throw off the shackles of the old ways of thinking, and strike out in new directions. He must dare to go down unmapped roads, and navigate the boiling seas of Uncertainty. He must be prepared to endure the mockery and derision of those who would belittle his efforts. But how does such a creative person come to this realization? What strikes the match of the divine fire? Does the conversion experience happen at once, in a flash, or is it an incremental process that takes place over a long period of time?

It seems to me that there is an interaction between two things: (1) a constant process of seeking and searching, that can take place over a long period; and (2) a more sudden "spark" that stirs the soul of the creative thinker, and lights his inner fire. Both of these things go hand-in-hand, and we do not see one without the other. Consider the example of that distinguished writer and reformer, Frederick Douglass, who faced the nearly insurmountable challenges of overcoming both mental and physical bondage. Most men can barely handle the servitude of the mind; but Douglass had also to contend with being physically imprisoned in an unjust system over which he had no control. In his 1855 memoir *My Bondage and My Freedom*, he credits his mother with instilling in him an early thirst for knowledge:

> I can, therefore, fondly and proudly ascribe to her an earnest love of knowledge…I am quite willing, and even happy, to attribute any love of letters I possess, and for which I have got–despite of prejudices–only too much credit…to the native genius of my sable, unprotected, and uncultivated mother…

But learning and knowledge were forbidden to him. He had to acquire literacy on his own, by copying letters and words from dictionaries, and by talking to whomever he could find. But his discovery that he was trapped fed his iron determination to win his freedom at any cost.

> When I was about thirteen years old, and had succeeded in learning to read, every increase of knowledge...added something to the almost intolerable burden of the thought, "I am a slave for life." To my bondage I saw no end. It was a terrible reality, and I shall never be able to tell how sadly that thought chafed my young spirit. Fortunately, or unfortunately, about this time in my life, I had made enough money to buy what was then a very popular school book, viz: the "Columbian Orator"...This volume was, indeed, a rich treasure, and every opportunity afforded me, for a time, was spent in diligently perusing it.

His unrelenting efforts led him to see the possibilities that the world offered him; he began to see that, if he could only escape the confinements of his present condition, he would have a chance to develop the qualities with which Nature and Reason had endowed him. The reader of his memoirs gets the impression that Douglass would never have attempted physical escape had he not first been able to liberate his mind from the pernicious beliefs that surrounded him on every side. This fact made him acutely aware of how systems of oppression operate and are sustained. The following passage should be read and reflected on by anyone trying to understand the servitude of the mind, and the abject breaking of the spirit:

> To make a contented slave, you must make a thoughtless one. It is necessary to darken his moral and mental vision, and, as far as possible, to annihilate his power of reason. He must be able to detect no inconsistencies in slavery. The man that takes his earnings, must be able to convince him that he has a perfect right to do so. It must not depend upon mere force; the slave must know no Higher Law than his

> master's will. The whole relationship must not only demonstrate, to his mind, its necessity, but its absolute rightfulness. If there be one crevice through which a single drop can fall, it will certainly rust off the slave's chain.

The converse truth of the last sentence above is that *if one drop of shining truth can fall up on a man's mental chains, he can begin the process of the liberation of his consciousness*. Another example of the unblocking of the mind is afforded by one of the most influential names in Islamic theology, Al-Ghazali. His full name was Abu Hamid Muhammad Ibn Muhammad Al-Ghazali (أبو حامد محمد بن محمد الغزالي) and he lived from about 1058 to 1111. One of his most famous works is a confessional treatise entitled *The Deliverance from Error* (المنقذ من الضلال); it is an intense self-examination of how the author was able to free his mind from what he believed was "error" and renew his faith in his life's purpose. What strikes the reader of Al-Ghazali's testament is its fervent sincerity; not since St. Augustine has an author so candidly revealed his faith. His profession was originally that of a teacher and scholar; but at some point, he suffered some kind of personal crisis that made him physically ill. He was unable to concentrate on his work, and lost faith in his personal direction. Finally, after an extended period of self-examination, he recovered himself, and undertook a new direction with a passionate sense of purpose:

> I remained for some little time speechless. Then the difficulty appeared to resemble the problem of sleep. I told myself that when one is asleep one believes all sorts of things and finds oneself in all sorts of situations; one believes in them absolutely, without the slightest doubt. When one wakes up, one realizes the inconsistency and inanity of the phantasms of the imagination. In the same way, one might ask oneself about the reality of beliefs one has acquired through one's senses or by reason. Could one not imagine oneself in a state which compares to being awake, just as wakefulness compares to being asleep?...My disease grew worse and lasted

> almost two months, during which I fell prey to skepticism, though neither in theory nor in outward expression. At last, God the Almighty cured me of that disease and I recovered my health and mental equilibrium. The self-evident principles of reason again seemed acceptable; I trusted them and in them felt safe and certain...To sum up, know that in the quest for truth one must strive for perfection, even to the point of seeking the unseekable. Primary truths have no need of being sought because they are present in the mind. What is present will disappear if you seek it, but one who seeks the unseekable will not be suspected of negligence in seeking what can be sought. [*Trans. by M. Abulaylah*]

To seek the unseekable: this ethic, perhaps, best encapsulates the process of mental liberation. There must be an ongoing, constant thirst for knowledge, a constant questioning of inherited beliefs, combined at some point with a spark that triggers a personal revelation. With some, the revelation of seeing the world in a different way arrives more suddenly. Anton van Leeuwenhoek was a self-taught Dutch businessman and amateur scientist who lived from 1632 to 1723. Living to the age of ninety-one, he spent forty of those years absorbed in scientific research. He came from a family of brewers in Delft; perhaps his observations of beer fermentation stimulated his curiosity about micro-organisms. Science was a hobby that became an all-consuming passion for him at some point in his adulthood; most of his 247 microscopes he made with his own hands. Leeuwenhoek's moment of revelation came in 1675 when, purely out of curiosity, he happened to examine a few drops of rain water that had collected in a pot a few days earlier. He was shocked to find the water swarming with micro-organisms, which he called "animalcules." Further investigation of other substances (e.g., saliva, semen, etc.) revealed an entirely unknown arena of life.

A similar episode of mental liberation came with physicist Max Planck's desperate attempt to find a mathematical model that would match his laboratory observations. The only way he could make the data "fit" the observations was to propose a radically new conception: the idea that light could only be emitted in distinct packets, or increments, which he called quanta. Herein lies the foundational observation and principle of quantum physics. It is not only scientists who experience such moments of inspiration, of course. I would be remiss not to mention here the English philosopher Thomas Hobbes's discovery of geometry. We are told that he once found a copy of Euclid's *Elements* lying open on a desk; what he saw fascinated him, and led him to work his way backwards in the book to the initial propositions. He was deeply impressed with geometry's logical structure and infallible reasoning, and longed to bring this way of thinking to philosophy. And should we not here mention Rene Descartes's observations of flies crawling around on his ceiling as he lay in bed sick as a young man, and how these observations caused him to speculate on mathematical models that might describe their movements?

But moments of inspiration are mirrored by moments of closure. There are some creative minds that suddenly shut down, perhaps under the influence of trauma or disillusionment. The Dutch scientist Jan Swammerdam (1637–1680) had an early period of productivity, then apparently burned himself out after completing a treatise on bees in 1673. He thereafter found comfort and renewed purpose in religious work. We may conclude from all these examples that the liberation of the mind takes place along two dimensions: *first*, there is a continuous, probing search for truth that can last for years; *second*; there is some kind of triggering spark that sets off a moment of revelation. Mental liberation is not a permanent end-state; it must be renewed and refurbished continually, as the mind easily slips into comfortable grooves and patterns, rejecting contradictory stimuli. Man begins his quest for freedom from the cradle, and it ceases only with the grave.

24. Ictus Animi: The Smiting Of The Mind

We are unlikely to arrive at any awareness of things while sitting within the confines of our domestic barricades. Enlightenment requires perception; perception, sensory input; and sensory input, direct experience with the world of the living outside our familiar habitations. The leisure of contemplation, and the enticements of philosophical reflection, allow for the refinement and processing of these experiences, but cannot serve as a direct substitute for them;

and unlucky is he who deludes himself into believing he has arrived at weighty insights from the contemplation of the four walls around him.

In one of his letters (*Epistulae* LVII), Seneca describes a trip he made from Baiae to the Naples. Baiae is gone now, having been reclaimed by the sea and the elements; but in Seneca's day it was a resort town for the wealthy on the north coast of the Bay of Naples. Seneca was thinking of making the trip by sea, which would have been faster and less arduous than an excursion by land. But he decided to travel by road instead, believing that a storm would be rolling in from offshore. The trip turned out to be an unpleasant one, leaving the philosopher covered in mud and dust; but this direct experience (literally "down in the mud") turned out to be a moment of revelation for him.

He wrote that "This darkness in fact gave me something that I might reflect on. I sensed something of an impact to my consciousness, and a conversion in thought without trepidation, which the novelty of this new experience and its filthiness had made (*Aliquid tamen mihi illa obscuritas, quod cogitarem, dedit; sensi quendam ictum animi et sine metu mutationem, quam insolitae rei novitas simul ac foeditas fecerat*)." It is no accident that Seneca chose to use the word *ictus* in this sentence: the word means a blow or a strike, which is a strong word to use for a moment of mental revelation. The experience of being down in the mud and the grime literally "smote his mind" (*sensi quendam ictum animi*) and pushed him into a new level of comprehension of his world. This *ictus animi*–this "smiting of the mind"–is what direct experience does to the consciousness.

And what was it that he became aware of? He says that became aware that it is absurd for us to fear the magnitude of the disasters that may befall us. Whether we are harmed by a tremendous force, or a force not so tremendous, the end result is the same: we are still being harmed. To use an analogy I remember from Cicero's *On Moral Ends*, a man who drowns in three feet of water is just as dead as the man who drowns at the bottom of the sea. In this example I am using, it is not so important just what lesson he learned from it; what is important is that he learned something by direct experience. He would have never had such a moment of insight had he kept himself locked away in a country villa. Isolation is for the processing and digestion of new experience; it is not for the generation of a new experience. Griminess and filthiness are essential ingredients of insight.

This is why, it seems to me, that a man should seek an environment where such experiences and stimuli can be found. Dr. Samuel Johnson, that eminent man of letters, always believed it was better for him to live in London, than to waste away his years stuffed in some book-lined cottage in, say, Cornwall. He wanted to be where the action was; he needed to walk the busy streets, to converse with friends and acquaintances, and to go out drinking and tavern-exploring until the early morning hours. This would not have been possible anywhere else. And what of human interactions? How can any knowledge of anything come to us when we are isolated? Do you really think that you can do everything yourself? Are you that strong, and that self-sufficient, that you do not need to make new friendships, or refresh old ones? It is our friends, and our intimate companions, who inspire us to continue the race of life; it is they who have the power to encourage us, or discourage us, as the case may be. Doomed is he who has no one to inspire him, and no one to encourage him. *O my brother, show me who you are, and who you could have been, if only someone had believed in you.*

I should say a few words on the subject of friendship, since it is a topic that the ancient writers love to dwell on. Perhaps I should use the word "deify," since some of them treat friendship as if it were some kind of "end state" that a man arrives at, and is then finished. Some–not all–of them make it appear that friendship is a static, fixed state, rather than the dynamic, fluid process that it really is. This is why I believe Dr. Johnson's views on the dynamic nature of friendship were more wise than the views of many other writers. Boswell tells us more in this regard:

> I have often thought, that as longevity is generally desired, and, I believe, generally expected, it would be wise to be continually adding to the number of our friends, that the loss of some may be supplied by others. Friendship, the "wine of life," should, like a well-stocked cellar, be thus continually renewed; and it is consolatory to think, that although we can seldom add what will equal the generous first-growths of our youth, yet friendship becomes insensibly old much less time than is commonly imagined,

> and not many years are required to make it very mellow and pleasant…

Men of affectionate temper and bright fancy will coalesce a great deal sooner than those who are cold and dull. The proposition which I have now endeavored to illustrate was, at a subsequent period of his life, the opinion of Johnson himself. He said to Sir Joshua Reynolds, "If a man does not make new acquaintance as he advances through life, he will soon find himself left alone. A man, Sir, should keep his friendship in constant repair."

No reasonable person can doubt, I think, the truth of these observations. And yet too often we slip into our self-imposed ruts, our routines that we believe are so important. Meeting new people, extending our hand to someone new, feels like an unwelcome imposition; for we cherish our comfort more than we do our health. Instead of traveling by boat, for example, we should, like mud-splattered Seneca, try for once to travel by land: the change in routine will do us good, and will be source of mental revelations. And since we are on the topic of friendships and new acquaintances, we can do no better than to relate the memorable first meeting between Dr. Johnson and his genial biographer, James Boswell. The meeting took place on May 16, 1763; Johnson was fifty-four years of age, Boswell only twenty-three. The pronounced age gap between them turned out to be an advantage, not a handicap; Johnson drew vigor from the younger man's vitality, and Boswell profited much from his mentor's wisdom. Boswell had long been an admirer of the older man's brilliant literary output, and longed to meet him. Yet he also felt some trepidation at approaching the great man, knowing Johnson had a formidable reputation for brusqueness. Like many public figures, he cultivated a somewhat blunt demeanor in order to keep the riff-raff at bay. Finally, Boswell found himself in a place where he would cross paths with his hero:

> At last, on Monday the 16th of May, when I was sitting in Mr. Davies's back-parlour, after having drunk tea with him and Mrs. Davies, Johnson unexpectedly came into the shop, and Mr. Davies having perceived from through the glass-door in the room in which we were sitting, advancing towards us, he announced his aweful approach to me…Mr. Davies

mentioned my name, and respectfully introduced me to him...I was much agitated; and recollecting his prejudice against the Scotch, of which I had heard much, I said to Davies, "Don't tell where I come from." [But Mr. Davies told Johnson this anyway, perhaps to have some sport with the younger man!]...

"Mr. Johnson (said I) I do indeed come from Scotland, but I cannot help it." I am willing to flatter myself that I meant this as light pleasantry to sooth and conciliate him, and not as an humiliating abasement at the expense of my country. But however that might be, this speech was somewhat unlucky; for with that quickness of wit for which he was so remarkable, he seized the expression, "come from Scotland," which I used in the sense of being from that country, and, as if I had said that I had come away from it, or left it, he retorted, "That, Sir, I find, is what a great many of your countrymen cannot help." This stroke stunned me a good deal; and when we had sat down, I felt myself not a little embarrassed, and apprehensive of what might come next...

I had, for a part of the evening, been left alone with him, and had ventured to make an observation now and then, which he received very civilly; so that I was satisfied that though there was a roughness in his manner, there was no ill-nature in his disposition. Davies followed me to the door, and when I complained to him a little of the hard blows which the great man had given me, he kindly took upon him to console me by saying, "Don't be uneasy. I can see that he likes you very well."

Johnson must have had, later that evening, a good laugh at the younger man's discomfort! But this is how it should be; the walls of friendship should not be so easily scaled. So began one of the most memorable, and fruitful, friendships in the history of English letters. Boswell went on to record every detail, every anecdote, and every piece of correspondence he could find on Johnson. His book is over one thousand pages long; but such is the vividness of his portrait, and the richness of his observations, that I will very much regret the day I finish it. They even traveled to the Hebrides together. And it all began on that one day in May of 1763. Had Boswell been the kind of man who liked to lock himself away in his attic, he would never have enjoyed the experiences he did, and literature would have been much more the worse for it.

If we wish to accomplish anything useful with our lives, we must shatter our old routines. And perhaps it is not just the routine that must be shattered: our own consciousness must be hit by that *ictus animi* of Seneca which I mentioned earlier. Seek out, and welcome, *ictus animi*. We must force ourselves out of the ruts and grooves of habit, and immerse ourselves in the redemptive springs of novel experience. The sledgehammer of reality always smashes the ethereal ice-sculptures of theory. The man alone, the man isolated in his hovel, can very easily convince himself of the superlative nature of his abilities: but unless these claims are tested in the world's fiery kilns and well-pounded anvils, and unless they can survive immersion in life's mud and grime, they will remain nothing but comfortable and pernicious delusions.

25. The Right To Evolve

Anyone who has ever cleaned out his basement or attic has certainly come across writings or photos from earlier years. We are likely to wince upon reading things we wrote ten, fifteen, or twenty years ago, to the same degree that we shake our heads in bewilderment at seeing old photos of ourselves. This is because our minds, and our consciousness, does not remain fixed and unmoved as we age; they are not like the Rock of Gibraltar. The things we believe when we were younger are not going to be the same things we believe as we get older. This is natural and predictable; only a fool would refuse to change his views as he aggregates years and worldly experience. This was the sentiment expressed by Dr. Samuel Johnson one evening in 1766, when he was fifty-seven years of age. Boswell, as always, reliably tells us the tale:

> Another evening Dr. [Samuel] Goldsmith and I called on him, with the hope of prevailing on him to

> sup with us at the Mitre. We found him indisposed, and resolved not to go abroad. "Come then, (said Goldsmith) we will not go to the Mitre to-night, since we cannot have the big man with us." Johnson then called for a bottle of port, of which Goldsmith and I partook, while our friend, now a water-drinker, sat by us. GOLDSMITH. "I think, Mr. Johnson, you don't go to the theatres now. You give yourself no more concern about a new play, than if you had never had any thing to do with the stage." JOHNSON. "Why, Sir, our tastes greatly alter. The lad does not care for the child's rattle, and the old man does not care for the young man's whore." GOLDSMITH. "Nay, Sir, but your Muse was not a whore." JOHNSON. "Sir, I do not think she was. But as we advance in the journey of life, we drop some of the things which have pleased us; whether it be that we are fatigued and don't choose to carry so many things any farther, or that we find other things which we like better."
>
> BOSWELL. "But, Sir, why don't you give us something in some other way?" GOLDSMITH. "Aye, Sir, we have a claim upon you." JOHNSON. "No, Sir, I am not obliged to do any more. No man is obliged to do as much as he can do. A man is to have part of his life to himself. If a soldier has fought a good many campaigns, he is not to be blamed if he retires to ease and tranquility. A physician, who has practiced long in a great city, may be excused if he retires to a small town, and takes less practice. Now, Sir, the good I can do by my conversation bears the same proportion to the good I can do by my writings, that the practice of a physician, retired to a small town, does to his practice in a great city." BOSWELL. "But I wonder, Sir, you have not more pleasure in writing than in not writing." JOHNSON. "Sir, you *may* wonder."

And of course the meaning of this delightful exchange is that we must be permitted to evolve, to grow, and to change our tastes.

One of the obstacles, perhaps hinted at in the preceding anecdote, are our friends, acquaintances, and society at large; the human mind likes nothing more than categorizing everything into neat boxes, and views with discomfort the idea that something safely classified may jump out of its imposed box. Those who know us do not really welcome our changes. Such evolution causes them to examine their own views and opinions, with results that may be distinctly unpleasant. The rock planted in the stream resents the waters that swirl by it. Yet all the best men make an effort to take stock in their own views every so often, to see if their opinions have stood the tests of time and experience.

The greatest men have been those who, while retaining a bedrock of unshakeable principles, still retain the ability to evolve. Their thinking has not ossified; their sentiments have not calcified into wearisome predictability. One of the best examples of this, as I see it, is Abraham Lincoln. One can never get enough of him; we constantly marvel at his near perfect balance of humanity, political acumen, and measured deliberation. Here was a man who was able to evolve over time, and grow into greatness. I have read several biographies of him lately, and each one has reinforced this point for me. Eric Foner's *The Fiery Trial: Abraham Lincoln and American Slavery* carefully traces the evolution of Lincoln's opinions on slavery, from his days as a young lawyer in the 1830s and 1840s, to the very end of his life. He always hated the institution, from the moment he happened to see slaves being transported on the Mississippi to New Orleans when a young man, but like many Americans he was not sure what to do about it. The problem was just too entrenched, the obstacles just too insurmountable.

Yet he retained a bedrock set of beliefs that served him well until he had the opportunity to make changes. His first impulses were to push for containment of the institution; and when circumstances created different realities, he responded to those as he felt necessary. Lincoln's impulse was to try to seek the middle ground on controversial issues; he disliked extremists of any type, believing that the best course usually was the path of moderation. But when faced with challenges that presented a threat to his basic, core principles, he never hesitated to act, and to act with resolution. This was Lincoln's way. Donald T. Phillips's *Lincoln on Leadership* speculates how Lincoln might respond to the challenges that the United States faces today: that is, the problems of foreign wars, health care, environmental issues, corruption in politics, and other issues. Drawing logical conclusions from the president's words–as found in speeches, conversations, and letters–the author convincingly shows how Lincoln would have remained true to a positive, optimistic view of humanity, while trying to seek a healthy middle ground between competing extremes. And when this stance was no longer feasible, he would not have hesitated to take decisive action to enforce the responsibilities of office.

The need to evolve in all aspects of our lives is a prerogative of existence. We cannot stay in place while the world changes around us. It has always been so; but today the need to define, and redefine, ourselves to the outside world seems more urgent than ever. Technology loves nothing more than to pigeon-hole everything, including us. The right to evolve is just that, *a right*: and rights that are not exercised are lost. One may ask, "How will I know when it is time to change my beliefs, or to reexamine my beliefs?" While there is not a single correct answer to this question, I have an idea about it that has proven useful for me. It is this: *if the original premises upon which our opinion is based have changed, then it is time for us to reexamine our opinion.* If we do not do so, we run the risk of having opinions that are based on wishful thinking or outright fantasy, rather than on reality.

26. The Sirens Seduced Not With Song, But With The Prospect Of Knowledge

Many readers, no doubt, have heard the Homeric fable about the Sirens. These were the alluring mythical creatures who, by using their advanced powers of song, were able to divert mariners who happened to sail by the rocks they inhabited in the Mediterranean Sea. Their voices were supposed to be so seductive that sailors could not resist them; and when they approached the Sirens' rocks to get a better look, they ran aground and were destroyed. This, at least, is what the Greek mythologists have told us. The Sirens most famously appear in the *Odyssey* (XII.180–200). Odysseus and his men sail by the Sirens' rocks, and the creatures–part female, part avian–call out to them, imploring them to come closer. Odysseus knows that no man can resist their temptations, so he orders his men to seal their ears, and has himself lashed to the ship's mast. He wants to hear the song of the Sirens, no matter what. The impression we are given is that there is a strong erotic element associated with the Sirens: perhaps they are meant to symbolize the temptations and perils that carnal pleasures represent for man. I think there is much to be said for this interpretation; and I had never heard of any other.

But our iconoclastic friend Cicero offers his own intriguing interpretation of what the Sirens and their songs really are meant to symbolize. His views are found in V.48–V.49 of *On Moral Ends*. And the more I have thought about his interpretation, the more I find it compelling. Cicero notes that man has an instinctive love for knowledge. He will put himself through all sorts of agonies to expand his awareness, increase his store of learning, and seek the causes behind things. It is, he tells us, part of what Nature has conferred on human beings to distinguish them from the unreasoning beasts. In the passage below, which is taken from my translation of *On Moral Ends* (V.49), Cicero provides us additional explanation:

> It seems to me that the poet Homer had something like this in mind when he imagined the songs of the Sirens. For it appears that it was neither the seductiveness of their voices, nor the uniqueness and variety of their singing, that used to divert unwary mariners; rather, it was because they claimed to have *a storehouse of special knowledge*. It was man's lust for learning that caused him to become ensnared by the Sirens' fateful rocks. This is how they called out to Ulysses (I have translated these relevant verses below, as well as others):
>
> *O Ulysses, great man of Argos, will you turn your ship*
> *And your ears, so that you can learn our sacred songs?*
> *For no one has ever passed through this blue-watered causeway*
> *Who could not first linger, held in rapture by our sweet voices,*
> *And having then satisfied his eager soul with all kinds of special music,*

> *Sail away much wiser back to his homeland's shores.*
> *We know well the dark truth of conflict and the devastation of war*
> *That the Greeks brought to Troy by divine command,*
> *And the secrets of all things manifested on this earth.*
>
> Evidently Homer saw that if a man could be mortally ensnared by some middling song, his fable would not be accepted. The Sirens are promising knowledge; and it is no wonder that this would be more precious to a lover of wisdom than his own country. To wish to know everything under the sun, with no regard for boundaries, is to wish to be counted among the meddlesome; but to be guided by the contemplation of great ideas to a genuine love of knowledge must be recognized as a mark of the greatest of men.

Cicero here is telling us that it was the tantalizing prospect of *special knowledge* that the Sirens dangled over the heads of the unwary, not the temptations of music or sex. *Man risks death for wisdom, not for enchanting songs.* Read the last sentence again in the quote above: "To wish to know everything under the sun, with no regard for boundaries, is to wish to be counted among the meddlesome; but to be guided by the contemplation of great ideas to a genuine love of knowledge must be recognized as a mark of the greatest of men." Is this not a sublime idea? Is this not a beautiful conception? I find it so.

Can anyone doubt the truth of his interpretation of the fable of the Sirens? I like his interpretation because it reminds us of an important truth about ourselves: *the idea that the man of action is driven by seek knowledge at all costs*. We read of many examples of those who have risked their health or lives for knowledge. Explorers, scientists, philosophers, and seekers of all types have gone to the far reaches of the globe in search of hidden, special knowledge. There must be something deep within us that causes us to do this; we will not go to such lengths for the sake of sensory delights. I remember learning an Arabic proverb some years ago: اطلب العلم و لو في صين, and this means, "Seek knowledge, even though it be in China." I do not know who actually said this, and for my purposes here, its origin is not important. I do not want to get into debates on authentic or false Hadiths, since such matters are beyond my knowledge. The point is that *someone* said it *somewhere*, and that it encapsulates a truth about human nature.

But to return to our topic. I like Cicero's interpretation of the song of the Sirens because it reminds us that man, for all his faults and foibles, was made for greater things than sensory delights. Physical pleasures are fine, when taken in moderation, but we have been granted special gifts by Nature that mark us out for nobler purposes. It is knowledge that we seek, and knowledge that we will risk our lives for. It is just as the French philosopher Blaise Pascal said, many centuries later: man's nobility comes from his *awareness* of things, even of his own suffering and death. The universe is passive, apathetic, and cold; and even if man happens to be destroyed by the universe, its victory will still be nothing in comparison to the greatness of man's persistence in the face of mortal harm. For man will *know* he is dying; but of its victory, the unthinking universe will forever remain unaware.

27. Avoiding Irritating Habits In Conversation

We are all acquainted with those people who have not sense enough to keep a conversation flowing smoothly. They have never been taught the conversational arts; they have nothing of consequence to talk about; and they try to compensate for these deficiencies by taxing the patience of their interlocutors. I have noticed a sharp rise in such boorish behavior in recent years; and it shows every indication of continuing its upward trend. I felt motivated to write a few lines on this subject, if for no other reason than to record my own displeasure.

Let us first deal with the up-talker. This is the person who can find no other way to end his sentences but with a rising vocal intonation. It was a speech habit once confined to young girls, and seems to have originated in southern California; but it is everywhere now, and has even captivated the minds of many younger men. I find it inexcusably effeminate in a man. Beyond this, it is an intrusive, aggressive, and discourteous form of speech: for it forces the other participant constantly to register his agreement to nearly every sentence he hears. The up-talking lilt at the end of every idea forces you to keep repeating, "Yes," or "Yeah," or "Hmm-hmm," over and over again. You are being shanghaied into participating in a dance you want no part of. This is why I call it rude and discourteous. The best way to deal with this sort of thing is to make no response at all. When the up-talker addressing you hits his bell-ringing lilt at the end of his idea, just look at him with an emotionless stare. Do not join in the charade. You are not obligated to humor his or her narcissistic preening.

The other irritating conversational habit that is enjoying a renaissance is the "conversationalist" who thinks he has the right to pepper you with staccato questions, one after the other. To him, grilling is dialogue. He does not understand that a conversation is like a dance: both parties must have something to offer, and both must be trained in the art of the dialogue. At times one man may lead; and at times another party may lead. It is a human interaction, one that arises out of a shared sense of respect and obligation. I think the Roman rhetorician Fronto said it best in a letter to the emperor Marcus Aurelius around A.D. 140:

> Unless discourse is adorned with seriousness of speech, it becomes openly impudent and shameless. [*Oratio nisi gravitate verborum honestatur, fit plane impudens atque impudica.*]

And this is certainly true. There are some people whose idea of a dialogue is to rattle off a series of vague questions, and then wrap up the sentiment with a one-word question like "Thoughts?" As if you are obligated to write a book report, or give a lecture, to him in response! It is a demanding, presumptuous pattern of behavior that springs from a lack of appreciation of the art of conversation. There is something seriously wrong with the sense of boundaries and social calibration that some people have; you almost feel mugged by their streams of verbiage. Rapid-fire questions are not conversation. A man feels put-upon, or put to the question, so to speak. This is exactly what Samuel Johnson meant when he exploded in anger one evening at one of his guests in London in 1778. His biographer James Boswell tells us the anecdote:

> He sometimes could not bear being teazed [i.e., pestered] with questions. I was once present when a gentleman asked so many as, "What did you do, Sir?" "What did you say, Sir?" that at last he grew enraged and said, "I will not be put to the *question.* Don't you consider, Sir, that these are not the manners of a gentleman? I will not be baited with *what*, and *why*. What is *this*? What is *that*? Why is a cow's tail long? Why is a fox's tail bushy?" The gentleman, who was a good deal out of countenance, said, "Why, Sir, you are so good, that I venture to trouble you." JOHNSON. "Sir, my being so *good* is no reason why you should *be so ill.*

I laughed out loud when I first read this. After seven hundred pages of Boswell, I felt almost as if I knew Dr. Johnson personally, and was one of his dinner-companions. I could understand his frustration and anger at being *put to the question.* We must be on our guard never to do this to a conversation partner. There is a right way, and a wrong way, to be a good participant in a dialogue. There is nothing wrong with asking questions, I want to emphasize. None of this should be interpreted as discouraging a person from asking sincere questions in pursuit of knowledge. It is just that it has to be done courteously. Plutarch, in his essay *On Listening*, said:

> Expressing approval, to be appropriate, also calls for care: the mean must be found, because too much or too little approval are both crass. A person who greets everything that is said with obdurate impassivity is a contemptible nuisance in the audience: he oozes hollow conceit and the deep-rooted self-aggrandizement of assuming he could improve on what is being said…[*On Listening* 13; *Trans. by R. Waterfield*]

So we must find a way of guiding the conversation forward, without seeming to be too imposing or intrusive. It is an art that can only be acquired with practice; and it takes a considerate, good-mannered person to carry it through. To be a good conversationalist, one should first strive to be a decent person. We do not need to be eloquent; it is a nice adornment if we can do it, but it is not necessary. Fronto himself says, in a short essay *De Eloquentia* (*On Eloquence*), sent to Antoninus Augustus around A.D. 162:

> You should act similarly when it comes to eloquence. You should not seek it out too much, or be averse to it too much: nevertheless, if a choice has to be made, you should very much more prefer eloquence to idiocy. [*Simile igitur in eloquentia servandum: non opere nimio concupiscas igitur, nec opere nimio aversere: tamen, si eligendum sit, longe longeque eloquentiam infantiae praeferas.*]

In other words, you should neither chase after, nor avoid, eloquence; but it is far better to be eloquent than to be an inconsiderate boor.

28. On Whether It Is Advisable To Change Religions

It is well-known that there is great variability in religious practices across the world. Climate, geography, and historical memory shape the outlook of man; and what may be routine and normal for one, may be seen as anathema to another. Yet this variability in practices does not mean that morals, or beliefs, are irrelevant; it only means that man has proven himself infinitely creative in adapting customs to environment. St. Augustine, in his *City of God* (VII.17), was making this very point when he quoted the Roman writer Varro (who was himself quoting Xenophanes of Colophon) with these words, when Varro was addressing the subject of the nature of the gods:

> Sed ut Xenophanes Colophonios scribit, quid putem, non quid contendam, ponam.

And this means, "But as Xenophanes of Colophon writes, 'I will set down what I think, not what I believe unambiguously to be true.'" In other words, no one can speak with absolute certainty when it comes to religious subjects. To elaborate on his point, Augustine later describes (VII.21) the sexually explicit religious rites of the pagan god Liber. According to him, phallic symbols were paraded around in public with shameless sincerity; and he tells us that the town of Lavinium in Italy assigned an entire month to this celebration. A woman of high standing in the community was also supposed to "place a crown" on the "shameful" phallus (*cui membro inhonesto matrem familias honestissimam palam coronam necesse erat imponere*). But Augustine should have been aware that these kinds of fertility rites and symbols are common in different parts of the world; they should be seen as harmless rites of the harvest, which persist here and there to this day. I remember the theologian Al-Ghazali made this very same point in the preface (تمهيد) to his personal testament *The Deliverance from Error*. He repeats a famous hadith, one that lodged itself in my mind when I first read it many years ago:

كل مولود يولد على الفطرة فأبواه يهودانه و ينصرانه و يمجسانه.

This saying means, "Every child is born with an innate character; yet it is his father who makes him a Jew, a Christian, or a Magian [i.e., Zoroastrian]." I know that there are certain interpretations of this saying, and I make no claims of expertise in the religious sciences of any faith. I can only repeat what this saying means to me, and that is: when it comes to religion, environment is the determinative influence. We adopt the faiths of our fathers, and are socialized to them as we grow to adulthood. What matters, it seems to me, is not so much a man's faith, but whether he behaves in socially responsible ways, respects his neighbor, and does not cause offense. Augustine tells us a pretty fable elsewhere in the *City of God* (XXII.8) about a man named Florentius, who was raised in Augustine's own city of Hippo.

This man–whose name was Florentius–was a poor tailor, but also very pious. One day he lost his coat, but did not have enough money to buy another one. Not knowing what else to do, he went to a church in Hippo called the House of the Twenty Martyrs and prayed for guidance. He did this in a loud voice, and some surly youths overhead him. They began to make fun of him and his misfortune. He left the church and began to walk along the seashore; there he saw a large fish lying on the beach. It was still alive, so he hauled it to a local fishmonger named Cattosus, and sold it to him. The cook began to prepare the fish by cutting it open, and found a gold ring in its belly. The cook generously returned it to the poor tailor, telling him that his prayers had been answered: "Look at how the Twenty Martyrs have clothed you! [*Ecce quo modo te viginti martyres vestierunt*]"

All things being equal, it is probably better to continue with the traditions in which we were raised, instead of adopting an entirely new set of religious beliefs. We become habituated to a certain set of rituals and symbols, and these things become firmly set as the years progress. I do not wish to criticize the conversion experience; I know that for some people, a clean break with the past is best for them. Religion is a matter of conscience, and no one should be forced to believe what he does not believe in. It is also true that matters of faith cannot really be fit into neat packages, or easily categorized. People change over time, and there are times when a sincere conversion is the best thing for them. Yet I find it difficult to imagine this sort of thing ever happening to me. As usual, our friend Dr. Samuel Johnson had something pungent to say on these matters. In April 1778, he was conversing with one Mrs. Knowles, who told him that an acquaintance of hers had converted to Quakerism. This woman had been known to Johnson, and he had been favorably inclined to her; but once he found out she had left the Church of England, he became offended by it. Boswell tells the rest of this unintentionally amusing anecdote:

> Mrs. Knowles at the same time took an opportunity of letting him know 'that the amiable young creature was sorry at finding that he was offended at her leaving the Church...and embracing a simpler faith,' and in the gentlest and most persuasive manner, [she] solicited his kind indulgence for what was sincerely a matter of conscience. JOHNSON (frowning very angrily). 'Madam, she is an odious wench. She could not have any proper conviction that it was her duty to change her religion, which is the most important of all subjects, and should be studied with all care, and with all the help we can get. She knew no more of the Church which she left, and that which she embraced, than she did of the difference between the Copernican and Ptolemaick systems.'

> MRS. KNOWLES. 'She had the New Testament before her.' JOHNSON. 'Madam, she could not understand the New Testament, the most difficult book in the world, for which the study of a life is required.' MRS. KNOWLES. 'It is clear as to essentials.' JOHNSON. 'But not as to controversial points. The heathens were easily converted, because they had nothing to give up; but we ought not, without very strong conviction indeed, to desert the religion in which we have been educated. That is the religion given you, the religion in which it may be said Providence has placed you. If you live conscientiously in that religion, you may be safe. But errour is dangerous indeed, if you err when you choose a religion for yourself.' MRS. KNOWLES. 'Must we then go by implicit faith?' JOHNSON. 'Why, Madam, the greatest part of our knowledge is implicit faith; and as to religion, have we heard all that a disciple of Confucius, all that a Mahometan, can say for himself?'

Perhaps this is the wisest position to take. Providence places us in a certain time, place, and circumstance, and it is our own task to (as Johnson states it) "live conscientiously" with those boundaries imposed by Fortune. I suppose there are always exceptions to every rule, but I would not venture to guess at them unless pressed forcefully on the matter. Some things are better left unsaid, and some topics better left alone.

29. On His Deathbed, Johnson Celebrates Youth's Vitality And Spirit

It is right that youth should celebrate its vigor. We do it a grave injustice by shackling its natural ebullience, by attempting to douse its fires with an excess of admonitions and restrictions. Let it, as far as health and safety will permit, taste the light of the open sky, the airs of unexplored mountains, and the swift currents swirling along tropical beaches. For in our elder years we will recall these liberating sensations with an intensity that sustains life itself.

To crush youth's healthy spirit, to shackle its innocence and daring with unreasonable rules and soul-killing punishments: these are unforgivable crimes. Is it any accident that, as Samuel Johnson neared death in 1784, he "repeated with great spirit a poem" that he had composed years before for a youth who had just achieved manhood? I do not think so. As a man's final hours draw near, he is pulled back decades to the recollections of his early years. This poem, says Boswell, was composed on the occasion of a young man's (Sir John Lade) coming of age; it was, he says, a poem "conveyed in a strain of pointed vivacity and humour, and in a manner of which no other instance is to be found in Johnson's writings." Some may see in these lines a satirical laugh at frivolous expenditure, and I suppose that may be one interpretation. But to me they are more than this. For my part I prefer to see them as a celebration of youthful effervescence and vitality. The verses are as follows:

Long-expected one-and-twenty,
Ling'ring year, at length is flown;
Pride and pleasure, pomp and plenty,
Great *****, are now your own.

Loosen'd from the Minor's tether,
Free to mortgage or to sell,
Wild as wind, and light as feather,
Bid the sons of thrift farewell.

Call the Betseys, Kates, and Jennies,
All the names that banish care:
Lavish of your grandsire's guineas,
Shew the spirit of an heir.

All that prey on vice or folly
Joy to see their quarry fly;
There the gamester, light and jolly,
There the lender, grave and sly.

Wealth, my lad, was made to wander,
Let it wander as it will;
Call the jockey, call the pander,
Bid them come and take their fill.

When the bonny blade carouses,
Pockets full, and spirits high–
What are acres? What are houses?
Only dirt, or wet or dry.

Should the guardian friend or mother
Tell the woes of wilful waste;
Scorn their counsel, scorn their pother–
You can hang or drown the last.

That a sick man in his seventies, on the threshold of death, would recall and repeat these lines fondly to those at his bedside, is a poignant thing. He never wrote anything wiser. Only one who had lived a full life could have composed such lines; and only one who harbored no regrets could have allowed his dying lips to utter them.

30. Eight Qualities Of The Man Of Understanding

One of the first and greatest classics of Arabic prose is the *Book of Kalila and Dimna.* It is a collection of fables told with an allegorical purpose, but it is presented with such wisdom, poetic eloquence, and engaging humor as to make it one of the treasures of world literature. Its pedigree verifies its merit. The stories it contains were originally derived from a Sanskrit classic called the *Panchatantra*, but a Persian scholar and translator named Ibn Muqaffa' (ابن المقفع), writing around 740 A.D., reworked the stories into something that was entirely original. In the book's introduction, our author gives us the fanciful explanation of how *Kalila and Dimna* came to Persia. Its wisdom was so valuable, we are told, that the Indian rulers guarded access to it jealously; eventually, however, the Persian Sasanid king Khosrow (also known as Chosroes Anushiruwan) sent a special envoy to the Indian principalities to see if he could procure a copy by stealth. The emissary he sent was a man named Barzouyeh, who was acquainted with the Indian languages and customs:

> Now Chosroes Nouschirewan, during the enquiries he made of the writings of the ancients, having received information of the book of Kalila and Dimna,

> became very impatient for its acquisition: for this purpose he sent Barzouyeh the physician on a mission to India, who having got possession of a copy of it by his skill and address, brought it away with him, and deposited it amongst the treasures of the kings of Persia. [*Trans. by W. Knatchbull*]

We may smile at the author's idealism in placing literature the subject of international intrigue; but there can be no doubt as to the book's brilliance. In rereading it recently, I was astounded by the richness of the language, the poetic descriptions, the engaging Oriental hyperbole, and the practical reality of the counsel. Consider the following passage, worthy of an aside in Cicero's philosophical works, which appears in the opening chapters:

> God has created man in his wisdom and mercy, has raised him to excellence and honor, and has put into his power the means of happiness in this world, and of avoiding punishment in the next: but the best gift of God to man is understanding, the source of everything that is good and profitable, the key to his happiness on earth, and his anchor through the stormy sea of life to conduct him into the haven of a blissful eternity. Understanding is the child of instruction and experience; its seeds lie hidden in the soul of man, and must be called into life by the nurturing hand of discipline and fortified by trial, as the sparks are struck out from the hard flint, before the fire, which lies concealed in the stone, can be produced. [*Trans. by W. Knatchbull*]

The passage that is the subject of this essay is the following. It describes the "eight different qualities" of a man of understanding:

> A man of sound understanding is distinguished by eight different qualities; by courteous and affable behavior, by a knowledge of himself, united with a strict and impartial observation of his own heart; by submission to lawful authority, and an endeavor to conciliate the good will of those who are in power;

> by great circumspection in his confidential communications; by becoming language and irreproachable conduct at the courts of kings; by secrecy, where his own interest is at stake, and fidelity in his engagements with others; by moderation in his discourse, so that no unpleasant consequence may arise from any hasty or intemperate word; and, lastly, by a prudent reserve and modest diffidence in delivering his opinion. And where these qualities are united in one person...they bring down blessings upon the head of him who possesses them.

These are Ibn Muqaffa's eight qualities of the man of understanding. Let us list them below for further discussion.

1. **Courteous and affable behavior**, united with self-knowledge.
2. **Knowledge of one's self**, so that a man is aware of his strengths and weaknesses.
3. **Obedience to lawful authority**, and the ability to use tact in the company of authority.
4. **Discretion**, or the ability to keep one's mouth shut, and one's business private.
5. **Proper language and conduct** in formal settings.
6. **Secrecy and fidelity** when one is dealing with friends, clients, lovers, or confidants.
7. **Moderation**, or the ability to keep a cool head. This is also called temperance.
8. **Reserve**, or the ability to conduct oneself in a way that is inoffensive to others.

The reader, in perusing this list, will be struck at how completely different this ethic is from what is currently taught in our schools. Conduct and character are all-important, and the mainstays of society; yet we are today taught by the media to scream our opinions in each other's faces, to disrespect tradition and authority, and to steamroll over anyone who looks at us crossways. These realities help to explain why our society currently finds itself in its present state. It seems to me that we should strive to cultivate the qualities listed above, and to unite them as far as possible within ourselves. The way to do this is through constant discipline and practice. We must disconnect ourselves from the modern media's unrelenting messages of moral corruption, destructive selfishness, and lies; we must look back in time to the wisdom of those who came before us, and implement this wisdom; and we must remove ourselves from dealings with people whose minds are poisoned by the modern ethic. At some point in every man's life, after the fires of youth have somewhat cooled, he must decide whether he wishes to be counted among the *men of understanding,* or among the *men of entertainment*. These are his two options. The *man of understanding* seeks to refine his soul in the cultivation of the ethic described above; while the *man of entertainment* seeks nothing more than constant sensory stimulation from his controllers. We must not delude ourselves, of course: the vast majority will certainly prefer entertainment.

But there will always be those who wish to penetrate to the heart of things, and to pursue the chalices of knowledge secreted from the unworthy. They know, deep in their hearts, that there are no short-cuts in life; that no amount of "life hacks," nootropics, pills, seminars, get-rich-quick schemes, and bombastic sleight of hand will help them. And it is they who will answer the call: so it has always been, and always will be. A man rises to honor and renown through the merits of his personal character; and although the unworthy man may temporarily occupy a place of distinction, he will not long last in this office. His fall is assured. It will inevitably come as a natural consequence of his base character and innate lack of virtue. The man of understanding can be assured he will eventually be rewarded for his labors. We reject evil by refusing to participate in it. We banish it by refusing to empower it. And we must fortify our souls and intellects for the great trials that will inevitably be brought down upon us.

31. At What Point Can A Man Be Called Happy?

The historian Herodotus (I.30) relates an anecdote involving a conversation between the Lydian king Croesus and the Athenian statesman Solon. Solon once found himself as a guest at Croesus's court. The king knew that Solon was renowned for his wise judgment and careful consideration of life's important questions. So he could not resist asking the Athenian a question that was troubling him. The question he asked him was this: "Who, Solon, was the happiest man you have ever seen?" It was expected for royal visitors to tell the king what he wanted to hear, of course. Croesus was expecting some words of flattery from Solon to reassure himself that he was living a meaningful life.

But Solon was not the type of man to act like a lackey before powerful men. He said a man named Tellus was the happiest man he knew; and as second-happiest, Solon named two men from Argos called Cleobis and Biton. All three of these men Solon considered "happy" due to the fact that they had all displayed virtue, courage, and character in the face of hardship. This to Solon was more important than frolicking around amid voluptuary pleasures which, he knew, were nothing but deceptive illusions. Yet Croesus was still chagrined to discover that Solon did not really place much value or importance in the sumptuous life of royals; his vanity was wounded, and he felt snubbed. Lashing out at his guest, Croesus demanded to know why he did not at least rate a place in the top three "most happy" rankings. Solon responded in this way:

> My lord, I know God is envious of human prosperity and likes to trouble us; and you question me about the lot of man. Listen, then: as the years lengthen out, there is much both to see and to suffer which one would wish otherwise. Take seventy years as the span of a man's life: those seventy years contain 25,200 days, without counting intercalary months. Add a month every other year, to make the seasons come round with proper regularity, and you will have thirty-five additional months, which will make 1,050 additional days. Thus the total of days for your seventy years is 26,250, and not a single one of them is like the next in what it brings. You can see from that, Croesus, what a chancy thing life is. You are very rich, and you rule a numerous people; but the question you asked me I will not answer, until I know that you have died happily. Great wealth can make a man no happier than moderate means, unless he has the luck to continue in prosperity to the end. Many very rich men have been unfortunate, and many with a modest competence

have had good luck. The former are better off than the latter in two respects only, whereas the poor but lucky man has the advantage in many ways; for though the rich have the means to satisfy their appetites and to bear calamities, and the poor have not, the poor, if they are lucky, are more likely to keep clear of trouble, and will have besides the blessings of a sound body, health, freedom from trouble, fine children, and good looks.

Now if a man thus favored dies as he has lived, he will be just the one you are looking for: the only sort of person who deserves to be called happy. *But mark this: until he is dead, keep the word "happy" in reserve. Till then, he is not happy, but only lucky.* Nobody of course can have all these advantages, any more than a county can produce everything it needs: whatever it has, it is bound to lack something. The best country is the one which has most. It is the same with people: no man is ever self-sufficient. There is sure be something missing. But whoever has the greatest number of the good things I have mentioned, and keep them to the end, and dies a peaceful death, that man, my lord Croesus, deserves in my opinion to be called happy. Look to the end, no matter what it is you are considering. Often enough God gives a man a glimpse of happiness, and then utterly ruins him. [*Trans. by A. De Selincourt*]

These were Solon's words to Croesus. They were not the words he wanted to hear, but they were the words he needed to hear. His point, of course, was this: it is not possible to evaluate a man's life until it has ended. No one can say whether a man is happy or miserable until he has sighed his last breath. Because fortune is ever-changing, and constantly setting up obstacles and challenges in our path, we cannot predict what impediments we will encounter. Or so it seemed to Solon. But is this really true? Do we need to wait until the end of a man's life in order to judge whether he is happy? Maybe we should see happiness as a mental state, a condition of the mind, that once attained, cannot be lost. The philosopher Epicurus believed that happiness, once attained, could not be lost merely because of physical pain or discomfort. In this view, we can say that happiness has nothing at all to do with externalities like health, wealth, family, and things like this. Some of the noblest words on this subject have been written by that great essayist, Michel de Montaigne. He treated this very question–that no man can be called happy until after his death–in book I, chapter 19 of his *Essais*. Probably speaking of his close friend Étienne de La Boétie, he says:

> Some deaths are brave and fortunate. I have seen death cut the thread of a man's days when he was on the point of magnificent achievement. In the flower of his age, he made so fine an end that I do not believe even his most ambitious and courageous designs attained a splendor equal to that of the moment that cut them short. Without moving towards it, he obtained his goal more grandly and more gloriously than he can have hoped or desired. And he gained by his fall a more ample power and fame than he had aspired to in his whole career. In judging another man's life, I always inquire how he behaved at the last; and one of the principal aims of my life is to conduct myself well when it ends–peacefully, I mean, and with a calm mind. [*Trans. by J.M. Cohen*]

I agree with Montaigne. As I see it, happiness is an internal change we make in our own minds, a change that cannot be ruined or degraded by the cruelties of fortune. We can say that happiness is a form of willpower, a form of mental resolution, in which we force ourselves to keep fighting the game of life until we draw our last breath. This is what I say: *happiness is the will to live; it is the will to stay in the arena until the curtain comes down on the last act of the drama.*

32. The Man Of Action Should Not Expect Gratitude From Others

We have recently discussed ways of handling a lack of appreciation. A certain independence of spirit–a soaring greatness of soul–is one of the main ways we can limit our expectations of appreciation from others. Consider again, if you need to, the verses of Ibn

Munir on this subject, which capture perfectly this spiritual independence.[11] As I see it, no more powerful statement of this ethic has ever been put into poetic form. This theme–the theme of ingratitude–presents itself in the lives of many historical figures. And this is predictably so, because we all know that human nature has not changed down through the centuries. The man of action, the man of achievement and ability, who seeks to rise above his immediate surroundings, will more often earn the antagonism of his peers than their warm considerations. Men do not like to be reminded of their shortcomings and faults; and truth, although it may be beautiful, is seldom popular.

The humanist Biondo Flavio, when he was composing his survey of Italy in the early 1450s, read in the naturalist Pliny that the mineral water springs near Liternum were especially redemptive. Biondo says that Liternum was located "on the part of the River Volturno facing Cumae." Pliny actually calls the springs "slightly acidic" (*Historia Naturalis* II.230), and gives the name of the springs as Lyncestis. In any case, Biondo actually visited this place, which is located in Italy's Campania region. He talked to locals there who told him that the water was good for curing all kinds of maladies. The water, he tells us, is so plentiful that it even seeps up among the ruins of buildings there.

Tasting it, he acknowledged that while it did indeed taste good, he could not really detect any benefit from it (*Italia Illustrata* VIII.25). It did not live up to the expectations generated by its reputation. So much for the legend of the marvelous waters, he thought to himself. Perhaps this is what the praise of others is like: desired in theory, but somehow unsatisfying when finally received. We may think we want or need the gratitude of others, but its acquisition brings us no real benefit in practice. Another purpose Biondo had in Campania was to locate the tomb of Scipio Africanus. Scipio had supposedly spent his voluntary exile in or near Liternum. Even in antiquity, the precise location of his tomb had somehow become lost. Seneca (*Epistulae* 86.1) claims to have spent time in the villa once owned by Scipio himself; and he seemed to think an altar there was actually Scipio's grave. The historian Livy, who lived less than one hundred years after Scipio's death, was also ready to believe that Scipio's tomb was located near Liternum.

---

[11] See the essay on Ibn Munir in Part II, below.

Notice that I said here that Livy was "ready to believe" the grave was in Liternum. Patriotic historian that he was, he was uncomfortable admitting that he did not know with certainty where the tomb was located. How could it be that a general and statesman as famous as Scipio–a man who had accomplished so much–had also been so neglected that his countrymen did not even know where he was buried? But this is in the nature of things. This is the fate of some great men. Even the location of the tomb of Alexander the Great, who conquered a good part of the known world, is lost today. With regard to Scipio, Livy says:

> Some say that Scipio died and was interred in Rome, and other say at Liternum; in both places, monuments and statues are on display. [Livy XXXVIII.56]

He did not know the precise location, and neither did anyone else. What an insult to a man who had done so much and sacrificed so much for his people! But there may have been specific reasons for the forgetfulness of Scipio's peers. To excel too much is to invite the resentments of others. Scipio turned his back on his peers, because they had turned their backs on him. They were unable to rise to the level of public responsibility and leadership that he felt was required for the health of the republic. The historian Valerius Maximus (V.3.2) tells us this:

> Repaying Scipio's great achievements with insults, his fellow citizens made him the tenant of a pathetic village and an empty swamp [*Cuius clarissima opera iniuriis pensando cives vici ignobilis eum ac desertae paludis accolam fecerunt*].

This was how they treated the man who had decisively defeated Carthage and brought Hannibal to heel. But Scipio was a fighter to the end, and he knew how to return a favor. He would not accept this shabby treatment without some response for posterity's sake. So before his death he gave instructions that his tomb should bear the following inscription:

INGRATA PATRIA, NE OSSA QVIDEM MEA HABES.

And this means: *Ungrateful country, you will not even get my bones.* Valerius has a great comment on this stinging epitaph. He says that Scipio "denied his ashes to her [i.e., Rome] whom he had prevented from becoming cinders."

So the man of action cannot look to others for recognition or approval. He cannot expect gratitude; and if he does get it, it will be short-lived. To illustrate this with another example, consider the career of the great Norman chief Tancred of Hauteville. He was oppressed by the burden of having twelve children by two wives, and resolved to seek his fortune in a new home. It is remarkable that the Normans were able to prosper in so many different countries and environments. Tancred first settled in Romagna, and he was hired by a local warlord there (Pandolfo, Prince of Capua) for his military prowess. The Normans performed wonderfully, but Pandolfo was a stupid and jealous man, and failed to show the uncouth, unrefined Normans any respect.

Instead of brooding about their fates, the Normans, once they realized Pandolfo's jealous games, simply moved on to greener pastures. They entered the service of Guaimar, another regional warlord. But inevitably, Guaimar's court officials began to whisper venomous words against the Normans as well. So Tancred and his men moved on, and this time found employment under the Byzantine emperor (who had holdings in Sicily) as a hired force to fight the marauding Saracens in Sicily. And this they did. Together the Normans and Greeks were successful in expelling the Saracens from nearly all of Sicily. But what happened then? Yes, the Normans became objects of jealously from the Greeks too; so they persuaded the Greek emperor Michael IV Paphlagon to let them settle in Apulia in southern Italy. They settled there and eventually built the city of Melfi in a well-fortified location. There they were able to fend off many attackers and build a permanent home for themselves.

We should learn from the behavior of the Normans, and from the "phantom of a vision" ethic of Ibn Munir, as we discussed earlier. When we are met with a lack of appreciation or a lack of respect, we must fold up our tents and move on to greener pastures. We should not wring our hands at the injustices of the world, for the world will pay little attention to our futile remonstrations. We do not perform great tasks for the applause of others; we do them for their own sakes, and because they are an expression of our characteristic fiber. Neither do we need the permission or validation of others; for our hearts are imbued with greatness of soul, with that inexpressible *magnitudo animi*, which has its own momentum and its own eternal logic. We write our own histories, and we inscribe the pages of our folios with the chronicles of our own great deeds.

33. Trust In Fate, Rely On Your Abilities, And Keep Moving

There are times in life when we need to have blind faith in forward momentum. We need cease the deliberations, the doubts, the equivocations, and the rationalizations. We should, instead, resolve to maintain a steady forward pace, trusting to our own abilities and the favorable intercession of Fortune. We may not have contingency plans for every eventuality, but we must press on with blind faith nonetheless. Momentum creates its own dynamic, and its own outcomes. It was precisely this principle that the great Spanish conqueror Hernán Cortés brought to bear in the early stages of the conquest of Mexico in 1519.

Conditions could hardly have been less favorable to Cortés. He and his men were isolated in a strange land, cut off from reinforcements and supplies from his countrymen. His mission had barely even been authorized by his superiors. Yet the cunning Extremaduran lawyer had a deep-seated faith in his own abilities, and an uncanny knack for exploiting opportunities that presented themselves. During the early stages of his march on Mexico City–which historian Bernal Diaz calls the "Tlascalan Campaign"–his men were troubled by the situation they found themselves in. They were worried that their captain-general had overreached himself; they did not understand his plans or motives and were shocked by his decision to burn his ships after arriving on the Mexican coast.

Diaz, who participated in the campaign, wrote decades later that a few of the other Spaniards in their party began to have grave doubts as to the strength of Cortés's judgment. They told their captain-general that he should "consider the condition we were in, wounded, thin, and harassed, and the great hardships we endured by night, as sentinels, watchmen, patrols, and scouts, and in continuous fighting both day and night." Even though they had enjoyed victory in every battle that had taken place since they had left Cuba, the men felt that their commander was tempting fate too much. Instead of pressing on to the Aztec capital, they said, might it not be better to go back to Villa Real, and wait among their Totonac allies? They could then build another ship and sail back to Cuba, and send for reinforcements. They chided Cortés with the fact that he had not consulted them at all before he burned his ships. Would it not have been better to save just one or two, in the event of an emergency? Even Alexander the Great and the most daring Roman commanders, the men insisted, would not have taken such an apparently reckless step. And by daring to attack such a large population as the Aztecs with no assistance, he was showing little regard for his own life and for the lives of his men. So it seemed to some of Cortés's men.

The captain-general listened patiently to these concerns and objections. He knew some of his men wanted desperately to go back to Cuba, where they had land, food, and women, and a life of comparative ease. He said he was well aware of the facts and dangers that currently presented themselves; there was not another military force of Spaniards in all the world that had endured as much and done as much as they had. According to Diaz, Cortés then spoke the following words:

> Why, gentlemen, should we talk of valorous deeds when truly Our Lord is pleased to help us? When I remember seeing us surrounded by so many companies of the enemy, and watching the play of their broadswords at such close quarters, even now I am terrified. When they killed the mare with a single sword-stroke we were defeated and lost, and at that same moment I was more aware of your matchless courage then ever before. Since God saved us from this great peril, I have every hope that He will do so again in the future. And I will say more, that in all these dangers you will find no negligence on my part; I shared every one of them with you. I wish to remind you, gentlemen, that since Our Lord has been pleased to help us in the past we have hope that He may do so in the future. For ever since we entered this country we have preached the holy doctrine to the best of our ability in every town

through which we have passed, and have induced the natives to destroy their idols…As for scuttling the ships it was a good plan, and if some of you were not consulted about it, as other gentlemen were, it was on account of my resentment at certain events on the beach, which I do not now wish to recall…

So, gentlemen, it would clearly be wrong to take a single step backwards, for if these people we leave behind in peace were to see us retreat, the very stones would rise up against us. They who at present hold us to be gods and idols and call us so would consider us cowards and weaklings. As for what you say about our staying among our friendly allies the Totonacs, if they saw us return without visiting Mexico [City], they would rise up against us too…And what would the great Montezuma say on hearing that we had retreated? That the whole expedition was a childish joke. What would he think of our speeches and our messages to him? So, gentlemen, if one course is bad the other is worse, and it is better to stay where we are, where the ground is level and thickly inhabited, and our camp is kept well supplied with poultry and dogs…We did not come here to take our ease, however, but to fight when the opportunity offered.

Therefore I pray you, gentlemen, kindly to behave like gentlemen, I mean those whose habit is to encourage others whom they see displaying weakness. From now on, keep the island of Cuba and what you have left there out of your thoughts, and try to act, as you have done hitherto, like brave soldiers. For after God, who is our aid and support, we must rely on our own strong arms. [*Trans. by J.M. Cohen*]

Taking even the smallest step backwards, Cortés knew, would have been fatal. It would have psychologically crippled his men, and it would have sent a disastrous message of vacillation to his native "allies." He knew that most of his advantage over his enemies was psychological, and that if he showed even a hint of weakness, they would swarm about him like piranhas. The only thing to do was to keep moving forward, and to let his momentum carry him all the way to the Aztec capital. Those who want constant assurances in life should remember that there are times when such guarantees cannot be given; that there are times when one must leap calculatingly into the unknown, trusting to Fate and to one's own capabilities. For unless these leaps are taken, a man will find himself in the same place throughout his life, quietly marking time until the twilight of his years.

34. On The Forgetting Of Offenses And Insults

It is a good thing for us to cultivate our aggressive spirit. Life requires participation, and participation demands endurance and adrenaline; and he who enters battle with a spirit of meek submissiveness is likely to get precisely what he asks for. All this is true. Yet the patient endurance of the pack-mule may be just as valuable as the explosive fury of the panther: the former triumphs by being able to endure, while the latter may find itself fatally exhausted once its initial burst of energy is spent. Life more often demands the ability to absorb punishment than the ability to deliver it to others.

Central to this idea of endurance is our ability to cultivate a thick skin. We are daily surrounded by distractions, nonsense, foolishness, and stupidity. We will find ourselves attacked, harried, and harassed by knaves and ankle-biters of all shapes and sizes. The attention-seeking culture in which we live guarantees us a steady stream of such exposure and treatment. This we cannot change; but we can change our own reactions to it. It seems to me–or at least it has been true in my own life–that it is vitally important to cultivate an ability to "let things go" that are not important in the larger scheme of things. We have to learn to distinguish what is important, from what is not important. Slights and insults will generate the fires of outrage: but we have to learn to distinguish the battles that matter from the battles that do not. This takes time, experience, and the cultivation of greatness of soul (*magnitudo animi*), about which I have spoken at length in the past, especially in *On Duties*.

Not every outrage can be rectified. Not every injustice can be righted. To spend our short lives fussing about and stressing over every single wrong will leave us with no life at all. No man ever gained from protracted litigation; and no nation ever benefited from protracted war: and these words are coming from someone who has been both an attorney and a military man. In the vast majority of situations, the sooner a conflict is settled, the better. This is so even if it leaves both sides feeling not quite whole. *In fact, it is my experience that the ideal settlement is the one that leaves both sides slightly dissatisfied.* Each would not have gotten everything it wanted, and this is a measure of justice. The pack-mule is wise in the ways of endurance and self-preservation. He will absorb a measure of punishment, and will never act out of malice. He knows when to put his head down, and move on. He is wise in his *conservation of energy*: he will not waste his time and energy on things that give him diminishing returns.

Consider some examples of this principle. King Pyrrhus of Epirus (318 B.C.–272 B.C.) was known for his skilled generalship and competent administration. He was also wise in the ways of men, knowing how to distinguish what was important from what was not. The Roman author Valerius Maximus tells us (in V.1 of his *Memorable Doings and Sayings*) an anecdote about the king that reveals this quality of forbearance. Pyrrhus once heard that some officials in the city of Tarentum (in southern Italy) had spoken evilly about him at some banquet. So he summoned a few of these people and asked them to account for their behavior. He asked them if they really had said what he had heard they had said. There was a long pause; no one wanted to respond to the king, fearing what his reaction might be. Finally, one of them spoke out (who had more honesty than prudence!). He said:

> If our wine had not run out, the things that were reported to you would have been trifles and jokes, compared to what we *would have said* about you. [*Nisi vinum nos defecisset, ista quae tibi relata sunt, prae iis quae de te locuturi eramus, lusus ac iocus fuissent.*]

Pyrrhus, upon hearing this, burst into laughter. So did everyone else, and all was forgiven. He had shown himself able to tolerate harmless criticism. By such *magnitudo animi* (greatness of soul), he was thereafter able to win over the people of Tarentum completely. They began to "thank him when sober and pray for him when drunk." Another example of this kind of warm humanity is found in an anecdote (also told by Valerius Maximus in V.1) about the Athenian tyrant Pisistratus. He was said to have a very beautiful daughter and on occasion walked her about the city. A passionate young man once strode up to his daughter and, overcome by emotion, attempted to kiss her. Pisistratus's wife was not amused; she urged the tyrant to have the young man executed for his impudence. He smiled and said,

> If we shall execute those who love us, what shall we do with those who hate us?
> [*Si eos qui nos amant interficiemus, quid iis faciemus quibus odio sumus?*]

And these surely must be counted wise words. It is this spirit of forbearance, this ability to let things go, that we have lost today in our culture. We now love to be offended at every imagined or real insult; we spin spider-webs of conspiratorial intentions on the part of our opponents, and feel the need to announce our grievances to the universe. It seems to me that there is a certain cruelty, a true lack of humanity, in this kind of mentality.

In this same spirit another story about Pisistratus is told by Valerius. The tyrant was once dining with family and friends. Present was a man named Thrasippus; intoxicated and agitated, he began to berate the Athenian leader to the shock of the others present. Pisistratus took the abuse in stride, and did not respond in kind. Thrasippus eventually stopped, but later on tried to leave the banquet. Pisistratus saw this and tried to stop him, thinking that the man was embarrassed by what happened and wanted to leave. Thrasippus then spat in Pisistratus's face, to the horror of those who witnessed the scene. The tyrant's sons wanted to retaliate, but he told them to stand down. The next day, once the effects of the wine had worn off and he realized what he had done, Thrasippus was overcome by a desire to kill himself. But Pisistratus visited him in person, assuring him that all was forgiven. In this way he displayed his greatness of soul.

In life we will always be able to find something to be outraged about, if we look hard enough. We will always be able to feel rage and hurt, if we poke around in the right places. But learning the art of "letting things go" gives us freedom. It allows us to be liberated from the chains of emotion. There are times when one must do something, and when one must do nothing. One does not need to right every wrong, or iron every rumple in our garments; let us learn the wisdom of living with rumpled garments every now and then. We may just find it to be a liberating feeling.

35. On Portents And Divination

The belief in portents, divination, and auguries was common before the modern era. We moderns, comfortably ensconced in our towers of science and "rationalism," are likely to view with extreme skepticism the notion that future events can be foretold. Such a view would appear to some as a superstitious relic from a less enlightened era. Or so we would like to imagine. The historian of late antiquity Ammianus Marcellinus had a few words to say about portents. In book XX of his history, he describes the Roman emperor Constantius's siege of the town of Bezabde in what is now southeast Turkey (modern Zabdicene). He was at the time engaged in a bitter struggle against the Persian king Shapur II, who had made moves to retake Roman Mesopotamia. For many days, Constantius's forces put the city to siege in the year 360, but were unable to take it. Thunder, lightning, and heavy rains then came, turning the ground around the city into dense mud, a fact that made military operations even more difficult.

Rainbows then appeared with frequency (XX.11.26: *Accedebant arcus caelestis conspectus assidui*). Ammianus is careful to explain the appearance of rainbows as a natural phenomenon. He does not believe they are miracles: he offers a very rational explanation of how they appear. He knows that water vapor in the air refracting sunlight is the cause of the rainbow (XX.11.26), although of course the spectral nature of refracted white light is not in his vocabulary. He associates rainbows with changes in weather patterns; but for Ammianus, they are not just a natural phenomenon. They were something more than this. They were an indication that the goddess Iris had been sent "when it was necessary to change the present state of things" (*cum praesentium rerum verti necesse sit status*).

Iris is not a very well-known goddess today. She was a harbinger—personified by the rainbow—sent by the more powerful gods to pass on signs of change: that is, when old things are replaced by new ones. A little bit later in his history (XXI.1), Ammianus goes into more detail regarding his belief in portents, auguries, and divination. Whether someone agrees or disagrees with this sort of thing is irrelevant: it mattered to him, and to nearly every other ancient historian. We cannot simply dismiss these things out of hand, just because they run counter to our modern sensibilities. Ancient man was not a fool: he did not have the techniques or tools of modern science, but his model of explaining the world did have a consistent logic to it, as someone who actually takes the time to read the original texts will understand.

The power of divination, Ammianus believed, was a kind of elemental spirit surrounding all things (*elementorum omnium spiritus, utpote perennium corporum praesentiendi motu semper et ubique vigens*). Under the right conditions, divination could reveal signs foretelling future events in one way or another. The goddess Themis had general control over such prophecies; she is the embodiment of the Divine Order of the world, a personification of the natural "balance" of the universe. For good reason Themis has been depicted holding scales: these are the universal scales of justice, and this gives her the power to detect disturbances in the natural order of things. Themis interpreted the rulings decreed by the "Fates" (i.e., things "fixed"). But how, according to Ammianus, are such prophecies revealed to men? It can happen in various ways. One way is through the trained inspection of the entrails of sacrificed animals. "The original instructor of this discipline is Tages, who according to legend arose suddenly from the earth in parts of Etruria" (XXI.1.10).

Another way divination can take place is when people become agitated and are moved to speak "sacred words" (*cum aestuant hominum corda, sed locuntur divina*). Under the right conditions, a person can literally channel a divine force, and speak convincingly of future events. The divine power of the sun (Ammianus says) can literally "light up" the right oracle, and cause a prophecy to be issued. This is why, he tells us, "the prophetic Sibyls [of Cumae] often say they are burning." Other things can trigger cosmic awareness, too: starlight, the right noises, thunder and lightning, or other natural phenomena. Yet another way prophecies are revealed is through the power of dreams. This is a powerful transmitter of fateful information, according to Ammianus, but the interpreters of dreams can easily be led astray.

Our intrepid historian anticipates that many people will laugh at the idea of divination and prophecy, and he has an answer for them. Belief in such supernatural occurrences was as much mocked in the ancient world as it is today. He knows that many people will scoff and say, "Well, if prophecy were indeed an art or a science, why can't an oracle predict things with consistency or accuracy?" His answer to this is:

> It is sufficient to point out that even a grammarian sometimes speaks incorrectly, or that a musician hits a note out of tune, or that a doctor is unaware of some cure: but even with all this, neither grammar, music, nor medicine have stopped in their tracks. Cicero has an appropriate comment on this subject: "The gods give us signs of future events; if an interpreter makes a mistake reading them, the fault lies not with the gods, but with the interpretation." [XXI.13]

This was Ammianus's response. As I said at the beginning of this article, we should not be too quick to judge and condemn previous eras for their belief in prophecies, auguries, and divination. Ancient man was not a fool, as I have said before. He did not have the same advantages we have today; he had to interpret the world in terms that were consistent with the corpus of knowledge he had available to him. Stated another way, his interpretations of the world more or less fit the accepted data at the time. And perhaps we can look at this matter another way. It may very well be that our "modern interpretations" of the world are not much more enlightened than Ammianus's. Perhaps it is only that we have discovered new terms, new names, and new concepts with which to cloak old ideas.

It may be that what Ammianus called "prophecy" or "divination," we today call psychic phenomena, psychoanalysis, dream therapy, or other unexplained mental phenomena. A cynic or a humorist might remind us that very little is new in history except arrangement. Or it may be that natural events can indeed give us clues as to what will come, if only we use our modern scientific instruments in the right ways. The volcanologist, the geologist, and the meteorologist are all "predicting" future events, and have to learn to read the signs available to them. There are valid arguments for each side. At the very least, we should not be too quick to claim the moral high ground over our ancestors. I will leave the final verdict on these matters, of course, to the considered judgment of the reader.

36. When To Wait, And When To Strike

There are times in a leader's experience when it will be prudent to watch and await developments. Sometimes more is to be gained by figuratively taking off one's pack, sitting down on the side of the road, and monitoring the flow of events, than by leaping into the fray. On the other hand, there are also just as many–if not more–times when decisive and speedy action is necessary to deal with a nascent problem. Knowing when to wait and when to act is one of those key questions that we all have to confront sooner or later. It is ultimately a tactical decision for which no firm rules can be laid out: every situation must be evaluated on its own merits. But if we study history, philosophy, and human behavior, we can gain insights that help us in our tactical agility. We will see, when reviewing the experiences of leaders and historical figures down through the centuries, that certain situations come up again and again. We will notice that certain human motivations are timeless. And we will see that the experiences of others may help us determine a course of action for ourselves.

We will consider the example of a king of the Alemanni (a group of Germanic tribes near the Rhine) named Vadomarius. In the year 361 A.D. he was an occasional antagonist of the Roman armies of Gaul, commanded by Julian, who had been elevated to the rank of Caesar in 355 by the emperor Constantius. Julian and Constantius were cousins; they were also deeply suspicious of each other. The emperor was jealous of Julian's charisma and popularity, and his mind was constantly oppressed by worries of how to deal with this dangerous potential rival. In 360 Vadomarius broke a treaty he had agreed to and ravaged some frontier regions controlled by the Romans. But Vadomarius and his brother Gundomadus apparently made a peace deal with Constantius. According to the historian Ammianus Marcellinus (XXI.3), the wily Constantius quietly enlisted Vadomarius as a "secret executor" of his schemes (*secretorumque taciturnum exsecutorem et efficacem mandabat*). The understanding between the two was that Vadomarius would, every so often, break the peace and make incursions into Gaul, with the purpose of tying down Julian with the defense of the province. Constantius wanted to keep his potential rival away from Constantinople, the seat and center of Roman political power. For him it was better to have his hated cousin tied down in the forests of Germany and Gaul, fighting to keep marauding Germans on the other side of the Rhine. This, at least, was the plan as Constantius saw it.

Vadomarius played his role to the hilt. He was a man "skilled in deception and fraud from an early age" (*ad perstringendum fallendumque miris modis ab aetatis primitiis callens*), according to our perceptive historian. And yet treachery usually has a way of revealing itself eventually. In 361, one of Vadomarius's messengers to Constantius was captured by Julian's men; he was found to be carrying a letter that revealed the extent of the collusion between the German leader and the emperor in Constantinople. The letter also contained derogatory remarks about Julian's qualities as a leader. This information, of course, was promptly relayed back to Julian, who was now confirmed in his belief that his cousin was scheming to have him put out of the picture.

Julian was an educated and cultured man, but also one of character, leadership, and hard-nosed practicality. He probably knew at this stage that, considering Constantius's perpetual bad faith and dishonesty, he would eventually have to rebel against his cousin and claim the throne for himself. But before doing this he would need to make his position in Gaul more secure. He resolved to have Vadomarius arrested and taken into custody. Julian sent a secretary named Philagrius to speak to the German king, who, suspecting nothing, was then invited to a banquet. Julian's secret instructions to Philagrius was to take Vadomarius into custody after the feast was over; and this he did. Julian had acted quickly to remove a double-dealing snake from the picture.

But Julian did not stop there. Besides arresting Vadomarius, he wanted to make an impression on the German king's men. So he crossed the Rhine at night and attacked them with ferocity; he received the surrender of some, and put others to the sword. The point was to teach them that they should behave themselves, and not create any more disturbances. "*Nothing was so favorable to an urgent project as was fast action,*" Ammianus tells us (XXI.5). So did Julian secure his rear as he prepared to revolt against his treacherous cousin in Constantinople. His men were ready; they liked him and would follow him anywhere. Julian "knew from hard experience how important it was to preempt and forestall an enemy during periods of volatility" (Amm. XXI.5.13). Readers may recall that this need for decisive action in the hour of decision was echoed in Sallust's *Conspiracy of Catiline:*

> By fussing over plans and postponing the day of attack, he believed they were squandering precious opportunities. In such an hour of peril it was action, not thought, that was needed; and if a few men would help him, he would mount a direct attack on the Curia despite the passivity of the rest...[*Cat.* XLIII]

The time had been right to act with speed and decision, and Julian acted. The natural question to be asked in these situations is, of course, this: how do I know when to wait, and when to act? The answer to this question is not an easy one. In fact it cannot be answered with finality, for each situation is unique and has to be dealt with in its own way. And yet it may be possible to offer some very general guidelines on this question.

Read widely in history, philosophy, and biography. As stated above, the same situations will come up over and over. If you can see how a great man handled himself in a certain difficulty, you will be inspired to do likewise. You will also learn about human behavior, and how to read people and situations. Reading philosophy is also important, as it trains the mind to think logically, directs the spirit to higher planes, fortifies the character, and provides a moral basis for life and thought.

When in doubt, it is usually better to wait. This rule may be disputed by many. But it seems true that even men considered "men of action" counsel prudence unless one has a good idea of what is going on. More damage and harm seem to come from intemperate speech or action than from caution and evaluation.

If a decisive step is being taken, behave decisively. If you are already committed to a course of action, you have crossed the Rubicon. It does no good to take mincing steps or half-measures. If you are already committed, behave as if you are committed. Flinching and squeamishness can become your ruin.

Develop an instinctive feel for people and situations. You must develop a sixth sense of when something is about to happen. You must be able to pick up on those subtle cues that tell us when to do one thing or something else. The only way this instinct can be trained is through experience. We must seek out ways to interact and associate with others, so that we can get a feel for group dynamics. Being in leadership positions is, of course, invaluable in this regard. Developing an instinct for situations also means that one must learn how to gather information. Good intelligence is a prerequisite for effective action.

Watch the right films. Some may scoff at this, but I am convinced that watching movies (the right movies, that is) is also a good way to train ourselves on how to deal with situations and personalities. Now I am not talking about the mindless dreck spewed out of most cinemas these days: I want to make this clear. I am talking about seeing the best and chewing on the right scenes and dialogue. In the era before cinema, plays and operas did this function, and they still do. Do not forget that Shakespeare was so popular in his time because he vividly portrayed characters that showed love, hate, treachery, loyalty, nobility, and the rest of the range of human qualities. These, then, are some thoughts about when to wait, and when to strike.

37. Separate Your Opponent From His Source Of Strength

When we are dealing with an opponent of substantial power, we should try to cut him off from his source of strength. If he can be made incapable of drawing on his strengths, he will be weakened; and so weakened, isolated; and if isolated, destroyed. Everything has a source of strength, whether we are talking about a person, an animal, a machine, a group, a nation. So the first step will be to identify this power source. Consider the fable of Antaeus, a figure from Greek mythology. He was the son of Poseidon and Gaia, the goddess of the Earth. According to the fable, Antaeus was a giant who inhabited Libya; he was notorious for challenging travelers who passed through his region to wrestling matches. No one was able to defeat him. The reason was that he was in physical contact with the earth, and his mother Gaia was thus able to give him special advantages. Antaeus exploited his special advantage over his opponents by killing them all. He even built a temple to his father Poseidon with a number of his victims' skulls.

But eventually Antaeus crossed paths with the wrong traveler. He encountered Hercules, and the goddess Athena had told Hercules the secret to defeating Antaeus. She told him to seize hold of the giant and lift him up in the air. This would remove him from contact with the earth, and deny him his source of sustenance and power. Hercules did precisely this; he lifted the giant in the air and squeezed the life out of him in a powerful bear-hug. And that was the end of Antaeus.

There are countless illustrations of this principle in history, of course, but for some reason this fable always comes to my mind. Another example can be found in the life of the emperor Julian in 361 A.D. He had just embarked on his course of rebellion against his malicious cousin Constantius, who was at that time wearing the royal purple. The historian Ammianus (XXI.9) tells us that Julian was moving quickly with his forces from Gaul to confront his cousin. Because Julian was a man of simple wants and means, he was able to move more quickly than many other commanders might have been able to move. He even liked to repeat the saying of the Persian emperor Cyrus, who, when on the march and asked by a host what kind of food he should prepare, answered, "Only bread, for I hope to eat near a stream." In this way he made clear that he needed only bread and water while on the march.

As Julian moved through the Alps, he knew he would encounter Constantius's men along the way. There was a government official named Lucillianus who was an important district leader near the city of Sirmium. Lucillianus planned on resisting Julian when he would pass through: his loyalties lay with Constantius. But Julian moved fast–so fast, in fact, that the historian Ammianus describes his march as similar to a "blazing dart" or a "meteor." He arrived at the town of Bononea in Pannonia (probably the modern Bonmunster) before anyone knew very much about his movements. Bononea was about nineteen miles from Sirmium.

Julian then summoned Lucillianus. It was at night or the early morning, and he was asleep. Julian had given instructions that his men should bring him by force if necessary. Lucillianus was terrified and thought he might be executed. But when he finally saw

Julian, he was given the chance to show his respects to the emperor, and quickly realized that he would not be harmed. Yet he still had an insolent tongue. He tried to make Julian doubt his course of action, and implied that Constantius had more support than did he. He told Julian, "My emperor, you have recklessly and rashly committed yourself with a few supporters to the provinces of someone else." Julian's response to this was:

> Save these prudent words for Constantius. I have shown you the insignia of imperial power not as an advisor, but so that you might stop quaking in fear.

And this ended the conversation; Lucillianus was taken away. Through such methods did Julian tame or remove his opponent Constantius's supporters. He understood that by detaching Constantius from his support network, he could be more easily isolated for the final blows.

38. The Guardian Spirit And The "Genii"

Most of us are familiar with the idea of the "patron saint" in Christianity. The doctrine is even found in branches of other religions. It is a comforting thing to believe that there is someone out there watching over us, and protecting us in an hour of need. I never used to give this idea much serious thought until recent years. But the idea predates Christianity; it was absorbed into Christianity from beliefs that came before it. The idea of the "guardian spirit" was a commonly-accepted one in the late classical world, as this passage from the historian Ammianus Marcellinus reveals:

> For the theologians maintain that there are associated with all men at their birth, but without interference with the established course of destiny, certain divinities of that sort, as directors of their conduct; but they have been seen by only a very few, whom their manifold merits have raised to eminence. And this oracles and writers of distinction have shown; among the latter is also the comic poet Menander, in whom we read these two *senarii* [verses]:

A daemon is assigned to every man
At birth, to be the leader of his life.

> Likewise from the immortal poems of Homer we are given to understand that it was not the gods of heaven that spoke with brave men, and stood by them or aided them as they fought, but that guardian spirits attended them; and through reliance upon their special support, it is said, that Pythagoras, Socrates, and Numa Pompilius became famous; also the earlier Scipio, and (as some believe) Marius and Octavianus, who first had the title of Augustus conferred on him, and Hermes Trismegistus, Apollonius of Tyana, and Plotinus, who ventured to discourse on this mystic theme, and to present a profound discussion of the question by what elements these spirits are linked with men's souls, and taking them to their bosoms, as it were, protect them (as long as possible) and give them higher instruction, if they perceive that they are pure and kept from the pollution of sin through association with an immaculate body. [XXI.14; *Trans. by J.C. Rolfe*]

Notice that Ammianus draws a distinction between the "guardian spirit" and the soul of the individual. The two are not the same thing. In the Roman religion there was something called the *genius*: an attendant spirit that each man possessed, and that accompanied him throughout his life. St. Augustine specifically equated it with the Christian concept of the soul:

> It is he, then, with whom is the dominion of all sowings. What is Genius? He is the god who is set over, and has the power of begetting, all things. Who else than the world do they believe to have this power, to which it has been said: *Almighty Jove, progenitor and mother?* And when in another place he says that Genius is the rational soul of every one, and therefore exists separately in each individual, but that the corresponding soul of the world is God, he just comes back to this same thing — namely, that the

> soul of the world itself is to be held to be, as it were, the universal genius. This, therefore, is what he calls Jupiter. For if every genius is a god, and the soul of every man a genius, it follows that the soul of every man is a god. But if very absurdity compels even these theologists themselves to shrink from this, it remains that they call that genius god by special and pre-eminent distinction, whom they call the soul of the world, and therefore Jupiter. [*City of God* VII.13; *Trans. by Cath. Encyclopedia*]

It is important to remember that the word *genius* is a Latin word, not an English one; its plural form is *genii*. We should not be confused by the fact that an English word has an identical spelling. The Latin *genius* has nothing whatsoever to do with superior intelligence or anything of that sort. It is a religious and spiritual term. But what is the connection between a guardian spirit and an individual man's *genius*? As the passage from Ammianus above suggests, it appears that the guardian spirit nurtures and protects each man's individual soul, guiding it along the right path in life, and helping it to reach a higher state of perfection. This makes sense in the context in which the passage appears. Ammianus is describing the elevation of the emperor Julian to the throne upon the sudden death of his cousin Constantius. The historian hints that the incident is the fulfillment of the intentions of Julian's guiding spirit.

I suppose the next question would be this: how do we find our guardian spirit, or know what it will be? Or can it even be found? I am not sure about the answer to this question. I can only rely on my own intuition and what I have read on these subjects (which is often ambiguous and contradictory). But I suspect that a guardian spirit cannot be sought out; it seeks you, and reveals itself to you, rather than the other way around. This to me has the ring of truth. In my life, I have been through enough hazards, scrapes, and dangers to feel comfortable with the idea of a guardian spirit watching over me. Whether this is "literally true" I neither know nor care to know. It matters only that the paradigm helps me make sense of some past experiences.

Now I know there are readers who will smile at what they believe to be superstitious relics that have no bearing on their modern lives. I suppose there are many who will see all of this as a comfortable delusion. Maybe they are right; but for my part I find it useful to explore the different ways that man has expressed his innermost thoughts on Fate, destiny, and the soul, even if some of those ideas run counter to accepted modern "orthodoxy." Sometimes great wisdom is hidden in unexpected places. Beyond this, man needs creative ways of wrapping his mind around abstract concepts; metaphysics and religion sometimes need to be tethered to comprehensible reality. Which paradigm we choose to describe the world is entirely up to us; and there is nothing wrong with believing two different things at the same time. Reality has many facets, many sides, and many faces.

39. The Symbols Of Power Are Not Substitutes For Power

Some are tempted to confuse the symbols of power with the reality of power. They are not the same thing. Power is the one thing that cannot be faked. For a time, perhaps, the bluffer can maintain an illusion of authority; he can go through his empty pantomime, imagining he is fooling everyone; but sooner or later, the truth will shine through. And then he will discover that the only one who has been deceived is himself. Symbolism, bombast, and slight-of-hand are no substitutes for the real thing. Some anecdotes from the historian Ammianus Marcellinus, so often mentioned in these pages, help us to reinforce this point.

In 362 A.D., soon after the emperor Julian had been elevated to the throne upon the death of his cousin Constantius, he was traveling near the city of Ancyra (currently known as Angora). Like many prominent public officials, he was constantly assailed by petitioners, office-seekers, and others from the general public. As you might imagine, it was the type of situation that would test any man's patience. Yet despite all this pressure, Julian maintained his impartial and judicious tone. Ammianus says that Julian was

> [A] more stern judge than Cassius or Lycurgus [famous law-giving figures from antiquity], and evaluated the evidence in his cases with legal neutrality, giving to each what was due to him, and never straying from the truth (*suum cuique tribuebat, nusquam a vero abductus*). [XXII.9.8]

Julian had a special dislike for those who spread malicious gossip about others. As a youth, he had often been the victim of such back-stabbers and trouble-makers, and these experiences made him acutely sensitive to the harm they could cause. On the other hand, he always tried to maintain his even-tempered judgment, never veering into overt rage. About this time he was approached by a man who made venomous accusations about some personal enemy. The accuser essentially accused his enemy of having committed treasonous acts, and wanted the emperor or one of his officials to do something about it. The actual transgression was this: the man was alleged to have made, and worn, a purple silk robe. Now, this may sound like a ridiculously trifling offense, but in those days the wearing of purple garments was reserved for the head of state only. The emperor could don the purple, and no one else. To attempt this was a crime.

Julian tried to dismiss the man and his complaint, believing it was nothing more than an attempt to remove a personal enemy on some trumped-up pretext. Yet the accuser persisted, and refused to take the hint. Julian then lost his patience with the man, and said this to him:

> I want a pair of purple shoes given to this dangerous big-mouth, so that he can give them to his enemy, whom he claims has a purple cloak. He will then learn what mere garments mean without real power behind them.

And with this, he had the man removed from his presence. Mere clothing–mere symbols–mean nothing unless they are backed up by true authority. From this we can extrapolate a general rule: the symbolism of power is not a substitute for real power. This may seem obvious, but it is not. If you follow the news on a daily basis, or interact regularly with your friends, family, and co-workers, you will find that many people are too willing to replace illusion with reality. They believe that bragging, bombast, or symbolism can be used to hide failure, to assert authority, or to confuse others. In time, they will discover the pure folly of this way of behaving.

Another example here is relevant (XXII.10). One time, Julian was presiding over a legal proceeding. Two parties were trying to adjudicate a dispute they had with each other. The plaintiff was a former court officer, and the defendant was a female citizen. When the defendant appeared in court, she saw that the plaintiff had (inappropriately) put on a belt (*cinctum*) that symbolized the authority of his former position. Apparently, the man thought that, even though he was now a private citizen, he might be able to score points with the judge by wrapping himself with this former symbol of authority. The woman protested angrily at the plaintiff's effrontery, believing that her opponent might be getting an unfair advantage. But Julian waved away her concerns. He said, "Continue with your case, woman. This man has belted himself in order to wade through the mud more easily; it cannot do any harm to your case." By this he meant to say that he, as an impartial judge, would not be influenced by the plaintiff's antics, or by the empty symbol of his power. He was capable of distinguishing real power, real authority, from an empty charade.

40. To Comprehend, You Must First Have The Desire To Comprehend

If you want to understand someone, you must have the desire to hear that person. You must have the willingness to open up your mind, to open up your heart, and be prepared to receive the communication that he or she is sending out. If this open-mindedness is not there, you will not hear the other person, even if he happens to speak your language. You will close your mind, and no words uttered by the other party will make any difference. If you have ever been a traveler in a foreign land, and you speak the language of that country, you may have encountered a situation where some person you are speaking to is not really hearing you. You may have all the words in your sentence in a grammatically correct form. Your pronunciation may be good. And yet the other person may be looking at you with furrowed brows, not comprehending what he is hearing. This is an example of a blocked mind: he can hear your words, but his eyes are telling him, "this is a foreigner." And he may be the type of close-minded person who cannot, or will not, open his mind or heart to a foreign person.

Conversely, you may have noticed the reverse. When you first began learning the foreign language in question, maybe your abilities were not so good. And maybe you encountered a kindly person who did not mentally "shut down" at the sight of you. They seemed to follow everything you were saying, even though your vocabulary and grammar were deficient. *More importantly, they adapted their speaking style to match your level of comprehension.* This is an example of how an open-minded person behaves, and stands in contrast to what we mentioned in the preceding paragraph.

So this is the point: when someone wants to hear you, he will make the effort to hear you. And when someone doesn't want to hear you, he will not hear you, even if you speak in a cogent way. His mind is not receptive to an encounter with a foreigner. This observation, I think, is an important one for us to make. When you encounter a foreign person who is trying to speak to you, you need to open your mind up and try to hear him. You have to make the effort. And if you find yourself a visitor in someone else's country, don't take it personally if someone mentally blocks you out. It is just the way things are.

I remember reading accounts of how the Romans and Greeks sometimes traded with the nomadic peoples of eastern Europe. Neither party spoke each other's language. But this is how they conducted business: each side would arrange their goods on the opposing banks of a river or stream that separated them. Each side could see what the other had. And they bartered by just pointing to various goods for inspection from one river bank to the other. Hardly a word would be spoken; and yet commerce was able to take place. Why? Because when two parties want to understand each other, they make the effort. They open their minds. It does not matter that they speak different languages. It does not matter that their habits, cultures, or ways are different. If the will to listen is there, then listening will take place. The historian Ammianus Marcellinus mentions this form of barter in an aside in his history. It is mentioned in one of the earliest Western references to the people of China (he calls the Chinese "Seres"). The quote below, written in the late 4th century A.D., is also one of the earliest Western references to silk. This is what he says:

> The Seres themselves lead a peaceful life, forever unacquainted with arms and warfare; and since to gentle and quiet folk ease is pleasurable, they are troublesome to none of their neighbors...There is an abundance of well-lighted woods, the trees of which

> [mulberry?] produce a substance which they work with frequent sprinkling, like a kind of fleece; then from the wool-like material, mixed with water, they draw out very fine threads, spin the yarn, and make *sericum* [the Latin word for silk] formerly for the use of the nobility, but nowadays available even to the lowest without any distinction…And when strangers, in order to buy threads or anything else, cross the river, their wares are laid out and with no exchange of words their value is estimated by the eye alone; and they are so abstemious, that they hand over their own products without themselves getting any foreign ware in return. [XXIII.6.67; *trans. by J.C. Rolfe*]

In the situation described above, two parties who had absolutely know knowledge of each others' language were able to communicate. There existed a desire to conduct commerce, and this desire enabled communication to take place. I remember, many years ago, spending some time in a certain Asian country. I was not fluent in its language, but I was able to handle myself in basic social situations. But many people there were not accustomed to dealing with foreigners on a meaningful level. Even if a perfectly fluent stream of words came out of my mouth (e.g., in a request for directions), sometimes the person standing in front of me could not connect the words he was hearing with the Western face he was seeing. His brain might shut down, and he would scurry away, unwilling to have his preconceptions about foreigners shattered; or he would simply stand there in mute incomprehension.

On the other hand, sometimes I would encounter people who behaved in just the opposite way. They went out of their way to try to understand, drawing the necessary inferences from words and context. Their minds were receptive to foreigners, and they had a desire to understand. And this made all the difference. It seems so me that we should make a conscious effort in our lives truly to listen to others. We should open our minds first, and then our ears second. Instead of looking for reasons *not* to understand someone, we should look for reasons to comprehend the *essence of his communication.* To do this, *we must rid our minds of fears, phobias, stereotypes, prejudices, and preconceptions, all of which are obstacles to communication.* If the will to comprehend is there, you will comprehend. The decision is yours.

41. The Boar And The Wolf Of Sant' Antonio

I will turn again to Biondo Flavio's geographical compendium of Italy called *Italia Illustrata*, which was published in 1453. Flavio traveled all over the Italian peninsula and recorded historical information, anecdota, and local customs of the Italian countryside in the late medieval period. During his tour of Tuscany, he found himself in the region near the city of Petriolo. Here there was a remote monastery dedicated to Sant' Angelo named the Eremo di Sant' Antonio in Val d'Aspra. Flavio describes the place as being at the top of an irregular road threading through forested hills. It was also an austere place, not lavish at all in its construction (*ut ad parum sumptuose et minus laute aedificatum te conferas monasterium*).

It was here that Flavio was told a story by the monks who resided there. The tale–an account of a fight between two animals and its aftermath–is related with such intensity that Flavio clearly meant it to convey some allegorical meaning. It was not unusual in those days for writers to cloak allegories in the form of anecdotes. But it seems the event actually happened; we will relate it here, and discuss its meaning.

On the grounds of the monastery was an abandoned garden covered in brambles and a large, coarse type of fern called bracken. Flavio tells us that this large, coarse plant produced a thick root that was actually edible. In times of famine, he says, it was not unusual for Italian peasants to dig up the fern, pound the roots into a paste, and make a kind of coarse bread with it. One day a large, five-hundred-pound boar began to enter the abandoned garden to dig up the fern roots and eat them, as these animals commonly do. The monks wanted to put an end to this dangerous nuisance, and sent for a professional hunter to rid them of the beast.

The hunter arrived at the monastery and spent some time observing the boar in the early morning hours through the narrow windows of the monastery. He was equipped with poisoned arrows for his task, and intended to use a crossbow (in Italian called a *balista*). Some of the younger monks and brothers assisted the hunter in his stalking and observation of the boar. One morning at dawn, they told him that they could see a wolf crouching in the garden, stalking the boar for himself. His body was pressed flat on the ground, and he was observing the boar with greedy intensity. But the boar was absorbed in his feeding, rooting around the ferns, tearing up the garden, and oblivious to what danger was near to him.

As the boar was doing its feeding, it would often raise up its hindquarters as it plunged its snout into the ground. In doing this, it would expose its large scrotum and soft underbelly. The wolf waited for his chance, and then struck with speed and intensity. It lunged for the boar's scrotum, bit down on it, and clamped its jaws shut like a vise. The boar roared out in pain, throwing its body this way and that all over the garden, tearing up ferns and brambles, and bleeding profusely. Frantically, it tried to swivel its tusks around to maul his attacker, but the wolf somehow was always just out of reach. The horrified brothers watched all this from their vantage point in the monastery, aware that they were witnessing a battle to the death. The garden was eventually strewn with so much gore and debris that, Flavio says, "one might have said that it was specifically arranged with these items for this event (*ut conserendo eius modi duello constratam praeparatamque fuisse quis dixerit*)." After about 30 minutes of brute struggle, the boar collapsed from exhaustion, with the wolf still locked on his genitals and underbelly. The wolf immediately began to feed on his kill, burying his snout in the boar's carcass with the same relish as the boar had shortly before feasted upon the bracken roots.

The hunter had been watching all this, of course, from his hiding place in the monastery. He then raised his crossbow, fitted with a poisoned bolt, and fired it at the triumphant wolf. The bolt found its mark, and the wolf writhed about in pain. The hunter quickly launched a second missile at the wolf, and this one finished him off. The monks, Flavio relates, were a bit disappointed by the wolf's speedy demise, as they had wished to "torture him to death while he was still half-alive." And with this comment, Flavio abruptly ends his story (*Sed hoc ad Petriolum satis*).

What is the meaning of this strange tale, and why did Flavio feel compelled to relate it in such gory detail? The answers are not entirely clear, but I will offer my own opinion. I think his intention was to warn readers (especially the princes and cardinals whom he knew would read his book) that blood begets blood, and cruelty begets cruelty. In effect, *that which you do to someone else, so that will be done to you.* The idea is that we should be mindful that there is always someone out there who is bigger and more powerful than we are; and that our own savagery will often be visited on us by someone of superior resources. There is an old Arabic proverb that relates this sentiment in a very clear way. The proverb reads:

الدم و الهدم الهدم.

Literally, this means "Blood, blood, and ruin, ruin!" The great German philologist G.W. Freytag, in his monumental 1838 (p. 477, Bonn ed.) treatise on Arabic proverbs *Arabum Proverbia,* states that this saying conveys the idea of "Beware lest you shed my blood, for my blood is your blood, and my ruin is your ruin (*Cave, ne sanguinem meum effundas, nam sanguis meus est sanguis tuus et ruina mea est ruina tua*)." And so this turned out to be in the fight between the boar and the wolf. For me this is one of those lessons that resounds more with the passage of years. Youth often believes itself invincible, forgetting that after every victory there is often someone more formidable hiding around the corner. We should not forget this. If only out of a sense of self-preservation, it is wise not to take too much delight in the shedding of blood, or the exercise of unjust power.

42. The Wrath Of Least Persistence

Everyone has heard the tired phrase, "path of least resistance." It represents a principle that I have no objection to. Of course there is no reason to make more work for oneself without good reason. No one is arguing with this idea; all things being equal, the shortest path to a goal is usually the best. But it occurred to me today to take this phrase and modify it a bit to create another principle, one perhaps equally valid, yet one far less frequently discussed. Let us consider this new phrase: *the wrath of least persistence.* What do I mean by this?

It seems to me that more damage has come from *failure to press our advantages, failure to pursue a defeated enemy, and failure to work diligently*, than has come from some momentous error of commission on our part. We have harmed ourselves more by our *inaction* than by our action; by failing to be diligent, by failing to pursue a defeated enemy, or by failing to press our advantage in some situation, we have been guilty of a lack of persistence. Fortune hates men who sit on their laurels. She despises those who, because of their own arrogance or indifference, prefer to sit comfortably and await developments, rather than seizing the moment for action. This is what I mean by the phrase wrath of least persistence. A failure of persistence on our part invites a wrathful retribution by Fortune.

Military history is littered with examples of generals who failed to pursue defeated enemies. It happens all the time. And it usually happens for one (or more) of these three reasons. One, the victor is utterly exhausted; two, the victor lacks (or thinks he lacks) actionable intelligence about his enemy; and three, the victor is convinced that his enemy is finished, thus relieving himself of his obligation to pursue. This usually ends up being a crucial mistake. Imagine what the coalition of Italians and Spaniards might have done to their enemy had they followed up their crushing naval victory at Lepanto in 1571 with a direct assault on Constantinople. But the best generals do understand the importance of pursuit. Julius Caesar and Napoleon always made a point of pursuing their enemies until they were totally defeated. "Your objective is Lee's army," U.S. Grant counseled a subordinate general during the final stages of the American Civil War. "Where he goes," Grant admonished, "you will go also." Other commanders were no less mindful. One example of this principle I like very much.

The historian Livy (XXV.37) relates that a Roman knight named Lucius Marcius (the historian Frontinus (II.10) calls him Titus Marcius) was tasked with taking over command of the remains of the armies of the Scipios in Spain in 212 B.C. With his forces, he once came across two camps of Carthaginians that were relatively close to each other. His men were tired and demanded a rest from the long marches that they had been subjected to; but he was not about to do this. He knew the enemy was celebrating a recent victory and had lowered its guard; so he wanted to attack the Carthaginians in the dead of night while they were unprepared. This Marcius did. He smashed the nearer camp, and slew its occupants to a man. His men then wanted him to take a rest, and resume the campaign on the following day. But Marcius was not willing to do this. He ordered his men, much against their will, to get themselves ready for action again. He attacked the second camp on the same night, and was victorious there also. This series of actions restored to Rome its control of Spain. Marcius had made use of a maxim that can even be found in the Old Testament (*I Samuel 30*):

> Then David said to Abiathar the priest, the son of Ahimelek, "Bring me the ephod." Abiathar brought it to him, and David inquired of the Lord, "Shall I pursue this raiding party? Will I overtake them?" "Pursue them," he answered. "You will certainly overtake them and succeed in the rescue."

Pursue them and you will succeed. There are so many examples of commanders allowing their enemies to slip through their fingers that we need hardly cite any of them here. Why does this happen so often? Arrogance has much to do with it. Insolence and pride blind men to the right courses of action, and emotion convinces them that they have assessed the situation correctly. Along these lines, Herodotus tells us that Xerxes was guilty of this many times during his ill-fated attempt to invade Greece. In book VII.8 of his *History*, Herodotus recounts how Xerxes assembled a number of dignitaries before embarking on his invasion. Xerxes told them this in his own haughty way:

> I have brought you together so that I might not seem to have used solely my own counsel before planning this expedition. But remember that your job here is not to advise me, but to obey.

With this arrogant and dismissive comment, the king revealed that he was not interested in listening to his experts; he was only interested in listening to his flunkies and relying on his personal delusions. The price he paid for this was a very high one. Even the great Hannibal, so often celebrated, was not perfect: he might have followed up his tremendous victory at Cannae with a direct march on Rome, but seems to have thought his enemy was already finished. Even when his lieutenant Maharbal told him that he knew a way for Hannibal "to dine on the Capitol in Rome" in a few days,

Hannibal did not take him seriously (Livy XXII.5.1–4). Even the greatest of commanders have made this error; and Fortune has made a point of punishing them for it.

If those who are the "least persistent" suffer the most "wrath" from Fortune, it should follow that the most diligent and persistent should win from Her the most favor. Valerius Maximus (VIII.7) tells us of a politician and orator named Roscius, who was famous for his theatrical gestures while he made speeches. To many people with no knowledge of how to craft speeches and arguments, it seemed that Roscius was acting randomly and carelessly. It seemed that just did things at the spur of the moment. But he was not some buffoon. He actually practiced each and every gesture he made during his speeches, so that the proper effect was produced on his audience. By his diligence and applied effort, he won the favor not just of the electorate, but also the friendship and respect of many influential men. Hard work in preparation for some task is the key to success in any field. Valerius has an eloquent way of stating this principle:

> These are the rewards of focused, anxious, and unrelenting study; and in this way can a modest actor find a praiseworthy place for himself among the rolls of such great men. [*Haec sunt attenti et anxii et numquam cessantis studii praemia, propter quae tantorum virorum laudibus non impudenter se persona histrionis inserit*]

This how to avoid the "wrath of least persistence." Those who are the least persistent will be punished by the wrath of Fortune. We should prepare, train, and taking nothing for granted; we should avoid arrogant behavior and close-minded attitudes; and we must constantly strive for knowledge in various fields. This–*this maximum persistence*–is the way to avoid to wrath of Fortune, and make her favorably disposed towards us and our designs. *Pursue them, and you will succeed.*

43. Why We Must Not Rely On First Impressions

It is often said that a man should rely on his first impressions of things when trying to form a final judgment. There is some merit to instinct; but it seems to me that reasoned deliberation will always provide more accurate results than the shifting sands of sense-perception. We cannot know all things, or even many things, at a glance. Julian, one of the greatest of the late Roman emperors, was an accomplished writer in his own right. In his *Panegyric in Honor of Eusebia*, a sincere expression of gratitude to the wife of his cousin Constantius, he writes the following lines:

> For there are two jars, so to speak, of these two kinds of human affection, and Eusebia drew in equal measure from both...

Now what was Julian referring to when he spoke of these "two jars" of human affection? The reference is to an aside in the *Iliad* (XXIV.525), where the poet says:

> For on this have the gods spun the thread for wretched mortals, that they should live in pain; and themselves are sorrowless.
>
> For two urns are set upon the floor of Zeus of gifts that he giveth, the one of ills, the other of blessings.
>
> To whomsoever Zeus, that hurleth the thunderbolt, giveth a mingled lot, that man meeteth now with evil, now with good.

So we have these two urns set before us, if you will, by Fortune. One is filled with evil things, and the other with good; and it will be our lot to sample from both of these urns, as Fate decrees for us. So there is no point in wasting time over injuries and the bad luck that we have suffered; it is all part of the arrangement that has been set in place since the beginning of time. The only way we can "shape" the outcome of events is to try to make use of our Reason, as Nature provides us, in such a way that we can overcome the deceptions and illusions of the senses. The failure to cultivate our powers of reason condemns us to the slavery of the senses. Julian makes this very point in another quote from the same panegyric mentioned above:

> For beauty alone, if it lacks the support of birth and the other advantages I have mentioned, is not

> enough to induce even a licentious man, a mere citizen, to kindle the marriage torch, though both combined have brought about many a match, but when they occur without sweetness or charm of character they are seen to be far from desirable.

Beauty alone is not enough: we cannot rely on the pleasurable sensations provided by our organs of sense in making important decisions like marriage. The fact that many people make this very mistake only reinforces the importance of the point. And if Reason is equally matched with the seductive call of the senses, we should always cast our vote in favor of Reason. One deceives; the other counsels. There was a custom at the Areopagus of ancient Athens that, during a trial by jury, if the votes were cast evenly for both the defendant and the plaintiff, the public would award the "vote" of the goddess Athena to the person who would have suffered the sanction, thereby acquitting him. An acquittal was symbolically secured by the intercession of Athena herself, who cast the "deciding" vote. This was the Athenians' way of saying that when things were evenly matched, the deciding vote should always be cast in favor of a merciful acquittal. In the same way, if our "first impressions" of something are exactly balanced by what our reason tells us, we should vote for reason. I think some will not agree with me on this, but I have found this rule to be a sound one.

But good judgment does not come automatically. It is not something that just settle on our head and shoulders like freshly-fallen snow. It comes about through diligent practice and experience, in the same way that the muscles of the body grow with productive and frequent periods of exercise. Good judgment also cannot be purchased at any price: *it comes about when good character works together with the guiding hand of Fortune*. Now no man can advance himself in years except through the passage of time. But even if we cannot buy years or experience, we can still learn from the experience of others. How can this be done? By listening carefully to those who have walked the path before us, and by a diligent study of history, which reveals the realities of human nature. The emperor Julian was entirely correct when he said:

> For many of those records of the experience of men of old, written as they are with the greatest skill, furnish to those who, by reason of their youth, have

> missed seeing such a spectacle, a clear and brilliant picture of those ancient exploits, and by this means many a tiro [i.e., a novice] has acquired a more mature understanding and judgment than belongs to very many older men; and that advantage which people think old age alone can give to mankind, I mean experience (for experience it is that enables an old man to talk more wisely than the young), *even this the study of history can give to the young if only they are diligent.*

So the lessons are there in the books of history, but only diligent study will allow us to unlock them and make them our own. And even here we cannot rely on first impressions: the same event in history needs to be examined from different perspectives and different angles, because truth is not one-sided. It may mean something different based on the perspective of the writer. Not only must we use different tellers of the same story, but we must also revisit the same story at different times in our lives. The same historical even may mean different things to us at different periods of our lives. This is because we ourselves become very different as we grow older. Appearances are deceiving; but this is because appearances necessarily involve the senses, and not reason. And the senses do not have a truth-telling style; this is the exclusive provenance of rational thought supported by either experience or diligent study. In the end, our goal is to increase our odds of receiving something from Zeus's urn of "good things" mentioned in the *Iliad* quote above, and avoiding something from the urn of evils.

44. Why We Must Seek The Divine Within Us

Upon his accession to the throne of Augustus in A.D. 364, the emperor Valentinian gave a short address to his troops. The speech is related in Ammianus Marcellinus's history (XXVI.1). The historian tells us that Valentinian appeared on an open expanse of ground and mounted a platform that had been arranged for this purpose; he was also wearing an imperial robe and a coronet. The speech itself was short and to the point. He began by thanking his men for their efforts in defending the provinces: at that time Rome's holdings were facing simultaneous incursions from Persia in the east and from Germans in the north. He then gave a few thoughts on what he believed was best for the maintenance of the common welfare (*quod conducere arbitror in commune*). Foremost in his mind was the choice of an appropriate colleague to help him in the task of governance.

In the period of the later empire, it was recognized that Rome was too large to be governed by one man. He knew he would have to contend with "huge volumes of worries" and "numerous changes in circumstances" (*curarum acervos et mutationes varias accidentium*). But the most important thing for him was the preservation and augmentation of "domestic concord," something that was so valuable that "even weak countries could make use of it to become strong." And this is undoubtedly true, as productivity and achievement can never be realized when a state is rent by factionalism, turbulence, and discord. But the most important part of his short address were these sentences:

> Fortune, the expediter of good plans, will hopefully give me a man of even-tempered character once I have done a diligent search, as far as I can do this and carry it through to completion. For as the wise men of old remind us–not only in matters of imperial power, where the greatest and most pressing dangers exist, but also in our daily and private affairs–*a stranger should only be joined in friendship once a prudent man has evaluated him. He ought not to be first joined, and then judged.* [XXVI.2].

Valentinian's meaning is clear. We should not consider someone a trusted friend or confidant until *after* such a person has shown himself to be worthy of the title "friend." We should not first consider someone a friend, and then only later put him through the evaluation process. In practice, of course, people often make this "evaluation process" a fast one; judgments are formed, and conclusions rendered, with the speed that expediency dictates. But you will eventually know the true character of something the longer you are in close proximity to it: the emperor Julian once mentioned (in his *Oration on the Cynic Heracleios*) the proverb "grape ripens against grape."

Yet it is not always an easy matter to know how useful these simple formulations are. To rule an empire is not easy; to run a business is not easy; and to rule a household is extremely difficult. With all respect to the emperor Valentinian, quoted above, we need something more than just simple formulas. This is because the crush of Fortune is sometimes too difficult to bear. If the average man, setting out on a journey, knew every possible danger he faced, he might be inclined to abandon the whole thing before his ship ever left port. This is the problem with simple advice and simple formulations: it often has the effect of discouraging a man, rather than encouraging him. Wise policy is good, but it may not be enough, as the emperor Julian says in his *Letter to Themistius*:

> For in such matters not virtue alone or a wise policy is paramount, but to a far greater degree Fortune holds sway throughout and compels events to incline as She wills…But a happiness that depends on the chances of Fortune is very rarely secure. And yet men who are engaged in public life cannot, as the saying is, so much as breathe unless she is on their side…Yet it is nothing wonderful to withstand Fortune when she is merely hostile, but much more wonderful it is to show oneself worthy of the favors she bestows. By her favors the greatest of kings, the conqueror [Alexander] of Asia was ensnared, and showed himself more cruel and more insolent than Darius and Xerxes, after he had become the master of their empire.

This primary role of Fortune in the affairs of men is a theme we have discussed here on many different occasions, and in many contexts; we have seen how Petrarch and Machiavelli tried to account for the role of Fortune in their own views of human affairs. The emperor Julian, whom I have just quoted above, presented his own interesting "solution" to the profoundly disturbing realization that we are not in control of everything in our lives. Julian quotes Plato's *Laws* [709a], where the philosopher says,

> God governs all things and with God, Fortune and Opportunity govern all human affairs: but there is a

> milder view that Art must needs go with them and must be their associate.

Julian went beyond even this. He thought that a man who was in charge of important affairs would inevitably become corrupted with authority; he would inevitably be filled with insolence and injustice. A Supreme Being, he believed, would therefore not allow human beings to be completely governed by themselves. Just as we humans do not allow goats and sheep to govern themselves, a Supreme Being would not want humans to be entirely self-governing. Placed over us, he says, are

> [B]eings of a more divine and higher race, I mean demons [which can be either good or bad]...God, since he loves mankind, has set over us a race of being superior to ourselves, the race of demons; and they with great ease both to themselves and us undertake the care of us and dispense peace, reverence, aye, and above all justice without stint, and thus they make the tribes of men harmonious and happy.

It should clearly be understood that when Julian speaks of "demons" he does not intend this word's modern, negative meaning. It is to be understood in its late Neoplatonic sense, colored by the theurgy of the philosopher Iamblichus: demons are intermediary "guiding spirits" between the worlds of Intellect and Soul. Cities and states that are not governed by some "divine spirit" are entirely left to the dangerous vagaries of Fortune:

> ...[I]n our day all cities that are governed not by a god but by a mortal man have no relief from evils and hardships. And the lesson is that we ought by every means in our power to imitate that life which is said to have existed in the days of Kronos: and in so far as the principle of immortality is in us we ought to be guided by it in our management of public and private affairs, of our houses and cities, calling the distribution of mind "law." But whether the government be in the hands of one man, or of an oligarchy or democracy, if it have a soul that hankers after pleasure and the lower appetites and demands to

indulge these, and if such a one rules over a city or individual having first trampled on the laws, there is no means of salvation.

So what Julian means by this, clearly, is that human judgment is not enough to protect us from Fortune. We must seek the intercession of "higher beings" to aid us in this task. "To me, at any rate," Julian said, "it seems that the task of reigning is beyond human powers, and that a king needs a more divine character, as indeed Plato too used to say." But we must still focus on the study of character and virtue; for by doing so we adhere to the last words of the philosopher Plotinus in his *Enneads*, when he implored his readers to "seek the gods within you." Self-study, then, almost becomes a *divine* duty, for it helps us to adopt divine aspects. The quote below perfectly summarizes his conclusion from a consideration of these questions, and deserves our careful attention:

> But to conceive true opinions about God is an achievement that not only requires perfect virtue, but one might well hesitate whether it be proper to call one who attains to this a man or a god. For if the saying is true that it is the nature of everything to become known to those who have an affinity with it, *then he who comes to know the essential nature of God would naturally be considered divine.*

All facets of our lives, and all phases of our lives, contribute to this effort. The diligent study of the virtues and character actually assists a soul in rising to higher plane of existence, such that it can take on certain divine aspects. And in this way, it may be shielded from the cruelties and randomness of Fortune. *We are men, it is true: but we can become men like gods.*

45. The Counsel Of Helios To A Noble Youth

There is a fable told in the Roman emperor Julian's oration *To the Cynic Heracleios* that is worth relating and discussing. The fable is rather involved, but we will extract its relevant parts here. The god Hermes once appeared before a youth who, though virtuous and good, was having some difficulties in life. Hermes said to the young man: "Follow me, and I will guide you by a better road. All you have to do is follow this winding and uneven road, where you see many other men stumbling and falling." The youth accepted this challenge. He armed himself with a sword, spear, and shield, and set himself to travel the road put before him. Eventually he came to the foot of a huge, craggy mountain. At this point, his guide Hermes said to him: "At the top of this vast mountain you will find the father of the gods. Make sure you worship and honor him with the greatest piety. You can ask of him whatever you wish."

And with this, Hermes vanished. The youth uttered a short prayer to Zeus, requesting his aid, and it was at this point that a feeling of divine ecstasy, a kind of trance, came over him. Suddenly he found himself before Helios, who in late antiquity (or at least in the writings of the Emperor Julian) came to be identified with the father of all the gods. Helios saw the boy and called in the goddess Athena for her opinion. She saw the youth's sword, spear, and shield, but could see he had no helmet. The youth told the goddess that he had no helmet, and that it was hard enough for him to have acquired what he had already. He said that he was not favored by his family or by other people he knew, and had received little or no help in life.

Helios then led the youth to a vantage-point on the mountain peak where he could see down to the world of mortals below. The king of the gods asked the boy what he saw. The boy said, "I see my kinsmen and friends going about their lives in blissful ignorance. A few are honest, but many are vicious and cruel. They live lives of dissolution and ignorance, unable to appreciate the divine spark that resides within them." Helios and Athena then bade the youth to return to earth, and gave him the following advice for him to carry out:

> The men you see often are asleep, and are often deceived. You must be sober and vigilant, so that you do not allow yourself to be taken in by flatterers who appear to be friends. A flatterer is like a smith who, though coming out of his forge, is dressed in white; he then tries to convince you of his lily-white purity while being covered with ash and soot from head to toe. You must also choose your friends

> wisely, and treat them as true friends. Remember that they are not your servants or orbiters. Your conduct towards them must be honest, generous, and noble: do not say one thing to them and do another, for this is the way of snakes. And treachery is the vilest of all deeds. Now depart with an elevated spirit. Know, O my son, that we, the gods of Olympus, will be with you at all times. Never become a slave to your passions, nor allow yourself to become a slave to someone else's passions.
>
> Take the armor with you that you have brought here; it will be useful to you. *But before you go, I will give you this torch. With it a great light will shine for you, and with the aid of this light, you will not crave the material things of the earth.* Athena will give you an aegis [an animal-skin or shield] and a helmet. Hermes here will give you a golden wand. Go to your homeland, then, and obey our laws, and do not allow anyone to misdirect you away from our commands. As long as you do so, you will be honored and respected. *And know also that your mortal body was given you so that you might carry out these commands. Remember that you have an immortal soul that comes from us; and that this soul can become something godlike.*

This was the advice given by Helios to the youth, as related by the emperor Julian. What is the meaning of this fable? Julian was a Neoplatonist in his inclinations; for him, the story was definitely meant to be allegorical. As he saw it, the man who followed the path of virtue was literally following a divine path. It was not an easy road, and not every man would be willing to attempt it. But for those who did, rewards of incalculable value might be earned. The man who undertook this mission would carry the symbolic items like the aegis, torch, sword, and helmet; these would protect him from the iniquities and evils of the world. But what was perhaps most important was Julian's attitude towards a man's corporeal form. In keeping with the spirit of late antiquity, the body was seen as inferior to the soul; it was nothing but an instrument to be used towards the attainment of divine qualities. As Julian himself would say later in his *Oration*:

> Now the true short-cut to philosophy is this. A man must completely come out of himself and recognize that he is divine, and not only keep his mind untiringly and steadfastly fixed on divine and stainless and pure thoughts, but he must also utterly despise his body, and think it, in the words of Heracleitus, "more worthless than dirt." And by the easiest means he must satisfy his body's needs so long as the god commands him to use it as an instrument. [*Trans. by W.C. Wright*]

This has a very strong Neoplatonic flavor. And for Julian it was conduct that mattered, not surface appearances or memberships in organizations. One did not become a good man by joining groups alone; he had to demonstrate his goodness by positive acts. In this regard, Julian quoted the philosopher Diogenes, who said:

> It is absurd to think that any tax-collector can share in the rewards of the next world if he simply becomes initiated into some group, while great men like Agesilaus and Epaminondas are fated to lie in their graves. [Diog. Laertius VI.39].

Actions are what count, rather than appearances. Every man must remember that he is similar to the youth who was counseled by Helios: as he makes his way in the world, he has special tools give him by the immortal gods. He must make wise use of these tools, and always remember that he carries within him a spark of that Divine Light imparted to his soul from the moment of his birth. This is that "torch" (or even that aegis of Athena) referred to in the fable above; and a man can choose to make use of this divine aspect and develop it to its full potential, or he can elect to ignore it. These implements symbolize the possession of the noble virtues. And to take up this torch, to wear the aegis of Athena, and to carry these things along the road of life: *this is the path of true glory.*

46. The Right Man In The Right Place Can Make All The Difference

There are times in history where the right man in the right place can make all the difference. Accidents of fate, the changing circumstances of fortune, and the randomness of events all conspire to turn predictability into uncertainty; yet a man of learning, vision, and character may, at times, interpose himself in the middle of these whirlwinds and by his actions change the course of history. It happens all the time. One of the precious few Mexican manuscripts that survived the Spanish conquest, the Codex Borgia has a mysterious and tortured history. The book is a collection of prophecies, and is also considered to be one of the finest representations of the Aztec ceremonial calendar.

Like many Mesoamerican antiquities, we know precious little about its history; it appears to have been sent back to Europe soon after the Spanish conquest, and somehow made its way to Italy during the eighteenth century. It may have been a gift from a Spanish clergyman to some prince or nobleman, who kept it among his personal effects. We do know that it was discovered among Cardinal Stefano Borgia's papers by famed explorer Alexander von Humboldt in 1805; he inspected the manuscript personally and claimed that "I believe the codex belonged to the family of the Guistiniani princes."

If so, the fact that the manuscript survived at all is a miracle. But this is how things sometimes are in history: at precisely the right moment, the right man comes along and transforms disaster into salvation. Cardinal Stefano Borgia (bearing that name so famous from Italian Renaissance history) came across the manuscript by pure chance. Borgia (1731–1804) was no ordinary cardinal, but a man of consuming antiquarian interests, prodigious linguistic abilities, and pronounced scholarly temperament. He so valued learning that he was known to sell even his own personal effects to buy books. He was proficient not only in the classical languages, but also in Amharic, Coptic, Armenian, and Hebrew. Such a man knew what an original manuscript was when he saw it. Perhaps if there had been more men like him, a far greater number of irreplaceable ancient Mexican artifacts would have been preserved.

Borgia happened to be walking around the palace of one of these princes, and saw some children playing with a vellum book containing strange symbols and colorings. Servants, unaware of the book's value, had given it to the children as a toy. But Borgia immediately recognized this weird manuscript for it for what it was, and saved it. The children had already destroyed the first and last of its pages; had he not appeared on the scene at that very instant, it is likely that the entire book would have been irretrievably lost.

But this did not happen. He took the manuscript himself, and housed it in his own museum. Whether he paid for it, I have not been able to determine; but if not, there was never an appropriation so justified.

He must have been a man of considerable political acumen as well, for Pope Pius VI appointed him to be the municipal head of Rome as Napoleon approached the city in 1798. Borgia even found time to establish a museum in Velletri, and made it his life's work to fill this space with valuable rarities from all over the world. Just before he died, he turned over his collection of manuscripts to the *Santa Congregazione di Propaganda Fide*. The book was displayed in the Ethnographic Museum in the congregation's palace from 1883, and is now in the Vatican Library, that vast storehouse of all things ancient. The book itself contains about 76 pages, and is folded into 39 sheets of animal skin; in length, it measures 10.34 meters. The subject matter of the book is religious and prophetic: it describes the origin and nature of some Aztec gods, as well as the deeds of Quetzalcoatl and his evil twin brother Xolotl.

Fate only needs the intervention of one good man. Sometimes this is all that is required: *the right man in the right place.* With the crush of modern life, and its attendant responsibilities, there is a tendency for us to think that our actions mean little. We are tempted to believe that nothing matters. Yet the story of the Codex Borgia's rescue from oblivion shows that this is not true. One man–the right man–can make all the difference. I was reading an article in a magazine yesterday about the exploits and tragic death of British explorer Henry Worsley. The author notes that Ernest Shackleton was an idol for Worsley, and that the former was known to be an incredibly capable leader of men. Shackleton knew how to get his men out of the worst scrapes imaginable. As one polar explorer put it, "For scientific leadership, give me Scott; for swift travel, Amundsen; but when you are in a hopeless situation, when there seems to be no way out, get on your knees and pray for Shackleton."

Absolutely right, I think. When the chips were down, and when disaster was hovering on the horizon, Shackleton was the man to call. And when precious books were perched on the edge of oblivion, Fate required the presence of Cardinal Borgia at just the right time. Is there some guiding hand of Fate that permits things to be so? I do not know. But of one thing I am certain: one man *can* make all the difference. *And when he is at the right place at the right time, he can move mountains.*

47. The Religion Of Mithras And Its Mysteries

The cult of Mithras remains generally unknown to the public, even, in many cases, to students of classical literature and ancient history. It will be useful to review its origins, doctrines, and the reasons for its extinction. It was an eastern ("oriental") faith of Persian origin. The god Mithras originally belonged to that complex pantheon of deities that can be found in the remote pasts of Persia and India. India, that eternal wellspring of religious faiths, was the ultimate source of Mithraism; the name "Mithra" appears in both the *Vedas* and the *Avesta*. Mithra (or "Mitra-Varuna") was held to be a god of light, a protector of truth and a deliverer from error. The worship of Mithra gradually percolated into Persia, where it became incorporated into Zoroastrianism and was assigned a position in that religion's cosmology.

Mithra occupied an intermediary place between the most elevated god Oromazes and the ruler of the realm of darkness Ahriman. From the beginning, the god was attended by a complicated series of rituals and ceremonial initiations, a feature that Mithraism would retain as it moved westward into the Greco-Roman world. The Greeks had a long tradition of contact with Persia and its customs, and it was only natural that aspects of that culture would begin to be felt in Europe. The primary means of dissemination of the cult of Mithra was through the military; Greek or Roman soldiers serving in the East came into contact with this strange "mystery" religion, were attracted by its rituals and masculine hierarchies, and brought it back home with them. As historian Franz Cumont writes, in his *The Mysteries of Mithra*, "The contact of all the theologies of the Orient and all the philosophies of Greece produced the most startling combinations, and the competition between the different creeds became exceedingly brisk." Over time, the pure Mithraism of India and Persia became blended and changed by Grecian and Roman elements; it added a strong Neoplatonic flavor, as well as Syriac and Assyrian colorings. It was also heavily influenced by Stoicism, as Cumont explains:

> Mysteries might possess for minds formed in the schools of Greece; philosophy also strove to reconcile their doctrines with its teachings, or rather the Asiatic priests pretended to discover in their sacred

> traditions the theories of the philosophic sects. None of these sects so readily lent itself to alliance with the popular devotion as that of the Stoa, and its influence on the formation of Mithraism was profound. An ancient myth sung by the Magi is quoted by Dion Chrysostomos on account of its allegorical resemblance to the Stoic cosmology; and many other Persian ideas were similarly modified by the pantheistic conceptions of the disciples of Zeno.

Since Mithraism tended to be a masculine religion, its practice took on the flavor of a secret society, with windowless temples dug into the earth, along with secret rituals that could only be revealed to initiates. Mithraism was combination of a Persian core mixed with Semitic rituals and adorned with Hellenic philosophical trappings in the form of Neoplatonism. This should not surprise us; all religions are in some ways composites of the environment from which they have evolved. With Roman expansion into Asia, the faith spread; the poet Statius mentions it in his *Thebiad* (I.717): *Persei sub rupibus antri Indignata sequi torquentem cornua Mithram.* It was a religion of soldiers, for its doctrines appealed to the masculine beliefs in sacrifice, redemption, and the acquisition of knowledge. Soldiers, like sailors, tend to be pious and superstitious, since so much of their lives depend on geography, the elements, and the randomness of fate.

What were the doctrines of this faith, the so-called "mysteries"? Because of its secret nature, we still to this day do not have a precise liturgy of Mithraism. It worshipped the four elements earth, air, fire, and water, and produced hymns in honor of the creative power of these elements. But the most potent of Mithraism's rituals was that surrounding the bull, a fertility symbol dating back to the dawn of history itself. Ancient man venerated the bull as a source of food, fertility, and the power of nature itself. The importance of the bull to the worship of Mithra is explained by scholar Franz Cumont:

> In the eyes of [ancient man], the capture of a wild bull was an achievement so highly fraught with honor as to be apparently no derogation even for a god. The redoubtable bull was grazing in a pasture on the mountain-side; the hero, resorting to a bold

> stratagem, seized it by the horns and succeeded in mounting it...Its conqueror then seizing it by its hind hoofs, dragged it backwards over a road strewn with obstacles into the cave which served as his home. This painful journey (*transitus*) of Mithra became the symbol of human sufferings. But the bull, it would appear, succeeded in making its escape from its prison, and roamed again at large over the mountain pastures. The Sun then sent the raven, his messenger, to carry to his ally the command to slay the fugitive.
>
> Mithra received this cruel mission much against his will, but submitting to the decree of Heaven he pursued the truant beast with his agile dog, succeeded in overtaking it just at the moment when it was taking refuge in the cave which it had quitted, and seizing it by the nostrils with one hand, with the other he plunged deep into its flank his hunting knife. Then came an extraordinary prodigy to pass. From the body of the moribund victim sprang all the useful herbs and plants that cover the earth with their verdure. From the spinal cord of the animal sprang the wheat that gives us our bread, and from its blood the vine that produces the sacred drink of the Mysteries....The seed of the bull, gathered and purified by the Moon, produced all the different species of useful animals, and its soul, under the protection of the dog, the faithful companion of Mithra, ascended into the celestial spheres above, where, receiving the honors of divinity, it became under the name of Silvanus the guardian of herds. Thus, through the sacrifice which he had so resignedly undertaken, the tauroctonous hero became the creator of all the beneficent beings on earth; and, from the death which he had caused, was born a new life, more rich and more fecund than the old.

This is the origin of the bull-sacrifice motif in Mithraism. Life is presented as a battle, and the continuation of life is dependent on sacrifice and struggle. The religion counseled resistance to carnal delights and sexual indulgence; this asceticism was probably a relic of its early Stoic influences. Mithraism also elevated dynamic action over passive contemplation, and courage over mercy. Good and evil were in constant tension with each other, its adherents believed, and only by constantly emphasizing good would a man be able to overcome the forces of darkness. This ethical code accounted for much of Mithraism's success. The new religion was remarkable in that it was able to adapt itself to a wide variety of environments and locales. There was a real possibility that it might have become the dominant religion of the Empire and of Europe. Temples to Mithras (*mithraea*) have been found all over the former Roman domains. Why, then, did the religion die out? Simply put, it could not compete with the spread of Christianity, which doomed many other Oriental cults of late antiquity (the cults of Adonis, Serapis, and Isis to name the most prominent).

Mithraism did not proselytize; and by forbidding women any role in the faith, it deprived itself of an incalculable source of potential power. Perhaps, too, Mithraism was too burdened with the weight of weird Indian and Persian gods that would have been bizarre to Roman, Greek, or Germanic sensibilities. It also must be said that Christianity persecuted all rival religions with a ferocity that was unmatched: mobs sacked temples to Mithras, slew Mithraic priests, and suppressed its liturgy on pain of physical retribution. Yet the influence of Mithraism is undeniable. Consider, for example, an ancient depiction of *Sol invictus*, the invincible Sun God of the Mithraic cosmology; it looks uncannily like the American Statue of Liberty in New York City, and must have had some substratal influence in its design. In history, nothing is ever really forgotten. A religion may die; but its art, ethic, and soul endure, in whatever incarnation human genius and sensibility see fit to generate.

48. Bad Character Will Inevitably Bring Consequences

The historian Ammianus, in describing the brief career of the usurper Procopius (326–366 A.D.), comments on the moral corruption inevitably caused by the abuse of power and privilege. It will have a familiar ring to those accustomed to the practices of contemporary politics:

> For in the midst of weapons of war and the call of the military trumpeteer, equality of condition makes dangers seem less burdensome. The power of martial virtue either obliterates what it confronts, or ennobles it; and death, if it results, is occasion for no feeling of shame. It causes an end to life but also an end to suffering. But when laws and regulations are perverted for impious schemes; when sitting judges hypocritically mouth the sentiments of Cato and Cassius while at the same time everything plays out according to the dictates of those who hold real power, and on whose whim are decided current questions of life and death; then the result is abrupt and mortal catastrophe. [*Res Gestae* XXVI.10.9]

The historian is reminding us that a state of war can lighten the burdens of danger, as it may promote a sense of solidarity born of shared hardships. But when a nation's laws and rules are abused by those in power for their own pernicious ends and "impious schemes," and when judges pretend to be fair and just while serving the interests of power at the expense of justice and fairness, then the ultimate result will be disaster. The reader will remember this theme from Sallust, also: moral corruption, hubris, and the perversion of institutions inevitably have consequences. And while the day of reckoning may be postponed again and again through whatever artifice may prove useful, there can be little doubt that a day of reckoning will certainly come. The personality of the emperor Valentinian I (321–375 A.D.) is similarly illustrative. Ammianus describes him as a cruel and arbitrary man from the early years of his reign. As much as he tried to keep his malevolence under control, it would bubble to the surface no matter how hard he tried to restrain it. It was almost as if he was poisoned by anger:

> Knowledgeable men define this anger to be a continuous, sometimes permanent, ulcer of the mind. They say it arises from a kind of defect in the mind, and say that the sickly are more prone to anger than the healthy, women than men, the elderly than the young, and the miserable than the lucky. (XXVII.7.6)

Anger is thus an "ulcer of the mind." And so may anger become bound up with a certain type of personality. Valentinian died when he was fifty-five years old from some kind of wasting disease that Ammianus describes vividly (XXX.6.4). It was almost as if his body and mind had been equally rotten, as often happens in such people. The historian makes it clear that Valentinian could never understand the wisdom of avoiding extremes. "He was unmindful of the fact that a ruler must avoid, as he would a mountain cliff, extremes of all kinds." [*Oblitus profecto quod regenti imperium omnia nimia, velut praecipites scopuli, sunt evitanda*]. (XXX.7.8)

To illustrate the importance of a ruler's avoiding extremes, Ammianus cites the example of the old Persian king Artaxerxes. He had an "innate even-temperedness" that corrected many of the harsh practices of his era. Instead of cutting off the heads of the convicted, he would often just cut off their turbans; and in lieu of cutting off their ears, he would often just snip off the threads dangling from their turbans. This moderation and mildness earned him the respect of most of his subjects. But Valentinian was cut from a different cloth; he did not respect this sort of ethic. There is a great saying of Cicero that Ammianus quotes on this subject; and it is wonderful for us that he does so, for the quote is not found in any of Cicero's extant writings:

> Having great power to save someone else has brought honor to many; but to have had too little power to destroy someone, has never for anyone been a cause for blame. [*Et enim multum posse ad salutem alterius, honori multis; parum potuissse ad exitium, probro nimini umquam fuit.*] (XXX.8.7).

And as time went on, Valentinian became more and more avaricious, more cruel, and more contemptuous of the rights of others. When his military campaign against the Parthians came to nothing, he found his treasury depleted. But instead of falling on the rich plutocrats who had profited from the war (as had the emperor Aurelian), Valentinian chose to resort to more and more cruelties. Restraint was not a word in his lexicon. Ammianus tells us that this corrupt emperor was completely unlike the Greek leader Themistocles, who refused to pick up a golden bracelet lying in plain view after touring a battlefield, knowing that it was not right that a leader should appear greedy for wealth. On seeing the ornament lying on the ground, he said to an attendant, "You may pick this up, since you are not Themistocles." Like many rulers of his type, he also resented and suspected men possessing greater ability or integrity than he. According the Ammianus, he despised those who were well-dressed, educated, or came from decent backgrounds (XXX.8.10); men of proven bravery he tried to belittle, knowing that he himself could never accomplish equal feats of valor. Being a man of low and base character himself, he assumed others were like him, and treated them accordingly.

He loved to ridicule cowards; and yet "he would turn pale when confronted with inconsequential frights." When confronted with proof that judges and officials he had appointed were unworthy of their offices, Valentinian would continue to protect and promote them. His first impulse was always to denounce, to punish, or to criticize; he was a man tormented by deep insecurities, who thought he could banish them by projecting them on to everyone else. Worse still, he did not know how to show compassion for the sufferings of others. Those who had been stricken by misfortune could expect no relief from an audience with him; he would send them away with platitudes at best, or punishment at worst. He had no knowledge or understanding of this idea:

> The ultimate purpose of a just authority–as the wise men teach us–is meant to be the usefulness and health of those who are ruled by it. [*Finis enim iusti imperii–ut sapientes docent–utilitas oboedientium aestimatur et salus*]. (XXX.8.14)

These were the negative character traits of the emperor Valentinian. Why do some leaders behave this way? The answer is that they do not know any other way to behave. They are immune to the lessons of history, the advice of others, or the commandments of right conduct. I think this quote by Ammianus best sums up this kind of mentality:

> It is not possible to fix the moral deviance of those who consider the things they most want to do to be the greatest virtues. [*Nil autem valet correctio pravitatum apud eos qui quod effici velint maximae putant esse virtutis*]. (XXVII.7.9)

Human nature is constant; character types and personalities have changed with glacial slowness down the centuries. If we encounter such men in the pages of history, we will be that much better prepared and equipped to deal with them in our own lives.

49. The Combat Of Sonnenberg And Sanseverino

It is right for us to celebrate great deeds of valor of ages past. By doing so we are inspired to achievement in our own affairs, and become connected to that electric current of masculine virtue that winds through the entire landscape of civilized, productive effort on this earth. It is good for us to be reminded of the feats of our predecessors; for if they fought, struggled, and overcame, then we know we have the ability to do the same. Let us now turn our attention to Italy during the waning days of the Renaissance.

The following account is described in Pietro Bembo's *History of Venice* (I.3). For some it is a long-dead tome; but for me, it is something very different. The year is 1487, and the Republic of Venice has a commercial domain that stretches across the Adriatic Sea, even pushing into the eastern Mediterranean. The shadow of war, however, appears from the north, in the Tyrol region of the Alps. As sometimes happens, conflict began for petty and trivial reasons. Sigismund, the cousin of the Holy Roman Emperor Frederick, was a local potentate there. As the historian Pietro Bembo describes him with subtle mockery, "He was not a bad man, but was the kind who readily listened to bad men" (*Homo non malus, sed qui facile malis hominibus crederet*). Venetian interests stretched into the Alps, and the republic's traders and businessmen conducted a brisk and profitable business there.

For reasons that had much to do with greed, Sigismund decided to pick a fight with the Venetians. He seized a group of Venetian traders on a flimsy pretext and confiscated their merchandise; he also took steps to seize Venetian mines and quarries in the region. The Germans then sent a military force under the leadership of Gaudenz von Matsch to occupy the territory of Verona. They assembled on the east bank of the Adige River and marched for about fifteen miles to the town of Rovereto, and promptly attacked the town. The Germans made use of a particularly novel incendiary weapon during this siege, a projectile machine that hurled iron canisters of flammable pitch (i.e., what would today be called "Greek fire" or napalm). It struck terror among the defenders and could only be resisted with great effort.

When news of these provocations reached the Venetian senate, a military force was raised in response. The local Italian commander in Rovereto was relieved, having been found insufficiently aggressive in his duties. He was replaced by a career soldier of proven worth named Roberto da Sanseverino, who accepted the command with enthusiasm. He headed for the Tyrol, accompanied by his sons, who were also military commanders. When Sanseverino arrived in the Alps, he found morale to be low and the forces there in disarray. Meanwhile, the Germans forces attacked the areas near Vicenza and Feltre and approached the borders of Friuli. These marauders, however, were beaten back with great loss of life on their part by a Venetian commander named Girolamo Savorgnam.

There then occurred an incredible incident that is the subject of this writing. Bembo tells the story with relish, and I will re-tell it with the same enthusiasm. Among the Germans engaged in this Alpine war was a brave young man named Georg Sonnenberg. He led a cavalry squad and was never known to shy away from a fight. Sonnenberg had heard that the Venetian commander's son, Antonio da Sanseverino, had boasted that he could defeat any German present in armed, man-to-man combat. We must remember that this was 1487, and individual combats were not unheard-of during war. Antonio Sanseverino said he was willing to fight it out with any German present, and would show the world how much the Italians exceeded the Germans in martial ability (*Se cum illo decertaturum proque sua parte ostensurum quantum belli gloria Itali Germanos antecellant*).

Thus the stage was set for a showdown between the heroes of two opposing armies. Sonnenberg sent a messenger (a military trumpeteer called a *tubicen* in Latin) to the Venetians stating that he would take Sanseverino up on his offer to fight. The latter readily obliged, and made the necessary arrangements. On the agreed day, the two mounted duelists met on a patch of ground that was situated precisely between both sides. On a given signal, they both charged towards each other, lances extended, ready to put their courage to the ultimate test. Besides lances, each man was armed with a sword and dagger.

The two mounted combatants collided in a furious crash that sent gasps of awe through the ranks of the observers on each side. Antonio's lance smashed against Sonnenberg's breastplate and splintered; his horse, confused and disoriented, crashed against a wooden fence enclosing the field, stumbled, and then collapsed to the ground. Antonio quickly leaped off, drew his sword and dagger, and prepared himself for the charge which he knew would now be coming. A knight was expected to know how to fight both mounted and on foot. A wooden post sunk into the ground he used as cover as he awaited Sonnenberg's attack. It had been agreed beforehand that the horses could not be stabbed or attacked; this was to be a man-to-man fight alone.

Sonnenberg hammered away at Antonio with ferocity, his swinging sword forming a glittering cage of steel around Antonio Sanseverino. But Antonio, skilled swordsman that he was, ably deflected the blows using both his own sword and the wooden post. And since both of their bodies were protected by helmets, breastplates, and leg armor, neither one of them could get in a killing blow. Finally, Antonio rushed at Georg Sonnenberg and was able to knock his sword out of his hand. But the German then seized a club he had in his saddlebag, hoping to bludgeon the Italian to death. At this point, the Italian taunted his mounted opponent, telling him in a loud voice:

> Why do you force me to fight alone against two: one protected by the rules of combat, another by foreign weapons? If you are a man, fight me fairly as an equal (*Si vir es, aequo Marte manum consere!*).

This was what Antonio said to Sonnenberg. Not wanting to look badly in front of his comrades, Georg Sonnenberg leaped down from his horse and lunged at the Italian, weapons drawn. Both of them were large men, tall and lean, and of about equal weight. It was not long before they were both rolling around on the ground, as the surrounding spectators remained transfixed by the spectacle. In time, however, the German was able to get the better of Sanseverino; a piece of the Italian's clothing had become snagged in Sonnenberg's armor, and this restricted his movement. Sonnenberg was able to stab his opponent repeatedly in the buttocks, the one place in his body that was not covered with armor. Bleeding profusely and unable to stand, Sanseverino now realized he had been beaten. There was nothing he could do at this point. At this point, Bembo tells us, he said to Sonnenberg: "You win, since Fortune wishes it to be so. But you win through circumstance, not through martial virtue."

He was wrong, of course. In battle, and in life, circumstance counts just as much as ability, and comprises an essential ingredient in the outcome of human events. Yet we may forgive this comment as the face-saving retort of a proud and noble combatant. Which of us, in similar circumstances, would behave any differently? To his credit, the German spared his life. Coming from a culture that prized bravery, he saw no point in killing the Italian, and believed that doing so would have violated the warrior's code. In fact, Sonnenberg brought the Italian back to his camp, accorded him honors, and saw to it that his wounds were attended to. This showed a greatness of soul–a certain *magnitudo animi*–that proved Sonnenberg to be a noble spirit as well as a fearsome warrior.

Bembo later tells us that Antonio Sanseverino made a complete recovery from his wounds. In fact, he re-entered the thick of the fighting soon after, even saving his father Roberto when he was surrounded by a group of Germans. Antonio threw himself into the thick of the fighting and fought off his father's attackers, giving the elder Sanseverino time to make his escape. This is the story of the combat between Sanseverino and Sonnenberg, two men of superlative masculine virtue. It was an age and an ethic different from our own. And they were, both of them, worthy of that ethic.

50. Ibn Zafar's Ideas On Revolutions

A careful reading of Ibn Zafar Al-Siqilli's ("The Sicilian") masterpiece of political philosophy *Sulwan al-Muta'* (سلوان المطاع في عدوان الأتباع, or *The Consolation of the Ruler in Dealing with the Hostility of His Subjects*) shows an emergent theory of political revolutions. In a previous article here we have discussed the fundamentals of the subtle Sicilian's treatise. We will now give the details of his ideas on how revolutions are born and take hold in a nation. Central to Ibn Zafar's view of revolutions is that they take place during times of affluence, ease, and excessive comfort. Such conditions corrupt the martial virtues, without which no nation can long expect to survive:

> It was said that revolutions are aimed against sovereigns whose crown was a hereditary right. Brought up in the midst of plenty, most are inclined to sloth and are persuaded that their capacity to govern is inherent in them. Moreover, most believed that the virtues of their illustrious ancestors applied to them without any necessity for exertion on their part. [*Trans. by J. Kechichian & R. Dekmejian*]

Such a corrupt sovereign will be endangered by four things: pride, anger, rapacity, and rebellion. When the masses sense that the sovereign is unsteady on his throne as a result of these weaknesses, revolts can take place:

> "Revolutions have their origins in *disappointment,*" was the reply, "and the audacity of the masses causes them to engage. The insolence of the great gives birth to revolutions (that are propelled by ideas), as well as the timidity of the rich, the confidence of the poor, the carelessness of those with plenty and the wakefulness of those who suffer."

Social classes consist of the elites at the top, then the middle classes of merchants and producers, and then the masses at the bottom. The masses are the most unthinking and blindly credulous of all these groups; they must be governed by fear and force. The ruler must never underestimate the role that the blind fanatic (the "revolutionary") can play in the spreading the idea of revolt. In this Ibn Zafar may have been thinking of the career of an Iraqi peasant named Hamdan Qarmat, who as the founder of the Qarmatian movement was a rebellious thorn in the side of the Abbasid Caliphate. Ironically, non-tyrannical rulers are usually more victimized by revolutions than are tyrants; as stated in the quotation above, revolutions are often the product of "disappointments," i.e., failed expectations. When leaders promise more than they can deliver, resentments brew, and insurrection seethes. Furthermore, populations accustomed to luxury will resent any impositions designed to curb their pleasure-seeking behavior. Above all, the rabble cannot be trusted. This is a constant theme that runs through Ibn Zafar's writings, and it was based on his study of history as well as his experience with Sicily's political life:

> The masses do not look upon the king as a member of the human family, but consider only his peculiar characteristics: his isolation, dignity, and the elevation of his office; therefore, they turn against him and unite with those who are on par with themselves.

Along these lines, Ibn Zafar offers this amusing pearl:

> Philosophers have said that there are four things that will cost you your life if confronted by violence: a king in his anger; a torrent that has burst its banks; an elephant during mating season; and masses in a state of excitement and tumult. They have said, moreover, that the measure which most resembles the forcible repression of the masses–when people rise in their fury–is that of treating smallpox with an ointment when it breaks the skin…Wise men have said that there are three kinds of human beings against whom, if tested, you could lose. These are the *pedagogue* (if you seek to test his learning while you are not a scholar); an *intimate friend* (because you would take advantage of him); and a *woman* (if you would marry her when you are advanced in age). These have given rise to the saying, "like those who test the stomach of a convalescent with heavy food."

What, then, is a ruler supposed to do in this minefield, where it seems that every step brings the possibility of ruin? He must in the first place base his actions on a combination of *competence* and *morality*. Possession of only one of these traits is just as fatal as having neither of them. Despite their fickleness and taste for violence, the masses have a kind of innate sense of justice that alerts them to malfeasance. The ideal ruler, the Sicilian tells us:

> [I]is he who fills the eyes of his people with glory, their ears with the sound of his praise, who inspires their understandings with reverence, and their hearts with affection...It is he who preserves the just from injustice, the monarch whose valor enables men, and whose moderation and generosity captivate their affection.

The ideal ruler should be able to project three kinds of "power": *inspirational power, ethical and moral righteousness, and blunt force when necessary*. He should project an image of himself as a servant of the people, ever ready to do their just bidding. Ibn Zafar was no dreamy-eyed idealist; he is fully aware that a ruler cannot long survive in the jungle of politics with good intentions alone. Problems in the body politic must be identified and dealt with proactively, lest they generate bigger, more complex problems. No ruler can do everything alone; having competent advisors is absolutely critical. In this Ibn Zafar is just as emphatic as Machiavelli, who considered the matter to be essential to success. It is interesting that both of these political thinkers–both of them having served in the halls of political power–realize that the ruler's choice of advisors is a window on his own character. Machiavelli stated bluntly that princes got the advisors they deserved: fools surround themselves with fools, and good leaders picked those who mirrored their own traits. One of the key traits of a good advisor is that he should put the leader's interests above his own interests:

> Amongst faithful and far-sighted counsellors, he is most deserving of attention whose prosperity depends on your own, and whose safety is tied to yours. He who stands in such a position, exerting himself for your interests, will likewise serve and defend himself while fighting for you.

True enough, but this is a prescription that is singularly hard to fill. In power, as in love, there is always a certain amount of chance involved. But the wise ruler can enlist Fortune in his service by keeping these principles in mind, and remaining constantly vigilant.

51. Some Battles Are Worth Fighting, Others Are Not

Historical opinion is often divided on the subject of famous military commanders. The good favor of historians may be divided with regard to their abilities, their judgments, and their battlefield results; and this favor can shift with time as readily as drifts of sand aggregate and dissipate in the desert. Douglas MacArthur is one example. Some see him as a brilliant strategist and tactician, using sophisticated combinations to outflank and out-maneuver his opponents; others see only a vain egoist whose achievements were obscured by his personal flaws.

What cannot be doubted is that MacArthur accomplished a great deal with little resources in the southwest Pacific theater during the Second World War. He was able to bypass the Japanese Empire's fortified island bases (like Rabaul), leaving them to wither on the vine, and strike at the enemy's more vulnerable points. This strategy stood in stark contrast to what the US Navy and Marine Corps were doing at the time, which was to make costly frontal assaults on islands that in some cases were of dubious value. When Okinawa was invaded, MacArthur privately told a confidant that he would have only taken half the island, and let the fortified southern half waste away from starvation and disease.

Perhaps the most famous lesson in economy of management is found in the career of Roman dictator Quintus Fabius Maximus, who was chosen by the senate to deal with the Hannibalic invasion during the Second Punic War. Hotheads in Rome were constantly agitating for a good general to take to the field and confront the wily Carthaginian. But Fabius knew better; he could see that Hannibal was a foe unlike any that his country had encountered before, and that any attempt to meet him on equal terms would end in disaster for Rome. The simple fact was that Hannibal was just too good of a general. So Fabius counseled for a prudent strategy of delay: shadow Hannibal all over the peninsula, harass him when possible, and let time, the lack of supplies, and normal attrition wear him down. The hotheads thought this policy was unbecoming of Rome's martial spirit, and pressed for direct confrontations with the invader. And the results at Cannae were catastrophic. One of the hardest lessons for us to learn is that there are battles that are worth fighting, and there are those that are not. Learning how to distinguish the two is one of the primary goals of maturity. We do not have unlimited energy, and we do not have unlimited resources. How, then, can we know when to engage, and when not to? *We must first make a realistic appraisal of our goals and resources.* You may think this is an easy thing to do. But this is not the case.

In my law practice, I have found that one of the most effective questions for prospective clients is this one: what is your goal? That is, what are you trying to accomplish here? This question has the virtue of cutting through all the excuses, daydreams, rationalizations, and wishful thinking. It clarifies things. And you would be surprised at how often this simple question is greeted with a blank stare, or how long it takes some people to answer the question. Why is this so? It is so because many people do not know what their goals and resources are.

And if we dig deeper, we find that the inability to articulate one's goal is based on an even deeper reality: the person does not know what his priorities are. He or she may have a mental laundry list of things they see as priorities; but they have not done the hard work of sifting out the "priorities" that matter, from the priorities that do not matter. And this is the heart of the problem. What is in your interest, and what is not in your interest? People and nations should be able to articulate a clear answer to this question. And yet we all know that many cannot do this. I suspect even high-ranking government officials in Washington could not give you a clear response to this question.

So the first problem is the lack of a clear understanding of *goals and resources*. But there is a second problem that degrades our ability to distinguish what battles should and should not be fought. This second problem is the problem of human emotion. It is emotion that often blind us from seeing where our priorities are. In the heat of the moment, our judgment may be affected by fear, pride, delusion, anger, or greed. We do not need to define these terms; their meaning is known to all. Their importance lies in the fact that they prevent us from seeing what is in our best interests. Under their influence, we make decisions that run counter to what is best for us. And this is why the man who can control his passions is more successful than the man who cannot; one is like a trained horse on a parade-ground, while the other is a wild mare, skittishly running here and there on the whim of the moment. So before you enter into some dispute, spend a good amount of time asking these questions: What is my *goal*? What are my *primary interests*, are what are not?

What are my *present and future resources*, and are they sufficient for the proposed challenge? Are my decisions *in alignment* with my proposed goals and resources?

These are the questions that a rational, reasonable man must ask himself. If your proposed decision or solution is not in alignment with your goals and resources, then the battle is probably not one that is worth fighting. I have previously written about the travels and career of the British traveler and philanthropist Jonas Hanway (1712–1786). In one of his books, he discusses the tragic absurdity of men fighting duels to the death for trivial reasons. He had personally witnessed a mortal duel between two young men in Germany, and thereafter never missed a chance to condemn the practice. His physical bravery was beyond question, as his life experiences demonstrate; it was just that he saw no point in risking his life without good reason. He considered the practice deeply immoral:

> To be reconciled to death is essential to a philosopher and a Christian, that is, in fact to be really no coward; but it is equally essential to these characters to refuse this criminal way of dying. It follows then, that these renounce the appearance of virtue for the reality of it. If the duellist acts contrary to this principle, he renounces the reality for the appearance. From hence we may observe how extravagantly absurd the conduct of those is, who offer incense to this capricious, cruel, lawless, stupid idol, opinion, dressed in the garb of honour, and under the disguise of a gallant spirit...The youth who has fought his duel, where no murder is committed, is some times more distinguished than the officer who has been in ten campaigns, has fought gallantly as many battles under a just command, and has truly served, nay perhaps has been one of a few who saved, their country. Thus the false courage which carries men to destroy the laws, and bring on anarchy and confusion, finds more respect than that which is employed according to the laws for the defense and preservation of the society, which can exist no longer than the laws.

Hanway tells us an amusing story of the one time he received a challenge to a duel. He thus describes the event:

> I once received a challenge. A certain manuscript of no consequence, clandestinely taken, and misrepresented, gave an alarm to a gentleman of the fighting sort; upon which I received a letter from him, conceived in these terms:
>
> *Sir,*
>
> *I understand you are the author of a paper subscribed ****, in which are initial letters that I presume mean me. As I always make it a point to resent affronts, I desire you will meet me at **** and bring your sword with you.*
>
> *I am, &c."*
>
> To which I answered to this effect:
>
> *Sir,*
>
> *In reply to your letter, the meaning of which I suppose is a challenge to fight with you: as I do not understand by what authority you call me to account, I will not tell you whether I am the author of any such paper as you mention, or not: but this I think my honour is concerned to tell you, that I never intend to do any man an injury; and if an offence does come, that honour also obliges me to make atonement, without putting my friends to the trouble of fighting: and for my part I ALWAYS MAKE IT A POINT NOT TO RESENT AFFRONTS, beyond the measure which reason and religion warrant. As to meeting you at *****, I have no inclination to walk in such weather as this, much less am I disposed to fight for nothing; but a sword I always wear, intending to use it upon every just occasion.*
>
> *I am, &c.*
>
> My antagonist was satisfied, and no doubt was glad to be excused fighting, as all men are except

> those who are intoxicated with wine, or what is much the fame, with anger; or quite deprived of understanding.

With this firm and measured reply, Hanway demonstrated that he understood the difference between battles that are worth fighting, and battles that are best ignored. Any fool can pick up a weapon; but the wise warrior will know when to draw his sword, and when to keep it sheathed.

52. The Importance Of Knowing What Boundaries Should Not Be Crossed

One of the characteristics of the fool is his inability to comprehend the idea of boundaries. He has failed to learn what rules of conduct can, and cannot, be broken. He flaunts his whims and desires without any care as to their consequences; he rates his own judgment above that of all others, and scorns the normative guidelines of social interaction. He believes that what he *wishes* to be done, in fact *ought* to be done, and reverse-engineers whatever rationalizations are needed to vindicate his behavior. In modern America we are regrettably familiar with this species. The strutting ass, the arrogant clown, the rich dullard, and other related personality types all exhibit this common behavior trait: *they are contemptuous of the rules of social and political conduct, and believe that these rules do not apply to them.* Once we understand this, their behavior makes some sort of sense. The Renaissance historian Pietro Bembo describes the following incident in his *History of Venice* (III.55) where the entourages of two competing diplomats encounter each other in the streets of Tortona in 1497:

> An incident took place at Tertona as follows. Venetian envoys, by chance encountering in the street two Florentine envoys who had come to [Emperor] Maximilian, orally greeted them. The Florentines continued on in an arrogant and uncouth way, without uttering a single word in response. They happened to meet them again on the next day, and refused to cede the way to the Venetian envoys; they physically accosted them with their entourage in a haughty manner. Morosini [one of the Venetian envoys] had

> a face of great dignity and was a strongly-built man besides; he told the Florentines, "Learn to give way to your betters!" [*Disce cedere maioribus!*]. He then shoved one of them with such force that he toppled over into the dirt.

The Florentine envoys had somehow never learned that the first lesson in diplomacy is *respect.* One is expected to behave like a professional even in the most tense of circumstances. Acting like a spoiled child never advanced the cause of any nation. In the example above, the Florentine ambassadors (who must have been very poorly trained or led) allowed their emotions to override their professional duties. Other examples are not difficult to find. The modern observer of domestic and international politics cannot help but wince as he watches the arrogant histrionics of certain United Nations ambassadors, people who arrogate to themselves the right to dictate the fate of foreign countries. Such people have no sense of boundaries, respect for others, or restraint. The spectacle would be shocking, were it not so routine; and as sure as the sun will rise tomorrow, the price for this behavior will eventually be paid. Pietro Bembo tells us another anecdote that ties in with this theme. The year is again 1497. Venice and France have been engaged in warfare against each other for some time.

> As the rumors and fears about Charles grew among the populace, Tristano Savorgnan, one of the leading men of Friuli, the brother of Girolamo and a man utterly devoted to the [Venetian] Republic, approached my father Bernardo Bembo, one of the Heads of the Council of Ten. He mentioned that he had a friend in Albania, a shrewd man with a very sharp mind who could be given any task with complete confidence. This man had for a very long time been on close terms with a relative of his who served in the bedchamber of King Charles [of France]. The Albanian ventured that he would leave for France and persuade his relative to do away with the king with poison that he would take with him, or, alternatively, that he would conceal the matter from his relative and kill the king himself, if the Council of

> Ten was prepared to offer him some reward for a deed of such moment. Savorgnan hoped and believed that the Albanian could bring the business to a quick conclusion. Although Bembo knew that such crimes were repellent to the magistrates, in accordance with ancestral custom and usage he nevertheless communicated the matter to the other Heads of the Ten, and they reported it to the Council. Summoning Tristano to him, Bembo gave him the Council's decision to the effect that the Republic had never used such schemes against its enemies, although it could often have done so, and was not about to start now. They feared Almighty God more than they feared the power of men, and, apart from that, those that planned to topple others through crime and sin were themselves brought low by their own wickedness. [*Trans. by R.W. Ulery*]

The Venetian authorities wisely decided not to engage in assassination. To their credit, they knew that this was a line that should not be crossed. Political murder is relatively easy to carry out; anyone opening the door to this sort of thing can expect it to be attempted against himself. Even among the jungle of states, armies, and diplomats, there are rules that govern conduct. Aggression will produce a response, and this response will often take forms that the aggressor cannot predict. And once the machinery of conflict has been set in motion, no one can predict what trajectory it may take. The wise man knows this; the fool cares nothing of it.

There are things that should be done, and there are things that should not be done, unless some compelling reasons exist. As stated above, one of the most alarming and pervasive features of our affairs today is the lack of restraint and moderation with which some conduct themselves. From the very top of our society to its bottom, there is a celebration of pride and arrogance as if this were some kind of virtue. But it is not a virtue: it is exactly the opposite. We must never forget that *the behavior of men and nations should be calibrated to serve the personal or national interest, not undermine it.*

53. Decisive Action In An Emergency Can Always Be Justified

There are some who take a relaxed view of human intervention in the events of Fate. They believe that nascent crises can be placed on the "back burner," so to speak, and left to stew in their own juices until a reasonable solution presents itself. They say that one should monitor developments, stay informed of the shifting winds, and act when one can be reasonably certain of a favorable outcome. There is some merit to this view. Every situation must be judged according to its own particular facts and circumstances; no universal rule of conduct has yet been crafted to deal with all settings and eventualities. Yet it seems to me that the need for action is directly correlated with the magnitude of the emergency: the greater the crisis, the greater the need to move quickly. I also suspect that many of us will deliberately downplay the seriousness of a situation in order to justify a decision to do nothing. The apostles of the "wait and see" approach also forget–or consciously ignore–the psychological effect that firm action can have in an emergency. *Action creates its own momentum, and shapes the course of events by virtue of its own inherent power.* Action activates the senses, fires the blood, suggests solutions, and imparts a sense of confidence. And this can make all the difference in conflict.

Lucius Furius Purpureo was a Roman politician and military commander. Serving in the office of praetor in 200 B.C., he was assigned responsibility for the province of Cisalpine Gaul in northern Italy. It is estimated that he had under him about 5,000 soldiers (allies of the Latin confederacy from all over Italy), a number that was inadequate for the task of defending the province. An emergency situation soon presented itself. An army of Gauls led by the Carthaginian general Hamilcar had laid waste to the province; their number was between seven or eight times the size of Lucius Furius's small force. Hearing that this Gallic army led by a hated Carthaginian was besieging the city of Cremona in Lombardy, Furius marched his men to the city and encamped about a mile and a half from its walls.

The two armies soon lined themselves up for battle. The superior discipline and organization of the Romans carried the day, as in so many other battles. The Gauls tried to envelop his lines, but Furius took effective and speedy countermeasures, using his cavalry and reserves at just the right moment. When he saw that the

Gallic center had been weakened through overextension, he ordered his men to concentrate and smash through it. This was the decisive point in the battle. The historian Livy tells us:

> And suddenly, after enduring tremendous slaughter in every part of their army, the Gauls turned their backs and fled back to their camp in total chaos. [*Ac repente, cum in omni parte caede ingenti sternerentur, Galli terga verterunt, fugaque effusa, repetunt castra.*] The cavalry chased them down as they fled; soon the legions followed them and assaulted the Gallic camp. Less than six thousand men were able to flee. Killed or captured were more than thirty-five thousand; around seventy military standards were also captured, along with more than 200 Gallic wagons filled with a large amount of looted goods. Hamilcar, the Carthaginian commander, was killed during the battle, along with three Gallic leaders of noble rank. [XXXI.21]

Roman losses came to about two thousand. The Gauls had suffered a calamitous defeat. Furius's small army had annihilated a force about *eight times its size*, a shocking outcome that few commanders in history have equaled. When the news of the battle reached Rome, a three-day festival was proclaimed. But political problems later developed, as often happens in the wake of great military victories. Furius understandably wanted to have a triumph celebrated in Rome in his honor. For those unfamiliar with the term, a triumph (*triumphus*) was more than just a military parade held for a victorious general. While there is no precise modern equivalent of a triumph, we can broadly say that it was a formal event that had both civil and religious significance. Furius thought he deserved one, and he was entirely justified in this. But the problem was that his achievement had attracted the anger and jealousy of the Roman consul, who tried to claim that Furius had "exceeded his authority" in attacking the Gaulish army!

How many times in history have we seen situations like this, where a brilliantly successful commander is suddenly assailed on all sides by opportunistic political figures or jealous rivals! It is an old story. Furius summoned the Roman senate to the Temple of

Bellona, explained his actions to the concerned senators, and asked to be allowed to enter the city in triumph. Livy says (XXXI.47) that Furius's sincerity made a good impression on the assembly (*Apud magnam partem senatus et magnitudine rerum gestarum valebat et gratia*). But the older senators were sceptical. As praetor (they noted) he was legally fighting under the consul's command, and he should have gotten approval from the consul before marching to Cremona and engaging the enemy. Some of these senators had been consuls themselves, and took a dim view of a subordinate who had acted with the scope and decisiveness that Furius had displayed. Livy clearly comes down on the side of Furius. He notes that some senators defended Furius by posing the following questions. If indeed Furius had exceeded his authority in attacking the Gauls, why had an army been entrusted to him in the first place? Should he have just sat where he was, as the flames of war were spreading from one place to the next, and waited for the consul to arrive? Finally Livy cuts to the core of the issue:

> The crises of war do not wait for the delays and stoppages of military commanders. *Sometimes you must fight not because you want to, but because the enemy forces you to do so*. The battle itself and the outcome of the fight ought to be evaluated. [XXXI.48]

In other words, sometimes one must react to the exigencies of the situation, and take decisive action to deal with the problem. And results matter, too: when the outcome is so overwhelmingly favorable, it practically justifies the action in itself. Because Furius made his case effectively, the senate as a whole was convinced; a full session voted to allow Furius his triumph. Livy notes that, either concurrently with this decision or after it, Furius also deposited a substantial sum in the treasury of 320,000 bronze *asses* and 100,500 silver pieces. (We may also note, with a cynical smile, that no assembly has ever been displeased by contributions to the governmental treasury).

Action, action, action, as Theodore Roosevelt used to say. If faced with a serious crisis, one should not look for reasons to prevaricate, delay, or pass the problem on to someone else. Inaction can easily slip into a fatalistic paralysis. Had the Aztec emperor

Moctezuma summoned his resources to deal with Cortes's expedition in 1519, he might have retained his throne; instead, he allowed himself to slip into a fatal lethargy. The fact that Mexico would have eventually come under Spanish rule anyway does not change the fact that Moctezuma's leadership was weak and indecisive. For my own part, I have adopted a simple rule to guide me in these sorts of situations: *in a serious crisis, always take action*. As Livy says, sometimes you must fight not because you want to, but because the enemy forces you to (*Et pugnandum esse interdum non quia velis, sed quia hostis cogat*). And it is generally better to explain later why you *did* act, rather than why you *did not* act.

54. The Tale Of The Two Ministers: Redemption Through Suffering

The following tale is told by Ibn Zafar al-Siqilli ("The Sicilian") in his political and ethical treatise سلوان المطاع في عدوان الأتباع (*The Consolation of the Ruler in Dealing with His Subjects' Hostility*). The story's purpose is to emphasize the importance that faith and endurance play in the fates of princes. We should note that Ibn Zafar does not advocate a passive resignation or inaction in the face of hardship. Instead he counsels us to do all we can to resolve our problems; but once one has exhausted his actionable remedies, he must submit himself to the workings of Fate. In this he is very much like the Stoic sages who preceded him by so many centuries.

We will now describe the tale of the two ministers (القصة الوزيرين). There was a ruler who retained two ministers to advise him on domestic and foreign affairs. They were very different in habits, philosophy, and temperament. One was renowned for his piety, good works, and abstinence from all forms of voluptuary pleasures; the other was a wily, cunning man of worldly affairs, who enjoyed a reputation for being strong and decisive. These two ministers, as one might expect, were often at odds with each other regarding the type of advice that they gave the king. Although the king appreciated the different perspective that each of them brought to his cabinet, he could not resist putting them to the test. (I note here, with a knowing smile, that this impulse is perhaps partly cultural; for Arab rulers of this era loved nothing more than to toy with their ministers). In any case, the king decided to fire one of his ministers. For him it was a matter of character. He believed that men of good character would give good advice, and that those of weak character would do the opposite. He also was crafty enough to understand that many men are able to conceal their true natures behind the facades of their professions and vocations; only by putting a man under extreme duress, the king knew, can one really discover their true constitutions. This is what the king did.

He first selected an appropriate prison for both of the ministers. He found some secluded dungeon that also had a hiding place where an outside party could observe those who were incarcerated there. The king directed his most trusted servant to secret himself in this dungeon's hiding place, so that he could not be seen by its occupants. The king told the servant that his intention was to throw both ministers in prison; the servant's job was to observe both ministers, and record everything they said and did. Once everything was prepared, he had both ministers arrested without warning and clapped into the prepared prison. It was a miserable place, and the initial shock to both of the ministers was terrible. The first day passed with very little of substance being spoken between the two ministers. Eventually, however, the worldly minister said to the pious one: "What is going on here? What do you think of our situation? How are we going to get out of this? I feel totally enraged by this situation. I am going to find out who did this to me, and see that he is punished." The pious minister responded calmly:

> I have confidence in the workings of God, for it is He who ordains all things. I have gone over in my mind all of my conduct in service to the king. I cannot recall ever having breached his trust or committed any offense. It is true that some of my advice may not have always been correct, but no man can be right all the time. Perfection is reserved for God alone. On the other hand, I do find that I have committed many personal sins. I have tried to examine my conduct daily, and have tried to comport my behavior with the teachings of the Almighty. Sometimes I have lived up to those teachings, and other times I have not. I believe my present situation is my punishment for not matching the conduct of the great teachers of the religious sciences (may God protect their secrets). We should

> accept the situation we are in now, and try to make the best of it. If we try to analyze it from a hundred different angles, it will only cause us further distress, and sap our will to survive.

The worldly minister, a man of money and business, did not know what to make of such statements. He did not know whether to laugh, or to feel pity for this deluded *faqir*. He considered them the utterances of a well-meaning but simple-minded fool. What did this woolen-cloaked, naive man know about how the world worked? These were the thoughts that went through his head. So he responded:

> No. I don't accept that. We have been the victims of some court conspiracy. Someone did this to us, and someone is trying to ruin us. We must write a petition to the king. We should make him an offer of money, in return for which he will set us free. I am rich and have resources, and we need to make some kind of financial offer to get out of this situation.

The pious minister heard this and shook his head. He rejoined:

> This is not a good idea. It would make you look guilty, like you had done something wrong. It would communicate culpability to the king; and it would be a way of forsaking your faith in God.

This was what the pious minister said. The two of them decided to drop the subject, since they were both at odds over it. After a day or so, a loaf of bread and some water was brought to them through a slot in the door of the dungeon. The worldly minister did not want to eat the bread, saying, "I think it's likely that it is poisoned." But the pious minister ate the bread, saying "I will eat and trust myself to God." He took the loaf, broke it open, and began to eat. And as he did so, he discovered that a red ruby had been baked into the bread. Shocked, the pious minister kept the gem in a safe place. Over the next few days, this pattern was repeated: a loaf of bread was delivered to the cell; the worldly minister refused to eat it; the pious minister did eat it, and discovered a gem concealed within.

After some days, the king ordered that the two ministers should be released from prison. He talked with the servant, who had heard and observed everything that had transpired in the dungeon. The king then sent for each minister, and questioned each of them carefully as to what they had seen and experienced. When the pious minister was questioned, he showed the king the rubies that had been in the loaves of bread, and said:

> Sire, it is not right that I should have these. I found them in the bread that was brought to me. I did not know what to do with them. I did not want to take the other minister's share.

The king, deeply moved, spoke these words with great care:

> By God! Know that the Almighty has granted you these riches. The other minister's lack of faith and endurance alienated him from His divine grace. So he has received nothing. Know, O my brother in religion, that worldly riches are for those who endure sufferings without surrendering to despair.
>
> By virtue of this experiment I have done, I have discovered that your colleague [the worldly minister] is inhabited by the demons of conceit, arrogance, and lack of faith. For when he was struck by disaster, all he did was try to blame others, make excuses, and look for ways to buy himself out of his problems. He even suspected *me* of trying to poison him. There was no soul-searching, no reflection, no desire to scrutinize his conduct. This is the mark of a vain, arrogant, and frivolous man; such men are worthless in a real crisis. They have no character, no moral fiber. You, on the other hand, resigned yourself to the Hand of God, and sought to review your own conduct in the light of present developments. You never sought to transfer responsibility on to anyone else. You did not curse the Universe. I conclude, then, that God has selected you to be my minister. You are not perfect, of course, but neither am I; perfection is an attribute reserved to Him alone. When

> calamity befalls us, we must trust in the designs of Fate, once we have done all we can. Life is a tempestuous sea, full of iniquity and torment; we must learn to deal with rank injustice in this world. But we must never surrender ourselves to despair, for this would be an offense against God.

This was what the king said to the pious minister. He had him reinstated to his full position, and banished the worldly minister from his cabinet forever.

55. The Final Act Of All Is Never Considered Late

It is a feature of human nature to try to control our environment. We wish to exert some kind of influence over the outcome of events, and thereby enhance our own feelings of security and comfort. Yet there are many times when human labor will fall short; it will prove itself to be incapable of dealing with a situation, or unable to weigh the nuances of an evenly balanced pattern of fact. When these situations come about, we must step back from the work-shop; we must move away from the work-table, the field of conflict, or the courtroom, and Fortune take over the guidance of events. This is not something that a man of action can easily do. Trained to act, to decide, and to intervene in the chain of causation, he will find it difficult to take a back seat and let another steer the vehicle. Yet it is a necessary skill to master. One cannot know everything; one cannot master all outcomes, or reduce them to an easy trajectory of predictability. I am not advocating a passive submissiveness to chance: that I want to make very clear. What I am saying, instead, is that once we have exhausted all of our available remedies, we must call on the assistance of the Ultimate Decision-Maker.

The final decision will always lie with Fortune, and her preferences may yet overrule the decisions of all lesser triers of fact and law. An old attorney once told me when I began practicing law, "You will win some you should lose, and you will lose some you should win." And so it has turned out to be. It is also true that equitable resolutions take time. They can take very much more time than we wish them to. But justice does not obey the dials on our clocks; it follows its own schedule, and it will not be rushed.

The following anecdote is a relevant illustration. It is found in both Ammianus Marcellinus (XXIX.2.19) and Valerius Maximus (VIII.1). There was once a woman of the Greek city of Smyrna who was arrested and tried for homicide. She was brought before the Roman proconsul Dolabella, a figure who apparently governed parts of Asia after Caesar's death. This woman actually confessed that she had indeed poisoned her husband and her own son by this man. She said that she did this out of revenge: the two murder victims had supposedly killed the woman's other son, who was from her previous marriage. Her confession presented the court with a problem. On the one hand, a double homicide had been committed, and the crime was a very serious one; but on the other hand, she had been acting from an understandable motivation. There were mitigating circumstances that argued for leniency.

She was ordered to re-appear before Dolabella several days later, but he and his judges could not find a satisfactory decision. Dolabella had reached the limits of his options; he did not know what his next step should be, or to whom he should turn. Finally an insight came to him: he referred the case to the Greek judges at the Areopagus, which was experienced in judging homicide cases. The judges there had a reputation for wisdom and equity. So he sent the case on. The subtle Greeks weighed the facts of the case and came to a remarkable decision. *They ruled that the case would be postponed for a hundred years; and that exactly a hundred years hence, she should re-appear before them with her accuser, at which time a ruling would be issued.* And so an equitable compromise was reached, after all other options had been exhausted. Regarding this ruling, the historian Ammianus adds this brilliant adage: *Ita numquam tardum existimatur, quod omnium ultimum.*

This sentence translates as, "Thus the final act of all is never considered late." What he means by this is that a postponement of even a hundred years from now will not be seen as late, since the postponement itself is serving the cause of justice. Justice can take time. It may even take a very long time. But as long as the final event in drama happens at some point in the future, it will not be considered "late," for it is an essential part of that continuum of justice.

According to Pliny (*Historia Naturalis,* XXXV.104) and Valerius Maximus (VIII.11), there was once a famous painter who completed an image of a horse. This artist wanted to show the viewer what this magnificent animal looked like after it had just completed a round of strenuous exercise. He got the idea to add foam to the horse's nostrils to help him in conveying the look of equine exertions. But try as he might, he was unable to get just the right look. He spent hour after hour in futile effort. His rage mounted steadily. He would apply some paint, and then scrape it off: nothing seemed to give him the picture he was aiming for.

Finally, in a fit of desperation and frustration, he grabbed the first thing within reach–a paint-soaked sponge–and flung it at his mural. The sponge just happened to strike the mural near the horse's nostrils, and, to his utter shock, gave him just the right color pattern and image he was looking for. So Fortune intervened to do what he himself could not do. The sponge landing on the mural at just the right place, in just the right configuration, was the last act in the painter's drama. *And the final act of all is never considered late.* When it comes, it comes; and its lateness does not diminish its impact or importance. Commenting on this story, Valerius says: *Quod ars adumbrare non valuit, casus imitatus est.* And this means: *Chance finally revealed what art was not able to create.*

56. Machiavelli's Principles Of Conspiracies

Machiavelli, in book III, chapter 6 of his *Discourses*, enunciates the principles of political conspiracies. He considers an understanding of them to be of primary importance. I intend to paraphrase his relevant points here, so that readers without access to the original text may have a better understanding of them. He begins with a point he considers self-evident:

> There is, on the other hand, no enterprise in which private persons can engage, more dangerous or more rash than is this [conspiracies], for it is both difficult and extremely dangerous in all its stages. Whence it comes about that, though many conspiracies have been attempted, very few have attained the desired end...There is, in fact, a golden saying voiced by Cornelius Tacitus, who says that men have to respect the past but submit to the present, and, while they should be desirous of having good princes,

should put up with them of whatever sort they may turn out to be.

Conspiracies are dangerous and usually fail; even a dolt as a ruler is usually better than chaos, and men should think twice about plotting to remove an imbecile from the throne. Here, then, are Machiavelli's observations on conspiracies:

1. Conspiracies may be formed against one of two targets: one's homeland, or against a specific ruler.

2. A ruler should try to avoid becoming a focus of hatred, for it is this which triggers most conspiracies. "A prince, therefore, should avoid incurring these personal reproaches, and since what he has to do in order to avoid them has been discussed elsewhere, I shall refrain from discussing it here…"

3. Fear or threats may lead men to enter into conspiracies against you: "The threat of bloodshed is more dangerous than is the shedding of blood. To threaten to shed blood is, in fact, extremely dangerous: whereas to shed it is attended with no danger at all, for a dead man cannot contemplate vengeance, and those that remain alive usually leave you to do the contemplating. But a man who has been threatened and sees that he must of necessity either do something or be for it, has been turned into a real menace for the prince, as we shall cite cases presently to show."

4. Another cause that makes men enter into conspiracies is "the desire to liberate their fatherland of which a prince has seized possession."

5. In history, it is shown that almost all conspiracies have been made either by men of standing or by men in close proximity to the prince. They are not made by the downtrodden, who are more preoccupied with the daily struggle for survival. "Consequently, since when their lives and property are not at stake, men do not entirely lose their heads, they become cautious when they recognize their weakness, and when they get sick of a prince confine themselves to cursing him, and wait for those of higher standing than they have to avenge them. So that, should one in fact come across somebody of this kind who has attempted such a thing, one should praise his intentions but not his prudence."

6. Those who conspire against you may more often be those on whom you conferred favor: "A prince, therefore, who wants to

guard against conspiracies, should fear those on whom he has conferred excessive favors more than those to whom he has done excessive injury. For the latter lack opportunity, whereas the former abound in it, and the desire is the same in both cases; for the desire to rule is as great as, or greater than, is the desire for vengeance."

7. Buffers must be created against the ruler and his friends: "Consequently princes should confer on their friends an authority of such magnitude that between it and that of the prince there remains a certain interval, and between the two, something else to be desired."

8. Conspiracies, to be successful, must pass through all three stages (initiation, the plot itself, and the period after the plot). Conspiracies fail because so few can navigate all three stages successfully. Most plots are revealed and crushed at the outset because of informers: "Now there may be one or two persons whom you can trust, but it is impossible to find such men if you reveal your plans to many people, for the goodwill they bear you must indeed be great if the danger and the fear of punishment is not to outweigh it in their estimation. Men, too, quite frequently make mistakes about the affection another man has for them, nor can you be sure of it unless of it you have previously had experience, and to acquire experience in such a matter is a very risky business."

9. Conspirators who wish to succeed should keep silent about their intentions until the last possible moment: "The first, the safest and, to tell the truth, the only [remedy against being discovered], is not to allow the [fellow] conspirators time to give information against you, and to tell them of your plan only when you are ready to act, and not before."

10. Only one other man should generally be trusted with information about a conspiracy. Confiding in any more than one other person tremendously increases the risk of being discovered: "A plot, then, should never be divulged unless one is driven to it and it is ripe for execution; and if you, perforce, have to divulge it, it should be told to but one other person, and this is a man of whom you have had very considerable experience, or else one who is actuated by the same motives as you are."

11. Changes of plans can be fatal to a conspiracy. It is usually better to keep to an old plan than to try to configure a new one: "I would here point out, therefore, that nothing so perturbs and interferes with anything undertaken by men as does their having

suddenly and without due notice to change their plan and to give up that laid down at the start…So that it is much better to carry out the original plan, even if one sees in it certain inconveniences, then it is to cancel it and thereby to involve oneself in a host of inconveniences."

12. Human indecision, irresolution, cowardice, or ineptitude can doom a conspiracy. It is very easy to make plans and plot strategies, but another thing entirely to follow through with them. When the time for action comes, not every man is up to the task: "Hence men should be chosen who have had experience in doing such deeds, and one should entrust them to no one else, brave as he may be thought to be. For when it comes to doing big things of which a man has no previous experience, no one can say for certain what will happen."

13. The role of fortune is paramount. Failure can come about through unforseen accidents or other intervening factors.

14. There is one great danger after a successful conspiracy has been conducted: "There is but one. It is that someone may be left alive who will avenge the death of the prince. There may, for instance, be brothers or sons or other supporters to whom the principality was expected to come. Survival of those who may wreak vengeance may be due either to your negligence or to the causes mentioned above." Machiavelli's recommendation for solving this problem, which he does not spell out specifically, is obvious.

These are the main ideas contained in Machiavelli's short treatise on conspiracies. In practice they are difficult to organize and keep hidden, and even more difficult to carry through to conclusion; but the wiser course for someone in a position of authority is not to provoke others into forming them in the first place. Vigorous and just leadership that continually measures the pulse of the people and responds accordingly is the best inoculation against such schemes.

57. François-René de Chateaubriand: An Apostle Of Romanticism

The nineteenth century literary, artistic, and intellectual movement we today call "romanticism" is not easily defined, but is generally acknowledged to embrace the following sentiments: an idealized view of the past, the emphasis of feeling and sentiment over rationality, a preference for exotic locales and peoples, and the primacy of emotion. One of the founders—perhaps the founder—of romanticism in French literature was François-René de Chateaubriand, whose memoirs I have just finished. He titled his book *Memories From Beyond The Tomb*, since they were specifically intended to be published after his death. The fact that Chateaubriand would never see the book's publication gives his words a strange poignancy, and a unique honesty. He would not have wanted it any other way. Born in Brittany in 1768, he came from an old aristocratic family, staunchly monarchist in its leanings, and decidedly Catholic in its outlook. If he was a romantic, he had every reason to be: his was a life as fully lived and as various in its experiences as any has ever been. As he himself announces:

> I have explored the seas of the Old World and the New, and trodden the soil of the four quarters of the globe. After sleeping in the cabins of Iroquois and the tents of Arabs, in the wigwams of Hurons and the remains of Athens, Jerusalem, Memphis, Carthage, and Granada, in the homes of Greeks, Turks, and Moors and among forests and ruins; after wearing the bearskin cloak of the savage and the silk caftan of the Mameluk, and after enduring poverty, hunger, thirst, and exile, I have taken my place, as a minister and ambassador, trimmed with gold lace and plastered with ribbons and decorations, at the table of kings, at the festivities of princes and princesses, only to fall once more into indigence and to taste prison life. I have had dealings with hundreds of notabilities in the armed services, the Church, politics, the judiciary, the sciences, and the arts. I possess enormous quantities of material, over four thousand private letters…I have had a hand in the making of peace and war…I have made history and had the opportunity to write it.

He served as an officer in the French army for a time, then lived in London from 1793 to 1800, wisely avoiding the worst of the French Revolution's terrors. Although he was a monarchist, he was not a reactionary, and believed the institution should be reformed rather than abolished; but Napoleon put an end to these pretensions, and Chateaubriand resigned from government service in 1804. He could not stomach the Corsican. Regarding the institution of royalty, he said, "Legitimate, constitutional monarchy has always seemed to me the gentlest and surest path to complete liberty." His writings on Christianity were influential across Europe and served as powerful intellectual rebuttals to the atheistic tendencies of the *philosophes* whom, he strongly believed, put far too much faith on reason and too little confidence in tradition. He seems to have begun his memoirs long before his death; they are carefully compiled and the overall feel is highly polished. Chateaubriand convincingly argues that a man's life is not just one life, but several separate "lives" laid end on end; all of us are "reborn" at certain points in our lives, and these natal resurgences mark the dividing lines between one phase and the next:

> When death rings down the curtain between me and the world, it will be found that my life's drama is divided into three acts. From early youth until 1800, I was a soldier and traveler; from 1800 until 1814, under the [Napoleonic] Consulate and the Empire, my life was devoted to literature; from the Restoration down to the present day, my life has been political.

Like all written recollections, his memoirs tell us more about the man than about his times. He reveals himself to be a perceptive observer of human affairs, capable at the same time of the tenderest sentiments and the sternest recriminations; he called marriage "the high road to all misfortunes" and seems to have known only conjugal coldness. He minimizes his ambition and, at times, his own responsibility for events in which he was intimately involved. But these are foibles common to all autobiographers, and may be readily forgiven; no one writes the story of his own life to indict himself. What redeems *Memoirs From Beyond the Tomb* is the surpassing beauty of the style, the evocative recollections of the famous people he has met (the meeting with George Washington is a masterpiece of portraiture), and the passionately romantic spirit girding the whole. This is a man living in his imagination, a man for whom the world of sense and perception must occasionally take a back seat to the world of emotion. Chateaubriand finds drama nearly everywhere, and internalizes it readily. This passage brilliantly mixes routine observation with soaring philosophical speculation:

> If my works survive me, I am destined to leave behind a name, perhaps one day, guided by these Memoirs, some traveler will come and visit the places I have described. He will be able to recognize the chateau, but he will look in vain for the great wood: the cradle of my dreams has banished like the drams themselves. Left standing by itself on its rock, the ancient keep mourns for the oaks, the old companions which surrounded it and protected it against the tempest. Isolated like that keep, I too have seen falling around me the family which graced my days and lent me its shelter: fortunately my life is not built on this earth as firmly as the towers in which I spend my youth, and man offers less resistance to the storms than the monuments raised by his hands.

Memoirs from Beyond the Grave can be taken as one of the greatest Romantic texts ever written. Every page pulses with the author's restless spirit; and even if we occasionally tire of Chateaubriand's outpourings, we never for an instant doubt his sincerity. His book is not well-known today, as literary fashions go in and out of style like the advancing and receding tides. But this is our loss, for in life it is clear that the world created by our own imagination is at least as "real" as the world of the senses. His message is as valid now as it was for his own day: we create our own reality, and tread the path of our deepest passions, whether realized or unrealized. Life is the lingering footprint marked by those steps.

58. Why We Study The Great Exemplars Of History

You may question why we seek to study the lives and deeds of history's great exemplars. When I say "exemplar" I mean a person of substance and distinction, a person of notoriety in some field of endeavor. There are many reasons for this; I will attempt to give a few of them here. The first reason is that to me there is nothing more instructive and edifying than the life of a man or woman of distinction. We human beings are not so differently composed that one of us cannot learn something valuable from a study of the other. When I examine the life of an exemplar, I like to ask myself questions like: What would I have done in this situation? How would I have solved this problem? Was his action reasonable or not? It is like a constant testing, a continuous dialogue, if you will, with the dead. If I am to emulate someone, I first want to know his motivations. And by exploring those motivations, I can reveal, in some small way, part of my own personality. *The laurels are bestowed on those who dare to achieve great things*

A second reason (which I suppose is related to the first) is that I enjoy keeping company with the very best of men. Who would not want to do this? We are surrounded in our ordinary lives with much of what is base, venal, and petty; and generally I have no desire to wallow in such personalities when I open the covers of a book. The book-cover is for me a time-machine: I can escape from the present moment, range across the centuries, and arrive at the precise point I wish. I can then sit down beside my exemplar and hear, from his mouth in his native tongue, what he has to say. If I want to be surrounded by the hum-drum banality of existence, I can easily do this by visiting any grocery store, or any of the numberless megastores that festoon the landscape of modern America. But I prefer to exercise my spiritual strength by escaping from these people every now and then, and keeping company with others.

Of course I recognize and acknowledge that history is made not just by individuals, but by forces, processes, and the tidal waves of fortune. Only a fool would deny this. Yet there are counterpoints to be kept in mind. Individuals both make history and are made by it; man and his environment are part of the same continuous feedback loop, and it is often not easy to tell who is influencing whom. Is the great man a product of his environment, or the other way around? Sometimes the examplar makes his environment, and at other times he is made by it. Like much else in life, it depends on the circumstances. I would also add another point to this: has anyone ever been inspired to great things by processes? By learning about impersonal forces? The study of great exemplars has the unique power of motivating and inspiring others; no one, on the other hand, has ever been moved to great deeds by learning about abstract, impersonal forces. This does not mean that they are invalid, of course; it only means that human nature, in its search for moral instruction, cries out for tangible, concrete examples as models of behavior.

A third reason why we study exemplars is that our world is in dire need of moral instruction. I have long been of the opinion–and have repeatedly stated as much in my books–that our modern educational system places too much emphasis on knowledge, and not enough emphasis on character. Moral development is learned through the diligent study of biography, history, and philosophy; for many centuries it was so. Religion provided a further underpinning of support for right conduct and right actions. School systems encouraged the study of such subjects, and students were encouraged to reflect on the lessons to be learned from the lives and careers of great exemplars. But these pillars of character have been steadily eroded under the influence of a pernicious mass media culture, a vulgarization of the mind, and an unrelenting glorification (in the West at least) of materialism. The mind becomes degraded, and the expected type of conduct soon follows.

I have seen first-hand how many people undertaken the study of virtue by pondering the lives of great exemplars. I know what change they can bring about. As Petrarch says (with which I completely concur) with a smile in a letter to Giovanni Colonna:

> Those who don't like to read about exemplars should not read about them. I am forcing no one to do so. And if you ask me, I would prefer to be read by only a few people. [*Quibus exempla non placent, non legant; neminem cogo; et si me rogas, a paucis legi malim.*]

Great deeds are infectious, just as are evil deeds. There is nothing more inspiring than seeing a man of character, a man of substance, giving expression to his inner *virtus*. It does not matter to me what his profession is: he may be a commander, a politician, an artist, a writer, a musician, an artisan, a tradesman, or a businessman. It does not matter. I also care nothing at all what his background, race, or religion may be. I could jab a finger at random on any map of the world, and see where my finger lands. Whether it be Cameroon, Italy, Burma, Indonesia, Paraguay, Sweden, Latvia, or the Congo, I could find men of substance and virtue there. It is our duty to sing their praises.

The great exemplars are a tonic for the sickness of the age. They are our cure for the general malaise that has gripped some of the more timid souls of our era. There is a current of defeatism, a feeling of helplessness, that can threaten to overwhelm the soaring eagles of our spirits. We must fight constantly against this negativity that shows its face in various forms. But no matter its mask, it is always the same Defeatism and Negativity standing before us. Fight this feeling; do not be rendered supine by it, and do not be cowed by what you see around you. Know that every man has within him the potential for greatness, and that this comes about as the manifestation of his own greatness of soul (Cicero's *magnitudo animi*, about which I have spoken before) which he himself can nurture, polish, and develop through effort. And if you are at times overwhelmed by feelings of futility, my response is the same as that so eloquently–and inspiringly–spoken by my cherished Francesco Petrarca in a letter written around 1350 to his friend Tommaso Caloiro. He tells us to throw off our anxiety, and cast our eyes on greater things that will always be pure and eternal:

> Let the past ten thousands years come back to us, let era be piled on top of era: never will masculine virtue be praised enough. General rules will never be sufficient to describe the love of God or the hatred of corrupt pleasures. The road will never be barred for men of sharp intellects to explore new things. Let us have cheerful spirits: we are not toiling away for no reason. Nor will those people who are born in the far future–just before the end of our own aging world–labor away in vain. We should be more afraid that men will no longer exist before the devotion to the study of human affairs has broken through to the essence of the Truth.

So go forth and be great, unhindered by timidity and fear, and master yourself.

59. Limits Must Be Imposed On Our Desires

Among the many problems that we are faced with today is the lack of restraint, the lack of moderation, that is actively supported and encouraged by our culture. If you have something, you are told that you deserve more. If you want something, you are told that you deserve to have it. If something stands in the way of your getting something you think you deserve, you are told how to obtain that thing you desire. Few people pause to think that what they crave may carry a heavy burden in the long run. A sensible person has to resist getting swept up by this current. It is not easy to do. You are surrounded by choices, by temptations, and by voices prodding you ever forward in the quest for permanent satisfaction. But knowing how to restrain oneself, and knowing when to stop: this is the safer course in the long run. Wise men have understood this, and have tried to put it into practice. There is an anecdote told about Scipio Africanus the Younger that relates to this point; it is found in the historian Valerius Maximus (*Memorable Doings and Sayings* IV.10).

When Scipio was serving in the office of censor, he was responsible for handling the details of one of the public religious ceremonies. As part of this ritual, an attendant was supposed to recite a formulaic prayer from the official register. It was an invocation in which the gods were asked both to increase the size of the Roman empire and to keep the state safe. Scipio did not like the tenor of this official prayer. He felt that its tone was greedy and grasping, and that it sent the wrong message to the people. He disapproved of an official prayer that asked the gods to increase the size of the empire. He said, "Our holdings are good and great enough; I pray only that the gods keep them safe in perpetuity." Scipio also ordered that the official prayer in the books should be changed in accordance with his new formula. Valerius tells us that from that time forward, Scipio's changes became permanent. The people agreed with him that it would be greedy to ask for more when the empire that they had was already so large; so from that point, the prayer only asked for the gods to keep the state safe.

Another example of how moderation was imposed on a people is provided by King Theophrastus of Sparta in the 8th century B.C. This anecdote is found in Valerius Maximus IV.15. The historian says that Theophrastus created the ephors as a way to check the power of the monarchy. When people told him that by creating this institution he was limiting the amount of power he could pass on to his own sons, he responded in the affirmative: he said that even though he would be passing on less power, that power would be more permanent and stable. He chose moderation, knowing that it would promote stability. Valerius says, "This was very well done, for power is only safe when it places limits on the men who wield it."

In our own day, the political elites and politicians pay little attention to these things, if any at all. They see no reason why any limit should be placed on their appetites; this is why we have military bases in nearly every country across the globe. This is why conspicuous expenditure is hailed as a virtue, and moderation seen as the mark of timidity. In due course, the price of all this will be paid. We cannot know exactly when or how, but there will surely be some kind of reckoning. Greed and avarice create their own momentum; it is not easy to stop the mad rush for physical or material pleasures once the sickness has taken hold of the mind. To sustain the momentum of greed, one has to become more and more aggressive, and more and more violent. It is a cycle of futility that leaves men and nations exhausted and broken; for as Petrarch said, in a letter to Paganino of Milan:

> Nothing violent lasts a long time [*Nihil violentum, diuturnum*]. Modest boundaries of a kingdom are easy to protect; an immense empire is difficult to obtain, and even more difficult to hold on to.

The only way to retain one's sanity is to impose some sense of moderation on ourselves. Insisting on more is the surest and shortest way to a man's ruin.

60. On Forming Our Own Judgments

When we need to form our own estimates of others, we should learn to trust our own judgments, and not be swayed by the criticisms or slanders of others. Behavior is better verified by observation, rather than by the rumors and innuendos of others. An amusing illustration of this principle is found in an anecdote related by Valerius Maximus (III.8.ext.6) about Alexander the Great. The great king was enjoying some leisure in Cilicia after a great victory over Darius. On a certain day the weather happened to be very hot, so he decided to take a swim in the river Cydnus. Shortly after this, he began to experience muscle pains and partial paralysis, to the extent that he was not able to walk of his own accord. His men were greatly worried about him, knowing that their fortunes were entirely dependent on him. He was taken to bed and his lieutenants called doctors in an effort to find out what the problem was; after some deliberation, one of the doctors (Philippus by name) made a medicinal liquid for the king to drink.

At about the same time that Philippus was offering the medicine to Alexander, a messenger arrived from one of Alexander's generals, Parmenio. The messenger bore a letter warning Alexander that the doctor Philippus had been bribed to administer poison to the king. When Alexander read the letter, he did nothing; he accepted the cup from Philippus, drained it, and then handed the doctor the letter he had just received. Alexander had such confidence in the people around him that he trusted his own judgment about the doctor. While this behavior may seem unnecessarily reckless, the story does contain an element of truth: we should not be too willing to accept the testimony of slanderers, gossips, or rumor-mongers. This was the point that Petrarch was trying to make in a letter to Niccola Acciaiuoli in which he counseled his friend against being too eager to listen to informers:

> Let him banish suspicions, deny the use of his ear to informers, brush back those who get too insistent, and punish those who refuse to stop such behavior. As the words of one emperor said: "A prince who does not discipline informers, empowers them [*princeps qui delatores non castigat, irritat*]."

In the vast majority of cases, we are better off not knowing malicious rumors, whether they are said about someone else or about us. They do nothing but poison the mind. It was for this reason that Julius Caesar is said to have burned an entire chest of letters written by his political opponents that came into his possession. He felt that reading such material would poison his mind and prevent the kind of reconciliation he hoped to build after he had secured his victory. This proved to be a wise step: for some things we are better off *not* knowing.

61. On The Remaking Of Character

One of the apparent corollaries of the maxim that "character determines fate" is that character is static and unchangeable. In the majority of cases this is undoubtedly true; but this truth should not be used as a license for us to lie supinely on our backs and let the swerve of the atoms in the void determine our future. As volitional beings, we must act. Forward movement is one of the imperatives of masculine virtue. The negative personality takes refuge in the apparent indifference of the universe; but the active man, the healthy man, is too busy with his own affairs to fret over such exculpatory abstractions. Each of us is responsible for his own fate. Having accepted this, we will now ask how character can be modified to suit the will.

Bodily Health. It was a common belief in the ancient world that a physical flaw or defect was the manifestation of a defect in one's personality. We cannot be sure they were wrong. Vices have a habit of warping the body of their bearer, and eating away at the health of the flesh; vice is not just a corruption, but a parasite. Health begins with the consumption of food and drink; we must take care to watch what we put in our stomachs. So much has been written about food and diet that little remains left to be said, other than to offer this simple suggestion: we should monitor our moods and bodily operations, and shun the foods and drinks that inhibit them. Exercise, of course, ties directly into this. It must be so ingrained, so essentially a part of us, that it becomes instinctive. If we cannot choose a career that imposes physical demands on us, then we must go out of our way to impose physical demands on ourselves. Not a single day should pass without some form of physical activity. Abandonment of personal hygiene and cleanliness is the first step on the road to Tartarus; no man can be taken seriously who believes more in dirt and grime than in sanitation. As the Roman medical author Celsus (one of the most sensible of men) says,

> A healthy man who is of sound body and master of his own affairs, ought to be beholden to no rigid rules. Neither should he need a masseuse or someone to rub him with oil. His lifestyle ought to give him varied settings: to be in the countryside, in the city, and more often on a farm. He ought to take to

> boats on the water, to hunt, to relax sometimes, and frequently exercise. Lack of activity is corrupting to the body, but labor makes it strong; the sedentary life makes a man old, but healthy activity begets an extended youth. [*De Medicina* I.1]

External Environment. Climate, scenery, and the people we interact with every day affect our mood and well-being. Some bodies are accustomed to the cold, and feel at home skidding and slipping on icy sidewalks; others, fearing for the circulation of their extremities, seek the languid softness of the globe's hotter regions. Environment is not just a passive landscape in which we move; it is a living, breathing participant in our lives. We are bombarded every hour of the day with its stimuli, and if these are not to our liking, we should take steps to change them. Frequent travel or permanent relocation can do wonders for the soul; and it is a mistake to think that we are always the same person wherever we go. The truth is that we are *many* people, and that every facet of our character vibrates at a different frequency depending on our external environment.

Friends. A life without friends, says Cicero in *On Moral Ends*, is a life of mortal terror. One man adrift alone in the ocean has no chance at survival; but place him in a raft with several others, and he at least has a fighting chance. But friends do not magically appear on our doorstep; we must make efforts to put ourselves into circulation. Frequency of contact is the mother of friendship. Our educational system, with its unremitting emphasis on the primacy of the individual ego, trains us hardly at all on how to make and keep friends. The modern man (and woman) is a thin-skinned, fragile creature; he is too quick to take offense, and too lacking in patience to tolerate the oddities of his fellows. It was not always so. But we should want friends who keep us in check, who prevent our runaway egos from crashing into the other cars on the human freeway. So if you want to have friends, learn to set aside your ego; learn to laugh at yourself and your foibles. Realize that you are only one human organism out of a countless multitude in the world, and that the world will little miss you when you are gone. Bottle the acid, quell the rage, and shut your mouth. Learn to listen more than to speak; remember that the world has heard many times before your brilliant opinions of it, and that the only thing different is the sound of the voice. We may not be able to pick our family, but we can pick our friends.

Love. Love can both move mountains and shape character. But what is love? This question was discussed at length in Chapter 35 of my book *Pantheon.* According to the mystic Plotinus (*Enn.* VI.9), it is that instinctive gravitational force drawing us to our creator (the One), the source from which we originally came. He tells us:

> I have seen a beauty wonderfully great and felt assurance that then most of all I belonged to the better part; I have actually lived the best life and come to identify with the divine; and...I have come to that supreme actuality, setting myself above all else in the realm of Intellect. [See *Pantheon*, p. 223].

Love is part of our eternal quest to know our true selves, a part of our desire to achieve union with the source that created us. A man cannot be said to have lived unless he has both loved and been loved. Even if we fail in our quests for friends or lovers, we will still in some way feel redeemed; for there is no pursuit so noble, no endeavor so eternal in its calling, that will yet bestow the laurels of the victor to the vanquished. The day we give up the chase is the day our souls begin to shrivel and die. Let us allow these elements, then, as the ingredients for the changing of our characters. How we mix them, season them, and knead them to expansion in our personal bakeries will be up to us. The positive man, the vigorous man, will not cower behind a barricade of complaints or timorous equivocations at the difficulty of undertaking the task. For he has long ago accepted the reality that life is for the living, and for the brave.

62. We Should Seize The Present Hour For Action

At the beginning of this month I bought the special director's cut of the Michael Mann film *Collateral*. I don't usually buy movies, having learned from past experience that it makes more sense to rent them. But every rule should have exceptions; and it is a good thing to collect those movies that transport you to a specific place or mood. And when you recall the mood, you revisit certain pleasurable sensations. There is just something about the way *Collateral* is shot, the way Los Angeles shimmers, that gives it a cool but intense patina.

There is a great scene in the film where the philosophizing hit man (Tom Cruise) hectors his captive cab driver, Jamie Foxx, about the necessity of not wasting time in life. Life is short, says Cruise; and one day, it is gone completely. Timid procrastination is not just bad policy, he tells him, it is an offense against life itself. Cruise is correct, of course; and we've heard this before. But having heard this, how many of us actually have the conviction to put this knowledge to use? How many of us seek refuge in our own comfortable excuses, delaying the hour of action until we have talked ourselves out of any action? Some things in life require planning; but some require blind faith. So much of the "life advice" tossed around by so-called experts really amounts to post-event rationalizations. What I mean by this is that for many successful people, the grand leap of faith was taken first–sometimes blindly–without reference to any "business plan." Only later was the laundry-list of preparation points written out. Many men like to believe that their success was due to their clear-headed powers of analysis, when more often it may be attributed to passion and circumstance.

I was reminded of this same point in another context yesterday, when reading through some letters of Petrarch. One dated March 21, 1361 caught my eye; in it, the great humanist urges the Holy Roman emperor Charles IV to visit Italy. With this as his starting point, Petrarch then manages to work into his letter many profound admonitions against delay and procrastination; these have lost none of their relevance and power since they were written. He says:

> Don't you hear the words of Virgil?
>
> *Every 'best day' of life for miserable mortals is the first to fly away...*
>
> Don't you hear the words of Lucan?
>
> *The hour may come when all the leaders are confounded; so prepare to die.*
>
> And in the same vein:
>
> *Oracles do not give me definite truth, but death is certain;*
> *The brave man and the timid both must be slain.*
> *Is it not enough that Jupiter has said so?*

Unless plans truly produce something in the way of action, thinking is toothless and worries are pointless. "Tomorrow I will begin; the next day, I will move!" I would ask, "Why not today?" Is the coming light more serene, and the present day more cloudy? The first day is the best, as you heard the greatest of poets say. The first day is here *now*, because we have nothing in the past except our memory, and there is no pondering about what is impossible. In the future there is nothing except oracles and the snares of false hopes. And even if this day and the next one are the same, who can doubt that this one is more *present* and more *certain*? It is in doubt whether the next day will come, or whether it will discover us; but we know that the present day, when it leaves, will not come back. Why are we always chasing after what is far away? Let us concentrate on the present, and work hard lest it flow away from us unused. This is expedient for everyone, but so very important to you, Caesar, that without it you will not be able to handle the affairs of your empire even using great industry or virtue…Why should you shy away, for what reason should you waste the present while obsessing about tomorrow? There is no place for tomorrow in the needs of the present [*Nullus in hodierna necessitate crastino locus est*].

Do what you have to do today: if something else comes up tomorrow, you or some other person will take care of it. There will be no scarcity of leaders for the times; and even if they are found wanting, you will never be held responsible for the ineptitude of another man. Make sure you are not found wanting in your own time. Tomorrow–which holds us in suspense and stresses us, and which we wait for as if it were imminently coming–has already gone by. *No day except the first day will not be the tomorrow of another day.* [*Nullus enim, praeter primum, dies non diei alterius cras fuerit*].

That last sentence is almost worth hanging on our bedroom wall. We can never hear words like this often enough. In the modern era, our lives have too often become comfortable arrangements of routine; and over time, we are lulled into a stupefying sense of regularity that can paralyze ambition and stifle creative designs for forward movement. We must never permit the seductive spiderwebs of complacency to entangle too completely our human drive to overcome obstacles, break through barriers, and surmount challenges. It is true that there is something worse than death: it is that grey, somnolent twilight zone in which life is physically lived, but has capitulated all vital force, all desire for healthy risk, and all masculine daring.

63. Getting A Point Across With Tact And Authority

One feature of great men is that they generally know how to handle themselves in a variety of situations. They tend to be flexible and agile; they will know when to scold, when to chastise, when to use the velvet glove, and when to use the hammer. Only the experience of life can impart this kind of wisdom. But we can at least prepare ourselves in some ways. One of these ways is to read the letters of such men. See how they interact with their peers. Study how they solve various problems or issues that fall on their desks. You will spend a good part of your life "putting out fires" at work and at home, so you might as well learn from the masters.

Those in positions of authority or responsibility will have dealt with all types of people. They will know how to express themselves in a way that gets their point across without alienating their addressee. These qualities–we can call them tact or diplomacy–are in short supply these days. I have learned a great deal by studying the correspondence of men like Abraham Lincoln, Seneca, Petrarch, and one man who may not be as familiar as these others: Libanius (c. 314–392 A.D.). He was a professional rhetorician and court official of the Eastern Roman Empire. He wrote one of the first "autobiographies" in history, but his chief importance for posterity lies in the voluminous correspondence which he maintained with a great number of people. More than 1500 of his letters survive, a vast corpus. Taken together, they show him to be a master of diplomacy and diction.

I like this letter below. Some background is necessary to put it in context. Libanius was a close personal friend and confidant of the emperor Julian ("Julian the Apostate") a zealously pagan emperor who had abandoned his early Christian upbringing in favor of the traditional deities of ancient Greece. For this, and especially for his open advocacy of paganism, he had earned the sullen wrath of the eastern Christian community. Julian led a military expedition to Persia and was killed while campaigning in 363. In the letter below, Libanius responds to an earlier letter written to him by a Christian named Julianus. In the earlier letter, Julianus had made some derogatory comments about the death of the emperor Julian. Libanius was stung by these remarks, but he did not respond in kind. He did not fly off the handle. Instead, he penned this measured, dignified response, which strikes the perfect balance between firm rebuke and formal courtesy.

> To Julianus:
>
> A fine letter from a fine fellow has been slow in arriving. As for the change of fortune that you say has befallen me, whereby I no longer have people to defer to me, I found it hard to realize that you were referring to the death of the emperor. I loved him no less than my own mother, and I was loved far more than those who really seemed to be. Anyway, I never employed my audiences with him to raise up some [people] to undeserved heights, or to depress others. Nor yet did I turn this into a traffic for gain, nor can it be alleged that I became a penny the richer from the imperial coffers, for I never asked for the return of all my grandfather's fortune which lay there, nor did I accept it when he pressed it on me. Even that paltry grant to Aristophanes was the consequence of an oration, not a request from me. So I concede that I am unfortunate in the loss of such a friend, but I have not lost any flatterers, for I never had any.
>
> My earlier friends are my friends now, and more pleasing to me now in their commendations of my conduct, which was not inspired to insolence by the accident of Fortune. By writing to me now you give me pleasure, as you did then. But had you wished to

> honor me in the same manner, you would have got a name for honoring a friend, not of truckling to fortune. [*Trans. by A.F. Norman*]

Libanius gets his point across very clearly. He defends the memory of the emperor Julian, and refuses to let Julianus's insult slide, but he does it in a diplomatic way. The stern hand is gloved in velvet. It seems to me that, if at all possible, we should try to emulate this ethic in our dealings with others.

64. "Italy Is Excellent In All Things"

The Roman engineer and architect Vitruvius believed that one of Italy's special gifts was its geographical location. The nation was so situated, he believed, to combine the positive aspects of both cool and warm climates. In his treatise *De Architectura* (VI.11), he notes that

> For in Italy the inhabitants are exactly tempered in either direction, both in the structure of the body, and by their strength of mind in the matter of endurance and courage. For just as the planet Jupiter is tempered by running in the middle between the heat of Mars and the cold of Saturn, in the same manner Italy presents good qualities which are tempered by admixture from either side both north and south, and are consequently unsurpassed. And so, by its policy, it curbs the courage of the northern barbarians; by its strength, the imaginative south. Thus the divine mind has allotted to the Roman state an excellent and temperate region in order to rule the world. [*Trans. by Frank Granger*]

We often forget how important geography and climate are to history. There is no doubt some truth to what Vitruvius says; we find the same sentiment echoed in Pliny's *Natural History* (II.189). Pliny talks about the need for a "tempering" of the extremes of cold and hot. Perhaps this is so of nations; but for individuals, personal preference is supreme. For my own part, I find myself becoming more and more concerned with climate as the years pass. One begins to lose enthusiasm for battling slicks of ice, blasts of arctic air, and the disturbing volatilities of temperature. There is no doubt in my mind that I intend to seek warmer climes in the years ahead. Cold for me oppresses the spirit; one desires to feel the sun beat down on the face, to be unimpeded by excessive clothing. An amusing anecdote reinforces the point. The scholar Petrarch sent a long letter to Pope Urban V in June 1366, the purpose of which was to convince him to move the seat of the papacy back from Avignon to Rome. He included a number of eloquent appeals to the beauty, fertility, and favorable climate of the Italian peninsula. There was also a humorous story that I will relate here.

Petrarch tells us that an earlier pope, Benedict XII, was once sent some impressively delicious eels from the Volsinian lakes. The pope could see that they were a great delicacy, and ordered them to be shared among the cardinals of the Curia. He kept only a small portion of the eels for himself. The cardinals ate them with gusto, and word quickly got around about how good they were. When a group was visiting the pope's residence a few weeks later, someone brought up the subject of the eels. Benedict, who was a man not only of great humanistic learning but also a jokester, said to all of them: "If I had known in advance how good the eels were, I certainly would not have shared them all with you. I never imagined that eels of such quality could be found in Italy." Upon hearing this, Cardinal Giovanni Colonna (a man whom Petrarch had worked under) got a bit incensed, even though Benedict had been joking. He said, "How is it possible that an educated man such as yourself, so learned in all things, doesn't know that Italy excels in all things?" Benedict's response to this jibe is not recorded. Petrarch went on say this about his country:

> The climate is most healthy and marvelously blended between chill and heat, which is the reason adduced by certain writers for the origin of Rome and her empire over the world, because it was so blended from opposites that it countered the trickery of the South with physical vigor, and suppressed the savagery of the North with its moral virtues, so that it was inevitable that the extremities would surrender to the middle, which shared in both their natures.

> Here there are lakes full of fish, such as no other region has in so small a space; there are rivers curving by the design of nature into most convenient bends in scattered places, so that a great part of Italy, Liguria and Venetia and Emilia and the Flaminian region scarcely have a distinguished place that is not accessible to a man calmly traveling along delightful waters. [*Trans. by Elaine Fantham*].

Well said, indeed. But we may concur with him that Italy excels in all things. Even in eels.

65. Why Worrying Is Pointless

For a good part of my life I used to worry excessively about things. When I was in college I worried about keeping up my grade point average and being able to complete Marine Corps Officer Candidate School; when I was on active duty I worried about doing my job well; when I started my law practice many years ago I worried about all the various thing related to establishing oneself in one's profession. And there are other examples of worrying that I need not rattle off here. All of this worry, all of this stress, was largely self-inflicted.

I won't go so far as to say that all worry is useless. In measured doses, worry serves an important function: it catalyzes the senses, focuses the energy, and prepares to body for struggle. It reminds us of important deadlines. It keeps us alert and attentive. Fear is a powerful motivator: we should not forget this. No species of animal is so irritating to me, and none so likely to induce contempt, as the carefree, happy-go-lucky slacker who cares nothing about his responsibilities. Such people need repeated kicks to the posterior. But even if some worry is good, excessive worrying is not good. It degrades the enjoyment of life, distracts us from accomplishing tasks, and warps judgment.

When a man takes stock in his life, he eventually comes to realize that most of the things he has worried about have never come to pass. I had this realization some years ago. I began to think about it, and I began to ask myself the question: why am I worrying about things in the first place? What is the origin of this impulse? These were the questions I was trying to answer. The more I thought about this, the more I was led to this answer: we worry because we think we owe a debt. What do I mean by this? Let me explain. I realized that the vast majority of the things I was worrying about were things I had no control over. They were external factors that I could not influence in any meaningful way. Why was I worrying about them, then? The answer is this. I thought that by tormenting myself, I could somehow pay a "debt" to the universe. *I subconsciously thought that my expenditure of "worry energy" might placate the god of Fortune, and make Her more favorably disposed to my predicament.* I don't think any of this is conscious thought: it all takes place below the surface of things. But it is there. It is an unconscious impulse.

This, for me, was the real reason I was worrying. I thought that I ought to worry. I thought that worrying would somehow help me. And I think there was another reason as well. *I realized that I was addicted to the "high" of worrying, if one can call it that.* We put ourselves in certain mental states because we enjoy the "rush" of feeling certain ways. We have conditioned our minds to fall into certain ruts of thought; and we like to return to these ruts and pitfalls, even if they are not healthy ones. So here are the two major reasons why we worry: (1) we believe we owe an emotional debt to the universe (or Fortune, whatever term you prefer); and (2) we seek the emotional satisfaction of burying ourselves in worry. The first reason arises out of fear; the second arises out of a desire for pleasure.

The problem with these twin causes of worry is that, with time, they take an emotional toll over us. They sap our energy and enjoyment of life. How can a man free himself from this monkey on his back? We must be realistic in the first place, of course. You are never entirely going to be free from worry, nor should you be. Any man totally free from worry or care would be a worthless derelict. Yet we can remove the worst of the tangle from the psyche's underbrush. The first step comes from realizing that we will never be exempt from bad things happening to us. We must realize this first. Disasters, tragedies, and misfortunes will befall us: this is unavoidable. I was reading these lines a few days ago in Lucan:

> Heu demens! Nullum belli sentire fragorem,
> Tot mundi caruisse malis, praestare deorum
> Excepta quis Morte potest?

And this means: *"You crazy fool! What god except Death can guarantee a man he will feel no crash of war or avoid the world's evils?"* He is telling us that we are crazy to think that we will get through life unscathed. Bad things will happen to us no matter what we do. The secret is not in worrying about these things, or even becoming neurotic about avoiding them, but in taking action to solve them when they happen. In the same vein of thought, my friend Petrarch said this in a letter to Pope Urban V:

> Sic est ergo: generosi animi pabulum ac delitiae sunt labores non propter se quidem, sed propter id quo non aliter quam per illos ascenditur.

This sentence says, "Thus it is: human labors are the nourishment and joy of the great soul not because of the hardships themselves, but because only through them can the soul achieve great things." We need struggle as part of our lives, our identity, our very existence. Embrace struggle and handle it: do not seek to avoid it or worry about it. Worrying about it is both self-indulgent and craven. I say it is self-indulgent because, as noted above, it represents a selfish desire to seek pleasure; and it is craven because it seeks to pay a debt to Fortune that she is not owed. She will extract Her own debt from you, in Her own way. Have no doubt about this! As I looked over so many phases of my life, I realized one inescapable truth: almost all of what I worried about never came to pass. It was all for nothing. It did not help me; in fact, it almost certainly harmed me. It prevented me from enjoying the moment. Worrying had been a thief, a pickpocket, a cheat: it had robbed me of life's pleasures. And when life is short, you must savor the pleasures that you can. Your trials will come anyway, whether you want them to come, or not. So it serves no purpose to worry about what you think will be your problems. Fortune decides this for you: She has the final say, not you. Do not be so arrogant as to assume you know best. You know only about yourself.

Appreciating these things is the way to begin to release yourself from worry. It takes confidence in yourself and your convictions. But what choice do you have? Do you want to remain a craven-hearted man, groveling before Fortune? Are you addicted to feeling depressed or stressed out? Fortune punishes most those who grovel before her: remember this. So by seeking out challenges, and handling those challenges, your feelings of confidence will grow. You will wean yourself from your habits of worry, and begin to savor the feeling of taking on difficult things and dealing with them. And in time, you will perhaps begin to see yourself as Joshua, who, during the Battle of Gibeon, asked God to stop the sun in the heavens (*Joshua 10:12*), so they could keep fighting during the daylight.

66. When Embarked On A Great Enterprise, Do Not Look Back

When you have begun a great project, press forward until it is completed. Do not look back; do not be distracted by the ambient noise of life, the doubting whispers of others, or the gnawing doubts that will inevitably bore their way into your consciousness. Nothing great was ever accomplished by half-measures; and the failure of grand ambition is still more inspiring than the cautious steps of the timid man. In a 1368 letter to Pope Urban V, the humanist Petrarch wrote the following words that I happened to read this morning:

> At qui se glorioso principio notum fecit, si id sponte destituat, infamiam non evadet...Nusquam substiteris: tempus breve, longum iter, lenit laborem operis spes mercedis. Nusquam denique in terga respexeris.

And this means, "He who achieves notoriety through a glorious project will not avoid disgrace if he voluntarily abandons it...Never pause: time is short, the road is long, and the hope of reward softens the weight of labor. Finally, never look behind you." We live in an age of samplers, braggarts, and buffet-pickers; lacking the fortitude to stay the course on any great project, such people are likely to give up and drop their packs at the first indications of hardship. This is their mentality; but this is not how character and greatness are forged. Why is it so important not to look back once you have begun a great enterprise? These are the reasons:

You will lose two critical things needed for the race: momentum and speed. No racing coach ever counseled a trainee to look back at his opponents while he was running a race.

Looking back can be psychologically crippling. Nostalgia and sentimentality have led many a man to ruin. Instead of being focused on the job at hand, you instead become consumed with the images and memories of the past. Even worse, doubts begin to grow in your mind whether you have made the correct decision. This principle of not looking back was, I believe, the origin of the famous myth of Orpheus and Eurydice. It is told in Virgil's *Georgics* IV.453 *et seq*. The gist of the myth is that Eurydice was bitten by a snake and died; her lover Orpheus went to Hades to beg for her return to the world of the living. This wish was granted him by Hades, but on one condition: she would have to walk behind him, and he could *not* turn around and look at her until they had both reached the light of the upper world. In other words, he had to exercise patience and discipline. This, however, he was unable to do. He could not resist looking back during the journey, and for this he forfeited his chance at happiness. At the very moment Orpheus looked back, says Virgil, "All his labor melted away, his deal with the stern tyrant [Hades] was breached, and the crash of thunder was heard three times among the waters of Avernus."

The same point is made in the Hebrew scriptures; we find in Genesis 19 the tale of Lot's escape from Sodom with his wife and daughters. Lot was ordered not to look back once he left Sodom. But for some reason, his wife either could not or would not listen to this counsel. She was turned into a pillar of salt. The text of Genesis 19 relates the story:

> As soon as they had brought them out, one of them said, "Flee for your lives! Don't look back, and don't stop anywhere in the plain! Flee to the mountains or you will be swept away!" But Lot said to them, "No, my lords, please! Your servant has found favor in your eyes, and you have shown great kindness to me in sparing my life. But I can't flee to the mountains; this disaster will overtake me, and I'll die. Look, here is a town near enough to run to, and it is small. Let me flee to it—it is very small, isn't it?...Then the Lord rained down burning sulfur on Sodom and Gomorrah—from the Lord out of the heavens. Thus he overthrew those cities and the entire plain, destroying all those living in the cities—and also the vegetation in the land. But Lot's wife looked back, and she became a pillar of salt.

The point made here is that sometimes we must make a clean break with the past. The ghosts of nostalgia can only haunt us for so long before they become impediments to advancement. It is a mistake to think that a multiplicity of options somehow produces happiness: it does not. It is more common that too many options only serve to confuse and demoralize us. A soldier is happiest on a long march when he only has the pack of the man in front of him to contemplate. He does not need to think about other options except moving forward and fighting. This is why Hernan Cortes famously burned his ships when he had arrived on the coast of Mexico and sought to conquer the Aztec empire.

One final illustration of this principle I will relate here. The military historian Frontinus tells us (*Stratagems* IV.1) that when the Roman general Q. Metellus Macedonicus was conducting operations in Spain, some of his units–five cohorts, to be precise–happened to fall back before the enemy. He was not pleased. He ordered the men to make out their wills, and sent them back into battle, with orders that they would not be received back into camp unless they were victorious. The only two options were victory or death. This is what I mean when I use the word motivation. So keep your head down, stretch out your legs, swing your arms, and keep moving with powerful strides: and do not look back.

67. Bequeath Your Problems To Those Who Deserve Them

There is an amusing anecdote related in Chapter 60 of Gibbon's *Decline and Fall*. The author is describing an encounter between Fulk of Neuilly (d. 1201), a mendicant preacher trying to win support for a Fourth Crusade, and Richard I Plantagenet of England. Fulk had been shopping his plans to various European monarchs, most of which were not interested in proving financial or material assistance to the project. Fulk was reduced to beating his fist on the doors of one country after another, only to be rebuffed. As Gibbon relates:

> The situation of the principal monarchs was averse to the pious summons [of Fulk]. The emperor Frederic the Second was a child; and his kingdom of Germany was disputed by the rival houses of Brunswick

> and Swabia, the memorable factions of the Guelphs and Ghibelines...Philip Augustus of France had performed, and could not be persuaded to renew, the perilous vow [of going on crusade]...Richard of England was satiated with the glory and misfortunes of his first adventure, and he presumed to deride the exhortations of Fulk of Neuilly, who was not abashed in the presence of kings. "You advise me," said Plantagenet, "to dismiss my three daughters, pride, avarice, and incontinence: I bequeath them to the most deserving; my *pride* to the Knights-Templars, my *avarice* to the monks of Cisteaux, and my *incontinence* to the prelates."

This was what Richard said to Fulk. And what he meant by this, beyond just humor, was that there were others more deserving of his vices than he himself. All in all, it was a witty and effective way to rebuff an overbearing scold like Fulk. But is there any deeper lesson here? Perhaps there is. Most of us are familiar with the old expression of the "monkey on my back." Having a "monkey on one's back" is equivalent to having a constantly nagging problem. As a practical issue of leadership, I have found from long experience that sometimes it is necessary to transfer the monkey on your back to someone else. If you are working in a large organization, or are dealing with customers or clients, you will certainly be familiar with this survival strategy. In the current climate we live in–our culture of blaming, lack of personal responsibility, and skirting obligations–there are many people who seek to transfer their problems to you. They want to pull the "monkey" off their backs and stick him on your back. Sometimes these proverbial "monkeys" get passed around like hot potatoes, as everyone frantically tries to shift responsibility for the problem to someone else. It is an old game.

I wish things were not this way, but the fact is that this is the kind of situation we often encounter. Do not allow other people's problems to become your problem. Remember the concept of the "dirtbag shuffle" that we spoke about here some time ago.[12] Make sure that you guard your "back" from those who would try to pin

[12] A reference to a podcast that appeared at *Fortress of the Mind* (qcurtius.com) on July 31, 2017.

their problems on your shoulders. In the example given above, Fulk tried to turn *his* problem (needing money for the crusade) *King Richard's problem.* And Richard cleverly deflected this effort. He dodged Fulk's attempt at emotional blackmail, and stuck the problem right back on Fulk, where it no doubt belonged. What Richard was telling Fulk was this: *if you want money for your little field-trip, go talk to the Templars, the monastic orders, and the prelates. I've already done my job and fulfilled my obligations. Your problem is not my problem. Now go.* Fulk was dismissed from the king's presence, with the monkey now firmly attached to his back.

68. Catching Birds In Anzio, Italy

The Italian humanist Biondo Flavio of Forli (1392-1463) was one of the great names of Renaissance humanism. His extensive *Description of Italy* (*Italia Illustrata*) collected anecdota and geographical information about every region of the country from ancient times until his own day. It was first published in 1451, but saw frequent additions and revisions until Flavio's death. Book II, section 7 of his treatise provides some details on how the natives of Nettuno (a town in the region of Lazio, south of Rome) go about netting birds. The passage attracted my attention for some reason, and I thought it might be worth relating; it may even be of interest to modern hunters. Flavio himself can provide the specific details:

> The sea there has lots of rocks, or rather gravel, and many excellent fish. Dense forests offer, as ever, good hunting of boar and deer. Fowling is of two sorts, depending on the time of year. At the first sign of spring, swallows and quail (now known as *quaglie* from their call) return together to Italy across the Tyrrhenian Sea. The people of Nettuno then cover the whole shoreline of old Anzio with continuous netting for a space of five miles. Each man sits on his own patch of ground, purchased at great expense, and with a pipe lures the quail as they arrive at night on to his own bit of the nets. When they are entangled in the nets in large numbers, the fowler picks up any that fall on to the sand beyond the net,

> exhausted by the long flight. I have heard that in a single month when the fowling was carried over several days, 100,000 of these little birds may be caught every single day.

Apparently this kind of "mass fowling" can be traced back to ancient times. Flavio notes that the quail in question are also mentioned in Pliny's *Historia Naturalis* X.65–X.66:

> These are the very quail of which Pliny says: "The quail always arrive before the cranes. It is a small bird, and when it has arrived, more generally keeps to the ground than flies aloft. Their flight is not without danger to mariners, for when they approach land they often smash into the sails of a ship, and that too always in the night, and the vessel often sinks. They will not fly when the south wind is blowing, as that wind is humid and apt to weigh them down…"

Flavio provides us more details about how the mass fowling takes place.

> They also catch birds at Anzio in the autumn. After they have flown over the sea, wood pigeons gather for a while in the woods of Anzio as they prepare to leave Italy. The expert fowlers of Nettuno hang up huge nets specially made for this sort of fowling at great expense. When they see a great number of pigeons gathered together and roosting in the trees, they terrify them by throwing stones and shouting, and make them fly off. In their flight the birds are forced into a great flock. When the fowlers see them above the snares of the nets they have spread, they sling small stones at them (either naturally white or coated with gypsum) with a great shout. Terrified by the whirring noise, the pigeons try to save themselves by dodging [what they believe to be] the hawks…which in their terror the imagine in the whirring of the slingshots. Flying as quickly as they can, they come near to the ground and thus distracted hurtle into the nets…Most of the present-day

> people of Rome catch wood pigeons for weddings and banquets, for these small birds are better in flavor and more nutritious than other cock pigeons. [*Trans. by Jeffrey A. White*]

One of the pleasures of reading old travel books and geographical surveys is that they provide us a window on the era in which they were written. They function as portable time-machines by freezing existence at the moment they were composed. It does not even matter if a travel book is "out of date"; the mind provides the scene and keeps it alive in our collective consciousness. Perhaps the natives of Nettuno today still practice some form of fowling; perhaps they do not. I do not know. But having read over Flavio's description of fowling above, I can forever revisit the scene of Renaissance Italian townsmen laying out five miles of netting along the shoreline, scaring birds *en masse* out of the trees, waving their arms and shouting at them, and pelting them with volleys of stones. The image remains forever fixed, suspended perfectly in time. Just like a hapless quail dangling in an Anzio net.

69. Even When Glory Departs, Something Always Remains

The Italian humanist Ciriaco de' Pizzicolli lived from 1391 to 1452. He is more commonly known as Cyriac of Ancona. While most humanists of his era were content to labor at their desks, he was unusual in that he sought to observe ancient monuments and inscriptions in person. He was, in fact, one of the very first to undertake a systematic survey of the surviving monuments of Greek antiquity in the Eastern Mediterranean; his work is of great value to the modern antiquarian, since many of the inscriptions and temples he sketched now no longer exist, ravaged by the cruelties of time and man. Ironically (or perhaps appropriately), his works themselves survive only in fragmentary form.

His multi-volume *Commentaries* were destroyed in a fire in the sixteenth century, having never found their way to print. But we do possess some extracts from his travel diaries, and these are better than nothing. They are strangely fascinating travel records, filled with philosophical asides on the transitory nature of glory and the enduring nature of virtue. One passage I read recently drives home the that even when a civilization's former glory has departed, some residue of that glory always remains. It may not be readily apparent. But it is still there. In the diary excerpt below, Cyriac describes his impressions when visiting the ruins of Sparta in 1447. He first begins with a sweeping panorama of disturbing decay:

> [E]ven though one must grieve to behold those noble, ancient, distinguished and richly adorned cities, now in our time in a state of utter collapse or demolition almost everywhere throughout the region, one must endure with an [even] heavier heart, in my opinion, the pitiable ruin of the human race...For that noble-spirited, renowned race of Spartans, once the memorable triumph of every kind of military valor, not only in Greece, but in Europe and throughout the whole world, [but] nowadays a people feebly and basely untrue to their breeding, seem to have fallen completely from that famous pristine moral integrity of the Laconian, Lacedaemonian way of life...[I say this] because, in these our days, those who dwell in the Laconian land, on the Spartan foothill of Mount Taygetus, in the town of Mistra (which has discarded its ancient name), men who practice a poor sort of agriculture or commerce or ignoble trades and every kind of worthless superstitious rite, are ruled by barbarians or by foreigners. For my part, however, I shall by no means pass over the following single exception, proving that, although the Lacedaemonians' much talked-of political excellence, military training, and the splendid contests of men and well-born women in the gymnasia has been abandoned and have fallen into disuse through neglect over a long period of time, *still, the nature of the place seems not totally to have waned, since it gives birth to human beings who are naturally honorable, able and suited to virtue.*

As evidence of this residual glory of ancient Sparta, Cyriac describes the physical prowess of an impressive local man:

> For today, while we were traveling from the village of Arcasa to Spartan Mistra, we saw among our companions a certain Spartan youth, tall of stature and quite handsome, George, called by the sobriquet *Chirodontas*, that is, "Boar's Teeth," because (they say) that once while hunting in the forest, encountering a fierce boar, he leaped onto its back, and pressing it down by sheer force, killed the prostrate beast; and they say that once he caught and held two men together under his arms and carried them several paces. In my case also, instead of reassuring me verbally, and as a physical statement of his honesty, he caught me up with his hands on the bank of a certain small river, held me under his arm, and deposited me safely on the farther bank of the stream. And at the next village, we saw that, brandishing an iron rod that was three fingers thick, he had split it into separate parts. [*Trans. by E.W. Bodnar*]

So while it was true that the monuments and architecture of old Sparta had decayed and was at present in ruins, Cyriac could see that some imprint of this departed glory still remained on the people and the place. And this is why we should never believe that our efforts in this mortal life are to no avail. No effort is ever wasted; for even if the physical monuments of human greatness eventually crumble into dust, some vestige of this spirit will live on forever. The residual glory is there, and always remains.

70. Adrastia: The Goddess Who Punishes Hubris And Arrogance

We have observed that one of the themes of ancient literature is the concept of Fate or Fortune. We find it first expressed in the plays and heroic poems of the Greeks; the idea then seeped into the writing of history and biography. Closely associated with this concept is the idea of divine retribution for offending the gods. Those who showed contempt for divine or human law would be humbled by the harsh blows of Fate: no man could expect to thumb his nose at the laws of the universe and get away with it. So Sallust reminds us that Catiline and Jugurtha went down in ruin because their blind hubris caused them to scorn the accepted laws of decency and human society. Livy and Polybius practically endorse the idea that Rome rose from nothing to rule the world because the gods had fated that it should be so. Tacitus and Suetonius chronicle every pernicious vice of the Julio-Claudian emperors to make the point that they deserved to go down in ignominious destruction. Cicero's philosophical writings are occasionally flavored by this idea as well.

The idea of Fortune or Fate as the arbiter of human destiny persisted for many centuries; we could even argue that the Catholic Church, through the writings of early Church fathers like Augustine, Jerome, Tertullian, simply substituted or imposed a new model on what had already existed before. In the Renaissance, the humanists (especially Petrarch, Machiavelli, and Guicciardini) enthusiastically endorsed the idea of Fortune. Yet for some reason modern man is uncomfortable with this idea; he likes to believe that he is in total control of his fate. He wants to believe his destiny is in his hands. More importantly, he recoils from any attempt to impose limits on his arrogance, greed, and desires. Anyone writing about the dangers of hubris today is not likely to find himself wildly popular. We live in an age of braggarts, big mouths, preening fools, and arrogant idiots; it is an age where ignorance is lauded and celebrated as wisdom, and the gutter is displayed to the public as something to be emulated. The price for all of this will inevitably be paid.

And this will be the cause of our undoing, if it has not already happened. One cannot just do whatever one wants in life. *You do not make your own rules.* You are not an emperor unto yourself; you are not an island of your own, isolated from the mainland of humanity. The Greeks of late antiquity had a goddess they called Nemesis, and her function was to deliver punishment to those who were guilty of hubris. She was the punisher of undeserved good fortune, and the chastiser of those who overreached themselves. Her name in Latin was *Adrastia*. You have probably never heard of her, and this very fact goes a long way to proving my point about the narcissistic streak of our modern culture. The best description of Adrastia is found in the Roman historian Ammianus Marcellinus. Writing in the fourth century A.D., he interrupts his narrative to remind us who really has the final say in human affairs:

> These and many other similar examples are often the operation of Adrastia, the punisher of wicked deeds and the patron of good deeds (and let us hope it is always so!). We may call Her by her secondary name, Nemesis. She is the subtle law of an inexorable higher power; as some men believe, She is located above the orbit of the Moon. Others maintain that She is a kind of general guardian over the fates of individuals. The ancient theologians have pictured Her as the daughter of Justice; and from a far-off eternity She looks down on all earthly affairs. As the queen of causes [*regina causarum*] and the arbiter and decider of human affairs, She handles the urn [for choosing lots] with its probabilities and causes fortunes to change, sometimes producing for us results that were very different from what we had originally intended.
>
> Many acts She twists into something very different. Restraining the always-expanding mortal arrogance with the chains of fate, and tilting the scales of gain and loss (as she knows how to do), She undermines and lowers the haughty necks of the arrogant. She elevates good men from the lowest rung of society to a blessed station in life. Tradition has provided Her with wings so that She might be able to visit anyone with all deliberate speed; and it gave Her a helm to grasp and a wheel under Her, so that as She runs through the elements, no one will ever forget that She commands the fate of the universe. [*Res Gestae* XIV.11; *translation mine*]

These are powerful words. For Ammianus, there was no doubt about who was really in charge of events. It was not man, with his pathetic, puny schemes that existed to feed his own ego; it was Adrastia, or Nemesis, who would decide who was rewarded and who was punished. Unearned good fortune would be punished; arrogance would be punished; hubris would be punished. Adrastia was the great equalizer, the dispenser of divine justice to those who would prefer to forget the laws of nature.

It seems to me that we have forgotten this lesson, much to our society's detriment. One of the benefits of classical studies is their ability to provide moral instruction and guidance; we learn to humble our pride, to live according to rules, to respect the rights of others, and to discipline ourselves to put our passion and greed in check. Yet much of this seems to be ignored today. One wonders what Ammianus would have made of this quote, attributed to Karl Rove, the advisor to president George Bush, in which he gave his views of how the United States should its foreign policy:

> That's not the way the world really works any more. We're an empire now, and when we act, we create our own reality. And while you're studying that reality—judiciously, as you will—we'll act again, creating other new realities, which you can study too, and that's how things will sort out. We're history's actors ... and you, all of you, will be left to just study what we do.

In Rove's view, a president should be able to do whatever he wants, whenever he wants to do it, and the consequences be damned. He "creates his own reality" and then the world just has to deal with that reality. It is a disturbing picture of hubris and incredible arrogance that can only end in tragedy and ruin. It goes without saying, of course, that people like Rove never have to deal with the direct consequences of their policies. Neither they nor their children serve in the military; they do not visit the places they destroy, or the communities they decimate. For them it is simply a matter of being able to do whatever one wants, without fear of repercussions or consequences. There are many national leaders today who have forgotten the ever-present reality of Adrastia (if they ever knew or cared about it in the first place). These leaders strut around on the world stage, beating their chests and talking loudly, creating havoc and consternation among their fellow men. Coddled and nurtured from birth as spoiled children, they care nothing for their duties of office, or for their responsibilities as citizens. But in a larger sense they are the leaders we deserve, for they reflect the state of the culture. A great humbling is unavoidable. The universe has a way of leveling things out, of imposing limits on greed, arrogance, and hubris. Either you will correct the problem yourself, or Adrastia will fix it for you. *Adrastia, would that thou comest, and that right soon.*

71. Cato's Advice On Purchasing A Farm

Cato the Elder (234-149 B.C.) is one of those legendary figures in early Roman history. Known for his stern, uncompromising vision with regard to personal morality, rules, and social obligations, his treatise *On Agriculture* (*De Agri Cultura)* constitutes the earliest complete Latin text that has survived. He was no stodgy country bumpkin, however. Plutarch called him "shrewd" and considered him the embodiment of the old Roman virtues. After a long political and military career he decided to devote himself to the arts of the soil and country living, and thought it would be useful to collect some of his best advice on rustic matters in one digestible volume. The book is an odd mixture of farming advice, food recipes, prayers, and life wisdom written in a terse and archaic style. We even detect, here and there, intimations of a sly sense of humor hiding behind the furrowed Catonian brow. At the outset of his book he gives us his opinions on how land should be purchased. Even after all this time, Cato's suggestions are sound and practical. Consider the following.

Buying. Do not be too eager to buy. There will always be time needed to examine the property in detail. A good parcel of land, he tells us, will satisfy us more and more with each examination (*Quotiens ibis, totiens magis placebit quod bonum erit*).

Neighbors. Be mindful of what the neighbors' properties look like. If the other people around you look bad, you should take note of this. Slovenliness has a way of spreading like an infection.

Climate. The climate of region should be generally good, and the soil free of problems. If possible, one should try to find a farm that lies at the foot of a hill or elevation and that faces south. Things that should be nearby are a water source or town. Being near the sea is also good whenever possible, as well as near well-used roads.

Location. It is better to be near other farms that have been in the area for a long time. Properties that change owners very frequently should be looked upon with suspicion.

Learn From Others. On the other hand, it is wise to show respect to how others solve problems: one should always try to learn from observing others (*Caveto alienam disciplinam temere contemnas*, or "beware of refusing to learn from others"). All other things being equal, it is better to buy a farm from someone who is good at what he does and is a good builder.

Luxuries. What is especially important is to avoid luxury and extravagance in buying land. Such frivolities can eat up a man's savings very quickly. Here is imparts a very sage piece of advice in his terse style:

> Know also that a farm is like a man; even if his resources be extensive, there is not much left over if he is lavish (*Scito idem agrum quod hominem, quamvis quaestuosus siet, si sumptuosus erit, relinqui non multum*).

The Master's Duties. The master of a farm must show good management (*De Agri Cultura* V.2). He should tend to his own business well, and keep his nose out of others' business. If he has workmen or hired hands, he should settle disputes among them quickly and with the most rigorous principles of justice. Punishments should be meted out in proportion to the offense, and no more. The servants should know their place, and should not consider the master's friends to be their friends. Servants and hands are more easily controlled and kept out of trouble if they are kept busy; how old is this timeless principle of management! His advice on finding a housekeeper clearly puts him in his era. The farmer's housekeeper should perform all her duties in an efficient manner (*De Agri.* CXLIII). She should be free of a taste for luxury and should hold the master of the house in high regard, even to the point of fear (*Ea te metuat facito*). She should not waste time going about as a social-butterfly or as a gossiper, but should be focused on the responsibilities of the household, which take precedence over all else. There is nothing more subtle and sophisticated as homespun wisdom honestly learned.

72. "Vanity Of Vanities, All Is Vanity"

Gelimer lived from about 480 to 550 A.D. and was the ruler of the Vandal kingdom in North Africa for four years from 530 to 534. The emperor Justinian aspired to restore Roman control over the region, and to this end sent his general Belisarius to expel the barbarian trespassers. This he did. Gelimer was also captured for good measure, and transported back to Byzantium as a prize of war. It was a Roman custom of the republic and early empire to allow victorious generals, back from their campaigns, to stage a "triumph" in the capital. This was essentially a mixture of parade and public procession where the victor would show the public the prizes of war, exotic animals, captured prisoners, and any other curiosities that might stimulate the fancy of a public hungry for spectacle. Such triumphs had passed out of fashion with the advent of a strong, centralized imperial authority. Emperors were not overly enthusiastic about seeing their generals lauded for things they themselves wanted credit for.

So for whatever reason, Justinian decided to break with precedent and award Belisarius a triumph. According to the historian Procopius (*Wars* IV.9), about six hundred years had passed since the last time a triumph had been staged in the capital. It was an unprecedented event. (In point of fact, the last non-imperial triumph, according to historian Anthony Kaldellis, was in 19 B.C. when Lucius Cornelius Balbus was granted one for his crushing of the Garamantes in Africa). Belisarius did not conduct the triumph in the traditional manner. Rather than ride in a carriage, he went on foot from his own house to the hippodrome; once inside he proceeded to approach the imperial reviewing stand to salute the emperor. About the spoils on display in the triumph, Procopius tells us:

> There was booty, including whatever is set apart by custom for imperial service, thrones of gold and carriages in which it is customary for the emperor's wife to ride, and much jewelry made of precious stones, golden drinking cups, and all other things that serve for the imperial table. There was also silver weighing many thousands of talents and all the royal treasure that was worth an extremely great sum...Among these were the treasures of the Jews, which Titus, the son of Vespasian, together with certain others, had brought to Rome after the capture of Jerusalem. [*Trans. by A. Kaldellis*]

Procopius says that when these treasures were put on display, a prominent Jew who had access to some imperial officials protested that the antiquities should be housed in Byzantium; their rightful place, he insisted, was in some appropriate facility in Jerusalem, the place from where they had been taken. Justinian was an extremely religious man–even by the standards of the day–and began to be concerned that the presence of the ancient Hebrew relics under his roof might subject him to some sort of divine curse. So he sent the treasures to Jerusalem under the care of some Christian legates.

Slaves were also paraded in the triumph. Gelimer himself, the deposed and defeated king, was among them; in those days, the defeated were made to taste the full bitterness of their condition by passing symbolically under the yoke (*sub iugum*). Gelimer and his retinue of slaves were brought into the hippodrome and made to circle the giant stadium before the roaring crowd. We may only speculate as to what thoughts were passing through his mind. Did he reflect on the transitory nature of earthly power and riches? Did he ruminate on the fickleness of Fortune, that had raised him up from nothing to be king of all the Vandals and Alans, only to hurl him back down to his presently abject condition? Did he take solace, perhaps, in the knowledge that those who cheered his downfall today might see themselves so judged by Fortune tomorrow?

We do not know. What we do know is that as he grimly circled the hippodrome, he paused before the box of the emperor and empress, high upon the reviewing stand. Justinian sat on an elevated seat with officials and spectators on either side. "He neither wept nor cried out," says Procopius, "but repeated again and again these words from Biblical scripture, '*vanity of vanities, all is vanity.*'" [*Ecclesiastes 1.1-2*] Most of the things we are convinced are so important will, in time, recede into the mists of irrelevance. Those who spend their lives, and their efforts, preoccupied with the minutiae of triviality will wake up one day to find themselves old and tired. And that which they once thought was so vital, is now revealed to be a cruel mirage.

73. Any City Can Be Taken

Any fortress can be stormed, and any city can be taken. It is a matter of using the correct tactics, combined with daring and imaginative leadership. Some citadels fall to guile, and others to brute force; still others yield to a combination of the two. We will consider the fall of Naples, an event that took place during the Gothic

War (A.D. 535-554). This was one of the emperor Justinian's wars to reassert imperial control over Italy from the occupying Goths. After Justinian's star general Belisarius conquered Sicily, he landed a force in Italy and began to advance on Naples in the spring of 536. After moving into position near the city, he summoned representatives of the occupying barbarians to call for the peaceful surrender of the city. The Goths refused; their representative, a man named Stephanus, gave Belisarius a response that bordered on insolent. Stephanus told the Romans that they were wasting their time. Belisarius answered in this way:

> Whether we acted wisely or not in deciding to come here is not a question we intend to put before the Neapolitans. But we desire that you consider carefully such matters as are appropriate to your deliberations and then act in accordance with your own interests. Receive the emperor's [Justinian's] army into your city, which has come to secure your freedom and that of the other Italians, and do not choose what will bring on you the most grievous misfortunes...But as for the Goths who are present, we give them a choice, either to array themselves hereafter on our side under the great emperor, or to go to their homes entirely free from harm. Because if both you and they disregard all these considerations and dare to raise arms against us, it will be necessary for us also, if God wills it, to treat whomever we meet as an enemy. [*Trans. by A. Kaldellis*]

But the Neapolitans put him off, offering one excuse after another. In the meantime they fortified the city heavily, and gave no intention of accepting his conditions. Time was short; he wanted to move against occupied Rome without delay but could not do so as long as Naples remained in enemy hands. And then fortune intervened, as it often does, to turn the tide of fate in his favor. Naples was supplied by an old aqueduct that led directly into the city. One of Belisarius's soldiers, an Isaurian, decided to explore it in order to better understand its construction. As the aqueduct approached the outer walls of the city, it narrowed as it came into contact with solid rock. The water-channel then became a narrow tunnel leading directly into the city. The entrance was not wide enough to allow a soldier equipped with weapons and armor to enter. But the Isaurian realized that if the tunnel entrance were widened, a force of men could gain entrance to the city by stealth.

Belisarius was greatly pleased to hear this news. He immediately ordered his men to begin work on the plan in the greatest secrecy. Rather than use chisels and picks–which might make a great deal of noise–he had the men use boring implements, rasps, and abrasive tools to grind down the entrance to the tunnel. Soon the work was done. Summoning Stephanus one last time, he gave him a final opportunity to yield the city to him and avoid bloodshed. He said:

> I have witnessed the capture of cities many times and am well acquainted with what takes place at such a time. They slay all the men of every age and, as for the women, although they beg to die, they are not given the gift of death but are carried off for outrage and suffer treatment that is abominable and most pitiable…When I see Naples falling victim to such a fate, as in the mirror of the cities that have been captured in times past, I am moved to pity it and you its inhabitants…I will be unable to control the fury of [my] men if they capture the city by act of war. While, therefore, it is still within your power to choose and act to your advantage, adopt the better course and avoid misfortune. For when it falls upon you, as it probably will, you will not justly blame fortune, but your own judgment.

This is what Belisarius said. When he was again rebuffed, he prepared to take the city by force. He had about four hundred men at night enter through the secret tunnel carrying weapons and lanterns. They also carried trumpets and noise-making devices to throw the city into terror once they had penetrated its interior. They also brought ladders and other climbing equipment. It was a daring and dangerous gamble, but if it paid off the city would belong to the Romans. The aqueduct was covered with a roof as it entered the city, so the raiders were not able to tell precisely where they were and how far they had gone. Eventually they found a gap in the roof of the aqueduct, and saw how far elevated they were above the city. Using ladders and straps, the soldiers climbed out of the aqueduct, and attacked a small garrison of Goths manning two watch-towers.

The trumpets were sounded, and Belisarius moved the bulk of his army to the part of the city wall that his men had already secured. His forces scaled the walls and made it into the city, and once there, overwhelmed the shocked population. When Belisarius later made his victory speech to his army, he concluded with these words: "And let the conquered learn by experience what kind of friends they have lost by reason of foolish counsel." The city was his, and fairly won. He moved quickly from there to Rome, which would prove to be the greatest prize of the war.

74. The Shortness Of Life, And The Second Death

There is a passage in Cicero's treatise *Tusculan Disputations* I was thinking about today while driving home from work. The passage begins as a parable, then closes with a glorious invocation to action. Cicero makes an analogy from nature observed near the River Hypanis, then draws some conclusions from that analogy. He says:

> By the River Hypanis [modernly, Bug], which empties into the Pontus from a part of Europe, Aristotle says that certain little animals are born which live for only one day. One of these animals that dies in the eighth hour of the day has reached an old age. One that makes it to sunset is extremely aged; even more so if it happens to be a day of the summer solstice. Compare our longest human lifespan with eternity: we may be compared with the same brief flourishing as these little animals. [*Tusc. Disp.* I.39.94].

To live for only one day! It is hard to imagine such a thing. But for some living things, it is a reality. It is all a matter of perspective. If a giant redwood tree (which can live for thousands of years) could speak, it might see us humans in the same way. We are the little animals, from the redwood's point of view. This is certainly true; the idea of the brevity of life was a favorite theme of the ancients, who in some ways were wiser than we. But while life may be short, the soul could be immortal; and this soaring idea found perfect expression in his short essay "The Dream of Scipio," which I liked so much that I could not resist including it alongside my translation of *Stoic Paradoxes*. I am digressing slightly. What I was thinking about today was what Cicero said in *Tusculan Disputations* just after the quote that I have presented above. He says this:

> Let us condemn, then, all stupidities–what gentler name may I attach to such nonsense? Let us place all power of right living in our soul's strength and greatness, in contempt and disregard for all human affairs, and in all virtue. For without doubt these days we are made effeminate by soft thoughts to the extent that if death hits us before we achieve the promises of the Chaldean oracles, we see ourselves as having been plundered of good things and as betrayed and robbed men. [*Tusc. Disp*. I.40]

I love this quote: it is Cicero at his best. Readers will by now recognize the reference to the "strength and greatness" of soul (*animi robore ac magnitudine*), a recurring theme in his writings. In the second sentence of the quote above, we should remember that when Cicero says "contempt and disregard for all human affairs" (*in omnium rerum humanarum contemptione ac despicientia*) he is referring to human affairs that are base and worldly. It is unbecoming for a great man to be obsessed with such trivialities. And consider the third sentence: what does it tell us? I have translated his phrase *Chaldaeorum promissa* as "promises of the Chaldean oracles." Today we might just say "fortune tellers." Cicero is telling us that we are not "entitled" to any assurance of an easy life. Some people these days, he warns us, have their heads so filled with "soft thoughts" that they consider themselves cheated and betrayed if they do not get everything they believe they are entitled to. This is an effeminate impulse, one unworthy of a broad-minded man.

I think there is a subject related to this topic, and wanted to mention it here as well. This is the idea of the variability of our reputations and images even after we die. We should first realize that during our lives we will be endlessly misunderstood and mischaracterized. People will do this either deliberately or through negligence: we should come to expect it. Why do people misrepresent others? Envy is one major reason: it victimizes anyone who tries to undertake great deeds. The common mob revels in ignorance and venal emotions, and instinctively feels uneasy with talk about talent and virtue. The person who has a great soul, the one who wishes to achieve great things, is attracted by such talk; but the gutter is deeply afraid of it.

So a man's fortunes are variable not only in his lifetime, but even after his death. His reputation may fluctuate over time after his death. Herman Melville died in utter obscurity in the 1890s. He was not really "discovered" as a profound writer until the late 1920s. His books were just not congruent with the mood of his times. So we die one death: our physical death. And then there is this other death, something that the humanist Petrarch called the "second death" (He says in his testament "My Secret Book": *quam non ineleganter in Africa tua 'secundam mortem' vocas*). In his poem *Africa*, he tells us what this "second death" is:

> Soon the tomb will collapse and the epitaph inscribed in marble will die;
> And with this, my son, you will suffer a second death. [Africa II.431]

This means that even after death, our reputations and memories will be impermanent. So we should be prepared to be misunderstood both during life and after it ends. Once we truly appreciate this fact, we will easily see how pointless it is to waste time on the frivolous and stupid nonsense we believe is so crucial. It is not. Once we see ourselves as akin to those little animals scurrying about on the banks of the River Hypanis, living for only one day, we will finally be free; we must, as Cicero tells us, place all power of right living in our soul's strength and greatness, in contempt and disregard for all petty human affairs, and in all virtue. This is the hard road to liberation. It is also the only one.

75. You Need Redundancy And Backup Systems

From the years 540 to 562, the Eastern Roman Empire under Justinian was engaged in a drawn-out struggle against the Sassanid

Persians under Chosroes (Khosrow). This contest is usually called the "Persian War." Many illuminating incidents that happened during this conflict I have used in previous articles here. Another one highlights the need for redundancy and "back-up" systems as security in times of trouble. We are aware of this principle when it comes to computing and software, but it can be applied to many other fields of activity. The following story demonstrates this principle. When Chosroes had captured the Syrian town of Petra, he immediately fortified it, believing that the Romans would make strenuous efforts to retake the town. Water resources were then (as now) a vital part of a city's defenses. He knew that one of the first things the Romans would do during a siege would be to cut the aqueduct bringing water into the city. So he devised the following plan.

He ordered a very deep trench dug, and into this trench he layered three water pipes successively. He first laid down one pipe, and then covered it with mud and gravel. Then he laid down another series of pipe-works, and covered those with dirt and sand. And then–above ground and visible to the unaided eye–he laid the third series of pipes. So now he did not just have one pipeline, but rather three independent networks of pipeline. When the Romans began the siege of Petra, they did not fully understand this. They cut the first pipeline, and assumed that doing so would bring the defenders to their knees. They were not thorough, and failed to make deeper investigation into the matter. As time went on, it became clear that the city was still somehow getting water; but the Romans could not understand how. By interrogating some captured residents of Petra, they finally realized that there was another water pipeline. So they dug down and found the second pipeline, and cut it; this, they thought, would be the end of the matter.

Yet the city still maintained its supply of water; and the Romans could never understand how. Chosroes had not even told the residents about the third pipeline: this was to be his state secret. Even if someone were captured, he would not be able to divulge something he was unaware of. When the Romans finally took the city by storm, they eventually discovered how they had been deceived by the three pipelines. They admired the care and diligence that Chosroes had taken to prepare such an elaborate back-up system. And now they showed the defenders that they were still Romans, and could compensate in ruthlessness what they may have lacked in subtlety. The Roman commander, Bessas by name, sent all the prisoners of Petra off to his emperor; he then razed the walls of Petra to the ground so that the city could never pose a problem for them again. From this story we can see the importance of thorough planning and preparation for any enterprise: and when it comes to security for things that matter, we must not rely on just one system. We must have several back-up systems in place. Redundancy is defense-in-depth; and this is security. This is the story of Chosroes's pipelines as described by Procopius in his *Wars* (VIII.12).

76. Machiavelli's Three Key Concepts

If a political scientist were asked who might be the most misunderstood writer of political theory, he would probably have the name of Machiavelli high on his list. To his name have been ascribed sinister motivations and calculated duplicity; and unscrupulous cherry-picking of his quotes has fashioned him into an ogre in the popular mind. Part of this may be unavoidable. In both *The Prince* and the *Discourses*, he had a tendency to draw sweeping generalizations accompanied by regrettable exaggerations. He was not the stuff of which great politicians or diplomats are made; he was too honest, too direct, to be trusted fully by the contemporaries with whom he had to rub shoulders. His portraits show him to have a keenly intelligent face, animated by a restless and nervous energy. In hindsight his enemies did him a favor by forcing him out of power: for it was the leisure time of exile that allowed him to write his earth-shaking books. Had he remained in court among the robed wielders of power, he would have become just another adviser, comfortable but forgotten. As he himself might agree: so it is that fortune turns a man's bad luck into golden opportunities.

He was not overly concerned with systematic theories. But there are, as Prof. Bernard Crick notes in his writings on Machiavelli, three "key concepts" that run through all his works: fortune (*Fortuna*), necessity (*necessità*), and virtue (*virtù*). I will discuss each of them here.

Necessity. By "necessity" he means political necessity: the idea that if a leader wants to accomplish goal X, he must use method Y. But a careful reading of his works shows us that necessity alone is not enough; the goal itself must be a good one. And for Machiavelli the goal was always order and stability. He was concerned with stable, republican governments governed by free men; he hated chaos and despotism. Living at a time when Italy was torn by factionalism and chaos, he looked with fondness on the golden age of Rome's ancient period of republican institutions. An active, participatory citizenry was one of the prerequisites for sound institutions promoting republican forms of government.

Fortune. There is no difference—to my mind—between Machiavelli's view of fortune and that view adopted by the ancient Latin writers on *fortuna*. They are precisely the same. Events are fluid and constantly changing; sometimes a man can control events, and sometimes he is controlled by them. We cannot insulate ourselves completely from this reality. There is a wonderful analogy in Chapter 25 of *The Prince* that sums up the role of fortune. Machiavelli likens fortune to an onrushing river pushing a wall of water before it: men can take some precautions to protect themselves from it in favorable times by building dams and dykes, but they cannot really prevent the wall of water from hitting them. This is fortune. The ancient writers said much the same thing. A careful reading of Plutarch, Sallust, and Polybius all support the role that fortune plays in making—and unmaking—notable personalities. It is not the same as fatalism or resignation: this point must be stressed very clearly. This would be going too far. Machiavelli describes fortune in *The Prince* as a fickle and temperamental woman who must be taken by force:

> [It is] necessary to beat and ill-use her...it is seen that she allows herself to be mastered by the adventurous rather than by those who go to work more coldly...She is therefore always, woman-like, a lover of young men, because they are less cautious, more violent and with more audacity command her.

We can do the best we can to try to master fortune, but the outcomes are not always assured. Chance can never be eliminated.

Virtue. Here again there is no difference between Machiavelli's idea of virtue and that held by the ancient writers. He means precisely what the ancient historians meant when they talked about virtus: masculine virtue or manliness. It is not easy to encapsulate in a few words. It means valor, manliness, ability, guts, will-power. And it is no accident that the Latin word *virtus* is related to the word for man, which is *vir*. But to what should this "virtue" be applied? Machiavelli makes it clear that virtue must be put to the service of the community. It should not be wasted in vain, narcissistic aspirations for glory: some kind of public service was the operative principle behind virtue. States or communities either have a spirit of "virtue" or they do not. Those possessing it will be better republics because each person will feel a sense of civic duty to the other. Without this bond of connection between citizens, a state will never fully congeal and will remain unstable. It is this "virtue" that can be a bulwark against the fickle vagaries of fortune. And herein lies its supreme importance. A man can impose his own will–to a certain extent–on fate by mastering his own character.

These are Machiavelli's three overriding themes that emerge from his books. It is probably true that one must read both *The Prince* and the *Discourses* together, since each complements the other. By keeping them in mind when we read his works, we will have a better appreciation of his purposes. At heart he was a man of order, a man of stability, a man concerned with restoring a sense of civic virtue in states beset by the machinations and schemes of self-aggrandizing princes and popes. In this sense, his message could not be more relevant to us today.

77. The World's Fury, And The Spirit's Repose

It should be a consolation to us to know that the world's mindless injustices and furies are of old date. Every age sees and experiences them, and every man finds his own way of adapting himself to the clamor and tumult around him. Some throw themselves into their work; others retreat into solitude; some find a balance between such extremes and navigate the white-crested waters of Fate as best they can. I was fortunate today to have found one of those little hidden literary gems that just begs to be polished off and displayed for others. Poring over the writings of the great humanist Francesco Petrarch, one finds so many bezels of wisdom that it becomes difficult to adjust one's gaze to their radiating brilliance. But there is one passage that so perfectly encapsulates the idea of the healthy philosophical mind accepting the cruelties of the world that I could not resist sharing it here. It is found among Petrarch's letters to his friends; this one is directed to one Stefano Colonna. Its message is one of spiritual empowerment: it reminds us that, amidst all the cyclones churning around us, it remains our own responsibility to extract peace and happiness from this life. Petrarch begins by taking for granted the permanent turbulence of the world, and the disturbing variability of fortune:

> A Roman emperor lasted out his years in prison subject to bitter servitude. The city of Rome itself saw Hannibal with his army standing before the Colline Gate. This might be borne more tolerably when compared with worse events, as the city was taken by Goths after many centuries, and had been captured by Senones before this. I conclude one thing from all these examples: in human affairs there is nothing so miserable that cannot happen even to those who are considered the luckiest.

If this is so, what can a thinking man do to maintain his sanity and dignity? In words that echo the tenderest and most intimate counsels of St. Augustine–and even, perhaps, the contemplative intensity of history's greatest mystics–Petrarch advises us:

> These things being what they are (you who is the best of men!), you see what you have to do...Do what some prudent men are accustomed to doing. Not the garden-variety man, but some pristine animals fearing contact with dirt. When they come out of their dwellings, look around, and see their places splattered with filth, they walk backwards on their feet and return to their dens. You also will find no place for peace and quiet in the whole world; go back to the confines of your room and stay within yourself. Stay awake with yourself; speak with yourself; be silent with yourself; walk with yourself; stand with yourself. Do not fret about solitude if you are with yourself: because if you are not with yourself, you will still be alone even if you are among other people. Make for yourself a place in the center

> of your soul where you may find refuge, experience joy, and where you may find repose with no one's interference…
>
> You may ask, "By what artistry may I accomplish this?" Virtue alone is able to summon all these things into existence [*Virtus sola potens est hec omnia prestare*]. Through virtue you will truly be able to live bountifully and happily wherever you want; when you are in the middle of evils [*in medio malorum*], nothing pernicious will have access to you; you will crave nothing except what produces happiness. Nothing will disgust you except what makes you miserable. You will know that no one becomes happy or miserable except through his own spirit.
>
> External things do not belong to you; everything you own is with you already. Nothing that belongs to someone else can be given to you, and nothing of yours can be taken away. The path of life you may select lies within your own power. The opinions of other people should be avoided and the wise counsels of the few must be followed. With an elevated spirit, Fortune must be looked down on. Know that she has more unthinking force than real strength, barks more often than she bites, and stands in your way less often than she yells at you; that she has no ability to control your property.
>
> Yet nothing is beyond her power; place no trust in her enticements; whatever has come to you is due to her intercession. To these thoughts, know also that if you should rise to a higher station in life, you should ascribe it to divine clemency. If you fall, accept it with a philosophic spirit: in fortune's kingdom, good men are defeated and bad ones are raised to high places. And understand, as the Psalmist says, the meaning of "in their final days." And remember that this is a road of labors, not a landscape of gifts [*Memorque viam hanc laborum esse non patriam meritorum*]. Farewell.

When you are feeling overwhelmed by the injustices of the world, and feel dislocated by the chaos swirling about you, take refuge in these sentiments. They are words to revisit often. If Petrarch ever wrote lines that surpassed these in wisdom, I have not read them.

78. Money Is Of Secondary Importance In War

Human nature being what it is, there will always be many different reasons why wars begin. All of these reasons ultimately find their roots in human passions: greed, the lust for power, or simply a desire to "put fortune to the test" (*fortunam temptare*) as the ancient Latin historians would say. But wars require resources, payrolls, and capable men. Governments try to balance these factors the best they can in order to increase their chances of accomplishing their goals. But it is not an easy matter: no one really knows how effective one strategy or another will be until the struggle is actually joined. And by then it may be too late if one side is found wanting. Some belligerents think they can compensate for unpreparedness in one area by emphasizing their financial strength; and out of this arises the delusion that money can win wars.

Was there any king who had more money than Atahualpa, the last king of the Incas? When the Spaniards came to Peru in 1531, they found a land rich beyond their dreams in metallic wealth. Gold was to be had in abundance. Yet Atahualpa thought he could leverage his money to preserve his life and the integrity of his kingdom. In this he was mistaken. The Spaniards captured and ransomed him; he offered to fill an entire room with gold and silver to secure his life. The gold was accepted, but he was executed anyway. The same point is made by Machiavelli in his *Discourses* (II.10):

> Among the other things that Croesus, king of Lydia, showed to Solon the Athenian was a treasure too great to count. Solon was then asked what opinion he had formed of the king's power, to which he replied that he did not think him more powerful on this account, for war is made with steel, not with gold, and if anyone came along who had more steel than he had, he could deprive him of his power…I assert, then, that it is not gold, as is commonly acclaimed by common opinion, that constitutes the sinews of

> war, but good soldiers; for gold does not find good soldiers, but good soldiers are quite capable of finding gold. If the Romans had chosen to wage war rather by means of money than by the sword, not all the treasure in the world would have sufficed in view of the great enterprises they undertook and the difficulties they had to encounter in them.

So there you have it. War is made with steel, not with gold. Related to this point is the idea that one cannot buy one's way into military preparedness: throwing money around is no substitute for military virtue. We see this principle illustrated today in the Middle East. No country is more rich in monetary resources than Saudi Arabia. They spend their petrodollars on the very best equipment and arms that money can buy. But the combat quality of their forces is woefully lacking. In any real fight, they would be unlikely to hold their ground for very long. All of their expensive hardware would become burning piles of metals, fit only to decorate the empty landscape. They have been engaged in a futile war in Yemen for several years now, and are no further along in accomplishing their goals than when they started.

There is more than one reason for this, of course; but behind them all lurk the perception that money can be a substitute for real power. They learned the same lesson in the Syrian war, which is still underway. They lavished huge sums on militias and proxy armies of dubious quality and reliability. And this rabble was routed in the end by the dedicated, cohesive fighters of Hezbollah and Iran, working in tandem with the Syrian government. Training, discipline, morale, and fighting ability will always defeat money. The United States has fallen into this trap as well. In its Indochina War of 1963-1975, it dumped huge volumes of money and material into an abyss. Its forces were very good, but it relied too much on money and logistics, and not enough on fire and maneuver consistent with its political objectives. Perhaps the war was unwinnable under any circumstances; and this may indeed be true. Yet the point about the addiction to monetary solutions stands. Machiavelli again:

> I repeat, therefore: gold is not the sinews of war, but good soldiers are. Gold is necessary, but it is of secondary importance, and good soldiers can get it for

> themselves; for it is as impossible for good soldiers to fail to find gold as it is for gold to find good soldiers.

When I listen to hearings in Washington that discuss issues of military preparedness, I hear very much about money, budgets, and equipment. I hear very little about how to create and sustain cohesive forces that can hold their own in a real fight against an equal force. We will discover the folly of this way of thinking sooner than we believe. In our personal lives as well we should be mindful of this principle. Moral forces matter more than money. Some people think that they can use money as a cover and as a substitute for taking real action in accomplishing a particular goal. I am not saying money is not important, of course; but in the hierarchy of importance, it must be placed where it belongs. You will not get in better physical shape by buying the most expensive pair of running shoes. You will not learn any language faster by tossing money around in uninformed bouts of expenditure. The attainment of goals is a matter of will, and strength of will cannot be bought for any price.

79. A Letter To A Graduate Student

I recently received an email that asked the following: "I'm very curious as to how you handle inner conflict when it comes to doing something that you know it's bullshit and you are just doing it because you feel pressured to do it. Recently I've been trying to apply for post-graduate degree and I filled in my CV and personal statement with so much bullshit…On top of that I'm studying courses in university that I have zero interest in because my parents were totally convinced that education is top priority for me like all other kids. How do I suck it up until I'm able to do my own thing in the future and how do I find a healthy way of releasing the stress that my gut is flushing my body with every time I do this kind of school work?"

Ah, the eternal question. How do I tolerate all the nonsense in my way until I can get to my final goal? Suppose we have two people. One is standing on a ladder, and one is standing on the roof of a building. The man standing on the roof can see a greater distance;

not because he is inherently better, but only because his vantage point gives him the ability to see a beyond his immediate environment. Sometimes this analogy is appropriate when giving advice. The first thing I would say is: go easy on your parents. What do you expect them to tell you? To be a professional loafer? If they are "totally convinced" that education is a top priority, then they can't be all bad or completely deluded. Why? Because education is indeed a top priority. Of course you have to navigate the waters to find the best options for yourself.

And if you think education is expensive–as the saying goes–then try ignorance. I don't subscribe to the school of thought that some people preach on this subject. "College is worthless!" "Abandon school!" "Live off your laptop in Dorkistan like me and sell vitamins!" No. That is not a good way to go about things. Yes, maybe there are some people who do this and hit paydirt. Chances are you won't be one of them. Anyone who thinks education is worthless should try hanging sheet rock for a living, or driving a cab. See how long it takes before you grow weary of that life. And this really is the point. Nothing is perfect. Nothing is even half-perfect. There are kernels of perfection here and there in life, embedded like raisins in a pudding. But for the most part, you will find the routine chores of existence. In everything.

The sooner you realize life is not about fun and games, the better. Life is not about traipsing from one "fun" place to another. This is how fools and effeminate shirkers think. You were not put on this earth to have fun. You were put here to build something with your life, to make a mark, to scratch your name on the Wall of Collective Memory. Yes, you will have some fun here and there. I am not against fun: I love it and savor it. But your thought should be focused more on (1) your duties and responsibilities, and (2) your soul. As things are right now, you are focusing too much on discomfort and pain you will have to endure. In your eagerness to avoid the pain of work, you are forgetting that it is that very pain that gives you the strength to succeed in life as you get older. It starts now. He who has the most endurance, wins.

To achieve your goal of graduating, yes, you will have to swallow your bitterness and bile and absorb the pain. This is how these things are. But what are your options? Join the ranks of all the other clowns and dunces who gave up because they weren't having "fun" from dawn till dusk? If this is not the right path for you, the universe will let you know in good time. The world will teach you. The world will tell you. But that time has not yet arrived. No intelligent person really knows what he wants to do until relatively late in life. Focus on your soul, your spirit, your duties. Nothing worthwhile was ever gained except through the most brutal struggle. Your society in which you were raised never told you this; or if it did, it did not drill the point home well enough. In Chapter 6 of *Thirty-Seven*, I wrote these lines:

> The world is a palestra of anxieties,
> A spectacle of wrongs and iniquities,
> And a vale of tears watering the rising
> Orchids of our discontent.
> It is a threshing floor of temptations for the unwary,
> And a churning sea, turbid with the color
> Of false hopes and virtues so inadequate
> In duration and amplitude.

Let me relate a story. The humanist Petrarch was climbing a mountain one day in the Alps with his brother. The mountain was located near Malaucène in France. It was not easy, as the mountain is steep and inaccessible. They came upon an old shepherd in the mountain; he tried to talk them out of reaching the summit. He told Petrarch that he had made the ascent fifty years earlier and had come back with nothing except torn clothing and an exhausted body. But the young men would not listen to him. So the shepherd pointed the way to the summit, indicating a certain narrow path. And Petrarch soon encountered real difficulties. It was a very hard road. He and his brother were soon torn and worn out from dealing with brambles and rocks that they could hardly continue. So he stopped to rest in a ravine. As he was sitting there, he said later in a letter to Dionigi of Borgo Sansepolcro:

> I forced these and other words on myself: "What you experienced all day in climbing this mountain, know that this happens to you and many others while seeking the blessed life. But it is not so easily noticed by men because, while the motion of the body is in the open, the movement of the soul is invisible and happens in private. This life that we call blessed is situated

> in a high place; and a narrow road leads to it. [*Equidem vita quam beatam dicimus, celso loco sita est; arcta, ut aiunt, ad illam ducit via*]. Many hills can be found here and there, and a man must walk from virtue to virtue with heroic strides. At the summit is the end of everything and the final destination of the road on which our hike takes place." Everyone want to reach this spot, but as Ovid says, "To want something is too little; you ought to lust after what you would do."

Petrarch then asks: what are the things that hold us back? The easy path: the path through earthly and base pleasures, which promise much but deliver, in the end, so little. He says that these thoughts inspired him to complete his journey to the summit of the mountain. He finally reached the highest vantage point, a place the locals called the "Little Son" (*Filiolum*). From this awesome crest, he could finally survey his scene in its entirety. He says:

> I was first of all moved by the unusual spirit of the air and the expansive view; I stood like one awestruck. I looked around: there were clouds beneath my feet. Now Mount Olympus and Athos were less incredible to me, since I was seeing in a less well-known mountain what I had heard and read about them. Then I turned my gaze to some parts of Italy, to which my spirit inclines. The frozen and snow-capped Alps…

These were the thoughts that filled Petrarch's mind. The road is a long one, and the journey will be filled with sharp rocks, uneven terrain, and nasty brambles. We will fall more often than we wish, and we will emerge scuffed, scratched, and battered. But the incomparable view from the summit moves the soul to awe; it is the natural dwelling of a lofty, independent spirit that has been tempered by struggle and sacrifice. This dwelling is its own reward, and needs no further justification.

80. How Benito Mussolini Took Power

Stalin biographer Stephen Kotkin spends several pages of his book discussing the lessons to be learned from Mussolini's seizure of power in Italy in the early 1920s. It was something that happened gradually, in stages, when institutions that should have been able to bring him to heel did nothing, either due to their own lack of resolution or tacit support of his power grab. Italy after the First World War was, like many European countries, rife with instability and factionalism. Mussolini's "fascist" party in 1922 had collected only 35 out of 500 seats in Italy's Chamber of Deputies; despite this apparent lack of popular support he was still asking to be appointed prime minister. He threatened to march on Rome himself with his private militia (*squadristi*) and take power with or without official permission. He had some support from the established institutions of the day: the monarchy, the army, the church, and big business. In the wake of the Bolshevist radicalism that was threatening Europe, the establishment was looking for a charismatic figure who might be able to restore order and bring the county some measure of stability.

In the end, these temptations proved too attractive to resist. King Vittorio Emanuele III asked Mussolini to become prime minister. He thought that by making him part of a coalition, he would be able to restrain the worst of Mussolini's excesses. The so-called "March on Rome" took place only *after* he had been appointed prime minister. Arriving in Rome by train–not marching along with his men–Mussolini then had his 20,000 blackshirts parade around the city like conquerors. This was the origin of the myth of his "seizure" of power: but there was no seizure. The myth was another of *Il Duce*'s shabby lies, designed to glorify himself and his movement; in fact, he was appointed by the existing powers, who thought they could use him for their own ends. In this they were only partially correct.

Besides being favored by the powerful institutions of the country, Mussolini was also aided at critical junctures by the ineptitude of his political opponents. In the elections of April 1924, Mussolini's party won 374 seats out of 535; this amounted to 66.3% of the popular vote. There then occurred an event that proved to be of great advantage to him. Giacomo Matteotti, a law professor at Bologna and the son of wealthy family from the Veneto, publicly denounced the fascists in strident terms, calling the vote a fraud and the result of intimidation and *squadristi* violence. With this step, he had signed his death warrant. He was abducted eleven days later, bundled into the boot of a car, and stabbed repeatedly; his body was found two months later, dumped on the outskirts of Rome.

It was never established whether Mussolini was involved or knew anything about the plot beforehand. He was certainly not above using violence, or encouraging its use, against political opponents; but such a reckless step probably was taken without his knowledge or approval. Despite this, he was able to use the crisis that the murder generated to consolidate his hold on power. Anti-fascist demonstrations escalated in the streets, general strikes were declared, and it seems that Mussolini would have to resign. But the king did not call for him to step down. His political opponents then committed a grievous error: they left the field of political conflict and walked out of the Chamber of Deputies. Trying to imitate the ancient Roman plebian practice of going to the Aventine Hill to protest measures taken by the nobility, the anti-fascist deputies probably thought that by walking out of the chamber they could pressure Mussolini to resign. In this they were sorely mistaken. The situation was getting more and more dangerous by the hour, until finally Mussolini (on January 3, 1925) threw down the gauntlet. In a dramatic speech, he "assumed responsibility" (whatever that meant) for the crisis and dared those present to remove him or indict him.

But nothing happened. By exposing his opponents as all talk and no action, he successfully called their bluff. He also refused to permit the deputies who had boycotted the session to return to the Chamber; by the middle of January, it was clear he had won. All political parties except the fascists were outlawed and Italy was on its way to becoming a dictatorship. This was how he consolidated his hold on power. In retrospect we can see how this happened: (1) the established institutions of the country (monarchy, church, army, and big business) more or less supported Mussolini and thought he was preferable to the communist alternatives; and (2) at the critical moment, his opponents failed to muster the requisite will to call his bluff. The institutions that should have acted as checks and balances on his power failed. And failed miserably. Readers will draw their own conclusions and lessons from this narrative of events. We may note also that this same "walking out" mistake was made by the Soviet Union in the early 1950s, when they thought that by boycotting the United Nations sessions on Korea, they could somehow prevent US military intervention in that country. This also turned out to be a delusion; for what the Americans did was simply to take advantage of the Soviet absence to vote for intervention in Korea under the flag of the United Nations.

On the political scene today, it is clear that some power elites believe that they can use unscrupulous, amoral demagogues for their own ends. They know very well that such demagogues are venal, lacking in restraint, and totally unsuited for office. Yet they do not care; they believe they can use the arrogance and stupidity of the demagogue for their own selfish ends, and for the ends of those who support them. In this they are mistaken. By putting partisan, factional considerations ahead of the national interest, they reveal themselves to be men without moral courage. They will find out, all too soon, just how serious was the mistake they have made. Institutions in a democratic republic cannot long survive a coordinated attack from those who inhabit them. When long periods of wealth, affluence, and ease condition a population for moral corruption, the citizenry is unable to see what is right before its eyes. It is unable or unwilling to call corruption and evil by their true names. It mistakes stupidity and arrogance for strength and tenacity; it more wishes to be entertained than to be informed and provided for; and it uses the nascent dictator as the secret mouthpiece of its dreams and malicious fantasies.

And it is the public that will suffer, just as it was the Italian people of the 1940s who suffered for the venality and crimes of their leaders. Mussolini was a con artist, a fraud, and a liar, but he would never have taken power had not the powerful elites in Italy looked the other way and collaborated with him for their own selfish purposes. Political factionalism and its associated moral cowardice, plutocratic control of economic life, the concentration of wealth in the hands of too few, and public ignorance combine to produce one outcome: the slide into authoritarianism. When in doubt, one should never leave the playing field until the last hand has been dealt, and the final card played.

81. Six Ethical Principles To Rejuvenate Societal Health

I read recently that a very rare animal was observed in the wild in the state of Iowa for the first time in over one hundred fifty years. The animal is called a fisher; I had never heard of it before, but the biologists tell us that it is a predatory mammal related distantly to the mink and the otter. The story reminded me of a similar one I had heard about some years ago, when a bird believed to have been long extinct was spotted in Arkansas. It is reassuring to know that some old things are still with us, and that the modern world can be resisted in some small ways. We find it unsettling to see "progress" expunge out beauty and life from the earth. It is the same way with ideas. Some ideas can lay dormant for a long time, quietly biding their time for more favorable conditions to reappear. And when they do, they are appreciated all the more. But it takes effort to keep ideas alive, just like it takes effort to preserve living things. Ideas, like organisms, need favorable habitats, as well as observers to appreciate their existence. When these conditions are not met, the ideas recede into the background, to hibernate until the veil of public ignorance has lifted.

The playwright Terence was wrong when he said in his *Phormio* (575) that "old age itself is a disease [*senetus ipsa morbus est*]." The better view is that of Petrarch, who said that old age amounts to an affliction of the body, but not of the mind: *esse senectutem morbum corporis, animi sanitatem.* And as we have said already, ideas can be like organisms. They may be old, but they still retain their vigor and truth. Age cannot taint–cannot wither–their validity. Old ideas need to be brought back and put into circulation, every now and then. Certain assumptions underlying our modern social system need to be re-examined. We are long overdue for a reconsideration of some of the assumptions we have been told since our earliest years. I made up a basic list of some things I believe modern American society has neglected for too long. It is not an exhaustive list; it is just a list of some things I see as important.

To prosper, man needs a sense of purpose, law and order, and a belief in himself. If you want to cultivate a strong, healthy youth, you must give them these three things. When I look at many young people today, they seem adrift, rudderless, and lacking in positive belief systems. The idealistic man wants to embrace an order, a hierarchy, and an ideology that is greater than he is. And once he finds this, he will defend it to the death. A man cannot believe in himself unless he first believes in something greater than himself. As Sallust says in *Catiline* (51.3): *Ubi intenderis ingenium, valet*: "when you make use of your talents, good things happen..."

There should be less emphasis on individual rights, and more emphasis on the common good. The era of unrestricted individualism is over. It is no longer enough for someone to say that he has a right to do whatever he wants. This contemptible concept of "I can do what I want as long as I am not hurting anyone" is a great evil. Who will be the judge of whether you are "hurting someone" or not? You? Unchecked greed and selfishness in our society masquerades as altruistic individualism; every man considers himself an emperor, and resents any control over his appetites. It never occurs to him that his appetites are fundamentally insatiable, and that by submitting to the common welfare he brings himself peace of mind.

There should be a greater focus on obligations than on privileges. Here it is the upper classes that have set tone. The super-rich in America have abandoned their sense of social responsibility; the poor and the middle classes sense this, and resolve to do the same. And the result is a chaos of individuals, all scrambling to get what they can before the resources run out. It truly is a despicable scene. The situation is so bad that even military journals are now using the term "plutocratic insurgency" to describe this phenomenon. In other words, the immoral plundering of the rich now constitutes a clear and present *security threat* to the well-being of our entire social system.

Parenting should be seen as a privilege, not a right. For too long, having children has been viewed as some kind of "right" that should never be questioned. And maybe this was not a problem in previous centuries, when land was plentiful and the world had much less population. But we are reaching the point where society should not be burdened with the task of raising and rearing children if the parents are unable–or unwilling–to do it themselves. Being a parent is a serious responsibility, not a frivolous part-time thrill. Those not able to handle the task should not become parents.

Moral instruction is critical. In previous ages, this function was performed by organized religions, family units, extended clans, trade associations, guilds, fraternal societies, and the like. The rise of the all-powerful state has eroded all of these traditional structures, and has replaced them with nothing except hedonistic propaganda that does nothing but increase state control over the lives of citizens. People do not automatically understand what is "good" and what is not: they must be trained by diligent study of classical texts, the lessons of history, and practical leadership. They must be thrown into adversity of all types, so that they can test their mettle against that of others. They must learn what it is like to both give and receive blows. Those who have been properly instructed in these matters from their earliest years will not need to be told to avoid behavior that corrupts the mind or body: they will sense it instinctively on their own.

Physical fitness is not just a matter of personal health, but a social obligation. Just as no one wants to associate with morally depraved people, no healthy person wants to associate with someone who refuses to maintain his body. There will always be differences in body types, but the pendulum of fitness has swung so far in the direction of degeneracy that it will take decades for the situation to correct itself. In the meantime, all of society will have to bear the cost of human selfishness and greed. He who fails to show any sense of respect towards his body directly insults his fellow-citizens; he is the epitome of selfishness and indolence. When placed against the panorama of history, one man is nothing. Man must begin to define himself by his cultivation of that ancient virtue (*virtus*) which molded the characters of so many great men before us. To live a long life means nothing if that life is marked by subservience, weakness, and moral depravity. Petrarch here tells us (how often do I lean on his wisdom!):

> The greatest citadel of your reasoning [he wrote to a friend] is that I should try to live as long as possible, for the joy of my friends and mostly for the solace of your old age; because, as you say, you desire that I should live longer than you...You want this, my brother, and some other friends also. It is a pious wish, but one opposed to my own wishes. For I want to die while you are in good health, and to leave behind me people in whose memory and words I will endure, by whose prayers I may be sanctified, and by whom I may be loved and longed for. I think there is nothing so pure, nothing so welcome for those about to die, except for a clear conscience...How would I want to live on among these current morals, which I am truly sad to see have gained currency? And what about the even worse things, the deformed and obscene actions of the most selfish of men, which I berate often in my writings and speech, yet about which I lack the ability to express in words my grief of soul and sadness? [*Epistula ad Iohannem Boccaccium*]

We are willing to work unceasingly towards our goals. There is a story that the Roman emperor Maximin (A.D. 173-238) was told that he was already great enough, and that he should relax a bit. His response was, "But truly, I will become even greater the more I work" (*Ego vero, quo maior fuero eo plus laborabo*). We say the same. Our renaissance will take time, and will proceed in stages. We cannot see the twists and turns in the road. But we will create this new man, this new image, out of the crucible of our own will. Ideas that have stood the test of time will always find ways of reasserting themselves. And like the reticent fisher, recently seen in Iowa for the first time in one hundred fifty years, ideas of worth will find ways of emerging from the shadows when conditions are right, and will make themselves visible. Until then, it patiently bides its time.

82. Why Every Man Should Read *Robinson Crusoe*

By any standard Daniel Defoe (1659?-1731) is one of the most remarkable authors in English history. In versatility, energy, and practical wisdom, few can claim to be his peer in life experiences or in skill with the pen. He came to writing by a circuitous route. After fathering seven children, he threw himself into business and politics; bankruptcy was the result in 1692, but his repayment plan would eventually compensate his creditors almost in full with an amount of 17,000 pounds. He was not a nobleman, and had to earn his bread. He entered the tile business, eventually running a factory in Tilbury; it is refreshing to see an author so firmly grounded in worldly economic reality. He read widely to sharpen his mind and increase his revenues; one of the books that came across his path was William Dampier's *New Voyage Round The World*, a volume published in 1697. This was the work that contained the story of Alexander Selkirk, the Scottish sailing master who had been marooned (not shipwrecked) on the Juan Fernandez Islands (four hundred miles west of Chile) for about four years. When Selkirk returned to England he related his story to a journalist named Richard Steele, who published the account in 1713. Defoe also apparently heard Selkirk's story directly from him.

In 1719 Defoe published the *Life and Strange Surprising Adventures of Robinson Crusoe.* It sold out four editions in only four months and has remained arguably the most popular novel in the English language ever since. Its descriptive immediacy, fidelity to detail, philosophical depth, and exciting scenes leave their impact on all readers. Never before had English readers seen a story like it. Instead of telling a tale of man against man, *Robinson Crusoe* deals with that far more common circumstance: man against himself. While most of us will never be shipwrecked on a deserted island, we will without doubt be faced with loneliness, isolation, and the grief of abandonment. How a man deals with these things, how he overcomes the voices of defeatism and despair, are what really concern us. And *Robinson Crusoe* tells us how to deal with these emotions.

The human emotion and detail of the book are incredible. We feel the rough sea pound our backs as Crusoe hangs on to a jutting rock for dear life on the beach right after the shipwreck; we share his isolation as he circumnavigates his new home and finds it deserted; we share his joy when he learns, after hard trial and error, how to bake a crude bread; we feel his trepidation and suspicion when he first sees strangers enter his weird Eden. This is almost the story of civilization itself, told entirely by one man: the slow, painful ascent from ignorance to ultimate mastery of one's environment. Few novels from this period are as relevant today. Who today does not struggle with self-mastery? Who today does not need to feel inspired to face life's onerous difficulties? Consider this moving passage, where Crusoe takes mental stock of the "good and bad" of his predicament:

> I now began to consider seriously my condition, and the circumstances I was reduced to; and I drew up the state of my affairs in writing, not so much to leave them to any that were to come after me – for I was likely to have but few heirs – as to deliver my thoughts from daily poring over them, and afflicting my mind; and as my reason began now to master my despondency, I began to comfort myself as well as I could, and to set the good against the evil, that I might have something to distinguish my case from worse; and I stated very impartially, like debtor and creditor, the comforts I enjoyed against the miseries I suffered, thus:

> **Evil**: I am cast upon a horrible, desolate island, void of all hope of recovery.
>
> **Good:** But I am alive; and not drowned, as all my ship's company were.
>
> **Evil**: I am singled out and separated, as it were, from all the world, to be miserable.
>
> **Good**: But I am singled out, too, from all the ship's crew, to be spared from death; and He that miraculously saved me from death can deliver me from this condition.
>
> **Evil:** I am divided from mankind – a solitaire; one banished from human society.
>
> **Good**: But I am not starved, and perishing on a barren place, affording no sustenance.
>
> **Evil**: I have no clothes to cover me.
>
> **Good:** But I am in a hot climate, where, if I had clothes, I could hardly wear them.
>
> **Evil**: I am without any defence, or means to resist any violence of man or beast.
>
> **Good**: But I am cast on an island where I see no wild beasts to hurt me, as I saw on the coast of Africa; and what if I had been shipwrecked there?
>
> **Evil**: I have no soul to speak to or relieve me.
>
> **Good:** But God wonderfully sent the ship in near enough to the shore, that I have got out as many necessary things as will either supply my wants or enable me to supply myself, even as long as I live.

If Crusoe can find some measure of relief by making a list like this, we should be inspired to do likewise in our own lives. We will probably find that things are not as bad as we think they are; and if they are bad, we will learn how to master them, just as Crusoe learns how to make weapons, fashion clothing, build his house, hunt game, and keep crows away from his vegetables. What is not generally known is that Defoe may have been helped in his creative endeavor by reading a translation of the Arabic philosophical classic *Hayy Ibn Yaqthan* (حي بن يقظان) by the twelfth century Andalusian philosopher Ibn Tufayl (طفيل بن). The title of this work literally means "Alive, Son of Awake" and is intended as an allegory for philosophical debate. In it, a feral child growing up alone on a deserted island gradually becomes aware of the higher truth of things. The book is an interesting mix of rationalism and mysticism, and remains one of the most remarkable literary productions of the medieval period. Its influence on later centuries (in both East and West) was due to its descriptions of how a man should think, and what questions he should ask himself, in order to progress in worldly knowledge to ultimate Truth.

Hayy Ibn Yaqthan was only available in Arabic until 1671; in that year it was translated into Latin by Edward Pocock. Three years later this Latin edition was translated into English by George Keith. So it is very likely that Defoe, enterprising journalist that he was, was familiar with Ibn Tufayl's work. None of this, of course, is intended to detract from the brilliance and originality of *Robinson Crusoe*. Even if Defoe may have been indirectly inspired by ideas that came before him, what he did with those ideas was entirely his own. Writers do not operate in a vacuum. We mention it here only to show that learned men of all cultures share certain things in common: intellectual curiosity, a restless search for the truth, and an ability to put in allegorical form the deepest cravings of the spirit. These overriding imperatives–springing from that Community of the Mind that knows no borders–finally transcend all languages, cultures, and faiths.

83. Fixed Fortifications Are Useless

Armies and states throughout history have sought to provide security by constructing fixed fortifications like fortresses, citadels, and walls. These projects inevitably end as dismal failures. Not only do they not provide security, but they do something even worse: they provide *an illusion of security* that encourages a defender to be overconfident and careless. And when this happens, disaster is only a matter of time. Walls and forts do not provide security; at most they can help channel avenues of approach for advancing enemies. For states are not protected by fortresses, but by the valor of their citizens. When the latter is lacking, the former are of no use. This point was well made by Machiavelli in his *Discourses* when he said the following (II.24):

> It must be borne in mind, then, that fortresses are constructed as a defense either against enemies or

> against subjects. In the first case they are unnecessary, and in the second case harmful…And if there ever was a time when [forts] were useless, it is now on account of artillery, for against its fire it is impossible to defend such small places where there are no embankments behind which men can retire…In no way, then, do fortresses help you, for you will lose them either through the treachery of their keepers, or by some violent attack, or by their being starved out. The ruler, then, who can muster a good army, can do without fortresses, and the ruler who has not a good army had better not build them. The best thing he can do is to fortify the city where he dwells, to keep it provisioned and its inhabitants well disposed, so as to hold off an enemy's attack till he can either come to terms or get outside help to relieve him.

Fortresses provide a false sense of security and become nothing but obstacles that an attacking army desires to overcome. This was true even in the days before artillery and air power. The historian Sallust describes in his *War of Jugurtha* (Ch. XCIV) how the Roman commander Marius took a fortress held by Jugurtha's Numidians that was supposed to be impregnable. It was a citadel at the top of a high elevation in the middle of the countryside of what is now Tunisia. The full story of this exciting event is related in Sallust. But essentially what happened was something similar to the capture of Naples by Belisarius during the Gothic War. One of Marius's men, a Ligurian who one day ventured out of his camp to hunt for water, noticed snails on the sides of the fortress's elevation.

As he collected these snails he discovered a route of ingress into the citadel, dangerous but accessible; returning to camp, he immediately informed Marius. With a hand-picked group of men he later infiltrated into the fort, taking the Numidians by surprise from the rear. The Roman "commando team" climbed the perilous sides of the plateau to reach the citadel, clambering over rocks and roots, and carrying shields made from animal skins that would not make noises when jostled. The fortress was captured and Marius was able to snatch victory from defeat "with the assistance of fortune," as Sallust tells us.

Another impressive example is provided by the fall of the Belgian fortress of Eben Emael to the German Army in 1940. The Belgians had constructed, at great expense, a huge fortress to protect themselves from invasion coming from the east. Their citadel at Eben Emael was intended to provide covering fire over a very wide area that, the Belgian command supposed, would block any invader from entering their territory. But this proved not to be the case. Hitler personally took an interest in the operation to take the objective; he himself apparently was the one to come up with the idea of using gliders to land troops on the roof of the fort and destroy the guns with "shaped charges," an innovation at the time. This brilliant operation may have been the most impressive of its kind in the entire war. Just as Marius's men used special equipment (shields made from animal skins) to maintain the element of surprise, the Germans opted to use silent gliders to land on the roof of the Belgian fort and take the defenders by complete surprise.

We will also recall that ancient Sparta did not have walls as did many other cities of its day. They wanted their security to be based on the competence of their army and not on the passivity of walls or blockhouses. As Machiavelli says, again in his *Discourses*:

> [F]or if the Romans did not build fortresses, the Spartans not only abstained from doing this, but did not permit their cities to have walls, because they chose to rely for defense on the virtue of the individual, and wanted no other. Hence, when a Spartan was asked by an Athenian whether the walls of Athens did not look fine, he answered: "Quite! Provided that it be ladies that live there."

It is a lesson that many have forgotten today; we must aim to free ourselves from this kind of thinking in all areas of our endeavor, not just in military affairs. Active engagement on the battlefield of life, and not passive inertia, must be our creed. The "fortification mentality" pervades entire sectors of political and military thinking in the West. The price of this folly will become apparent in due course. Security is not conferred on a society by inanimate objects like forts, machines, or walls, but only by the valor and readiness of its men.

84. The Inscrutable St. Patrick

The first modern, comprehensive biography of St. Patrick was written by the scholar J.B. Bury, who was for many years a professor of history at Cambridge University. As in every work by this great author, it is thoroughly sourced and documented, and yet retains a readability and freshness that makes it timeless. He relates this fable that supposedly happened during the foundation of Armagh in A.D. 444. Patrick laid his eyes on a hill named Macha and desired to acquire it to construct a monastery. The local king, Daire, refused this request, and gave the saint another parcel. One of the king's men later brought a horse to graze in a field owned by the monastery. Patrick asked him not to do this, but he was rebuffed. The following day, the horse was found dead. The king's man told Daire that the saint was responsible. The king then ordered a group of men to capture Patrick and slay him.

But soon after, the king was stricken with an illness. His wife was superstitious, and believed that it was some sort of curse that had come about from trying to kill a holy man. She begged Daire to call off the assassins; she also told the king to seek the saint's blessing. This he did. Men went to Patrick and told him that the king was sick. So the saint consecrated some water and first sprinkled it on the dead horse. The horse was instantly revived, apparently from the dead. Some of the water was also brought to the king, and it restored him to health as well. The king was grateful for the gesture and desired to repay the saint. He had a large bronze vessel–very expensive–brought to the saint. Patrick said only this: *Gratias agamus*, which in Latin literally means, "We give you thanks." But the king, ignorant of the language, only heard something that sounded to him like *gratzacham*. The taciturn Patrick said nothing else to the king.

When Daire returned home, he became more and more peeved at this inscrutable religious man. He ordered a few of his servants to bring back the bronze vessel, which the ascetic Patrick apparently could not appreciate. When the men brought back the bronze vessel, the king asked his men what Patrick's response had been. "He only said one word to us, and it was *gratzacham.*"

The king now was amused. "What kind of man is this? He says *gratzacham* when he gets something, and *gratzacham* when he loses something. This must be a good word." He then went right away to pay Patrick another visit, and this time he delivered the bronze vessel in person. "Please keep this, holy man, for you are a steadfast and solid-minded man." And he gave Patrick this vessel, as well as the land that the saint had originally wanted. This was how the saint demonstrated that patience, and a dash of inscrutability, are more effective than bellowing and bombast.

85. The Three Rings

An interesting fable is found in one of the published lectures of the late historian J.B. Bury. Some investigation into its lineage shows that it is of very old date, and has appeared in various literary sources. One was Boccaccio's *Decameron*; another was the medieval chronicle *Gesta Romanorum*; and yet another was from Lessing's drama *Nathan der Weise*. In most essentials, the stories agree with each other, and I will reproduce it here. The Moslem ruler Saladin desired to extort a sum of money from a wealthy Jew named Melchizedek, who also had a reputation for being very wise. Saladin had been waging wars for many years and was eager to find new sources of loans. Saladin was crafty, and devised a stratagem to trap Melchizedek. He said to him the following: "You are known to be a patient and honorable man. Let me ask you the following question." Melchizedek immediately became uneasy; trying to offer advice to absolute rulers like Saladin was always a risky proposition. But he heard the sultan out.

"Of the three major religions–Christianity, Judaism, and Islam–which one do you believe is the most true?" Startled by this impossible-to-answer trap, the wise man thought for a moment. He then offered this response.

"Excellency, your question reminds me of a situation I once heard about in these regions. There was a wealthy old man who had in his possession a gold ring of great value.

"In his will, the old man stated that whichever of his sons was in possession of this ring upon the old man's death would be able to inherit his estate. He gave the ring to one of his sons. And in this way the ring was passed down from one generation to another.

"But the ring eventually came to be owned by a man who had three sons whom he each loved equally. He could not decide which son to give the ring to. So he told each one of them privately that he would give him the ring. Then he went to a jewelry maker and had two duplicate ring made of the original ring. The duplicates were exact copies of the original. The rings were eventually presented to each son.

"When the man died, each of the sons claimed title to the father's estate. Each one of them had a ring to prove their title. But no one could tell which one was genuine, and which one was not. All three of them sued each other, and the suit is still ongoing. So it is with the three religions, excellency. No one can say for certain who has the monopoly on the truth. God grants us knowledge, and this same knowledge is revealed in different ways to different peo-plc."

Saladin was greatly pleased by this subtle and sophisticated answer, and became close personal friends with Melchizedek. He received his loan, which he paid back promptly with interest. The point of the parable is to emphasize the need for tolerance among different points of view. No one can claim absolute infallibility in most things, or even in many things. The forward movement of knowledge–and therefore of civilization–is dependent on the conflict among competing ideas. When this competition of ideas ceases, the waters of knowledge run dry, or are diverted into pools that become stagnant and fetid.

Any orthodoxy which demands that we prostrate our intellects unquestioningly before it, and deliberately seeks to suppress, shame, or marginalize competing views, is unworthy of our respect. It should, on the contrary, bc attacked that much more vigorously. Experience has shown that coercion of opinion is a disastrous road for any society to take. Man's natural mental laziness, and fear of things that are new and different, will mean that those who advance new ideas will be treated at first with scorn and contempt, sometimes even worse. Freedom of thought is not achieved by accident. It is not arrived at through wishful thinking. It must be won through the advancing of competing and offensive viewpoints. Those viewpoints that seem to the lazy mind to be most objectionable are often the most necessary for the forward progress of knowledge and social health.

86. Petrarch Reflects On The Causes And Cures Of His Depression

The Renaissance literary figure Petrarch met his fame and success with ambivalence. On the one hand it was the fulfillment of what he had worked for, but on the other, it left him with deep feelings of unease. These feelings eventually ripened into outright contempt for those who could not understand the origin of his malaise. These kinds of feelings are common among many driven, goal-oriented people. To help himself cope with his depression, Petrarch wrote an intensely personal dialogue called *The Secret Conflict of My Thoughts* (*De Secreto Conflictu Curarum Mearum*). Likely never intended for publication, it is set in the form of an imaginary dialogue between one "Franciscus" (certainly the author himself) and a historical figure he greatly admired, St. Augustine. The dialogue, in three books, is a catalogue of his worries and cares. It must have been therapeutic for him to set down on paper the thoughts on life and career that so oppressed his mind. He says in the book's introduction:

> You are my Secret Book, and this is what I will call you; and when I am preoccupied with higher things, just as you recall whatever has been said secretly, so you will remind me of it privately.

In Petrarch's time, depression was considered a sickness of the mind (which, in a way, it is). The Latin word for it was *accidia*, which can be rendered as "anguish"; another term used for it was *aegritudo animi* (sickness of the soul). In book II of the dialogue, Petrarch and his conversation partner St. Augustine probe to find the source and solution to the depression:

> Augustine: A deadly sickness of the mind has taken hold of you, which the moderns call "accidia" and the ancients called "mental sickness."
>
> Franciscus: I am in horror at the very name of this sickness.
>
> Augustine: No doubt, as you have been stricken by this disease for a long time.

Franciscus goes on to say that his depression torments him day and night; its attacks come often, but are brief. What especially seems to trouble him is that he has begun to take some sort of "perverse enjoyment" (*atra quadam cum voluptate*) in his misery. Modern experts on depression today tell us that this sort of thing is not uncommon: the mind gets used to being miserable and actually prefers this state. Augustine presses him to say why he is depressed. Is it the loss of physical goods, some sort of physical pain, or is it bad luck? When Franciscus gives evasive answers, he is pressed still further. The best answer that he can seem to give is that he feels overwhelmed by events and "threats" that he feels are surrounding him. Petrarch dramatically illustrates what he means:

> It is as if I were enclosed on all sides by innumerable enemies, for which there is no way to flee, and no hope of mercy or solace; everything swarming over me, the siege-engines surrounding me, and the infiltration tunnels dug under the earth; the towers are vibrating, the siege-ladders are standing against the walls, ramps are leaning against the walls, and fire rising through the floor…

Few authors have described the dread caused by depression so vividly as Petrarch does here. Finally, the source of Franciscus's depression seems to be identified: *he is not happy with his lot in life*. But Augustine puts things in perspective for us. What makes us depressed, he says, is our tendency to focus on ourselves and then to compare what we have to what others have. Such bean-counting sets us up for feelings of misery, because not everyone can be on top. So when we do not get what we want, we become resentful. What makes men so foolish, Augustine continues, is the fact that we do not appreciate just how miserable the men on top are themselves! If we really knew what great fame and fortune entailed, we would not desire it, he says. Instead, we should follow the advice of Seneca, when he says that when we obsess about how many people are "ahead" of us, we should be mindful of how many of them are also "behind" us. To be truly grateful for what we have, we should consider all those who are less fortunate than we are. The best strategy for us would be to:

> Finem constitue, quem transire ne possis quidem si velis.

Which means, "Set a limit for yourself, which you can't cross even if you want to." Once we recognize that our desires and longings tend to increase without limit, the only sensible thing to do is to impose strict limits on what we want or need, and then hold ourselves to those boundaries. Left unchecked, the desires tend to spiral out of control, dragging us this way and that, and causing us misery. But Augustine gives him even more food for thought. Can any man hope to live a life free from anxiety? Who can totally claim to be "living for themselves"? Not many. All of us are enmeshed in obligations to various things and to various people. It is often sadly true, as Lucan tells us, that "the human race lives for only a few." Instead of stressing about things over which we have no control, we would do better by being angry at our own lack of wisdom. This is what we should be focusing on. The study of wisdom, says Augustine, is the one and only thing that can make us truly wealthy and free.

87. The Soviet Union's Philosophy Of Weapons Design

The Soviet Union is no more, as everyone knows. Its political system proved to be unsuccessful; it was incapable of adapting to the challenges of history. But this should not blind us to the fact that in some things the Soviet Union was very successful. One of these things was in the design of weapons of war. Soviet weapons were all designed around a very specific operative philosophy: *simplicity, reliability, and mass production are paramount in war.* This attitude took precedence over all other considerations. This is the heart of the Soviet weapons design philosophy. From its experience in the Second World War, Soviet planners and engineers realized–often in sharp contrast to their Western counterparts–that fancy, complicated designs may be fine for the parade ground, but they will be failures in real war.

Consider the Soviet small arms of the Second World War, such as the PPSh-41 and the PPS. These weapons were not as sophisticated as the German small arms. They had limited ranges and were relatively crude. But they could be produced in almost any machine-shop. They often had chromed barrels, which reduced wear and tear and cut down on the need for maintenance. These were tough weapons that could endure mud, dirt, grit, ice, and water.

They were so simple that nearly any illiterate peasant could learn how to use them. And they could be mass-produced on a huge scale.

Consider also the Soviet T-34 tank. Many authorities consider this the very best tank produced during the war. The Soviet Union produced this tank in huge numbers, while the Germans turned out surprisingly few Panzers and Tiger-Koenig tanks. Only about 4800 Panzer tanks were built; as for the vaunted Tiger-Koenig, only about 485 were produced. How many tanks did the Soviets build? The answer is this: about 102,000 tanks, and of these, about 70,000 were T-34s. The fact is that the T-34 was not only the most powerful tank in the world, but also one of the simplest to produce. There is a lesson to be learned here. When the German generals first encountered the T-34, they were shocked at its effectiveness and urged the high command to copy the design. But the Germans had a different design philosophy. They were too focused on complicated designs that may have been visionary on paper, but were unsuited to the realities of the war. The famous Kalashnikov assault rifle, one could argue, is in reality a simplified, super-durable version of the German MP-44.

This design philosophy permeated all of Soviet military planning. If weapons engineers were faced with a multitude of designs, all of which were effective, they would invariably choose the design that was the simplest. This even held true in aircraft design. When the West first had a chance to examine the Soviet MiG-25 aircraft, they did not think much of it. But it was the fastest combat airplane in the world in its day, and had the highest rate of climb. It was suited for mass production in wartime by being deliberately simple to roll off the production lines. Steel was chosen for its construction, rather than titanium. Soviet designers also would often produce two versions of a weapon. One version would be exclusively for themselves; its capabilities and details would be secret. A second version–called the "monkey-model" would be produced for export. This would be a bare-bones, simplified version of the already simple design. But it could be mass-produced on a huge scale. Many people in the West did not understand this philosophy. They laughed at what they considered the "crudity" and "simplicity" of Soviet weapons. But they were mistaken. For this was not a weakness, but a strength. Soviet planners understood that war is not a game of sport shooting. War is not a game of cricket. The designs that win wars are the ones that are reliable and tough, and that can be produced quickly. Victor Suvorov, in his *Inside the Soviet Army*, tells the following revealing anecdote:

> I once saw a film comparing a Soviet and an American tank. A driver was given both models to drive and was then asked, "Which one is better?" "The American one, of course," said the driver. "It has automatic transmission, whereas in the Soviet tank you have to change gear, which is not easy in a heavy machine." He is quite right–if you see war as a pleasant outing. But Soviet designers realize that any future war will be anything but this. They consider, quite correctly, that if there are mass bombing attacks, if whole industrial areas are destroyed, if long-distance communications break down, mass production of tanks with automatic transmission would be out of the question...Accordingly, there can be only one choice–the ordinary, non-automatic transmission.

The convenience of the driver matters nothing at all. Simplicity, reliability, and the ability to accomplish the task at hand under duress were the controlling principles.

88. Only The Offensive Brings Victory

I have very much enjoyed the writings of Victor Suvorov. I wish I could meet and speak with him. He served for thirty years as an officer in the Soviet Army before defecting to the West in the 1980s. In his book *Inside The Soviet Army*, he tells the following anecdote:

> On day in Paris, I bought a book published in 1927 on the problems of a future war. The author was sober-minded and reasonable. His logic was sound, his analysis was shrewd and his arguments unassailable. After analyzing the way military equipment had developed in his lifetime, the author concluded by declaring that the proper place for the tank was the

> museum, next to the dinosaur skeletons. His argument was simple and logical: anti-tank guns had been developed to the point at which they would bring massive formations of tanks to a complete halt in any future war, just as machine guns had completely stopped the cavalry of the First World War. I do not know whether the author lived until 1940, to see the German tanks sweeping along the Paris boulevards, past the spot at which, many decades later, I was to buy my dusty copy of his book, its leaves yellowing with age.

We can see Suvorov's point. But it is a point that needs to be made. I have read many articles in military literature making the same argument: that the tank in 2016 has little role to play on the battlefield, and that air power and sophisticated anti-tank weapons make the tank a steel coffin. The tank, they claim, is obsolete. It is amusing to see such writings. I smile when I read them. Usually the writers of such things have never experienced the full power of a tank. And there is a difference between writing about something in an office, and experiencing it up close in a personal way. When I was in the Basic School for Marine Corps officers in 1990, one routine exercise for us was to crawl with our equipment under a tank while its engine was idling. The tank was stationary. We crawled under it from the back to the front, through the muck. It sounds easy, and physically it was not especially challenging, even with all our gear.

But the experience itself was very, very sobering. Its engine roared like an enraged dragon. One sensed the awesome power of the metal behemoth. One twitch of its treads in one direction or another, and you would be ground to pulp. No one made any jokes about that exercise. And this is the essence of the difference between theory and practice. The tank is an engine of war. It is an engine of conquest. It is designed to attack. Make no mistake about this.

The tank is not going anywhere. It is a predator, and it is designed to destroy obstacles and occupy ground. We have become too addicted to our drones, our computers, our airplanes, and our other fancy gadgets. We have forgotten what truly brings victory in a contest between two opposing forces. Defensive weapons are always representatives of a passive mindset. Offensive weapons promote an active mindset. If we were to deploy a lot of anti-tank weapons to cover an area, we would have to disperse them to some extent. And the tank attack would of course hit us in the weakest area. Would aircraft be able to contend against an attack by hundreds, maybe even thousands, of tanks? I don't think so. And remember that tanks have defensive features of their own. They are not just inert containers running on treads.

Since tanks are offensive weapons, they decide the time and place of the attack. They can survey the enemy's posture, and divine his weaknesses. They call the shots. They can bring to bear the moral factors of conflict. I am not saying anti-tank weapons are useless. I am saying that the day of the tank is not over. Soviet generals understood this. They comprehended that the only thing that produces victory in war is the taking of the offensive. You have to seize the initiative and hammer your enemy with multiple blows. You have to force him to respond to your moves. Three days ago, I conducted a trial in federal court where I was representing the plaintiff. I set the terms of the engagement. It was I who decided what issues to talk about, what exhibits to introduce and talk about, and how to move from one issue to the next. So the principle is the same. By taking the initiative, I increased my chances of success.

Soviet military planners understood the need for taking the offensive. The Soviet Union did not spend much time or effort focusing on "anti-ballistic missile defense systems." They were not interested in protecting their ICBM silos from attack. Why? The answer is simple. The best protection for a nuclear missile in the event of war was to use it immediately, they believed. They did not comprehend the American logic that a nuclear war might start gradually and escalate slowly. Under Soviet doctrine, the best way to win a war was to destroy your opponent immediately. And the best way to do that was to hit him with a nuclear strike immediately. If this sounds terrifying, I am sorry. But this is the truth. Victor Suvorov claimed that a Soviet strategic offensive would unfold in five stages.

First Stage. A 30-minute nuclear strike by the Strategic Rocket Forces would be directed at the enemy's command posts, strategic lines of communication, storage depots, submarine bases, aircraft, and anything else of strategic value.

Second Stage. This would last between 90 and 120 minutes. It would be a massive air attack by the Air Armies of all fronts and by the Long-Range Air Force. The attack would take place in multiple waves. These nuclear-armed aircraft would finish off anything the first stage did not destroy.

Third Stage. This would last only about 30 minutes. It would be further attacks by local rocket brigades and air forces; it would finish off anything left over from the first two stages.

Fourth Stage. This stage lasts 10 to 20 days. It would consist of massive tank attacks by concentrated tank armies, coordinated to inflict the maximum damage. The goal in this stage is to find and exploit an opening in the enemy's fronts. Once the opening has been found, the tanks rush in and keep moving.

Fifth Stage. This final stage lasts about a week. The breach in the enemy's defenses has been achieved, and the tank armies are blasting through to the enemy's rear.

Even though these "stages" may not take place quite as the planners expect, they give an idea of the Soviet understanding of the importance of offense. This is not a defensive strategy. It is designed to overwhelm an enemy in the shortest possible time with the maximum amount of force. If we wish to be successful in conflict, we must think about what matters, and what does not matter. Having an offensive mentality is what produces results. When our minds are crippled with defensive thinking, we are unable to see the hidden moral factors that truly drive the flow of history.

89. The Seven Sleepers

We all desire to retain a sense of connection to the past. It is part of human nature. Too sudden a break with tradition can produce something very much like insanity; in individuals we call this a broken mind, and in nations we call it revolution. And both of these reactions are destructive. And at the same time, we need to feel we can project ourselves into the future, somehow. We want to escape the limitations of this frail physical life, with its miserly duration and inconstant rewards. This may be one of the reasons for the popularity of stories relating to time-travel. We want to know what life was like in the past, and what it may be like in the future. Man in olden days did not think in terms of Wellesian "time-machines" or other contrivances of science fiction. He thought more in terms of Rip Van Winkle fables. But the purpose was the same:

the chance to give modern man a taste of contact with his progenitors.

We consider the legend of the Seven Sleepers, found in Chapter XXXIII of Gibbon's *Decline and Fall.* The story is originally Roman, but found its way into Arabic lore after the seventh century. In his own typical way, Gibbon tells us: "Among the insipid legends of ecclesiastical history, I am tempted to distinguish the memorable fable of the Seven Sleepers; whose imaginary date corresponds with the reign of the younger Theodosius and the conquest of Africa by the Vandals." The story in its original form is found in Gregory of Tours's *De Gloria Martyrum*; he apparently translated his version from an undisclosed Syriac original. The essence of the story is this. During the reign of the emperor Decius (A.D. 249–251), seven noble youths of the city of Ephesus sought to escape the emperor's furious attempts to suppress Christianity. They secreted themselves inside a cave near the top of a mountain.

Minions of the emperor located them and had the entrance of the cave sealed with heavy stones. The youths then fell into a deep sleep that, we are told, lasted for one hundred and eighty-seven years. One day a random person happened to remove the stones from the cave's mouth and, when rays of light penetrated the interior, the young men awakened, apparently unharmed after all this time. They were not aware that they had slept so long. One of their number, a boy (adult?) named Iamblichus, decided to go into town to buy some bread for the remaining six in the cave. Everywhere he looked, he was shocked to see Christian crosses and other religious paraphernalia. He could not understand why the pagan gods were no longer publicly worshipped.

When the boy went into a bakery, the owner and all the patrons were startled by his antique dress and archaic speech. When he went to pay for his bread, the proprietor was incredulous to receive a coin dating from the reign of Decius. Word of the stranger soon circulated, and Iamblichus was hauled before a judge to explain himself. Soon the bishop of Ephesus, local notables, and eventually the current emperor (Theodosius) visited the cave, and were convinced of the truth of Iamblichus's story. The six youths there related their story with sincerity; and once they had told it, they died peacefully in the presence of all. This is the legend of the Seven Sleepers. Even today there is a cave near Ephesus that is said to be the original cave of the Seven. The tale was so popular that it persisted for centuries in the Near East. We even find an Islamic version of it in the Qu'ran (*sura* 18), along with the addition of a dog in the fable (Al-Rakim). Gibbon also tells us that a version of the tale even appears in Scandinavian literature (cf. Paul of Aquileia's *De gestis Langobardorum*). Why does this story, and others like it, have such a hold on the imaginations of so many separate traditions? Gibbon explains:

> We imperceptibly advance from youth to age, without observing the gradual, but incessant, change of human affairs and, even in our larger experiences of history, the imagination is accustomed, by a perpetual series of causes and effects, to unite the most distant revolutions. But, if the interval between two memorable eras could be instantly annihilated; if it were possible, after a momentary slumber of two hundred years, to display the new world to the eyes of a spectator, who still retained a lively and recent impression of the old; his surprise and his reflections would furnish the pleasing subject of a philosophical romance.

And so it is. We stretch out our arms, and extend our fingers, to catch hold of some as-yet uncongealed future; hoping, in some small way, to project our present consciousness into realms of future events, and thereby achieve immortality. It is a delusion, but it is the noblest of all delusions.

90. The Courage Of Andreas

In the year 530 the Eastern Roman (i.e., Byzantine) Empire was engaged in a limited frontier war with its traditional enemy, the Sassanid Persians. The two great empires had a long history of border clashes, as each constantly was testing the resolution of the other. One of the engagements that took place in this year was the Battle of Dara, and it was fought in what is now eastern Georgia in the Caucasus mountains. An anecdote is told about the battle by the historian Procopius (I.13). At the beginning of the battle, the forces of both the Persians and the Romans were content to remain in fixed positions. One Persian soldier rode out in front of the Roman defenses, seeking to engage the enemy commander in one-on-one combat. But no one would take him up on his proposition.

No one, that is, except one man named Andreas. This unknown combatant was not even a professional soldier. Procopius tells us that he was an attendant of one of the Roman generals whose name was Bouzes. Andreas was the proprietor of a wrestling school and gymnasium in the city of Byzantium; he had been brought along on the campaign as a kind of "personal trainer" for the top Roman generals.

He accepted the Persian's challenge. "This man alone had the courage, without being ordered by Bouzes or anyone else, to go out of his own accord to meet the man in single combat," as Procopius relates it. The historian does not speculate on the reason. Perhaps Andreas was offended by the arrogance of the enemy soldier; perhaps he was bored with the heat and flies of the area and needed some way to relieve the tedium. We do not know. Men in action have their own reasons for doing what they do, about which we cannot presume to speculate.

So Andreas accepted the challenge. Then he walked up to the surprised Persian–mounted on his horse–and drove his spear into his right breast. He tumbled down from his saddle. And while he was writhing on the ground, Andreas drew a dagger and "slew him like a sacrificial animal as he lay on his back, and a mighty shout was raised both from the city wall [of Dara] and the Roman army." Now the Persians were incensed at this outcome, and sent another of their champions against the Romans to try to make good the situation. This man was strong and large, but not as young as the first Persian; grey hair had started to appear around his temples. He also rode in front of the Roman positions, waving a whip, and challenging another of their number to personal combat. And here again Andreas accepted the man's challenge when no one else would. He had to do this secretly, as another general named Hermogenes had told him not to engage in such fights.

The Persian and Andreas were both on horseback, and charged each other with lances ready. Each lance struck the breast-plate of the other, and both were deflected. The riders were hurled from their mounts and fell to the earth with great commotion. The two horses collided bodily and also fell to the ground. Andreas and his opponent both tried to get back on their feet, knowing that speed in doing so would ensure survival. But Andreas was more agile and flexible than the Persian, and he recovered himself with great speed. As his enemy was on one knee, Andreas drove his spear into him, wounding him mortally:

> And then A roar went up from the wall and the Roman army, as great, if not greater, than before. The Persians broke their phalanx and withdrew to Ammodios, while the Romans, raising the paean, went inside the walls; for already it was growing dark. Thus both armies passed the night. [*Trans. by A. Kaldellis*]

This was how Andreas, the wrestler with no military experience, accepted the challenge of personal combat and killed two of the enemy host.

91. The Engrossed

Seneca had a word for men who were consumed with the chase after worldly riches and pleasures to the exclusion of everything else. He called them *occupati*, the past participle of the verb *occupare*. They were so busy in this obsessive, single-minded pursuit of the phantoms of prosperity that they never properly set aside time for themselves. The word *occupati* means engrossed, preoccupied, or obsessed. And I think this word is a fitting description. We all know people like this. They think they have the world all figured out. That is, until they're lying on a hospital bed from a heart attack. They spend all their time amassing wealth, without any thought of how they might enjoy it. The higher they climb on the social or economic ladder, the more furious the pursuit of wealth and pleasure becomes, until they are teetering on the top of the totem pole. And then comes the fall: which it always does. And the higher the height, the greater the fall. Marilyn Monroe–a far more astute observer of human behavior than is generally believed–once said, "gravity catches up with all of us." It does.

It usually does no good trying to explain things to The Engrossed. They will smile their little Cheshire-cat smiles at you, smug in the knowledge that it is you who is deluded. Philosophy, they think, is a waste of time. All that matters is to accumulate as many things as one can, and that is all. Everything else is just conversation. And when I hear this sort of talk, I do not respond. Because I know that the world will teach them far more effectively than I can. *The Engrossed do not appreciate the omnipresence of Death.*

It goes without saying that The Engrossed do not understand the concept of time. Time has three divisions: past, present, and future. All of them have their purposes. The Engrossed do not read many books, and for this reason they have little sense of history. And having no knowledge of the past is like walking through life with a blindfold on. One gets no sense of the real depth of things, or how things in the world interrelate to each other. The present is in many ways nothing except the past rolled up into one large bundle that we carry about on our backs. Sometimes you have to stop and see what your knapsack holds. Our sense of mortality forces us to confront these truths. The eighteenth-century traveler Constantin François de Volney, who had ruminated over many a ruin of vanished empires in the Middle East, understood well the tomb's power to mock our mortal pretensions. In his philosophical classic *Meditations on the Revolutions of Empires*, he warns us (in American president Thomas Jefferson's translation):

> O Tombs! What virtues are yours!...You punish the powerful oppressor; you wrest from avarice and extortion their ill-gotten gold, and you avenge the feeble whom they have despoiled; you compensate the miseries of the poor by the anxieties of the rich...Aware that all must return to you, the wise man loadeth not himself with the burdens of grandeur and of useless wealth; he restrains his desires within the bounds of justice; yet, knowing that he must run his destined course of life, he fills with employment all its hours, and enjoys the comforts that fortune has allotted him...You free the soul from the fatiguing conflict of the passions...You thus impose on the impetuous sallies of cupidity a salutary rein!

So the first step in extricating yourself from the ranks of The Engrossed is to read. You almost certainly have heard the saying about how we cannot choose our family or our birthplace. This is true. But we can choose what books we read. If we want to be surrounded by good things, we have to read good books. Books are time-machines. They can transport us back across centuries or millenia of experience; we can converse with the greatest minds who ever lived, and take them as our teachers. We can explore the South

Seas, the Arctic regions, the steaming Amazonian jungles, and the mysterious waters of the Nile, whose source lies in the deepest heart of Africa. We can stand there, along its turbid shore, and listen to the reeds sway in the wind, as they sigh one into the other.

These great men of the past can teach us both how to live and how to die. We will begin to realize how the most precious commodity is time, and that to squander it in useless pursuits is the height of folly. Wasting away the weekends in idleness then seems more like a crime than it does bad judgment. It is because our time here is so brief that we must make the most of every moment. Associating with clowns or fools does nothing to advance this purpose. We may not be able to choose our family or birthplace, but we can certainly choose our friends in books and in real-life. *The fount of knowledge nourishes the soul of the seeker.* My bookshelves are filled with intimate friends, I am proud to say; they are all friends of proven worth. I speak with them often. And I practice the same principle with flesh-and-blood friends. I do not like to waste time with bad people; they do nothing but drain one's energy and offer nothing in return. The Engrossed only care about themselves and what you can do for their frantic pursuits of ever-receding goals. I can certainly pick my friends arranged on my bookshelves, and I always pick the best. They neither hound nor oppress me with nonsense.

One of the best pieces of advice from the original film *Rocky* was when Sylvester Stallone tried to counsel a young girl in his neighborhood. She was hanging around a group of kids who were headed nowhere. He told her, *Hang around good people, and you'll do good things. But hang around idiots, and you'll go nowhere.* If you remember, she did not like to hear this advice. The Engrossed only respond to the sound of their desire's music. The other way to climb out of the pit of The Engrossed is to have the right sort of job. For me it makes no difference what a man does. The important thing is that his job should provide the means to support himself in a reasonable way, and that it should allow him some leisure. Now when I say leisure, I do not mean leisure to squander oneself in chasing after self-destructive, illusory pleasures; I mean the leisure to spend some time in speculative thought. To be free, a man must be able *to think.*

This is the reason why The Engrossed are so enslaved. They spend all their time and effort on that material goods treadmill.

They spend all their time during their waking hours slaving away for no good end. And at the end of the day they are nothing but spent, dry husks. There is nothing left of them. I am not saying that a man should not try to reach the top of his profession; I am not saying that wealth is necessarily evil. Far from it. I applaud it and have been fortunate in my own life to achieve material success. But wealth is nothing unless it is put to the service of wise and prudent goals. And even when you have it, you will realize that it wears on you, slowly but surely: you spend much time preserving and maintaining it, and fret over its loss.

The Engrossed also sin against time itself. We have already observed that time is the past, present, and future. The Engrossed only live in the present, with no thought to either the past or the future. The past to them is irrelevant; and the future, they believe, will take care of itself. And as life and its inevitable hardships close in on them, they are left bewildered. Only too late do they find out the truth of things. Some of them never do. Some men do not want to be edified. The ideal job to me is the job that a man enjoys doing, provides him a reasonable income, and give him the opportunity for speculative thought. The Engrossed are the way they are because they never think about what they are doing, whether by choice or by necessity. They never think about life and how it might best be lived. And they certainly never think about death, which is far closer and more intimate a presence in our lives than any of us would care to admit.

But this is how it is. The Engrossed share much in common, in point of fact, with the slave. Slaves were always kept busy. Slaves were never encouraged to read: most were even forbidden to learn how to read. And there is a reason for this. The reason is that a thinking slave is dangerous. A man who thinks–who can engage his cerebrum–is a man who will eventually begin asking dangerous questions. These questions may lead to subversive answers. I was talking to someone recently who was trying to impress me with the quantity of material goods he had, with his status-symbol toys, and similar such things. It was clear that he was from the ranks of The Engrossed. He noticed that I was not much impressed with his litany of luxuries. My inner reaction was actually more like pity than anything else, although I did not overtly show any emotion. I thought to myself, the *occupati* are all the same. Their lives are battle-grounds between the competing spirits of Enlightenment and

Self-destruction. The avoidance of ruin will depend on each man's ability to keep his negative, acquisitive urges in check until Wisdom can accomplish her positive work.

92. The Giving And Receiving Of Advice

Advice requires two participants. One must offer it; and another must receive it. If it is offered without first having been solicited, it generates resentment, however small and incremental. And if it is requested, the counselor must yet take care not to overstep his boundaries, for fear of providing insight that is too pungent. So advice is problematic both in origin and in delivery. Francis Bacon, in his essay *On Counsel*, identified three "inconveniences" in the asking of advice. They are:

1. That the person asking for advice may see his secrets uncomfortably revealed.

2. That the person asking for advice may perceive that his authority or status is somehow lowered.

3. That the person asking for advice may receive bad guidance, which may be more in the interest of the person offering the advice than in the person receiving it.

From my own experience in providing guidance and advice to people in distress, I can say that these hazards are very real. The first two numbered items above are another way of saying that the person seeking advice may feel a sense of shame, or a loss of dignity, in asking for help from another. In my experience, men seem more susceptible to this problem than women. Men, especially elderly men, do not like to ask for help, even when they are in dire need. There seems to be some misplaced sense of pride that springs into action, like a watchful sentinel guarding an inner sanctum, which prevents them from permitting the messenger of advice to enter. A misplaced sense of pride is the downfall of many men. For it obscures the judgment, and blinds a man from taking positive action at the early stages of a crisis, and by delay, so harmfully narrows the range of constructive solutions. Men are in the habit of shouldering many burdens, and may find it difficult to drop their bags of bricks and allow themselves to be helped. For as the statesman Richelieu once observed, a key virtue in any sovereign is the capacity *to allow himself* to be advised by his ministers.

Pride, in this situation, is an enemy, rather than a friend. Women, on the other hand, seem better able to focus on solving the problem at hand, without being bothered by wounded pride or status. These are generalizations, of course, but ones based on personal observation. The third point noted above is a common fear among those seeking guidance, but I have found that it is a hurdle that is easily overcome. Trust either exists, or it does not. The asking for guidance does not even take place unless the bonds of trust and respect already exist. Bacon overlooked the fact, however, that there are hazards in advice-giving not only for the recipient, but also for the giver. The dangers of advice-giving for the giver are these:

1. The advice-giver will be blamed if things do not unfold as the advice-seeker plans.

2. The advice will be distorted by the recipient in comprehension and in execution.

3. Some advice-seekers resent having to ask for advice, seeing a request for help as some sort of sign of weakness.

The first of these drawbacks is the most powerful of the three. Human nature is such that it often confuses aspirations with assurances; and unless the advice-giver successfully manages the expectations of his client, he may find himself the focus of ire when things do not turn out as the advice-seeker expected. The second of these drawbacks is not as powerful as the first, but still can be a problem. Advice-seekers like to cherry-pick the shiny fruit from the basket of advice, and discard that which does not comport with their comfortable delusions. And finally, as is noted in the third point, people often do not like to be seen in a vulnerable state, and may secretly resent their dependence on another for guidance. Need and gratitude are not always in accord with each other. If I could have my way, I would wish for this as the best piece of equipment for the aspirant advice-giver: the Cap of Hades. What is this? In classical mythology, the Cap of Hades (called in the Renaissance the "Helmet of Pluto") conferred invisibility on its wearer. It was given by the Cyclops to Hades, the god of the underworld, during the war between the gods and the Titans. The possessor of such a fantastic article could then give his advice, don his cap, and then walk away from his solicitor, safely cloaked in a mantle of invisibility.

93. Petrarch Reflects On Ignorance And Happiness

The great humanist Francesco Petrarca (Petrarch) had opportunity to reflect on the fact that the more he gained in knowledge and experience, the less and less certain he became of his own judgments. These thoughts were recorded in an essay called *On His Own Ignorance And That Of Many Others* (*De Sui Ipsius Et Multorum Ignorantia*). Some of these observations are incredibly frank. He begins by noting that:

> Concerning ignorance, wisdom, and other things, the wise man should be the one pronouncing judgment. He should be "wise" in what he proposes to judge. An ignorant person cannot judge ignorance as musicians judge music, or as grammarians judge grammar. With certain things, abundance brings a dearth of critical faculties, and practically anyone can judge such things better than the person who possesses them. No one understands disability less than a disabled person, who is numb to his disability and cannot see what offends the sight of a non-disabled person. The same logic applies to all other defects: no one is a worse judge of ignorance than the ignorant. [*De Ignorantia* III.30]

And as one gets older, he notes, the very idea of knowledge becomes more and more elusive. For all his learning, Petrarch often feels like he is put on show as a clown, a buffoon meant for the amusement of the powerful. To make this point, he tells the story of a man named Liberius. Liberius was, according to Petrarch, a military man who was persuaded (or forced) by Julius Caesar to perform as a mime (i.e., a buffoon or clown). It was an insulting recommendation, probably meant to degrade him for one reason or other. Liberius did not "bear this treatment in silence" (*quam iniuriam ipse quidem non tacitus tulit*), but instead protested with these words (which are taken from the writer Macrobius):

> So, I have done my job for twice thirty years without complaint,
> And left my station as a Roman knight,

> But stand before you now as a clown.
>
> Without doubt, I have lived one day longer than I should have! [III.35]

So poor Liberius ended his days as a clown, forced to hop and dance to the tune of the rich and powerful. Petrarch notes that he has spent his life in scholarly pursuits, and has sought the patronage of the rich and the powerful. He achieved great notoriety. But it seems all to have come to nothing. He says, in a startling admission,

> And so I seem to have met the same end as Liberius. I lost my position after having turned sixty years of age. But unlike Liberius, I was not transformed into a clown...I became something even worse, an ignoramus. But this is how things go. This is the outcome of all my studies, work, and my burning of the midnight oil. Judges far more intelligent than I have ruled that I am ignorant. Even though this fact hurts, it must be said (*dolendum forsitan, sed ferendum*). [III.39]

Fame, he goes on to note, is not an easy thing to manage, "especially literary fame." He longs to shed this burdensome robe of fame, and live a quiet, unadorned life, far from the crash and roar of the mob, and the cloying attentions of idiot kings and princes. He agrees with Seneca that it is better to be thought of as a good man, than as a learned one. One can sympathize with Petrarch for these admissions. As a mendicant scholar, he was often dependent on the patronage of powerful figures to earn a living. He could not often say what he really believed, or expressed what he really felt. Add to this the natural feelings of perspective that come with old age and experience. One is less impressed with novelty and excitement, and more impressed with constancy, character, and virtue.

After a time, he must have found it exhausting and humiliating to have to "perform as a clown" as Liberius was forced to in the anecdote mentioned above. And yet this is fate of all wise men, to some extent. Everyone, to some extent, has to play ball. To some extent, we are all dancing to the tunes set by others. It is all a matter of degree. It is all a matter of what one can tolerate. And despite his protestations, I doubt Petrarch would have changed anything in his life, had he the opportunity. I am not so sure I believe Petrarch. He sounds a bit like a tired old man who has had enough of the arena of conflict. This is natural, I suppose. But men must do what is in their natures. The secret, inner spirits drive them forward, with a calculated assurance. They go forward, strive, and act, based on the spirits that dance inside them, and animate them. We are all puppets of these hidden wire-pullers.

Some men crave knowledge, wisdom, and understanding, even if it ultimately condemns them to some form of psychological exile from their fellows. They are compelled to seek the truth, even if their vast knowledge makes them feel more and more vulnerable. I do not know if I am a wise man, but I do know that I would not turn away from the quest for knowledge, in order to embrace the comfort and security of ignorance. For it is the ignorant man, and not the fallen good man like Liberius, who is the real clown. Liberius may have had to dance to Caesar's tune temporarily, but in the end Caesar could never strip him of his goodness, his virtue, or his knowledge. I would not shirk the seeking of knowledge in order to make others feel better. I would not stop learning, probing the inner nature of things, out of fear of what I might find. I would always choose knowledge over ignorance. If knowledge maketh misery, then I shall embrace my misery, knowing that ignorance is an even worse hell, and a more inescapable prison. We go forward because we must go forward. *Sic res eunt*, as Petrarch says: *This is how things go*.

94. Pure Talent Is Never Enough: The Case Against Leonardo Da Vinci

Everyone thinks of Leonardo da Vinci as the paragon of Renaissance virtue. He could paint, design, and use intuition as an aid to creativity, when he felt like doing so. But a closer look at the record paints a picture of a chronic procrastinator, a man of dubious reliability, and an idler who was more preoccupied with his daydreams than with perfecting his craft. He had genius, of course. But that is never enough. Harness, discipline, and application are far more important.

Laudatory writings about him list his "interests" as evidence of his greatness, but conspicuously fail to mention that he contributed almost nothing of worth to all of these ancillary fields that he was "interested" in. No one doubts his incredible genius; but we cannot overlook his very meager output. Genius locked away in unpublished notebooks is genius wasted. He is primarily known for his painting. But in practice, he seemed more interested in solving the technical problems of composition than in the actual execution of a work. It seems he used assistants to fill in large parts of his paintings based on instructions he provided. Even worse than this was the pitifully small number of works that he produced in his lifetime. For a painter of his caliber, the final count is not at all impressive. The *Mona Lisa*, his most famous painting, took him about 15 years to finish; and his *Virgin on the Rocks* took even longer, perhaps 20 years. These facts are indicators of a mind unable to focus, or to discipline itself, to the task at hand. One of his most famous paintings is *The Last Supper*, which Leonardo was hired to paint for the refectory of the Convent of Santa Maria della Grazie in Milan. In its technical details, the work is incredible, of course. There are precise geometric proportions that underlie the work, and the viewer's attention is kept focused (as it should be) on the faces of the disciples present.

But Leonardo had to be hounded night and day by his patrons. He worked in short bursts of activity, followed by periods of inactivity. It was the same story with nearly all of his works. He would be commissioned to get some project done, and would then settle into a predictable pattern of behavior. An initial burst of energy would quickly fizzle out, and Leonardo would then putter along in fits and starts until his employers lost patience with him. An observer (Matteo Bandello) who actually watched Leonardo working on *The Last Supper* recorded that the artist would on occasion work all day without taking a break (even for meals), and then promptly lapse into inactivity that might drag on for several days. Leonardo had to be badgered relentlessly in order for anything to get done. Worse still, for all the glowing praise that has been showered on him for his supposed technical wizardry, he executed the painting incompetently. For a painter of his commission, this was simply inexcusable.

Leonardo had chosen not to use the tried-and-true method of fresco painting, almost certainly because it would have required him to work efficiently. In fresco painting, the paint is applied directly to wet plaster, so that when both dry, they form an inseparable union with each other. A fresco painter cannot waste time; he must move quickly to get the project done. Instead, Leonardo opted for a method that was completely unsuited to the task. He used tempera paints on a base of gesso; this ensured that the paint did not adhere deeply to the wall surface. Within less than a hundred years after Leonardo completed work, it was described by one viewer as "completely ruined." One can only imagine how this must have frustrated and enraged his patrons, who were paying him well to see meaningful results.

But Leonardo was impervious to the criticisms of others; living in his own world, and without a family to support, he could afford to spend his days wandering around the Italian countryside, pondering nearly everything that arrested his fancy. There is nothing wrong with this, of course; it has been the catalyst for productive genius since the beginning of time. But at some point, speculation must give way to application. Thought must be set aside in favor of execution. And this was where Leonardo faltered, over and over again. To provide another example of Leonardo's inability to get things done, we can point to the immense statue of a horse that he planned to construct. It was intended as an equestrian monument to Francisco Sforza, and has also been called the "Gran Cavallo" (Big Horse). As usual, he pored over every detail lovingly, as he was especially fond of animals. More than seventy tons of bronze were actually allocated for its casting. Leonardo completed a huge clay model of the horse in 1492, but this model was destroyed by invading French military forces in 1499. They used it for target practice.

Thus the Gran Cavallo remained like so many of Leonardo's abortive projects: unfinished and eventually forgotten. Leonardo's fame as a Renaissance polymath rests almost entirely on his voluminous notebooks, which were discovered long after his death. In these impressive collections, he records drawings and designs for all sorts of subjects: engines of war, agricultural inventions, natural history, geology, the activity of animals, mathematics, and similar subjects. We acknowledge his great abilities, of course. *But is "interest" in a subject area enough for one to claim recognition in that field?*

Where are the tangible fruits of his labors? Where are the actual inventions? And did these notebooks even exert any influence in history? The answer must be a resounding negative. Beyond their curiosity value, the notebooks do not contain any hidden engineering "secrets," nor were they the catalyst for any future discoveries. Popular mythology here as entirely obscured the reality of the situation. Leonardo never saw fit to edit or publish his drawings or speculations. The reason why was that he was simply too lazy to endure the arduous drudgery of putting a book together. It was easier to speculate. Even the drawings are much overrated in their inventive power. If we wish to find a polymath who actually has achievements to his credit, Benjamin Franklin cuts far more impressive a figure than does Leonardo. Leonardo had no practical experience with mechanics, metallurgy, or engineering, and this is evident in his drawings. Almost all of them are impractical, or would not work as he intended them to do. Even his notebooks do not seem to have inspired many later engineers or inventors. They have value in shedding light on Leonardo's personality, but beyond this, there is little that the world has gained from them. His fame rests largely on the romanticized image of him that later centuries would confer on him; but this halo obscured more than it revealed.

Some biographers have made exaggerated claims about these notebooks, finding in them evidence of "scientific researches" that "foreshadow" or "anticipate" or "inspire" the work of actual scientists centuries later. The very fact that historians have to resort to such vague qualifiers is testimony to Leonardo's inadequacy as a true scientist. It is true that Leonardo made significant and original investigations in anatomy (especially in the workings of the valves of the heart) and fluid dynamics; but these observations were never distilled into identifiable hypotheses that could be evaluated by others. Kepler, Tycho Brahe, Copernicus, and Galileo are rightly called scientists because they arduously collected data and then performed the labor of synthesizing that data into hypotheses. Leonardo failed in three of the most important duties of a scientist: the systematic recordation of data, regular collaboration with like-minded peers, and the dissemination of verifiable results. He was an artist with scientific inclinations, but he was not a scientist. What is so frustrating about Leonardo's scientific researches is that he lost interest in them at precisely the moment when intense concentration and labor were needed to reap the fruits of his experiments.

Leonardo published not one book, either during his life or posthumously. When he died in 1519 at the age of 67, he had only completed 15 paintings. This is a pitifully small number for an artist of his caliber. Contrast this to the inexhaustible energy of Michelangelo, who worked himself to death and slept with his boots on, eager for the start of a new day of work. *Genius is not enough*: it must be sharpened to a fine point by diligent application, discipline, and relentless work. And this Leonardo was maddeningly unable to do. There is an Arabic proverb that emphasizes the critical difference between thinking about something, and implementing something:

من تفكر اعتبر و من اعتبر اعتزل و من اعتزل سلم

And this means, He who thinks about things, takes examples from them, and he who takes such lessons, separates himself from other men; and he who separates himself from others, is saved (an adage from Freytag's *Arabum Proverbia* (III, no. 2395): *Qui de rebus cogitat, exemplum ab iis sumit, et qui exemplum sumit, ab hominibus se separat, et qui se separat, salvus est*). Stated another way, *cogitation and observation are not enough*: we must put our lessons into practice, and actually *produce results*.

95. Selection And Supervision Are Critical In Any Great Enterprise

I have lately been rereading Candace Millard's excellent *River of Doubt*, a narrative of Theodore Roosevelt's ill-fated sojourn through the Amazon in 1914. As is well known, the expedition was plagued by a lack of adequate food supplies and equipment. This fact nearly caused the entire project to unravel once it was deep in the Amazon. What strikes the reader is just how cavalier and inept Roosevelt was in handling the planning phases of the undertaking; I say this as a fervent admirer of the President in nearly everything else he did. But one must accept the faults of our heroes; we cannot turn a blind eye to their shortcomings, and gloss over obvious failings. Roosevelt's original plan was to conduct a moderately ambitious journey, with a select group of men, through the lands and rivers of several South American countries, including Brazil. It was intended to be an expedition that would observe the geographical and natural life of the regions it passed through. And this is all well and good: for it aligned with the ex-President's lifelong interests in natural history and geography. But the problems began with the implementation of the scheme.

Chief among these problems was a man named Father John Zahm. He was a Catholic priest and an instructor at Notre Dame University who was an interesting man in many ways: he had (supposedly) traveled widely in South America, published a book defending evolution (a big deal in those days), and was not without a certain avuncular charm. But he was also what we would today call a bullshitter. His claims of jungle exploration appear to have been greatly exaggerated; he was ignorant of the Spanish and Portuguese languages; he was in his sixties; and he had never been involved in an actual exploratory expedition. Worse still, he had an entitled and privileged attitude that became more and more manifest as the expedition progressed. As an example, he actually expected to be carried over rough terrain by native porters. But he had Roosevelt's ear, at least at first, and the president did not see anything wrong with indulging his delusions.

Zahm should have had no place on the expedition. His only credentials were that he knew Roosevelt, and had somehow convinced him that he was knowledgeable and competent. But Zahm was not the only problem. When he was tasked with equipping the expedition, Zahm turned to someone who had no experience in tropical exploration, a sporting-goods store clerk named Anthony Fiala. Zahm just invited Fiala into the group. Fiala was forty-four years old in 1913, and a cloud hung over his head. He had commanded a polar expedition several years earlier, and it had ended in disaster; he had failed to distribute the expedition's food and equipment supplies, with the result that half of the group's food stores had been lost in one accident.

This was not all. Fiala's only expedition "experience" was in a part of the world (the arctic) that had nothing to do with the Amazon. Fiala had no understanding of the type of food needed for Roosevelt's expedition. He burdened it with all sorts of idiotic and unnecessary luxuries, instead of the high-calorie survival fare that was really needed. As one reads of the planning phase of the expedition, one is shocked that no one thought to consult someone who had actually made tropical explorations. All of this might have been tolerable if the Roosevelt expedition had kept to its original plan of seeing known rivers and regions. But this is not how things developed. As the launch date approached, Roosevelt changed the entire character of the expedition: persuaded by others, he decided to explore an unknown Amazonian tributary known as the River of Doubt. This decision turned a reasonably challenging enterprise into an extraordinarily challenging one. No one knew anything about the River of Doubt, and the expedition would be venturing entirely into the unknown. It was not a place for amateurs, or even semi-professionals.

Roosevelt himself must accept responsibility for the shortcomings and mistakes that nearly cost him and his team their lives. It was one of his traits to see only the good in others; he often could be blind to the failings and character traits of those whom he worked with. Zahm was not an explorer, and he had no business getting within a hundred feet of the expedition; Fiala was little more than a clerk, and should have stayed in his department store. The fact that Roosevelt could not see these things is very much to his discredit. He had an unlimited supply of enthusiasm, grit, and optimism; but these things are not enough when facing an important enterprise. As commander, he had a responsibility to make sure that the right man was in the right place, and that he was not leading his men over a cliff. He was far too trusting of those who did not merit his trust, he did not supervise those he had chosen, and he was blind to the realities of what he would be facing.

All of this, it must be said, is surprising in Roosevelt. He knew how to put the right man in the right place, and understood the importance of professionalism. When he redesigned the coinage, he put Augustus St. Gaudens in charge; and when he built the Panama Canal, he made sure to put the task in the hands of America's best corps of engineers. So he knew how to get a job done. Yet somehow all of this experience failed him when planning the Amazon expedition. What we conclude from all this is that passion *is not enough*; a leader must have a streak of hard calculation, of careful planning and diligent preparation, in order for an important undertaking to succeed. A commander must look into the backgrounds and track-records of those in whom he places his trust. Delegation must never become an excuse for surrendering this duty of responsibility. He cannot be swayed by sentimentality or friendship in the construction of a team; and he must independently verify all claims of proficiency and achievement. Lives depend on meticulous preparation. The priority must always be the successful accomplishment of the mission, not the indulgence of the egos of others.

96. The Pitfalls And Vices Of Old Age

We are afflicted by different vices in different periods of life. While much energy is spent in discussing the pitfalls and failings of youth, it is just as important to be mindful of the pitfalls of old age. It seems to me that these are especially difficult to correct if not identified for what they are; and just as ivy may slowly encroach on a neighboring plant and choke the life out of it, so may the vices of old age bring what may once have been an admirable life to a miserable conclusion. This was what the humanist Paolo Giovio meant when he made this comment in the third dialogue of his *Notable Men and Women of Our Time* (*De Viris Et Feminis Aetate Nostra Florentibus*):

> I truly believe that these opinions are much mistaken. Old men evaluate the women of this era with debilitated eyes; frail and afflicted with physical shortcomings, they cannot appreciate what seizes the attention of young people's fervent and vigorous observation. Satisfied with their own lives, they seem to hold on tightly to the remembrance of long-lost pleasures. Images of pleasurable things, stamped on more ingenuous senses, still flash sharply in their minds; they visualize the things they see now with the same pleasure-criteria [*persimili iucunditate repraesentant*] they used when looking at things they once saw long ago, and intensely loved. [III.10]

This observation is an accurate one. Time moves forward, but the retained images in our minds of past pleasures endure. The harsh judgments of the old may very well be an attempt to resurrect these lost sensations, and bring them back to reality. But we cannot do this; we must find new pleasure, new enjoyments, and new images in life. The miseries of old age are most acutely felt by those men and women who have refused to carve out new pathways for their lives; they remain motionless in time, while the hourglass continues inexorably to empty. This is why it is so important for us to try to find new directions and meaning as our lives move advance. We cannot remain motionless: there must only be *forward, forward.*

Let me say here that objective advances and declines in standards and taste do happen. By any objective standard, there are periods of progress and decline in history, and I am not trying to say that all opinions of the old should be dismissed. It is unquestionably true that historical standards in education, morals, taste, virtue, fortitude, and character are not evenly distributed; there have been eras of great flourishment, and eras of conspicuous debasement. I think the pitfalls of old age can be identified as one or more of the following categories:

The failure to stay current with contemporary developments and trends. A society consists of its members, and it is incumbent on each member to stay abreast of current developments. A person cannot bury his or her head in the sand and pretend that the world does not exist. I see many older people who spend too much time pining away for how things used to be, instead of taking a good hard look at how they are now. This sort of perspective will inevitably lead them to make flawed judgments in things. We cannot, and should not, shut our eyes to developments in culture, news, politics, literature, and entertainment; I say it is a duty of each of us to stay current in these fields, at least to some degree.

The failure to carve out a new defining purpose. All of life changes as a person grows in age. What may once have been a goal, now may no longer be a goal. New objectives come to replace the old, or *should* come to replace the old. I have found that the happiest, and most productive, older people are those who have found a way to carve out a new life purpose for themselves as they retire from work. The most miserable elderly people are those who have never spent any time cultivating any independent interests. They sit at home, imprisoned in their houses, and fail to take action to improve themselves. What they refuse to understand is that it is *their* responsibility to take action; no one is going to come knocking at the front door. It is they who must find their own new mission. I recently saw a biographical film of heavyweight fighter Mike Tyson in which there were clips played of his original trainer, Cus D'Amato. The old man bluntly stated that training Tyson was what had given him his life's new purpose; without this, he added, "I would probably have nothing to live for."

The failure to interact with the young. This is a terrible shortcoming, as it seems to me that the young and the very old are admirably suited for each other. Youth benefits and blossoms when it comes into the warming rays, and nurturing waters, of old age's (we hope) wisdom and experience. And old age is invigorated and sustained by contact with the powerful Odic forces of the young; yet there must be a willingness on both sides for this interaction to take place. I believe it is up to the older party to initiate this sort of contact, as youth is often so distracted and impetuous as to be unable to accomplish this.

The failure to maintain physical fitness. Freshness of mind and perspective is engendered and promoted by a healthy constitution. Much has been written on this subject, and I can only add that vigor of body is a requirement for vigor of mind. If good habits have not been cultivated since youth and middle age, then it is inevitable that old age will become a torment of aching limbs and bodily malfunctions. A doctor cannot wave a magic wand and cure a patient's lack of discipline; it is the patient who must take charge of his or her own health. I can do no better here than to quote the Persian physican Rhazes (Abū Bakr Muhammad ibn Zakariyyā al-Rāzī), when he said the following in his great *Kitab al-Mansuri fi al-Tibb* ("Book on Medicine for Mansur," or كتاب المنصوري في الطب):

> When you can cure by a regimen, avoid having recourse to medicine; and when you can effect a cure with a simple medicine, avoid employing a compound one.
> With a learned physician and an obedient patient, sickness soon disappears.
> Treat an incipient malady with remedies which will not prostrate the strength.

The failure to appreciate the perspective of the young. It is often said that ossification of thought is a natural consequence of old age, but this is not something that I really believe. Of course, there is some natural slowing down of the machine; the fires of youth eventually come to be moderated by the cooling winds of painful experience. I am convinced that nothing prevents men and women in their eighties and nineties from enthusiastically listening to new perspectives and adopting new approaches. Lucretius tells us that life is nothing but flux and change, and we must come to believe this: nothing stands still. Even if youth is wrong, we must give them a fair hearing, if only to act as the brake to the car's gas pedal. As I see things, these are the major moral vices of old age.

97. Hercules And The Apple Of Athena

One of the fables of Aesop concerns Hercules and Athena. One day, Hercules was proceeding along a pathway in the mountains when he spotted an apple lying on the ground. Irritated at its presence, he decided to smash it with his club; and when he tried to do so, the apple doubled in size. Shocked, he swung his club at it again, this time determined to crush it completely. But he had misjudged the situation, for the apple now swelled to such size that it blocked the mountain pass through which he intended to travel. He did not quite know how to deal with this situation; he was in the habit of solving problems by bludgeoning them. Suddenly, the goddess Athena appeared before him, amused at his predicament. "It is no use to go on like this, comrade," she counseled him. "What you are experiencing is what it is like to become embroiled in conflict with others. If you leave matters alone, you can proceed with your life as before; but if you decide to engage them, they explode in front of you, hampering your progress." This is what the goddess said to Hercules.

Now we know this is sound advice in many situations. It normally serves no purpose to spend one's time engaged in petty squabbles with others. The conflict takes on a life of its own, and soon becomes unmanageable, dragging us down while wasting time and effort. Most of us have experienced this sort of thing in our lives. But with all due respect to Athena, can it really be said that one should never engage in conflict? And if so, when should we enter the fray, and when should we avoid it? These are the types of questions we really need answered. No one can go through life while avoiding conflict completely; there will be many times when we must respond to unjust or unfair attacks. What we really need to know is: *when should we desist, and when should we engage*?

The answer, of course, is not an easy one, and will always depend on the situation. Some miscalculate, and abstain when they should defend themselves, while some do the opposite, pointlessly expending energy in futile bickering. I think it should go without saying that one must fight back if one's vital interests are being threatened: if one is being unjustly accused, maligned, or attacked. We would even expand the scope of this zone of critical interest to include our close personal family members. So then the question becomes being able to identify one's vital interests. Some things should be ignored, and some must be addressed with vigor and ferocity.

The Renaissance humanist Giovanni Pontano (1426-1503), in his treatise *On Speech* (*De Sermone*) identified a number of different classes of speech personalities: *the flatterers, the affable, the urbane, the adulators, the gasping, the insipid, the prolix, the contentious, the verbose, the triflers, and the taciturn.* The experience of being able to identify these various personality types will assist us in deciding whether someone is worth responding to. An insignificant fool with no influence or significance is probably not worth a response, even if he attacks a vital interest. Here, as in so many other things in life, an observance of the mean is needed: *one must aim for a balance between defending one's legitimate interests, while letting insignificant irritations slide*. Some people love to get involved in pointless disputes. We must learn to identify such types, and understand their motivations. Pontano calls them the "contentious" (*contentiosi*), and describes them in this way:

> The complete opposite of adulators in their endeavors appear certain contentious men, whose nature and also endeavor are not only not to speak to please or gratify others, but on the contrary to oppose them and, nowhere or in any situation, to fear to offend anyone by speaking. Indeed, they both sow disputes willingly and eagerly take up ones sown by others, and rejoice in fostering and keeping them going. [*De Sermone* I.18; *Trans. By G. Pigman*]

But it is not just a matter of knowing personality types; we must have an understanding of *how* words and actions can threaten vital interests. I would suggest that the following zones of interest should be considered vital: reputation, honor, employment, close family members, and spouse or other loved ones. An attack on any of these zones of interest is significant and deserving of a response, as long as the other party is significant. Even when one does respond to an attack on a vital interest, one should only engage in this type of conflict for the minimum time needed to make one's point, and not a second longer. For no one has ever benefited from protracted conflict. This is one of the pitfalls that traps many; they make their point effectively, but then they refuse to let the matter rest. They feel a need to continue making the point over and over again, with the result that any goodwill they might have earned from others is quickly dissipated. Fight your corner, say your peace, and stand your ground; but once this has been done, comb your hair, straighten your collar, dust off your shirt, and keep walking.

98. What Are We, After All?

I was recently reading some of Cicero's letters to Atticus, and came across this sentence in one of them:

> Quid enim sumus, aut quid esse possumus? Domis an foris? [*Epistulae* XIII.10]

And this means, *What really are we, or what can we be? At home or outside the home?* Cicero's statement is made in the context of his shock over the death of a man he knew–named Marcellus–who had been murdered in Greece. The murderer was someone Marcellus believed was a friend; and yet things turned out as they did, where one friend was slain by another. Many centuries later, Petrarch voiced the same sentiments in the following words:

> Quid sumus? inquam; quam gravi, quam tardo, quam fragili corpore, quam caeco, quam turbido, quam inquieto animo, quam varia quamque incerta volubilique fortuna!
> [*Letter to Socrates*, c. 1349]

This means, *What are we? I ask. How heavy, how slow, how delicate is the body; how blind, darkened, and turbulent is the mind; how various, uncertain, and volatile is fortune!* Can anyone who has lived past the age of forty doubt for one second that this is true? Yet the variability of fortune is not the subject that I want to discuss here. I prefer to comment on something else, something derived from Cicero's sentence I have quoted above: *What really are we?* Do *I* know who I am? Do *you* know who *you* are?

Consider the experiences you have in foreign lands. Have you ever noticed that the people who know the least about a famous city are those who have lived their lives in that city? Is anyone more ignorant of Roman history than the Romans themselves? I am ashamed to say it, but in many cases you will find this to be true: ask a denizen of some famous city about some historical event or place in that city, and observe the gaping, blank stares from the other party. You can almost hear him thinking, *Oh, here we go, another one of these foreigners. Don't they know we have to earn a living? Who cares about things that happened fifty, one hundred, one thousand, two thousand years ago?* Well, I certainly do not sure I agree with this view. They *should* know their past. They should never stop thinking about the past; none of us should stop thinking about the past. Who would want to put out his own eyes or ears, or amputate one of his limbs? Even the Romans have lost their sense of identity, and all the world slides into somnolence.

But forget cities: consider ourselves. What do we really know about who we are? I know my thoughts and actions at the present time. And I believe I know my actions that took place ten, fifteen, or twenty years ago. Maybe even farther back. But here is the problem: when we recall past events, we are recalling them *now*, in the mind we have *now*, in the imaginative capacity we have *now*. But doesn't our mind change over time? Doesn't our personality change and evolve over time? I submit to you that I cannot have an accurate recollection of past events for this reason: I cannot grasp how my mind worked many years ago. I can recall events, but I cannot recall the workings of my mind. I will never be able to project my present mind back through time, across the years, to understand what I was like, say, in 1993. I cannot do this. Our memories are not reliable. I have tried to do this, but it is not really possible. It is not a matter of trauma; it is a matter of evolution. An organism hurtling through space and time cannot force itself backwards in time, to learn about its own thoughts. At best, it can catch glimmers of those thoughts, suspended like ghostly fragments in time, perpetually subject to obliteration through the encroachments of time's swirling mists.

And if you are being honest with yourself, you will also find out that you cannot do it, either. It is very frustrating, but it is true. Our personalities change over time; the very structure of our minds changes. Try it and you will see. Have you ever noticed that that it is almost impossible to think back many years ago, and to try to remember what you were actually thinking or feeling at that time? You cannot do it. This is because your current mind, your present mental composition, always gets in the way. I cannot reconstruct my mind from 1993, because my mind has changed. Therefore I can never really, truly remember what was going through my mind decades ago; that is, what I was thinking or feeling. You may think you can do this, dear reader, but I am convinced that this is only your present mind speaking for your old mind. The old mind is gone, and gone forever. It has been irretrievably replaced. If you want proof of this, you can easily prove it to yourself. Begin to keep a journal, and record your observations in it year by year. Then go and read it after five or ten years have elapsed. You will be disturbed at your own observations, your concerns, your various thoughts. Why is this? Because you have changed: you are reading something written by someone else.

So, if this is so, we must ask: who are we, really? Am I the man of 1993, 2002, 2010, or 2019? Or am I a composite of all of these? The answer is that you are the you of the present moment; but your present moment stands on the shoulders of all those moments that came before. You have evolved and developed, and you will continue to do so. This reality presents us with a conclusion that should inspire hope. For if it is true that there is no fixed "us," and that we change dramatically over time, *then it must be true that we can, through the power of the will, remake ourselves as we wish.* The iron can be recast, reheated, and forged into a new and different implement. Man has the power to remake himself in the image he chooses. Can there be any more inspiring knowledge than this? The dissatisfactions of the past can be swept aside, if only we can summon the strength to do so. And so I would say to my friend and companion Cicero: "Consul, you ask who are we, really? I say that we are who we make ourselves to be."

Let no man ever say he is trapped by the past, that he is a prisoner of fortune's fickle dictates; for he always retains within himself the power to break the Chain of Fate, and cast a new metal, a hardier metal of a more resilient composition.

99. Camels, Eyes Of Needles, And An Old Proverb

Readers are likely to have heard, in one form or another, the New Testament proverb, "And again I say to you, it is easier for a camel to go through the eye of a needle than for a rich man to enter the kingdom of God" (Matthew 19:24). The saying is an old one, and probably was in common currency centuries before its alleged utterance by Jesus. I find proverbs and adages interesting, as they contain not just worldly wisdom, but information about the culture and period in which they were composed. This point was recently impressed upon me while reading a forgotten bit of nineteenth-century travel literature, the Rev. F.J. Arundell's 1834 memoir *Discoveries in Asia Minor*.

I have a romantic fondness for old travel literature; from it we learn not just how societies operated in previous eras, but also how the arduous exercise of travel was conducted. Arundell relates the following observations (in Ch. 5) on the use of needles as he moves with his party through a remote part of Turkey:

> As we were ascending the hill, I saw something shining along the road, which proved to be one of the needles used by the camel-drivers for mending their camel-furniture. It was about six inches long, and had a very large, very long eye; it had evidently been dropped by one of the conductors of the caravan which was a little way ahead of us...The association of the needle with the camels at once reminded me of the passage which has been considered so difficult to be illustrated: "It is easier for a camel to pass through the eye of a needle, than for the rich man to enter the Kingdom of God."...Why should it not be taken literally? The needle, from its constant and daily use, must have held a prominent place in [ancient man's] structure of ideas and imagery; and we know how fertile the imaginations of these camel drivers were in furnishing us with proverbs and legendary tales...Why may not the impracticability of a camel's passing through the eye of his needle, even a common camel, much more the double-hunched gentleman of Bactria,

> have been a common expression to denote impossibility? How valuable the needle must be to the poor camel-driver, may be inferred from its loss. Should he have been so improvident to have had only one, the loss of it would be one of the greatest he could suffer, and when traveling through the desert, might even endanger his personal safety.

These comments help us understand how the adage of the camel and the needle's eye could have been created. In the modern era, we visualize a needle as something diminutive, something tiny and disposable. But to the dweller of the arid regions of the Middle East, it was something more significant. Arundell says that the needle he observed was about six inches long, with a large eye: this is an enormous needle. From this we can understand how a proverb might be crafted around the needle: it was a significant piece of equipment for a caravan-driver, and perhaps for all desert-dwellers.

We do not imagine such things when we hear ancient proverbs. We hear the word "needle," and immediately imagine some tiny sliver of metal, something entirely unworthy of serious contemplation. Yet, had we actually seen a real desert needle, we would better be able to appreciate not only the proverb, but the lives of the ancient dwellers of these regions. And in this little anecdote, so well-related by our Rev. Arundell, we can understand the importance and value of *travel*. Travel enables us to relate disparate things with each other; it assists us in making rational sense of this immeasurably complex world. Travel liberates, and explicates.

I am sure that there must be a specific Arabic word for this sort of large needle (rather than the generic إبرة), but I do not know what it is. Arundell goes on to speculate, equally plausibly, that there might be another origin of the "needle" proverb. In ancient times, obelisks were sometimes colloquially referred to as needles, and would be erected near the entrances to towns and cities. If two such "needles" were placed close beside each other as a portal, it would not be possible for a heavily-loaded pack animal or man to pass through them. Such a "rich man" would have difficulty passing through the "eye" of the two "needles." Language is our repository of culture, wisdom, and elegant truths.

100. The Chain Of Fortune Links The Fates Of Men

The British invasion of the Dardanelles in 1915 is a text-book example of how wishful thinking and imagination can override sound judgment and careful planning. The idea of knocking Turkey out of the war with an amphibious landing at Gallipoli, followed by a march on Istanbul, was in principle strategically sound; but as a practical matter, the British simply lacked the tools and leadership for the job.

Modern amphibious landing tactics had yet to be developed. The British had no proper landing craft, and were forced to rely on exposed wooden boats; they had no armor (tanks); they had no air support; they had inadequate naval gunfire support; with no frogmen teams, they had not done proper hydrographic surveys of the landing zone; they had not studied the strength of the currents near the beaches; and worst of all, they had dramatically underestimated the resolve of their enemy. The early Ottoman campaigns in the Sinai and the Caucasus had been utter disasters, and had convinced the Entente powers that Turkey would quickly fold when attacked directly. In this, they turned out to be very much mistaken.

The primary advocates of the Gallipoli campaign were Lord Kitchener and Winston Churchill. While personally brave, these men knew nothing of amphibious landings; their experiences in war had been limited to colonial adventures and the Boer War. It was the Japanese Army in the 1930s that would make great strides in developing amphibious landing tactics; the famous "Higgins boat" landing craft was modeled on Japanese designs observed by US Marine general Victor Krulak in military engagements in China before the Second World War. Without air support, naval gunfire, or armor, the invasion force was guaranteed to become bottled up on the Turkish beaches, and exposed to unrelenting fire until it was withdrawn. The British did not even have the element of surprise, as was used in Inchon in 1950 or during D-Day in 1944.

Modern concepts of combined arms had not yet emerged. They separated naval and infantry operations, instead of using them in unison to generate maximum force and momentum. Experience has shown that the only way to make an amphibious landing succeed is to hit the beaches with overwhelming force, and then immediately move forward without stopping for any reason. This never happened at Gallipoli. They first tried to force the Dardanelles using a naval attack; when this failed, the Turks were alerted to the inevitability of a landing somewhere along the coast. And they were prepared for the invaders.

For the Entente powers, the invasion had the aspect of an adventure; but for the Turks, it was a matter of survival. The difference in priorities is evident from the words of Col. Mustapha Kemal—a commander at Gallipoli who would later go on to become the founding president of the Turkish republic—who told his men:

> I don't order you to attack, I order you to die. In the time which passes until we die other troops and commanders can take our places.

Let us now take our leave of these technical matters, and direct our attention to the role of Fortune in human affairs. The following story appears in Eugene Rogan's *Fall of the Ottomans*. It reinforces an idea I have long subscribed to, which is that the fates of men are linked by the Chain of Fortune.

Private Robert Eardley was serving at Gallipoli with the Lancashire Fusiliers. In August 1915 his unit conducted an attack on Turkish lines near the Krithia road; he survived the attack and managed to reach the Ottoman trenches relatively unscathed. Leaping into the enemy trench, he saw a British soldier with bayonet fixed standing over a fallen, wounded Turk. The soldier was hot with the heat of battle, and wanted to plunge his bayonet into the man. "Here, you get out of my way," he told Eardley. "He has killed my mate and I am going to stick him." Eardley, feeling pity for the fallen foe, was persistent. He managed to talk his comrade out of killing the wounded man. He said: "Put yourself in his place, chum. One never knows...Don't do it. That's a good fellow." The soldier eventually accepted this argument and relented, storming off with a scowl. Eardley remained with the wounded Turk in the trench.

The two of them could not speak each other's language, but they did manage to communicate in a primitive way. Eardley dressed the enemy's head wound, gave him some water and tobacco, and propped him up in the trench with his coat. "I could see by his eyes that he appreciated the kindness," he would later write. Soon afterward, however, the tides of battle had turned. An Ottoman counterattack drove the British back to their original lines. Eardley was left to cover the retreat, but was captured by Turkish infantry as they retook the trench. As he looked over the parapet of the trench, he was pierced by the fixed bayonet of an attacking Turk. He wrote: "I felt a sharp piercing sensation—a burning feeling at the back of my left shoulder. I knew I had got the bayonet…I distinctly felt the thrust and drawing out." He passed out from loss of blood as dozens of Turks overran his position. When Eardley regained consciousness, he found himself surrounded by enemy soldiers with fixed bayonets, their eyes ablaze with hate.

They began to lower their bayonets and move steadily toward him. He was sure that he had come to the end of the road. Then, suddenly, he heard a voice crying out from among the enemy gathered before him. A Turkish man with a bandaged head, jabbering unceasingly in his native language, leaped between Eardley and the rest of the soldiers. Although he was still weak, he wrapped his arms around Eardley, covering him with his body, while gesticulating wildly with his comrades. In his dazed state, Eardley finally realized: this was the same man whose life he had saved in the first attack.

A Turkish noncommissioned officer finally arrived on the scene, and the wounded Turk explained the situation to him. Eardley could not understand what was being said, but it was clear that the Turk he had saved was now trying to save his life. After a few minutes of discussion, the noncommissioned officer said to Eardley in broken English: "English, get up. No one will harm you. You would have died if only for this soldier. You gave him water, you gave him smoke, and you stop bleed. You very good Englishman." He then patted Eardley on the back. As he was being led away into captivity, Eardley shook hands with his savior, with whom he could not communicate. But all that needed to be said was said with their eyes, and with their physical touch. "I shook hands with this Turk (and would give all I possessed to see this man again). As our hands clasped, I could see he understood, for he lifted his eyes and called 'Allah' and then kissed me. I can feel this kiss even now on my cheek as if it was branded there or was part of my blood." The two men parted, and never saw each other again. In such ways, and through such fortuitous interventions, are the fates of men linked by the all-powerful Chain of Fortune. It links all human affairs with its own unfathomable logic, which we dare not disregard.

101. On Choosing Between Alternatives

Many times in life we will be faced with a choice between two or more alternatives. As we weigh each option, it may become difficult to know which choice is best; the strengths and merits of each possibility cancel each other out, and we are left only with indecision. But I have come to think that this is for the most part an illusion: that there is always some factor that recommends one selection or the other. There is always a reason to choose one thing over another. It is our obstinate will that prevents us from seeing this clearly.

We know what needs to be done, but are reluctant to commit ourselves to a decision. Asking for advice sometimes helps, and sometimes does not; our friends will more often than not tell us what they think we want to hear. This is why we must find some way of imposing objectivity: that is, to look at the problem from a neutral, dispassionate perspective. Our task must be to find the deciding factor that will sway the decision one way or the other. And there always will be this deciding factor, no matter how close the two choices may be in appeal. One will always be preferable. There are some who say that, when in doubt, it is better to do nothing. I have found this to be a decent idea, and have used it now and then. But the problem is that, when I look deeper into myself, I find that it worked only in situations when I did not want to take any action anyway. My honest goal was procrastination, despite my excuses to the contrary. Procrastination garbed in royal purple is still procrastination. There will be times when some action of some sort needs to be taken.

Herodotus tells a story (VI.51-53) that illustrates this point. Sparta in ancient times had a custom of appointing dual, co-equal kings. Presumably this arrangement was meant to check the power of one with another, to prevent the possibility of a tyrannous aggregation of authority; we find a somewhat analogous system with the Roman republic's custom of having two consuls ruling together. According to Herodotus, the Spartans believed that when they originally settled in their present territory, the name of their king was Aristodemus, the son of Aristomachus. His wife Argeia gave birth to twins.

Soon after the birth, Aristodemus died. At that time, we are told, the Spartan custom was to have the eldest son made king. But this was not easy to determine, since both infants looked exactly alike and were of the same size and shape. The city elders asked Argeia, but she cleverly begged ignorance; she told them that the two boys looked indistinguishable to her also. Of course this was just a ruse, for a mother always knows the difference, but she was hoping that both sons might be made co-equal kings. At this point the Spartans were at a loss about what to do, so they sought the guidance of the Delphic oracle. The priestess told them, in typical opaque fashion, that they should make both boys kings, but should give greater honor to the eldest. The problem was that they could not decide which boy had been born first.

The problem was solved by a man from Messenia named Penites. He suggested that someone should watch the mother, and see which boy she fed and washed first. If she usually kept to a certain order, they would be able to tell which boy had been born first; but if she varied the order, then it was probably true that even she did not know which boy was eldest. So with this guidance in mind, the Spartans did as Penites suggested, and kept the mother under observation, without telling her what they were doing. They eventually saw that she would wash and feed the two boys in the same order, and naturally concluded that the one who received priority was the eldest. This boy was selected to be king, and was brought up at public expense. He was named Eurysthenes, and his younger brother was named Procles.

This, in any case, is the tale as related by Herodotus. For me this story conveys the point that there is always some way to choose between two very close alternatives, if we can only bring some objectivity to bear on the problem. Notice how, in the tale, the intervention of a neutral observer was required to make the determination: Argeia claimed she was unable to tell which of her boys was the eldest; so the Spartans had to deploy the services of a neutral observer. And I think this point holds true for very many things in life: we must find some way of stepping outside the problem, of getting outside the issue. Why is this so difficult to do? It is difficult because our judgment is clouded by passions, cupidities, preconceptions, and prejudices. These emotions lie to us, and tell us those things we want to hear. And this is why it is so important to discipline the passions, and to harness our latent powers of objectivity: it is the only way to pull away the obfuscating tangle of vines and brambles that prevent our penetration of the Thickets of Wisdom.

These thickets allow entry only to those with the right tool–the right machete–that can hack a way through.

102. The Merciful Filtration Of Memory

James Boswell, in his 1785 memoir *Tour to the Hebrides*, makes the following psychological observation:

> I have often experienced, that scenes through which a man has passed, improve by lying in the memory: they grow mellow. *Acti labores sunt iucundi* ["Past work is pleasant to recall"]. This may be owing to comparing them with present listless ease. Even harsh scenes acquire a softness by length of time: and some are like very loud sounds, which do not please, or at least do not please so much, till you are removed to a certain distance. They may be compared to strong coarse pictures, which will not bear to be viewed near. Even pleasing scenes improve by time, and seem more exquisite in recollection, than when they were present: if they have not faded to dimness in the memory. Perhaps, there is so much evil in every human enjoyment, when present–so much dross mixed with it–that it requires to be refined by time; and yet I do not see why time should not melt away the good and the evil in equal proportions; why the shade should decay, and the light remain in preservation.

I have noticed something similar with my own memories. Time planes down the jagged edges, and the bitterness of past events seems to melt away, leaving only the good. Why is this? Like Boswell, I "do not see why time should melt away the good and the evil in equal proportions." It is almost as if we have had some mysterious blessing conferred on us by Fortune: that only what is pleasant and good remains of the past, while the rest is banished from the consciousness. It must be some kind of defense mechanism, some biological necessity of survival; for perhaps the human mind would lose its balance if it remained constantly aware of life's iniquities and acerbity. I do not know. The loss of memory is no doubt an evil; but the filtration of memory must be counted as a good. It is not something that even requires conscious effort on our part; the unceasingly active mind performs this task on its own. The soul has this ability to adopt whatever form as may be needed for survival. As Ovid says,

> The spirit wanders, coming now here and now there,
> And adopts whatever form it wishes.
> From animals it moves into human bodies,
> And from our bodies to the animals,
> But at no time does it die. [*Metam.* XV.165-168]

There are some who make it a point of pride to say, "I will never forget." But when you probe beneath the surface of such statements, you will often find that such motivations are ignoble. Their desire never to forget arises from a frantic attempt to control that which they have no right to control. They wish to impose their will on others, and force others to feed an insatiable sense of grievance. How can this be counted a good thing? I say we should forget some things, and perhaps many things. Not all loss is tragic: some loss is merciful, and is to be embraced by the rational mind.

We should be grateful that we have this power of memory-filtration. Read the memoirs of those who have suffered: examine the writings of those who have been confined to prison camps, those who have endured catastrophic injuries, or those who have been witness to unspeakable events. You will find, if you look closely enough, some fond remembrances from even the most evil of times. So Hans von Luck, confined to a Russian prison camp at the end of the Second World War, proudly relates how he learned to knit stockings to earn extra income; or we hear of the Depression-era farmer in the American midwest, who engagingly recalls how he shoveled dust and dirt from his living room while mired in poverty. Time has filtered out the memories of the uncertainties, terrors, and insecurities. I can only think that if the gods truly wished to punish a man, they would take away his powers of forgetfulness.

103. What You Wish To Avoid, Fortune Compels You To Do

It often happens that we are forced to accept what we wish to avoid. Avarice, for example, defeats itself; and the miser who in futility clings to every penny finds himself compelled to part with greater sums than he might otherwise have spent. The health fanatic who obsesses about every morsel of food that goes into his mouth, or cup that is pressed to his lips, finds himself harassed by ailments and bodily infirmity, while the moderate enjoyer of pleasure scarcely has a need to visit the physician. The athlete fixated on avoiding injury brings it down upon himself. It is nothing more than a form of pride, a manifestation of the unreasoning human Will: this Will we have to control the universe. But Fortune does not allow such presumption on our part. There is a kind of balance in Fortune, you see, a balancing of the scales, that prevents our foolish desires from assuming undue importance. We are put in check by these Scales of Adrastia. I recently read another amusing example of this in Boswell's *Tour of the Hebrides*. The work is a travel journal of their visit to the Scottish highlands in 1773. Boswell and Johnson were discussing the amusing fate of a Scottish miser who did not have the wisdom to let go of his pennies.

This miser once was visited by a friend, an Irish harper. The harper performed for him, but the miser, as Boswell says, "could not find it in his heart to give him any money." Instead, the miser gave the musician a harp-key, which is a tool for tuning the instrument. The miser thought this key was of middling value; but it turned out to be ornamented with gold and silver, and contained a precious stone as well. It was worth between eighty and one hundred guineas. When the miser eventually discovered its value, he tried to take it back, but the harper refused. Boswell then relates his dialogue with Johnson on the matter:

BOSWELL. "I do not think O'Kane [the harper] was obliged to give it back." JOHNSON. "No, sir. If a man with his eyes open, and without any means used to deceive him, gives me a thing, I am not to let him have it again when he grows wiser. I like to see how *avarice defeats itself; how, when avoiding to part with money, the miser gives something more valuable.*" Col said, the gentleman's relations were angry at his giving away the harp-key, for it had been long in the family. JOHNSON. "Sir, he values a new guinea more than an old friend."

And here can be found an illustration of what we said above. Those who cling too tightly to their obsessions, those who seek to impose their unreasoning Will on the workings of Fortune, are reminded of their folly. The fool conserves his water while his house burns; he sets himself up as Fortune's equal, blind to the fact that he controls very little. Extremity in anything is never good, for it defeats its own purposes; moderation in all things is far wiser, and less costly. Loosen your grip, and you will find Fortune's judgments less harsh! Fateful irony is Fortune's way of restoring the balance in things. Modern man is in desperate need of periodic reminders that it is not he who runs the Universe; his arrogance has become unchecked, and knows few boundaries. We can try to evade this truth; and if it be thrown out the front door, it reenters through a side-window. *Quod evadere velles, fortuna te facere cogit*: what you wish to evade, Fortune compels you to do.

104. The World's Smallness, And The Permanence Of Noble Actions

The world is a much smaller place than we are aware. Things we do, actions we take, can have far-reaching effects that come back to us in ways we can never imagine. While events, places, and the flowing rush of time are shifting and transitory, the power of virtue is such that it transcends time and place. I was reminded of this recently after reading the Second World War memoirs of Col. Hans von Luck, a German commander who fought in all the major theaters of the European war.

He also served in North Africa was very close to Erwin Rommel, that tragic figure whose stature only seems to increase with time. Von Luck relates the following story about the capture of a fellow officer named Major Willi Kurz. Kurz is described as a "highly decorated commander admired by all and with whom I had bonds of true friendship." Von Luck only learned of this story in 1986, when he had a chance to meet his old friend again in Toronto, Canada; both of them were, of course, old men by that time, but certainly knew something about survival and tenacity. As the war was winding down in 1944, Kurz found himself in the hands of the Americans, who had overrun his sector in the Western front. He was detained along with many of his comrades, grateful, no doubt, that they had not been captured by the Russians.

A few days after his capture, Kurz was standing around the courtyard of the detention center, talking with some people. Suddenly, an announcement came over the camp's loudspeaker: "Major

Willi Kurz, report to the gate!" A military police detachment appeared to retrieve him; they told him he was to be taken for an interrogation. He was brought before an American officer. The passage below describes, in Kurz's words (as related by Von Luck), what happened next:

> I still wore all my medals and insignia of rank. On stepping into the large room I saw American officers lined up on either side to form a long aisle, down which I was led to a huge table, at which sat a general and a row of senior officers. A court-martial, I thought, but what for? As I arrived at the table, the general and his officers stood up.
>
> "Are you Major Willi Kurz of the 21st Panzer Division?"
>
> "Yes, I am." I still didn't know what was going on.
>
> "Did you belong to Regiment 125 under Colonel von Luck and were you in action at Rittershoffen, in Alsace?"
>
> "Yes, that is so. They were probably the hardest fourteen days I went through on any front." Were they going to punish me now for Rittershoffen?
>
> "I am the commanding officer of the 79th U.S. Infantry Division, which fought against you in Rittershoffen; these men here are my staff and behind you my officers have formed an aisle in your honor. In the name of all my officers and men, and myself, I should like to show your regard and appreciation for the brave conduct of your men. We owe you our respect."
>
> I was speechless and struggled to hold back my tears. After the heavy fighting at Rittershoffen and the last difficult months and my wound, now suddenly this great gesture by our enemy. I finally pulled myself together and replied.
>
> "May I also express our respect for you, General, and your division. We admired your courage and the doggedness with which you defended the villages of Hatten and Rittershoffen, although three

> of your battalions were encircled at times for days on end. We were particularly impressed by the way you finally managed to disengage, by night, without our noticing. When you had gone, we were all of the opinion that in Rittershoffen there had been no victor and no vanquished. In the morning after your withdrawal, my commander, Colonel von Luck, played a chorale on the undamaged organ of the church, at which our men and the sorely tried civilians were moved to tears."
>
> "In the next few days," the General resumed, "I should like you to talk over with me and my officers how you on the German side conducted the engagement at Rittershoffen, what your problems were, and your tactics. I believe we can learn something from you."

This is the moving anecdote of Willi Kurz as it is related by Von Luck. I cannot help but be affected by this story; out of all the carnage and devastation of the war, there emerges moments of true chivalry, worthy of some engagement between combatants of the medieval period. Kurz's exemplary conduct had not gone unnoticed; it was remembered, and it made a big difference in his treatment as a captive. We may be only creatures of flesh and blood, of corporeal substance; but such substance can produce things of great value. Plutarch reminds us of this in the following quote from his essay *On Moral Virtue* (4):

> And they say that Zeno on one occasion, going into the theater when *Amoebeus* was playing on the harp, said to the pupils, "Let us go and learn what music can be produced by guts and nerves and wood and bones, when they preserve proportion and time and order."

Now what Plutarch meant to illustrate by this quote was this: even bodies composed of lowly corporeal substance are capable of producing the most sublime, beautiful things. So it is with us; the music generated by each man is his conduct, and how he reveals himself to the world. Each man's music is generated by the vibrations of his soul; and that music may be either sonorous and sublime, if his soul is good, or it may be foul and wretched, if his soul be corrupt. Three influences drive the soul forward: power, passion, and habit. And if these three components are under the restraint and guidance of reason, the natural result is an unbalanced, corrupt soul, capable of nothing but evil. Right conduct always confers greatness on those who practice is. The medieval Arabic writer Al-Mustanjid once wrote to the epistolary Ibn Rabada,

> If you aspire to command, act uprightly; then, even if you wish to reach the heavens, you will succeed. The [Arabic letter] *alif* (ا), one of the written letters of the alphabet, is placed at the head of the others because it is upright.

These words are most assuredly true. Great actions reverberate more loudly in a small container, than in a larger one; and no one should doubt that the world we live in is a small one. We all know many anecdotes that confirm this. Colonel Von Luck was himself captured by the Russians in 1945 and was shipped off to a prison camp in the Caucasus. There he once had the opportunity to speak to the camp commandant. This commandant asked him where he had fought in Russia, and with what units. Von Luck recalled the conversation as follows:

> "In the middle sector, with the 7th Panzer Division, via Smolensk and Vyazma to Klin and Yakhroma, north of Moscow."
>
> "Tell me about Yakhroma," he went on, "exactly when were you there?" [said the commandant]
>
> I was surprised by is interest but told him. "In December 1941 I advanced with my tank reconnaissance section via Klin to the Moscow-Volga canal and was able to cross it, the first unit to do so, at Yakroma, about 30 to 40 kilometers north of Moscow. I can well remember how we went into a little Russian inn to get warm. On the table stood the steaming samovar and an almost untouched breakfast, which we ate up with a good appetite." I was interrupted by a roar of laughter.

> "That was my breakfast. I was a colonel in the reserve and during your surprise attack I had to leave Yakhroma and my breakfast rather abruptly. So small is the world, *polkovnik*, now you are here as a prisoner of war, and I am the boss of this town, in which I found myself at the end of the war…"

See, reader, how these two men crossed each other's path as enemies at one time, and then, some years later, met again in entirely different circumstances! So small is the world! And yet this fact should serve as an encouragement and an incentive. For it reminds us that we can truly make a difference in this world through great deeds of character, and through the nobility of virtue.

105. Taming The Soul's Turbulence

In our lives we often encounter people whose behavior seems to make no rational sense. I am referring to people who do things that seem to be against their own self-interest: those who say one thing, but do something else. We ourselves can fall into this trap on occasion. It is almost as if there exists some morbid consciousness in all of us, a voice calling out for us to exactly what we should not do. Different ages and eras have interpreted this negative aspect of the soul in various allegorical ways. For me it is enough to acknowledge its existence, its omnipresence, and its destructive power. There is a certain turbulence in the soul which can manifest itself in varying degrees of tumescence; at times it is a moderately placid sea, and at other times it is all white-capped, billowing waves, battering the hull of our ship. Petrarch wrote a letter in 1354 to Giovanni Aghinolfi (Giovanni of Arezzo) in which he stated:

> We suffer from the bad acts we have done, and adverse consequences often fall back on the head of him who commits such acts. We are not kept down by others, nor is it right that we should be…
> [*Patimur mala quae fecimus, et saepe in caput auctoris poena revertitur. Non aliunde premimur, nec oportet…*]

Petrarch then goes on to quote the title of a work by John Chrysostom that reinforces this point: *No One Can Be Harmed Except by Himself* (*Nisi A Semet Ipso Neminem Laedi Posse*). Now of course we all know that this is true only to a certain extent: outside oppression can exist, and one can very much be harmed by others. But if we think about this, and carefully examine our own life and the lives of others who are experiencing problems, we can easily see that Petrarch's point is true more often than it is not true. We are the creators and authors of most of our problems, and it is for us to remedy such problems. To take a different position as a matter of faith is to surrender control of one's free will—insofar as it exists outside of Fortune—and amounts to abandoning the responsibilities of life.

I was watching a documentary the other day about the construction of a massive sarcophagus to house the radioactive remains of the Chernobyl nuclear reactor. When the reactor exploded in 1986, its destructive debris was spread over a wide area. The reactor itself was entombed in a hastily assembled edifice that almost immediately began to fall apart. The site constantly emits gamma rays and other radiation, and the only way to prevent a recurrence of the problem is to enclose it once again in an immense, permanent dome. This "shell," if we may call it that, will contain and suppress all the waves of poison emanating from the ruined and exposed reactor core.

I mention this in order to make the following analogy. We can see the distressed soul as akin to this ruined reactor: it is constantly emitting harmful radiation, and can contaminate others who spend too much time within its range. It is this toxic nature that causes such people to do things that are obviously against their better interests. Now, you may say, "The reason why so-and-so does things against his own interests is because he has a drug addiction problem. It is a chemical matter, and not a moral or ethical matter." And my answer to this would be: "Yes, this may be true as far as that goes, but what made him become a drug addict in the first place? What agony of soul, what inner turbulence and instability, caused him to seek relief in drugs in the first place?" It is clear that if we go to the root of most personal problems, we can find some lack of alignment in the soul's constitution, which in turn manifests itself as a moral or character problem. I think this is why St. Augustine said the following words in his *Confessions* (VIII.9):

> Therefore there is no grotesque division between "wanting" and "not wanting," but rather a sickness of the mind. When it is voluntarily raised up, it does not rise up completely, but is dragged down by one's habits. Thus there are two wills, since one of them does not control everything, and what is present in one is absent in the other.
> [*Non igitur monstrum partim velle partim nolle, sed aegritudo animi est, quia non totus assurgit, voluntate sublevatur, consuetudine pregravatur, et ideo sunt duae voluntates, quia una earum tota non est, et hoc adest alteri quod deest alteri.*]

So we have a sickness of the mind at work. The better instincts do not "rise up" completely, because they are dragged down by the negative forces of habit. This explains why we often do things that are against our own interest. There is not just one tugging influence on the soul: there are, in fact, two forces competing for the soul's direction. We have the will, and we have the force of habit. Habit is like inertia: it carries a certain momentum of its own, and wants to resist any kind of positive change. So how can we learn to restrain this rebellious soul, this soul that spews out harmful rays like the melted core of the Chernobyl reactor? The answer is that it must be tamed by individual force of will: the will must, like the shell entombing that reactor just mentioned, demonstrate its dominance over it. It must smother the soul's destructive, negative aspects. And this grappling, this wrestling, can take years of effort. I have used the language of conflict in describing it, because conflict is exactly what it is.

In Virgil's *Georgics* (IV.387 *et seq.*), the poet provides a most relevant image along these lines. Cyrene tells Aristaeus that "in the Carpathian gulf of Neptune" there exists a soothsayer named Proteus, who goes about in a chariot drawn by fish and horses. Cyrene tells him that he must seize this Proteus, put him in chains, and make him reveal his secrets:

> For without force, he will not give up his secrets;
> and you will not sway him with prayers.
> Use decisive force and clap him in chains,
> His hollow tricks will eventually be broken around these.

Persuasion and mind games only work up to a certain point. You cannot subdue a radioactive force with benedictions and prayers. You must house it, contain it, and entomb it under a sarcophagus. This is the method that must be used in taming and subduing the wayward soul. It will resist attempts to control it, of course. There is that competing force of "habit" that Augustine mentioned in the previous quote, and this force pulls the soul in the opposite direction. Some will be successful in mastering themselves; some will be moderately successful, and some will not be successful at all, and will remain a slave to their own baser natures. A man does not change until he wants to change: until he wants to clap his Proteus in chains, and force this imp to submit. Some have the strength to accomplish this; and some do not even wish to try. In the end, each person must decide for himself, and live with the consequences.

106. Be A Horseman, Not A Rider

Philo of Alexandria, in his essay on agriculture (*De Agricultura*), points out that there is a difference between an ordinary tiller of the ground, and an actual farmer; and that there is also a clear difference between a shepherd and someone who just tends to sheep. In the same way, he tells us, there is a great difference between a rider of a horse and a true horseman. This difference exists not just in the experience and habits of he who sits atop the horse; the difference lies in their respective carriages, manners, and degrees of ability to control the animal carrying them along. Along these lines, Philo says:

> Therefore the man who gets on a horse without any skill in horsemanship, is correctly called a rider, and he has given himself up to an irrational and restive animal, to such a degree that it is absolutely inevitable that he must be carried wherever the animal chooses to go, and if he fails to see beforehand a chasm in the earth, or a deep pit it has happened before now that such a man, in sequence of the impetuosity of his course, has been thrown headlong down a precipice and dashed to pieces. But a horseman, on the other hand, when he is about to mount,

> takes the bridle in his hand, and then taking hold of the mane on the horse's neck, he leaps on; and though he appears to be carried by the horse, yet, if one must tell the truth, he in reality guides the animal that carries him, as a pilot guides a ship. For a pilot too, appearing to be carried by the ship which he is managing, does in real truth guide it, and conducts it to whatever harbor he is himself desirous to hasten. [XV.67]

So we have this analogy of the rider and the horseman. But to what purpose, this analogy? It is clear that he intends us to see this as a description of the soul. "The horses are appetite and passion…of a slavish disposition, and rejoicing in all kinds of crafty wickedness…And the rider and charioteer is one, namely, the mind." When a man mounts a horse with competence, confidence, and ability, he is a horseman; when he does so with inexperience, carelessness, or lack of respect for the horse, he is then nothing but a rider. An incompetent cannot keep control of the reins; they fall from his hands, and the horse wanders this way and that. The rider may even be thrown off, injured, or trampled, or dragged along to his death behind the horse.

In this analogy the horseman represents the mind, and the horse represents the baser passions and appetites. He who can make use of his mind correctly, can control his baser instincts, and thereby steer his mount in ways that are productive. But the undisciplined fool, who lacks experience, does not guide his appetites: he is guided by them, and these quickly lead to his own ruin. We see this truth played out with inevitability all the time; all we have to do is look around, and observe. Now we are often told that a man's choices in life are indicators of his fate. What is often not mentioned, or what is mentioned obliquely, is that what we choose *not to do*, is often more important that what we affirmatively choose *to do*. What we avoid can be of momentous consequence. For you will often find, as you go through life, that many others around you will try to pull you into their habits and schemes. You will be encouraged to let your horse–that is, your appetites and passions–roam free. You will be told that you do not need to become a horseman, and that being a plain rider is good enough. Others will try to make you a participant in their dramas, going so far as even to try to clothe you in their costumes, and write your stage dialogue, as if you were some sort of Elizabethan dramatic actor.

For corruption and frivolity love association; they cannot exist except by drawing others into their nets. But in allowing this to happen, you set the stage for your own ruin. Every ship, caught in the grip of a tempest, can only sustain the force of so many waves; and after this, it will become upended and sink below the waves. Philo quotes an ancient writer–he does not say who it is, and I cannot locate the source of the quote–who advises:

> I will never engage in such a contest as that in which he who wins is more dishonored than he who is defeated. [*De Agricultura* XXIV.107]

The meaning of this quote is made very clear: "Do you, therefore, my friend, never enter into a contest of evil, and never contend for preeminence in such practices, but rather exert yourself with all your might to escape from them. And if ever, being under the compulsion of some power which is mightier than yourself, you are compelled to engage in such a strife, take care to be defeated without delay." The man who desires to live well must refuse to participate in contests of evil. He must refuse to follow paths of iniquity and evil that he has been encouraged to follow. The prisons, the asylums, and all the miserable corners of this earth are populated with souls who were either unable or unwilling to refuse such invitations. They voluntarily chose to follow destructive paths, either through indiscipline, ignorance, or foolishness; and they were forced to endure the consequences, just as the inexperienced horse rider found himself thrown off his mount and crippled.

So you must refuse to participate in such evil contests and games. To be "defeated" in them is an honor; and he who is so defeated is actually a conqueror. Those who "win" at such games are no more than fools living on borrowed time; you should imagine the crown of laurels on his head to be composed of nothing more than the excrement of a beast. Your conduct should announce to the world, "I do not participate in contests of evil and corruption. Crown these other men your Kings of Corruption, praise them to the skies, and observe how goes the trajectory of their lives!"

So abandon all these unworthy contests: they are pursuits not worth pursuing. Direct your energies towards finding worthy endeavors for your time and effort; and although the path of virtue is a constant effort, know that it is the path of true freedom. Although no man is an island, he yet finds it necessary, in this modern age, to dig entrenchments around his fortress, and to man his own watch-towers: for no one else will perform this function for him. No man can escape his confinement within himself, and so therefore must acquire the skills to master himself, and become a *true horseman*, instead of a *rider*. I find it relevant, in this context, to close with a few lines from a song mentioned by Boswell in his *Tour of the Hebrides*:

> Every island is a prison
> Strongly guarded by the sea;
> Kings and princes, for that reason,
> Prisoners are, as well as we.

107. On Hospitality

In taking the measure of a man's cultural refinement, we must examine the degree to which he is practiced in the art of hospitality. And when I say *art*, I mean this in a literal sense. The arts are not inborn; they must be studied and honed with constant use. A culture that teaches its members how to treat guests is a confident one; it is a culture that has, to some degree at least, liberated itself from the oppressions of acquisitiveness and greed, and has embraced some aspects of the communitarian ethic. It is also a culture that understands the value of *reciprocity*: the idea that a good turn done for one today, may mean a good turn done for oneself tomorrow.

This is one of the reasons why hospitality was so prized among the Arab bedouins of old. They understood that in a harsh environment, goodwill begets goodwill, and that the man who grants a favor today may himself need one at some point in the future. The desert is a landscape unsuited to individualist effort, and survival hinges on the activity of tribes, families, and clans: human courtesies have always originally evolved for some practical reason. And yet this art seems to be in serious decline now. Both the giver and the recipient of hospitality today appear to be unsure of themselves; they do not know quite what they should be doing. It is either this, or they simply do not care. The rule is not universal, of course; I have been fortunate to have entertained guests, and to have been entertained by hosts. But the creeping rise of vulgarity in our society has not spared any of the old arts. You see people who show up to an invited home with no concept of how to handle themselves; it never enters their minds, for example, even to bring a token gift. And when they are in the position of having to host others, they exert no effort at all to make their guests feel welcome or comfortable.

For me the cardinal rules of a guest are: to bring some kind of gift to the host's home (I prefer a bottle of decent wine), not to overstay one's welcome, and not to cause offense with uncalibrated speech or actions. For a host, my rules would be: to put in some basic effort to clean one's house and make it presentable, to have some kind of food or drink available, and to engage the guest in some kind of meaningful interaction. One does not invite someone over one's house and then abandon him on the sofa to play video games in the next room, or leap about with a dog in the back yard. Along these lines, I remember a recent comment in James Boswell's *Tour to the Hebrides*, a travel account of his and Samuel Johnson's trek through the Scottish highlands in 1773. Boswell astutely noted the following comment by his friend:

> He [Johnson] was angry at me for proposing to carry lemons with us to [the Isle of] Skye, that he might be sure to have his lemonade. "Sir," said he, "I do not wish to be thought that feeble man who cannot do without any thing. Sir, it is very bad manners to carry provisions to any man's house, as if he could not entertain you. To an inferior, it is oppressive; to a superior, it is insolent."

I thought that this comment by Johnson showed a high degree of sensitivity to the feelings of others. It is acute, and it is perceptive. He was aware that showing up at a host's house with a bag of lemons, as if they were some kind of indispensable medicament, would be perceived by a host as strange and irritating. The fact that he would think in this way demonstrated he was a refined, civilized man. Yet I can imagine that not many people today would be this courteous. They would bring the lemons, and the host's feelings be damned. They would see themselves as the center of attention, and would use the lemons as the vehicle by which they could garner even more attention.

People were so much more refined in ages past. You catch glimpses of the old ethic when you are exposed to literature. They were both more formal, and less formal, at the same time. The French writer François-René de Chateaubriand, when he was visiting the United States in the early 1790s, was granted an audience with George Washington. Chateaubriand was not an important man, yet Washington readily ate dinner with him; and the record of their meeting portrays the president as a perfect host. He is polite, but not ingratiatingly so; he is formal, yet somehow still avuncular; he is experienced and worldy, yet neither boastful nor long-winded. It is difficult to imagine any public figure being able to strike this balance today. Compared to our ancestors, we seem much like savages when it comes to the refined arts.

Hospitality can on occasion turn to hostility. A good example of this can be found in the career of Hannibal, during the period of his life after the defeat at Zama. The great Carthaginian general found himself branded an outlaw, and forced on the run, once the fortunes of war turned against him. After the Second Punic War, he fled to King Antiochus in Syria, whom he tried to enlist in a war against the Romans. Antiochus even made plans to land an army in Italy, but these plans came to nothing; he was routed in the end, and Hannibal had once again to take flight. This time he stopped in Crete to seek asylum with the Gortynians; but the canny Hannibal sensed something was wrong with the behavior of his hosts.

He was carrying a great deal of money with him, and news of this had leaked out. He correctly suspected the Cretans of planning to rob or kill him. As always, he discovered a ruse to extricate himself from this situation. As the historian Cornelius Nepos tells the story, he got hold of several large *amphorae* (earthen jars), and filled them with worthless lead ingots; he then topped them off with a layer of gold and silver coin, so that upon cursory inspection the jars appeared to be filled with money. With several prominent Cretan citizens as witnesses, he deposited these jars of "money" at the temple of Diana, which was a secured facility. Guards were posted at this temple, not so much to keep intruders out, but to prevent Hannibal from coming back and claiming his funds. Now Hannibal also had a number of small hollow bronze statues with him, and these he secretly filled with his real money; he then dumped these items in the courtyard of his house. So when he slipped away from Crete, he was able to take the apparently worthless statues with him as baggage, while abandoning the jars of lead at the temple.

The Cretans thought they had gotten the better of Hannibal when they heard he had left the island; but upon opening the *amphorae*, they were enraged. So did the great Hannibal punish the greed and malice of his hosts. *Sic conservatis suis rebus*, says Nepos: *in this way he preserved his valuables*. Not every refuge is offered for noble motives; not every host is altruistic; and not every man whose lips move in friendship harbors good intentions in his heart. It seems to me that, if hospitality is to mean anything at all, it must be based on good faith: no gesture that is done with a malignant heart can ever be called hospitable; and as Cicero has told us, no action can ever be called morally good that is based on expediency alone.

108. The Armor Of Virtue

The Hellenistic philosopher Philo of Alexandria made this compelling analogy in his essay, *Every Good Man is Free* (*Quod Omnis Probus Liber Sit* V.26):

> I have before now seen among the competitors in the pancratium, at the public games, one man inflicting all kinds of blows both with his hands and feet, all of them with great accuracy of aim and omitting nothing which could conduce to victory, and yet after at time fainting and desponding, and at last quitting the arena without the crown of victory; and the other who has received all his blows, being thoroughly hardened with great firmness of flesh, and being touch and unyielding, and filled with the true spirit of an athlete, and invigorated throughout his whole body, being like so much iron or stone, not at all yielding to the blows inflicted by the other, at last, by the endurance and resolution of his spirit, defeating the power of his adversary so as to obtain a complete victory. And the condition of the virtuous man appears to me very much to resemble that of this person. For having thoroughly fortified his soul with strong and powerful reasoning, he so compels the man who is offering him violence to desist from weariness, before he himself can be compelled

> to do anything contrary to his opinion of propriety. But perhaps this is incredible to those who do not know by experience that virtue is of the character that I have mentioned, just as that other case would be to those who have never seen the combatants in the pancratium. But nevertheless it is strictly true.

The physical contest called the pancratium was an ancient sport that combined boxing and wrestling. I suppose its closest modern equivalent would be our "mixed martial arts" contests of today; there were few rules to these bouts except that biting and eye-gouging were not allowed. Now what Philo is emphasizing here is the fortifying power of virtue. A man's mastery of the masculine virtues protects him and shields him from the iniquities of the world, in the same way that a hardened fighter can absorb with resilience the blows of his opponent. The converse of this point is beyond dispute, as experience shows: he who pays no attention to the cultivation of the virtues is like a man who enters a plague ward in a hospital without having received any immunization for the disease. He is entirely exposed to harm. Virtue is a stabilizer, a rudder, and a guiding light: "For as folly is a light thing easily tossed about in every direction, so, on the contrary, wisdom is a well-established and immovable thing of a weight which is not easily agitated."

And this is the reason why the wicked man, or the foolish man, is so vulnerable to the injustices of Fate. We should not be surprised at all that the truly wise man is far outnumbered by fools, wicked men, and lazy men. The majority will generally prefer indolence and amusement to industry. The virtuous man radiates goodness like a phosphorescent source; he emanates his qualities as the sun emits its rays. Whatever is beautiful, is exceedingly rare. Another reason why virtuous men are so rare is because they often find it more conducive to their peace of mind to withdraw from the main currents of society; they grow tired of the constant distractions and absurdities that are distressing features of modern life. The Greeks of antiquity talked about their "Seven Sages" or "Seven Wise Men"; and the fact that they felt the need to number them with digits less than those found on two hands, shows us just how few in number such men truly were.

Such wisdom, of course, was not confined just to the Greeks. Philo also talks about an Indian philosopher—he calls him a "gymnosophist," indicating that he probably also practiced yogic exercises—named Calanus, who was also mentioned by the historian Arrian in his history of Alexander the Great. When the Macedonian king was in India, he heard the reputation of this great Indian thinker, and desired Calanus to accompany him on his campaigns. When Calanus refused this invitation, Alexander was incensed, and threatened to take him along by force; he was not accustomed to being refused. Philo says that Calanus sent Alexander a letter explaining himself in the following way:

> Calanus to Alexander, Greetings.
> Your friends are endeavoring to persuade you to apply force and compulsion to the philosophers of the Indians, though not even in their sleep have they beheld our actions. For you will be able indeed to transport our bodies from place to place, but you will not be able to compel our souls to do what they do not like, any more than you would be able to make bricks or timer utter words. We can cause the greatest troubles and the greatest destruction to living bodies. Now we are superior to this power... there is no king nor ruler who will ever succeed in compelling us to do what we do not choose to do. And we are in no respect like unto the philosophers of the Greeks, who study speeches to deliver to a public assembly...our speeches which are short have a power different from that of our actions and secure for us freedom and happiness.

This is what Calanus wrote to Alexander the Great. While defiant, his words nevertheless have a noble ring; for nothing is more slavish than the debasement of flattery. He did not fear this powerful foreigner, who had brought all the world under his sway; if anything, he was all the more dismissive of the Macedonian. His attitude towards the impetuous Greek was something like, "Look at you, Alexander. You are not much more than a temporary irritant to our land; in a few years, you will be gone. But we, and our teachings, will still remain." And so it proved to be.

Along these lines a story is told of the Greek philosopher Diogenes the Cynic. There are many anecdotes circulating from antiquity about his wisdom and calmness of mind, his *tranquilitas animi.* He was once captured by bandits who refused to offer him much food. He did not beg his captors for more nourishment, but endured his lot with measured determination. He then learned that he was to be sold as a slave, along with some other captives. Diogenes's fellow captives were crushed by this news, but he gave them heart, saying, "Let go of being miserable. Take what fortune deals you, and adjust." When Diogenes was brought up to the slave auction block, he was approached by a prospective purchaser. This rich man asked Diogenes, "So, what do you know?" The philosopher's response was, "I know how to govern men." This answer shows us just how great a man Diogenes was: he knew that wisdom and virtue were the keys to the governance of men, and he valued these things above all others. This was what he meant by his response.

No one can doubt the truth of this. Great men, men of wisdom and virtue, have something within them that radiates outwards like an inner light; external circumstances cannot extinguish this light. If anything, such adversity makes it shine even more brightly. And this is why we must always seek the company of such noble men, and shun any kind of association with the baser, meaner types. When Jason was putting together his crew of Argonauts, he made a point of selecting only the best, noblest, and most courageous types of men; he had no desire to pollute his band with the inclusion of pleasure-seekers or braggarts. He wanted only noble souls with him, not selfish individualists. For such types of men add nothing to the pursuit of great enterprises.

When we make the pursuit of masculine virtue our goal, we hammer out, plate by plate, our own personal suit of armor. It protects us from the blows and wounds of fate, just as Philo observed in the combats at the pancratium. Know that we are the blacksmiths of our souls. It is a lifelong task. We forge the metal, we temper the steel, we pound the rivets, and we hammer the plate. Let this be the focus of our training and education. This armor of virtue protects us, stiffens the resolution of the soul, and grants us the capability to pursue all noble and transcendent purposes.

109. The State Of Common Life

In 1773 Samuel Johnson and his friend James Boswell made a journey through some of the more remote parts of Scotland. Each of them wrote his own account of the journey, and I am currently absorbed in reading Johnson's impressions in his *Journey to the Western Islands of Scotland.* As always, he stimulates and fascinates: his eye for detail is superb, and like the best of writers he combines wit, dry observation, and philosophic pronouncements. He was in his early sixties when he undertook this journey; his friend Boswell was decades younger. One has to admire the hardiness of the old man. We cannot really say that Scotland was wild in those days, but travel to the Hebrides could not be described as a comfortable outing. At one point the pair pass through Bamff, which I assume to be a town; there Johnson notes that Scottish windows are so constructed that they cannot be opened or closed with ease. He labels them "incommodious," and from here proceeds to this comment:

> But it must be remembered that life consists not of a series of illustrious actions, or elegant enjoyments; the greater part of our time passes in compliance with necessities, in the performance of daily duties, in the removal of small inconveniencies, in the procurement of petty pleasures; and we are well or ill at ease, as the main stream of life glides on smoothly, or is ruffled by small obstacles and frequent interruption. The true state of every nation is the state of common life.

This last sentence is what resonates. How often do we overlook this fact! Outside the courts of kings or the offices of presidents and senators, the rhythm of life goes on as it always has; people work, play, and divert themselves with the amusements that their purses and constitutions may so tolerate. It has always been so; while Ptolemy III Euergetes fretted about copying the works of the great Greek tragedians for his vast library, so the Nile's taxed and harried *fellaheen* continued on with their labors, much as their ancestors had done for centuries, if not millennia. While the pen dances across the page, so the scythe continues to swing and reap.

History emphasizes the unusual or the extraordinary, since most of life remains so ordinary and usual. And perhaps more is to be learned in the shops of history's merchants, ironsmiths, butchers, and artisans, than in the rostra of an empire's capital. What is clear is that we should focus our efforts on what is *of routine concern,* rather than on what may be glamorous or extraordinary. True progress is made by doing consistently what is laborious and boring. No truth is less welcome, but no truth is so vital to comprehend. The art of doing what has to be done, day in and day out, is the true art of living: this is the obedience to the Universal Will. Most of life is spent doing things we do not really wish to do. But we do them for those jewel-like moments when our inner wish-fulfillments may be indulged. And I suppose a corollary to this is that we should not complain when the drudgeries and muddiness of life intrude on our serenity. As Seneca says,

> Quaedam in te mittentur, quaedam incident. Non est delicata res vivere. [*Epist.* 107]

That is, "Some things are sent your way, and some things just happen. The art of living is not a delicate affair." We all know this to be true, of course. No one disputes this. To state it is an easy matter: what is far more difficult is to adjust ourselves to it down to the marrow of our bones. Herein lies the real problem. I am as guilty as anyone in this regard—I struggle with it constantly. If I were to speak honestly, I do not know if I will ever be able to accept life's slings and arrows with a serene smile. Is there anyone who does this? What I do instead is trudge forward like a mule: that is, I recognize that the dull labors of life constitute the foundation of life; and if I wish to enjoy my moments of bliss, I must put my head down, take comfort in my harness and yoke, and pull my plow as the whip cracks over my head. It does no good to fight this sort of reality; you can try to wriggle and writhe this way and that, but there is always the same old yoke hitched to your body.

This really is what maturity comes down to: accepting the distinctly unglamorous realities of life. This does not mean that we have to give up the simple joys: on the contrary, they assume an even greater importance. I am constantly seeking diversions in so many things: writing, translating, painting, exercising, traveling, and associating with those whose company brings me joy. My threshold of satisfaction has been adapted to my circumstances. I find joy in the simple things: the sight and smell of decaying leaves; the feel of an old book, the hoverings of the hummingbird, the gastronomic pleasures of the body, and the satisfaction of a task carried through to ultimate fruition.

But there must always be an acknowledgment of where one's duty lies. Life is not about frivolous time-wasting; it is a serious business, filled with serious consequences for the transgressions of fools or miscreants. We wish that this were not the case; we pine for the excitement of novelty, the allurements of the fantastic. And of course the modern culture feeds and nurtures this illusion: everything in life is supposed to be pleasurable, exciting, and stimulating. But it is not so. Every man must decide for himself if he wishes to accept these realities, or ignore them.

The greatest of men are those who patiently go about their labors with quiet deliberation, slowly and steadily building a life for themselves and their families. If you have ever been inside a cave, you will know that some of the most beautiful sights in them are the stalagmites and stalactites that respectively emerge from the floor or dangle from the ceiling. They took a great many years to form, and they were formed drop by drop, flowing with an unrelenting and inexorable consistency.

110. The Moderation And Control Of Anger

Anger is an insidious thing. It can twine and wind its way around the soul, like ivy over some physical impediment, and slowly throttle our more beneficent instincts. This creeping control does not happen all at once; it happens gradually, imperceptibly, one gradus at a time. When speaking to someone on the phone, I often find my voice gradually rising with a surplus of emotion. You can barely notice it happening, but it happens still. Anger then finds a ready opportunity to intrude itself. Anger is also deceptive: it makes us believe we are taking action to solve some problem, when in fact we are doing nothing to solve the problem. Anger is a liar. He is a deceiver.

So many of the popular prescriptions for controlling anger do not seem to be effective. I think this is because they treat anger as one discrete emotion, separate from all of the other emotions. But operating on the psyche is not really the same as a doctor performing a physical operation on a body: we cannot just make a few incisions with a scalpel, or probe around with a forceps, and remove that which ails us. The mind does not work like this; it is not a collection of fishing lures in a tackle-box, or an assortment of Snap-

On tools in a mechanic's chest. Yet Galen, that most profound of medical practitioners, was correct when he said:

> Medicine is, then, one of the productive arts, not simply as house building, carpentry and weaving are, but like the art that restores an adversely affected house and repairs a torn cloak...For it does not fashion the model for itself, but having seen the whole accurately through anatomy, it attempts to restore what is damaged.[13]

In order to understand the mind, we have to consider the mind as a whole, not as an assortment of separate things. I remember reading recently in Jack London's *Cruise of the Snark* of a fishing method he observed among the South Sea islanders. They called it "stone-fishing." The natives would find a shallow lagoon somewhere and arrange their canoes in two parallel lines facing each other across the lagoon. The lines of canoes would then approach each other; and the first man in each canoe would smack a large, flat stone against the water, which was tied to a long cord. I suppose that the shock of the stone hitting the water would cause any fish in the vicinity to flee in alarm into the lagoon. And as the two lines drew together, the fish would become trapped in a vice whose jaws were snapping shut; women on the shore would then wade into the shallow lagoon and collect the fish en masse. This was stone-fishing. And it seems to me that we should approach the examination of the mind in this way: we have to surround it and engulf it, rather than try to pick out individual fish. We have to "herd" the mind and all its components, and embrace it as one large school of fish, so to speak.

Anger is an agitation of the mind brought on by several causes. The first of these causes is failed expectations. Anger takes root and finds ready ground for flourishment when our aspirations have not been satisfied. Aspirations for what, you ask? Well, they can be for anything: love, life, work, whatever. It does not matter. Another cause is infirmity: either immaturity in years, or some physical affliction. It is no accident that anger finds more fertile ground among those who are immature or infirm. The young, the old, and the sick

[13] *Constitution of the Art of Medicine*, 20.

all find themselves confronted with dashed hopes or ruined expectations. They either cannot process what is happening to them, or they are unwilling to do so. Those who are weak or immature lash out at others in impotent expressions of rage. As Plutarch tells us,

> For as a swelling is produced in the flesh by a heavy blow, so in softest souls the inclination to hurt others gets its greater strength from greater weakness...So from the very great pain and suffering of the soul there arises mainly from weakness anger, which is not like the nerves of the soul, as someone defined it, but like its strainings and convulsions when it is excessively vehement in its thirst for revenge.[14]

This is one of the reasons why expressions of anger are so unbecoming to a man of good character: they reflect some hidden deficiency, some festering weakness, that has not yet been mastered. And yet it can be so difficult to banish expressions of anger; if I were honest, I would have to say that it will remain a lifelong task. One does not simply squelch it, and be finished with it. I have to trim my ivy, my weeds, and my trees frequently throughout the year. Why should it be any different with the maintenance of my soul? How can avoid my obligations of self-reflection and correction? But how does one go about doing this? The following remedies for anger I have found to be most effective.

Love. If we cannot banish anger entirely, we can at least try to replace it with an emotion just as powerful. And no one can doubt love's transcendent power in all things: its ability to conjure solutions from nothing, its ability to transcend space and time. Leo Tolstoy thought that Abraham Lincoln was on a par with Alexander the Great and the other truly great men of history; and he believed this because Lincoln's triumphs were based on the search for what was best in human nature. To see how his ideas developed and matured from the time he was a frontier lawyer to the time he was elected to his second term as president, is to chart the growth of a profound maturity in philosophical thinking. I don't think we have even as yet fully understood it, or grasped its implications. As Tolstoy wrote, it will probably take us another five hundred years to understand Lincoln fully.

[14] *On Restraining Anger*, VIII.

Plutarch tells us a good anecdote on love's spiritual force in his essay *On Love* (XXV). There was a rebel in Galatia named Sabinus who had failed in his rebellion. He had a beautiful wife named Herois. He decided to take refuge in some of the caves that festooned Galatia, and took one of his servants with him, a man named Martialis. He then sent Martialis to tell his wife that he had poisoned himself and died. When Herois heard this news, she wailed and wept bitterly; but then Martialis told her that the news was untrue, and that they had needed her to make an outward display of genuine grief. She gradually began to live a double life: she would visit Sabinus and spend time with him in his subterranean cave, and then would go about her business as a "widow" in her regular life. Nothing could dissuade her from living this double life: she saw it as her obligation.

She eventually helped disguise Sabinus by shaving his beard, dyeing his hair, and modify his appearance, so that she could take him to Rome and seek a pardon for him. At some point she even became pregnant with his child, but managed to conceal it for a time by putting on a small amount of corpulence as camouflage. She is said to have given birth to two sons in Sabinus's cave. But her efforts at obtaining clemency for Sabinus were not successful; we are told that the emperor Vespasian had her cast into the arena, where she met her end. "For during the whole of his [Vespasian's] reign he did no more savage act," says Plutarch. "Nor could gods or demons have turned away their eyes from a crueler sight. And yet her courage and bold language abated the pity of the spectators, though it exasperated Vespasian, for, despairing of her safety, she bade them go and tell the Emperor, 'that it was sweeter to live in darkness and underground than to wear his crown.'"

This is what I mean by love. This is the level of emotion required to banish anger. Any expression of sincere emotion will redirect our energies from that which is base and evil, to that which is good and wholesome. It is difficult, if not impossible, to suppress a powerful emotion; *but we can replace one emotion for another, and train our mind to rearrange itself in how it focuses its attentions and expends energy.*

Plain Living. Anger thrives when we indulge too much our appetites. More always begets the desire for more, as we know; and this in turn inflames expectations that cannot be met. The major reason why it is so difficult for most to live plainly is that our entire society is set up to promote the opposite of this. You cannot escape it; you cannot avoid it. Yet you must fight it again and again, for the battle is one for your soul. You cannot afford to lose this battle. The rational man must find ways of shutting his eyes and ears to the corruption and poison he finds himself plunged into. Plutarch says that a lawyer named Satyrus, when pleading a case, asked his friends to stop up his ears with wax so that he would not be roused to anger when his enemies shouted abuse at him.[15] We must do what is necessary to shut out negative stimuli that might cause us to be inflamed with anger. If you are upset by listening to the news, which deliberately tries to inflame people with anger, then do not listen to it. Listen to audio books instead. Talk to friends instead. Exercise instead. When I go on walks these days, I have even taken to averting my eyes from scenes and sights that anger me. If I do not want something in my field of vision, I do not let it enter my field of vision. You have a right to control what you see, hear, taste, and smell. If we cannot easily control our emotions, we can at least brake, bank, and check what enters our senses.

As I bring these thoughts to a close I suppose I should also say that we cannot expect complete victory in this. No human emotion can be amputated, only moderated, channeled, and controlled. There is no one walking around in a permanent state of tranquility and bliss—at least no one who is normal. We cannot expect the impossible. We must try to beautify what we have; we must try to make order out of chaos by harnessing anger. We should try to create something that will stand erect and clean amid the sundry chaos. It is like the poet Wallace Stevens said in "Anecdote of the Jar":

> I placed a jar in Tennessee,
> And round it was, upon a hill.
> It made the slovenly wilderness
> Surround the hill.
> The wilderness rose up to it,
> And sprawled around, no longer wild.
> The jar was round upon the ground
> And tall and of a port in air.

---

[15] *On Restraining Anger*, X.

111. Burst Away From The Shore, And Head For The Open Ocean

The Latin poet Claudian lived from about 370 to 404 A.D. He was born in Egypt but as an adult associated himself with the imperial court at Rome. One of his more famous works is the unfinished epic "The Rape of Proserpina" (*De Raptu Proserpinae*). The poem contains a short prologue which I render as follows:

> The one who first created the ship and
> Sliced through the boundless liquid expanse,
> And churned the curling surf with makeshift oars,
> Who dared commit his fragile ark to the fickle winds
> And who by his enterprise revealed routes not allowed by Nature,
> Entrusted himself, hesitating at the first placid waves,
> Clutching the shore's length in a trouble-free route.
> Soon the voyager summons the will to test vaster bays
> And let go the land, beginning to unfurl his sail to Notus's soft wind.
> Yet where bit by bit his rising boldness grew
> And his heart banished paralyzing fear;
> Now he broke out, roaming the sea's open space,
> Navigating with the stars in the heavens,
> And conquered the Aegean and Ionian tempests.

This is not a poetic passage shrouded in ambiguity. We know precisely what Claudian is saying here, and it is an important message. He is describing man's halting, fitful progression from timid, shore-hugging traveler to full-fledged navigator of the open seas. Man, he says, first began with the most rudimentary of ships. He was unsure of himself. The winds, the waves, and the dangerous shoals around him were terrifying realities. His boats were flimsy, his oars rude and unfinished, and his navigation skills uncertain. He dared not venture out too far from the comfortable shoreline, for unknown dangers likely awaited him. His impulse was to stay close to the shoreline, lest he be stricken by some nautical disaster. Yet slowly, steadily, he became more self-assured. He was willing to take on greater and greater projects. With the assistance of his own ingenuity (Claudian uses the word ars, or artistry), he gradually gained enough courage to seek "vaster bays."

And this is what we may call *progress*. Soon he had the audacity to open up his sails to "Notus's soft wind" (Notus is name given to the south-wind). Finally, man had gained the conviction to break out into the open sea, and conquer the tempests that would be waiting for him far from shore. In simple but elegant language, Claudian's short poem encapsulates the spirit of exploration. He is really describing man's Robinson Crusoe-like transformation from frightened novice to master of his environment. One can imagine the history of exploration to be exactly like this. The anthropologists tell us that the Polynesian islands were settled in this way. It seems amazing to us today to imagine how such vast distances in the Pacific could have been traversed by men with supposedly "primitive" technology. But it is not difficult to imagine when we appreciate that human progress is incremental and agglutinative. Each generation added to what came before it. Small journeys increased the store of information that later generations used. Basic observations of the stars, winds, currents, and tides congeal into a profound understanding of the island chains scattered over the Pacific. Voyages became bigger, better equipped, and much more regular. And so were the islands of the Pacific settled.

It turns out, in fact, that the navigational systems of the ancient Polynesians were quite sophisticated. They had "charts" constructed which showed a deep understanding of celestial navigation, currents, tides, and the natural world. Certainly the Scandinavian explorers of the Dark Ages had their own methods of navigation, of which we now know little. Where there is an open space, mankind will expand to fill it. Perhaps we overestimate the need for "technology" in exploration; what really seems to matter is the desire to explore, that pestering curiosity which compels man to answer the call of the waves.

The same thing happened in the ancient Mediterranean. We begin to understand that travel and exploration are not just motivated by economic interests; instead, they spring from some elemental desire in the human consciousness to burst the boundaries the present habitat. And I think all organisms share this biological imperative: to expand to the outwards limits of every habitat. This is why it is certain—despite all economic and financial hurdles—that the human race will eventually colonize other planets. As our capacities grow, so will our biological imperatives. But that is for the future, and it does not yet affect us directly.

Our responsibility now is to cultivate our urge to explore. It is our purpose to slough off our land-bound coils, and head for the open ocean. Nothing matters more than this, for herein lies the essence of both progress and survival. If our ship is not crashing forward through the surf with salty foam drenching her undulating bow, we must know we are doing something wrong. We must, as Claudian says in his last lines above, banish all paralyzing timidity and break out into the open sea; we must allow our vessel to cleave the white-capped waves, and find routes to new opportunities; and, using the stars in the heavens as guides, we will master the ocean's squalls, and arrive triumphant at new destinations. *Burst out of your confines, O seeker, and forge a way ahead!*

112. The Dolphin Of Hippo

Pliny the Younger described in one of his letters a story noted both for its sadness and its revelatory quality on a characteristic of human nature. The letter was written to the poet Caninius Rufus (IX.33), and in it Pliny recounts extraordinary interactions between a boy and a dolphin. I am not quite sure whether the word "friendship" would be appropriate in this context, but one could say that the relations between the two looked very much like this.

The event occurred near the city if Hippo in North Africa, which is now located in Tunisia and known as Bizerte. Pliny says that near Hippo was a small lagoon that led to the sea, and that the area was frequented by the local people as a place for swimming, fishing, and playing games. Boys would often swim far out from shore to test their strength against the currents and waves. One young swimmer once ventured our farther than usual, and was approached by a curious dolphin. The dolphin began to circle him, rolling around in a playful manner as if trying to communicate something; it seemed fascinated by this terrestrial animal that was bold enough to explore the watery regions of the earth. At some point the dolphin made physical contact with the boy, allowing him to straddle his back and ride him through the surf. The mischievous animal carried the boy some way out to sea, then brought him safely back to shallow water. People on shore watched all this with shocked fascination.

Soon the story had made its way around the town. People imagined that the workings of some sea-god were in evidence, and they could not get enough of the tale. The next day another group of boys swam off shore, among them the boy who had ridden the dolphin the previous day. The dolphin promptly recognized his young companion from the previous day, and performed his usual water-frolics, as if demanding additional play time. The dolphin grew tamer as its contacts with humans grew more frequent. Other swimmers made contact with it and touched it. As Pliny says,

Crescit audacia experimento,

Which means "their boldness increased with habit." Eventually the dolphin found the boy whom it had originally invited on its back, and carried him through the waves again; other boys would follow the pair through the water, yelling out words of surprise and motivation. Now I suspect that some readers may think this story is without basis in fact. But there are many documented cases of dolphins interacting in a highly intelligent manner with us humans. Pliny's uncle, the naturalist Pliny the Elder, records several instances of such contact (*Hist. Nat.* IX.8.26 *et seq.*). He tells us of dolphins who allowed themselves to be petted, fed, even ridden. One such dolphin, he says, carried a boy in Italy across a bay to school at the city of Pozzuoli.

Other examples of human contact with dolphins include the many instances where dolphins helped fishermen direct schools of fish into their nets. We can see from these stories that it is reasonable to assume a factual basis for the legend of Arion. Those familiar with tales from mythology may recall that Arion was a skilled musician who was captured by pirates; and before the marauders killed him, he asked to play a song on his harp. This he did; and the sonorous chords attracted a school of curious dolphins. Arion then leaped into the sea, and was carried safely ashore at Cape Matapan in Greece, then called Taenarum or Ταίναρον.

But to return to our story. These interactions with the dolphin at Hippo grew in frequency and intimacy. It would even swim right up to shore and linger with the townspeople, allowing itself to be touched and stroked. And then bad things began to happen. Pliny tells us that the local governor, a man named Octavius Avitus, stupidly rubbed scented oil on the dolphin, perhaps as a way of asserting some misguided sense of authority. Then as now, political figures love to grandstand and thrust themselves into situations where they can gain some personal benefit from it. And their intercession never seems to do any good. In this case, the dolphin was alarmed by the pouring of perfumed oil on its back, and left the area for a time; but it did eventually return.

All these bizarre occurrences made Hippo an object of fascination. People from all over visited the town to see its uniquely tame dolphin. Suddenly the town lost its quiet, sleepy character and became burdened with the annoyance of what we would today call "eco-tourists." Someone in the municipal government—Pliny does not say who it was—decided that the dolphin, this miracle of nature, should be killed as a way of "solving" the problem of unwanted visitors. And so it was done.

Reading this denoument to the story filled me with an inexplicable anger and sadness. For it points to something that no student of history can fail to notice as he casts his attention down the centuries: man has a powerful dark side, a capacity for evil that is every bit as strong as his capacity for good. There is something irrationally bestial in man's nature, we must admit, some warped sense of unreasonable ownership, that makes him think he is lord of the world, and may do as he pleases to it and every living thing within its borders. Not content to dominate his fellows, he seeks to extend his sovereignty over every other form of life. No one matters but him; everything in the world exists to serve his sense of convenience and comfort. I am sure readers can recall their own stories of such callous cruelty on the part of humans towards our fellow inhabitants of this world. What malicious ingredient is in our nature, what secret lust to control and dominate, compels us—as if we were animated with the blind assurance of a sleepwalker—to strive not just to be lord, but to be the dispenser of life and death over all? The historian Edward Gibbon noted:

> There is nothing perhaps more adverse to nature and reason than to hold in obedience remote countries and foreign nations, in opposition to their inclination and interest. [*Decline*, Ch. XLIX]

But I am not so sure that this lust to conquer and control is so "adverse to nature and reason." If one looks at history and at current events now, one could just as easily remark that this sadistic desire to control is about as natural in man as is the instinct to procreate. But we must never forget that just because some desire in us is *natural*, that does not mean the desire is *right*. Moral goodness, as Cicero tells us in *On Duties* and *On Moral Ends*, can never have any connection to expediency. And yet such tales as this one weigh heavily on the consciousness. It is easy to agree with the view of Themistocles, who, when he was approached by a man who promised to teach him secrets on how to improve his memory, said: "I would sooner learn to forget, than how to remember."[16]

Sometimes the pain of experience is too much to bear. It is not for us to tamper with or destroy our fellow creatures as it may suit our convenience; we do not have this unrestricted freedom of action, nor may we presume to exercise it. It is not for us to arrogate this judgmental authority to ourselves. On these matters I find myself lately in alignment with the somber sentiments of Lord Tennyson expressed in these verses from his "Tears, Idle Tears":

> Fresh as the first beam glittering on a sail,
> That brings our friends up from the underworld,
> Sad as the last which reddens over one
> That sinks with all we love below the verge;
> So sad, so fresh, the days that are no more.

113. Grave Offenses, And Little Thanks

In a letter to Titinius Capito, the Roman official and career lawyer Pliny discusses the idea of writing a book of history. Of particular concern to him was the choice of topic: he was uncertain whether he should treat an ancient or a modern subject. Valid arguments existed for both options. An older subject might allow for a more considered perspective, far removed from the passions of immediate memory; whereas the treatment of a current subject might inflame unreasonable emotions in his readers. Pliny has serious doubts about choosing a subject that might be within the living memory of his readers. He summarizes his feelings with this sentence:

[16] *Acad.* II.2

Graves offensae, levis gratia. [*Epistulae* V.8.12]

And here we can see how the sententious brevity of the Latin language can express an idea that might take two or three times the volume of English verbiage. Literally the sentence reads, "Serious offenses, meager in thanks." What he means is that, when writing about a modern topic, he might anger many while receiving little in the way of thanks. One can understand Pliny's sense of hesitation. But it seems to me that he might have overlooked the fact that there are arguments that can be made for both sides. In the very same letter, he quotes Thucydides; and even a brief moment of reflection might have reminded him that the great Greek historian wrote his work very much within the living memory of his contemporaries. He conducted countless interviews with people who had been present during the momentous events he so vividly describes. He visited the scenes of the action, and he walked the ground where such events took place.

In the twentieth century, the American historian William Shirer certainly benefitted from having been a correspondent in Berlin during the 1930s; his history of the Third Reich, composed decades later, is imbued with a pungent sense of emotion that could only have come from personal experience. Bernal Diaz, who served with Hernando Cortes during the latter's campaign of conquest against the Aztec Empire in the early 16th century, wrote his precious work when he was an old man in his eighties. His driving motivation was to correct the many misconceptions and lies that had begun to surround the career of his former commander, of whom he speaks in the most reverential tones. Because of its clarity and immediacy, his *History of the Conquest of Mexico* has become a precious document, something irreplaceable in every respect.

Clearly there is much value in proximity; and Fate confers a special authority on those historians who are close to historical events and have the ability to translate that authority into cogent writing. For me, one of the most unforgettable images in a work of history is the Ammianus Marcellinus's description of his escape from the city of Amida, which had been subjected to a long siege by the Persian king Shapur II. The account is found in XIX.8 of his history. Ammianus says that, as he was making his way through the rocky terrain away from the fallen city, he encountered a ghastly sight: a horse dragging the torso of its former rider. The cavalryman had gotten his arm entangled in the reins, and had fallen off; unable to extricate himself, he had been battered to his death on rocks and sand for many miles. Such is the compelling power of being witness to momentous events.

But there are valid arguments on the other side as well. Perhaps the removal of an event from the passions and bile of the era can promote a seasoned, rational maturity in historical writing. Edward Gibbon's history is perhaps the best example of this: he takes us across many centuries, locales, and dynasties, and benefits from a sweeping rationalism that animates the whole. There is feeling here, but it is deployed in the service of a philosophy of history, rather than as a rapier with which to skewer unfavored personages. And is there not much to be said for this? Who can say when historical immediacy crosses the line into bias and slander? It is true that Procopius's *Anecdota* gives us many gossipy details about Justinian and Theodora, but one cannot escape the feeling that the writer remains a scorned court official who is revenging himself with his pen. The writer Sidonius Apollinaris, writing around 460 A.D., expressed a thought similar to what Pliny observed in the quote mentioned earlier. He says,

> Telling lies is despicable, but speaking the truth is dangerous…it is the type of work where little thanks comes from mentioning the good, and reference to notorious events causes a great deal of outrage. [*Epistulae* IV.22: *Turpiter falsa, periculose vera dicuntur…Est enim huiusmodi thema vel opus in quo bonorum si facias mentionem, modica gratia paratur, si notabilium, maxuma offensa*.]

Without doubt, he who wishes to chronicle modern events must have a measure of courage. But this measure of fortitude need not be confined to modern studies. We live in an age of rampant politicization: there are many who wish to interpret historical events through the filter of their own prejudices and preconceptions. To some degree this has always been so, of course; bias is an unavoidable fact in studies of all types. But there seems to be now a greater willingness by some to depart entirely from what used to be generally accepted principles. Unable to accept the past as it is, there are some who seek to "re-imagine" it in ways that serve their own interests. And this is where I might have to disagree respectfully with

Pliny and Sidonius: it seems to me that it takes just as much thankless courage, and focused discipline, to write about events in the remote past, as it does to write about current events. No matter the undertaking, courage and discipline remain the timeless constants in all human endeavors. So know that *he who is bold, and possessed of the conviction of rectitude, will never for long be lacking in fortune's favor and enduring gratitude.*

114. Hercules On Oeta: Immortality Through Virtue

As I have gotten older I find that reading plays brings more enjoyment than it did in earlier years. Tragedies especially: the unformed mind has not yet been sufficiently battered by the winds and waves of fortune against the rocks, and is equipped with a merciful immunity to the pathos of existence. And yet, as the years roll on, beards and barnacles begin to replace the smooth, supple surfaces of youth; scars and aches accumulate; and the omnipresence of tragedy dawns on the maturing mind with a startling rapidity. The mind then calls for a tonic: it requires the writer to make sense of all this chaos, all this pain, and all this suffering. The struggle must be dignified with a sense of universal justice, and an ethic of enduring goodness. So the tragedian steps forward, and with his stylus attempts to perform this task.

The plays of Seneca were apparently intended for reading only; we do not hear of them having been performed in classical times. Some critics have not warmed to them, but I find them much underrated. The longest tragedy Seneca wrote—indeed, the longest tragedy to survive from antiquity—is his *Hercules on Oeta.* It is customary to extoll the dramatic skills of Euripides, and one cannot disagree with this custom. But of Seneca's dramatic skills we hear nothing at all. I find him easier to read than the Greek tragedians; his characters seem to be more fully painted, more completely fleshed-out. We are not offended by his verbosity, or his adages and maxims that accumulate page after page; in fact, we long for more of them. Seneca's characters say what is on their mind, and rely less on interpretive choruses to filter their sentiments. The effect is one of passionate immediacy, of seething emotion, and of bitter truths revealed.

The reader needs to be aware of the background to Hercules on Oeta. Hercules is married to the volatile Deianira, and is traveling through Greece, as heroic demigods are wont to do. When the couple come to a river (the River Evenus), Hercules permits a centaur named Nessus to carry Deianira across. But Nessus is treacherous, and tries to steal Hercules's bride for himself; the enraged Hercules then kills the centaur with poison-tipped arrows, made lethal when Hercules dipped their points in the toxic blood of the Lernaean Hydra. Nessus dies, but makes one last attempt at revenge: he tells Deianira to save some of his own now-poisoned blood, to use it as a future weapon against Hercules should he ever be guilty of marital infidelities. He then dies. At some point in the future, Hercules becomes enamored with the beautiful Iole, from the city of Oechalia. Her father Eurytus makes the mistake of denying the hero his daughter, whereupon the enraged Hercules lays the city to waste, killing Iole's father and brother. He forcibly carries off Iole and sends her to his domicile, where his wife also lives. This act, of course, arouses Deianira's unmitigated jealously and sense of betrayal. Powerful verses abound. In Act I, we read the following lines:

Vitam qui poterit reddere protinus,
Solus non poterit naufragium pati. [I.117]

Only someone who is willing to surrender his life can endure a shipwreck: meaning that the horrors and tragedies of life can only be endured by someone who refuses to become too attached to it. Elsewhere the sentiment is more personal:

O quam cruentus feminas stimulat furor,
Cum patuit una paelici et nuptae domus. [II.233]

What bloody fury arouses women when a single house is opened for a wife and a mistress, a sentiment that requires no explanation. And so Deianira will have her revenge on her husband. She informs the audience:

Maximum fieri scelus
Et ipsa fateor, sed dolor fieri iubet. [II.331]

I confess it to be the worst possible crime, but my anguish commands that it be done. She is inflamed with rage and betrayal, and this emotion must take its course. By the end of the play's second act she has resolved to poison Hercules; so she sprinkles some of Nassus's saved blood on a robe, and sends it to her husband using a messenger. Deianira's female assistants, of course, express their approval of the plan and willingly cooperate. In act three Hercules has donned the robe, and been fatally affected by the poison; Deianira has now begun to regret her actions, knowing that her revenge was too extreme. But it is too late: just as Hercules permitted his passions to override his judgment when he destroyed Oechalia, so has Deianira allowed her rage to trigger a fateful chain of uncontrollable events. She contemplates—then carries out—suicide as Hercules is brought home, close to death. When he becomes aware that his death had been prophesized, he suddenly finds comfort and relief; his death thus acquires a new meaning, and is embossed with the seal of divine will. This knowledge allows him to face his end with Stoic calm and courage, and he asks that a funeral pyre be built for him on Mount Oeta.

In the final act, we hear a description of the hero's fiery funeral on Oeta. The only remaining question is whether his spirit has ascended to heaven, to dwell among the gods, or has instead been consigned to the underworld. We learn the answer when Hercules's spirit appears before his mourning mother Alcmene, to assure her that he now dwells among the gods. Despite his human faults, Hercules's life was more characterized by virtue than by evil, and this is enough:

> Virtus in astra tendit, in mortem timor [V.1971]

Virtue moves us towards the stars, and fear to death. Stated another way:

> Sed locum virtus habet inter astra. [V.1564]

That is, *virtue has a place among the stars.* This is the same sentiment we find expressed in Cicero's essay *The Dream of Scipio*: that is, a man's great deeds will assure him immortality. It has always been so, and it always will be so.

115. The Cultivation Of A Sense Of Humor

To be lacking in a sense of humor is a true misfortune. I would not go so far as to call it an offense against others; but it certainly is a detriment to oneself. Social media seems to magnify our sense of self-importance; and when self-importance escalates, so does our sense of grim momentousness. There is nothing wrong with being serious, of course, up to a certain point. But there must be some kind of pressure-value to release the steam-engine's expanding vapors. And if the first duty of the philosopher is to be clear, then certainly his second obligation is *not to take himself too seriously*. The truly wise know when to laugh.

Now I know that there will be many who say that a sense of humor cannot be cultivated: they will say that one either has it, or one does not. There is some merit to this view. Not everyone who practices at the piano will reach the same level of ability. Not every golfer's swing will be equally effective, if equal amounts of time have been invested in developing them.

Humor is the product of many things: a sensitivity to one's surroundings, an ability to master timing, and the ability to detect a certain incongruity in the world's workings. What do I mean by incongruity? The humorist must be able to detect those myriad inconsistencies in life where the reality departs from the ideal; he must be able to articulate this lack of congruence to an audience in a way that amuses it, rather than depresses it. It is an art form, make no mistake. But that does not mean that one cannot *develop or refine* a sense of humor. And from what I see on Twitter and other social media sites, many of us are in desperate need of *learning to lighten up*. Deal with serious topics, by all means. Discuss them, debate them, and roll around in them; but remember too that life is short, and every minute spent inveighing against the world's evils is one less minute learning to appreciate beauty or truth. Baldesar Castiglione, writing around 1527 in his Renaissance classic *The Book of the Courtier*, had this to say about a sense of humor:

> Therefore everything which provokes laughter exalts a man's spirit and gives him pleasure, and for a while enables him to forget the trials and tribulations of which life is full. So you can see that laughter is

> most agreeable to everyone, and the one who inspires it at the right time and place deserves every praise. But what laughter is, and where it is to be found, and how it sometimes takes possession of our veins, our eyes, our mouth and sides, and sometimes seems about to make us burst, being uncontrollable no matter how hard we try, I shall leave to Democritus to explain; who, even if he should promise to find the words, would not be able to.

The pursuit of any art requires diligence and application, and humor is no exception. The aspiring humorist must acquaint himself with the humor styles of different countries and cultures. This is so because humor varies widely from continent to continent, and from country to country. What is funny in England may not be funny in Japan; what is amusing to an Italian may not be so mirthful to a Scandinavian. Some humor is universal, and some is not. Above all, I think, the cultivation of a sense of humor requires this: *humility*. One must humble oneself. One must have the ability to step outside his self-created world, and reflect on that fact that he does not really control as much as he would like to believe. Humor is submission: submission to the goddess Adrastia, or Fortune. Only when we reach this level of philosophic reflection will be truly be able to see the pathos that lurks behind all human affairs.

The humorist must be a master of imagery and metaphor. He must above all know language: puns, metaphors, nicknames, alliteration, and hyperbole must all be arrows in his quiver. He must be a master of irony, and this takes a certain level of seasoning and experience. Practical jokes are a different matter; these rely on the ability to enjoy another person's discomfort. With practical jokes, execution is especially important; taken too far, they can easily become sadistic. One must have a sense of restraint to carry them off effectively. The practical steps that can be taken to develop a sense of humor are the following:

1. **See what other humorists have done.** Learn about humor by starting with historical humor and working up to the present day. Read books, poems, plays; see movies. You will see how some things have changed, and some have not. Exposure to comic works, books, films, and television shows will sharpen your senses.

2. **Travel widely, and observe human nature.** You will develop a sympathy for the plight of the common man, who does his best to survive in a world where things are always more difficult than they appear.

3. **Stop taking yourself so seriously.** It is not good for your health. Unrelenting negativity, or unrelenting positivity, quickly become tiresome. Realize that no one is infallible, and that perfection is not a quality reserved for humans. Have the confidence to make mistakes. Have the confidence to realize that you do not control the world. Have the confidence that no everyone will agree with how you see the world.

4. **Calm down.** Stop shouting. No one wants to hear a wide-eyed maniac screaming into a camera. No one wants to listen to someone drone on for hours about their favorite conspiracy theory. It may be important to you, but it is not important to others.

These for me are some practical ways of cultivating a sense of humor. Like any good spice, it must be used sparingly. Too much humor will make a man look like a clown; too little makes him look like a warmed-over corpse. I cannot resist the chance to include a few of the jokes and anecdotes described by Baldesar Castiglione in his book. Here are a few of them.

> Duke Federico was [one day] discussing what should be done with a great load of earth that had been excavated for the foundations of this palace, which he was then building, and he remarked: "My lord, I have the perfect answer for where it should go. Order a great pit to be dug, and then it can be put there without any further ado." And to this the Duke Federico replied, not without laughing, "And where will we put the earth that comes out of the pit?" Responded the abbot: "Have it dug so large that it will take both loads." And even though the Duke kept insisting that the larger the pit was made, the more earth there would be to dispose of, the man could never get into his head that it could not be made big enough to take the two loads…

Castiglione tells us that the following comment was once made about a certain court official: "He lacks nothing except money and brains." He also relates an anecdote about a greedy official who said this: "I have thought of [a way] in which we can find a large sum of money without too much bother. The first is as follows. Seeing that we have no more profitable source of income than the customs levied at the gates of Florence, and we have eleven gates altogether, let us *immediately have built another eleven, and we shall double our revenue*."

Elsewhere he describes this hilarious comment by Lorenzo de Medici to a "very tedious clown" who kept badgering the great man about pointless trifles. One morning, this buffoon found Lorenzo in bed, sleeping late. The fool said to him, "Sir, you are still sleeping here, while I have already been to the New Market and the old, and outside the San Gallo Gate and around the walls for exercise, and I've done a thousand other things besides, while you are still here sleeping!" Lorenzo glared at the fool and said, "What I have dreamed about in an hour is worth more than what you have done in four."

116. On Living Near The Ocean

Although I do not live near the ocean now, I grew up in a small town that was close to it. The spirit of place enters imperceptibly into one's bloodstream; and one gets used to the tang of rotting seaweed, the early morning salt mist, the relentlessly shifting dunes, and the omnipresent screams of the gulls. I have found that being near the ocean is restorative of health. Allergies are swept away. The roar of the crashing waves takes on a certain soothing rhythm; and this pulse augments that of our own hearts, raising them to crescendos of emotional power. And yet at the same time the ocean is concealing something. The last line in Melville's *Moby Dick* said it best, I think.

> Then all collapsed, and the great shroud of the sea
> rolled on as it rolled five thousand years ago.

I do not think it was any accident that Melville chose to use the word *shroud* when describing the sea. A shroud is something that covers or conceals. But conceals what? The word carries a vague sensation of death: that is, a body wrapped in a *shroud*. A shroud of death, an emblem of mortification. He knew what he was saying, and he knew what he was getting at. At another place in *Moby Dick* he mentions that beneath the ocean's apparently placid surface "pants the heart of a tiger." The cabin-boy Pip falls out of one of the boats during a whale chase; left floating alone in the endless expanse of the sea, he loses his mind. Anyone who does not feel a shudder of horror when looking into the depths of the sea has not understood it properly. It is not a place for man. He does not belong here. He is born of the sea; but he climbed out of its primeval slimes aeons ago, and was not meant to return. He cannot go back, and he should not go back.

But this is a very different thing from living near the ocean. He can feel its essence and power when he is near it; and he can draw on its strength and primeval ferocity. He can listen to the pounding of that tiger's heart. But he must always be conscious that he can never really achieve union with it. There is no union with the sea. There is the sea, and there is you, and this is as it should be. So we have this cautionary dualism: there is the ancient, perilous essence of the ocean, this tiger's heart, and at the same time there is this rejuvenating energy of the sea. There is this inexplicable allure that calls us to it. It both provides, and destroys. There is kindness, and there is cruelty of the most savage sort: the fire can both sustain and destroy. And it seems that too much exposure to the ocean has some kind of degenerative effect, as well. You cannot quite put your finger on it. But it is there. You see it with those old mariners. The grizzled visages of those who have spent too much time with the ocean do not really convey wisdom: it is rather that the life has been sucked out of them, leaving a desiccated human husk. There are no places so degenerate as some of these obscure seaside communities. The odors of decay and ruin hover about them.

This kind of dualism is not unusual. It is just that we do not see it for what it is, most of the time. There is an episode from Rome's Samnite War in 321 B.C. that is another example of this kind of dualism. The historian Appian tells the tale in his *Samnite History* (Ch. 3). The Samnites, an Italic people against whom Rome had waged constant war, won a victory against the upstart Romans. The Samnite victor's name was Pontius. He asked his father for advice after he had crushed a Roman army and taken tens of thousands of them as prisoners. Pontius did not know whether to put the prisoners to death, sell them into slavery, or release them. His father gave him this advice:

> My son, for a great enmity there is but one cure–either extreme generosity or extreme severity. Severity terrifies, generosity conciliates. Know that the first and greatest of all victories is to treasure up success...Vanquished by benefits only, they will strive to surpass you in respect of this deed of kindness...If this does not suit you, then kill them to the last man, not sparing one to carry the news...[*Trans. by H. White*]

One could either act with extreme cruelty, he says, or with extreme benevolence. The old man's advice was to slaughter the Roman prisoners. But this was something that Pontius was quite unwilling to do. He feared the wrath of the gods for such a cruel deed. He also thought that such an atrocity would make peace between the two peoples nearly impossible to achieve. At the same time, he was not willing to let them go with just a slap on the wrist. To err on the side of kindness was also dangerous: the Romans were in the habit of exploiting every opportunity, and they might see such a gesture as a form of weakness. So Pontius sought a middle ground between these two extremes of generosity and cruelty. His decision was to confiscate all their arms and equipment, and then force them to "pass under the yoke," which was an ancient ritual of humiliation where the defeated had to pass under the upraised swords of the victors.

And this is the same kind of duality we referred to earlier. The idea of the ocean's ability to deliver savage retribution, and at the same time, life-sustaining power. It is good to draw warmth from its fires. But at the same time there are limits. There are limits to what can be done, and to what benefits that it can provide. To appreciate the ocean, to draw from its strength, a man must pass under its ritual yoke. He must walk *sub iugum*. He must accept its duality, and submit to it without complaint.

117. The Sword Of Mars

The humanist Poggio Bracciolini wrote a long letter to his friend Niccolo Niccoli in November of 1430. The letter contained the following words:

> Now surely our citizens ought to be persuaded by experience, the real teacher, that they have no gift for the art of war, since they have never seen a line of battle drawn up or a fort. For what is more ridiculous than for a people to be in charge of a major war who have never performed the tiniest bit of warlike duty? But in reality men who have never so much as seen the blade of a sword give orders from their safe retreat to the actual commanders in the war as to how forces should be deployed and attacks made, towns stormed, and the enemy driven back. [*Trans. by P.W. Gordan*]

Poggio was trying to point out the absurdity expecting men who had no military experience to be able to direct wars. He was correct in this, of course; but he might have been even more correct if he had extended his admonition to say that those with no military experience should never be in a position *to oblige* their nations for war. Someone sitting in a political assembly (e.g., a senate or parliament) should have a clear idea of what they are voting for, should they ever vote to enter a war. They should have a basic understanding of what conflict is. They should themselves have had some experience with the armed forces, for only in this way will they be able to grasp the meaning of armed struggle.

One can only imagine what Poggio would have thought of our current state of affairs. I remember reading somewhere–I cannot remember where–that the current members of the US Congress have almost no collective military experience of any kind. In the nineteenth and early twentieth centuries, they did; but those days are long past. Not only do they have no military experience, but they make sure that their sons and daughters stay as far away from the armed services as possible. The children of President Reagan did not serve, as far as I am aware. The children of President Bush (Bush I) did not serve in any meaningful capacity. The children of President Clinton did not serve. The children of President Obama did not serve, and neither did the children of President Trump. And yet all of these emperors–for that is what they really are–blithely obliged their nation to extended conflicts in foreign lands, to wars that have no end and were never meant to have any end.

This is not all. The children of these emperors–Bush I's sons, Clinton's daughter, and presumably at some point Obama's daughters–still have the nerve to parade themselves before the public to build their "brands" for eventual elected office. The hypocrisy and the arrogance would be breathtaking, were it not so routine. How is it that we accept this? Have we become so numb, so hypnotized with the allurements of pleasure, that we have forgotten the basic obligations of the statesman?

It was not always so. During the days of the Roman republic, each elected consul was expected to have a lengthy period of military service under his belt before assuming the responsibilities of office. He would have had a long track record of campaigning. He would have lived in the field with his men. He would have seen first-hand what war meant. He would have grown accustomed to hardship, to entrenching fortifications, to seeing blood and death on a regular basis. And this knowledge would have given him a keen appreciation for the sacrifices involved in committing the nation to war. To further cement the ties of responsibility, each consul was assigned a province that became his personal obligation. If something went wrong, he would be held accountable. Compare this to the system in place now in the United States, where everyone in Congress has an opinion, but no one is responsible for anything. These are men and women not only without courage, but individuals lacking in basic human decency.

I wish to say a few more words on this subject. The fifth century Roman diplomat Priscus (c. 415–c. 425 A.D.) once had occasion to visit the court of Attila the Hun. His account of this visit is highly readable, and can be found in the first volume of J.B. Bury's *History of the Later Roman Empire*. According to Priscus, Attila believed that he had been destined for military power because of the discovery of something he called the *Sword of Mars*. According to this legend, a cowherd once saw one of his animals limping and bleeding. When he retraced the steps of the animal as shown by the drops of blood that had been left on the ground, he discovered that the cow had stepped on an iron sword. The cowherd brought the sword to Attila, who pronounced it the fabled Sword of Mars described by the Greek historian Herodotus (IV.62):

> Every year a hundred and fifty wagon-loads of sticks are added to [a] pile, to make up for the constant settling caused by rains, and on top of it is planted an ancient iron sword, which serves for the image of Ares [Mars]. Annual sacrifices of horses

> and other cattle are made to this sword, which, indeed, claims a greater number of victims than any other of their gods.

Whether Attila really believed that the sword was the one described above, or whether he was just humoring local customs in a politically astute manner, the reader will have to decide for himself. For my part I do not think it really matters what Attila believed. The point is that he took warfare seriously, and was willing to symbolize its importance with the *image of a sword.* There was a physical image that would be impressed on the minds of his people and himself. It strikes me that we do not really do this now. War now assumes a sanitary, abstract, and ethereal aspect to those who wage it; to them, it is never reduced to any concrete symbol. Why not? Would this kind of ritual drive home the seriousness of war? Another sword-worshipping ceremony is described by the historian Ammianus Marcellinus (XXXI.2). In talking about the customs of the Alans (Halani), he says that they would drive a naked sword into the ground (*gladius barbarico ritu humi figitur nudus*) and perform rituals before it. The sword took the place of an altar or temple.

All of these examples show that war was taken seriously by these ancient peoples. It was not an abstraction cloaked in the sanctimonious, hypocritical speeches of parliamentarians. By our definitions, these people may have been "crude" or "barbarous"; but at least their leaders never asked them to do things that they themselves had not done. They rode with their men; they campaigned with their men; and they fought and suffered with their men. Everyone knew what the rules were. The leaders who made the decisions had a personal stake in the outcomes of their decisions. And this made all the difference. The Sword of Mars symbolized an explicit contract the leader had with his people: he would have the power to wage war, but would accept this trust with the deadly seriousness that it deserved. *Reverence made war sacred; and being sacred, it could not be disrespected without consequences to the leader.*

118. Coming Full Circle

As a man hopefully grows in experience and knowledge, he will begin to notice a curious thing. The knowledge that he continues to acquire, and the sights that he continues to see here and there, subtly redirect him back to where he first departed. It is almost as if some grand cosmic joke is at work. Now when I say we return to where we first started, I do not mean that we return as *ignorant* as when we first left. We have grown, matured, and become more complete; there is no going back to the old ways and old days. And yet, as knowledge grows, we begin to long for the places of our youth: the sights and sounds of our younger days, and the pleasant connections to eras past. Wisdom reduces all things to their essentials.

We see this sort of thing in travelers. They range about the world, and see many sights and places; and yet in the end they prefer to settle quietly in their own homelands. The more things they have seen, the more they realize that they belong home. Everything begins to look like everything else. Travelers grow tired of the endless inconveniences of travel. Sights, sounds, and smells blend into one sensory experience that has been experienced one time too many. You can see the fatigue, the world-weariness, in their faces. Perhaps there is such a thing as seeing too much. Plutarch was the intimate of famous men and emperors; and yet, in the end, he chose to settle in his hometown of Chaeronea. I believe he even became mayor of this town when he was advanced in years. When someone asked him why he preferred to live there, he said that he thought it was the place where he could do the most good. In his writings he ranged over the ages, and examined the lives of great men; yet this modest Platonist chose to remain in his provincial hometown.

As I write these paragraphs I am reminded of a fable by Ibn Muqaffa that will be my pleasure to tell. He says that there was once a religious man who always seemed to be granted what he asked for. One day, as he was sitting alone on the seashore, a bird flew by with a mouse in its claws. The bird–it was a bird of prey called a kite–dropped the mouse. The old man wrapped the mouse in a leaf and brought it home, thinking he might be able to keep it as a pet. Soon his intention changed. He desired that the mouse be changed into a girl, and for this he prayed. The prayer was granted. He presented the girl to his wife, and told her that the girl was his adopted daughter. He raised the girl to womanhood; and when she became mature, he told her that it was time for her to think of marrying. The choice of husband, he said, was hers.

The girl said she preferred a husband of great strength. The man said, "Maybe you would like to choose the sun." So he spoke to the sun and said, "I have a young woman looking for a strong husband. Would you like to marry her?" The sun looked brightly down on the man and replied, "Maybe you should be looking at someone stronger than I, for my rays are not all-powerful. They are blocked by the cloud, who can prevent my light from reaching the earth."

So the old man then spoke to the clouds, and made the same proposal to them. But the clouds deferred also. They said, "Talk to the wind. He is stronger than us, for he has the power to push us all over the sky." Then the old man spoke to the wind. The wind sent him to speak to the mountain, because the wind knew that the mountain could stand firm and fixed against the strongest gales that the wind could offer. Exasperated, the man finally spoke to the mountain. And the mountain said, "You should talk to the mouse, for the mouse must be stronger than I am, since I always have to offer the mouse a place to live in my crevasses." The old man finally offered his daughter to the mouse. But the mouse replied that it would be impossible for him to marry her, since his little house would be too small for her. So after hearing this, the old man thought that it would simply be best to have his daughter changed back into her original form, a mouse. This wish he now made, and it was granted. His efforts had led him right back to where he first began.

119. Whether A Man Can Change, And How He May Change

Can a man change, or are his personality traits so fixed that external circumstances are incapable of adjusting them in any significant way? This is a question that finds enthusiastic advocates for both answers. The cynics–or as they prefer to be called, the "realists"–tell us that personality does not change. Our knowledge contracts and expands, but the core of our being remains immutable. We may become more polished in our presentations, or more adept at concealing our intentions, but in the end it is still the same old "us." We are here, and we have not changed.

The idealists take a different view. They say that, while it is not common, it is possible for a man to change if he truly wants to change. External circumstance, some transformative trauma, or the force of will can cause this to come about. For my own part I do believe it is possible for a man to change in fundamental ways, but that it is not very common. I remember an amusing tale told by Aesop, which makes this very point. Before relating this story, we should note that in ancient times, domesticated ferrets were sometimes kept as pets in Greece. Cats were far less common as domestic pets than they are now.

A female house-ferret, Aesop says, once became infatuated with a certain young man. The ferret pleaded with the goddess Aphrodite to change her into a young girl; and the goddess, amused by this request, granted it without delay. The young man laid eyes on this new creation and became enthralled with her. He decided to take her home with him. When this passionate couple made their way to the bedroom, Aphrodite decided to toy with them a bit. The gods, of course, love to do such things to us humans. She wanted to see if this newly anthropomorphized ferret really had changed in its nature, or whether it was just the same being with a different skin. Aphrodite released a mouse in their bedroom to see what would happen. The newly minted "girl," immediately upon seeing the mouse scurry across the floor, leapt at it aggressively and began to chase it around the room. The shocked young man could do little more than gape in amazement as this took place. Aphrodite was now confirmed in her theory that people do not change, and elected to turn the girl back into a ferret.

Aesop is making a point, and the point is well taken. But changes to personality can take place: they may be rare, but they do happen. The impetus for such change seems to be a traumatic event of some kind. My favorite example along these lines is Ignatius Loyola. He was born in the Basque region of Spain in 1491 and occupied his youth with soldiering and brawling. These frivolous escapades came to an end in 1521 when a cannonball shattered his leg during a French attack on Pamplona. Incompetent medical care left him nearly crippled; one leg was now shorter than the other. He was forced to undergo a long period of rest and recuperation in a castle, during which time he consumed his hours with reading and reflecting on how he had lived his life. A powerful sense of guilt overcame him. As Fate would have it, there were only two books in the castle "library": a life of Christ, and a collection of short biographies of saints called *Flos Sanctorum*. His first reaction in reading these books was contempt and boredom. But then, over time, he began to see things in a different light. The stories grew on him. He began to see that these warriors of religion could be just as brave, and just as self-sacrificing, as the lance-wielding knight. He would eventually forsake his earlier ways and become a soldier in the service of God, and he would go on to found that most influential of religious orders, the Jesuits.

Now I know that there are some who will say that Ignatius had not changed at all, but had simply redirected his impulses in new directions. But is this not the essence of change? What is wrong with a man channeling his energies in new ways, and for nobler purposes and goals? To deny that change is ever possible is to deny the possibility of redemption. There is a scene of dialogue in the 1997 David Mamet film *The Edge* where Anthony Hopkins and Alec Baldwin, both trapped in the wilderness, discuss whether it is possible for a man to change. Hopkins asks Baldwin whether it is possible for a man to change. Baldwin replies with something to the effect of "why would it not be possible?" Hopkins then makes the point that he never knew anyone who actually *did change* their life, but that if he ever made it home, he would start his life over.

While there may be arguments both ways on whether a man can change, I am very sure that a man can grow into a great responsibility. What I mean by this is that a man can rise to the occasion that Fate places on his shoulders. My favorite example of this is the life of Abraham Lincoln; the biography by Ronald C. White has been especially instructive. One can never read enough about him, or see enough documentaries about him. His life is filled with an unlimited amount of practical guidance: the struggles of his early youth, his burning ambition to make a name for himself as a lawyer in Springfield, his mastery of local and then national politics, his dismay at being caught up in the most shattering war in his nation's history, his struggle to articulate his views on slavery, and his agonized attempts to bring the war to a swift conclusion. One begins to have an immense respect for his masterful ability to blend caution with boldness, and decision with patience.

Lincoln's views on slavery, for example, evolved greatly during his life, as is recorded in Eric Foner's excellent *The Fiery Trial.* Like many of his generation, he saw slavery as an evil, but he did not quite know how to deal with the problem. He danced and danced around the issue, as did many of his contemporaries, hoping that it would somehow go away. He tried to occupy the moderate middle ground, promising that his only goal was to "preserve the Union." But the problem would not go away. Sometimes Lincoln's efforts to deal with the issue (e.g., the now-embarrassing "colonization" proposals) expose his shortcomings; but they at least give us a window on a mind struggling to find solutions to a problem that no one before him had been able to solve. As the war ground on, and as the casualties mounted, Lincoln took greater solace in his reading and reflection. He could see that there would be no going back to the old system. The war had now come to stand for something else. He came to see himself as an agent of change, and that the only answer to the slavery question was permanent abolition by constitutional amendment. The old nation could never be returned to: the war had changed everything. A new United States, a new nation, would arise from the ashes and ruins of the old.

The growth and development of Lincoln's views on slavery and many other questions are fascinating objects for study. As I see things, his career proves that a man can grow into a role. A man can rise to the occasion and achieve greatness by mastering his environment. It is not an easy process, of course; it can come about only when the greatest humility collides with the greatest external shock. As these two opposing forces collide, something new, something pure, is finally born. In an address to Congress on December 1, 1862, at a time when the outcome of the war was not at all clear, Lincoln challenged his colleagues to set aside their old ways and think in bold, new terms. Victory was impossible, he told them, without letting go of the "dogmas of the past":

> The dogmas of the quiet past are inadequate to the stormy present. The occasion is piled high with difficulty, and we must rise to the occasion. As our case is new, so we must think anew, and act anew.

Herein lies the secret of change. A man must rise to the occasion in which he finds himself. He does this by showing a willingness to set aside those "dogmas of the quiet past" that are no longer applicable. We cast off the old, and collide with the new: and out of this violent fusion is born a new man, and a *new Ideal.*

120. The Five Protecting Companions

Our trusted friend Ibn Muqaffa provides us with the following advice which I have committed to memory:

> For there are five things, which any one may call his friends, which are his surest support on every occasion, his protecting companions in his journey through life, and the source from which he may draw the supply of his natural wants. The first of these is the knowledge of how to guard against evil; the second are virtuous habits; the third, freedom from doubt; the fourth, generosity of character; and the fifth, good conduct.

It will be useful for us to say something more about each of these protecting companions.

1. **The knowledge of how to guard against evil.** I find that this knowledge is very much underestimated. Most advice centers around how to extricate one from pernicious situations; but little or no attention is given to avoiding evil before it insinuates itself in one's life. Prevention is easier than remedial cures, as we know. One of youth's major shortcomings is its inability to detect trouble in its formative stages. A man must develop a nose for it. He must have all his senses actuated to the detection of evil well before such evil latches on to him. Some have an innate ability to ferret out trouble; some much less so. To develop this skill, I find that a man must learn to detach himself from his surroundings; he must develop a kind of extra-corporeal sensitivity, an eye-in-the-sky awareness that is able to look down on events with studied dispassion. For it is emotion that blinds us to reality; it is our own ego that obscures the sight of danger.

And yet evil is unavoidable in life. One cannot get along in the world without some jostling with it. The man of sense will detect it, learn to compartmentalize it, and will not hesitate for a moment to deal with it if circumstances so require. But at the same time, he will never forget what it really is, and will not hesitate to sever his connections to it at the first opportunity. For evil cannot really be reformed; malice has a way of concealing itself in a dormant state for a long time, only to renew itself at some future date. In such cases it is wise not to be near it. Statements of affability and friendship cannot be trusted in these situations. Conciliation in the short-term, but termination in the long-term: this is a prescription for dealing with evil.

2. **Knowledge of virtuous habits.** We have discussed this topic many times in these pages. Readers should consult *On Duties* and

On Moral Ends for detailed examinations of these matters. But I would like to mention several virtuous habits that I think are of the highest importance: and these are thrift, good judgment, and diligence. By thrift I mean the saving of money, and the ability not to waste it. In our modern era of increasing control and shrinking options, a man must do all he can to preserve his independence and mobility. A store of lucre means freedom; for no bondage is so restrictive as the inability to move from one place to another. Money should not be hoarded for its own sake, or to satisfy voluptuary desires, but to serve as an arsenal of freedom. He who travels and sees the world liberates his mind, and prevents its confinement within the boundaries of parochialism. The second quality, good judgment, is something that can only be acquired from experience and contact with the world. It is uncommon to see a youth with an intrinsic sense of judgment. Seasoning and experience are its prerequisites.

Now with regard to diligence, I can say that it is absolutely essential. We live in an era of short attention spans, endless talk, and abortive efforts; few have the ability to concentrate with single-minded intensity on a project over a sustained period of time. We are more likely to see that most common feature of our age, the internet braggart, endlessly talking and planning, but always coming up short in the way of verifiable accomplishment. And on this subject, it will not be out-of-place here for me to relate another anecdote from my friend Ibn Muqaffa.

He tells us that there was once a religious man who used to receive a daily supply of olive oil and honey from a certain merchant. The man would consume a certain quantity of it every day, and put the remainder of the oil and honey in a jar and hang it from a nail on his wall. One day he was leaning back in his couch with a walking-stick in hand, dreaming about the market prices of oil and honey. He thought to himself, "I will sell what I have in this jar, and with the proceeds I will buy some goats. Each of these goats will produce a kid every six months. Soon I will have a good number of them." According to his mental calculations, he would have a huge number within a few years. And he thought to himself, further, that he could then sell some of these goats and buy a few head of cattle. With this cattle he could till more land, and buy more land, then hire more workmen to help him, and then sell additional plots of land. With the proceeds from such sales, he would be able to buy a larger house, and increase the estate of his family.

These were the religious man's pleasant thoughts as he reclined in his couch. And yet he allowed himself to indulge in even more fancies. Once he had increased his estate, he dreamed, he would be able to marry a beautiful woman, who could then help him raise a family. He would have several children, and he would raise them to become learned and quick-witted. And if, he thought to himself, any of his children disappointed him, he would not hesitate to discipline them with his staff. As he imagined this, he raised his staff vigorously in the air for emphasis. The top of his staff struck the ceramic jar of oil and honey that was hanging on the wall, and promptly shattered; and its contents ran over his head and body. He felt precisely like the fool he was. From this story we are advised not to speculate on goals, but to take action on them. Idle fantasizing and talking mean nothing, and soon bring men to ruin.

3. **Freedom from doubt**. Here again is an underappreciated quality. Modern man is crippled by anxiety, stress, and worry. There are many reasons for this: the lack of support men receive from society today, the lack of clear direction and purpose, and an educational system that destroys their natural instincts and inclinations. He who walks with the purpose and assurance of a conqueror will find he is nearly alone. If you cannot find someone who believes in you, you must believe in yourself. You must become your own supporter. It is always that glimmer of doubt that holds a man back at the crucial moments. We must train ourselves to banish those negative and self-defeating thoughts. Confidence is not easy to come by; I find that it is one of those things that is not a permanent condition. Sometimes we feel it, and sometimes we do not. It is not an end-state that one arrives at and resides forever. It can be snatched away in an instant: and this is why we must constantly be working to reinforce it.

4. **Generosity of character**. This is equivalent to that intangible *magnitudo animi* (greatness of soul) I discussed in Cicero's *On Duties* and *On Moral Ends*. A man must possess that elusive, intangible quality of "greatness of spirit" if he is to leave his mark on the world in a positive way. It is not easy to define. I see it as a mixture of charisma, generosity, humanity, justice, and goodness, all rolled into one aggregated quality. While it is not easy to define, it is very easy to discern in the lives of history's great men, whom we have here studied so often.

5. **Good conduct**. Practical application is the cement that binds together all the qualities mentioned above. For something to make

a difference, it must not only be discussed, it must be practiced. Good conduct is nothing more than acting in the right way, that is, acting in a way that is consistent with what we have described above. On this subject, I do not need to say any more.
These, then, are our five protecting companions.

121. Generosity Should Be Bestowed With Care

There is a scene in the movie *The Wild Bunch* (1969) where Ernest Borgnine and William Holden are discussing the making of promises. Holden says, "We gave our word." Borgnine angrily responds, "That ain't what counts. It's *who* you give it *to*!" Now we can agree or disagree with this statement, but it was meant to call attention to a point that should not be denied: our generosity should be extended only to those who are capable of receiving it without hostility or vituperation. "For it is unwise," says the philosopher Ibn Muqaffa, "to despise either man or beast, small or great, without having examined their utility, which is the proper rule for the conduct to be observed towards them." And by the word "utility," he really means "character." A fable that illustrates this principle may be found in this same writer, which I will relate here.

There once fell into a pit a goldsmith, a serpent, a monkey, and a tiger. None of them were able to get out of the pit, and they all waited patiently for someone to arrive who might help them. Soon a traveler came along; he stood over the pit and looked down into it, and resolved to extract the man and the animals from it. He lowered a rope into the pit, and the monkey–because he was so agile–seized it and swung himself out. The rope was lowered a second time, and the snake wound himself around it, and escaped. Then the rope was lowered again, and the tiger grabbed it with his teeth and climbed his way out of the pit. When the three animals were out, they asked the traveler not to let the goldsmith out of the pit. The animals were suspicious of the nature of man, and were wary of him as an ungrateful beast.

The monkey told the traveler that he lived near a city called Nawadarkht; the tiger said he lived in a nearby forest; and the snake said he lived in a nearby city. The animals told the traveler that they would help him if he was ever in need of aid, and that he only had to ask them. The traveler did not listen to their advice about the goldsmith, however; he decided to pull him out of the pit. The goldsmith came out, and thanked the traveler for the good deed. He said that he lived in Nawadarkht, and if the traveler ever found himself in this city, he should try to visit the goldsmith's house. Then all parties went their separate ways.

Sometime after this, the traveler found himself visiting the city of Nawadarkht. He encountered the monkey he had rescued; the monkey was happy to see him, and fetched some fresh fruits for the traveler to show his gratitude.

The traveler then went on his way. He soon met the tiger whom he had rescued. The tiger, to show his thankfulness, went away to get something for the traveler. He actually went off and killed the daughter of the king living at Nawadarkht; he removed her jewelry and brought them to the traveler, not telling him where the items had come from. The traveler also recalled that the goldsmith lived in this city, too, and he wished to pay him a visit. This he did. Now when the traveler entered the house of the goldsmith, the goldsmith recognized the jewelry that the traveler had: he had made it for the king's daughter.

The goldsmith immediately suspected that the traveler had somehow stolen this jewelry, and thought he could ingratiate himself with the king by reporting the theft of his daughter's valuables. He told the king's retainers that a thief and murderer was at his house. The traveler was seized, tortured, imprisoned, and prepared for execution. As he was being led away, the traveler remembered that the animals had advised him not to rescue the goldsmith from the pit. "How I could have avoided this miserable death, if only I had listened," he repeated to himself. The serpent, who happened to be nearby, heard these words, and tried to think of some way he could help the traveler. The only thing the snake could think of was seeking out the king's son and biting him. This the snake did.

The serpent also had a sister who was a genie: that is, a spirit. The serpent told the genie what was happening, and asked the genie if she could somehow help the traveler and save him from execution. The genie visited the son, in an invisible form, and told the son that he would not be cured of the poison unless the condemned traveler uttered some magic spell over him. In other words, the son would not be saved unless the son interceded to save the traveler from execution. Then the serpent visited the traveler in prison, gave him some leaves that could serve as a snakebite anti-venom, and told him to pretend to use these leaves when he would be called to save the king's son. He should, said the snake, make a boiled drink out of the leaves and encourage the son to drink the potion, which would cure him.

So the king's son told his father that a nighttime voice had told him that the imprisoned traveler would be the doctor who could help him. The king ordered the traveler to be released from confinement. The traveler did as the snake instructed. He told the king's son to drink a decoction made of the leaves. The boy actually recovered, and the king was extremely happy. The king took the traveler aside and asked him to tell his full story, and relate how he had come to be in this situation. The traveler told the king everything. Then the king thanked the traveler for all his efforts, and gave him some lavish presents. But the king was not yet finished. He ordered the goldsmith to be found, arrested, and thrown in jail. He commanded that the goldsmith should be executed for having falsely accused the traveler of murder and theft, and for showing such ingratitude after having been earlier rescued from the pit by the traveler. The goldsmith was put to death.

And so here we may compare the gratitude of the animals towards the one who saved them, with the ingratitude of the goldsmith towards to one who had saved him. It is undoubtedly true that we must select with care the objects of our benefaction, to ensure that we do not incur the negative consequences of others' treachery. And here the words of Ibn Muqaffa are relevant:

> Two descriptions of persons may be said not to see: *the blind man*, and *he who is without understanding*. For as the blind man does not behold the firmament of heaven and the stars, nor what is near and what is far off, in the same manner he who is deprived of understanding can neither distinguish what is praiseworthy from what is dishonorable, nor the good from the bad.

122. Only The Brave Will Find Redemption

There are two things that a man must learn to accept in life: the inherent ambiguities in choosing between alternatives, and the omnipresence of suffering. Consider the story told about Socrates in

Diogenes Laertius's *Lives of the Philosophers* (II.33): a young man asked the philosopher for his advice on whether he should get married. The old man told him that there were good arguments both for and against the proposition, and that he would regret whatever decision he made. "If you do not get married," he said, "you may be lonely and your bloodline will die out; if you do get married, you may be henpecked, beset by financial strains, and dubious in-laws. You may also have to tolerate bad children."

I think the point Socrates was trying to make here was this: since you will have regrets no matter what you do, you might as well just do what you believe is best at the time, and have the confidence that you will meet all future challenges as they present themselves. In other words, there are times in life when we can do no better than act, and then adjust course as needed. He did not counsel a timid retreat from life's responsibilities; instead, he wanted his pupils to have the confidence to attack the challenges and obstacles they would inevitably encounter. He who fusses too much about his health and safety can never rise to greatness. It is an idea that would be capably expressed centuries later by Sir Thomas Browne, when he said:

> He that is chaste and continent, not to impair his Strength, or terrified by Contagion, will hardly be heroically virtuous.

And this, it seems to me, is a very healthy posture to have. But it requires a certain degree of bravery, a certain amount of fortitude, to hear these lessons, and to act on them. It does us no good to obsess about the burdens and heartaches we bear. The Roman writer Valerius Maximus tells us (VII.2) that the Athenian statesman Solon once found one of his friends stricken by grief. He took his friend to the citadel (the Latin word he uses is *arx*, which would refer to the Acropolis), and told him to look down on the houses in the city. "Think to yourself," he said, "of all the tragedies in all the households, among all the people, that are below those roofs. Think of how many there were in the past, how many there are now, and how many there will be in the future. When you do this, you will not mourn your own tragedies, as if they were uniquely your own. What you feel now, was also felt, and will be felt, by countless others." This was the lesson in perspective that Solon gave.

To grieve too long, and with too much intensity, is unmanly. We cannot become too caught up in our own insular worlds. It may often be that a drastic change in circumstances that we initially consider to be tragedy, instead turns out to be a saving grace. This was the meaning behind a certain statement of the philosopher Anaxagoras, as it is recorded by Valerius Maximus (VIII.7). Anaxagoras had left Greece for a long time; when he returned, he found that all of his possessions had been dissipated, destroyed, or lost. He did not waste much time in grieving for these things. His response was:

> Non essem ego salvus, nisi istae perissent.

This means: *I would not have been saved, if these things had not perished.* What he meant by this was that his willingness to give up his comfortable life, and his willingness to lose his material possessions, was what had given him the strength to travel abroad and seek knowledge. And it was the seeking of this knowledge that had allowed him to achieve the great things he did. *For him to achieve greatness, a certain old part of him had to "die," so to speak.* This spirit of seeking knowledge is one manifestation of bravery; perhaps it is the subtlest and most enduring form of bravery. Once this spirit has been grafted into a man, he will carry it with him until the end of his days. The philosopher Isocrates is said (*Val. Max*. VIII.7) to have composed his book *Panathenaicus* when he was ninety-four years of age; even at that advanced stage of his life, he was still seeking to keep his mind fresh and active. What admirable vigor of mind, even though he carried so many decades on his back!

Valor is recognized by all, even by one's enemies. Herodotus (II.102) relates the story of the Egyptian king Sesostris who cruised along the coast of the Red Sea in search of tribes to conquer. He later assembled a large land army and sought further extensions of his domains. When he would overcome a nation who had resisted him, Sesostris would erect monuments describing the details of his victory; but when he occupied nations who submitted to him without ever putting up a fight, his stone markers would additionally be inscribed with the image of a female vagina. What he meant by this was that those who failed to resist him, were not even worthy of being called men. In the crassest terms, he thus announced to the world the femininity of his enemies.

And so there is always hope, no matter how wayward we may have been earlier in our lives. The courage to move forward, to fight through one's mistakes and detours from the proper road: this is the distillation of valor. I will relate one final anecdote, as I recall it from Valerius Maximus (VI.9), which tells us how the philosopher Polemo discovered the proper road for him in life. You may recall the name of Polemo; some of his ideas were discussed in Cicero's *On Moral Ends*. When he was young, Polemo of Athens was something of a hellraiser. He was the type of young man who loved to thumb his nose at authority, drink, carouse, and otherwise do things to upset the established order. Once, after a night of partying, he was walking home, his head still throbbing from the effects of his drunken revelry the night before. Courtesans had doused him with perfume, and his head was crowned with garlands (*sertis capite redimito*).

As he wandered through the streets of Athens, somehow Polemo passed by a lecture-hall and began to hear the voice of the lecturer. He paused; there was something about the sonorous voice of the speaker that gripped his attention, even through his hazy level of alertness. The instructor was Xenocrates. As if he was guided by some invisible hand, Polemo entered the lecture-hall and sat down among the rest of the students. His intention was to disrupt the lesson with heckling and insincere questions; and in fact, he did make some comments along these lines. But Xenocrates was not perturbed; as good teachers are able to do, he sensed something in the young man that was worth his effort to correct. So he immediately changed the subject of his lecture, and began to talk about modesty, temperance, and character.

This had the effect that Xenocrates knew it would have. All good men, deep within them, have a yearning to discuss great things, and to perform great deeds; they need only the right spark, the right teacher, to kindle this spark into a sustainable fire. The good know when they have erred, and instinctively feel shame at their misconduct. Xenocrates knew this, and this was why his words had the effect they did. It was from this point that Polemo's conversion to the pursuit of wisdom can be dated. He threw away the garland on his head, ashamed at how he had been living until that time. Valerius Maximus says:

> And he was saved by the truly nourishing tonic of one speech: he changed from a notorious profligate

into an eminent philosopher. His soul visited the regions of infamy, but it did not live there. [*Uniusque orationis saluberrima medicina sanatus, ex infami ganeone maximus philosophus evasit. Peregrinatus est huius animus in nequitia, non habitavit.*]

In time, Polemo would even succeed Xenocrates as scholarch of the Platonic academy. And it was this very conversion event in this lecture-hall that set him on this path. Polemo had the bravery to listen, and the courage to change. We may all have visited the "regions of infamy" in our lives; such peregrinations are the natural consequences of a turbulent soul seeking direction. *But as long as we do not live in those regions in perpetuity, we carry within ourselves the potential for resurrection, and ultimate triumph.*

123. On Each Side Swords, And On Each Side Corpses

The Battle of Zama essentially concluded the Second Punic War, that terrible contest waged by Rome and Carthage for control of the western Mediterranean. It took place in 202 B.C. near the town of Zama in what is now Tunisia. The commanding generals were Hannibal on the Carthaginian side, and Publius Cornelius Scipio on the Roman. The historian Livy (XXX.30) relates a fascinating exchange between these two great commanders that took place on the eve of the battle. As is well known, it was customary for historians in antiquity to put speeches in the mouths of their protagonists. It was a tradition that dated back to Herodotus and Thucydides, and was continued by the Roman historians. How closely such orations corresponded with what was actually said on any occasion, is open to debate; perhaps some of them are reasonably accurate, but embellished by writers eager to show off their rhetorical training. But the speeches served a purpose, even if they were not precise stenographic records: they helped readers (or listeners, if a book was read aloud) get a sense of what was going on in the minds of the characters. But to return to our story.

It was Hannibal who suggested the conference; Scipio agreed to the proposal. Both generals moved their respective camps closer together, so that the meeting might take place somewhere equidistant between them. Scipio positioned himself near the town of

Naraggara, because a water-source was only "a javelin's throw away (*intra teli coniectum erat*)." Hannibal chose a place that was about four miles away from this. The conference spot picked was one visible from all sides, so that neither party would have to fear a sneak attack. Each general was accompanied by an interpreter. And then they met. Livy somewhat excitedly calls the two men "not only the greatest commanders of their era, but on the same level as any of the kings or generals of every nation in history before that time (*Non suae modo aetatis maximi duces, sed omnis ante se memoriae, omnium gentium cuilibet regum imperatorumve pares*)."

It was Hannibal who spoke first. He was glad, he said, that Scipio was the commander from whom he had to seek peace terms. It was a cruel joke of Fortune, he noted, that he had many years before met Scipio's father on the field of battle, and had bested him; now he was forced to come to that man's son in defeat. It was too bad that the two nations had gone to war. Although the past was an unbroken litany of mistakes, disasters, and misfortunes, Hannibal remarked—in a statement worthy of a philosopher—that

> The events of the past can be more easily condemned than corrected. [*Praeterita magis reprehendi possunt quam corrigi*]

At this point Hannibal dons the cloak of a philosopher, and brilliantly harangues his opponent on the transitory nature of Fortune. He admitted that his country had overreached itself. "We so tried to acquire the property of others, that we ended up fighting for our own (*Ita aliena adpetivimus ut de nostris dimicaremus*). Hannibal told Scipio that he had lived a long life, and that his successes and failures had taught him it was better to follow reason than take one's chances with fortune (*Iam secundae, iam adversae res ita erudierunt ut rationem sequi quam fortunam malim*). And here Hannibal took note of his opponent's youth and string of good luck. With perhaps a hint of bitterness, he tells Scipio:

> You are today what I once was at [Lake] Trasimene and Cannae…I too was once blessed by such fortune…although the gods may give us good judgment in good times, we should be thinking not only about what events have happened, but also

> about what can happen. Even if you forget everything else, I am clear proof of what happens to those who fail to appreciate the role of fortune…The most favorable fortune should be trusted the least [*Maxime cuique fortunae minime credendum est*].

Hannibal finally got to his point. Considering fortune's uncertain dice, he told Scipio, it was better to seek a negotiated peace whose terms were certain, than to take one's chances on the battlefield. Peace terms are in the hands of man; but the outcomes of war are decided by fate. He urged Scipio not to gamble everything on the uncertainties of battle; to do so, he said, would be to risk everything he had so far achieved in life:

> On each side there will be swords, and on each side there will be corpses. Nowhere less than in war do actual events respond to our expectations. [*Utrimque ferrum, utrimque corpora humana erunt; nusquam minus quam in bello eventus respondent.*]

It was far better, Hannibal reasoned, for Scipio to conclude peace on reasonable terms, than to take his chances in an armed contest. With this, the Carthaginian concluded his statement. Yet Scipio was not much moved by these sentiments. He gave a polite and perfunctory response, but nothing worth quoting here. He and Hannibal were unable to agree to terms, the battle was eventually joined, and Hannibal was decisively defeated. So things apparently worked out well for Scipio. Scipio's good fortune at Zama does not diminish the power of Hannibal's cautionary words. I find them to be profound, and a compelling testimony. We pay far too little attention to the realities of fortune's power: a string of successes will inevitably be met with a string of crippling defeats. Hannibal's words could only have been uttered by a man who had both scaled the heights of glory, and felt the despair of abandonment and looming defeat. There is a degree of maturity and seasoning that is a prerequisite for certain kinds of knowledge; we cannot feel the truth of some things in our bones until those bones have been broken and battered by fortune.

Many times as an attorney I have represented clients in criminal or civil cases. In nearly every case, there will come a point where a

proposed resolution of the matter is up for consideration; it is then the job of the attorney to counsel his client on the available options, and to suggest what he believes is in his client's best interest. If the relationship is a good one, and if the client trusts his counselor, he will take this advice to heart; but there will be rare cases when a client cannot see the danger lurking around the corner.
Managing risk is an art, and a necessity. It often happens that a settlement, however imperfect, is a far better choice than rolling the dice at a trial, where uncertainties abound, costs balloon, and risks dramatically increase. In these situations, the words of Hannibal become the voice of reason whispering in our ears: *On each side there will be swords, and on each side there will be corpses. Nowhere less than in war do actual events respond to our expectations.* Recklessness and indiscretion are calamity's surest friends. He who tempts fortune too often, is visited with precisely the outcome he deserves.

124. Never Surrender What Is Most Important

There is a fable in Aesop that involves the behavior of the beaver. In ancient times, beavers were often hunted for the scented oil, known as *castorea*, that was found in sacs near its genital area. The beaver liked to rub its hind parts against trees and logs, thereby possessively marking them with his scent; and this scent apparently had to humans a pleasant aroma, reputed to be evocative of vanilla. The ancients mistakenly thought that this valued aromatic came from the beaver's scrotum, rather than from special internal sacs adjacent to the genitalia.

Aesop says that the animal understood the reason why it was hunted by humans, and that when it was pursued, it would stop to bite off its "genitals" and fling them at his pursuers, thereby saving its life. The legend on its face sounds ridiculous, but it had a long life. We find it in Pliny's *Natural History* (VIII.47.109), where he says of the beavers of the Black Sea region: *Easdem partes sibi ipsi Pontici amputant fibri periculo urgente, ob hoc se peti gnari; castoreum id vocant medici.* Herodotus's description of the Scythian regions of eastern Europe (IV.109) alludes to the medicinal utility of beaver genitalia; he says that the testicles of these animals are "useful for treating the diseases of the womb." Illustrated bestiary manuscripts in the Middle Ages contained depictions of this strange self-mutilation legend. In Latin there are two words for beaver, *castor* and *fiber*; the Greek word for this animal was *castor*, and there is a Sanskrit word that is essentially the same, *kasturi*.

I do not know the origin of this particular myth; perhaps beavers did make some impulsive or panicked movements when pursued that might cause hunters in those days to conclude that the beaver was severing his valued organ. What we do know is that Aesop was attempting to use this example of animal "behavior" to make a moral point. He was trying to warn his readers that, if one had to choose between saving one's life and saving one's valuables, one should unhesitatingly choose to abandon material goods. Of course this is sound advice, and a point made by many writers both ancient and modern. But Aesop's point gets muddled in the telling. The fable is rather opaque, and one could easily propose alternative interpretations. I would even go so far as to say that Aesop missed a more important lesson: by this I mean that a man should never surrender or abandon what defines him, or what is most important to him. Aesop picked an exceedingly bad example when he chose the genitals of the beaver as something that could be approvingly abandoned to save its life. For what symbolizes the physical male of the species, what enables the male to pass on his genetic inheritance, more than its genitalia? Material goods are something very different; they can always be replaced, but the male organ cannot. We do not even need to use an example as extreme as the genitals. A man's integrity and honor can be said to constitute his essence; all he really has in this world is his good name. And this should never be "bitten off" and surrendered to the enemy. For once this happens, he has nothing left. So I would propose that we turn Aesop's fable on its head, and try to correct it: *I say that a man should never surrender that which constitutes his essence.*

We can illustrate this point better by considering an example from history. In the 1750s, the Marquis de Pombal rose to power in Portugal. He was a man of uncommon energy and resolution, and he had a modernization vision for the country that was single-minded and obsessive. The Jesuit order had long dominated education and politics in the country; Pombal saw them as a reactionary clique that was blocking much-needed reforms. He resolved to move against them at the earliest opportunity. The Portuguese king, Joseph I, was no match for him; in short order, Pombal enlisted the king in his plans, and used this royal approval to pursue his agenda.

An alleged assassination plot against Joseph was used as the pretext to launch a long-intended persecution of the Jesuits. A decree bearing the king's signature was issued in September 1759 that confiscated all Jesuit property in the kingdom, and expelled every member of the order. It was a shocking and unprecedented move; the deportations were carried out immediately, with many old and infirm priests bundled off to Italy and Brazil. Other clerics and nobles were thrown into prison on trumped-up charges of conspiracy and treason, without any legal recourse or opportunity to appeal the verdicts against them.

But the tide would soon turn. Joseph died in 1777, and his successor, Maria I, was a pious and traditional sovereign. Under her the traditional religious orders recovered their influence; she wanted to prosecute Pombal, but was dissuaded from this upon discovery that the former king had endorsed all of his programs. On the day of Joseph's burial, Maria ordered the release of eight hundred political prisoners. Most of these wretched men had been rotting in dungeons for twenty years or more; they were malnourished, clothed in rags, and could barely walk due to the tortures they had endured. Some were nearly blinded by daylight, as their eyes had become accustomed to years of operation in darkness. And here we arrive at the purpose of my relation of this incident. There were five men who refused to leave prison until they had been officially declared innocent of treason and conspiracy. Their names and their integrity were so important to them, that they were willing to continue their confinement until they had been vindicated.

To me this shows an incredible force of will, and an unshakeable integrity of character. Think of the resolution that this decision must have taken. Broken in body, they remained unbroken in soul. And this is the kind of ethic that, I think, we need to cultivate today. In the face of danger, in the face of injustice, these men refused to abandon what to them was most precious: their integrity and their good names. This is the point that Aesop should have made. No man needs the advice of a sage to remind him to give up his wallet to save his neck during a robbery. What he does need, however, is to hear that he should remain undaunted in the face of existential threats. *Once a man voluntarily surrenders his ideals, his essence, his manhood, he is irretrievably lost.* When Pombal's political prisoners stepped out of confinement, it was a march of triumph; and they refused to move one muscle until the lies against them had been retracted.

That which is most important, that which is most vital—namely our integrity, our honor, and our good names—must never be bitten off and tossed before the aggressor, like these legendary beavers of old. *Know, then, that that which is our essence must be gripped with the raw conviction of life itself, because it is the very essence of this life.*

125. Petrarch Counsels A Ruler On The Ends Of Power

Giacomo Bussolari was born to a poor family in Pavia, Italy around 1300. A natural gift for oratory augmented the modest opportunities available to him; and he found in the Augustinian order a vehicle for the expression of his ambitions. During the 1350s he was a leading figure in the city, even rising to command the city's military during conflict with the Visconti in 1356. Yet Fortune was to turn against him, as so often happens; by 1359 the Visconti had mounted a successful campaign against Pavia, and Bussolari was ignominiously deposed.

Imprisoned in 1360, he was freed only thirteen years later, by which time his claws had lost their sharpness. He ended his days in apparent contentment on the island of Ischia, where his brother Bartolomeo was a bishop, dying in 1380. He should have counted himself lucky, for there are many worse ways to end one's days. The humanist Petrarch wrote Bussolari a letter of admonition when he was on the ascendancy at Pavia. The old scholar knew what was in store for Bussolari, and felt it was his duty to make an effort to rein him in. We may gauge the success, or lack of success, of these efforts by observing the Augustinian cleric's dramatic fall from power to the darkness of a dungeon; but at least Petrarch tried to mollify the worst expressions of Bussolari's arrogance. Petrarch's letter is a long one, but it contains timeless leadership advice, perhaps never needed more than our own modern leaders. This advice we will now discuss. Recognizing that Bussolari had an unquenchable will to power, Petrarch begins with this warning:

> You will understand—unless I happen to be wrong—that there is no place here for ambition and bragging, and no place for an irrational and shameful tyranny. Whenever your lust to dominate others starts to

> burn, I do not say "gaze upwards at the heavens" (as well-educated and reasonable men do when egged on by temptations), but redirect your eyes on your own self, and in turn think closely about your shoes, belt, and cloak. You will see nothing about yourself that displays imperial purple, but everything that indicates a service to Christ, not a kingly authority over men.

Instead of thinking of your own power and omnipotence, Petrarch warns, think of your own duties and obligations. Remember who you are, and where you came from; never assume airs that you have no right to assume, and do not become intoxicated with your own grandiosity. His letter continues in no ambiguous terms:

> If you are avid to control others, order around those who comfortable with a servile role. Control, my good brother, control the willing; but do so in peace, which alone can raise up the small, bring together the dispersed, and revive the feeble. Wield authority, but in a city that is intact, or since this cannot be done now, rule more gently among the city's ruins, and do not think what is maimed should be even more maimed by your implacable barbarity. [*Dominandi avidus, servire cupientibus impera; dominare, frater, dominare volentibus sed in pace, quae sola quidem et parva augere potens est et dissipata colligere et exsanguia refovere; dominare, sed integra in urbe, sive, id iam quoniam fieri nequit, his ipsis in ruinis dominare placatior, nec laceram iam amplius lacerandam implacabili censeas feritate*.]

If you must indulge your lust to dominate, at least channel that lust against those wretched creatures who seem to enjoy being dominated. The healthy majority, Petrarch says, should be let alone. Govern a state that is whole and healthy; but if you have already caused severe damage to the nation's institutions, at least have the consideration to be mild among the ruins, and cause no further harm. Finally, Petrarch says,

> Do not build a temple to Mars, as Julius Caesar is said to have considered doing near the end of his life.

Instead of building shrines to wasteful and futile wars, Petrarch says, a leader should instead focus his energies on improving the lives and conditions of his people. These achievements are more lasting, and more worthy of a great leader, than the illusions created by fleeting military adventures. When I visited the ancient town of Cumae near the Bay of Naples, I remember looking out across the Tyrrhenian Sea towards the island of Ischia, where Bussolari spent his final days. I thought about his fate, a man whose name is almost forgotten today. He once ruled Pavia like a tyrant; and then, one day, it was all gone, and his city lay in ruins. Along these lines I suppose we can say that life is both too short, and too long: it is too short to make full use of the lessons we learn along the road, and too long for us to want to relive life's pains and sufferings.

There is a passage in Herodotus (VII.45) where the Persian king Xerxes is described as watching his vast invading army cross the Hellespont into Europe. As he observes his endless numbers of ships and men, all busily absorbed in their tasks, his eyes (we are told) began to fill with tears. Xerxes's uncle Artabanus, standing beside him, asked the king the reason for this outpouring of emotion. "I was musing now on how short is human life, and the pity of it pierced me through," Xerxes said. "All these men are here before us, all so focused on their purposes, and yet, in a hundred years' time, not a single one of them will be alive." Artabanus's response was one truly worthy of a philosopher. He told Xerxes that, even though life was short, mortals experience such sufferings that no wise man would wish for an unnaturally extended life. "So numerous are the misfortunes that befall us, and so terrible the diseases that afflict us, that life in all its brevity still seems long," he said.

History has not recorded Bussolari's response to Petrarch's sharp chastisement. One suspects that it fell on deaf ears, as the words of philosophers often do when they try to advise temporal rulers. Plato was unable to win over Dionysius of Syracuse, who had the philosopher enslaved for a time; Voltaire was eventually run off by Frederick the Great; and Bussolari ignored Petrarch, believing him to be fit only for the world of books. Alas! He would eventually realize his mistake. But by then it was too late. Petrarch's wisdom likely came to Bussolari during his thirteen-year prison term, or when he was winding down his days in exile on the island of Ischia, alone and forgotten.

Such is the inevitable fate of all those who grasp blindly for power, heedless of their obligations and limitations.

PART II:
THE WISDOM OF THE NEAR EAST

Author's Note

The primary source for the essays in Part II is the multi-volume *Biographical Dictionary* (وفيات الأعيان وأنباء أبناء الزمان) of Ibn Khallikan. His full name was Shams Al-Din Abu Al-Abbas Ahmad Ibn Muhammad Ibn Khallikan, and he lived from 1211 to 1282. His work is a compendium of biographical sketches of notable medieval Arab and Persian figures in the fields of politics, jurisprudence, theology, philology, literature, poetics, military science, and philosophy. The only complete English translation of Ibn Khallikan was carried out by the Irish orientalist William McGuckin de Slane (1801—1878). De Slane's work, sponsored by the Oriental Translation Fund of Great Britain and Ireland and printed in Paris in the 1840s, is nothing short of magnificent. It required years of effort, and embraces four thick volumes, each one filling nearly eight hundred dense pages.

As someone who has trudged through all four volumes, however, I can assure the reader that De Slane's translation in its current form cannot be described as accessible to modern readers. This fact is hardly his fault. Linguistic conventions and styles have changed dramatically since the 1840s, and the text is desperately in need of modern formatting and typesetting. Adding to the difficulty is the fact that Ibn Khallikan was writing for a Muslim audience seven hundred years ago; the modern Western reader without a basic grasp of Arabic culture will find his references and allusions to be meaningless. He makes no concessions to his readers, and is quite willing to bury his points under mountains of irrelevant detail. The patience needed to read the original text is in short supply in our impatient modern era.

Yet there are treasures hidden in these intimidating roughs, and I believe his writings are a precious legacy that merit the attentions of a modern audience. My goal was to compose short essays that present the source material in a coherent, digestible form. Unless otherwise indicated, the indented quotations from Arabic writers in these essays were translated by De Slane. In some cases, I have made minor changes in his punctuation or spelling to conform to modern usage. Citations to De Slane's translation are given in brackets as the volume and page number of the 1843 Paris edition. A bracketed citation in an essay will apply to each indented quotation in that essay, unless otherwise indicated.

1. Be The Phantom Of A Vision: The Wisdom Of Ibn Munir

In medieval times there was a Syrian poet known for his acrid wisdom in verse, as well as for his distaste for dealing with nonsense. Time and convenience has mercifully shortened his lengthy name (which we will not trouble the reader with here) to Ibn Munir Al-Tarabolusi, or more commonly Ibn Munir. He was born at Tripoli in Lebanon in 1080 and, after receiving a good education, settled in Damascus. There he quickly landed a reputation for penning biting satires against various judges and political figures. This did nothing, of course, to help him win influence in high places. According to his biographer Ibn Khallikan, the son of the *atabeg* (local governor)[17] of Damascus even had Ibn Munir imprisoned for a time.

Gradually a philosophy took shape, and it was one based on an uncompromising self-reliance. One of his verses (*qasidas*) distills his independent worldview in nearly perfect form. For me it is just about the most effective summary of self-reliance ever put into verse. Consider these lines:

> When a man of noble mind perceives that he is neglected, his resolution should be to depart for another land.
>
> Thus the moon, when waned away, strives to attain to its full, and succeeds by changing its place.
>
> Shame on your wisdom if you consent to drink of a troubled source when the bounty of God fills the very deserts.
>
> During the course of your life, you sat in listless idleness and rivaled your camels in indolence; why not take them, and pry into the secrets of the desert?
>
> Depart and you shall gain luster, like the sword which, when drawn, shows on each side of its blade the ornaments which were hidden by the scabbard.
>
> When life forsakes the body, count it not death; the only death is to live in humiliation.

[17] *Atabeg* is a word of Turkish origin. It signifies a local governor appointed by the caliph.

Devote your life to the deserts, not to poverty! As long as God permits you to live, let it suffice you to deserve his favor.

Despise the vileness of Fortune's gifts, when they draw near to you, remain not in inglorious ease, *but be as the Phantom of a Vision which appears and departs.*

Fly, even during the noontide fires, from those on whom you rained honey, and who reaped for you colocynth.[18]

Fly the deceitful wretch in whose heart the plantations of friendship are badly rooted, and who, if you show him sincerity, will misinterpret your conduct.

Ah, how well I know the world and its people! With them it is a crime for merit to be perfect. They are formed in Nature's basest mold: the best of them, if I say a word, will repeat it; and if I keep silence, will report to others what I never said.

When Fortune thinks to cast me down, my haughty spirit bears me up even to the stars. I impress upon my mind the discourse of grave events, though it be darkly uttered; I tend my camels, but I fatigue them also on the failure of vegetation.

The declaration which I make is plain and clear as the light of morning; then follows a firm resolution which executes my will, as the edge of the sword slays the victim which it encounters. [I.139]

What Ibn Munir here is saying is that if we feel neglected and unappreciated, it is our responsibility to make for greener pastures elsewhere. Some people will misinterpret your kindness for weakness. Some will denigrate your contributions or achievements. You may feel as if you are casting your pearls before swine. The worst fate for a man is to live in humiliation among people who denigrate him. We should act like the *Phantom of a Vision*, an airborne spirit, who knows when to move on. If we befriend people and get nothing in return, we should avoid those people. And no matter what, we

[18] A bitter gourd found in the Eastern Mediterranean.

should not be discouraged by the arrows that Fortune shoots at us. We know that he lived life on his own terms, and never chased notoriety or publicity as did many of poetically inferior contemporaries. He apparently died in Damascus in 1152 and was taken to Aleppo for burial; his tomb was said to be near a hill outside the city called Mount Jaushan. Yet even in death he was unrelenting, and not without a mischievous sense of humor. On his tomb, we are told, were inscribed these words:

> Let him who visits my tomb be assured that he shall meet with what I have met with.
>
> May God have mercy on him who visits me here and says to me: '*May God have mercy on you*!'

2. The Ointment Of Abu Ayyub

It is unwise to incur the wrath of a powerful man, if such a situation may be avoided. Sometimes it can; other times it cannot. Even being in the proximity of power can be perilous, as authority has a way of coloring everything in its field of vision with suspicion. An illustration of this principle appears in Ibn Khallikan's *Biographical Dictionary* on the life of the court official (*wazir*) Abu Ayyub Al-Muryani, who served the second Abbasid caliph, Al-Mansur. Things started out amicably enough between Abu Ayyub and Al-Mansur. Before Al-Mansur ascended to the throne, Abu Ayyub had saved him from a rival named Sulaiman Ibn Habib. It is said that Sulaiman Ibn Habib had a grudge against Al-Mansur, and wanted him out of the way. Abu Ayyub helped his friend Al-Mansur escape from the jaws of this predicament. When Al-Mansur became caliph, he had Sulaiman Ibn Habib executed and promoted his apparent friend Abu Ayyub as a key court official. Yet gratitude is not normally an emotion that moves the crown. We may remember the words of Sophocles, quoted by Plutarch in his *Life of Pompey*:

> He who enters a tyrant's door
> Though free before
> Shall be owned by him
> Forever more.

For some reason–we do not know precisely why–Al-Mansur's feelings for Abu Ayyub underwent a gradual but profound change. Perhaps the caliph was secretly troubled by the fact that he knew he was unconsciously in Abu Ayyub's debt for his having saved his life earlier. Or maybe it was something else. Whatever the reason, Abu Ayyub felt the change. He never went into the presence of the caliph without secretly being in fear of his life. Yet each time, he emerged unscathed. Other court officials began to joke that Abu Ayyub possessed some magic "ointment" that protected him from the wrath of the caliph. The story became a running joke around government circles in Baghdad: the expression *Abu Ayyub's Ointment* came to mean an all-purpose protective from bad luck. When a man once asked Abu Ayyub why he always felt such apprehension when coming into close contact with the caliph, he related the following parable by way of explanation.

> It is said that a falcon once said this to a rooster: "There is no animal more ungrateful than you."
>
> "Why so?" said the rooster.
>
> "Because your masters, humans, brought you into this world, took care of you, fed you, and protected you from the elements and from other predators. And yet every time a person comes near you, you run about, cackling and squawking like a maniac, and raising up a huge ruckus for no reason. This to me looks like the behavior of an ingrate."
>
> The falcon continued. "As for myself, humans took me from the wild when I was an adult. They trained me, and for them I catch small game and bring it back to them." The rooster thought about this, and then said the following. "That may be true. But how many falcons do you see turning on a spit over a fire or grill? How many falcons are consumed by man? If you had seen as many falcons roasting on a spit as I have seen chickens, you would be just as apprehensive at the approach of your master as I am." [I.596]

This is the parable that Abu Ayyub related to the man. I wish I could say that this story ended happily, or at least somewhat happily. It does not. Eventually Abu Ayyub's luck ran out; even his famed ointment could only protect him so much. The caliph eventually demoted him and ordered his property to be confiscated. He died, impoverished and broken, in 770 A.D.

3. Seek It, And It Recedes; Ignore It, And It Comes To You

The biographer Ibn Khallikan relates the following anecdote about a man named Abu Amir Orwa Ibn Uzaina, a scholar and poet who died around A.D. 736. Not much is known of his life except that he was a member of the Iraqi tribe of al-Laith. It illustrates the importance of not chasing things in life too much. From personal experience I can attest to this principle's soundness. When I was younger, there were times when I would try too much to chase things or control events. These efforts would leave me exhausted and frustrated. But I found that when I relaxed and just focused on doing my "due diligence," then things seemed to go well for me. The Andalusian poet Mohammad Ibn Idris is quoted has having made the same point in one of his verses, which read as follows:

> The favors which you pursue are like your own shadow.
> Follow them, and you cannot catch them;
> Turn away from them, and they will follow you.

But let us relate the anecdote about Ibn Uzaina. He once set out from the Hijaz to visit the court of the caliph Hisham Ibn Abd Al-Malik in Damascus, Syria. The caliph was a patron of the arts and a lover of fine things, and was much addicted to poetry. He asked Ibn Uzaina, "Are you, sir, the author of the following lines?":

> I am not inclined to wastefulness, and I know that He who is my purveyor.
> Will come to my assistance.
> If I strive to attain his favors, my efforts fatigue me; and if
> I abstain from seeking them, I receive them without undergoing any toil.

The poet replied in the affirmative. The caliph (and caliphs loved to toy with people) said, "Well, I see that you do not practice your own words. For you have come all the way from the Hijaz to seek favors from me." The poet blushed and said, "Yes, commander of the faithful, you have reminded me of those words which I should not have forgotten." He left the court and then departed back for the Hijaz the next day. But the caliph too began to feel uncomfortable. That night, as he lay in bed, he began to think about the incident. He said to himself, "That poet is a skilled man and a clever wordsmith. It is unwise to offend such men who wield the power of the pen. I might be exposed to his satires." The next day he asked about the poet but learned he had already left Damascus. "Well," he said to himself, "I will show him that favors can come chasing after him." So the caliph had a messenger sent in pursuit of Ibn Uzaina. This messenger tracked him all the way from Damascus to the Hijaz. He then came calling at the home of the poet and knocked on his door. When the poet answered, the messenger presented him with the money. Ibn Uzaina smiled and said:

> See how the caliph has demonstrated the proof of my words. I toiled for hours on that poem and was called a liar. But when I remained silent and returned home, favor sought me out.

These are the words of Ibn Uzaina on the wisdom of not chasing frantically after favors.

4. A Fool Is Put In His Place

The following anecdote is related in Ibn Khallikan's short biographical profile of the philologist and rhetorician Al-Said. His full name was Abu Al-Said Ibn al-Hasan Ibn Isa Al-Raba'i. Verbal abilities are highly prized in cultures with rich literary traditions, and this tale bears testament to this fact. Al-Said was born in Mosul but raised in Baghdad and, after completing his education, moved to Spain (Andalus) around A.D. 990 to seek additional opportunities. He quickly gained a reputation for being fast on his feet in verbal sparring and in repartees with opponents. He was a favorite of the powerful minister Al-Mansur, who served the Andalusian ruler Ibn Al-Hakam. We are told that Al-Said did his job well at court but kept asking for more and more money, something that did little to help him gain friends. He composed a book called *Al-Fusus* (roughly meaning "bezels" or "gems") and was paid five thousand dinars for it, but the work was not favored by the public, which found some of the content objectionable due to its off-color content.

Enough of these preliminaries. During one of his journeys he visited the city of Denia and was invited to a public event hosted by the governor, a man named Muwafiq Mujahid Al-Amiri. One of Mujahid's court flunkies was there, a man named Bashar. Bashar happened to be blind, a fact that has key significance in this story. He knew of Al-Said's reputation for verbal ability and could not resist challenging him in public. The governor advised Bashar against this, however, knowing that it is unwise to toy with such men in the presence of an audience. "Do not attack his man who is so quick with his words," he warned Bashar. But Bashar had read Al-Said's books and thought he could best him in public. He would not listen. What happened next is told by Ibn Khallikan, whom we can almost hear laughing as he writes these words:

> "Ya Said!" called out Bashar.
>
> "At your service," replied Al-Said.
>
> "Tell me, what does the word *jaranful* signify in the dialect of the desert Arabs?"
>
> Said, who knew that he himself had invented the word and that it did not really exist in the language, remained silent for some time, and then replied, but without any equivocation or periphrase: "The *jaranful* is one who has sex with blind men's wives and not with other women. He services them with sex on a regular basis."
>
> Bashar, on hearing this, was covered with shame and confusion, whilst every person present burst into laughter. [The governor] Mujahid then said to him: "I told you to abstain, but you would not listen." [I.633]

In such ways are fools put in their places. Another story about Al-Said relates to an incident when one of his literary detractors threw his book into the sea off the coast of Spain. The detractor then penned the following verse:

> The *Fusus* sinks into the sea, and so does everything heavy.

Not to be outdone, Al-Said replied to this verse using the very same rhyme and measure as his detractor, and bested him by punning off the title of his book:

> The *Fusus* has returned to its element; it is from the bottom of the sea that pearls [*fusus*] are taken.

Al-Said eventually left Spain during a period of political turbulence. He died in the year 1026 in Sicily, but his epitaph, unfortunately, has not survived.

5. Abu Al-Hasan On The Fleeting Nature Of Earthly Riches

During the Abbasid caliphate of Al-Mutawakkil there lived an imam named Abu Al-Hasan Ali Al-Askari, surnamed Al-Hadi ("the director"). He was born at Medina in A.D. 829 and died in 868. The Shia considered him one of the twelve imams; he was the son of Muhammad Al-Jawad and the grandson of Ali Al-Rida. He was widely known as an honest man, learned and fearless. But men of ability have a way of antagonizing others merely by their existence; they attract suspicion and jealousy in their very movements. For a base and wicked man loathes nothing so much as the sight of his precise opposite. It cannot be otherwise.

Thus it was that some malicious person passed word to the caliph Al-Mutawakkil that Abu Al-Hasan had stockpiled quantities of books, weapons, and other items for the use of his followers. Or perhaps it simply was that the caliph wanted to take the measure of him. In any case, the king sent some soldiers from his guard to fetch Abu Al-Hasan and bring him before him. The soldiers did as instructed; they found the imam "alone and locked in his room, clothed in a coarse hair-shirt," prostrate and praying on the floor. We are also assured by our historian that there was "no other carpet between him and the earth than sand and gravel." Ibn Khallikan tells us:

> He was carried off in that attire and brought, in the depth of the night, before al-Mutawakkil, who was then engaged in drinking wine. On seeing him, the

> caliph received him with respect, and being informed that nothing had been found in his house to justify the suspicions cast upon him, he seated him by his side and offered him the goblet which he held in his hand. [II.215]

Perhaps to toy with him, the caliph offered the imam some wine to drink. "Commander of the faithful!" cried Abu Al-Hasan, "a liquor such as that was never yet combined with my flesh and blood; dispense me therefore from taking it." The caliph dropped the matter and then asked the imam to deliver some lines of poetry for his and the room's amusement. The imam had not memorized much poetry but did the best he could under the circumstances. He repeated these lines of poetry in a clear, flowing tone:

> They passed the night on the summits of the mountains, protected by valiant warriors, but their place of refuge availed them not.
>
> After all their pomp and power, they had to descend from their lofty fortresses to the custody of the tomb. O what a dreadful change!
>
> Their graves had already received them when a voice was heard exclaiming: "Where are the thrones, the crowns, and the robes of state?
>
> Where are now the faces once so delicate, which were shaded by veils and protected by the curtains of the audience hall?
>
> To this demand, the tomb gave answer sufficient: "The worms," it said, "are now reveling upon those faces; long had these men been eating and drinking, but now they are eaten in their turn." [II.215]

This was the parable that he related to the caliph Al-Mutawakkil and the others present. And when he had finished speaking, a pall of silence fell over the gathering. Some rustled nervously; but no one could speak. Beads of sweat began to break out on some, and now on others; and many were afraid for Abu Al-Hasan's safety. They worried that the caliph, filled with indignation, might give the imam a harsh rebuke for his impertinence. Yet this is not what happened. We are told instead that tears appeared in Al-Mutawakkil's eyes; these became plainly visible to all present. Others attendees also wept. Once the caliph recovered his composure he asked the imam if he owed any monetary debts. Abu Al-Hasan's answer was yes, and the amount of the debts was about four thousand dinars. "See to it that this man is paid this sum of money," the caliph instructed an attendant. We are also told that Al-Mutawakkil invited the holy man to move to a town called *Al-Askar*, which in Arabic means army or military. It was in this way that the imam acquired his surname. He died there in A.D. 868.

6. The Wisdom Of Mercy From Ibn Hazm Al-Zahiri

We turn now to those founts of wisdom who have lessons to teach us. Abu Muhammad Ali Ibn Ahmad Ibn Sa'id Ibn Hazm (أبو محمد علي بن احمد بن سعيد بن حزم) is known to history as Ibn Hazm Al-Zahiri. Born in Cordoba, Andalusia (Spain) in 994, he achieved enduring fame for his incredible intellectual achievements in a number of disciplines, including jurisprudence, theology, philosophy, and poetry. He even composed a manual on love known as *The Ring of the Dove* (طوق الحمامة). Here was a man of substance, a man who could appreciate the virtues of the passions as well as those of the mind. According to Ibn Khallikan's biographical portrait (my source for information in this article), Ibn Hazm's ancestors originally came from Persia. Our intrepid biographer says this about him:

> His knowledge was of the most varied kind, and although he, as his father before him, had held an exalted post in the vizirate and the administration of the empire, he manifested the utmost deference to worldly advantages. His profound humility equaled the greatness of his talents; the number of works composed by him was very considerable; and, possessing a large collection of books, formed by himself, on the Traditions, traditional information, and original subjects, he had also a memory richly

> stocked with such information as could only be supplied by oral transmission. [II.288]

Most of his works have been lost to history. My source for the anecdotes in this article is of course Ibn Khallikan, and I believe he himself took the anecdotes from one of Ibn Hazm's lost works called *Niqat al-Arus* (نقاط العروس) or "Trifles of the Bride." Lost works are the torment of the historian, and the amusement of Fortune. Another source Ibn Khallikan used was the work of the scholar Al-Humaydi (1025–1095). One of Ibn Hazm's favorite sayings–one he inherited from his father–was the following line, which could have come from the pen of a Roman Stoic:

> If you wish to pass your life in wealth, adopt such a mode of life as will not cause you discontent if reduced to an inferior station.

In other words, do not be too attached to material possessions. Al-Humaidi records the following story in his work *Extracts on the Learned Men of Andalusia* (جدوة المقتبس في تاريخ العلاماء الاندلس), a collection of anecdota about the scholars of Spain which Al-Humaidi wrote entirely from memory. Men in medieval and ancient times had better memories than we moderns; memorizing large amounts of information was then part of the educational process. In any case, here is the story.

Ibn Hazm's father served the Spanish Umayyad vizier Abu Amir Al-Mansur (938-1002). His name is Spanish is given as Almanzor. One day, Al-Mansur was attending a public gathering (as leaders commonly do) with his attendants and security detail at his side. He was unexpectedly approached by an old woman who was trying to petition him for the release of her son. The son had been jailed for some offense. Al-Mansur took the petition and scanned his eyes over it. When he had finished, he exclaimed, "By God, now I remember this man. You have reminded me of him." Now seething with anger, he wrote on the petition that the man should be crucified. The Arabic word he intended to write was يصلب, which means (in its passive form) "let him be crucified."

Al-Mansur handed the written order to Ibn Hazm's father, who then passed it on to the guard detail. When Al-Mansur went to check on the matter, he was shown the paper by Ibn Hazm's father.

Although the vizier thought he had written يصلب, it turned out that there was a different word on the paper. The word was يطلق, which means "let him go free." Al-Mansur fumed at the error, struck out "let him go free" with his pen, and then handed the paper back to Ibn Hazm's father (whose name was Abu Omar Ahmad, we should note). But the same thing happened again, to the vizier's mounting rage. By the time the paper made it to the guards, it had somehow become a release order. The word يصلب had again been transformed into the word يطلق. Whether this was due to Al-Mansur's hand, or to the intercession of another's, no one could tell. When the vizier was confronted with the changed word for the third time, he said:

> Be it so. Let him be released in spite of me. When God wills that a man should be set free, I have no power to stand in his way.

So it was done. The anecdote is meant to illustrate the importance of mercy and forbearance in our dealings with others. Another tale along these same lines is told regarding Ibn Hazm's son, whose name was Abu Rafi Al-Fadl. He was working for the most powerful of Spanish leaders at the time, Al-Mutamid Ibn Abbad, whose court was at Seville. One day the caliph called in some of his trusted advisors (of which Al-Fadl was one) and put to them this question:

> I have lately become suspicious of one of my uncles, Ibn Ismail Ibn Abbad. I suspect he has been plotting against me. Are any of you aware of a caliph who has executed an uncle for conspiracy against a caliph?

Al-Mutamid was looking for some precedent or justification for putting his uncle to death. At this point, Al-Fadl was brave enough to step forward and say:

> May God's assistance never fail you! We know of none who put his uncle to death for conspiracy against him, but we know of one who pardoned his uncle who had revolted against him. It was Al-Mamum, specifically, who forgave Ibrahim Ibn al-Mahdi.

When everyone heard this, the court fell silent. Making such pronouncements to a ruler was always a risky proposition. But when the caliph heard the statement, he was greatly relieved. Ibn Khallikan's text tells us that the caliph "kissed him [Al-Fadl] between the eyes." He threw his arms around Al-Fadl, embraced him, and then ordered that his uncle should be treated with respect and courtesy. Thus did the caliph demonstrate the importance of mercy and forgiveness in dealings with others. We are told by Ibn Khallikan that even though Ibn Hazm was a man of incredible ability, he made many enemies because of his ceaseless disputes with political officials over various matters. It is a pattern that is not without precedent in history. He is said to have quarreled with so many people that eventually no one wanted to deal with him. The sovereigns of several Spanish principalities removed him from his official positions. Ibn Hazm retired to the town of Labla (now Niebla) in Andalusia, and died there in June of 1012.

7. The Wise Sayings Of The Poet Al-Tihami

The Arabic poet Abu al-Hasan Ali Ibn Muhammad Al-Tihami (? – 1025) is said to have taken the name *Tihami* in one of two possible ways that may hint at his family's origins, according to our trusted chronicler Ibn Khallikan. *Tihami* was used both as an informal name for the city of Mecca, and as a name for the mountains between the Hijaz and Yemen. But it is not clear which of these geographic references apply to our poet. We do know that most of his life was lived in Syria. That he was an artist of consummate skill is attested to by the Andalusian poet and historian Al-Bassam (1058-1147) whose massive work ذاكرة في المحاسن اهل الجزيرة ("Record of the Merits of the People of Iberia") compiled information about the great Arabic Andalusian poets. Al-Bassam offers the following evocative comment, rich in imagery, about Al-Tihami's verses:

> He was renowned for his abilities and possessed a cutting tongue. Between him and all the varied modes of expression the path was free; his poetry indicated as clearly the talents which had fallen to his lot, as the coolness of the zephyr denotes the

presence of the morning; and it disclosed his exalted station in science as plainly as the tear-drop reveals the secret of love. [II.335]

There are many elegant verses in Al-Tihami's repertoire; too many, in fact, to list here. I will repeat some of the best which Ibn Khallikan records as coming from his *qasidas* (poems), along with a brief comment as needed.

> When the lips of the flowers on the hills and those of our mortal beauties were smiling, I asked my friend which were the fairest to the sight: "I know not," said he; "all of them are anthemis blossoms." [The anthemis flower is white, and often compared in old Arabic poetry with a woman's teeth.]

One of his longer poems was composed after the death of his son. Stricken by grief, he wrote a long poem to express his anger and contempt for the world. Some extracts taken from it are these:

> I pity those who envy me, because hatred burns within their bosoms. They see God's kindness towards me, and thus their eyes are in paradise, whilst their hearts are in hell...
>
> [The world] is composed of turbid elements, yet you hope to find it free from dregs and sediment! He who requires of time what is contrary to its nature, is as the man who seeks in water for a firebrand.
>
> He who expects what is impossible, builds his hopes on the brink of a tottering sand-bank.

Regarding the chasing of women, he said this:

> How often have I warned you against the land of Hijaz, for its gazelles [girls] are accustomed to make its lions [men] their prey.
>
> You wished to pursue the hinds of Hijaz; but, unfavored by fate, it was *you* who became *their* prey.

Here are some of his saying on human relations and general wisdom:

> In the company of noble-minded men there is always room for another. Friendship, it is true, renders difficulties easy. A house may be too small for eight persons, yet friendship will make it hold a ninth.
>
> If Time, who is the father of mortals, treats you ill, then do not reproach his children when they do the same.

These last two maxims are without doubt words to live by. But Al-Tihami himself came to an unfortunate end. Because of his fame he was asked to intervene in political matters. Although this sort of thing is always a perilous proposition for artists or idealists, he agreed to do so. He was asked to carry some documents as a secret messenger between two quarreling political factions. When he arrived in Egypt to complete his mission, he was discovered, confined to jail, and later executed for conspiracy.

8. Resources Can Come In Unexpected Ways: The Bounty Of Imad Al-Dawla

Imad ad-Dawla Ibn Busway (A.D. 891—949) was the founder of the Buyid Dynasty in medieval Persia. His name in Persian is given as Ali Ibn Buya, but he is more commonly known as Imad Al-Dawla ("pillar of the state"). Ibn Khallikan's short sketch of his life contains the story related here; this story in turn is taken from the historian Al-Mamuni. It reminds us of the fact that, sometimes in life, a bit of good fortune can provide us with all we need. The world, somehow, has its own way of providing for us; and if we persist long enough, some problems eventually solve themselves.

When in 934 Imad Al-Dawla captured the city of Shiraz, he was hard-pressed to pay his soldiers. Then as now, it was never a good thing to have unpaid, battle-hardened soldiers in your midst. But his coffers were empty, and he would need time to replenish them. He was apprehensive at the prospect that some mutiny might break out. To contemplate what to do, and to try to devise a solution, he went alone to his bedchamber and laid down. Looking up at the ceiling, he spotted a snake emerge from a small hole and move to another part of the ceiling. Concerned that it might fall on him, he called some attendants to bring ladders and try to catch the serpent. While they were searching for it, the workmen discovered a compartment between the ceiling and the roof of the building. Secreted inside the compartment was a cache of money and expensive clothing, valued in the thousands of dinars. He thus was able to distribute this money to his men in the short-term and stave off discontent.

He then used one of the pieces of fabric recovered to make a garment for himself. He inquired and found a tailor in Shiraz who carried a high reputation for competence. Imad Al-Dawla summoned this man–who was deaf–to ask him to work for him. But the tailor mistakenly thought he had been called on account of some unrelated matter. Some time previously, the tailor had been asked to watch over some items that his former master had entrusted to his care. Thinking that this was the reason for his summoning, the tailor suddenly blurted out that he had only twelve chests of value at his house that he was holding. Imad Al-Dawla sent some people to investigate. The trunks did indeed contain a sizeable amount of money, and this was used to pay off his soldiers in full. So it was that his needs were provided for by the intercession of fate.

9. Language Mastery As A Secret Code

Mastery of language is indeed a powerful tool. This is especially true when the speakers hail from the same cultural background, and can make use of all those subtleties that would be lost on the non-native. This point is brilliantly illustrated by an anecdote told about Ali Ibn Munqidh, who became emir of the district of Shaizar in northern Syria in 1081. His surname was Sadid Al-Mulk, and this is how I will refer to him in this article. We will see that words effectively deployed can literally save lives. This story is adapted from Ibn Khallikan's short biographical sketch of Sadid Al-Mulk.

Sadid Al-Mulk was such a good leader that he acquired great renown in his time. Many of his descendants became noted jurists, military men, and scholars; he was the grandfather of the famous poet Usama Ibn Munqidh (1095-1188). Observers in his day often commented on his penetrating intellect and ability to detect the slightest hints about mood and intention. How sharp he was, we will now relate. Before Ibn Munqidh (Sadid Al-Mulk) became lord of the castle at Shaizar, he used to make frequent trips to the city of Aleppo. (The governor of the city at that time was a man named Taj Al-Muluk Mahmud Ibn Salih Ibn Mirdas). One time Sadid Al-Mulk had to leave Aleppo and go to Tripolis in Syria; its emir Jalal Al-Mulk Ibn Ammar let him stay in his palace there. The governor of Aleppo, Ibn Mirdas, then asked one of his secretaries to write a flattering letter to Sadid Al-Mulk, asking him to come back to Aleppo.

But the secretary was an honest man and happened to be a friend of Sadid Al-Mulk. He suspected that his boss, Ibn Mirdas, had nefarious plans in store for Sadid Al-Mulk if he came back to Aleppo. So he contrived a plan to warn his friend in the most subtle way possible. As he was finishing writing the letter, he came to the standard formula in Arabic, *In sha' allah*, meaning "if God wills it." But as he wrote the letter *n* in the first particle *In*, he wrote the Arabic *shadda* mark over the letter *n*. This is a diacritical mark in Arabic that means a consonant is to be given emphasis or "doubled."

When Sadid Al-Mulk received this letter in Tripolis as he was relaxing with the emir Ibn Ammar, he showed it to his friends. They all commented on how elegant it was, and how it seemed to express a sincere desire to have Sadid Al-Mulk return. But he, being more perceptive any other man, detected something wrong with the letter. So he wrote a response. In his response, Sadid Al-Mulk used the following phrase: *I, your humble servant, who am grateful for your kindness.* The Arabic word for "I" is أنا (*ana*). But under the first letter he wrote the vowel mark for the "i" sound, and above the second letter he wrote the mark (*shadda*) of consonant duplication. Thus the word *ana* became *inna*. This is difficult to convey clearly in English, but the idea is that the words looked outwardly similar but were linguistically different. When the secretary of Ibn Mirdas received Sadid Al-Mulk's reply, he knew that his secret message had found receptive ears. He said to himself:

> Now I know that he truly understood what I wrote.
> For I gave him a clue, and he answered with something that confirmed his understanding.

And this his what the two men meant by their word-games. They were both referring to different Koranic verses. Each verse carried meaning. When the secretary first wrote to Sadid al-Mulk and transformed the *In* into *Inna*, he was referring to the following Koranic words: *Inna 'l-Mala yatamiruna*, etc. (*Verily, the great men are deliberating concerning you, to put you to death*...). And with his own response using the word *inna*, Sadid al-Mulk was referring to the following verse: *Inna lan nadkhulaha abadan*, etc. (*We will never enter therein while they stay in it*...).[19]

The quotes are from suras 28:20 and 5:24 of the Qur'an. In this way were these two men able to communicate in secret using their shared knowledge of Qur'anic scripture. With this coded language the secretary was able to warn off Sadid Al-Mulk from returning to Aleppo and facing possible imprisonment or death. This is the story as told by the biographer Ibn Khallikan, from whom I have adapted it. Words can inspire, illuminate, and save.

10. How Al-Fadl Al-Barmaki Learned Generosity

Al-Fadl Ibn Yahya Al-Barmaki (A.D. 766—808) was a government official who served the most famous of all the Abbasid caliphs, the great but mercurial Harun Al-Rashid. Besides serving in several administrative posts (such as governor of Khurasan), he was also trusted enough to tutor Harun's young son and heir Al-Amin. Although he later fell out of favor with the caliph, many stories are told of his generosity and kindness. It is said that Al-Fadl once got himself into trouble with excessive partying and hunting. His father, the famous patriarch Yahya Al-Barmaki, wrote a letter to him advising him to correct his behavior; the letter closed with the following wise lines:

> Pass the day in the pursuit of honors and bear with patience the absence of your beloved. But when the darkness approaches and veils our vices, pass the night to your satisfaction, for night is the clever man's day. How many are the men whom you think devotees, that play strange games in the face of the night! It [night] lets down the veils of darkness around them, and they spend their hours in pastime

[19] II.362.

and enjoyments till morning. The fool exposes his pleasures to public gaze, and all his watchful foes denounce the scandal. [II.487]

By this Al-Fadl's father seemed to be telling his son to maintain proper conduct when exposed to public view; enjoyment is best enjoyed away from the prying eyes of the public. One of Al-Fadl's sayings was "The joy of the man who receives a favor is not equal to mine in granting it." While he enjoyed a reputation for great generosity, he also was known for his brusque manner and blunt directness. When a friend asked him how he came to be so, his reply was: "I learned this manner from a man named Omara Ibn Hamza." When pressed on further details, Al-Fadl told the following anecdote.

"Many years ago my father was a tax-collector in a province in Persia. Through the bankruptcy of some business he owed the state a great deal of money. The total owed to Baghdad was about 3 million dirhams. As he was unable to come up with the money, he was taken into custody and brought to the capital. My father had no way of coming up with the money, and faced very real trouble from the caliph.

"At that time I was a young boy. My father told me to go and see a man named Omara Ibn Hamza. I and many other people knew that a great enmity existed between Ibn Hamza and my father; yet I was told to approach him, explain the dire circumstances my father was in, and ask for a loan until such time as it could be paid back. I was certain that my father was a deluded fool. What man would loan his personal enemy any money at all, never mind 3 million dirhams?

"But my father said, 'You must go to him anyway. Perhaps God will subdue him and open his heart up to pity.' So I advanced unwillingly to Omara's house; I was certain that I would be rejected with scorn. When I entered his house, I found him reclining on a sofa, his beard and hair perfumed with civet and musk.[20] I offered my greetings to him, but he made no response. I then explained the

[20] There is an interesting point of etymology in this line that I cannot resist mentioning. The verb غلف is used here, and it normally means "to wrap" or "enfold." But it can also mean the act of perfuming a beard with civet-musk (غالية, *ghalia*). In Arabic the word for a civet-cat (a type of cat) is قط الغالية (*qit al-ghalia*). This same word has passed into the Portuguese and Spanish languages as the word for civet-cat: *gato de algalia*.

purpose of my visit, to my great chagrin. He only grunted a bit, and then said, 'We will have to see.'

"I left his house with a burning sense of humiliation. I was furious at my father for exposing me to such humiliation, and angry as well at Omara for what I took to be his condescending arrogance. But when I returned to our house a few hours later, I found several loaded pack-mules with attendants waiting near our door. I asked what they were there for, and the attendant told me that Omara had sent us the money. My father and I were incredulous, and could not believe that Omara had behaved so generously.

"Soon my father was reinstated in his post, cleared up the problem with the uncollected taxes, and recovered his financial situation. He soon had a great deal of money and wanted to pay Omara back for the loan he had so generously granted us. So I returned to his house and found him there at rest. When I explained the purpose of my visit and our family's desire to repay him, he cut me off, saying 'By God, what is this? Am I your banker now? Go away, and keep the money!' When I returned to my father and told him what had happened, he was astonished. This was how I learned both generosity and brusqueness."

So things can be in life. It is not possible to predict all things, and it is not possible to divine the intentions of others. Sometimes those we believe to be our enemies may actually have hidden reserves of goodwill, the sources of which are beyond our powers of comprehension. The following lines of poetry were later composed regarding Al-Fadl's generosity. Ibn Khallikan says that they were written by either by Marwan Ibn Abi Hafsa or Abu Al-Hajna:

> The power of doing good and of harming is in the hands of princes, but the Barmakids [the family of Al-Fadl] do good and harm not. If punishment is to be inflicted, that duty is imposed on others; but to them all good is justly attributed. When you do not know the origin and ancestry of a man, examine his acts; when the roots are swollen with moisture, the sprouts flourish and the crop is abundant.

These are wise words, and rightly spoken. The last line in the quote above makes use of a clever pun in Arabic that is lost in translation. The word for "moisture" in the last sentence (ندى, *nada*) can also mean “generosity,” thus allowing the poet to play on both ideas with the same word.

11. Using Ingenuity To Accomplish Your Goals

Those who are resourceful will find ways of carrying out their purposes. They will not be deterred by momentary setbacks or obstacles. The lazy man or the dullard will take refuge behind the natural obstructions that life places in his path and, using such problems as excuses to avoid work, take comfort in his failures. In his mind, failure was inevitable. This way of thinking can be found in many people; they never advance far in life because they are not willing to hunt for creative solutions to problems. Obstacles must be bypassed, smashed through, vaulted over, or avoided altogether. To amusing anecdotes taken from Ibn Khallikan’s biographical works help to illustrate this point. The first story is derived from the entry on Abu Abdallah Al-Masudi, a Shafite jurisconsult who was a native of Marw (Merv). Al-Masudi studied under a master named Al-Kaffal. One day Al-Kaffal was conducting a class for his law students on perjury. The topic of discussion was how perjury may committed or avoided. Someone posed the following hypothetical:

> Suppose a man swears that he will not eat eggs. Then imagine he approaches someone else and says, “I will eat whatever food you are carrying.” Out of his pocket, the man promptly produces an egg. What should the promissor then do? How can he avoid perjury? [II.637]

This was the rhetorical problem; it reminds me of the type of rhetorical exercise found in Seneca the Elder’s *Controversiae*. Al-Kaffal was unable to propose a solution to the riddle. Al-Masudi, sitting in the classroom, came up with the following solution:

> Let the man make a biscuit out of the egg, and then eat that. He will then have eaten what the other man was carrying, yet not have broken his oath to abstain from eggs.

This is indeed a clever way of threading the needle and solving the problem. (The jurisprudent Abu Hanifa later would advance his own solution: he said that the egg could be hatched, and the raised chicken could be eaten later. But I prefer the first solution to the problem).

The second anecdote is taken from the biographical sketch of the judge Abu Ali Al-Tanukhi. The point of the story is to illustrate that one must find imaginative ways of carrying out one's designs. A fabric merchant had traveled a long way to the city of Medina in order to sell some women's veils. He had some pack animals loaded with these articles of clothing and was seeking purchasers; but he had no success. The merchant persisted in asking around and was led, by one way or another, to a somewhat sketchy character named Miskin Al-Darimi. He was famous for his poetry and for his womanizing in his youthful years. But he was now old, and he had given up his licentious ways to become devoutly religious. But he still enjoyed a reputation for bawdy humor. But the merchant persisted in asking for the old poet's help in trying to sell the load of veils. Al-Darimi finally consented and wrote these words, which he released to the public:

> Say to a beautiful woman in a black veil,
> "What design have you formed against a pious devotee?
> He just secured his genitals for prayer
> When you sat in ambush for him at the door of the mosque!" [II.583]

(Meaning, of course, that the sight of the woman would have produced physical arousal, and shown outwardly through his garment.) The sexually suggestive lines had the desired effect. When these lines were circulated, people assumed that Al Darimi had fallen back into his old habits of sexual license; everyone thought that he had become infatuated with a woman who wore a black veil. Suddenly, nearly every woman in the surrounding neighborhoods wanted a black veil, and Al-Darimi's merchant friend was able to sell his inventory at greatly inflated prices. In this way did the merchant come up with a clever way to turn his load of unwanted goods into goods that were highly desirable and ultimately profitable. He found a creative solution to his problem.

12. Sometimes It Is Not Advisable To Question Authority

While it may be good in some instances to question inherited tradition and authority, there are many times when one should not. Free-thinking individualism has its place, but there is an equally valid place for respecting the power of authority and tradition. This point is amusingly illustrated in the two anecdotes presented below. They are related in De Slane's edition of Ibn Khallikan's encyclopedia, but the first tale is originally found in the Egyptian historian Al-Maqrizi. Ahmad Ibn Tulun (c. A.D. 835–884) was the founder of the medieval Tulunid dynasty that ruled Egypt and greater Syria from 868 to 905. He had been a slave early in life, yet rose to become a ruler in fact as well as in name. It is remarkable that soldier-slaves so often rose to the highest positions in medieval and early modern Islam; the historian finds repeated examples of this unexpected social mobility. In any case, Ibn Tulun had a reputation for being a stern task-master, a man who tolerated no dissent and was determined to modernize the civil and military structures of his lands.

Once Ibn Tulun had ordered the completion of an aqueduct in Egypt. For some reason, rumors began to spread that it was not "lawful" to drink the waters coming out of the aqueduct. The likely explanation seems to be that some of the emir's clerical enemies were trying to embarrass him. To solve the problem, Ibn Tulun called on a doctor of jurisprudence from the Shafite sect named Mohammed Ibn Abd Al-Hakam. The emir sent a slave to fetch Al-Hakam in the middle of the night from his house.

"What does the emir want with me?" he asked the slave nervously.

"We are supposed to meet him in the desert. That is where he is waiting for you," was the reply.

"By God! For what purpose?" said Al-Hakam.

The slave would only say, "Just avoid making any remark about the aqueduct."

Now more terrified than ever, Al-Hakam mounted his horse and went by a public road with slave into the desert. At length he began to see torches in the distance; the two riders finally came to a meeting place in the desert. A section of the new aqueduct was also nearby. Ibn Tulun was present, with his retainers, all of whom were carrying torches. Al-Hakam dismounted and saluted the emir, who did not return the salute. This was a bad sign, and the poor doctor was by now thoroughly petrified. Neither was it encouraging that an ominous silence had now fallen over the group. Pleasant things usually do not happen in such situations, to say the least. But suddenly an idea came to him. Al-Hakam broke the silence and spoke as follows:

> O emir, your messenger here has seriously fatigued me! I have ridden a long way and am in dire need of a drink! [II.619]

One of the emir's pages offered him water, but he said, "No, please allow me to draw it myself." He then drew some water from the emir's aqueduct, and drank so much that he felt he would nearly burst. When he was finally done, he looked at Ibn Tulun and said: "May God quench your thirst at the Rivers of Paradise! I have drunk to my fill, and I do not know which to praise more: the excellence of the water, with its purity and sweetness, or the wonderful appearance of the new aqueduct!" The emir looked at Al-Hakam for a moment and then said, "I will need you at some point, but now is not the time. Thank you for your courtesies; you may now withdraw." He then ordered his retinue to assemble, and they made preparations to depart. The doctor also left. On the way back to his residence, the slave said to him, "Sir, you have hit the mark!" To this Al Hakam answered, "May God reward you! Were it not for you, I might have perished!"

We will close with one final anecdote. A student of the Shafite jurisconsult Al-Tirmidhi (c. A.D. 824– 892) once was asking him to explain a nuanced point of theology. The student did not accept the explanation provided by the master. The problem being discussed involved an abstruse point about the descent from one plane of consciousness to another. The master was growing tired of explaining himself, and finally told the student:

> The descent is intelligible; the manner how is unknown; the belief therein is obligatory, and the asking about it is a blamable innovation. [II.620]

This response abruptly ended the discussion.

13. The Wisdom Of Fakr Al Din Al Razi

Fakhr al-Din Al-Razi (1149–1210) was a Persian theologian and philosopher whose fecundity was only surpassed by his depth of understanding of various disciplines. He is credited with over one hundred works, although it is likely that this number was considerably higher. Learned in astronomy, philosophy, theology, chemistry, and a variety of other subjects, he was also said to have been a man of great humanity and understanding. His inclinations were rationalist and scientific; for this reason he found more to his liking in the natural sciences than in airy theological speculations. Like Plutarch, the biographer Ibn Khallikan believed that more could be revealed about a man's character in a few anecdotes than we might expect. He says:

> Fakhr Al-Din was the pearl of the age, a man without a peer; he surpassed all his contemporaries in scholastic theology, metaphysics, and philosophy. He composed instructive works on many branches of science, such as a commentary on the Koran containing an immense quantity of rare and curious observations; it is a most extensive work, but he left it unfinished; the explanation of the opening *sura* alone fills one volume... He was the first who introduced the systematical arrangement so remarkable in his writings, and which had never been employed by any person before his time. He preached with most impressive effect, both in Arabic and Persian; in the midst of his exhortations, feelings of compunction would draw floods of tears from his eyes. [II.671]

According to his biographer, one of Fakhr Al-Din's wisest pronouncements on intellect and reason was this gem, which could easily have come from the mouth of St. Augustine:

> Human reason can reach only to the extent of its chain; the utmost efforts of mortals mostly serve to lead them into error. Our souls and our bodies are at variance, and the sum of our worldly enjoyments is

> but bane and evil. Though we pass our lives in investigation, all we can collect may be reduced to this: ***it is said***, or ***they say***. How many men, how many empires have we seen flourishing, and which rapidly disappeared; how many mountains to the summits of which men have ascended, who are now gone, and the mountains remain.

In other words: all knowledge is limited by human perception. We can know inherited tradition, and we can rely on the testimony of our physical senses, but our powers of reason have outward boundaries. On his good nature and kindness, the following anecdote is told by the poet Ibn Onain. One day Fakhr Al-Din was delivering a lecture out-of-doors to a group of students in the city of Khowarism. Snow had begun to fall and the air had become very cold. A pigeon flew by, pursued by some bird of prey, and landed near the learned professor; it was disoriented from the cold and by shock. After the lecture was over, Fakhr Al-Din took it in his hands and physically calmed the animal down until it was able to be released back into the air. After watching this dramatic scene of rescue, the poet Ibn Onain composed the following verses in commemoration to praise Fakhr Al-Din:

> Son of the generous!...Son of those who protected the unfortunate when their souls trembled under the sword and the gory-pointed spear!
>
> Who told the dove that your mansion was a sanctuary, and that you were an asylum for the timorous? It came to visit you when its death was near, and you bestowed on it new life, in saving it from destruction. Could it receive such presents as men obtain, it would leave thy hand, bearing off a large donation.
>
> It came with its complaints to the Solomon of the Age, whilst death gleamed at it from beneath the wings of a rapacious, vigorous bird attracted by the sight—-no, by the shadow—of food, and it fled before him with a trembling heart.

In the city of Herat, he was said to have spoken the following maxim about life and fate during one of his lectures:

> A worthy man is despised during his lifetime, but when removed by death, his loss is severely felt.

It is a saying valid for any age, and any culture.

14. The Wise Sayings Of The Philosopher Al-Turtushi

Abu Bakr Al-Turtushi (ابو بكر محمد بن الوليد الطرطوشي) was a political philosopher and doctor of the Malikite sect. He was but one of that avalanche of philosophers, poets, writers, scientists, and theologians produced by the energy and brilliance of Andalusian Spain in the medieval period. Many–probably most–of these Andalusian writers are completely unknown today in the West, a fact that I have made efforts to change in previous articles here.

He was born in 1059 in the maritime city of Tortosa, and took his surname "Al-Turtushi" from that city, which is now in Catalonia. He received the rudiments of education in Zaragoza under the guidance of several great teachers, among them a noted philosopher and rhetorician named Abu Al-Walid Al-Baji. Like many scholars of his day, he traveled widely, eventually reaching Damascus and Baghdad. He would eventually come to reside in Alexandria, Egypt. The biographer Ibn Khallikan, probably suppressing laughter as he wrote, tells us:

> [Al-Turtushi] studied also, in his native place, the science of arithmetic and the art of calculating inheritance shares. [II.684]

His most enduring work was a treatise called *Siraj al-Muluk* (سراج الملوك, "The Lamp of Kings"). He is also credited with a book entitled "The Lamp of Guidance" (سراج الهدى). As far as I can determine, neither one has ever been translated into English. His biographer Ibn Khallikan tells us that he lived a life of asceticism and self-mortification, yet he understood human nature, and realized that more could be achieved by indirect teaching and counsel than by blanket moral prohibitions. He wisely refused to condemn too strongly the charms of women and wealth. In this he resembled the Greek Neoplatonists like Plotinus. He once said the following to his students:

> When two advantages are offered to you, one of them worldly and the other spiritual, seize on the latter, and you will obtain them both.

This is wise counsel for any occasion. He is also said to have made a habit of reciting these lines:

> God possesses intelligent servants who have renounced the world through fear of temptation. When they considered it and discovered that it was not a fit abode for the living, they took it for an ocean, and made of their good works a ship.

What Al-Turtushi meant by this was that, while the world may often be a wicked and difficult place, we must still try to construct our own personal "ark" in his life, and within it live as best we can following the dictates of our own conscience. He was an eminently practical philosopher as well. The following amusing lines are attributed to him by more than one source, and show a hard-headed, realistic business sense unbecoming for a philosopher:

> When you wish to advance an affair for the success of which you are anxious, let your messenger be blind, deceitful, deaf and dumb—spare every other messenger, and employ that one which is called *money*.

Sometimes a few lines of humor can make a point better than a hundred pages of text. He died, says Ibn Khallikan, in Alexandria in June 1126, and "was buried in the Wala cemetery, near the New Tower (*Burj Al-Jadid*), and to the south of the Green Gate (*Al-Bab Al-Akhdar*)." Al Turtushi also went by the surname *Ibn Abi Randaka*. The name "Randaka" seems to have been derived from the Spanish words *renda-se aca*, meaning "render" or "come here." Spain's rich past should never cease to amaze us.

15. The Wise Sayings Of Ibn Al-Sammak

The biographical encyclopedia of Ibn Khallikan–that deep well of collective anecdotal wisdom–has an interesting entry for one

Abu Al-Abbas Muhammad Ibn Sabih. His surname was Al-Mazkur, but like many famous figures it is his nickname that posterity recalls best. This nickname is Ibn Al-Sammak, which literally means "son of a fish-monger" in Arabic (the word for fish is samak, سمك). It is not clear where this name came from; perhaps he had a fish-merchant as an ancestor.

Ibn Al-Sammak was a native of the city of Kufa in today's Iraq, and was a prominent figure in the Ijl tribe. He was a rhetorician and speech-writer of great skill, and there are many stories told of his proficiency with the spoken and written word. Linguistic skills (both oral and written) are highly prized in the Arab world; to a degree not fully appreciated in the West, it is a culture that elevates beautiful writing and speech to an art form. We will relate some of his sayings, as well as the stories told about him. The translations of Al-Sammak's sayings here were done by McGuckin de Slane, with his characteristic artistry and competence. One of his sayings was this:

> Fear God as if you had never obeyed him, and hope in him as if you had never disobeyed Him. [III.27]

It is said that Al-Sammak had once made the acquaintance of the famous caliph Harun Al-Rashid. A tale is told of the interaction between these two men. When Harun was close to death, he began to have doubts as to whether he would ever enter Paradise. He was conscious more and more of the evil deeds he had committed in his life. Troubled by these persistent fears, he summoned several doctors of theology and consulted with them; but alas, this was of little use, for three of these doctors had the temerity to inform the caliph that he would not enter Paradise. In desperation, the caliph told Al-Sammak to be brought before him. The following exchange then took place between the two.

Al-Sammak asked, "Have you ever had the occasion, O Commander of the Faithful, to commit an offense against God, and refused to do so from fear of offending Him?"

"Yes, doctor, it is true," replied the caliph. "When I was young, I set my eyes on a servant girl who was associated with one of my ministers. I lusted after her and wished for sexual union with her. I had a clear chance to do this once, but then reflected on the fact that fornication is a serious offense. So I restrained myself and turned my thoughts elsewhere."

"The let the caliph rejoice," said Al-Sammak. "For you are one of those who will enter Paradise."

"But how can you possibly know this just from this story?"

"I know this from the words of God himself. For he tells us this: *Whoever shall have dreaded appearing before his Lord and shall have restrained his soul from lust, verily Paradise shall be his abode.* [Qur'an, Sura 79:40]

Of course the caliph was greatly comforted by this reply. On another occasion, Al-Sammak went to a city official to intercede on behalf of a man who needed some help. The man had done something to offend the official, and someone had asked Al-Sammak to use his influence to get the man out of trouble. When Al-Sammak approached the official, he spoke these words of exquisite eloquence:

> The beseecher and the besought will feel honored if the request for which I come be granted, and disgraced if it be refused. Choose, therefore, for yourself the honor of giving, not the shame of refusing; and choose for me the honor of obtaining, not the shame of being refused.

On hearing this, the official was so overwhelmed by Al-Sammak's hypnotic words that he gave him everything he asked for. One of his well-known sayings was:

> He who, being inclined to this world, is sated with its sweetness, shall be drenched with the bitterness of the other world, though he abhors it.
>
> By which he meant that those who are too fixated on voluptuary pleasures will eventually pay the price for this behavior.

We should end this profile on a humorous note. It is said that one day Al-Sammak was discussing some abstruse subject with another person. Within earshot was an attractive woman who could not help overhearing the gist of the conversation. Noticing this, Al-Sammak approached her and asked her what she thought of his comments. This was the exchange between the two of them:

She replied that it would have been good, were it not for the repetitions. "But," said he, "I employ repetitions in order to make those understand who do not."

"Yes," she replied, "and to make those understand who do not, you weary those who do."

Al-Sammak died around 799 A.D. in Kufa.

16. Sometimes One Must Speak Indirectly

There are times when one's communications must be protected from the unwelcome attentions of third parties. The richness of a language's vocabulary, and its embedded metaphors and cultural allusions, are powerful assistants to this end. I was recently reminded of this when reading an anecdote related by that most ponderous and loveable of biographers, Ibn Khallikan. We have related many of his stories and wise sayings here in past articles. The story I am about to relate here is linguistically oriented; it can tell us much about the power of speech in the hands of those who can deliver it with nuanced subtlety. It will be of interest to any enthusiast of language, philology, and culture.

This story is found in Ibn Khallikan's biographical sketch of the life of the grammarian and philologist Abu Abdallah Al-Yazidi. His birth date is not given, but he died in October of 922 A.D. at the age of eighty-two and three months. He is said to have belonged to the tribe of Adi Ibn Abd Al-Manat (Al-Adawi), and authored numerous works on language and rhetoric. In his day it was believed that the purest form of Arabic was spoken by the bedouin of the desert, who were supposed to be uncorrupted by contact with sedentary city-dwellers. It was considered almost obligatory for a scholar to spend some time interacting with the bedouin in order to acquire knowledge of their classical style of speech. Al-Yazidi did just this, and was able to acquire a thorough knowledge of "pure" Arabic, as well as many amusing and interesting anecdotes told by the bedouin.

The following story is one such anecdote. There was once a desert Arab who was smitten with the beauty of a woman in his region. As a gift, he decided to send her thirty sheep and an animal skin filled with wine. Animal skins, of course, were used as vessels for carrying water and other liquids. The man sent one of his servants to deliver the gift to the woman. Along the way, however, the servant drank some of the wine, and killed and ate one of the sheep. This had been strictly forbidden, of course. When the servant arrived with the items, the woman could sense from the servant's demeanor that something was wrong. She, wise in the ways of human nature, sensed what he had done. As the servant was leaving to return home, he asked the woman if she had any message to convey to his master (the man who had sent her the gift of sheep and wine). She told the servant to convey this message:

> Give your master my salutation, and tell him that our month was *mahaaq* (محاق). Tell him also that Suhaim, the keeper of our sheep, arrived here with a bloody nose (*marthum*, مرثوم). [III.59]

This cryptic message made no sense to the servant, but he dutifully carried it back to his master. When the master heard it, it immediately made sense to him. He seized a cane and threatened the servant with a beating unless he revealed what he had done. The servant did so, and the man pardoned him with a peal of laughter. What was the meaning of this strange communication from the woman to her suitor? We must analyze the Arabic words to find out. It is a message of real sophistication:

1. The word محاق (*mahaaq*) literally means a "waning of the moon." Used by the desert Arabs of the medieval era, it meant *a month which has no moonlight on its last day*. By saying "the month is *mahaaq*," the woman wished to convey that the servant arrived with 29 sheep instead of 30, which is what a *mahaaq* month would look like.

2. The word سحيم (*suhaim,* a diminutive form meaning "little black") was a common bedouin name for a water-skin. It was called "little black" because such skins were often coated with black pitch or resin to make them more waterproof.

3. The word *marthum* (مرثوم) means a person whose nose is broken and bleeds. Another derivation from this word, according to Ibn Khallikan, is the word *ratham* (رثم), which means a white spot on the upper lip of a horse.

Thus the woman was able to use linguistic metaphors to inform the master that the servant had stolen a sheep (arriving with 29 sheep instead of 30) and some wine (arriving with a "broken nose" in the sense *that he had broken into the water-skin*). The reader can be assured that it was not an easy task to decipher the precise meaning of the woman's message. The words and their nuances of meaning are archaic. I consulted three authoritative lexicons of modern written Arabic (*Al-Munjid*, *Al-Mawrid*, and Hans Wehr's dictionary of modern written Arabic), but none of them contained the words *ratham* or *marthum*. This seemed strange to me, but apparently the usage is so antiquated that it can only be found in the classical dictionaries. But consultation with a native speaker of the language confirmed that these meanings, while very arcane, are valid. All languages have such subtleties of vocabulary and metaphor. The greater one's mastery of these things, the more effective will be his or her communication. For in life it is not always possible to speak openly or candidly.

17. On Meetings And Separations: The Wisdom Of Two Scholars Of Al-Andalus

We have paid a price for the media age. Yes, it is true that we have access to an immense volume of information (or mindless trash, depending on one's perspective); but the average person is now so deluged with tsunamis of inanity that it is a full-time responsibility just to sift out what is of value from what is not. Some are not able to do this–or do not want to do it–and as a consequence swim in mental sewage; others are able to do it, and can ascend to the loftiest heights of knowledge and perception. Every man makes his own choice as to which world he prefers to inhabit.

I mention all this only to point out how pleasing it can be to read the words and anecdotes of the literati from olden times. Their writing had a refinement and civilized quality that is lacking today. The pace of life was slower; people had more time to read, to reflect on things, and to focus on interpersonal relations. People actually spoke to each other, and were judged on the quality and gentility of their speech. They listened to each other, too, rather than just waiting for their turn to speak. One misses this sort of thing, and is constantly reminded of it when poring over long-forgotten volumes from centuries past. But all this just makes the old books that much more precious. They are our connection to a lost world: a time machine, as it were. Let us consider a few anecdotes from two Arabic scholars of old Andalus in Spain. The subjects treated are separations and meetings. The first anecdote is from the life of the historian and scholar Ibn Qutiyya (ابن القوطية); his birthdate in Seville is unknown, but he died in Cordoba in 977 A.D. He is remembered today for an extensive history of Islamic Spain. The biographer Ibn Khallikan provides us more details about Ibn Qutiyya:

> He was one of the ablest philologers and grammarians of the age, and possessed extensive information in the Traditions, jurisprudence, and history; he also knew by heart a fund of curious anecdotes, and, by the quantity of poetical pieces which he transmitted down and of historical facts which he discovered, he outstripped every competitor. In the history of Spain he displayed the highest acquirements, and was so fully acquainted with the biography of the emirs, jurisconsults, and poets who flourished in that country, that he used to dictate, from memory, all the facts concerning them...The eminent abilities of Ibn Qutiyya were accompanied by a spirit of profound piety and an assiduous attachment to the practices of devotion; he displayed also considerable talent as a poet, but he afterwards renounced that occupation, although his poetical compositions were remarkable for correctness of style, perspicuity of thought, the beauty of the exordiums and the grace of the transitions. [III.90]

Such were the impressive abilities of Ibn Qutiyya. The following anecdote is told of him. A scholar named Al-Tamimi was once out riding his horse, on his way to his country villa near the foot of the Cordova mountains. He happened to meet with Ibn Qutiyya, who was returning from his own villa that he owned in the area. Al-Tamimi recognized him and knew he was a man of erudition and humor, so he jokingly tested him with this greeting:

> From where do you come, incomparable man? You
> who are the sun, and whose sphere is the world?

Ibn Qutiyya laughed and responded in this way, without any hesitation:

> I come from a hermitage where the devotee can enjoy solitude, and where sinners may commit their sins in secret.

This reply showed a sense of refinement and humor, and it delighted Al-Tamimi, who later wrote, "I was so highly delighted with his reply, that I could not forbear kissing his hand and praising him, and invoking God's blessing on him; he was moreover my old master, and, therefore, deserved these marks of respect."

The next anecdote concerns the philologer and grammarian Abu Bakr Al-Zubaidi, who was a native of Cordoba. His biographer Ibn Khallikan tells us he was born in Seville and died in Cordoba in 989 A.D. Of his reputation we are told:

> He surpassed all his Spanish contemporaries by his knowledge of syntax, rhetoric, and curious anecdotes; besides which, he was well versed in biography and history. The works which he left us are a proof of his extensive learning...[among them are] a treatise on the incorrect phraseology of the vulgar; the *Wadih* (plain treatise), a highly instructive work on grammar; and a treatise on the grammatical forms, which has never been surpassed.

Al-Zubaidi was renowned for his wise teachings, sayings, and stories. Among them I have selected the following sayings, which relate to our theme of meetings and separations. He also very much appreciated the charms of women. He carried on a passionate affair with a girl in Seville named Salma, whom he was forced to take separations from on account of his work. During one of these enforced separations, he wrote her the following lines:

> My dear Salma, I take it not to heart. Separation must be endured with fortitude. Think not that I bear your absence with patience, unless it be with the patience of a man in the pangs of death. God has not

> created a torture more excruciating than the moment of goodbyes. Death and separation appear to me the same, except that the former is accompanied by the wailing of the funeral mourners. Promptly severed as we were, though once closely united, reflect that every meeting leads to a departure, that the boughs divide into branches, that proximity tends to remoteness, and union to separation.

On the same subject of separations from those we are fond of, he would often say the following:

> To be poor in one's native country is like living in a foreign land; a foreign land with wealth is home; the earth is all the same; mankind are brothers and neighbors.

This is a wise statement, and no less true today. Finally, I cannot resist quoting Al-Zubaidi on the subject of knowledge. He said:

> A man must be judged from his intelligence and discourse, not from his equipage and dress. A man's clothing is not worth a straw if he possesses a narrow mind. It is not long sittings in the professor's chair which can procure learning, wisdom, and intelligence.

18. The Wisdom Of Ibn Zafar Al-Siqilli And Abu Bakr Al-Khowarizmi

The writer and scholar Ibn Zafar Al-Siqilli lived from 1104 to about 1170. The cognomen *Al-Siqilli* ("the Sicilian") was given to him because he was born on the island of Sicily. There are a number of important works credited to his name, the most famous of which is a book of ethical and political philosophy called *Consolation for the Master Who Suffers From the Hatred of His Servants* (the Arabic title, written in the rhyming prose commonly used at the time, is (سلوان المطاع في عدوان الأتباع). In English, this work is often referred to simply as the *Sulwan al-Mutaa'*. The book was composed in

1159, during the time of the second Norman king of Sicily, William the Bad. Sicily (*Sakalliya*) had been an Arab emirate from A.D. 831 to 1091. Those who have read his work have commented on it favorably; it has been accurately described as a kind of predecessor of Machiavelli's *The Prince*. Here we have the remarkable fact that, hundreds of years before that subtle Florentine, an Arab Sicilian lays out the basic principles on how a ruler should control his subjects. The fact that he is nearly totally unknown in the West today also tells us much about the absurd dearth of modern, annotated English translations of many (if not most) Arabic literary classics.

The biographer Ibn Khallikan tells us that Ibn Zafar endured a hard life accompanied by constant poverty. His early life was spent in both Sicily and Mecca. According to Ibn Khallikan, he was in such dire need that in the city of Hamat, he was forced to marry his daughter to a man of a lower social station than his daughter's; and when the bridegroom left the city, he sold his bride as a slave somewhere else (although this act was forbidden by law). Despite these miseries, Ibn Zafar has left behind one quote of such penetrating wisdom that it must be quoted here, and reflected on by readers. He wrote:

> A man's misfortunes correspond to his merits; and, by his patience under affliction, his share of merit may be known. He who has but little firmness in facing what he apprehends, will have but little chance of gaining what he hopes for. [III.107]

A man's abilities and personal characteristics determine, in many ways, his misfortunes. The more of a fool a man is, the greater his bad luck will be. We turn next to an equally memorable personality. Abu Bakr Al-Khowarizmi was raised in Syria, in the region of Aleppo, but traveled widely and died in Nishapur in A.D. 993. He is described as one of the best poets of his era, as well as an accomplished philologist and grammarian. In time his fame preceded him, and he was highly sought after by political figures of his day. The following anecdote is told of his meeting with a local ruler, and says much about his reputation for wit and linguistic subtlety:

> It is related that having gone to see the Sahib [the word *sahib* was an honorific title] Ibn Abbad, who

> was then holding his court at Arrajan [a medieval city in southwestern Iran], he requested one of the chamberlains to announce to him that a literary man desired permission to enter. The chamberlain took in the message, and his master replied: "Tell him that I have bound myself not to receive any literary man unless he know by heart twenty thousand verses composed by the Arabs of the desert." [the Arabic spoken by the bedouins was, by common consent, considered the purest]. The chamberlain returned back with this answer, and Abu Bakr said: "Ask him if he means twenty thousand verses composed by men, or twenty thousand composed by women?" This question was repeated to the Sahib, who immediately exclaimed: "This must be Abu Bakr Al-Khowarizmi! Let him come in."

However, the meeting of the two men was not as congenial as it might have been. Apparently they had a falling-out. It is said that after leaving the Sahib Ibn Abbad, the poet composed the following lines about the ruler:

> Praise not Ibn Abbad when his hands shower forth generosity so as to shame the rain-cloud. Such acts are merely the suggestions of his fancy. He grants, but not from liberality, and he refuses, but not from avarice.

Ibn Abbad did not forget this insult. When Al-Khowarizmi died, Ibn Abbad made the following comment:

> I said to the caravan returning from Khurasan: "Is your Khowarezmite dead?" and they answered: "Yes."
>
> On this I said: "Inscribe these words upon his tomb: "*May the curse of the Almighty light upon the ungrateful!"*

The other following sayings are attributed to Al-Khowarizmi:

I see that, when wealthy, you pitch your tent close to us, and that, when you are in want, you visit us seldom. It is with you as with the moon: when her light is diminishing, she delays her visits, but when it increases, she remains with us long.

O you who longs for draughts of pure wine, but who, occur what may, will never break the seal of the paper in which your money is rolled up: know that the purse and the goblet cannot be filled at the same time. *Empty then your purse, that you may fill your goblet.* [III.110]

The points of these two quotes should be obvious. The first is a ridicule of those fair-weather friends who only care about appearances. The last one is a caution that one must sometimes spend money to enjoy the good things in life.

19. Ibn Zafar's Principles Of Power And Success

We have previously mentioned the political philosopher Ibn Zafar Al-Siqilli ("The Sicilian"), who lived from 1104 to about 1171. Very little is known of his early life; his entry in Ibn Khallikan's *Biographical Dictionary* reveals little more than a few sad anecdotes. We do know that he was born under the Norman rule of Sicily, and received a good education in Mecca in Arabia. A period of wandering followed, which ended around 1150 when he secured a teaching position in Aleppo, Syria. When war broke out in Syria, Ibn Zafar moved back to Sicily; some years later he moved back to Syria, ultimately residing in Hama, where he died around 1172.

Sicily at the time was rent by factionalism and political turbulence and, much as Machiavelli embraced strong leadership as an antidote to political selfishness, this reality must have been a formative influence on Ibn Zafar's thought. We should recall that Sicily was conquered by the Aghlabid rulers of North Africa in A.D. 827; their rule over the island was followed by that of the Fatimids, who in turn lost power in 1052. An interregnum period of chaos paved the way for the Norman conquest of the island, which took place gradually from 1061 to 1097. It is a fascinating fact that the pragmatic Christian king, Roger I, kept Muslims as office-holders in key positions of authority in both the government and the military. Thus in Norman Sicily there would have been both Europeans and Arabs serving alongside each other in government, something very rare in Europe at the time.

The English translators of Ibn Zafar's work call this period "a unique milieu of Christian-Muslim symbiosis and coexistence." Sicily, like Andalusian Spain several centuries later, became a "bridge for cultural transmissions between the Muslim World and Christian Europe." Ibn Zafar was a highly-regarded writer of enormous fecundity; we are told that his works eventually filled thirty-two volumes. Time has erased most of these learned reams, but one masterwork has come down to us, a fascinating treatise called سلوان المطاع في عدوان الأتباع, which translates clumsily as *The Consolation of the Ruler in Dealing with the Hostility of His Subjects*. We will call it here by the first word in its title, the *Sulwan*. Let us examine this fascinating tome, which deserves to be recognized as one of the great achievements of medieval political philosophy.

He dedicated his book to two patrons: the first edition of the work was inscribed to an unknown Syrian ruler, a "noble king," who was facing a rebellion. The second edition in 1159 was dedicated to a Sicilian Muslim leader named Abu Al-Qasim Al-Quraishi, a man whom Ibn Zafar apparently knew personally. Abu Al-Qasim was a military commander in the Norman government; and it is likely that he would have known Latin as well as his native Arabic. Perhaps Ibn Zafar's book was intended to help Abu Al-Qasim navigate that delicate tightrope between the Arab and the Norman communities. If so, he could hardly have received a better aid for his balancing-act. Yet it is important to emphasize that the *Sulwan* is not written exclusively for princes; anyone interested in the psychology of power and human relations will find it to be an indispensable guide.

We will address only the highlights of Ibn Zafar's theories here; later articles will discuss these topics in greater depth. He begins by laying a broad theoretical framework within which a leader should operate. Considering the stresses and strains placed on men of authority, Ibn Zafar takes it for granted that a leader must be a man of extraordinary character; with Oriental hyperbole, he imagines him as "more singular than the sphinx, more marvelous than alchemy, and rarer than red gold." But before specific strategies of government can even be devised, a ruler must understand the following give principles that buttress sound governance:

Trust in a higher power (تفويض). The word (*tafweed*) literally means "delegation" and derives from theology. The competent leader must place his trust in a higher power. All of existence derives from the One Being, and no successful ruler be able to do anything without recognizing the importance of faith in human affairs. Moreover, faith is an unmatched tool for shaping and molding the minds of subjects to the virtues of loyalty, work, and acquiescence. On a personal level, the precepts of faith will enable a good prince to differentiate a good cause from a bad one, and will hopefully permit him to avoid the latter. As Ibn Zafar says,

> He who has waged great injustice shall not flourish.
> He who is strengthened by malice shall not endure.
> He who is raised to the throne through violence shall not reign.

Fortitude (تأسيس). This word derives from the same Arabic word that means "base" or "foundation." A man who lacks personal courage is worthless; his character must be foundational enough to enable him to chart a course and remain on it despite the storms of fortune. Courage may not be the only virtue, but it is that virtue which makes all the other irrelevant if it is found wanting in a man. Disasters and calamities will naturally happen to all of us, but our true measure of worth lies in how we handle them. Ibn Zafar had no illusions about men, however. Consider this sober estimate:

> There are three kinds of subjects. The first are worthy individuals who are faithful and who recognize the superiority of the ruler. They acknowledge the importance of the care that is devoted to him, and feel the burden of his responsibilities. Their affection towards the ruler may be recognized by their graciousness and courtesy. The second group includes good and bad individuals who must, therefore, be held in check by a combination of gentleness and severity. The third is the populace that always supports those who advocate causes without questioning either their words or actions. They side without knowing friend from foe. They must be governed through fear, without harsh treatment, and tough punishment without excessive rigor.[21]

---

[21] J.A. Kechichian & R. H. Dekmejian, *The Just Prince*, London: Saqi Books (2003), p. 253. Quotes herein are from this translation.

Patience (صبر). Western political thinkers consistently underestimate the value of patience. As Ibn Zafar describes it, he makes it almost seem as an extension of fortitude; and in a way, this is not inaccurate. Patience consists, he tells us, of three elements: forbearance (which promotes mercy); vigilance (which is self-protection and survival); and courage (which is self-explanatory).

Contentment (رضا). This is a distinctly Arabic concept, something that is sorely missing from Machiavelli and later Western political philosophers. Deriving from theology, "contentment" is an idea meant to put a ruler's mind at ease if he has done his best to achieve his goals. No leader, Ibn Zafar sagely advises, will be able to do everything, or even most things, that he would like to do. A good leader must have the ability to set aside his anxieties and frustrations, and focus on the tasks at hand. If he cannot do this, his mind will always be in turmoil, and he will eventually lose confidence in himself. He says:

> It is better to govern with contentment than to be governed by it. *Incline yourself to contentment before you are compelled to it by necessity.*[22]

Temperance (زهد). This concept revolves around self-denial. Wealth and power are fleeting, Ibn Zafar tells us. There will be times when the burden of responsibility becomes too great a burden. If so, a prudent and wise ruler will know when to step down and leave office. "Let him who longs to obtain power know how to abdicate," he counsels. No ruler can be truly great unless he knows how to walk away from the pressures of office once he has done all he can do. These, then, are the five general points Ibn Zafar begins with in his *Sulwan.* He recognizes that they are idealistic and, in many situations, short on specific guidance. The Italian political theorist Gaetano Mosca (1858-1941) noted that Ibn Zafar's ideas alternated between both "Machiavellian" and "anti-Machiavellian" advice. But as translators Kechichian and Dekmejian note, Ibn Zafar's most basic "maxim of power" may be summarized with the following formula:

تدبير + حيلة + قوة = Victory

---

[22] *Id.* at 75.

Represented in English, this formula is:

> Power (*quwwa*) + Stratagems (*heela*) + Planning (*tadbiir*) = Victory

Each of these three elements occupies a key ingredient in ultimate victory. Necessary at the outset is the need to have good advice from wise counsellors:

> It was said that "counsel is the mirror of the intellect." If, therefore, you would like to know the capacity of anyone, ask for his advice. It was also said: "The best counsel is that which has been proven by reflection, and adopted after mature deliberation." And: "Counsel is the sword of wisdom. If a sword is the keenest and has been sharpened with the best care, and its blade most diligently polished, then surely the counsel which has been the most frequently deliberated and the longest weighed will be better than all others." And: "The counsel which is delivered in haste is worthless."[23]

These are some of the rudiments of Ibn Zafar's leadership principles. The well here is very deep, and we will draw from it again in future articles. Like any profound thinker, it is impossible to do justice to the views of this subtle Sicilian in a few pages; but we have our foundation, and one must start somewhere. Future discussions will focus on the details of the general principles outlined above.

20. The Life-Affirming Philosophy Of Al-Salami

The name Muhammad Al-Salami (محمد السلامي), who lived from A.D. 948 to 1003, is nearly unknown in the West, but occupies a prominent position in medieval Arabic poetry. The genius of his metaphors, the richness of his turns of phrase, and the elegance of his diction can be felt even through the fog of translation; and we

[23] *Id.* at 162.

will do our best to pay him homage here. The anthologist Abu Mansur Al-Tha'alibi called him:

> [I]ncontrovertibly the best poet of Iraq. And his right to that rank is sufficiently evinced by his merit. The opinion which we have expressed concerning him is supported by a sure testimony, that of his poems; and the beauties of his compositions which we have here inserted are a delight for the eye, a charm for the heart, and a satisfaction for the mind. [III.119].

He was born in Baghdad in 948 and at some point in his youth moved to Mosul. Like many great poets, he showed promise at an early age; his biographer Ibn Khallikan, perhaps with oriental hyperbole, claims he began composing verses at the age of ten. Poets in those days engaged in verbal battles with each other, much like modern rappers might duel in "freestyle" competitions. Al Salami was a master of the insult and the invective, and if provoked, he could deliver a withering barrage of verbiage. On one occasion a competitor named Al-Tallafari tried to denigrate him; Al Salami responded with these brutally vulgar lines, of which Aristophanes would have been proud:

> Al-Tallafari aspired to my friendship, but the soul of a dog would despise such friendship as his. His character is repugnant to mine, and my actions scorn to be joined with his. My noble art comes from my mouth, but his worthless art is found in his ass…and I am not the right man to try to penetrate this.

His biographers tell us that at one point he visited the court of Al-Sahib Ibn Abbad in Isfahan (in Persia), and recited a poem that contained the following sublime verse:

> We abandoned ourselves to sin, when we found that forgiveness was the fruit of crime.

This line encapsulates the same thought expressed by the caliph Ibn Ma'mun, who once said, "If criminals knew what pleasure I take in pardoning them, they would strive to gain my favour by committing crimes." Also similar is line by the famed hedonistic poet Abu Nuwas, who announced, "You shall gnaw your hands with regret, for the pleasures which yon avoided through fear of hell." One of the best anecdotes about Al Salami concerns the time he visited the court of Adud Al-Dawlat lbn Buwaih at Shiraz in Persia. For this visit, he was given a letter of recommendation to be presented to one of Ibn Buwaih's ministers. This document without doubt ranks among the most refined and elegant letters of recommendation ever written. The text is as follows:

> Your lordship knows that the traders in poetry are more numerous than the hairs of the head, and that those persons are much less so whose jewels, when offered as presents, can be confidently taken as the workmanship of their own genius, and whose embroidered tissues, when presented to a patron, can be considered as wrought on the loom of their own imagination. Now, among the persons whom I have put to the test and approved, whom I have tried and chosen, is Muhammad Al Salami, the originality of whose talent surpasses expectation and hastens on in the career of excellence, tempting the ear to hearken with attention to his compositions and the eye to peruse them.
>
> Mounted on the steed of hope, he is induced to visit Your Excellence, in the expectation of being admitted into the band of his fellow-poets and attracting notice by sharing their good fortune. I have, therefore, dispatched to you, in his person, the emir of poets, escorted by the train of his accomplishments, and I have adorned that vigorous courser of eloquence with the harness which becomes him. This, my letter, serves him as a guide towards the regions watered by the showers of liberality, or rather as a conductor towards the ocean of beneficence. Therefore, if your lordship judge proper to take into consideration these words of mine in his favor, and to let them be the means of procuring your consent to his wishes, you will, I hope, execute what you resolve.

What eloquence! We are told that, once Al-Salami arrived in Shiraz, he recited these excellent verses to the king:

> To reach you, a man who made the sight of your palace the term of his camel's journey, crossed the wide-extended desert. I, my courage in the depths of darkness, and my sword, were three companions united like the stars of the constellation of the eagle. I encouraged my hopes with the sight of a king who for me would replace mankind, of a palace which for me would be the world, and of a day of meeting which for me would be worth an eternity.

The prince (Adud Al-Dawla) was greatly impressed by the poet. For him the poet composed a large number of works; among many great passages, the lines below stand out for their unashamed advocacy of life's pleasures. They encapsulate the poet's views of life better than any other passage:

> I roused my boon companions as the dog-star passed above us, and the moon in the expanse of heaven seemed like a pond in the midst of a meadow.
>
> "Awake!" said I, "Hasten to drink of generous wine, for this world is a mere illusion!"
>
> The spy now sleeps from fatigue, and pleasure has awakened! Satan prompted us to sin, and we all declared him an excellent counsellor.
>
> We lay prostrate on that battle-field of pleasure which is shunned by vultures and beasts of prey.
>
> The blooming flowers of our meadow were female cheeks, and female waists were its pliant shrubs.
>
> *The enjoyments of life are always best bidden when the veils in which false modesty shrouds us are rent away.*
>
> The cup-bearers passed the goblet around, and offered it to the guests, as the falcon offers the game to the sportsman.

> The virgin liquor comes disguised by the admixture of water, concealed in it as the soul is concealed in the body.
>
> The red surface crowned with bubbles seems like a cheek receiving a kiss.
>
> We, at length, sunk in prostration, but we had then before us the chords of the lute for our imam to direct our devotions.

Al-Salami believed that life should be enjoyed to the fullest, and that to do so, we must remove what he called the "veils of false modesty." The key line in the passage above, it seems to me, is this one: *The enjoyments of life are always best bidden when the veils in which false modesty shrouds us are rent away.* I doubt whether Epicurus could have said it any better. One cannot begin to love until those false masks of modesty are removed to expose the natural patina of sincerity that lies beneath. So it is in the creative process as well: we cannot begin to express ourselves artistically until we set aside those crippling inhibitions, and strike out into uncharted lands.

21. Reversal Of Fortune: The Fate Of Mu'tamid Ibn Abbad, Ruler Of Seville

Al-Mu'tamid Ibn Abbad (المعتمد بن عباد) lived from 1040 to 1095 and was the last ruler of the Abbadid kingdom of Seville. He was raised under the fold of royalty, and enjoyed the pleasures and good fortunes that come to young princes. In 1069, upon the death of his father Abbad Al-Mu'tadid, he inherited the dominion of Seville; his domain included a large part of southern Spain. An Arabic chronicler described the young king in this way, according to the biographer Ibn Khallikan:

> [H]e was gifted with a handsome face, a body perfect in its proportions, a colossal stature, a liberal hand, penetration of intellect, presence of mind, and a just perception. By these qualities he surpassed all his contemporaries; and moreover, before ambition

> led him to aspire after power, he had looked into literature with a close glance and an acute apprehension; so that by his quick intelligence, he acquired an abundant stock of information, noted down without serious study, without advancing far into its depths, without extensive reading, and without indulging in the passion of collecting books of that kind...He composed also pieces of verse remarkable for sweetness, containing thoughts which the natural turn of his disposition enabled him to attain, expressing perfectly well what he wished to say, and displaying such excellence as caused them to be copied by literary men. [III.183]

Seville had acknowledged itself as the vassal of the King of Castile, Alfonso VI. At some point Al-Mu'tamid found it inconvenient to continue paying tributes to the Christian king, and refused to continue doing so. This prompted a military response from Alfonso. Al-Mu'tamid asked the Almoravid rulers in neighboring Morocco for assistance, and they gladly agreed. The Almoravids were successful, perhaps too successful; crushing the Christian army in the Battle of Sagrajas in 1086, they decided to occupy all the Islamic territories in Spain for themselves. Thus Al-Mu'tamid, who had called upon the Moroccans for help in preserving his kingdom from Castilian attack, now found himself a prisoner of the Almoravids. Calling upon other states for military help, it seems, is often a dangerous request. So Al-Mu'tamid was shipped off to the town of Aghmat in Morocco in chains, to spend the remainder of his life as a prisoner. He had lost everything, and turned to his one consolation, poetry. Recalling his days of comfort and splendor, he wrote:

> Early in the morning, when I stopped to say farewell, standards were waving in the court of the castle, and we wept blood;
>
> So that, by the shedding of red tears, our eyes appeared like wounds.

Of him another poet, named Ibn Labbana, penned the following verse:

> The heavens shed tears, evening and morning, over
> the noble princes, the sons of Abbad.

While he was in captivity in Morocco, Al-Mu'tamid found much time to reflect on the transitory nature of earthy riches, glory, and the pleasures of the flesh. He endured his privations with Stoic resolution, but would allow himself to grieve in his verses. Some of them are masterpieces of sorrowful reflection, as the following lines:

> For the shade of my once triumphant banners I have
> received in exchange
> The ignominy of fetters and the weight of chains.
> The irons which I once used
> Were the pointed lance and the sharp, thin, and polished sword;
> But both are now turned into rusty chains, grasping
> my leg as lions grasp their prey.

One historian described his confinement with these words:

> Torn from his country and stripped of his possessions, he was carried off in a ship and deposited on the African shore as a corpse is deposited in its place of burial; the pulpits of his states and the throne deplored his absence; those who once visited his table or his bed of sickness went near him no more; he remained alone in his grief, uttering deep-drawn sighs and pouring forth tears as a conduit pours forth water. None were left to console him in his solitude, and, instead…he now saw nought but strangers. Deprived of consolation, hopeless of the approach of friends, debarred from the aspect of joy, he called to mind his native abodes, and that thought made him long for home; he saw in imagination the splendor of his court, and that image raised his admiration…

More poignant still were the words of the poet Ibn Labbana, who described Al-Mu'tamid's reversal of fortune with a philosophic grace worthy of Seneca:

> Each thing has its appointed hour; each wish, a time for its fulfillment.
> Fortune has been immersed in the dye of the chameleon, and the colors of its various states are always changing.
> We are chessmen in the hands of fortune, and sometimes the pawn may check the king.
> Cast off the world and its inhabitants; the earth is now tenantless; men worthy of the name are dead.
> Tell the creatures who dwell here below that the secret plan of Providence above is now concealed at Aghmat.

The biographer Ibn Khallikan tells us that Al-Mu'tamid was once visited in prison by his daughters, who had also fallen far from the positions they once held. They had been reduced to spinning wool in the region near Aghmat, and were desperately poor. The sight of them was almost too much for him to bear. He wrote the following anguished lines later, which are directed to himself:

> In former times festivals made you rejoice; but now, a prisoner in Aghmat, a festival afflicts you.
> You see your daughters hungry and in rags, spinning for hire and penniless.
> They went forth to salute you, with down-cast eyes and broken hearts; they walk barefoot in the mud,
> As if they had never trod on floors strewed with musk and camphor.
> Not a cheek of theirs but its surface complains of drought misery,
> And is never watered but with sobs and tears.
> Fortune was once obedient to your command;
> Now it has reduced you to obey the commands of others.
> *He who, after you, lives rejoicing in the exercise of power,*
> *lives in the mere delusion of a dream.*

Those who strut so arrogantly on the stages of power would do well to reflect on these last lines. Power is the most fleeting thing in the world; and its loss will be that much speedier if untempered by modesty, justice, and restraint. Al-Mu'tamid died in prison in 1095. He had lost his kingdom and his fortune, but retained his dignity. This endured beyond his grave, and his poetry gave it immortality.

22. Until You Can Change Things, You Must Endure Them: The Wisdom Of Ibn Tumart

The founder of the Almohad movement–a puritanical reformist school originating in North Africa–was a man named Ibn Tumart (أبو عبد الله محمد ابن تومرت). The historians tell us that he was a Berber from the Atlas Mountains in what is now southern Morocco, and that he lived from 1080 to about 1130. The biographer Ibn Khallikan relates numerous anecdotes about him that center on his strictness and piety. As is often the case with such anecdotes, however, we may sift through them and find something useful for our own lives. Religious reformers are not meant to be jolly or genial; and it is decidedly more pleasant to admire them from a safe distance than to be forced to live according to their prescriptions. Yet they too have a purpose and place in history. They can set in motion regenerative forces that sweep away the collective rot of generations, and so help to rebalance societies that may have become too corrupted with luxury. Ibn Khallikan describes the austere reformer in this way:

> Pious and devout, he lived in squalid poverty, subsisting on the coarsest fare and attired in rags; he generally went with downcast eyes; smiling whenever he looked a person in the face, and ever manifesting his propensity for the practices of devotion. He carried with him no other worldly goods than a staff and a skin for holding water. His courage was great; he spoke correctly the Arabic and the Maghrib [Berber] languages; he blamed with extreme severity the conduct of those who transgressed the divine law, and not content with obeying God's commandments, he labored to enforce their strict observance; an occupation in which he took such

> pleasure that he seemed to have been naturally formed for it, and he suffered with patience the vexations to which it exposed him. [III.206]

Naturally such men make rulers nervous. Ibn Tumart gradually made a name for himself as a strident believer in the reform of rulers and society. And if he could not reform them, he was determined to replace them. He soon acquired a reputation in Morocco for fearlessly speaking out against practices that he believed violated divine law. A local ruler, hearing of his zeal, took the advice of one of his advisors and summoned Ibn Tumart before him to provide an explanation for his conduct. When Ibn Tumart arrived at court, the king politely but firmly asked him to account for his words and actions. Ibn Tumart freely admitted his preachings, and went on to demand an explanation from the ruler himself as to why *he* tolerated such abuses. The preacher spoke with such emotion and intensity that the king was moved to tears. Yet the king's advisor (a man named Ibn Wuhaib) detected a will to power behind the mendicant's pious facade. He also knew that it was wise not to take too hard a line with such men; they seemed to thrive on repression, which only made them grow stronger. So he told the king:

> I am afraid that this man [Ibn Tumart] will do you harm, and my advice is that you imprison him and his companions, and assign to them for their support the daily sum of one dinar. This will secure you from his evil intentions; and, if you refuse doing so, *he will cost you all the money in your treasury, and your indulgence will have profited you nothing.*

The king agreed, but Ibn Wuhaid also told him this:

> It would be shameful for you, after having wept at the exhortations of this man, to treat him ill in the same sitting, and disgraceful for you who possess so great a kingdom to show your fear of a man who does not even possess wherewithal to appease his hunger.

So the king, not wanting to give Ibn Tumart the upper hand, wished him well and dismissed him. But as he left the king's presence, Ibn Tumart kept his face directed towards the king. Afterwards, some people asked him why he had never turned his back on the king. His response was this:

> My intention was to watch vanity as long as I could, until the time comes that I may change it.

This story, according to Ibn Khallikan, was taken from a work entitled كتاب المغرب في اخبار اهل المغرب (*Kitab al-mughrib fii akhbar ahl al-Magrib*), which may be loosely translated as *Unusual Book on the History of the People of the Magrib* [i.e., Morocco]. It contains a wise observation. Ibn Tumart reminds us that *if we do not have the power to change what is bad, it is more prudent to keep a trained eye on the subject, until the time arises when one may take corrective action.* Sometimes conditions are just too difficult, and the times are just not right. In these situations, one must bide one's time. But patience has never been a common virtue; and it has become even less common in our own era of instant gratification. Everyone wants everything *now*. Ibn Khallikan relates some of Ibn Tumart's memorable sayings. Here he counsels a cleansing austerity:

> Strip yourself of the world and its passions; for naked you came into the world.

The following quote I like very much, and was favored by Ibn Tumart. It is actually a verse from the classic poet Al-Mutanabbi:

> When you strive after much-desired glory, cease not to aspire until you reach the stars.
> For in both a mean and in a noble undertaking, the taste of death is quite the same.

The meaning is obvious: death in a wretched enterprise is the same as death in a glorious one, so we might as well aim high. The following quote of his (also from Al-Mutanabbi) gives an idea of his aggressive spirit:

> He who knows the times and mankind as well as I do, should quench without remorse his lance's thirst for blood.
> He would meet no mercy from them if they got him into their power; to hurl destruction on them is not then a crime.

And with regard to his independent spirit, Ibn Tumart used to say the following:

> I become not one of them by living among them;
> sandy earth is the gangue in which gold is found.

This last beautiful quote requires some explanation. The word *gangue* means the worthless material in which a valuable mineral ore is hidden.

He was a severe man; but dynasties are not founded by weak-minded men. He would eventually engage in open revolt against the Almoravid rulers of the Magrib. The Almohad dynasty he spiritually founded would eventually extend over all of North Africa, as well as Andalusian Spain, and would last until 1212. He reminds us that when we lack sufficient resources to bring about the changes we want in our lives, it is wise to keep our eyes on the problem until such time that action may become effective.

23. The Hand Of Ibn Muqla: Do Not Envy Those Who Wield Power

There was once a government official and literary figure of the Abbasid caliphate in Baghdad named Abu Ali Muhammad Ibn Ali Ibn Muqla Al-Shiraz. He is known to history as Ibn Muqla, and he lived from about A.D. 885 to 940. According to his biographer Ibn Khallikan, Ibn Muqla began his government service career as a tax collector in the city of Fars. He was famous as an innovator in calligraphy and the literary arts; and he (or his brother) is credited with having refined a particular type of calligraphy called خط المنصوب (*khatt al-mansub*, or "well-proportioned line"). But things did not turn out very well for Ibn Muqla as he moved through the halls of power. He unwisely became involved in various political intrigues; one of them did not go as planned, and he was thrown into prison. Worse still, a vengeful rival ordered his hand to be amputated. This punishment was actually carried out. One of the doctors who attended Ibn Muqla during this terrible ordeal later related this anecdote:

> I went to see him [Ibn Muqla] when he was in that state, and he asked me news of his son Abu Al-Husain. I informed him that he was concealed in a place

> of safely, and these words gave him great comfort. He then began to lament and weep for the loss of his hand. "I labored," said he, "in the service of the caliphs and twice transcribed the Koran. Yet they cut it off [my hand] as if it had been the hand of a thief." I endeavored to console him, saying that it would be the last of his afflictions and that no other mutilation would befall him. To this he replied by the following verse: *When a part of you perishes, weep for the loss of another part; for one part is near to another.* [III.271]

According to Ibn Khallikan, Ibn Muqla somehow managed to devise a way to write by using the stump of his hand. Yet the loss of a hand is the loss of a hand, and he often gave vent to his grief. What particularly embittered him was the ingratitude he experienced from those he believed he had served loyally. The following verses are credited to his name, and attest to these feelings of betrayal:

> To act thus I was not weary of existence, but I trusted to their good faith and lost my right hand.
> To obtain worldly rank, I sold to them my spiritual welfare, and they deprived me of one and of the other.
> I used all my efforts to preserve their lives, but mine they did not preserve.
> After the loss of my right hand, there is no pleasure in life; my right hand is gone! Depart you also, O my soul!

The following saying is perhaps the wisest of his that has come down to us. It expresses his relief at not having to be in the position of a man of power. Such a station, he knew from bitter experience, often carried with it more curses than blessings:

> When I see a man in an exalted station mounted on the pinnacle of power, I say within myself that favors must be appreciated at their just value. What a service he has rendered me by taking that place of power!

Here are some of his other aphorisms:

> When I love, I risk death. And when I hate, I inflict it.
> When pleased, I favor. When displeased, I punish.

The Abbasid poet Ibn Al-Rumi (A.D. 836–896) eulogized Ibn Muqla with these penetrating lines:

> If the pen be master of the sword before which all necks are humbled and to whose edge nations are obedient,
> Recollect that death also, death which nothing can resist, follows from words traced by the pen of fate.
> It is thus that God has decreed, from the time in which pens were first made.
> He decreed that swords, from the moment they received their edge, should be servants to the pen.

Ibn Muqla died in prison. When you see someone in a position of power and authority, do not envy that person. Remember that his position may be more of a gilded cage than you can appreciate. Do not think, *how I wish I could be like him.* Instead, remember the fate and the words of Ibn Muqla, who lost his hand trying to gain access to power. Reflect on his fate, and say to yourself: what a favor that man I envy has done me by occupying that position. For he has saved me from certain peril.

24. The Lesson Of Rhazes

Abu Bakr Muhammad Ibn Zakariyya Al-Razi (known in the West by his Latinized name Rhazes) is considered one of the most original and accomplished of the medieval Muslim physicians. An impressive list of achievements is linked to his name: he pioneered the study of pediatrics, ophthalmology, synthesized laboratory acids, composed treatises on smallpox and measles, wrote voluminously in a number of scientific fields, and had extensive practical experience with treating patients. He was born in 854 A.D. in the town of Rai in Persia, and was educated in Baghdad's extensive network of hospitals. His biographer Ibn Khallikan describes him in the following way:

In his youth, he played on the lute and cultivated vocal music, but, on reaching the age of manhood, he renounced these occupations, saying that music proceeding from between mustaches and a beard had no charms to recommenced it. Having then applied himself to the study of medicine and philosophy, he read the works on these subjects with the attention of a man who seeks to follow the author's reasonings step by step; and he thus acquired a perfect acquaintance with the depths of these sciences and appropriated to himself whatever truths were contained in the treatises which he perused...Another writer says: "He was the ablest physician of that age and the most distinguished; a perfect master of the art of medicine, skilled in his practice and thoroughly grounded in its principles and rules. Pupils traveled from distant countries to receive the benefit of his tuition." [III.312]

Rhazes's great treatise *Kitab Al-Mansuri* (كتاب المنصوري) contains a wealth of practical advice and was used as a standard text in European medical training for many centuries. Some of his sayings are still valuable, among them the following:

> When you can cure by a regimen, avoid having recourse to medicine; and when you can effect a cure with a simple medicine, avoid employing a compound one.
> With a learned physician and an obedient patient, sickness soon disappears.
> Treat an incipient malady with remedies which will not prostrate the strength.

In his own charming way, our faithful guide Ibn Khallikan ignores nearly all of Rhazes's scientific and medical accomplishments, choosing instead to repeat amusing anecdotes about his life. Like all anecdotes in Arabic literature, it houses a moral lesson, even if the story itself may be apocryphal. The following story, says Ibn Khallikan, is related by the Spanish historian of medicine Ibn Juljul in his work *Generations of Physicians and Wise Men* (طبقات الأطباء

(والحكماء). It is said that Rhazes, when he was an old man, composed an extended treatise on alchemy and decided to present it to one of the Saminid kings named Abu Salih Al-Mansur, a prince of Khorasan, who was known to be an enthusiastic patron of the arts. He was also a man of subtle cunning, and had a nose for chicanery. Al-Mansur was greatly pleased on being presented with this work, and said to the old philosopher:

> Your work on alchemy is exceedingly fine. I am going to present you with a gift of one thousand dinars. And I would like you to reproduce for me the thing you have described in this treatise.

Rhazes must have grown nervous at hearing this, for he tried to stall the prince by saying as follows:

> That, sire, is a task for the execution of which ample funds are necessary, as also various implements and drugs of genuine quality; and all this must be done according to the rules of art. So, the whole operation is one of great difficulty.

But the monarch was not to be put off. He told Rhazes, "Everything that you need will be furnished to you, so that you can bring about what you describe in this book. You will want for nothing." Seeing that there was no way to wriggle out of what he was asked to do, he confessed to Al-Mansur that he would not be able to do it. The prince said to him sternly:

> I should never have thought a philosopher capable of deliberate falsehood in a work represented by him as a scientific treatise, and which will engage people's hearts in a labor from which they can draw no advantage. I have given you one thousand dinars as reward for this visit and the trouble which you have taken, but I shall assuredly punish you for committing a deliberate falsehood.

With this, he hit Rhazes on the head with a whip and then sent him off to Baghdad "with a stock of provisions for the journey."

This blow caused one of his eyes to swell, but Rhazes refused to have the boil lanced. The reason, he said sadly, was that he "had seen enough of this world." He died soon after this. Whether this pretty fable is true or a contrivance, we will let the reader decide. Few would be able to doubt the validity of the tale's moral, which is that we should pay scrupulous attention to what we write, and not put out demonstrable nonsense. It is a lesson that unfortunately seems to have been lost on a great many.

25. The Justice Of Malik Shah, Son Of Alp Arslan

Malik Shah I lived from about 1053 to about 1092, and was the sultan of the Seljuk Turkish Empire from 1072 to 1092. His name in Turkish is given as *Melikşah;* and he succeeded his father, the renowned Alp Arslan. According to his biographer Ibn Khallikan, Malik Shah was famous for his sense of justice and equity; he was said to have been untiring in his efforts to correct wrongs that were in his power to cure. So known was he for this trait that some Arabic historians took to calling him الملك العادل (*al-malik al-a'adil*), which means "the just king." He also focused his attention on public works, canals, agricultural projects, and buildings; a large mosque in Baghdad called "The Sultan Mosque" (الجامع السلطان) was constructed under his direction. As Plutarch tells us, sometimes an anecdote can tell us more about a man's character than many pages of historical narrative can. We are told that the sultan was fond of hunting; but over time his appetite for this diversion began to wane, and he told one of his ministers:

> I fear that I may have offended Almighty God by the shedding of the blood of animals for pleasure, rather than for food. [III.445]

After having said this, he resolved to give a gold dinar in charity for every animal he killed on the hunt. And when he began to think of all the animals he had killed in the past, he gave an additional sum of ten thousand dinars as a form of compensation. Around 1087, as he was passing the city of Kufa, he had a tower erected that was made of all the horns and hooves of the deer and onager he had killed; this became known fittingly as the Minaret of Horns

(منارة القرون, *Minara al-Qurun*). Once when Malik Shah was on the march and waging war against his brother Tukush, he paused to say his prayers at a small house of worship. He was with one of his viziers, a man named Nizam Al-Mulk. After they had finished, the sultan asked his minister what he had prayed for. Nizam Al-Mulk replied:

> I prayed for God to assist you in overcoming your brother and granting you victory.

To this, the sultan responded:

> That is not what I prayed for. I asked only that God should grant victory to whichever one of us could provide a better life for the people whom we serve.

This was the kind of thinking that animated the mind of the sultan. But the best anecdote I have been able to discover about the Just Sultan is the following tale. One day the sultan encountered a poor man, a native of Al-Sawad (Al-Sawad is an old name for southern Iraq, which means "the black land" on account of the soil color). The man was weeping and seemed to be broken in spirit.

"What is the matter, brother? Why are you crying?" said Malik Shah.

"O Commander of the Faithful!" said the Iraqi. "I have lost what little money I have in the world. I bought a melon for a few coins, but several Turkish soldiers took it from me. And now I have nothing."

Hearing this stirred the sultan's innate sense of justice, and he began to become angry. "Be still," he told the man. "Let us see what can be done." So he told one of his attendants that he was in the mood for a melon, and commanded him to scour the camp to find one for him. Off went the attendant to carry out these orders. Soon the attendant returned with a melon.

"Where did you get this from?" the sultan asked the attendant.

"It was given to me by one of your viziers, who had it in his possession," was the reply.

"Go and fetch this vizier, and bring him to me," ordered Malik Shah.

When the startled vizier appeared before the sultan, the king asked him in a stern voice, "Where did you get this melon, sir?"

The vizier could sense the monarch's displeasure and knew he needed to be fully honest with his sovereign.

"The melon, sire, was brought to me by my pages," said the vizier nervously.

"Go and find them, and bring them here without delay, sir," ordered the sultan.

The vizier now knew that they were all treading on very thin ice at this point, since discipline in the Turkish army was known to be extremely strict. He knew that his pages would at the very least be subject to a flogging, possibly worse. So he told them to lie low and vanish for a time. When the vizier returned to the sultan's presence, he informed him that he could not find his pages. Malik Shah, then, turned to poor Iraqi man and said to him, "This vizier of mine, the man you see before you now, I am going to give to you as your slave. He has failed to produce the men who stole your property, and so he himself will now suffer the consequences. Take him as your slave. If he wishes to purchase his freedom from you, that will be a matter between the two of you. I shall not get involved in that matter. For now, however, he is your slave until such time as you decide otherwise. If you let him go, by God, I will strike off your head."

And with this, he dismissed the astonished persons standing before him, and they were led away by guards. Outside the tent, the vizier negotiated with the poor Iraqi man to buy his freedom for a price. The vizier agreed to give the native of Al-Sawad three hundred gold dinars in order to buy his freedom. The parties were then led back into the presence of the sultan. The Iraqi told the sultan,

"Commander of the Faithful, I have agreed to let your vizier buy his freedom for three hundred dinars."

"Are you now satisfied that justice has been done?" said the sultan.

"More than happy, sire," was the emotional reply.

"Then go now, brother, and may God be with you."

26. The Wise Sayings Of Al-Muhallab

The Arab military commander Al-Muhallab Ibn Abi Sufra (المهلّب بن أبي صفرة الأزدي) was born around A.D. 632, but not much is known of his early life beyond anecdotes. His biographer Ibn

Khallikan tells us on good authority that "His surnames Al-Azdi, Al-Ataki, [and] Al-Basri indicate that he descended from Al-Atik, member of the tribe of Al-Azd, and that he was a native of Basra." We are also told that he was distinguished for his generosity and graciousness. His military prowess was beyond question; he defended the city of Basra so effectively from its enemies that some took to calling the city "The Basra of Al-Muhallab." He served as a general under Mu'awiyya, the first caliph of the Umayyad dynasty. His major fault, his biographers relate, was his willingness to repeat falsehoods. The trait became so noticeable that jokes began to be told about it; the colloquial Arabic phrase راح يكذب ("he is going to lie", *rah yakdhab*) even made the rounds of the leadership circles of his day. The historian Ibn Kutaiba, in his work *Kitab Al-Maarif*, has this to say about Al Muhallab's habit of mendacity:

> As for me, I shall say that, of all men, Al-Muhallab was he who feared God the most, and that he was too noble, too generous to tell lies; but he was always engaged in war and the Prophet has said: 'War consists in stratagems and deceit.' He used to address the Kharijites in equivocal terms, saying one thing and meaning another, so as to keep them in dread, and that was why they called him the liar and said that he went about telling falsehoods. [III.509]

This is certainly true, for war does consist entirely of stratagems and deceit. Al-Muhallab was fond of quoting one of the Traditions that describes the circumstances under which it is permissible to lie. He would say:

> Every lie shall be written down as a lie (by the recording angels), with the exception of three: *a lie told in order to reconcile two men, a lying promise made by a man to his wife, and a lie in which a man, when engaged in war, makes a promise or a threat.*

However, according to the historian Ibn Khallikan, it was not beyond Al-Muhallab to fabricate Traditions in the service of his military purposes. One saying about him ran thus: "You would be a man perfect in every way, did you only speak the truth." We cannot be certain how far we can trust the accuracy of these old tales; probably he was no worse–or no better–than any other fighting general when it came to honesty. Battles are not won by playing fair. What should not be doubted was his bravery; he lost an eye during the siege of the city of Talakan. But he was philosophical about this, and showed true wisdom by saying this:

> Though I lost my eye, I have preserved my life, and that–thanks be to God!–will contribute to make me forget my mishap. When the cause of God is to be defended, our cavalry must endure fatigue; and when missiles are thrown about, some eyes must be blinded.

One cannot expect to emerge from a fight unscathed. We would do well to remember this point. When he was nearing death, he told his son that he should choose a minister (*hajib*) for his prudence, and a secretary (*katib*) for his elegance of style. The reason is that "a man's *hajib* is his face, and his *katib* is his tongue." He died in A.D. 703 in Marw, in Khorasan, and was survived by a great many sons. Many fine poems were composed upon his death as a way of honoring him. One especially fine *qasida*, written by Ibn Jabir, is quoted in part below. Ibn Khallikan calls it "one of the finest and most brilliant *qasidas* ever composed." It contains some wonderful images, and its opening lines are as follows:

> Say to the caravans and to the warriors setting out for battle, say to those who depart in the morning and those who, in the evening, hasten to arrive.
> Generosity and manliness are now shut up in a tomb at Marw, near the high road.
> On passing by, sacrifice to its inmate a camel of noble race and many a rapid steed. Sprinkle the blood on the sides of his tomb, for he was a shedder of blood and a slayer of victims.
> After the hour of noon, draw near unto his tomb and the flag of commandment which waves over it and invite those who pass by as hunters do when roasting venison.

> In pursuing the foe and in returning from battle he was a father to his troops, but now, he lies engaged as a pledge, in a grave among the tombs…
> All the land was shaken by his fall, so that our very hearts remained not unscathed. They suffer even now, for he was the noblest man that ever walked on earth; he smiled at the arrows shot against him by the bowmen…
> The pulpits are empty in which he presided at the prayer; his saddles have been removed from the backs of all his spirited mares and high-mettled steeds…
> Warfare will never have an abler man than Al-Muhallab: he makes it produce its effects by means of chosen horses, thin in the flanks, rapid in crossing plains and deserts.
> In the hour of grief, his cavalry rallies around him, and the sides of the horses are white with copious sweat.
> To this mighty prince, bearer of a diadem, his friends look up with joy, whilst the eyes of the envious are cast down before him.
> True standard-bearer of war I when he marches against the foe, good omens are for him and bad ones for his enemies. [III.512]

This poem, we are told, rhymes in the letter "h." Could warrior in death ever receive a finer eulogy?

27. Ibn Qalaqis On The Importance Of Travel

The poet Nasrallah Ibn Abdallah Al-Qalaqis (نصر الله بن عبد الله القاضي الأعزّ ابن قلاقس) was born near Alexandria, Egypt in 1137. He was a master of language and a composer of many exquisite verses, and was also an intrepid traveler. The name by which he is generally known (Ibn Qalaqis) is derived from the Arabic word for *colocasia*, a plant cultivated in his day for its medicinal qualities. His biographer tells us (with a twinkle in his eye) that "He had so little beard that his face was quite bare and, for that reason, verses were composed against him, which I abstain from mentioning on account of their indelicacy." One wishes that these lampoons might have been preserved, if only to see how little insults have changed over the centuries. Here is an example of his love poetry, as it is quoted by the biographer Ibn Khallikan. It demonstrates the unchangeable nature of love's frustrated affections:

> What harm would it do that gazelle [maiden], were she not to leave us,
> And were she to hear one wounded lover condole with another?
> What harm to one whose society is a paradise, were she not to see him whom
> She rejected suffering from torments like those of hell?
> As long as I courted her, that slender waist, like to a pliant branch in a garden,
> Enfeebled my body by the passion it inspired in me,
> So that I became a mere breath, like the zephyr of that garden.
> She, with the beauty-spot on her cheek, slumbers, neglectful of her sleepless lover….
> Why should a gazelle [maiden] not remain with us?
> I allowed her to anger me uncontrolled, for a man should be mild
> When angered by his fellow-creature. [III.537]

He traveled a great deal, and seems to have been constantly on the move. He studied in Cairo and Yemen; in 1169, he relocated to Sicily for a time. He believed that travel was of critical importance, and memorialized its praises in his poems. One of his sayings about travel was this: "Men are very numerous, but I am destined to keep company with only sailors and caravan-drivers." Travel in his day was not the luxurious experience it is in our own time; but he retained a sense of humor despite its travails. In August of 1168, he was aboard a ship that wrecked soon after leaving port, and all his possessions were lost. He returned destitute to his patron, a local governor, and recited these lines to him:

> When we departed, generosity called us back, and we returned to your residence;
> Returning from evil ways is highly meritorious.

Fortunately this miserable experience did not dampen his enthusiasm. In another *qasida*, he said the following about the world-changing benefits of travel. The analogies are unforgettable:

> Travel, if you wish to acquire real worth;
> It is by travelling that the crescent becomes a full moon.
> Water, whilst it runs, acquires good qualities; when it settles, it becomes corrupt.
> It is by removing from their place that precious pearls pass
> From the sea to the necks of the fair.

He died in 1172. Every culture receives the same divine rays of wisdom; but the prisms through which those beams of light are refracted may be different, making this light manifest itself in varying colors to different sets of eyes.

28. Treachery Ensnares Some, But Is Defeated By Others

Every man who goes about his business must be attuned to the realities of his surroundings. He should not close his eyes to what lies within his field of vision; and he must not delude himself by rationalizing the treacherous intentions of others. The prudent man will not see plots and conspiracies everywhere, for this is the mentality of a craven fool; but he will still maintain a healthy alertness and awareness of his environment. Such a policy might have saved the life of the camel in this tale from Ibn Muqaffa that we will now relate.

A lion once lived in a wood with a number of companions. The closest of these were a wolf, a crow, and a jackal. One day a camel driver passed along a road near the wood, and one of his camels wandered off into the wood. The camel became quite lost and eventually ran into the lion. The lion asked him what he was doing there, and the camel explained his predicament; the lion assured him that he would be protected by him, and that he need fear nothing. The camel, of course, was quite relieved to hear this, and thanked the lion profusely.

One day while out hunting the lion was seriously injured by an elephant. He was able to hobble back to his den, but needed to regain his strength and nurse his wounds. During this time he was unable to hunt, and so unable to eat. The wolf, the crow, and the jackal were used to eating the lion's leftovers, and so began to grow thin themselves. Everyone was worried, and no one was really certain what should be done. The lion told his friends to try to look after themselves. So the wolf, the crow, and the jackal had a conference to decide the best course of action. They soon reached the same conclusion: the camel should be killed and shared among the others. The jackal said that this ruse would be difficult, since the camel was enjoying the protection of the lion. "Do not worry about this," said the crow. "I will get the lion to agree to our plan." So he set out to speak to the lion.

The crow approached the hungry lion and stated what he, the jackal, and the wolf had agreed to. He noted that the camel was not contributing much to the group, and that his body could easily feed the rest. The lion was outraged at this proposal. "How could you speak to me of this?" he told the crow. "The camel is under my protection, and has done nothing to us to deserve such treatment. It would be pure treachery to kill him." The crow told the lion that he understood the guarantees that had been provided the camel, but that in some situations the good of the group outweighed the good of the individual. Sometimes, he said, a family had to be sacrificed for the good of a tribe, and a city sacrificed for the good of a nation. Finally, the crow offered these sly words: "Do not worry, O king, of your involvement. I can arrange for taking care of the camel without your being linked to it." The lion did not respond to this statement; and once the crow noticed this, he knew he had to opening he needed to pursue his scheme further.

So the crow went back to his friends and told them what had happened. He suggested that they convene a meeting in the lion's den, along with the camel. The crow explained how they should conduct their charade. Each of them–the jackal, wolf, and the crow–would pretend to offer himself up to the lion as food for his hungry mouth. When each of them did this, the other two animals would voice objections on cue. So the meeting was called, and all attended. The crow began by noting how guilty and tortured he felt by seeing the lion in his hungry condition; he then offered himself to the lion as food, so that his king would stay alive. At this suggestion (and on cue, as previously arranged), the jackal and the wolf scornfully stated that a crow would be nothing more than a snack for a lion, and that the crow's offer was essentially useless.

Then it was the jackal's turn. He mouthed the same platitudes about loving the lion, and feeling honor-bound to sacrifice himself to him for all that he had done for the jackal. But here the crow and the wolf interjected: they noted that the jackal's flesh was exceedingly poor, oily, and bad-tasting. So this plan was shelved. Then it was the wolf's turn. He offered himself up to the lion, but the jackal and the crow nixed this idea, too; they said that there were strong superstitions against eating wolf flesh. To do so would risk a curse of death.

Now remember that the camel was present at these proceedings. He had heard the statements of each of the parties. Not wanting to look ungrateful in front of the others, and believing that the others would intervene to protect him, he spoke to all. He said that his flesh was healthy and plentiful, and that it was safe to eat. He further stated that he had appreciated all the help the lion and the others had given him. Once this was said, and to the camel's mounting alarm, the other animals agreed with him. The wolf, jackal, and crow nodded their heads in agreement, and the lion sat in silence. And then the wolf, jackal, and crow attacked the camel and killed him. Such is the tale of the wolf, jackal, and crow, as it is told by Ibn Muqaffa. The camel failed to see the net closing in on him, and proved to be incapable of detecting the schemes of his smiling enemies. Contrast this tale with the second one below.

There was once a merchant who dealt with metals. He had an inventory of a hundred pounds of iron in his warehouse. He was leaving town for a few days, and asked his friend to take care of watching his affairs during his absence. When he came back, however, he found that the iron had vanished. He asked his friend what had happened to it; and his friend replied, in all sincerity, that mice had eaten it. The merchant played along with this charade, not letting on that he knew the friend was taking him for a fool. "Yes, brother, I had heard that the mice in our city have huge appetites, and very sharp teeth!" This and similar statements were what he told his friend. A day later, the merchant happened to see his friend's son walking along a street. So he seized the son, restrained him, and took him to his house.

Soon the merchant's friend was consumed with fear and worry. He asked the merchant, "Do you know anything about my son's disappearance? Have you seen him? What could have happened to him?" The merchant looked at his one-time friend and told him with a straight face, "I believe he was carried off by a falcon! In a region like this, where mice can eat iron, there is no doubt that a falcon could carry off a young lad." Once he heard this, the merchant's friend confessed his theft and his lies, made restitution, and asked for the return of his son. This was done.

When one is confronted with treachery, it is often necessary to take immediate action to avoid falling into the traps of another. Friendship must be tested by time and experience to be durable and resilient; and we must more often consider the *actions* of men than the sweetness of their words. Comradeship and love are products of the heart; they do not spring solely from the movement of another's lips. As Ibn Muqaffa has wisely noted:

> The society of the good is productive of corresponding advantages, whilst the fellowship of the wicked is attended by very opposite results, in the same manner as the zephyr which fans the aromatic shrub becomes impregnated with its delicious smell, whilst the wind which has passed over a corrupt substance, carries pollution on its wings.

29. The Eloquence Of Ali Ibn Al-Athir

Ali Ibn Al-Athir (علي عز الدين بن الاثير الجزري) was an Arabic historian, poet, and scholar who served for a time under Saladin. Born in 1160 in the city of Jazeera Ibn Omar (the modern Turkish town of Cizre), he received his education there and in Mosul, Iraq. From an early age, he showed an uncanny aptitude for literary work, composing verses and prose with fluent ease; he was soon able to master the essentials of grammar, philology, rhetoric, and law.

How he was able to accomplish this feat he explained in a poem called *Al-Washi Al-Markum* (*The Flowered Silken Tissue*): "I learned by heart an immense quantity of ancient and modern poetry…I committed to memory all the poetical works of [three important authors] and often studied them through during a number of years, till I obtained the faculty of expressing correctly my ideas and succeeded in acquiring such habits of application as became for me a second nature." Here is direct testament to the utility of memorizing passages of good literature. To write well, we should make an effort to read and digest as much as possible from the best exemplars.

His writing abilities suggested a career as a government secretary; and in 1191 he boldly approached the court of Saladin to ask for an appointment. After some time he left to work for the governor of Damascus, Al-Malik Al-Afdal, and eventually rose to the rank of grand vizier. He discovered, however, that political fortunes can shift quickly. When a change of power took place in Damascus, Ibn Al-Athir was forced to leave on short notice; his biographer tells us that a friend hid him in a trunk which was smuggled out of the city. He then relocated to Cairo to join his master.

He remained in the service of Al-Afdal until 1211, when he accepted a post with the governor of Aleppo. This job did not work out, and he moved to Mosul, determined to stay there. He was considered one of the greatest writers of letters and official correspondence of his era. He composed a famous work in two volumes on the proper composition of letters called *Al-Mathal Al-Sair fi Adab Al-Katib wa Al-Shair* (*The Current Proverb, Dealing With the Literary Information Needed for the Writer of Prose and Verse*). He is said to have read this work in public upon its completion. Specimens of his poetry show him to have been a master of imagery. Consider the following verses describing a moment of physical attraction:

> Between the sands of Al-Jaza and the river of Al-Akik dwells a person whose charms her lover can never forget.
> He gathered the plunder of the bee [honey] off the lips of that maiden whose motions are so graceful, and whose teeth so bright.
> If her forehead were not a paradise, it would not have produced those charming curls.
> How painfully cool the water of her lips! I shall complain of its poignancy even to those who censure me.
> Strange that in our mutual love, she who is my friend should act towards me like an enemy!
> Let my life be the ransom of that gazelle whose slender waist works the same effect as the pliant lance.
> [III.545]

Another one of his lines that I like very much is this one, which is a proverb in itself:

> Three things give joy: a cup, a bowl and a goblet.
> When the wine-skin is pierced for them, it is pierced for the dispelling of cares.
> How much pleasure, indeed, can a cup, bowl, or goblet bring!

Here is a beautiful line he composed in Egypt to describe the life-giving River Nile:

> Sweet in its waters, like the gatherings of the bee [i.e., honey];
> Red in its face, so I knew it had slain sterility.

And here is an evocative line he wrote after seeing the stripped corpses of soldiers slain in battle:

> They were stripped, but the blood, shining on their bodies with a scarlet hue,
> Made them appear as if they were clothed.

Ibn Al-Athir also wrote an extensive history in eleven volumes called *The Complete History* (الكامل في التاريخ). It is strange that his biographer Ibn Khallikan spends so little time discussing this work, preferring to describe Ibn Al-Athir's poetical prowess. But *The Complete History* is an important work of historiography, as it summarizes many earlier histories that are now lost. It has also been cited as an important source for medieval Persian history. He died in Mosul in 1233.

30. Vanity Brings Waste And Ruin

According to his biographer Ibn Khallikan, a Christian physician of Baghdad named Ibn Al-Talmid who practiced there around the year 1100 spoke the following words of advice:

> A prudent man should wear such clothes as may not draw upon him the envy of the lower orders, or the contempt of the higher. [III.603]

What he meant by this was that we should not dress, or show wealth, in such a way as to antagonize those who have the power to do us harm. Vanity leads to trouble. It is not just a matter of displaying ostentation. Vanity can express itself in displays of arrogance or emotion. How this can happen is related in the following tale from Arabic literature known as the "Boots of Hunain." The story has several versions, I am told; but the following version is the one I am familiar with.

An Arab of the desert entered an Iraqi town in search of goods he needed to purchase. He entered a market-place, dismounted from his camel, and began to haggle with a merchant there named Hunain over a pair of boots. The back-and-forth bargaining there did not go well, and the two men were unable to agree on a price. The bedouin became very condescending and furious with Hunain, and began to call him vile names, mocking him in a most insulting manner. The merchant swallowed his anger, and the bedouin left in a fury; he made some other purchases then got on his camel and rode away. The more Hunain began to think about this incident, the more offended he became. He decided to take his revenge.

Hunain took the boots and took them to a road by which the bedouin would have to pass. He set one boot on the ground along the side of the road, and then set the other boot along the road some distance from the first one. He then hid by the side of the road. As the bedouin rode by, he saw the first boot and said, "Look! Here is one of the boots of Hunain. If I see the other, I will take them." When he saw the second boot, he dismounted from his camel, tied it to a bush, and picked up the boot. He then left his camel and walked back along the road to retrieve the first boot. While he did this, Hunain, who had been hiding, stole the untended camel and all the goods that were loaded on it. The bedouin had to walk back home with nothing but the new boots on his feet. When someone asked him what he had gotten in town, he said, "the boots of Hunain." His vanity and arrogance had turned Hunain into an unnecessary enemy, and this carried certain consequences. The expression "the boots of Hunain" has come to mean disappointment in general, but I think the real significance of the story is its warning about the dangers of vanity. The bedouin created trouble for himself for no other reason than it *made him feel good* to be rude and insulting.

Another tale from Ibn Khallikan reminds us of the same lesson, but this time with even more tragic results. This tale concerns the family of the famed poet known as Al-Farazdaq. Al-Farazdaq's real name was Hamman Ibn Ghalib (همام بن غالب), and he lived between 640-730 A.D. The poet's father Ghalib was a well-known chief of the tribe of Tamim; and he was noted for his deeds of generosity and kindness. One year, the people of Kufa, Iraq were stricken by a famine, and a number of them left the city to live in the surrounding countryside. These refugees gathered together near the desert of Al-Samawa, which in those days was about a day's journey from Kufa. Ghalib ordered a camel to be slaughtered, and a dish prepared called *tharid*, which involves bread soaked in broth. His purpose was to try to help the people of Kufa who were in need of food. He sent some of the food to another tribal leader in the area, a man named Suhaim, who was the leader of the Banu Riah.

Instead of being pleased with this gift, Suhaim was angered and offended by it. When the dish was brought to him, he threw it on the ground and growled at the bearer, saying, "Do I look like I need Ghalib's food? If he kills one camel, I can kill one myself." At this point there followed an escalating series of livestock killing. The second day, Suhaim slew two camels, and Ghalib did likewise; the next day after this, it was three, and then four. Each chief, trying to save face among his people, tried to outdo the other in generosity. But it was not about generosity any more. It was about glory and pride. Long-submerged feelings of jealousy now came to the fore, and neither one of them could stop.

The famine was eventually over and the people of Kufa went back to their city. Suhaim's people continued to say to him, "You have shamed us! Why could you not get the better of Ghalib? We would have supplied you with all the camels you needed. For every one he killed, we could have given you two of them." Soon after this, he decided to slaughter three hundred camels. He presented the meat to his people to eat, acting like some great benefactor, and said, "This is for you…eat it!" Somehow, word of this little drama reached the ears of the caliph in Baghdad, who at that time was Ali Ibn Abi Talib, a man known for his sternness.

Hearing of the facts of this tribal squabble, he became more and more angry. He issued his own ruling, and said: "It is not permissible to eat this meat, for the animals were not slaughtered for the purpose of legitimate consumption, but rather to satisfy your vanity and ostentation." So the meat was collected and cast away like so much refuse; it became the nourishment of "dogs, eagles, and vultures." In this way did human vanity cause a tremendous amount of waste and ruin. Pointless squabbling benefited no one. It attracted the attention of the powerful, and the powerful are actuated by their own motives.

31. Thinking On One's Feet: A Lucky Escape For Ibn Abi Muslim

We all know that the ability to think on one's feet is an important skill. There may even be times when this ability makes the difference between survival and execution. The amusing anecdote that follows appears in Ibn Khallikan's biographical sketch (IV.200) of a government official and administrator (مولى) named Yazid Ibn Abi Muslim, who served under an Umayyad governor of Iraq named Al-Hajjaj Ibn Yusuf (c. 661—714 A.D.).

Ibn Abi Muslim was appointed by his patron Al-Hajjaj to handle the administration of the land-tax (*kharaj*) in Iraq. But Al-Hajjaj eventually died, and his successors did not much care for Ibn Abi Muslim. Such falls from favor are not uncommon in the corridors of power. One of these successors was the caliph Suleiman, who removed Ibn Abi Muslim from office on suspicion of graft, and in his place appointed a man named Yazid Ibn Al-Muhallab. Abi Muslim was thrown into prison; he was eventually brought before the caliph in shackles, with a wooden collar (جامعة) binding his neck and hands. He is described as presenting a terrible appearance to the irritated ruler: ugly (دميم) and disheveled. The dialogue between the caliph and the accused ran thus:

"Are you Yazid Ibn Abi Muslim?" said Suleiman.

"I am," said the other. "And may God guide the Commander of the Faithful!"

But Suleiman was not amused. Glaring at his prey, he said, "May the curse of God be upon him who entrusted you with a position of responsibility!"

"Commander of the Faithful! Do not wish for this. You are seeing me now that things have turned out badly for me. But if you had seen me during better times, you would admire me, instead of scorning me."

Suleiman, not being used to such responses, said, "A curse be on this man, who has such a pointed tongue and fast answers! Tell me, Yazid, is your old patron Al-Hajjaj still falling down into hell, or has he reached the bottom of it already?"

"By God, Commander of the Faithful! Speak not in this way. For Al-Hajjaj was a friend to your friends, and a foe to your foes. He shed his blood for you, and on the Day of Resurrection his place will be on the right hand of Abd Al-Malik and the left of Al-Walid [two Umayyad caliphs]. You may place him where you think fit."

There was something about this quickly-delivered, cogent answer that caught Suleiman's attention. He paused for a moment to think, and then said, "By God, how devoted this man is to the memory of his former patron. It is men of such loyalty that make good administrators."

But one of the caliph's attendants, seeing where things were headed, whispered to Suleiman, "Sire, you should get rid of this man. Do not spare him." Ibn Abi Muslim saw what was happening and grew incensed. He asked to know the name of this devious courtier who was maneuvering to have him executed. Upon being told, he said angrily, "By God, I've been told that his mother didn't always have her ears hidden by her hair."

A punishment for being a prostitute in that era was the cutting off of the hair. So by this comment, he was calling the courtier's mother an ex-prostitute. When the caliph heard this retort, he became convulsed with laughter, and ordered the prisoner to be released. He later ordered an investigation into whether Abi Muslim had been guilty of misconduct or graft; but no evidence of this could be found. This knowledge confirmed his belief that the man had been unjustly accused.

32. The Wise Sayings Of Ibn Zabada

Abu Talib Ibn Zabada was born in Baghdad in 1128 and lived his early life there, although his biographer Ibn Khallikan says his family was based in Wasit. He is described as a poet, jurisprudent, and administrator of exceptional talent and wit; his letters were said to be singularly refined. "His epistles," says Ibn Khallikan, "are remarkable for the graces of their style, the elegance of their thoughts, the beauty of their ornaments and the delicacy of their allusions. In drawing up dispatches, he paid more attention to the ideas than to the cadence; his letters are elegant, his thoughts just, his poetry good and his merits are so conspicuous that they need not be described."

He served in a governmental post in Basra until 1179, and in 1187 was appointed mayor of the palace (*ustadh al-dar*) in Baghdad. "His conduct was exemplary," says his admiring biographer, "and the line of life which he followed most praiseworthy." These are not easy feats in any era. I find some of his sayings to be profound, and deal with themes I have written about in other contexts and circumstances. Here he admonishes:

> In times of trouble [i.e., times of decadence], the worthless are raised to such eminence that the affliction is general. When tranquil water is agitated, the dregs rise from the bottom. [IV.129]

By this he meant, of course, that during times of stagnation and malaise, the worthless are honored with distinction. This saying describes how he shows his resilience during times of struggle and adversity:

> People never find me more firm than when I am in the power of sudden misfortunes. It is thus that the sun does not display all his force till he enters into the Mane of the Lion.

In the quotation above, the phrase "Mane of the Lion" is a poetic term used by the Arabs for a feature on the lunar surface; presumably it means that the sun does not display its full force until such time as it is eclipsed by the moon, or when the moon "highlights" its luminescence. The poet Al-Mustanjid once wrote to Ibn Zabada the following words of advice, which are worth remembering:

> If you aspire to command, act uprightly; then, even if you wish to reach the heavens, you will succeed. The [Arabic letter] *alif* (l), one of the written letters of the alphabet, is placed at the head of the others because it is upright.

This is timeless leadership advice. Another piece of guidance, again written to him by Al-Mustanjid, is this:

> Envy not those who are viziers, even though they obtain from their sovereigns, by the favor of fortune, more than they ever expected. Know that a day will come when the solid earth shall sink from under them as it used to sink before them through awe. Aaron, the brother and partner of Moses, would not have been seized by the beard, had he not been his brother's vizier. [*See* Quran 20:94]

There is an anecdote told about Ibn Zabada that he was so highly valued that "no other example is known of a person having a vizirate [i.e., a high-ranking government office] sent to him." When the caliph's emissaries visited Ibn Zabada to tell him of his appointment, one of them said prophetically to him:

> While a great man is living, people hope in him and fear him; but no one knows what is concealed in futurity.

And this is certainly true. He died in 1198, and a funeral service was held for him in the castle at Baghdad. He was buried near the tomb of Musa Ibn Jaafar.

33. The Wisdom And Generosity Of Yahya Ibn Khalid

Yahya Ibn Khalid (يحيى بن خالد) was an influential figure during the tenure of Abbasid caliph Harun Al-Rashid. We do not know the precise date of his birth, but he was the son of Khalid Ibn Barmak, a memberof the powerful Persian family known as the Barmakids. The third Abbasid caliph, Al-Mahdi, tasked Yahya Ibn Khalid around 778 A.D. with the education of his son Harun. Yahya must have perceived the seeds of greatness in the young Harun, for he tried to convince the fourth Abbasid caliph Al-Hadi to elevate Harun to a high position of leadership. This was a mistake. Al-Hadi had his own son in mind for the position, and so tossed Yahya into prison; but Fate would eventually smile on Yahya.

Harun was eventually made caliph, and he turned out to be perhaps the greatest of all the Abbasid rulers; he released his former tutor from jail, and made him a trusted advisor and vizier. It was a mark of Harun's respect for his teacher that he always referred to Yahya as "father." This lasted, says Ibn Khallikan, "until he [Harun] overthrew the Barmakids. Being then irritated against Yahya, he imprisoned him for life [in 803 A.D.] and put to death his son Jaafar." Then as now, being too close to the throne was always a perilous proposition. Many stories are told of Yahya's wisdom, which we will reproduce here with pleasure. His biographer Ibn Khallikan provides us a deluge of them, of which we will siphon off the best. Some of his maxims are as follows:

> Three things indicate the degree of intelligence possessed by him who does them: the bestowing of gifts, the drawing up of letters [i.e., writing], and the acting as ambassador.
>
> Write down the best things which you hear; learn by heart the best things which you write down; and, in speaking, utter the best things which you have learned by heart.
>
> This life is a series of vicissitudes, and wealth is given to us as only a loan; let us follow the models of virtue offered by our predecessors and leave a good example to those who come after us.
>
> As for the man to whom I have done no good, I have always before me the choice of doing so or not, and as for him to whom I have done good, I am engaged to serve him for the future. [IV.103]

The following anecdote is told of Yahya by a grain merchant, and it demonstrates the vizier's modesty and unwillingness to accept gifts that he had not yet earned:

> I traded in grain at Medina and had in my hands one hundred thousand dirhams which has been lent to me in order that I might make them productive.

This money I lost and then I went to Iraq for the purpose of seeing Yahya, the son of Khalid. Having sat down in his antechamber, I entered into conversation with the servants and door-keepers, and asked how I could get to see him. They answered: "When his dinner is taken in to him, no one is prevented from entering; we shall then admit you." When the dinner was brought, they let me in and seated me with him at the same table. "Who are you?" said he, "and what do require?" I told him and, when the dishes were removed, we washed our hands; after which I went over to him with the intention of kissing him on the head, but he drew back from me.

When I retired and reached the place where the guests mount their horses on departing, a servant came to me with a purse containing one thousand dinars and said: "The vizier wishes you a good evening; he bids you help yourself out of your difficulty with this and requests you to come to see him tomorrow morning." I returned to see him the next morning and sat down to table with him, and he began to question me as he had done the day before. When the dishes were removed, I went up to him for the purpose of kissing him on the head, but he drew back from me. On my going to the mounting-place, a servant brought me a purse containing one thousand dinars and said: "The vizier wishes you a good day, bids you help yourself out of your difficulties with this and requests you to return tomorrow." I took the money, retired, and, the next day, went again to see him. He then gave me as much as I had received the two days previously. On the fourth day, I went to visit him as I had done before, and he then allowed me to kiss him on the head. "I did not at first permit you to do so," said he, "because I had not rendered you a service which entitled me to that mark of respect. But now, I have been of some use to you."

Here are some of Yahya's additional sayings, which I have collected from the turgid mass of information provided by Ibn Khallikan. All of them were attested to by witnesses:

> Spend when Fortune turns towards you, for her bounty cannot then be exhausted; spend when she turns away, for she will not remain with you.
>
> The benefactor who reminds a person of a service rendered dilutes the value of that service; and he who forgets a favor received is guilty of ingratitude and neglect of duty.
>
> The sincere intention of doing a good action and a legitimate excuse for not doing it are equivalent to its accomplishment.
>
> In adverse fortune, wiles and stratagems lead to perdition.

This last aphorism I find particularly wise. Here is a very edifying anecdote about Yahya, and shows his understanding of how power and influence should be perceived. One day, Yahya was out riding with the caliph Harun Al-Rashid. A man appeared before the caliph and said to him, "My mule is dead." Upon hearing this, the caliph commanded that the poor man be given five hundred dirhams. But Yahya signaled the caliph to dismount, and then took him aside. "Father!" said Harun. "You made a sign to me about something I do not understand." Yahya said in response, "A caliph should never lower himself to mention so small a sum of money, even as a gift. When it is necessary to give, it is better to give five thousand, or ten thousand. Harun said to him, "So what should I have done in this situation?" Yahya said, "Simply offer to get him a new mule."

Here is another anecdote that relates to Yahya's generosity and wisdom. He once had a trusted personal secretary whose son was to be circumcised. People of all classes and stations made preparations to be present at the ceremony. It was customary for attendees to present gifts and similar offerings. One of the secretary's friends was in adverse financial circumstances, and could not offer a lavish gift like many of the other people going to the ceremony. So he filled to bags: one with salt, and the other with perfumed potash. He then attached a note to these bags, which said:

> Sir: My means preclude me from doing what I wish and the narrowness of my fortune prevents me from engaging in a competition with the wealthy. Fearing, however, that the register of our gifts should be closed before the inscribing of my name therein, I send you some of that which, at the beginning of a repast, brings good luck and a blessing, and of that which concludes the repast by its perfume and cleansing quality. In so doing I bear with patience the pain which my inability gives me, and support the anguish of not having the power to execute my intentions. But, as long as I find not the means of filling my duty towards you, I shall offer, for my excuse, this word of almighty God: *No blame shall be incurred by those who are weak, or by the sick, or by those who find not wherewithal to contribute.* [Qur'an 9.92]

Now when Yahya arrived at the celebration, his secretary showed him all the gifts that he had been given. He also showed the vizier the two bags, and the note that came with them. Yahya was much moved by this elegant and honest letter. He ordered that the bags should be emptied and their contents distributed to the guests; he then had the bags filled with money, and returned to the man who had sent them. This was how he repaid the man's honesty and good faith efforts.

34. The Life, Travels, And Literary Works Of Yakut Al-Hamawi

In some recent researches I have discovered one of the more interesting travelers and scholars of the medieval Islamic world. I have been encouraged to review what sources are available; and the more we learn, the more impressive his story becomes. His name is Yakut Al-Hamawi, and his career and achievements tell us much about the geographical and social mobility of the age in which he lived. His career also confirms the truth of the adage that a man of ability will always find a way to rise to the top, regardless of the obstacles placed in his path.

His full name was Yakut Al-Hamawi Al-Rumi (ياقوت الحموي الرومي); the "Rumi" (i.e., Rome) epithet was a reference to his Greek origins.[24] "Al-Hamawi" refers to city of Hama, the place where he was manumitted by his master. He also was known by the moniker Shihab Al-Din (شهاب الدين), which means "flaming torch" or "shooting star" of religion. He was born in Constantinople in 1178, and his biographer Ibn Khallikan says that he was "carried off as a captive" as a youth and brought to Baghdad to be sold as a slave. We do not know his original Greek name; if it is known, I have not been able to discover it. His master, one Askar Ibn Abi Nasr lbn Ibrahim Al-Hamawi, was a merchant who knew commerce, and only commerce; he needed someone to manage his accounts, keep his records, and perform other secretarial duties. Yakut's master sent him to school, had him educated in a number of disciplines including literature, mathematics, and grammar, and encouraged his growth. He became entirely Arabized and lived in Baghdad for many years, married, and fathered several children.

His education gave him the ability to travel widely as a secretarial assistant to commercial expeditions. He acquired a familiarity with the Arabian Gulf and Oman and learned how to function on his own. As often happens in such situations, there was an inevitable break with the less-educated master; this occurred around 1200, and the two of them went their separate ways. To earn a living, Yakut secured work as a copyist, a profession that brought him into contact with many books, which his curiosity caused him to devour with enthusiasm. We are told that he migrated to Damascus in 1216, and there was nearly killed in a dispute with a stranger over some points of religious doctrine. An arrest warrant was issued for him, but he escaped to Aleppo; from there he went to Karbala, Mosul, and Khorasan. From there he moved on to Merv, and then to the province of Khawarism, and decided to settle there; but Fortune had other plans for him. The Tatars invaded Khawarism in 1219 and our unfortunate Greek barely escaped with his life. Ibn Khallikan says the following about this incident in Yakut's life:

---

[24] To the Arabs, the Byzantine Empire was "Roman."

> He [Yakut] fled as naked as when he shall be raised from the dust of the grave on the day of the resurrection, and arrived at Mosul, after suffering on the way such hardships and fatigue as would even tire a narrator before he could describe them all. Deprived of every resource, in want of even the vilest food and the coarsest clothing, he remained for some time at Mosul and then went to Sinjar.

Such are the ways of Fortune; but he survived, and continued. Yakut eventually settled in Aleppo and remained there, more or less, until his death in 1228. It was probably here that he put in final form his many literary works. The largest of these was the four-volume historical work *Irshad Al-Alibba ila Marifa til-Udaba'* (*Guide of the Intelligent to an Acquaintance with the Learned*). Perhaps his most famous work was the *Mua'jam Al-Buldan* (*Dictionary of Countries*), a compendium of geographical information about the various regions and peoples Yakut had visited. He also composed lengthy works on the lives of poets and literary men, as well as chronicles and genealogies of various Arabian tribes. One of the most interesting pieces of his writing is this extract of a long letter he wrote to a vizier of the governor of Aleppo after he had escaped the Mongol invasion of Persia. The letter describes his experiences and anguish, in high literary language, at having witnessed the ravages of the Mongol invasion. It is a long letter, but so full of character and historicity that I cannot resist quoting it at length. It is also a masterpiece of philosophical reflection on the folly of vanity and the ultimate power of Fortune in controlling events:

> Your *mamluk* [humble servant] Yakut Ibn Abd Allah Al-Hamawi, wrote this letter from Mosul, in the year 617 [i.e., A. D. 1220-1], on his arrival from Khawarism whence he was driven by the Tartars, may God destroy them! He sent it to the presence of his sovereign lord...[This account] is addressed of what has passed in Khawarizm and of what has happened to this writer. It offers a slight indication of the manner in which he began and ended his career on taking leave of Your Excellency. He shrank from

the idea of submitting it to your appreciation; such was his respect and veneration for your dignity and such his repugnance to offer you a document so unworthy of your exalted merit…I feel encouraged to present this notice to my honored master and to a judgment which will show how exalted it is by perusing it and treating its imperfections with indulgence. For I am not a professed writer. Every person who fingers dirhams should not be taken for a money-changer, neither is the man who acquires a pearl to be considered as a jeweler. Here follows my statement…

When your humble servant left your noble presence and departed from the abode of unsullied glory and exalted merit, he intended to conciliate frowning Fortune and draw milk from the udder of this age, wicked and unruly as it is…For he was seduced by the idea that changing place brings grace, that passing into a foreign land brings wealth to hand, that dwelling with one's friends disgrace and pain upon us sends, and that the lover of home who stirs not apace, is distanced in the race. Mounted on the steed of hope, your servant rode off to a distant land, and placed his foot in the stirrup of peregrination with every company that offered; he crossed the valleys and the hills till he nearly reached the Sudd; but perfidious Fortune did not befriend him, neither did the times, now run mad, treat him with kindness. I was like a mote in the eye of Fortune or a bone in her throat; so, to get rid of me, she deluded me in promising to fulfil my wishes and finished by casting me into the snares of death…

He stopped not long in any land before he set out for another; his person was with his fellow travelers but his mind was far distant. One day, he was at Huzwa; another, at Al-Akik; another, at Al-Ozaib, and another, at Al-Khulaisa…The frowns of ill-luck drew smiles from cruel time, and I ceased not to blame Fortune and reproach her with her errors, till, instead of getting wealth, I was satisfied in reaching home. And, during all that, your humble servant tried to pass away those days and to get over them; deluding himself with the hopes of sustenance, covering his head with the veil of endurance and self-denial, arrayed in abstinence and in scanty fare, but not resigned to the wearing of such clothing.

The place where I stopped was called Marw Al-Shahjan, which latter word, according to the explanation given by them, means the soul of the sultan. I found there some works treating of the sciences and of literature, volumes composed by men of intelligence, and, whilst I studied them, I forgot family and country, and thought no longer of sincere friends nor of my home. Among them I discovered some stray volumes which I had long sought for, and some works which I had ardently desired. To them I applied with the avidity of a glutton and, having assigned to them a place from which they could not easily depart, I began to browse in these gardens, to admire the beauty of their form and of their contents, to let my eyes rove freely over these pasture grounds, to enjoy these detailed accounts, these compendiums, and to think that I should remain in that quarter till I became a neighbor of those who repose under the earth…

So things continued till the catastrophe arrived by which Khorasan was over whelmed with ruin, with evil all-destroying and with desolation. Now, I declare on my life and by Allah that it was a country beautiful in all its parts, charming in all its regions; a fertile garden enjoying an air pure and languishing mild, and in which the trees inclined their branches with delight at the singing of the birds. In it the rivulets shed tears whilst each flower smiled at the other; the breath of the zephyr was sweet and the temperature of the climate healthy. Never shall I forget those delightful arbors and those trees sinking under the weight of their foliage. The southern gales bore thither its wine-skins filled with the liquor of the clouds; the meadows drank the wine of the dew,

> and on the flowers were formed drops like pearls fallen from the string...It is, in a word, and without exaggeration, a copy of Paradise: there was to be found all the heart could wish for, all that could enchant the sight. Encircled with its noble endowments, it offered, throughout all its tracts, a profusion of rich products to the world. How numerous were its holy men preeminent for virtue! How many its doctors whose conduct had for motive the conservation of Islamism! The monuments of its science are inscribed on the rolls of time; the merits of its authors have redounded to the advantage of religion and of the world, and their productions have been carried into every country...
>
> The people of infidelity and impiety [i.e., the Mongols] roamed through those abodes; that erring and contumacious race dominated over the inhabitants; so that these palaces were effaced off the earth as lines of writing are effaced from paper, and those abodes became a dwelling for the owl and the raven: in those places, the screech-owls answer each other's old friends who enter there are filled with sadness; Iblis [the Devil] himself would bewail the great catastrophe... We belong to God and to God we shall return! It was an event sufficient to break the back, to destroy life, to fracture the arm, to weaken the strength, to redouble sadness, to turn grey the hair of children, to dishearten the brave, to blacken the heart, and to stupefy the intelligence. Then did your humble servant turn back and retrace his steps. Filled with grief, he sought a friendly retreat where his mind might repose in security.

It is an impressive letter, filled with the anguish of one who has barely escaped a conflagration. But history will remember him for his *Dictionary of Countries*, the rough draft of which was completed in 1224. He died without having had the chance to revise and polish the work; it nevertheless remains a masterpiece of geography and ethnography produced at a time when Europe was accomplishing nothing of importance in these disciplines. His biographer, Ibn

Khallikan, closes his account of Yakut's life with a sentence of understated but moving poignancy:

> In the beginning of the month of Dhu Al-Kaada, 626 [September 1229], I arrived at Aleppo for the purpose of pursuing my studies. This was subsequent to Yakut's death; and I found every one speaking in his praise, extolling his merit and his great literary acquirements. It was not therefore in my destiny to meet with him.

Ibn Khallikan had arrived in Aleppo too late to meet the great man, but the tales of his deeds were on the lips of all.

35. Al-Farra And The Three Obligations Of Respect

Abu Zakariyya Yahya Ibn Ziyad is one of the more famous of the early Arabic grammarians. Known to history by his moniker Al-Farra, he was born in the city of Kufa around A.D. 761 and received an intensive education there in rhetoric, law, and theology. His biographer Ibn Khallikan calls him "the most eminent of all the doctors of Kufa and also the most distinguished by his knowledge of grammar, philology and the various branches of literature." An early story told of him indicates the notoriety he achieved in linguistic knowledge. He resolved to enter the service of the caliph Al-Mamun, and approached the palace doors a number of times in an attempt to gain entrance. One of the caliph's learned advisors, Abu Bishr Thumana, went to question this young man who desired royal service. He made the following observations on Al-Furra:

> I saw a person in the attire of a literary man. So I sat down beside him and commenced putting to the test his knowledge of philosophy. Finding that he was in that branch an ocean of learning, I tried him in grammar and discovered that he had not his parallel. I then examined him in jurisprudence and perceived that he was a good legist and well-acquainted with the conflicting opinions of those people. I ascertained also that he was an able astronomer, a learned

> physician, and well-versed in the history of the Arabs, their battle-days and their poetry. On this, I said to him: "Who are you? You must be Al-Farra." He replied: "I am he." [IV.63]

In this way did Al-Farra gain admittance to the palace. He established a reputation as a linguistic scholar who had few equals. One of his peers said of him that "Were it not for Al-Farra, pure Arabic would no longer exist; it was he who disengaged it from the ordinary language and fixed it by writing." Another anecdote that shows his knowledge of speech registers is the following. One time, in the presence of the caliph Al-Rashid, Al-Farra was discoursing on some subject. One of the caliph's attendants, always anxious to try to demean a rival, pointed out that Al-Farra made a few grammatical mistakes in his speech. Al-Farra responded in this way:

> Commander of the faithful! It is in the nature of the desert Arabs to employ correctly the final inflexions, and in the nature of those who inhabit fixed abodes employ them incorrectly. When I am on my guard, I do not commit errors, but when I return to my natural habit, I commit them.

Al-Rashid, having a sense of humor, was greatly pleased by this answer. When Al-Farra came into the service of the caliph Al-Mamun, the latter wanted him to prepare a detailed and extensive reference work on the correct use of the Arabic language. He had special rooms on the palace grounds set aside, and appointed copyists and secretaries to ensure that Al-Farra had everything he needed. The work took many months, but was finally completed. The grammarian named his opus كتاب الحدود, or "Book of Limits" (*Kitab al-Hudud*). The word حد (hadd) means boundary or limit, and the titles conveys the purpose of the work as laying out what is correct and what is not. The caliph ordered the book to be extensively copied and distributed.

The high respect that the caliph had for Al-Farra is indicated by the fact that he wanted his two sons to be tutored by him in the correct use of Arabic. The following story is the best one associated with his tenure as a royal tutor. One day, Al-Farra desired to move from one room to another, and the two princes wished to bring their teacher his slippers. In the East in general, teachers are held in very high regard, especially in this era. So the two princes argued with each other on who would have the honor of bringing Al-Farra his slippers. Unable to agree, each prince brought one slipper. Now it is in the ways of kings to have ears and eyes everywhere in his palace; and soon the caliph heard about this little incident. He decided to use it as an opportunity to check on the moral development of his sons.

The caliph had Al-Farra brought before him. He then said to him, "Teacher, who is the most honored of all men?" To this question Al-Farra gave the reply, "I know of no one more honored than the Commander of the Faithful."

"No," replied the caliph. "It is he who, upon arising, was able to get two successors of the Commander of the Faithful to compete for the honor of carrying his slippers."

"Commander of the Faithful!" said Al-Farra, "By God! I would have prevented your sons from doing this, had I not wished to dissuade them from some honorable duty they had conceived in their minds. I did not wish to discourage them from trying to achieve a certain estimation in the eyes of others. We know from tradition that lbn Abbas held the horses of Al-Hasan and Al-Hussein. When he was doing this, someone asked him why he was doing this, since he was their elder. Ibn Abbas replied, 'You fool! *No one can appreciate the merit of people of merit except a man of merit*.'" This was the brilliant answer that Al-Farra gave the caliph. The caliph was deeply moved by this answer, and was unable to speak for a moment. Then he said this:

> Had you prevented them from carrying the slippers, I should have inflicted on you the penalty of censure and reproach, and should have declared you in fault. That which they have done is no debasement of their dignity. On the contrary, it exalts their merit, renders manifest their excellent nature and inspires me with a favorable opinion of their character. *No man, thought great in rank, can be dispensed, by his high position, from three obligations: he must respect his sovereign, venerate his father, and honor his teacher.*

This was what the caliph said. He then rewarded them all. To Al-Farra he gave twenty thousand dinars, and to his sons, he each gave ten thousand dirhams. There are other anecdotes told of Al-Farra, but this one to me is the most instructive. His biographer says that he lived to the age of sixty-three, which would date his death to A.D. 824.

36. The Wisdom And Recklessness Of Ibn Al-Sikkit

The birthdate of the philologist and grammarian Yacub Ibn Al-Sikkit (ابو يوسف يعقوب ابن السكيت) is not known with certainty, but 800 A.D. is a reliable estimate. His father enjoyed notoriety and prestige in court circles, and may have conferred on his son some access to the corridors of power. The sobriquet "Al-Sikkit" was given to him because of his taciturnity, for the Arabic verb *sakata* (سكت) means "to be silent." However, as the reader will soon discover, he was evidently not silent enough.

Al-Sikkit resided in Baghdad for most of his adult life, where he was employed as a tutor to the son of the Abbasid caliph Al-Mutawakkil. His most famous work was an exhaustive philological and grammatical treatise called *The Correction of Language* (اصلاح المنطق); his biographer Ibn Khallikan calls it "an instructive and useful work, containing a great quantity of philological information, and there does not exist, as far as we know, a treatise of the same size and on the same subject." One of Al-Sakkit's sayings was the following:

> Ibn Al-Sammak used to say: He who knows mankind humors them [i.e., people]; he who has not that knowledge thwarts [i.e., fights with] them, and the main point, in humoring mankind, is to abstain from thwarting them. [IV.293]

What he meant by this, of course, is that it is usually not wise to engage in pointless disputes with others. Al-Sikkit, however, seems to have been unable to apply his valid advice to himself. He was warned by his friends not to take on the job of tutoring the caliph's sons, apparently knowing that the philologer had a problem controlling his tongue. One anecdote relates that the caliph was with his two sons one day, and saw Al-Sikkit walking by. He asked the scholar, "Tell me, Yacub, who do you like more, my own sons, or the sons of Ali, Al-Hasan and Al-Husain?" Al-Sikkit recklessly answered by praising the sons of Ali, and remaining silent on the character of the caliph's sons. The caliph then ordered his Turkish guards to seize the hapless tutor, throw him down, and "tread on his belly." This incident allegedly occurred in A.D. 858 or 859, and caused Al-Sikkit's death several days later; but conflicting stories are also given on how he met his death, so we cannot be certain of its veracity. He has left us much sage advice; one of his best sayings was this:

> I desire things which I cannot possibly obtain as long I remain in apprehension of what destiny may bring about. Travelling as a merchant in search of riches is not travelling and fatigue; it is your remaining in a state of misery that is really traveling [i.e., fatiguing].

Other notable quotations of his are the following bits of worldly wisdom:

> A man may be punished for a slip of the tongue, but is never chastised for the slipping of his feet. A slip of the tongue may cost him his head, but a slip of the foot is cured by repose.

> There are persons who love you ostensibly with a love not to be diminished; and yet, if you ask them for ten farthings [i.e., a bit of help], they would refer their dear friend to the bounty of the all-knowing God.

His poetry was said to have been elegant and intense. The following beautiful lines are attributed to him:

> When the heart is filled with despair, and the widest bosom is too narrow
> To hold the grief which invades it, when afflictions have lodged therein
> And taken up their dwelling, when you find no means of escaping from

> Misery and perceive that all the address of the most experienced is useless,
> Assistance will come to you, whilst you are in despair, as a favor from the
> Bountiful being who hears the prayers of the wretched.
> When misfortune has reached its height, deliverance is at hand.

As we have noted above, there are different accounts given of how Al-Sikkit met his demise. All of them, however, turn on the fact that he incurred the angry disfavor of the caliph Al-Mutawakkil. In one account, the caliph is said to have been insulting the characters of Al-Hasan and Al-Husain, who are revered in Shia Islam. Al-Sikkit is supposed to have responded angrily, "Kanbar, Ali's slave, was a better man than you and your sons." The enraged caliph then, we are told, ordered the philologist's tongue to be plucked out. According to Ibn Khallikan, this event took place when Al-Sikkit was fifty-eight years old. In another rendition of this story, the caliph had ordered Al-Sikkit to perform a certain task, which he had refused to do; the caliph then ordered him to be flogged, and the scholar died several days later from complications. As Ibn Khallikan says, "Only God knows which story is true!" What is certain is that Al-Sikkit, despite his abilities, was either unable or unwilling to apply his own sound advice, and hold his tongue in the presence of the powerful.

PART III: TRAVEL AND EXPLORATION

View of Timbúktu, from the Terrace of Dr. Barth's House.

1. John Ireland: Captured By Cannibals In The South Seas

We have related incredible tales of suffering, adventure, and endurance. The little-known account of the adventures of John Ireland ranks high on the list of harrowing stories of nineteenth century explorations. The world was a larger place then, vastly less explored than now, and some places in the remoter regions of the globe were as isolated as they had been for thousands of years. Just how isolated and remote, the reader here will soon discover. In September 1833, young John Ireland was in England, helping outfit the ship *Charles Eaton* for her voyage to Australia. The ship left in December of that year with a cargo of lead and calico; it also carried around twenty-five young boys and girls of the Emigration Society. They reached the Isle of Wight on December 27, but were then detained for a short time to conduct repairs on the ship. They finally left England in February 1834, and crossed the Equator in March. After rounding the Cape of Good Hope, the ship finally reached Sidney (as it was spelled then) in New South Wales on July 13, 1834.

For trade purposes the ship captain then decided to sail for China. On August 14, the *Charles Eaton* entered the Torres Straits, which separates Australia from Melanesian New Guinea. Readers should understand that in the 1830s, New Guinea and the islands near the Torres Straits were almost totally unknown to Europeans. Navigational charts gave a general sense of where things were, but accurate data about oceanic depths and reefs was not available. Mariners had to find their way around with a mixture of dead-reckoning and intuition. However, the *Charles Eaton* soon ran into disaster when the ship hit a reef and began to break up. In the account Ireland later wrote of his experience, he tells us:

> It was happy for us that the upper part kept together as it did, though there was so much danger from the water rising, that everyone expected to be washed over. There was plainly to be heard above the din of the wind and sea, the horrible groaning of the planks forming the sides of the ship, between which the water rushed as through a sieve; and as they were one by one broken away from the ill-fated vessel, we felt that we were approaching near and nearer to a death

> from which we could not hope to escape, unless by some merciful interposition of Divine Goodness we should be rescued from our watery enemy.

Realizing that the situation was hopeless, the ship's captain gave orders to abandon ship. The passengers began to stock the lifeboats and make preparations to set out for land, taking with them as many of the ship's stores as they could. The best that the crew could do was to construct a primitive raft; they then loaded it with casks of water and prepared themselves for the Verdict of the Sea. By this time young John Ireland was close to despair. Seeing all his dreams dissolve into nothing around him, he could do little more than try to survive as best he could. Half-starved and parched with thirst, he began to paddle along with the other survivors of the wreck. They spend the night on a reef; early the next morning, the raft set out again, and this time spotted a canoe filled with "ten or twelve native Indians [i.e., Melanesian islanders]." Using sign language, the natives offered to transport the shipwrecked survivors in their canoe. After hesitating at first, the survivors finally decided to accept; they were desperate and felt that they had little to lose. In this, as we will shortly see, they were very much mistaken.

They soon reached a small island that, Ireland says, "the natives called Boydan." Once the survivors were on shore, the natives began to "show signs of their ferocious disposition." Leering at their captives, they seemed to take a delight in their sufferings and fear. Everyone present now began to realize what was in store for them. They began to pray, and, exhausted from their ordeal and lack of food, they lay on the ground and went to sleep. The natives seemed to encourage them to do this. Gradually, however, the natives began to congregate around the survivors with war-clubs. Ireland relates what happened next:

> About as near as I can guess, an hour after I had been asleep, I was awoke by a terrible shouting and noise. I instantly arise, and on looking round, I saw the natives killing my companions by dashing out their brains with clubs. The first was that was killed was Mr. Ching, and after him his companion, Mr. Perry; the next victim was Mr. Major, the second officer.

> The confusion now became terrible, and my agitation at beholding the horrid scene was so great that I do not distinctly remember what passed after this. The last person that I recollect seeing alive was Mr. Clare; who, in an attempt to escape, was overtaken and immediately murdered by a blow to the head.

Such was the horrifying fate of the survivors of the *Charles Eaton*. By one of those miracles of Fortune, however, Ireland and another boy named John Sexton were spared. Ireland comments in his narrative on the natives' curious mixture of violence and tenderness: "I have frequently seen them fly into a rage, and then recover themselves in a moment, becoming quite calm, as was the case with the man who tried to take my life." However, more disturbing sights were in store for Ireland. He watched in shock as the natives lined up the decapitated heads of his dead shipmates, and begin to eat their eyeballs and pieces of flesh cut from their cheeks, all the while "shouting most hideously." Ireland and Sexton were handed over to one of the natives, apparently to become some kind of servant or slave. The natives then divided up what was left of the possessions of the dead. The two boys were then taken to another neighboring island, where the native women lived. They observed a strange native religious ceremony whereby the severed heads of their companions were tied to a pole, and every morning a native would stand below them and blow into a large seashell.

Ireland tells us that he was initially very ill-treated by the natives; they would deprive him of food, and the native women would often tie him to a tree and administer beatings with bamboo canes. He and Sexton were ordered to collect firewood and do other chores; when the work was not up to native satisfaction, they were beaten. They would also accompany the natives on spear-fishing forays in the ocean. For a while they (Ireland, Sexton, and two boys named George and William Doyley) stayed at a place they later learned was Darnley's Island.

Eventually they were moved to a new location called Murray's Island, which was only about two miles across and contained between seven and eight hundred people. The boys came under new masters who were much kinder and willing to teach them practical skills. Ireland relates how he and the other boys quickly became proficient in the Melanesian language used by the natives, on account of "having no one else to speak to except natives." They also learned practical skills such as hunting and fishing.

Ireland also noticed that after a few months, their light skin was nearly as brown as the skin of the natives; they could only be distinguished from them by the "light color" of their hair. The boys spent much time on Murray's Island, and Ireland records in detail their customs, habits, weapons, and tribal practices. Their diet primarily consisted of fish, coconuts, yams, and bananas. By this time Ireland had gone completely native; his ears had been pierced, and native women had hung wooden and grass ornaments from the, as well as on his neck, wrists, and ankles. Perhaps the natives saved his life out of curiosity; or perhaps this is nature's practical way of replenishing the gene pool among island cultures who are often cut off from outside intercourse.

After about a year on Murray's Island, the natives decided to go on a trading voyage to New Guinea, and took Ireland along with them. During this trip, he eventually encountered one of his own countrymen, who asked him where he had come from. He would eventually learn that the man had come from a ship that was sent out to search for the *Charles Eaton*. This was how Ireland was ultimately rescued. His final goodbye with his master (who was named Dupper) was emotional; the old Melanesian islander had become literally a father to Ireland, and the affection was apparently mutual. Dupper wept and hugged his "son," unwilling to let him go until the last minute. But there was nothing he could do. Ireland bequeathed his possessions to Dupper's natural son, and left with a ship bound for England. Ireland sailed back to Sidney and there immediately became a local celebrity. He gave a narrative of his experiences to the governor of the colony, Sir Richard Bourke. He quickly recovered his health (he had apparently been afflicted with vitamin deficiencies or tropical ulcers). And after this, he returned to England, having been gone for more than four years.

2. Heinrich Barth: An Incredible Explorer And Ethnographer

The name Heinrich Barth is almost unknown today. But he is without doubt the greatest explorer that Germany produced in the nineteenth century, and probably even in the twentieth. Not only did he penetrate completely unknown regions of Africa, but he kept a meticulous record of his travels, to such an extent that his published works are still useful to scholars today. Even in his own day he did not receive the recognition that he deserved; central Africa was then so unknown even to educated Europeans that a balanced appraisal of his work was not possible at the time. Yet a review of his life and travels leaves little doubt that he must be ranked among the bravest and most resourceful of all explorers of the African continent.

He was born in Hamburg in 1821. His father was a merchant and trader, and possibly imparted a love for travel and foreign languages in his son. The young Heinrich distinguished himself in his early schooling by showing a passion for hardship and foreign lands: as a teenager he had already begun to teach himself Arabic, and to master his body with a rigorous physical fitness regimen. Enrolling in the University of Berlin in 1839, he basked in the aura of Alexander von Humboldt, Carl Ritter, and August Boeckh, brilliant instructors in the fields of geography, biology, and philology. By this time he had also mastered Latin, and became well acquainted with classical literature; a trip to Italy further reinforced these classical inclinations. We get a taste of his Stoic character when, in May 1842, a massive fire in Hamburg severely damaged his father's business, and also totally destroyed Heinrich Barth's personal library (which was extensive even as a student). His comment on this tragedy, worthy of Simonides, was this:

> One's only secure possessions are those which he carries within him. Wealth? Can be gone in a second. Outward joy? Breaks as easily as glass. But inner strength and refinement can never be taken away–they only disappear when one ceases to exist, making them superfluous.

He received his university degree in 1844, after completing a dissertation on the commercial activity of the ancient Greek city of Corinth. He had no job prospects; yet he audaciously proposed to undertake an extended journey around the Mediterranean's shores. He believed that the resulting book from such a trip would attract the attention of professionals. He had no money, but his father generously agreed to finance Heinrich himself: on top of everything else, he was blessed with supportive and broad-minded parents. Before setting out for the trip, he spent some time in London perfecting his mastery of spoken and written Arabic, which he knew would be an essential tool. From 1845 to 1847 he traversed North Africa, then moved up through the Levant into Syria and Turkey, finally ending in Greece. There was some element of risk involved: he had been robbed by bandits near Egypt. He published a book about these experiences in 1849.

This trip would set the stage for what would prove to be the pivotal experience of his life. We must first keep in mind that the African continent in the 1840s was largely *terra incognita* to Europe; indeed, the source of the Nile was not even known until the late 1850s. Explorers who proposed to penetrate beyond the Sahara into the heart of the continent would have been viewed in the same way as astronauts are today. A British explorer named James Richardson had received a commission from his government to conduct an expedition into central Africa; he needed men of proven worth and experience, and Barth offered his services. He was accepted; besides all the other languages he knew, he was also fluent in English. He freely acknowledged the debt he owed to those who came before him. In his monumental five-volume record of his expedition, *Travels and Discoveries in North and Central Africa*, he would write nobly:

> In matters of science and humanity all nations ought to be united by one common interest, each contributing its share in proportion to its own peculiar disposition and calling. If I have been able to achieve something in geographical discovery, it is difficult to say how much of it is due to English, how much to German influence; for science is built up of the materials collected by almost every nation, and, beyond all doubt, in geographical enterprise in general none has done more than the English, while, in Central Africa in particular, very little has been achieved by any but English travelers. Let it not, therefore, be attributed to an undue feeling of nationality if I correct any error of those who preceded me. It would be unpardonable if a traveler failed to penetrate further, or to obtain a clearer insight into

> the customs and the polity of the nations visited by him, or if he were unable to delineate the country with greater accuracy and precision than those who went before him.

For the journey he would call himself "Abd al-Karim Barth Al-Inglisi." It was not, of course, a good idea to appear too conspicuously foreign. Among his many notebooks, he wrote the following epigraph in Arabic, perhaps as inspiration for the road ahead:

> Knowledge is power.
> Because science is
> The confidante in the wilderness,
> The companion in a foreign land,
> The storyteller in solitude,
> The guide in joy and sorrow,
> The weapon against the enemy,
> And the ornament for friends.

The expedition left France and arrived on the North African coast. In 1850 Barth and his comrades crossed the Sahara (an extremely arduous feat in that era), and arrived in the city of Agadez in what is today Niger. But the years 1851 and 1852 would bring disaster, as the deaths of the two other principals of the expedition, Richardson and Adolf Overweg, left Barth on his own. But in some strange way, this may have been exactly what Barth's life up to this point had led to: for years, he had cultivated his self-sufficiency and independence. He was by now an experienced traveler, able to record everything that mattered about a region: language, climate, biology, topography, and ethnic details.

From this point Barth was on his own. He logged about 12,000 miles of travel in what is now Cameroon, Chad, and Timbuktu, patiently recording every observation that mattered. His fluency in Arabic was put to good use, as that language was (and is) the *lingua franca* of the Islamic world; yet during his time in central Africa he also managed to learn several regional tongues, specifically Hausa, Fulani, and Kanuri. Curiosity about travelers goes both ways; not only was he interested in the customs of the diverse peoples he encountered in Africa, but the same peoples were of course intensely interested in him. Who was this tall, pale-faced stranger with his baggage trains, books, and strange scientific and medical instruments? Barth records the following amusing anecdote, which shows that humor and curiosity are universal:

> The princesses also, or the daughters of the absent king, who in this country too bear the title of "mairam" or "méram," called upon me occasionally, under the pretext of wanting some medicines. Among others, there came one day a buxom young maiden, of very graceful but rather coquettish demeanor, accompanied by an elder sister, of graver manners and fuller proportions, and complained to me that she was suffering from a sore in her eyes, begging me to see what it was; but when, upon approaching her very gravely, and inspecting her eyes rather attentively without being able to discover the least defect, I told her that all was right, and that her eyes were sound and beautiful, she burst out into a roar of laughter, and repeated, in a coquettish and flippant manner, "beautiful eyes, beautiful eyes."

Finally, on August 28, 1855, after an absence of five years and five months, Heinrich Barth returned to Tripoli in North Africa. He had been gone so long that London assumed he had perished. In Hamburg, German officials awarded him a gold medal. Tragically, however, his achievements became obscured in a swell of professional jealousies, conflicting national prides between England and Germany, and simply bad timing. Frustrated with the lack of recognition for his achievements, he applied himself to write his testament to posterity, the 3,500-page *Travels and Discoveries in North and Central Africa*. (Mercifully, an abridged one-volume version was also prepared, from which the quotes in this article are taken). Barth strikes a note of pride in his discoveries:

> Thus I closed my long and exhausting career as an African explorer, of which this narrative endeavors to incorporate the result. Having previously gained a good deal of experience of African travelling during an extensive journey through Barbary, I had embarked on this undertaking as a volunteer, under

> the most unfavorable circumstances for myself. The scale and the means of the mission seemed to be extremely limited, and it was only in consequence of the success which accompanied our proceedings that a wider extent was given to the range and objects of the expedition; and after its original leader had succumbed in his arduous task, instead of giving way to despair, I had continued in my career amid great embarrassment, carrying on the explorations of extensive regions almost without any means. And when the leadership of the mission, in consequence of the confidence of her majesty's government, was entrusted to me, and I had been deprived of the only European companion who remained with me, I resolved upon undertaking, with a very limited supply of means, a journey to the far west, in order to endeavor to reach Timbúktu, and to explore that part of the Niger which, through the untimely fate of Mungo Park, had remained unknown to the scientific world.

He was eventually awarded a post at the University of Berlin. He continued to travel, visiting the Balkans extensively in 1865. In November of that year he died suddenly, possibly the result of an intestinal disease he had contracted in Africa. Barth's biographer, Steven Kemper, speculates in his book *A Labyrinth of Kingdoms* that the cause of death was the result of years of hard living and poor diet while on the march. An autopsy also revealed a bullet lodged in his thigh, a relic from an encounter with bandits. He was only forty-four years old. But his achievements and his books live on, and they assure him immortality.

3. The Incredible Life And Explorations Of John Ledyard

Of all the explorers and travelers that have populated these pages, few are as fascinating and as little-known today as the American adventurer John Ledyard. He lived from 1751 to 1789, during the seminal years of American history; and his travels across the globe (especially in Russia and Siberia) mark him out as a man who deserves far more recognition than he has received from posterity. In fact, as I was researching his life in preparation for this article, I could hardly believe that his name had sunk into such undeserved oblivion. Let us give him his due now. Who was this man? An acquaintance described him in this way:

> To those who have never seen Mr. Ledyard, it may not, perhaps, be uninteresting to know, that his person, though scarcely exceeding the middle size, was remarkably expressive of activity and strength; and that his manners, though unpolished, were neither uncivil nor unpleasing...His genius, though uncultivated and irregular, was original and comprehensive. Ardent in his wishes, yet calm in his deliberations; daring in his purposes, but guarded in his measures; impatient of control, yet capable of strong endurance; adventurous beyond the conception of ordinary men, yet wary and considerate, and attentive to all precautions, he appeared to be formed by Nature for achievements of hardihood and peril.

He was born in Groton, Connecticut; his grandfather was a native of Bristol, England, and had come to America as a merchant. His father was involved in maritime commerce in the West Indies, but died young at the age of thirty-five. This left the weight of the household responsibilities to fall on his mother, a woman of strong character and conviction. Ledyard's biographer Jared Sparks tells us, in his *Life and Travels of John Ledyard*, that his mother rose to the challenge:

> It may be supposed, that misfortune did not weaken her parental solicitude, nor make her neglectful of her high trust...In the marked features of his eventful life, eccentric and extraordinary as it was, full of temptations, crosses and sufferings, may often be traced lineaments of virtues, and good impulses, justly referred to such a source, to the early cares and counsels of a judicious, sensible, and pious mother.

Not having many options, Ledyard enrolled in Dartmouth College in the spring of 1772. The college had been recently been founded with the intention of educating and converting local Indian tribes. Ledyard thus prepared himself for missionary work. He did not like the work; the poverty and general wretchedness of the Seneca and Oneida tribes deeply disturbed him. In a letter to his benefactor Dr. Eleazer Wheelock, he wrote:

> Many of them for a month past have eat but once a day, and yet continue to work. From week to week I am obliged to go eeling with the Indians at Oneida Lake for my subsistence. I have feasted and starved with them, as their luck depends on wind and weather. If it should be asked, why they do not support me, the answer is ready, they cannot support themselves. They are now half-starved. Some of them have no more than two quarts of corn. I fear my appearing in such a servile, beggarly manner, will very much disserve the design in view; but I must desist, must go down to the lake for eels this day, and return to-morrow to hill the corn and potatoes. Flour and milk with a few eels have been my living. Such diet, with my hard labour abroad, doth not satisfy nature...My poor people are almost starved to death. I am grieved to the heart for them.

He soon grew to despise missionary work. Yet his experiences with the Indians did ignite a latent passion for native cultures and foreign travel: and this was the theme that would dominate his life. His restlessness and active nature unsuited him for school discipline, and his chafed under the restrictions placed on him. He took to traveling on his own, and in 1773 he left college for good. At this point he decided to plunge head-first into a life of travel. His biographer admirably explains this decision in this way:

> [P]overty stared him in the face; and at the age of twenty-two he found himself a solitary wanderer, dependent on the bounty of his friends, without employment or prospects, having tried various pursuits and failed of success in all...Poverty and privation

> were trifles of no weight with him, compared with the irksome necessity of walking in the same path that all the world walked in, and doing things as all the world had done them before. He thought this a very tame pursuit, unworthy of a rational man, whose soul should be fired with a nobler ambition.

He enlisted as a merchant seaman on a cruise bound for Gibraltar and the Caribbean. This further whetted his appetite; but on a later voyage he deserted in England and was impressed into military duty with the British Navy. This was a common practice at the time; naval duty was not popular (due to privation and strict discipline), and recruiters had to fill the rolls however they could. Nevertheless this experience Ledyard made the best of; he eventually had the chance to join the crew of the most noted explorer of the day, Captain James Cook, from 1776 to 1780. This epic cruise with Cook took Ledyard all over the Polynesian regions of the Pacific, the Aleutian Coast, Alaska, and Hawaii. In adventures too detailed to recount fully here, Ledyard was one of the first (if not the first) Americans to make detailed observations on the Alaskan coast.

In Hawaii (then called the Sandwich Islands), he was awestruck by the lush beauty of the islands, and attempted several expeditions inland. He even attempted to summit Mauna Loa, but was unsuccessful. The expedition ended on a tragic note with the death of Captain Cook, who was killed when relations with the islanders collapsed. The expedition returned to England, and Ledyard, still serving with the British military, was sent to Canada. There he promptly deserted and returned to Dartmouth after an absence of about eight years. He wrote an account of his travels in 1783 called *Journal of Captain Cook's Last Voyage*, a well-written memoir, which has the distinction of being possibly the first written account describing Hawaii that was published in North America. With the end of the American Revolutionary War in 1783, Ledyard tried his hand in various commercial and trading ventures, none of which amounted to anything. In 1784, he visited Paris to meet another restless, disgruntled veteran of the Revolution, John Paul Jones. One of his major purposes was to plan an expedition that would explore the Pacific Northwest, then still very much *terra incognita*.

In Paris Ledyard met both Jefferson (serving there as a US ambassador) and John Paul Jones, both of whom were remarkable men of energy and vision. It is amazing that the young United States was able to produce so many men of distinction in those days.

At this point Ledyard's plan (with the backing of Jefferson, Jones, and several other notables) was among the most ambitious and audacious proposals in the history of exploration: *he now wished to travel across Russia from West to East, across Siberia and the Bering Strait, move down through Alaska, cross the entire continental United States, and arrive back on the east coast of America!* Such a proposal would be extremely impressive in 2017; in the 1780s it defied belief. And so off he went. We regrettably cannot follow Ledyard on all his adventures in Russia and Siberia. But they are extremely interesting for the student of exploration or Russian history; we have few reliable accounts of native customs in Siberia and the Russian far East, and Ledyard's travels fill a critical gap in our knowledge of the region.

Remarkably, he was able to discern the common ancestry of the American Indians with the Asiatic peoples of Siberia and eastern Russia, a fact that has now been confirmed by DNA evidence. Ledyard wrote the following perceptive words to Thomas Jefferson, which hint at further anthropological discoveries (global human diffusion) to come in a later century:

> I am certain, that all the people you call red people on the continent of America, and on the continents of Europe and Asia, as far south as the southern parts of China, are all one people, by whatever names distinguished, and that the best general name would be Tartar. I suspect that all red people are of the same family. I am satisfied, that America was peopled from Asia, and had some, if not all, its animals from thence. I am satisfied, that the great general analogy in the customs of men can only be accounted for, by supposing them all to compose one family; and, by extending the idea, and uniting customs, traditions, and history, I am satisfied, that this common origin was such, or nearly, as related by Moses, and commonly believed among the nations of the earth. There is, also, a transposition of things on the globe,

> that must have been produced by some cause equal to the effect, which is vast and curious. Whether I repose on arguments drawn from facts observed by myself, or send imagination forth to find a cause, they both declare to me a general deluge...

But foreigners traveling in remote regions frequently come under suspicion, even when they have official permission to be there. Ledyard was arrested in Irkutsk by the personal order of Empress Catherine the Great and taken into custody. The charge was apparently that he was a "French spy." He was packed off to Moscow for a perfunctory hearing, and then deported from the country. The real reason for Ledyard's expulsion? Catherine did not want an informed American to learn too much about Russia's far eastern holdings, which at that time included Alaska.

An observer named Count Segur (who spoke to Catherine himself) claimed that her pretext for arresting him was an intention to save Ledyard from possible death in the wilds. "Possibly this pretext of humanity," Segur wrote, "advanced by Catherine, only disguised her unwillingness to have the new possessions of Russia, on the western coast of America, seen by an enlightened citizen of the United States. The above, however, were the reasons she advanced to me."

So Ledyard found himself back in London in 1788. But the relentless explorer had new vistas in mind: Africa. He assembled the men and supplies for such an expedition, and arrived in Alexandria soon after. He was able to explore parts of Egypt and even sent letters to Thomas Jefferson describing his experiences and findings. But here tragedy struck. He likely contracted some sort of disease in Egypt; his biographer only identifies it as an "attack of bilious complaint." As a remedy, Ledyard began to take doses of vitriolic acid (now called sulfuric acid); whether this was administered by himself or by a local doctor, we do not know. The dosage was too great, and he died, despite an attempt to save him with a dose of tartar emetic. He was only 38 years old. We do not know the exact date of his death, but it was probably near the end of November 1788. He was buried in Cairo, probably along the banks of the Nile, but the location of his grave remains unknown. Covered up by the silts and sands of time, as so much in human history, Ledyard's achievements remain the only funerary monument to his memory, and these live on wherever men continue to celebrate heroic deeds.

4. Carsten Niebuhr: Sole Survivor Of The Danish-Arabian Expedition

Of the German explorers of the eighteenth century, the only man whose accomplishments rival those of Alexander von Humboldt is Carsten Niebuhr. His extensive travels and surveys in the Near East and India resulted in specific geographical data, surveying information, and historical insights. This was no dreamy wanderer; this was a trained professional, a man who was tough, hard-bitten, and practical, with the astuteness to process what was going on around him and commit his observations faithfully to paper. If he is little-known today–as are so many of these great explorers we have enshrined here–the fault lies with us, not with him; for as the sole survivor of the so-called "Danish-Arabian Expedition," he proved himself not only as a scientist, but as a tenacious fighter.

His origins were modest, as are those of many great explorers. He was born in 1733 in Lower Saxony to an agrarian family. Access to education for him was not easy, but he did learn the value of hard physical labor; perhaps it was these early years before the plow that forged the iron constitution his body would display in future travels. He did show an aptitude for surveying and map-reading, and as he grew to adulthood his services were sought by local notables in the area. The mid-eighteenth century was a period of religious revival in Europe as well as in the American colonies; there was a hunger for accurate and modern information on the regions described in the Bible. The Ottoman sultans were in general favorably disposed towards permitting foreigners access to their domains, as long as they secured permission in advance. Motivated crowned heads in Europe did not take long to respond to such windows of opportunity.

Through one of his colleagues, Niebuhr received word that Frederik V of Denmark was assembling an expedition to Arabia, Syria, Egypt, and other parts of the Near East. The subtle Danish king prided himself on being a patron of the arts and sciences, and was determined to expand the outer limits of the current knowledge of the Middle East. Having nothing else to do, Niebuhr resolved to apply for the position of surveyor. In preparation, he polished his skills at the University of Goettingen, and applied himself to the study of the Arabic language. He would never achieve the dazzling proficiency in Arabic that we find in John Lewis Burckhardt or

Richard Burton; but Niebuhr was good enough, and he more than made up any shortcomings in this area with other equally important skills.

By 1760 the members of the expedition had been chosen. They were: Peter Forsskål, a Swedish naturalist; Frederik Christian von Haven, a Danish linguist and philologist; Niebuhr himself, who would act as surveyor and geographer; Christian Carl Kramer, a Danish physician; Georg Wilhelm Baurenfeind, a painter and artist (in the days before photography, artists were part of every well-equipped expedition); and Lars Berggren, a Swedish soldier and orderly. Frederik's instructions to his men were to "make as many scientific discoveries as possible," and, most importantly, to refrain from any conduct that might arouse the antagonism of the "native Mohammedans." In other words, they were to act in a modest, humble manner, and not as arrogant imperialists or conquerors.

The expedition left Europe in January 1761, and made for Alexandria, Egypt. From here the team traveled to Suez, then Jeddah in Arabia, and then into Yemen (Hadramaut), which was at that time was a very remote corner of the Arab world. But disaster struck in Yemen; two members of the expedition died in May 1763 (von Haven and Forsskål), probably from malaria, although the record is not entirely clear. We must understand that Europeans at that time did not appreciate the need to adopt local clothing and mannerisms. In addition, modern knowledge of vitamin deficiency diseases, dehydration, and malnutrition were entirely lacking. Among the team members, only Niebuhr seemed to thrive. He was a tough, lean German of peasant stock who was used to physical privation.

More importantly, however, he had the humility and canniness to watch how the Arabs dressed and conducted themselves in the desert, and quickly set about imitating them. This amused the locals, of course; but the bedouins respected him, and gave him an extensive wardrobe of native garb, as well as foods more suited to the climate, such as dates, dried meats, and thick cheeses. Niebuhr's account of his travels was translated from German into English in the early 1790s. It makes for interesting reading today, as it contains a wealth of personal observations that scrupulously strive for objectivity despite the obfuscating fogs of cultural conditioning. Here he describes some social habits of his hosts:

> The Arabs are not quarrelsome; but, when any dispute happens to arise among them, they make a great deal of noise. I have seen some of them, however, who, although armed with poignards, and ready to stab one another, were easily appeased. A reconciliation was instantly effected, if any indifferent person but said to them, Think of God and his Prophet. When the contest could not be settled at once, umpires were chosen, to whose decision they submitted...Notwithstanding this coolness, on which the people of the East pique themselves, the Arabs shew great sensibility to everything that can be construed into an injury. If one man should happen to spit beside another, the latter will not fail to avenge himself of the imaginary insult. In a caravan I once saw an Arab highly offended at a man, who, in spitting, had accidentally bespattered his beard with some small part of the spittle. It was with difficulty that he could be appeased by him, who, he imagined, had offended him, even although he humbly asked pardon, and kissed his beard in token of submission.

Here Niebuhr describes the basic dress of the region:

> The ordinary dress of the Arabs is indeed simple enough; but they have also a sort of great-coat, without sleeves, called *Abba*, which is simpler still. I was acquainted with a blind taylor at Basra [in Iraq], who earned his bread by making *Abbas*; so that they cannot be of a very nice shape, or made of many pieces; In Yemen they are worn only by travellers; but in the province of Lachsa, the *Abba* is a piece of dress commonly used by both sexes.

The expedition next sailed from Yemen to Bombay. En route, two more members died (Georg Baurenfeind and Lars Berggren); and once the ship reached India, the physician, Kramer, also died, leaving Niebuhr now completely alone. It was a similar situation that African explorer Heinrich von Barth would encounter in later decades. Niebuhr decided to press on, oblivious to the hardships and determined to carry out the commission entrusted to him by the Danish king. After spending a little over a year in Bombay in preparation, he traveled overland through Persia, then what is now Iraq, Syria, and Palestine, Cyprus, and Israel. He transcribed the famous "Behistun Inscription" in 1764 (which helped pave the way for the later decipherment of cuneiform script), and finally reached Constantinople in February 1767.

From here he sailed back to Copenhagen in triumph; it had been an incredible odyssey, exceeded in romantic danger only by its practical utility. Rarely has one man's travel yielded so much in practical detail; Niebuhr's maps are masterpieces of utility, and were used for generations. Plant and animal specimens, as well as Arabic and Persian manuscripts, were also brought back and are still used to this day. His explorations also provided precious ethnographic and historical information for later scholars. Before they died, the other members of the team did their jobs wonderfully, and Niebuhr (in contrast to the behavior of some later explorers) was careful to give them the credit that they deserved.

Of Niebuhr's absolute dedication to scholarship there can be no question. Not only did he risk his life (and devote ten years of it) during the expedition, but he was forced to commit his personal resources to ensure that his books and maps found print. As often happens in such situations, royal interest in the expedition waned quickly after Niebuhr returned to Copenhagen. The government was willing to finance his efforts from that point only grudgingly. The voluminous output of his findings stretched into six volumes, most of which Niebuhr had to pay for himself. And yet it was all worth it: all the suffering, all the financial expenditure, and the lives of the men who had been lost. For here, for the first time, was hard, tangible information about the Arabic-speaking regions of the East, as well as antiquarian data on the ruins that dotted western Persia. All later travelers would stand on the shoulders of their achievements. Niebuhr died in the city of Meldorf in 1815 at the age of 82.

All in all, the Danish-Arabian expedition was a triumph of Enlightenment faith in science and observation, wedded with iron determination, luck, and sustained effort. It was imbued with a spirit of genuine curiosity and scientific objectivity; and there was not a shred of the cultural friction that has too often marred the record of European contact with the region. To this day, it remains perhaps the most productive expedition to the Middle East ever carried out.

5. Charles Sturt's Australian Explorations

The student of the history of exploration and discovery cannot fail to notice certain recurring patterns in the lives of great explorers. Many of them come from modest or poor backgrounds; many have military experience; many are driven by an inner conviction that they are destined for great achievements; many have a high tolerance for pain and hardship; and some of them have combative or disputatious natures that make them difficult to get along with. Not all of these generalizations are found in every explorer, of course. But it cannot be denied that a certain personality type is well-suited to a life of exploration.

We will consider here the life of Charles Sturt, one of the most important leaders of land expeditions in Australia. I expect Australian readers well acquainted with Sturt's career will review this article with tolerant smiles, noting how much information I have of necessity omitted. But it should be kept in mind that the names and events of Australian exploration are almost totally unknown (even in the English-speaking world) outside of Australia. This obscurity is a fate that has sadly befallen many of the great names we have described in these pages. It is my goal to help correct this situation. We will be accomplishing something, I think, just by providing a taste for the interested reader of some great deeds in the history of this fascinating land, that is both a continent and a country.

He was born in Bengal in colonial India in 1795, the son of a British judicial official. At an early age he was sent to England for schooling; an attempt to enroll in Cambridge University in 1812 did not meet with success, primarily due to his family's financial circumstances. So, like countless young men before him, he chose the military as a way to seek glory and professional security. He saw service in the wars of his era, traveling to Canada and back. As a captain, he was appointed to escort convicts to Australia; in 1827 he arrived at Sydney, and this was the start of his enduring fascination with the country. Here, he believed, was a place he could make his mark, without being burdened by the stifling rules of social caste and lineage that would always be present in Europe.

Sturt developed an interest in riverine exploration as the key that would unlock the secrets of Australia's interior. We must remember that, in his era, the interior of the continent was practically a blank slate. Sturt's experiences in Canada's wilds had led him to believe that rivers were the arterial vessels of any land, and that he who mastered the rivers would master the country. Fed by rumors and stories he heard from the natives, Sturt also believed there was a large "inland sea" in the center of the continent, and he was determined to locate it. The governor of New South Wales, Sir Ralph Darling, recognized him as a man of ability and resourcefulness, and agreed to sponsor an expedition to explore the Macquarie River. Completed in 1829, this early expedition whetted his appetite for additional forays. That year he set out on an epic journey of exploration of the Murray and Murrumbidgee Rivers.

The results of these explorations was his book, *Two Expeditions into the Interior of Southern Australia during the years 1828, 1829, 1830 and 1831.* We are gratified that these early explorers felt compelled to record every detail of their travels. Interesting are some of his revealing thoughts on his emigration to a new country:

> But to sever the links of kindred, and to abandon the homes of our fathers after years of happy tranquility, is a sacrifice the magnitude of which is unquestionable. The feelings by which men are influenced under such circumstances have a claim to our respect. Indeed, no class of persons can have a stronger hold upon our sympathies than those whom unmerited adverse fortune obliges to seek a home in a distant country. Far, therefore, be it from me to dispute a single expression of regret to which they may give utterance. It must, however, be remembered that the deepest feelings of anguish are providentially alleviated in time. Our heaviest misfortunes are frequently repaired by industry and caution. The sky clears up, as it were: new interests engage the attention, and the cares of a family or the improvement of a newly acquired property engross those moments which would otherwise be spent in vain and unprofitable regrets.

Here Sturt relates the formidable heat of Australia's climate, which he experienced near Buddah Lake:

> The sun's rays were too powerful even for the natives, who kept as much as possible in the shade. In the evening, when the atmosphere was somewhat cooler, we launched the boat upon the lake, in order to get some wild fowl and fish; but although we were tolerably successful with our guns, we did not take anything with our hooks...As soon as the sun dipped under the horizon, hundreds of birds came crowding to the border of the lake, to quench the thirst they had been unable to allay in the forest. Some were gasping, others almost too weak to avoid us, and all were indifferent to the reports of our guns.

Sturt's work was greeted with excitement in England, for his explorations confirmed the fact that the country was a unique habitat unlike any other in the world. In 1835 he returned to Australia from England and occupied himself with farming a large tract of land; after settling in Grange, South Australia, he was appointed Surveyor-General there. But the call of exploration continued: he undertook an expedition on the Murray River in 1839, and continued to obsess about the possible existence of an inland sea in central Australia. In 1844 he finally got his chance to search for an inland sea.

With a party of men he advanced into what is now Sturt's Stony Desert and the Simpson Desert, but was unable to continue, due to extreme heart and his debilitation by scurvy. He took a break from exploration for a few years, returning to England in 1847 but coming back to Adelaide in 1849. His later years were marred by personal tragedy and disappointment: one of his sons died in India, and he was unsuccessful in attempts to seek government positions he believed he deserved. He died suddenly in 1869, primarily due to the mileage he had put on his body by years of hard traveling. But he left behind him a legacy that would inspire the next generation of discoverers. So does the spring of courage nourish all those who visit its waters. His books live on as testament to his fortitude. I believe we can give him no better epitaph than these stirring words which he wrote in 1849 in his *Narrative of an Expedition into Central Australia*:

> To that man who is really earnest in the performance of his duty to the last, and who has set his heart on the accomplishment of a great object, the attainment of which would place his name high up in the roll of Fame; to him who had well-nigh reached the topmost step of the ladder, and whose hand had all but grasped the pinnacle, the necessity must be great, and the struggle of feeling severe, that forces him to bear back, and abandon his task. Let any man lay the map of Australia before him, and regard the blank upon its surface, and then let me ask him if it would not be an honourable achievement to be the first to place foot in its centre.

Great men do not abandon their goals at the first sign of discomfort or trouble. They press on, fortified by an inner conviction that gives them the moral right and duty to push beyond ordinary limits; and, by so doing, they mark the upward progress of knowledge and civilization.

6. The Remarkable Travels Of Jonas Hanway

Travelers and explorers march on; and I march on with my retellings of their adventures and philosophies. I suspect that few readers will have heard of the great English traveler and philanthropist Jonas Hanway; yet his career and worldview embodies many of the values we have extolled here, as we will understand later in this article. Hanway's journeys in Russia and Persia alone make him worthy of inclusion among any list of great itinerants; but, when these experiences are combined with his expansive moral and ethical philosophy, we have the ingredients of true greatness. The world needs more men like him now.

He was born in 1712 in Portsmouth, Hampshire, and his father died when Hanway was but a child. His family was not especially wealthy, and he imbibed an industrious, enterprising ethic at an early age. When the was seventeen, he was sent to Lisbon, Portugal to become an apprentice in a mercantile house. This experience whetted his appetite for foreign languages and foreign travel. At this passionate age, he was also not immune to the charms of Iberian femininity, and he carried on an affair with a local girl whom he wished to marry. But, alas, his romantic experiences ended badly; perhaps her family did not accept him. We do know that the experience permanently colored his outlook. He forswore the idea of marriage, and remained single for the rest of his life. Perhaps the greatest philanthropists all nurse some secret wound.

Hanway steadily mastered the essentials of commerce and business. He departed for Russia in 1743 to serve in a commercial house, and was soon assigned to represent the firm in the Caspian trade. He was appointed the agent of the Russia Company in Persia. He resolved to go to Persia himself, and set out from Moscow with an interpreter and some assistants, along with various commercial samples. He first proceeded down the Volga and then took a ship to Astrakhan, and from there went to Yerkie. Finally, on December 3, 1743, he arrived at Lanjaron, Persia, after having crossed the Caspian. He reached Astrabad on December 18.

At Astrabad he secured the protection of the local leader, Nazir Aga; he asked to be allowed to leave with his merchandise (cloth and assorted manufactured goods) to the city of Meshed. He was now using camels for transportation. Danger now intervened. Hanway found himself in the thick of a local insurrection that flared up without warning, and as a comparatively wealthy foreigner he would be an easy target for the local dispossessed. Rebels seized his merchandise and placed him under house arrest. The Turcoman rebels, as is customary in Persia, exceedingly polite, but left no doubt that he was their prisoner. He was able to conceal 160 gold on his person, but lost the rest of his cargo to Fate.

Local sympathizers helped smuggle him out of Astrabad, so that he might avoid the indignity of being made a captive servant. From this point he traveled in disguise through remote pathways of northern Iran, masquerading as a poor Russian. He had a chance to inspect the ruins of Ferhabad, once the seat of the ancient Persian kings. After almost getting involved in a shootout, he paddled along the Persian coast in a canoe with a few tough comrades as far as Teschidezar. The shah heard of his difficulties and sent an outfitted horse to Hanway. With this he proceeded to Balfroosh; but Turcoman rebels were all over the countryside, and he soon found himself in even worse straits than before. By this time he had lost nearly everything: his companions, his supplies, and his horse. Even his clothing was in tatters, hanging like rags from his body and giving him the appearance of a vagabond.

By some miracle he found kindly villagers who were willing to help this strange "Russian" who could barely speak Persian. By the first week of March he reached Casbin, nearly blind from the glare of snow on the ground, and joined a detachment of soldiers. He finally was able to secure an audience with the shah, and petitioned for compensation for the loss of his goods in Astrabad. Shah Nadir agreed, and Hanway left him at the end of March. He was impressed by thc bcauty of Iran, commcnting on:

> [T]he falls of water from the rocks, the stupendous mountains, far higher than any he had seen in Europe, rising gradually one above another, some with their summits covered with snow, and others concealing their heads in the clouds, formed a delightful scene. The vines were full of foliage, the orange-groves perfumed the air with their fragrance, and the gardens were in full blossom.

By April he was back in Astrabad. Payment as promised was slow in coming. But the new local leader offered him compensation in female slaves, that might, he was assured, be sold for a handsome profit. Hanway politely demurred. He was then laid low by the plague for several months; this bout with disease nearly killed him. After various adventures too numerous to mention here, he was able to make his way out of Persia, arriving back at the Volga by September 13. By December 22, he had arrived back at Moscow and too safety. And yet Fate, as we have so often observed here, works in strange, unexpected ways. In Moscow he found letters waiting for him that announced he had become the beneficiary of a very large (and totally unexpected) inheritance. "Providence was thus indulgent to me," he would later say, "as if it meant to reward me for the sincerity of my endeavours." He returned to St. Petersburg in January 1745, and stayed there for five more years, watching his fortune increase through the benefits of trade.

He returned to London in October 1750 and decided to give up all commercial pursuits. He was by now a changed man. Some fundamental change had taken place in him, which must have had its origins in the near-death experiences he had in Persia and Russia. He grew to despise arrogance, cruelty, and the exploitation of the weak, and resolved to struggle against it for the rest of his life. He turned out one pamphlet after another, advocating for things that we today take for granted. He proposed the paving of all of London's streets; he founded the Marine Society, which promoted maritime trade; he pushed for the founding of hospitals, orphanages, and rehabilitation houses for reformed prostitutes. He even advocated for the rights of chimney-sweepers, who in his day endured terrible physical hardships. Not all of his reforms were successful; for some reason he believed tea-drinking was harmful and advocated–unsuccessfully–for its limitation. This great Englishman died on September 5, 1786. By this time he and his good works were known to all in London. One biographer described him with these words:

> His last moments were those of a Christian and a philosopher, calm and tranquil, indicating the firmest reliance on the mercy and goodness of God, and a consciousness of a life honestly and usefully spent...When he endeavoured to sooth distress, or point out to any wretch who had strayed the comforts of a virtuous life, he was peculiarly impressive; and everything that he said had an air of consideration and sincerity...

In the course of preparing this article, I was fortunate to come upon a concise summary, in essay form, of Hanway's ethical philosophy. It can be seen as the lessons he learned from his extensive travels and near-death experiences, and it is taken from his book *An Historical Account of the British Trade over the Caspian Sea* (1753). As Hanway sees things, each member of society has a responsibility towards his peers; and no nation can long survive as a free state if the privileged few shirk that responsibility. Moral corruption matters, too: when a people lose sight of virtue, a slide into "libertinism" is inevitable, and this quickly causes political freedom to dissolve into authoritarianism:

> The ravages of time, the ruins of cities, the desolation of countries, the tyranny of kings, the folly and

> iniquity of subjects in selling themselves like beasts to the slaughter; with all the pernicious effects of arbitrary power, must, in a serious mind, draw reflexions on the uncertainty of human affairs. By tracing these events, as near as possible to their source, the heart will be lifted up to the great author of nature, and adopt a consistent principle concerning the general law of his moral government, by observing how vice is ever productive of misery. Though the dispensations of his providence are oftentimes incomprehensible, yet this ought not to weaken a steady persuasion, that virtue is in every region, and under every government, acceptable to him; "that what he delights in must be happy," however the face of things may appear...The present and future happiness of individuals, as well as the felicity of the state, are all intimately dependent on each other. True politeness is but humanity refined, which ultimately centers in charity; public love is but the fame charity adapted to the dignity and prosperity of the community of which we are members... Do we not rather vie with each other, not who shall be wisest, but who shall excel most in vanities and expensive follies; and thus deviating from the great principle laid down, at least, prepare a way for ruin?

Has any man learned as much from his travels, and put such humanistic knowledge to practical use? The length of the quote above may be forgiven by virtue of its timeless relevance. Hanway's words on the responsibilities of all citizens resonate just as powerfully today–perhaps even more so–than when they were written in the 1750s. This is greatness of soul–in Cicero's words, *magnitudo animi*–in living and applied form. We acutely feel the loss of men like him in our own era.

7. The Strange Travels Of Pietro Della Valle

Pietro Della Valle was an accomplished traveler as well as a literary figure in his own right. Other great names of Middle Eastern exploration came after him, but he was one of the very first pre-modern Westerners to gain first-hand experience in the region. As the reader will discover, he was also undoubtedly the most eccentric. He was born in Rome on April 11, 1586, to a distinguished family that was able to provide him with a good education. Developing a flair for literature at an early age, he thirsted for the glories of the sword as well as the glories of the pen; and to this end, he signed up for adventure with a Spanish fleet in 1611 on an expedition to the North African coast.

The expedition accomplished little, and Della Valle returned home in disappointment. He then experienced miseries of a different kind, those related to the dashed hopes of love. His biographers relate that he sunk into a deep depression after having been rejected by a woman he was pursuing; and, to revive his spirits, he resolved to travel far beyond the borders of his country. So it is that the great enterprises of men often owe their beginnings to those tumescent emotions so fundamental to his nature. His plan was to explore the famous cities and regions of the East, beginning with the Ottoman domains, and then moving on to Persia and India.

His ship left Venice in June of 1614 and sailed for Constantinople. His first order of business after reaching the Ottoman capital was to acquire as thorough a knowledge of Turkish as he could. This was not difficult for him, as he had demonstrated a facility with the classical languages in his youth. Once one already knows a language or two, acquiring another one becomes less difficult. He was also able to taste coffee for the first time in his life; the beverage had not yet become fashionable in Europe. When an epidemic of the plague broke out, however, he found it advisable to relocate to Egypt. After arriving in Alexandria, he saw the sights of ancient and modern Egypt in and around Cairo. From there he moved through the Sinai and on to Jerusalem. It was at this time that he began to formulate a new plan: a trek across the desert wastes from Jerusalem to what is now northern Iraq. In those days, such a journey required thorough preparation. In September 1616, he and his small caravan left Aleppo in Syria for Iraq. They had to take care to avoid certain routes, as some bedouins in that proud age took it as a point of honor to relieve well-equipped strangers of their possessions. They reached the banks of the Tigris near the end of October. The day before they entered Baghdad, however, the party was robbed during a night raid, and Della Valle found himself facing severe hardship.

At some point during his stay he became acquainted with a prominent local Nestorian (Assyrian) Christian. The man's eldest daughter was a beautiful girl named Sitti Maani, and our passionate young Italian, now so far from home, found himself swept away by her charms. He was fluent in Turkish, but possessed little Arabic; but this seemed to be enough, and the two became married. A dangerous problem developed for him when one of his party murdered another member after a dispute; fearing that the local pasha would detain all the foreigners and hold them all accountable, Della Valle and his men concealed the body and left the murder unreported.

He then set out to explore the ancient ruins in the area, as well as parts of Kurdistan. He left Baghdad in January 1617, this time bound for Persia. Ispahan he found much more to his liking than the Ottoman domains; Persia was more densely populated, had better accommodations, and presented less of a personal risk for foreign travelers. His wife was with him, too, as well as her sister. His party moved from Ispahan to the Caspian Sea, and around this time he faced another serious problem. His wife Maani, after having been insulted by a local Persian man, recklessly ordered one of her servants to give the man a verbal dressing-down. He took things too far, a fight broke out, and the Persian was killed in the ensuring brawl. Worse still, he turned out to be a military officer.

Della Valle used all of his diplomatic skills to resolve the situation with a local magistrate, and the affair was patched up, probably with the assistance of a monetary payment to the dead man's family. There was nothing to do but keep moving, and in 1618 he presented himself to the court of Shah Abbas. The shah received him cordially, but paid him little mind; his attentions were focused on fighting the Turks, with whom he was engaged in a contest for control of the Iraqi provinces (a joust that continues to this day). After a victory over the Turks, the shah took his leave to Casbin; Della Valle could sense that his presence there served no purpose, so he returned to Ispahan. Sickness and fatigue had taken their toll on him, and he longed for a period of rest.

Further disappointments awaited. Maani was by now pregnant, and in no condition to travel, but she and Della Valle insisted on visited the coastal regions of Persia that were often afflicted with pestilence. This turned out to be a serious mistake. It was not long before they both came down with fever; he recovered, but she did not, dying at the age of twenty-three. So he was left alone in a foreign land. And it was at this point that he began to reflect on the transitory nature of all earthly riches. He sunk into a deep depression that rendered him nearly immobile for months. And when he emerged from it, he would be a changed man.

The experience must have permanently damaged his psyche, for at this point he took a step that cannot be considered rational under any circumstances. Unable to part with his beloved, he arranged to have her embalmed, encased in a coffin, and fitted in a trunk that he continued to carry with him on his travels. Corpses in Islam are considered unclean, and his action must have been greeted with horror by his servants; but his mind was made up, and it was done. The grisly task was accomplished through the assistance of several old women Della Valle hired for the purpose. They removed the organs from the body and filled it with camphor and other preservatives; it was then set out to dry for seven days and nights in the open air. During this time, he kept an armed vigil over the body to prevent its being carried off by wild animals. At this point he decided to continue with his travels, rather than return to Italy. In January 1623 he boarded a ship and headed for Surat and Goa in India.

After various adventures in India, he boarded a ship from Goa to Muscat in November 1624. From there he moved up the Arabian Gulf to Basra. In May 1625 he set out for Aleppo, finally resolved to return home. After long journeys he finally returned to Rome at the end of March in 1628. He had almost lost the corpse of Maani to bandits in the Syrian desert. But, after explaining to them the contents of his chest, they were touched by his piety and devotion, and lessened their demands on him. In Alexandretta, he had to conceal his wife's embalmed body from the authorities; such a cargo would never be permitted aboard ship, so Della Valle secreted it between bales of cotton.

On his return to Rome he gained an audience with Pope Urban VIII. He was the talk of the town for some time; during a funerary mass he held for Maani, he burst into tears and was unable to continue with his address. He still had sufficient means to live the remainder of his days in comfort, but the evidence suggests that his experiences had loosened his hold on reality. He remarried, apparently to a Georgian girl that had returned with him on his travels; yet she could not soothe the fires that burned within him. He killed his coachman in a dispute, but the record is silent as to the specific details. While he was not prosecuted, his fellow Romans gave him a wide berth thereafter. When he died in April 1652, he was not a favored citizen. His wife moved to Urbino, and his children were banished from Rome. We cannot say that he was a good man; but the evidence suggests that he was daring, and that his contributions to geographic knowledge were significant. The personal attributes of this strange traveler remind us that while travel can open new horizons for the soul, it can never really expunge that soul's inherent defects. He remains both a pioneer, and a cautionary tale.

8. Adam Johann Von Kruzenstern Circumnavigates The Globe

In these pages we have given the great explorers of Britain, Germany, Australia, the United States, and some other nations their due. We now discuss the life and career of Russia's most accomplished nineteenth century explorer and adventurer, the Baron Ivan Fyodorovich Kruzenshtern (Иван Фёдорович Крузенштерн). Like many of the names celebrated here, his is virtually unknown in the West today, a fact that may intimate just how far we have departed from the adventurous, daring spirit of those who came before us. He was born in Estonia in 1770 as Adam Johann Ritter von Krusenstern; as his name suggests, his ancestors had originally come from Sweden. A military career in the Russian navy turned out to be his calling; perhaps a proximity to the ocean imparts a dosage of salt water in every man's veins. Russia had explorers before, of course, but most of them (e.g., Behring, Tchirikoff, Spangberg, Laxman, Krenitzin) had been focused on explorations near the waters of the Russian Empire's vast domains. Perhaps the terrestrial immensity of Russia itself kept its people so preoccupied that they had no energy left over for the kind of international ventures that the Western Europeans undertook. In any case, Kruzenstern was the first Russian to lead a scientific expedition that spanned the globe.

When one wishes to learn, one seeks out the best. Kruzenstern served in the British Navy in 1793 and remained there, learning what he could, for six years. His experience in the Far East, especially in China and the Aleutian Islands, convinced him that geographical knowledge of the area was woefully underdeveloped; Czar Alexander I agreed with him, and in 1802 commissioned him to explore the little-known coast of what is now Alaska. His two ships, named the *Nadiejeda* and the *Neva,* left the port of Cronstadt (near St. Petersburg) in August 1803. They visited the Canary Islands and Brazil, then passed through the Straits of Magellan and pushed into the Pacific.

In the South Seas his powers of observation became more finely honed. Here he describes some warriors and weapons of the Marquesas:

> The members of these clubs are distinguished by different tattooed marks upon their bodies; those of the king's club, consisting of twenty-six members, have a square one on their breasts about six inches long and four wide...The two Europeans whom we found here, and who had both resided with them several years, agreed in their assertions that the natives of Nukahiva were a cruel, intractable people, and, without even the exceptions of the female sex, very much addicted to cannibalism; that the appearance of content and good-humor, with which they had so much deceived us, was not their true character; and that nothing but the fear of punishment and the hopes of reward, deterred them from giving a loose to their savage passions...Their weapons are invariably adorned with human hair, and human bones are used as ornaments in almost all their household furniture; they also often gave us to understand by pantomimic gestures that human flesh was regarded by them as a delicacy.

We may allow for some hyperbole in the above passage. Kruzenstern's biographer Jules Verne, quoting this passage in 1881, regarded his description as somewhat exaggerated, as perhaps it was. Man and his cultures are products of geography, climate, and other circumstances; and we cannot be too quick to deliver verdicts on the social customs that result from these influences. Verne gave a fair assessment when he noted, "We must not, therefore, blame these representatives of humanity for not having risen higher. They have never been a nation. Scattered as their homes are on the wide ocean, and divided as they are into small tribes, without agricultural or mineral resources, without connexions, and with a climate which makes them strangers to want, they could but remain stationary or cultivate none but the most rudimentary arts and industries. Yet in spite of all this, how often have their instruments, their canoes, and their nets, excited the admiration of travelers." Kruzenstern proceeded across the Pacific and explored parts of Kamchatka and Japan. Regarding Satsuma, he noted:

> The whole country consists of high pointed hills, at one time appearing in the form of pyramids, at others of a globular or conical form, and seeming as it were under the protection of some neighboring mountain, such as Peak Homer, or another lying north-by-west of it, and even a third farther inland. Liberal as nature has been in the adornment of these parts, the industry of the Japanese seems not a little to have contributed to their beauty; for nothing indeed can equal the extraordinary degree of cultivation everywhere apparent.

But his visit to Japan was not entirely pleasant. Expecting to be accorded the same privileges as the Dutch, who were already there, he found himself isolated and shunned when he put the *Nudiejeda* ashore at Nagasaki. Japan at this time practiced a strict policy of isolation, and foreigners were not welcome. He then surveyed the western coast of Japan and edged toward the Korean peninsula. At Sakhalin, he recorded observations on the Ainu people, an indigenous people of Japan: "The Ainos are rather below the middle stature, being at the most five feet two or four inches high, of a dark, nearly black complexion, with a thick bushy beard, black rough hair, hanging straight down; and excepting in the heard they have the appearance of the Kamtschadales, only that their countenance is much more regular."

In October 1805, Kruzenstern headed towards Europe. He visited Macao in China on the way there, then finally arrived back at Cronstadt in August 1806. His written record of his explorations was translated into English several years later. He was one of the first Westerners to provide detailed descriptions of the little-known regions near Japan and Kamchatka; before him, many navigators had to rely on the uncertain accounts of shipwrecked sailors. He was elected to the Russian Academy of Sciences, made an admiral in 1841, and then died five years later. One of his hopes was that Russia would follow-up his expedition with others like it; this, unfortunately, did not happen, for variety of reasons. Russia in the mid-nineteenth century was grappling with social change and political instability, and not enough attention was paid to Kruzenstern's warnings that the Russian Far East would be an important region in the decades to come. Perhaps he was too far ahead of his time. But he was the first Russian to circle the globe, and he had dared to push the outer limits of geographic knowledge.

9. The Life And Travels Of Leo Africanus

The diplomat and traveler now known as Leo Africanus was born Hasan Ibn Muhammad Al-Wazan Al-Fasi (حسن ابن محمد الوزان الفاسي) in the early 1490s in Spanish Grenada; of the exact date we are not certain.This period was not a favorable one to be an Andalusian Arab in Spain, as the last vestiges of the old caliphate were being pushed off the Iberian peninsula by the nascent Castilian kingdom. When Granada passed into Christian hands, Leo's family found it expedient to move to Fez in Morocco, and there he received a good education.

He completed his studies as a teenager and managed to get himself appointed a secretary, with a salary of three gold dinars per month, to a merchant enterprise that sent caravans all over north Africa and the Middle East. Together with his uncle, he visited various commercial centers in the region, and was even based in Timbuktu for about four years. Travel in those days–as now–was fraught with danger, and Leo learned first-hand how local leaders could be just as rapacious as bandits in extorting bribes and ransoms from travelers perceived to be wealthy. It is difficult to plot the precise course of his travels during this period, as we only know what he prefers to tell us; and this, in the fashion of a true diplomat, is often less than candid. But it is clear enough that he visited Constantinople, Egypt, Arabia, and likely made the obligatory pilgrimages there.

His importance to history begins in 1518 when his ship was captured in the eastern Mediterranean by Spanish raiders. This era was one of heightened naval warfare between the Spanish and Italians on one hand, and the Ottoman Turks on the other; but religion determined which camp a person belonged to, and any Christian or Muslim caught by the other side could expect to be sold into servitude, either as a servant or galley-slave. Leo was on his way to Rome, but at some point he must have deeply impressed his captors with his erudition and knowledge of the remote places in Africa, such as the Berber regions of the Atlas mountains and Timbuktu.

Of course he was literate in Arabic, but he probably by this time also knew at least the rudiments of Latin and Spanish. It is also highly likely that he could speak Turkish and some of the Berber dialects. In any case, there is no doubt that he was extremely adept at languages, and knew how to talk to people. Someone with his background would have been highly valuable both to the Spanish and the Holy See; in today's jargon, he might have been considered an "intelligence asset." At some point during his stay in Rome, he secured an audience before Pope Leo X, a man of broad learning and wide interests. The fact than an Andalusian Arab was able to accomplish such a feat at that time is clear evidence either of his extreme value or his persuasive skills. The most likely explanation stems from the alarm felt in Rome at the unstoppable advance of the Ottomans, who were poised to attack Rome itself. Someone who could bridge both cultures would have been in high demand. In any case, he must have said the right things to the papal legates, for the pope set him free, provided him a pension, and arranged for his conversion to Christianity.

For several years he traveled up and down the length of Italy, perfecting his mastery of Italian. When Leo X died in 1521, Leo Africanus found himself without an advocate in high places, and he realized it was time to lie low for a while. He may have helped support himself by teaching the rudiments of Arabic and medicine (Western medicine would not surpass Islamic medical knowledge until later). He must have been working on his travel masterpiece all this time; with the support of the papacy, he published his travel memoirs in 1550 under the Italian title *Della Descrittione Dell'Africa et Delle Cose Notabili Che lui Sono, Per Giovan Lioni Africano.* The original manuscript was written in Leo's native language of Arabic, and then dictated in an Italian that was far from polished. The Arabic original has apparently been lost; we are told that it was once located in the private library of Vincenzo Pinelli (1535-1601), but, if so, it has since disappeared.

The book was extremely popular for its time, as it dealt with remote regions in Africa that were almost totally unknown to Europeans. The book went through many editions and was translated into Latin, French, and English; like his famous predecessor Ibn Battuta, Leo Africanus has come under suspicion for not actually having visited every place he describes, or for embellishing his descriptions with hyperbole. The modern verdict is that Leo is a reliable chronicler, who knew what he was talking about and had been to most of the places described in his account. He may have incorporated descriptions and details from other travelers, but this was in keeping with the practice of the time. It is also likely that he intended his book to be a general geographic survey, rather than a strict travel itinerary. Here, for example, is an interesting and valuable description of the destruction wrought by locusts in the West African kingdom of Guinea:

> The countrey [Guinea] in most places is destitute of trees that beare fruite: neither have the greatest part of the inhabitants any haire on their bodies, save onely a thicke tuft growing upon their heads...Unto these naturall miseries of the place, you may add the insupportable mischiefs which are here done by the locustes: for albeit these creatures do infinite harme likewise in all the inner parts of Africa; yet seemeth it that this countrey of Ghinea is their most proper habitation; whither they do often resort in such innumerable swarms, that like a mightie thicke cloud they come raking along in the skie, and afterward falling downe, they cover the face of the earth, devouring all things that they light upon. Their comming towards any place is known two or three daies before by the yellownes of the sunne. But in most places where they haunt, the poore people are reuenged of them by killing and drying them in the aire for their foode: which custom is commonly vsed by the Arabians and Ethiopians; and the Portugals also haue found vessels full of them vpon the coast

> of Cambaia, where they do the like mischiefs. They which have eaten of them affirme that they are of a good taste, and that their flesh (so much as it is) is as white as that of a lobster.

Of Leo's later life we know little. His value to the Italian authorities probably waned as the threat from the Ottoman Turks declined; and after the publication of his magnum opus in 1550, there was no real reason for him to maintain a high profile. We may surmise that he lived out his final years in Italy, teaching Arabic to learned Italians and reminiscing about his earlier years. It has also been conjectured–without any hard evidence–that Leo left Rome after its famous sacking in 1527 by Charles V and ultimately returned to Morocco. We simply do not know; we do not even know if he ever married or remained a bachelor. We do know that he was resourceful, intelligent, and possessed of a keen ability to ingratiate himself with those around him. These are admirable skills in a diplomat or merchant; and even if we cannot plot the precise trajectory of his later life, we can be sure that he would have found some way to survive in style. One historian has given perhaps the definitive statement on his character:

> Perfectly at home anywhere, and always "lovingly" entertained, ready to be African or Granadian, Moslem or Nazarene, as best suited the circumstances of the case, keen to note everything, and capable of telling what he had seen in a pleasant fashion, to trader or lawyer, soldier or judge, diplomatist or priest, each in his turn, with equal readiness, Leo Africanus must have been a pleasant companion to travel with, and of all men the best fitted to traverse the interior of Africa.

His importance to the history of exploration lies in the fact that he provided, long before the great age of African exploration in the 19th century, coherent and reasonably reliable accounts of Saharan and sub-Saharan Africa. His career also attests to the inherent value of men who can bridge the distance between two different cultures, and can serve as a living conduit between the two.

10. René Caillié: To Timbuktu And Back Alive

The modern traveler has little conception of the hardships and expense that were involved in the journeys of ages past. Surrounded by comfort, his every whim catered to by a global tourism industry, he is blissfully unaware of the suffering and danger necessarily involved in travel to remote regions of the globe before the modern consumer age. His chief preoccupations are the adjustment of his body to new time zones, the temperature of his air-conditioning, and the quality of his accommodations. Perhaps it is well that this is so: for nothing so unbalances the complacent mind than the realization that its perspective is based on narrow, parochial experience. Knowledge can both liberate and destroy.

The French explorer Auguste René Caillié was born in 1800 at Mauzé in the department of Deux-Sèvres; like many of the great travelers we have studied, he was possessed of a restless spirit and was orphaned at an early age. His education was rudimentary, but this mattered little. He had imagination, and that was enough. The fires of exploration and adventure were lit in him as a boy after reading the novel *Robinson Crusoe*; from this point, he read everything he could acquire about African exploration. He tells us in his *Travels Through Central Africa To Timbuctoo*:

> Geographical books and maps were lent to me: the map of Africa, in which I saw scarcely any but countries marked as desert or unknown, excited my attention more than any other. In short, this predilection grew into a passion for which I renounced everything: I ceased to join in the sports and amusements of my comrades; I shut myself up on Sundays to read all the books of travels that I was able to procure. I talked to my uncle, who was my guardian, of my desire to travel: he disapproved it, forcibly representing the dangers which I should incur at sea, and the regret which I should feel far away from my country and my family—in short, he neglected nothing to divert me from my project. My resolution, however, was irrevocable; I still insisted on setting out, and he made no further opposition. All that I

> possessed was sixty francs, and with this trifle I proceeded to Rochefort in 1816, and embarked in the brig *La Loire*, bound to Senegal.

So it is with young men, and so it should be. With only sixty francs in his pockets, Caillié set out to see the world. Our era is too smothering of its young men; instead of encouraging their healthy and vigorous energies, and pushing them to seek what is beyond the horizon, we constrict and neuter them with shame and debilitating guilt. But that is a subject for another place. Once in Senegal he joined an English expedition that was heading for the mouth of the Gambia; his party then penetrated as far as Bondou. He returned to Bordeaux and then headed back to Senegal again. He joined another, larger expedition: it contained seventy men with over thirty loaded camels. The party left Gandiolle in Cayor in February 1819, and soon encountered difficulties in the desert; the leader had failed to bring a sufficient supply of water, and the group was tormented by thirst.

Caillié contracted fever on this expedition and had to return to France. But in 1824 he was able to return to Senegal equipped with both experience and heightened resolution. With his contacts there, he was able to secure the means to study Arabic and the Islamic religion with some local communities. These people–who were known as "Bracknas"–were understandably suspicious of his motives and of his activities in the country; but he apparently won them over enough to reach a decent working relationship. According to him, the Bracknas were divided into five social classes: Hassanes (warriors), Maraboutir (clerics), Zenagues, and Laratines (slaves).

In 1825 he returned to St. Louis and began to save money for future explorations. He amassed around two thousand francs, collected assistants, and told them he had been born in Egypt to Arab parents, but then been taken to France to be raised. It would not have been advisable for him to attempt to reach Timbuktu as a Christian foreigner. His goal now was to reach the fabled city and return alive, something that no other European Christian had yet accomplished. The city had been known as a center of Islamic learning in medieval times, but current geographic and ethnographic information about it was lacking. In April 1827, Caillié began his trek. He first crossed the region inhabited by the Foulahs and the people of Fouta Djallon. His party then crossed the Ba-Fing, a tributary of the Senegal River, which has a very swift current. In May 1827 he crossed the Tankisso River, a large waterway that was connected to the Niger River system. On June 11, he reached the Niger, at Couronossa. It was an intimidating river, described by Caillié as around 900 feet wide. After many adventures, too numerous to recount here, he neared Timbuktu. When he finally laid eyes on the city, his impressions were these:

> The sky was of a dull red color on the horizon; all nature seemed melancholy; profound silence prevailed, not so much as the song of a bird was heard. And yet there was something indescribably imposing in the sight of a large town rising up in the midst of the sandy desert, and the beholder cannot but admire the indomitable energy of its founders. I fancy the river formerly passed nearer the town of Timbuctoo; it is now eight miles north of it and five of Cabra.

But he had little time to waste. The traveler must take advantage of the opportunities that present themselves, especially when one's survival is at stake. Less than a week after he arrived in Timbuktu, he received word that a large caravan of 600 camel was heading for Talifet. Since the next one would not be departing for another three months, he made haste to join it. It left on May 4, 1829, and reached El Arawan after enduring real suffering from the heat and sandstorms. The caravan left El Arawan on May 19 and set out for Morocco; he was now crossing the Sahara from south to north. By now he was enduring real suffering; a fall from a camel had given him a painful injury that refused to heal. His Moorish companions took delight in ridiculing him, taking pleasure in his ignorance of desert travel. But as an old Arabic proverb says, the caravan always moves on, despite the barking of dogs or the swirling of insects. It eventually reached Marabouty and El Harib, but Caillié was still suffering greatly.

The caravan finally arrived at Fez in August 1829, and then moved on to Rabat. His funds had by now run out and he was unable to buy anything substantial to eat. He subsisted primarily on Islamic charity and on the generosity of a few Moroccan Jews he met who, shocked by his disheveled and haggard appearance, took pity on him. Eventually, by a combination of craftiness and luck, he was able to secure his way aboard a ship to Tangiers. There he made contact with a French government official named Delaporte, to whom he revealed his true identity. From there Caillié finally reached Toulon, France, where he could hardly believe he was still alive. He had accomplished something that no European had done before him: to travel to Timbuktu and return home alive. Others before him had reached the city, but none had come back alive.

Both the French and English geographical societies had long wished for an expedition to the city, but Caillié had pulled it off on his own, using nothing but his own abilities and daring. He had added a great deal of information to European knowledge of the West African regions, and for this the French Geographical Society awarded him 10,000 francs and the Cross of the Legion of Honor. He died young at the age of 38. It is right that we should remember these brave men who suffered and died in the quest for glory and knowledge. It was an age of heroic exploration. The day we cease to honor men like René Caillié is the day we become unworthy of our patrimony.

11. Starvation On The High Seas: The Ordeal Of The "St. Le Jacques"

Perhaps it is well that the modern traveler remains serenely unaware of the extraordinary hardships endured by his itinerant ancestors. For if he knew what travel in the pre-modern era truly entailed, he would be rightfully consumed by a sense of shame and inadequacy. His concerns are whether he will have the chicken or the pasta aboard Delta Flight XYZ bound for one city or another; his ancestors, however, were grateful just to get a few moldy biscuits and rum during some miserable transoceanic ordeal. Perspective is everything, or nearly everything.

We turn now to the topic of early Brazilian exploration and travel. The Frenchman Jean de Léry (1534–1613) is a now-forgotten name from that age; but he was one of the first explorers of that dense, green land, and his name deserves to be better known. Born in Bourgogne, he was a Huguenot minister who emigrated to Brazil in 1556 to establish the first Calvinist colony in South America. He and his party set up a habitation on one of the islands off the coast of Rio de Janeiro. Infighting and the treachery of the colony's leader scuttled the plan, so Léry left to live on the mainland among the Tupinamba Indians. He learned Indian habits and customs from first-hand observation, including the grisly practices of inter-tribal warfare and cannibalism. He eventually returned to France and became a minister, although he apparently never was truly able to reintegrate himself back into French life. His experiences in the New World had affected him permanently; he participated in some military campaigns but died of disease in 1616 at the age of 79.

He left behind a valuable account of his travels and experiences in Brazil named *History of a Voyage To Brazil, Also Called America*, published in 1578. Its Latin title was *Historia Navigationis in Brasiliam, Quae et America Dicitur*; a French translation appeared the same year, but it was apparently not available in English until the early 1990s when Janet Whatley published an excellent translation. It is a wealth of ethnographic, geographic, and travel information; Léry describes the land of Brazil in detail, along with the customs and habits of the Indians. He also provides his readers with shipboard details about his voyage across the Atlantic both to and from Brazil, a practice that was not common in his era. During the trip from France to Brazil, he gives entertaining descriptions of how the crew harpooned dolphins, speared sharks, and used gaff-hooks to capture sea tortoises. I have chosen to describe his terrifying experience with starvation aboard ship on his journey from Brazil back to France, which took place in the spring of 1558.

The ship *Saint Le Jacques* left Brazil in January 1558 with a cargo of lumber, pepper, monkeys, parrots, and various other commodities. There were about 45 passengers aboard. After a week at sea, the ship began to take on water; the captain permitted some of the passengers who feared the ship would sink to return to Brazil using a smaller vessel that was with them. But the leak could not be completely repaired, and after about seven weeks at sea, the water-logged *Saint Le Jacques* was not even halfway to France. Some of the crewmembers advised eating the parrots and other animals aboard; others thought the ship should make for Cape St. Roch, where they might be able to replenish their supplies.

Things did not improve. The mate and the navigator fought with each other, and forgot that their first responsibility was to bring the vessel safely home. Things were so bad that in March 1558 the mate forgot to reef the sails while on watch during a storm, with the result that the ship capsized. Most of the cargo was lost, and the crew were only able to right the ship by cutting away the rigging. At this point the ship could only be navigated with extreme difficulty. More disasters followed. The ship's carpenter negligently removed a wooden plug in the ship's hold that was holding back the seawater, with the result that the hold flooded; the captain ordered a large quantity of Brazilian precious woods to the thrown overboard in an effort to lighten the ship. The leak was eventually plugged.

As the *Saint Le Jacques* crossed the Tropic of Cancer, they passed through a very dense patch of seaweed; it was so thick that they had to practically hack their way through it. Soon after this, another misfortune hit the ship when the gunner, trying to dry a batch of gunpowder on deck in a metal cauldron, caused it to burn; as the flames shot skyward, the sails and rigging caught fire, causing serious damage. At this point Léry must have thought that the ship was cursed. The worst was yet to come, however. The best navigators have an instinctive "feel" for the sea, and can guide a vessel even without the aid of maps and charts. Léry's ship did not have a navigator of this caliber; by the middle of April, it was clear that they were far away from the Spanish coast, and their supplies were running out. Biscuits were rationed, but these had become little more than lumps of crumbs by now.

Passengers hoarded what few parrots were left. Two men died of starvation and were flung overboard. Léry tells us that a seaman named Nargue went insane with hunger and thirst, and actually *ate the eyeballs* of the dead men before they had been thrown overboard. Nargue himself died soon after. Léry's experiences in Brazil must have mentally prepared him for the horrors he witnessed aboard ship; he had witnessed war, killing, and cannibalism before, and this must have helped alleviate the shock of his predicament.

The weather did not cooperate with the doomed ship either. Rough seas prevented the crew from fishing, and added the miseries of seasickness to their starvation. The men scraped and boiled the skins of an animal Léry called "Tapirous sou," and this seemed to give them some nourishment. The cabin boys ate candles and boiled pieces of horn taken from their lanterns. They boiled and ate every piece of leather they could find, even the bindings of books and the coverings of boxes. They then set out to hunt down every rat they could find. Rats, when caught, were boiled whole, and eaten in their entirety, including the intestines and bones. The men were by now mere skeletons, lacking much energy to do more than lie around the deck and dream of nourishment. Some men tried to gnaw on the Brazilian woods that were still on board, but this was of course useless. The specter of cannibalism began to hover about the ship. But salvation was close at hand.

On May 24, 1558, someone sighted the coast of Bretagne; it turned out that they were close to Rochelle. At first no one wanted to believe that land had been sighted; by now no one had any faith in the navigator. On the 26th of May, the burned, half-sunk vessel arrived at the port of Blavet. We are told that some of the starving sailors, after putting ashore, ate to sudden excess and died of shock. But most of the crew survived, and lived to tell the tale.

12. Captain George Francis Lyon's Explorations In Africa

There is a certain type of Englishman who is not content with confinement in any one locale. He seeks new vistas, new challenges, and the chance to test his mettle against geography, climate, and the decrees of Fortune. We have chronicled a number of such men in these pages. To this list we must add the name of British naval officer George Francis Lyon (1795–1832), who enjoys perhaps the unique distinction of being known for exploratory achievement in two very different climatic conditions: the polar regions of the Arctic and the desert expanses of northern Africa.

Not much of significance is recorded of his early life; his memoirs of his African travels omit extensive biographical details. In 1818, he was tasked by Second Secretary of the Admiralty Sir John Barrow to discover the source of the Niger River in central Africa. He was to be accompanied by the surgeon Joseph Ritchie. The expedition was able to take advantage of the good relations that the British Consulate enjoyed with the Arab authorities in Tripoli. On March 25, 1819, Ritchie and Captain Lyon departed from Tripoli with Mohammad al-Mukni, the Bey of Fezzan. Lyon was fluent in Arabic, and the expedition was not disorganized; but they underestimated the difficulties involved in crossing the Sahara from north to south. Lyon interestingly describes the articles of clothing taken on the expedition:

> *Sidrea.*—A waistcoat fitting tight to the body, without any opening in front, having only holes for

> the neck and arms. It is pulled on in the same manner as the Guernsey frock used by seamen. *Farmela* is a second waistcoat, open in front, and having broad gold lace and buttons, but no button-holes. It hangs over the *sidrea*.
>
> *Zibboon.*—A jacket, the sleeves of which are embroidered. These first three dresses are confined round the waist by the band of the trowsers, which come outside them. A broad belt of silk or gold is then passed round the body. Over the jacket is an embroidered waistcoat without sleeves, called *Bidfiah*. All these dresses may be of different colours, the most brilliant and gaudy being chiefly in request. On walking out, a hooded cloak of very finely spun white wool is thrown over all, and on great occasions a cloth one of the same form, bordered with rich gold lace, is used. This cloak is called *Bornouse*. The trowsers are immense, and of silk or cloth, according to the pleasure of the wearer…

The expedition got as far as Murzuq, located in the Fezzan region of what is now southern Libya. There Ritchie died on November 2nd, worn out by the harsh desert conditions. Lyon himself also had fallen ill from the privations of the journey. The sultan who was with them, Mohammad al-Mukni, began to confiscate the expedition's supplies, believing both men to be as good as dead. Captain Lyon recovered, however; although he was unable to continue into the interior of Africa, he spent his time wisely in southern Libya, observing the customs and practices of the Tuareg people, who at that time were nearly unknown to Europeans. Lyon seems to have been the first European to document in detail the customs, language, and culture of the Tuareg. Thus the expedition proved to be a successful one, even if it failed in the design for which it was originally contemplated. Consider these morsels of information:

> A great article of commerce is the fat which the shepherds procure from the sheep they kill. They cut it from every part of the body, salt it, and lay it by until a large quantity is collected, when, whether putrid or not, they boil it, until it bear some resemblance

> to the grease used by tallow-chandlers; it is then poured into skins, and is fit for use. In the interior it sells at about a shilling a pound; but at Tripoli it is much cheaper. It is put into almost every article of food by the Arabs, and though not very savoury, we soon became accustomed to its taste. It is called *shahm* [شحام?]...There is great variety in the manner of dressing meat, which is stewed, boiled, or baked; but for journeys the Arabs have a very good way of preserving it, by cutting it into thin slices, drying it in the sun, and afterwards stewing it in fat...There is a species of dandelion, very bitter, and exuding a white juice, which is much liked by the sheep as well as their masters. The taste at first is very unpleasant; but I soon became accustomed to it.

Lyon's account of his travels is an impressive document. It is precise, lucid, and free of the type of fanciful depictions that mar so many other travel records of the nineteenth century. He did not explore the Sudan, but he did collect a great deal of valuable anecdotal information about the region. Physical danger was a very real issue; Lyon frequently remarks that it was an absolute necessity for him and his party to adopt local dress and speak Arabic at all times, for had they been detected as foreigners, they would immediately have fallen under suspicion. On his journey back to Tripoli, he observed raging flash floods that had the power to sweep a man away in an instant:

> Our tents were no sooner pitched than very heavy rain came on, in a tremendous storm (called *Gherra* [غرة?] by the Arabs): thunder and lightning close to us. The noise was tremendous, and the wadey before us was quickly filled with a roaring torrent, sweeping all before it: happily, the tents were on a rising ground, which prevented them from being washed away. The mountain torrent continued all night. I had often heard these storms spoken of, but always imagined that the accounts given of them were much exaggerated; I now found that the description did not at all come up to this night's tempest.

He almost died of thirst in the return trek across the desert; he seems also to have been suffering from some unspecified illness, perhaps malaria. "Weak and exhausted as I was, and with no alternative but to drink, or, as I thought, to expire, I was about to catch and swallow the nauseous draught, when, at that moment, I perceived my trusty Arab ascending a hill, and advancing towards me. Those only who have experienced the agonies of suspense, or the torments of parching thirst, can conceive my sensations when he joined me, bringing the wished-for beverage." But he reached Tripoli. He finally left the city in May 1820, bringing with him a camel intended as a gift for King George IV. Upon reaching England, he was quarantined, he tells us, for twenty-five days. He finally arrived in London on July 25, 1820. He would later suffer from bouts of ophthalmia–a legacy of his arduous desert travels–and feared he might lose his eyesight. His travel memoirs, *A Narrative of Travels in Northern Africa in the Years 1818, 1819, and 1820*, was published in London in 1821. Lyons lived a full and eventful life. He would later go on to command an Arctic expedition in the vicinity of Hudson Bay, and collected valuable information about the Inuit peoples residing there. He was elected a fellow of the Royal Society in 1827, and died in 1832. Man is mortal; but his achievements endure forever.

13. George Forster Travels Overland From Bengal To England

Little is known of the early life of British explorer George Forster. His travel memoirs, published in 1808 after his death, were edited by persons who apparently never considered that such information would be of interest to readers. We can thus only rely on what we find in scattered letters and journals. He was probably born around 1750 and at some point joined the East India Company as a young man; he would eventually be posted to Madras to work as a writer. Around 1782 he was granted leave to return to England; and for some reason–perhaps it was just a taste for adventure–he decided to make the return trip by land through Afghanistan, Central Asia, and Russia.

We know that at some point he acquired a knowledge of the Persian language and Islamic customs. He probably also had a functional command of Hindostani and Arabic. Then, as now, Persian could be used as something of a *lingua franca* in Afghanistan and some parts of central Asia. Forster set out on his journey from Calcutta on May 23, 1782. By the end of June he was on a boat in the Ganges, headed towards Rajmahal. From there he proceeded to Monghee and Patna, which he reached by July 5. By the end of July he was in Benares. Here Forster lingered for a time, and absorbed himself in the study of Hindu antiquities, which in that region were very plentiful. Satisfied with his inquiries, he set out for Allahabad in early December. By this time he had adopted the dress of a native Georgian; like most European travelers in these regions, he knew it was ill-advised to appear too distantly foreign. At Rampoor he was able to see the Himalayan Mountains near the Tibetan border in their full glory.

At Najebabad he joined a caravan (*kafilah*) that left that city on February 14, 1783; and as an additional precaution he hired a Kashmiri servant who knew the region and its people. A moment of panic occurred as the caravan was passing through mountainous country near Lolldong; he sat down under a tree to smoke a pipe, drifted into sleep, and awoke to find that the caravan had left without him. After several hours of panic, he found some villagers who were able to help him rejoin his companions. He reached the frontiers of the Punjab (a city named Bellaspoor) in March; moving through the region, he was nearly killed during a chance encounter with a body of Sikh cavalrymen. He reached Jummoo in April, and replenished his funds at a bank with a letter of credit he had with him. Setting out again into the mountains with his Kashmiri servant, his shoes were soon reduced to tatters by the sharp rocks he was forced to scale; soon he could do little more than wrap his feet and shins with bindings soaked in oil. But arriving in Kashmir in May was worth the suffering, for in the spring and summer months it is said to be a place of great beauty.

While he was in Kashmir he was nearly exposed by a prying Georgian he encountered. This man, closely observing the mannerisms and personal habits of Forster, pronounced him a Christian, and not a professer of Islam.

Forster, realizing the danger that this knowledge would put him in, cornered the man and told him that should he reveal to anyone what he knew, he (Forster) would see to it that his family's estate in Benares was confiscated by the British government (the Georgian lived in Benares). Forster knew he could not enforce this threat, but the bluff worked, and the Georgian held his tongue thereafter. He left Kashmir in early June accompanied by a Persian youth he had hired as an assistant. He crossed the Indus on July 10, and then made for Peshawar. For additional security he agreed to travel with a local man who had some knowledge of Pashtun dialects and ways. Security in many of the areas he traversed was so bad that it was more advisable to travel by night than by day. On August 2nd his party reached Kabul.

Until this point in his travels, Forster had avoided any encounter with sickness or bodily injury. Yet like many travelers in forbidding regions we have previously discussed, he now found himself plunged into the miseries of affliction. In Kabul he was seized with a fever, and trembled with nausea for several days; his body was covered with red sores, and he had difficulty holding down food. Whatever the disease was (perhaps cholera or the plague), it seemed to dissipate after about several weeks. This misfortune was followed soon after by another one equally dangerous, but in this case one of his own making: he foolishly revealed himself to be a Christian, and so had to endure the mockery and scorn of nearly everyone who crossed his path. In October he finally arrived in Kandahar, which at that time was a populous and thriving city. By the end of January 1784, his caravan had nearly reached the shores of the Caspian Sea, having traveled through Khorasan.

At Baku he boarded a Russian frigate bound for Astrakhan, and arrived at that city at the end of April. From there he traveled to Moscow, then St. Petersburg, and then finally England. He reached his homeland at the end of July 1784, after an epic journey that had taken over two years. After arriving in London he proceeded to collect his notes and observations on Hindu antiquities, and published them in 1786 under the title *Sketches on the Mythology and Manners of the Hindoos*. His precise activities between 1786 and 1790 are difficult to trace; whatever record he may have left has either been destroyed or is not yet discovered. We do know the was back in Calcutta in 1790, preparing for publication the first volume of his *Journey from Bengal to England*. Tragedy then intervened. His superiors sent him to the city of Nagpoor in Gundwarra, where he died in February 1791. It is not clear what the exact circumstances of his death were. His memoirs would eventually be published six years later by his literary executors in the form of travel letters, but they were either unwilling or unable to include any specific details on how the author met his end.

The merit of the work is beyond doubt; Forster's feat was an incredible one, hardly duplicated in the annals of travel and exploration. His observations are clear-headed, free of hearsay and nonsense, and sympathetic. Little was known in the West of Hindu customs and religious practices before Forster published his first-hand observations after returning from his travels. What is even more remarkable is the fact that he undertook his journey without any official sponsorship; he simply planned them and carried them out, using his own ingenuity, linguistic ability, and resources. We will close our account of George Forster and his travels using the unique and poignant valediction with which he ends his *Journey from Bengal to England*:

> Having now brought you to the close of a long journey, the performance of which was chiefly derived from a vigorous health, and a certain portion of perseverance, I bid you an affectionate farewell; and I trust, that you will never have cause to impute to any of the various facts which have been brought forward in the body of the letters, the colour of passion, or the views of interest…The opinions deduced from them, given by a man slenderly conversant in the higher classes of science, and who has yet much to seek in the abstruser page of human life, I freely commit to your censure, as also the manner of writing, which, I fear, will be judged offensive to the chasteness distinguishing the language of the present day.

We find nothing offensive in him, only wonder and inspiration.

14. Antonio De Ulloa's Daring Explorations In South America

Antonio de Ulloa y de la Torre-Giral may have been Spain's greatest explorer of the eighteenth century. The hardships he endured certainly merit his inclusion on any list of that century's great cultivators of geographic knowledge. He was born in Seville on

January 12, 1716; and like many accomplished travelers, he received a thorough education in the traditional disciplines. He came from a family with a naval tradition, and young Antonio was eager to follow in these footsteps.

After joining the Spanish Royal Navy in 1733, he was provided a unique opportunity: the chance to participate in a joint French-Spanish expedition to South America for the purpose of measuring some degrees of meridian near the equator. It was essentially a surveying project to measure degrees of latitude, and the knowledge thereby gained would be used to compose a more accurate idea of the earth's dimensions. The expedition came to be known as the French Geodesic Mission. De Ulloa must have been a man of singular ability to have been entrusted with such a responsibility; and as we will see, the confidence his superiors placed in him was entirely justified. Once the necessary permissions were secured from Louis XV of France and Philip V of Spain, the expedition headed for Quito, then part of the province of Peru. De Ulloa would be assisted by another Spaniard, George Juan; and both of them were appointed lieutenants.

In May 1735 the expedition left Spain and reached Cartagena on July 9. De Ulloa and Juan had been instructed to wait there until the French members of the expedition arrived; but this took much longer than expected. The French did not appear until November, having been delayed by all the usual encumbrances and impediments of travel in that era. After November 15, the French-Spanish team headed to Porto Bello in Panama, and then ultimately to Guayaquil, in what is now Ecuador. As they moved up the River Chagre; and de Ulloa was shocked by the lush vegetation and exotic animals he could see every minute of every day. They reached the Pacific side of Panama on December 29, where de Ulloa conducted astronomical surveys. They then set sail from the Pacific to Guayaquil, which was reached on March 25. They then traveled by river from Guayaquil to Caracol. This riverine journey was a difficult one; lacking adequate protection against the mosquitoes, they endured constant torture:

> We had provided ourselves with quetres and mosquito-cloths; but to very little purpose: the whole day we were in continual motion to keep them off; but at night our torments were excessive. Our gloves

> were indeed some defense to our hands, but our faces were entirely exposed; nor were our clothes a sufficient defense for the rest of our bodies, for their stings penetrating through the cloth, caused a very painful and fiery itching. The most dismal night we spent on this passage, was when we came to an anchor near a large and handsome house, but uninhabited; for we had no sooner seated ourselves in it, than we were attacked on all sides with innumerable swarms of mosquitoes, so that we were so far from having any rest there, that it was impossible for a person susceptible of feeling to be one moment quiet.

At Caracol they abandoned the river and continued on with pack mules, following the river Ojibar. By good luck they encountered Indians who were friendly, and who helped them construct shelters at night out of efficient local materials. By now the expedition was moving into high-altitude areas; the weather became colder, and the terrain more and more mountainous. De Ulloa was glad they had brought mules, for these animals proved to be most adroit in navigating the precipitous mountain trails. They eventually reached the province of Chimbo, and were welcomed by a group of Dominican monks; and from here they pressed on through the desert of Chimborazo, where they suffered greatly from the cold and wind. But they eventually reached Quito–it had taken them about a year–where they were received by the local authority, Don Dioneso de Alzedo y Herrera.

De Ulloa spent the rest of 1736 making observations and measurements near Quito, especially on the plain of Yaruqui. At some point a decision was made to split the party in two, with De Ulloa and a few men going to the summit of Pichincha, and the other half going to the summit of Pambamarca. Climbing these mountains proved to be an incredibly difficult task: they lacked good mountaineering equipment and provisions, and had no defenses against the cold. But they had a sense of duty, and that was enough:

> The wind was often so violent in these regions, that its velocity dazzled the sight, while our fears were increased by the dreadful concussions of the precipice, and by the fall of enormous fragments of rocks.

These crashes were the more alarming, as no other noises are heard in these deserts; and during the night our rest, which we so greatly wanted, was frequently disturbed by such sudden sounds...Our feet were swelled, and so tender that we could not even bear the heat, and walking was attended with great pain. Our hands were covered with chilblains, our lips swelled and chopped, so that every motion, speaking and the like, drew blood; consequently we were obliged to observe a strict taciturnity, and were but little disposed to laugh—an extension of the lips producing fissures, very painful for two or three days together....Our common food in this inhospitable region was a little boiled rice, with some flesh or fowl, which we procured from Quito; and instead of fluid water, our pot was filled with ice; we had the same resource with regard to what we drank; and while we were eating everyone was obliged to keep his plate over a chafing-dish of coals, to prevent his provisions from freezing.

It was only with great persuasion and threats of punishment that De Ulloa could prevent his Indian guides from deserting him. From 1737 to July 1739 the expedition lived this difficult life; but they accomplished what they had set out to do. De Ulloa has also been credited with being one of the first observers to write an accurate description of the metal platinum, which he observed in Ecuador. In 1740, De Ulloa and his George Juan were recalled to Lima by the Spanish viceroy to help prepare defensive works there; war had just broken out between Spain and England and there were fears that the coasts might be raided by the British Navy. After 1744 it finally became possible for De Ulloa to return to Europe; he and some other men boarded two French ships bound for Brest by way of Cape Horn. Along the way his ship was diverted to the French settlement of Louisburg in North America; after he arrived the city fell to the British and he was detained.

De Ulloa relates, however, that he was treated with great courtesy by the British, who had a particular admiration for daring explorers and adventurers. He got along so well with them, in fact, that he decided to go to London. Martin Folkes, president of the

Royal Society, took an interest in him and his work, and was prepared to sponsor him; he was even made a fellow of the Society. "Actions like these," says De Ulloa, "convinced me of the sincerity of the English, their candor, their benevolence, and disinterested complaisance. I observed the tempers, inclinations, particular customs, government, constitution, and policy of this praiseworthy nation, which in its economical conduct and social virtues may be a pattern to those who boast of superior talents to all the rest of mankind." Perhaps so, but it seems likely that the British were also eager to gain access to his scientific data and observations, which were of course extremely valuable.

He finally left England in 1746 and made his way to Madrid. It had been eleven years and two months since he had first departed Spain for South America. His scientific observations were published in 1748 and he was accorded all due honor by the Spanish crown, and he retained his connection to the navy. In fact he was appointed governor of Louisiana in 1762, a territory that had recently been conveyed to Spain by France as a consequence of its defeat in the Seven Years' War. Things did not work out well for him there, however; the local population of French colonists had no desire to be linked to Spain, and he found it prudent to return home. His memoirs of his travels in South America were translated into English and entitled *A Voyage To South America.* The rest of his life was spent in quiet scholarly pursuits; he died in July 1795 on the Isle of Leon.

15. A Humanist Visits The German Baths

The Renaissance humanist Poggio Bracciolini wrote a fascinating letter to his close friend Niccolo Niccoli in May of 1416 while on one of his book-hunting expeditions to remote monasteries Germany. While in Germany he had an opportunity to visit the baths near Kaiserstuhl, and he has left us a detailed description of the experience. On the first day of his journey, he traveled twenty-four miles along the Rhine to reach the town of Schaffhausen, and from there he continued on foot for another ten miles to reach a castle called Kaiserstuhl. Poggio believed that it must have once been a Roman camp, since it occupied a favorable vantage point overlooking the river. From here he reached the town of Baden; and about half a mile from this town was a villa which contained a collection of baths. There were both public and private baths, and they numbered about thirty in all. The baths were also segregated by social class, and a fence separated the men from the women.

> It is comical to see decrepit old women as well as younger ones going naked into the water before the eyes of men and displaying their private parts and their buttocks to the onlookers. I have often laughed at this extraordinary sight, calling to mind the carnival, and I have privately wondered at the simplicity of these people who do not stare, suspect evil, or speak it.

Inside the private houses were other baths where men and women would congregate and have drinks together; and above the bathing pools were walkways where bathers could stand and "gossip," as he says. Anyone in attendance could be seen naked by anyone else, and it was not a problem or cause for concern. What is amusing about these passages in Poggio's letter is to take note of the cultural differences on display; here Mediterranean conservatism is sharply contrasted with the more frank bodily attitudes of the northern climes.

> In many places the entrance to the baths is the same for men and women, so that it often happens that a man and a half-naked woman or a woman and a naked man come face to face. The men wear nothing but a leather apron, and the women put on linen shirts down to their knees, so cut on either side that they leave uncovered neck, bosom, arms, and shoulders.

In the baths people would gather to have picnics or drinks, "with the tables floating in the water." Poggio was asked to attend such a picnic in the baths but says he did not feel comfortable doing so; the reason was not due to the nakedness of the bathers, but because (he says) he could not speak German. According to him, the Germans considered "undue modesty" at the baths to be a "sign of cowardice or provinciality." A man was hardly considered worth anything if he was afraid to be seen naked in front of others. Here I can say that I noticed this same attitude in the public baths of Japan and Korea, with which I have had some personal experience. Poggio says that he had two other male friends with him who had a good time at the baths; but as for himself, he could not feel at ease. "For me it seemed ridiculous that a man from Italy, ignorant of their language, should sit in the water with a lot of women, completely speechless, while the day was wasted by everyone's drinking and nibbling." Poggio further relates that men could see their wives being "handled" by strangers and were not at all disturbed by it. Some of the bathers visited the pools three or four times per day, singing, dancing, and drinking. The young German women particular fascinated Poggio. Here he describes an evocative scene:

> It is very pleasant to see girls already ripe for a husband, already of marriageable years, good-looking and well-born and in manner and form like a goddess; for when they play on instruments, they draw their clothes slightly behind them [to display their bodies?], floating along the top of the water, until you might think they were winged Venuses. It is customary for the women, when men gaze down on them, to ask the men in fun for alms. And so the men throw down pennies, especially to the prettier women, which they catch sometimes in their hands, and sometimes in their outspread clothes, pushing one another, and in this game they even sometimes uncover more hidden parts of their bodies.

Poggio himself was more than willing to toss pennies in this game. Near the baths were fields where other games could be played. A kind of ball-game was played where men and women would throw around a ball "full of bells" to one another; the first person to catch a ball thrown to a group was considered the winner. One can imagine what other types of Epicurean games would have inevitably been played, but our humanist does not venture to describe them. He says that many people, both nobles and common folk, would travel up to two hundred miles to visit the baths, and that it was a form of recreation for them. Beautiful women would appear in their best clothing, some even with maids and valets. Everyone's goal was to "flee from gloom" and seek enjoyment.

Poggio's experience at the baths prompted moments of philosophic reflection. He found himself regretting his own countrymen's habits of jealousy, calumny, and scandal, and wishing his people could learn to enjoy life with a bit more ribaldry. "I often envy them their calm and I hate our perversity of spirit, for we are always searching, always hunting, always turning sky, earth, and sea upside down in order to make a fortune, content with no gain, appeased by no money." Perhaps it is so. But I could not help thinking, after reading Poggio's letter, that every traveler thinks these thoughts when experiencing the customs of another country for the first time. It is only our own delusion to believe every other group of people is having more fun than we are. The truth is that all are struggling to balance the responsibilities of life with those pleasurable diversions that relieve our omnipresent toils. For me the real value of Poggio's letter was the light it cast on how life was actually lived in the late medieval period. It is comforting to know that the average person in 1416 was just as concerned with trying to enjoy life as we are now. Then, as now, the average man went about his life and work, and indulged in as much extravagance and play as his economic circumstances and geographic mobility would permit. *Plus ça change, plus c'est la même chose.*

PART IV: HISTORY, LANGUAGE, AND LITERATURE

1. The Grave of Suleiman The Magnificent

I remember reading news agency's report that the tomb of Suleiman the Magnificent had been discovered. Suleiman, who lived from 1494 to 1566, is now nearly unknown in the West; but he was, in the words of one eminent historian, "the greatest and ablest ruler of his age." The general consensus seems to be that he remains the greatest of all the Ottoman sultans. In the Muslim world, Suleiman is known as "Qanuni" or "the Lawgiver," for his efforts at reforming the complex Turkish legal code. The name "Magnificent" was actually affixed on him by Western admirers who eyed possessively the extent of the vast Ottoman domains, which in his day stretched from Algiers to Baghdad. He also took pains to adorn his cities in splendor; the famous "Forty Arches" aqueduct was completed at his bidding, as well as countless public buildings, mosques, and public squares. His rule also oversaw a flowering of cultural and artistic achievements.

He was, in embarrassing contrast to the European states of his era, more tolerant of foreign religions than his Christian counterparts. He did not molest Christian or Jewish communities, and promised the unfettered practice of all faiths in his domain. A Catholic Cardinal would write, "The Turks do not compel others to adopt their beliefs. He who does not attack their religion may profess among them what religion he will; he is safe." There is ample evidence that some Christian communities actually preferred to be under Ottoman rule, as the Turks, bewildered by the proliferation of Christian sects, were more even-handed than Christian princes. We may contrast this picture with what was going on in Western Europe at the same time, where Protestants and Catholics were slaughtering each other with dedicated enthusiasm.

This picture is not quite perfect, of course, for Suleiman had the vices of all leaders trying to keep together a vast and unwieldy collection of peoples. Corruption and lassitude certainly thrived in Turkish lands, and we miss that commercial vitality that characterized the freewheeling merchant spirit of Holland or Venice in the same period. While Suleiman did not abandon himself to the sexual corruption of the harem to the extent that some later sultans did, he did devote his attentions to elevating his favorite concubine (Roxelana, or "The Laughing One," also known as Khurrem) to the palace. And he was as addicted to war as any prince of his era.

When he died at the age of 72, he was personally leading an army of over 200,000 men to punish Maximilian II, who had held back the tribute his father promised the Turks. Maximilian also had the temerity to attack Ottoman outposts in Hungary. The Turks actually won the battle of Szigetvar, but the loss of over 30,000 men in the campaign made its continuance inadvisable. Suleiman's army–and his corpse–reversed course and rode quietly back to Constantinople. He was dead, but in 1568 Maximilian resumed payment to the sultans; and the Turkish navy still controlled the Mediterranean. One might argue that Suleiman had accomplished his objective.

Suleiman died in 1566 while his army was engaged in military operations near Vienna. Part of his remains were buried in what is now Hungary; but when the Hapsburg rulers retook the area in the 1680s, Suleiman's mausoleum was razed, and its location eventually became lost. It is a familiar story in history, and has been repeated over and over. After many years of searching for the actual grave site, a joint Hungarian-Turkish team seems finally to have found the location of the old mausoleum. On participant in the dig stated: "Tools of [16th-century] daily use like coins, knives, potsherds, pipes [were found]; architectural fragments…and the layout of the buildings in relation to each other support written and pictorial documentation and technological analyses. So we can say that we unearthed Sultan Suleiman the Magnificent's tomb."

The great men of European history continue to exert a hold on the minds of their descendants. Their ghosts still haunt the quiet and forgotten fields of the old continent. And Europe's complex and turbulent relationship with the Islamic world–characterized by admiration and disdain in equal measure–seems to get more intriguing every year. The relics of history are everywhere around us; and there is nothing that ages so well as departed glory. The story is not just in the stones of fallen buildings or temples: it is everywhere. We need only to listen, for a story can be heard everywhere. As the Arabic saying goes:

لكل مقام مقال

And this means, "A discourse is for every place."

2. The Greatness Of Alp Arslan

The first of the Seljuk sultans was Togrul Beg. Of him Edward Gibbon said, "It would be superfluous to praise the valour of a Turk; and the ambition of Togrul was equal to his valour." This is a supreme compliment, and entirely true. By the time of his death in 1063 he had firmly laid the foundations for the Seljuk Empire in the Middle East and Central Asia. He was succeeded by one of the greatest of the of Seljuk kings, Alp Arslan. This honorific ("valiant lion") is an affectionate title by which he is known to posterity; his real name was Muhammad Ibn Dawud Chaghri. Gibbon here tells us:

> The name of Alp Arslan, the valiant lion, is expressive of the popular idea of the perfection of man; and the successor of Togrul displayed the fierceness and generosity of the royal animal.

He expanded on the conquests of his predecessor, enlarging Turkish domains by wile and lance. The Byzantine Empire in those days was hard-pressed to maintain its frontiers; and that job would become even harder once Alp Arslan took the field in search of territories to submit to him. The Greek emperor, Romanus Diogenes, was his equal neither in military nor personal virtue. In 1071 the sultan marched at the head of a force of over one hundred thousand men towards eastern Anatolia. Near the city of Manzikert, his forces collided with the Romans in one of the most decisive battles of medieval history. Before the battle, Romanus had treated Alp Arslan contemptuously, refusing his offers of peace. Gibbon tells the tale:

> Had he listened to the fair proposals of the sultan, Romanus might have secured a retreat, perhaps a peace; but in these overtures he supposed the fear or weakness of the enemy, and his answer was conceived in the tone of insult and defiance. "If the barbarian [Romanus said] wishes for peace, let him evacuate the ground which he occupies for the encampment of the Romans, and surrender his city and palace of Rei as a pledge of his sincerity. [Ch. LVII, *Decline and Fall*]

Battle was then joined. The result was that "the Asiatic provinces of Rome were irretrievably sacrificed." Romanus himself was captured by the sultan; by some accounts, he was subjected to having the sultan's foot placed symbolically on his neck to drive home the reality of his defeat. (This was in keeping with the custom of the day; the emperor Justinian II had done the same thing to his rivals Leontius and Apsimar). And yet, as many historians have averred, the medieval Islamic princes usually exceeded their Christian counterparts in the chivalric graces: they broke their word less often than did the Frankish and Byzantine kings, and considered it a moral duty to show respect for the defeated.

> From the divan Romanus was conducted to an adjacent tent, where he was served with pomp and reverence by the officers of the sultan, who, twice each day, seated him in the place of honour at his own table. In a free and familiar conversation of eight days, not a word, not a look, of insult escaped from the conqueror; but he severely censured the unworthy subjects who had deserted their valiant prince in the hour of danger, and gently admonished his antagonist of some errors which he had committed in the management of the war.

Romanus and Alp Arslan actually dined together, and the Turkish sultan asked his counterpart what sort of treatment he expected to receive. Romanus said, "If you are cruel, you will take my life; if you listen to pride, you will drag me at your chariot-wheels; if you consult your interest, you will accept a ransom, and restore me to my country." When the sultan asked the emperor what he himself would have done had their situations been reversed, Romanus replied honestly–but insolently–that he would have had the sultan lashed. At this Gibbon says, "The Turkish conqueror smiled at the insolence of the captive; observed that the Christian law inculcated the love of enemies and forgiveness of injuries; and nobly declared that he would not imitate an example which he condemned." In the end he had Romanus ransomed.

His empire would eventually cover much of Western Asia. But even great men can fall victim to the terrible fickleness of fortune, as we have observed so often in these pages. And in the end, he was struck down in a bizarre assassination. He had condemned to death a particularly obstinate military enemy named Joseph the Carizmian. Joseph, upon hearing his sentenced pronounced, drew a dagger and rushed the sultan; Alp Arslan asked his bodyguards not to interfere, knowing he was an extremely skilled archer. But while trying to draw his bow on the assailant, the sultan's foot slipped, and the killer's dagger found its mark. Joseph was immediately killed by the sultan's retinue. Gibbon rises to great eloquence in describing his final words and legacy:

> "In my youth [began Alp Arslan's final words] I was advised by a sage to humble myself before God; to distrust my own strength; and never to despise the most contemptible foe. I have neglected these lessons; and my neglect has been deservedly punished. Yesterday, as from an eminence I beheld the numbers, the discipline, and the spirit of my armies, the earth seemed to tremble under my feet; and I said in my heart, surely thou art the kind of the world, the greatest and most invincible of warriors. These armies are no longer mine; and, in the confidence of my personal strength, I now fall by the hand of an assassin."
>
> Alp Arslan possessed the virtues of a Turk and a Musulman [Muslim]; his voice and stature commanded the reverence of mankind; his face was shaded with long whiskers; and his ample turban was fashioned in the shape of a crown. The remains of the sultan were deposited in the tomb of the Seljukian dynasty; and the passenger might read and meditate this useful inscription: *O ye who have seen the glory of Alp Arslan exalted to the heavens, repair to Maru, and you will behold it buried in the dust!* The annihilation of the inscription, and the tomb itself, more forcibly proclaims the instability of human greatness.

This last sentence, oft forgotten by the insolence and myopia of power, forms an unanswerable commentary on all human affairs.

3. Unusual Battle Injuries In Ancient Combat

The historian Procopius relates some unusual combat injuries of the Gothic War, which took place from 535 to 554 A.D. as part of the emperor Justinian's attempt to bring back the Italic peninsula and its environs back into the Roman fold. A few incidents stand out as worth of relation here. In our modern age of firearms and high-velocity projectile weapons, we forget that battlefield wounds from swords, javelins, and spears had their own bizarre qualities. In the spring of 537, Justinian's general Belisarius sent his commanders Martinus and Valerianus to a place called the Plain of Nero near Terracina, which is about 75 kilometers southwest of Rome. The Roman forces engaged the Gothic occupiers at close quarters:

> But as they continued, they began at last to be filled with rage against each other. The battle then settled down to a fierce struggle in which many of the best men on both sides fell, and support came up for each of the two armies, from the city and the camps. When they mixed with the fighters the struggle became still greater. The shouting that filled the city and the camps terrified the combatants. But finally the Romans by their valor forced back the enemy and routed them. In this action Koutilas [one of Belisarius's men] was struck in the middle of the head by a javelin, but he kept on pursuing the enemy with the javelin still embedded in his head. After the rout was finished, he rode into the city about sunset with the other survivors, the javelin still in his head waving around, an extraordinary sight. In the same encounter Arzes, one of Belisarius's guardsmen, was hit by one of the Gothic archers between the nose and the right eye. The point of the arrow penetrated as far as the neck behind, but it did not show through, and the rest of the shaft projected from his face and shook as he rode. When the Romans saw him and Koutilas they marveled greatly that both men continued to ride, paying no heed to their wounds. Such, then, was the course of events there. [*Wars* VI.2. *Trans. by A. Kaldellis*]

But removing such projectiles from the body was never an easy matter. When foreign objects enter the body, the tissues can "close" around it, forming a seal; trying to remove the object is a matter of great surgical skill. If it is done in too much haste, the patient can experience massive blood loss and trauma. What could be done about the wounds of these fighters. Procopius relates:

> When all had returned to the city, they attended to the wounded men. In the case of Arzes, although the physicians wished to draw the weapon from his face, they were for some time reluctant to do so, not so much on account of the eye, which they supposed could not possibly be saved, but for fear that, by cutting the membranes and tissues that are very numerous in that region, they might cause the death of one of the best men of Belisarius's household. But afterward one of the physicians, Theoktistos by name, pressed on the back of his neck and asked whether he felt mush pain. When the man said that he did feel pain, he said, "Then you yourself will be saved and your sight will not be impaired." He made this declaration because he inferred that the barb of the weapon had penetrated to a point not far below the skin. So he cut off the part of the shaft that showed outside and threw it away, and cutting open the skin at the back of the head, at the place where the man felt the most pain, he easily drew out the barb, which with its three sharp points now stuck out behind and brought with it the remaining part of the weapon. [*Wars* VI.2.25]

But things did not go as well for Koutilas, who had the javelin embedded in his head. The surgeon who was caring for him drew the weapon out of his head, perhaps unwisely; when this happened, Koutilas fainted. The membranes began to be inflamed, and he died of acute phrenitis soon afterward. Another hero, a soldier named Bochas, also died of his wounds that day. He had been hit in the breastplate with about ten enemy spears, but had stood firm. But a slashing sword wound to the thigh that severed his muscles there ultimately led to his death. In some ways, battle medicine has changed much since antiquity. But the basic principles are the same. Another notable incident is recounted several pages later. This is something that Procopius, who was present with the army, must have witnessed at first hand. A soldier named Traianos was struck in the face with an arrow "above the right eye, not far from the nose." The iron point penetrated inside his head and disappeared inside his skull. The barb was long, but not securely fastened to the arrow's shaft; this made the shaft drop to the ground almost immediately.

> Traianos, however, paid no heed to this at all, but continued killing and pursuing the enemy. But in the fifth year after this, the tip of the iron barb of its own accord began to project visibly from his face. This was now the third year since it has been slowly but steadily coming out. It is to be expected, then, that the whole barb will eventually come out, although not for a long time. But it has not been an impediment to the man in any way. [*Wars* VI.5]

We can now understand why the Greek physician Galen spent so much time writing about treating inflammations and fevers. It seems that a foreign object entering the body is sometimes not the direct cause of death. Rather, death comes from the collateral effects of such wounds, in the form of infections, fevers, and inflammations. Galen says the following with regard to such inflammations:

> Therefore, in the case of a seething inflammation, it must be cooled to a degree that is appropriate to eradicate it altogether or to prevent it from increasing. And because too much heat excites pain and also draws something to the affected part, what happens is that the inflammation is increased by both of these factors...Therefore, since the whole principle of the treatment of inflammations lies in evacuating the excess blood of the inflamed part, this evacuation is thought of in a twofold way: the transfer of blood contained in what is inflamed to other parts, and the evacuation of the body externally. [*Method of Medicine* XIII.6; *Trans. by I. Johnston*]

Even today we see these sorts of wounds. I remember a client who was a police officer told me about a crime victim he once witnessed. The man had been stabbed in the head with a knife and was able to speak and walk about normally with a knife in his head. But when the doctors tried to remove it, his head tissues became inflamed, and he died. So much, then, for these matters.

4. The Fate Of A Collaborator

At one point in the Gothic War during the reign of Justinian, the Romans (or as we would now call them, "Byzantines") under Belisarius were besieging a Gothic garrison at the town of Osimo in Italy. The blockade of the town was very effective, and the inhabitants had been reduced to eating almost anything to stay alive. But they were hoping to get some relief from the siege; their plan was to beg the Gothic commander Vittigis at the city of Ravenna to come to their aid. The problem was to get a message out of Osimo to Ravenna. Some of the Goths realized that they could corrupt one of the Romans who was standing guard near the city at a checkpoint. His name was Burkentius; the fact that he was of Gothic ancestry himself may have contributed to his infidelity. The Gothic spies approached Burkentius and promised him a sum of money if he would deliver a message for them to Ravenna. He accepted the sum of money and delivered a sealed letter to Ravenna, which basically begged Vittigis for relief.

Vittigis promised the garrison at Osimo relief, but would give little in the way of specifics. He paid the treasonous messenger Burkentius more money, and sent him on his way back to Osimo. When he rejoined his unit in Osimo, Burkentius of course concealed that he had acted as a messenger for the enemy, offering as an excuse that he had gone to Ravenna for medical treatment. He was then placed back on guard duty, as before. So the Gothic garrison at Osima held on, refusing to surrender, and was encouraged by Vittigis's promises of relief. Eventually Belisarius realized something was wrong; there was no real reason, he thought, why this garrison should be putting up such stout resistance. There must be some reason he was unaware of. What hopes were they hanging on to? What information did they have? To find out, he resolved to do what today would be called a "body snatch": that is, capture alive a Goth from Osimo and interrogate him about why the garrison was holding out for so long.

Using some of his Slavic troops, who were experienced in laying ambushes, Belisarius ordered one of his men named Valerianus to capture and question one of the enemy. From this he was able to discover that the Goths had corrupted and bribed the Roman guard Burkentius. The remainder of the tale is best told in the historian Procopius's own words:

> When he interrogated the prisoner about what basis of confidence and what assurance the Goths could possibly have that they were so absolutely unwilling to yield to the Romans and voluntarily enduring the most dreadful suffering, the barbarian told Valerianus the whole story concerning Burkentius, and when he was brought before him he proved his guilt. When Burkentius perceived that he had been already found out, he concealed nothing of what he had done. For that reason Belisarius handed him over his comrades to do with as they wished, and they not long afterward burned him alive, with the enemy looking on. Thus did Burkentius profit from his love of money.

This is the story as it is told by Procopius, in his *Wars* (VI.27).

5. Theodore Roosevelt Brings Big Business To Heel

A central tenet of Theodore Roosevelt's leadership was the idea that no one should be above the law. He was deeply troubled by excessive concentrations of wealth in the hands of a few; such a situation was, he knew, inimical to the interests of a democratic republic. He did not begrudge a man his wealth fairly earned, but he believed that the accumulation of vast treasure should not come at the expense of the public good. The super-rich could not plunder at will and, at the same time, expect the public to operate under a different set of rules. What especially galled Roosevelt was the arrogant way that the "captains of industry" of his day expected to reap all the benefits of the American economic system while feeling bound by no reciprocal duties to it.

The economic picture of the United States at the turn of the twentieth century was for many a grim one. Industry and manufacturing were controlled by a very few hands, and (as now) the majority of the nation's capital was aggregated in the hands of a very few. There was no regulation of Wall Street; that would not come until 1933, when the Great Depression made it impossible to ignore. There was no central bank. Some historians have noted that it was a "toss-up" whether Roosevelt or financier J.P. Morgan was the most powerful man in the country. Morgan was a cold-eyed and ruthless figure with a skin condition that made the surface of his nose appear as a mass of warts; but this seemed only to enhance his intimidating countenance. He had a brilliant mathematical mind, and was able to keep track of numbers and figures to an extent that astounded his assistants. He did not, however, believe that he owed the public anything; to the extent that he ever even thought about such things, he liked to believe that monopolies were actually "good" for the country. But so believes every monopolist of every era.

In our day, the major levers of power in the United States are the internet, the media, the arms industry, and the industries connected with information and entertainment. In Roosevelt's day, the linchpin industries were railroads, mining, and steel. Sooner or later, Roosevelt knew, he was going to have to confront the plutocratic monopolies in the United States and try to break them up. A failure to do so would leave the control of the country in the hands of economic forces that would seek to enrich itself at the expense of everything else. And once Roosevelt set his mind on something, he was not the kind of man who would back down from a fight. He would soon find his opportunity to engage these dark economic forces.

In 1901, railroad men James J. Hill and Edward Harriman solicited the support of J.P. Morgan (as well as J.D. Rockefeller) to form a corporate entity called the Northern Securities Company. Northern Securities was essentially a huge holding company that held the shares of several different railroad companies. If this arrangement were allowed to continue, it would enable Northern Securities to monopolize the rail transport system for most of the western United States. When Roosevelt found out about it, it seemed to him as practically a declaration of war against the public good. In 1902, he ordered his Justice Department to initiate legal proceedings against the Northern Securities behemoth and break it up; it was a combination in restraint of trade, and it had to go.

But how could this be done? What legal mechanism could be used to take the fight to J.P. Morgan? The weapon found was the Sherman Anti-Trust Act of 1890. While today it seems a routine matter to use this kind of tactic, the situation was entirely different in the early 1900s. The federal government had never used the Act in the way it was proposing to use it now. In the few times that the Act had actually been used, courts and judges were unwilling to give it much teeth. Even in situations where obvious monopolies existed (as in the 1895 antitrust case against the American Sugar Refining Company), the courts dragged their feet and failed to take decisive action against corporate interests that were acting "in restraint of trade." In February 1902, Roosevelt's attorney general filed suit against Northern Securities. It was a risk, and a big one; there was no legal precedent for what Roosevelt was doing, and no guarantee he would succeed. If he failed, it might embolden big business even more.

But something had to be done. There was no advance notice, no chummy, back-slapping phone calls of the type that happened in the wake of the financial meltdown of 2008. According to some accounts, J.P. Morgan was informed of the suit while enjoying a sumptuous dinner with friends; infuriated by the news, he sought an audience with Roosevelt himself. "If we have done anything wrong, send your man to my man and they can fix it up," Morgan told Attorney General Philander Knox. "We don't want to fix it up…we want to stop it," was Knox's acid reply. Morgan basically communicated to the White House that the issue should be amicably resolved and that he was willing to reach some reasonable accommodation. Roosevelt was polite but firm. He let it be known that he could not be bought off; his goal was not to settle with a financial slap on the wrist but to end the abusive practices of the arrogant plutocracy. When the case finally wound its way up to the US Supreme Court, Roosevelt narrowly won by a 5 to 4 vote issued in March 1904. Northern Securities Company was dissolved. The Court's written opinion duly noted:

> It cannot be said that any State may give a corporation, created under its laws, authority to restrain interstate or international commerce against the will

> of the nation as lawfully expressed by Congress...But to the end that effect be given to the national will, lawfully expressed, Congress may prevent that company, in its capacity as a holding corporation and trustee, from carrying out the purposes of a combination formed in restraint of interstate commerce...[Northern] Securities Company is itself a part of the present combination; its head and front; its trustee. It would be extraordinary if the court, in executing the act of Congress, could not lay hands upon that company and prevent it from doing that which, if done, will defeat the act of Congress. Upon like grounds, the court can, by appropriate orders, prevent the two competing railroad companies here involved from cooperating with the Securities Company in restraining commerce among the States. In short, the court may make any order necessary to bring about the dissolution or suppression of an illegal combination that restrains interstate commerce. All this can be done without infringing in any degree upon the just authority of the States. The affirmance of the judgment below will only mean that no combination, however powerful, is stronger than the law or will be permitted to avail itself of the pretext that to prevent it doing that which, if done, would defeat a legal enactment of Congress is to attack the reserved rights of the States.

Roosevelt's victory in *Northern Securities v. United States*, 193 U.S. 197 (1904) was used as a legal precedent for breaking other monopolistic restraints of trade. The message went out from Washington that corporate abuses of power would be rolled back with a firm hand.

Sadly, one cannot help comparing Roosevelt's moral courage with the behavior of two recent occupants of the White House, presidents Obama and Bush. During the financial crisis of 2008-2009, when fear gripped Wall Street, President Obama called a handful of bankers to a meeting in March 2009. The concentrated power of the financiers, as well as their greedy practices, had caused the crisis; yet the American president greeted them with smiles and compliments. He talked tough, telling them that "the only thing between you and the pitchforks is my administration," but in the end the response was toothless. Nothing changed. The plutocracy got everything they wanted: bailouts, unrestricted promises, and blank checks. All of them kept their jobs, their positions, their outrageous salaries and bonuses, everything. The American taxpayer was left to foot the bill. Congress did next to nothing in the way of meaningful reform. If Theodore Roosevelt had lived to see this charade, I believe he would have had nothing but scorn for the moral cowardice of Presidents Bush and Obama.

Victories once won do not stay won unless they are fortified and renewed with each successive generation. We live in an era now where the super-rich have surpassed their Gilded Age predecessors in venality and avarice. They care nothing about the public good; they believe the public exists to serve them. They snort in contempt at the very suggestion that they should accept any restraints on their appetite for money and power. They begrudge the public the basic necessities of human life, health, and advancement. Congress and the presidency are firmly in their pockets. Things have gotten so bad that some military analysts have started to call this state of affairs what it is: *a form of insurgent warfare waged by the super rich against the public.* The time will come–very soon–when the need for drastic reform will become too compelling to be papered over with smiles and benedictions. And when this day does come, the plutocracy will be brought to heel once again.

6. Fray Bernardino de Sahagún: The New World's First Ethnographer

Little known today is the courageous Catholic friar, linguist, and ethnographer Fray Bernardino de Sahagún. He was born in Sahagún, Spain, in 1499 and drank deeply from the well of Renaissance humanism that had been washing over Europe for several decades. Mastering Latin at an early age, he startled his instructors with the intensity and depth of his observational powers. He arrived in Mexico (New Spain) in 1529 with a group of Church prelates whose job it would be to convert the natives to Catholicism.

Like the best clerics of his era, he was a man of contradictions; an ardent believer in the faith, he nevertheless believed the customs and traditions of the native Mexicans should be shown great deference and respect. Soon after arriving in Mexico, he applied himself to the mastery of the Aztec language, Nahuatl, and achieved a level of fluency in that tongue that was equaled by none of his peers. As he traveled extensively in the Mexican countryside and interacted with the natives, he came to realize more and more that the mass "conversions" to Catholicism were in many respects superficial; Mexico, he realized, had its own customs that were deeply-rooted in the life of the people.

He was not a cubicle dweller, content to wall himself up in his study. Adopting the views of the classical Latin writers and Renaissance humanists, he believed that a man of learning should involve himself with worldly affairs if he could be of some use to his society. He drove himself to exhaustion in providing relief to the Indians in 1545 when a plague decimated the countryside. Hundreds of thousands perished; Sahagún himself supervised the burial of thousands of infected corpses, nearly dying himself in the process. "Providence," said a biographer, "wished to preserve him for many more years to the benefit of his contemporaries and future generations." As he traveled and administered to the Indians, he collected as much information as he could about the language, customs, and geography of old Mexico. Sahagún recognized quickly that older Aztec women in particular were repositories of the cultural history of the native people; a rich oral tradition existed of stories, legends, medicinal remedies, food preparation, and poetry. All of this he absorbed and recorded for posterity.

In this he had to proceed cautiously, however, and cloak his intellectual interests under the guise of advancing the cause of the official faith. To show too much interest in native ways for their own sake was something his unscientific contemporaries would not have understood, and it would have exposed him to accusations of heresy. He thus had to present his research as efforts *to refute* the native faith. He presented his investigations as a means of educating his countrymen "so that all the confessors [priests] would have knowledge of the idolatrous rites, the superstitions and sins" of the indigenous Mexicans. His goal was to produce a vast compendium of knowledge that covered history, language, geography, and religious information. He labored on his *magnum opus* night and day, rewriting it three times, until it was finally ready for review by Church authorities in 1569.

It was called *Historia General de las Cosas de la Nueva España,* or *General History of Things in New Spain*, and at 2400 pages was a landmark in ethnography. Informally known as the Florentine Codex, it was the fruit of sixty years of observation and study. This was no dry tome cobbled together by regurgitating the work of others, but an entirely original product of the author's own field-work. Written in both Spanish and Nahuatl, the manuscript was densely packed with information on Mexican religion, language, history, and folkways. Not since Ibn Khaldun's *Muqaddima* several hundred years before had a work of comparable sociological depth appeared. His examiners were impressed, but worried. They recognized the originality of the work, but were uneasy with praising the effort too highly. (The book is now available in both English and Spanish).

With typical clerical subtlety, they pronounced it "contrary to [the vows of] poverty to spend money writing such papers and therefore ordered the author to dismiss the scribes and write what he wished with his own hand only." In other words, Fray Bernardino (who was then seventy years old) was told he would have to copy his books by himself, without help from scribes or copyists. More disappointments would follow. When a copy was finally produced after five years of labor, King Philip II of Spain, fearing too wide a dissemination of Mexican cultural knowledge, decreed that "[I]t is not advisable for this book to be printed nor should it circulate in any wise in those parts…because thus the interests of God Our Lord and our own are best served." Sahagún found himself effectively gagged by both Church and state. A manuscript copy of the book was carried back to Spain, and was buried in obscurity for decades. In 1780 a copy was recovered in a Franciscan monastery in Toulouse; and in 1793 a copy was found in the Laurentian Library in Florence, Italy. But it would take a long time for scholars to examine the volumes and gain an appreciation of their contents. Sahagún was unique in his time for insisting on conducting original field research among the Aztecs; with his fluency of Nahuatl, he could interact directly with any man, woman, or child who could provide him with grist for his pages.

His work was neglected and unappreciated in his day; he would have to wait more than two hundred years after his death for the recognition that he richly deserved. He is said to have died of the grippe in 1590 at the age of ninety-one. Refusing medical treatment, he told his attendants, "Go away, you little fools, leave me in peace because my hour has not yet come." He expired several days later and was buried in the cemetery of the San Francisco Monastery in Mexico City. One source I consulted for this article states that the cemetery itself was obliterated during the Mexican Revolution of the early twentieth century, making the current location of his remains unknown. Time and circumstances were not kind to the good friar. But his brilliant book is the real monument to his life, and this will live forever.

7. Charles Étienne Brasseur de Bourbourg: An Early Pioneer In Mesoamerican Studies

We have previously discussed the career and work of Fray Bernardino de Sahagún. Another major pioneer in the study of early Mexican antiquities was the intense French abbé Charles Étienne Brasseur de Bourbourg (1814–1874). He remains another name nearly lost to history, but a good case can be made that without his work, we would know far less than we do about the culture of old Mexico and Guatemala.

Like his role model and idol Champollion (the French orientalist who used the Rosetta stone to decipher Egyptian hieroglyphics in 1822), his imagination was fired at an early age by stories of foreign travel, exotic languages, and decaying civilizations. Growing up near Dunkirk, France, he soon found it too confining for his personality or tastes. He would later say that he chose to study Mesoamerica after reading an article in the *Journal des Savants* on Palenque culture of Mexico. For a boy without family connections, the only realistic way to travel and live abroad was to join the Catholic clergy, which he did in 1844. Soon he was off to Quebec; but he brutal winters there quickly cooled his passion for the New World. He preferred to be in Mexico, and by 1847 he got his wish, serving in the French Legation in Mexico and later as an ordinary priest in two small towns in Guatemala.

Even with little money, he was able to indulge his intellectual passions. He chanced upon a Quiché–Spanish dictionary during one of his travels; and in the library of the College of San Gregorio in

Mexico he was able to locate a previously lost Nahuatl manuscript which is now known as the Chimalpopoca Codex. By this time he was fluent in the Mayan language, and was able to translate the Mayan sacred scriptures (the *Popol-Vuh*) into French. He would also later discover another precious manuscript known as the *Memorial de Sololá,* a lost work written in the Kaqchikel language by Francisco Hernández Arana Xajilá in 1571 (and later finished by his grandson in 1604). These were all significant discoveries, any one of which might have earned him lasting fame in the annals of Mexican antiquities.

But Brasseur de Bourbourg would press on. One of his most impressive feats was to finance personally an actual performance of an old Mayan stage play. When he heard that the Mayans of the town of Rabinal had still preserved the knowledge of how to stage one of their traditional dramas (the *El Rabinal Achi*), he found a way to finance the construction of the original costumes and set designs, and then had the natives perform the drama. He would later say:

> After mass, the natives built a stage under the arches of the churchyard, which very soon was filled with quite a multitude. A chair was prepared for me on the platform [to watch the performance].

But without doubt his greatest discovery was to unearth in 1862 one of the lost keys of Mexican ethnography, Fray Diego de Landa's monumental *Relación de las Cosas de Yucatán.* This work, a fascinating collection of first-hand observations and researches by one of the more controversial figures of early New Spain (Diego de Landa), was only an abridged version of the original; but there was still enough there to make the discovery a revolutionary advance in the study of Mayan hieroglyphs. Very little was known about Mayan glyphs at the time, and the book at least gave basic information about the Mayan calendar, holidays, religion, and other cultural matters. It was not a Rosetta stone, but it was at least a place from which work could begin.

Like any great pioneer moving through lands where none have trod before, he made a fair share of errors. Letting his imagination get the better of him, the credulous abbé de Bourbourg saw connections between the Mayans and the ancient Egyptians where none existed; but these flights of fancy were forgivable mistakes in a man passionately devoted to his subject. He would redeem himself in 1866, however, when he discovered a precious Mayan codex now known as the Troano Codex. While on a visit to Madrid, he had heard about a Mesoamerican artifact that had been purchased by a professor named Juan de Tro y Ortolano.

Upon examining it, he immediately realized that it was almost unique (only three Mayan codices have survived). De Brasseur was not able to read the codex: he mistook its contents, seeing it as a record of ancient mythology and natural phenomena. But here, at least, is an appreciation for the culture, and a willingness to begin the laborious task of unlocking its secrets. De Brasseur's record is on balance entirely positive. He devoted his life to the interests that the was passionately devoted to, and never lost sight of what he believed his life's purpose was. He was willing to endure poverty, hardship, and ridicule to bring an entirely unknown past to light. If he occasionally stumbled over his own excitement, we must smile favorably and see these sins as the forgivable consequences of isolation and the lack of predecessors in his field. His work would stand as a sign-post, pointing the way for the generations of linguists and ethnographers that would come after him. Sometimes imagination, enthusiasm, and daring count for a great deal in scholarship.

8. The Emperor Julian Cleans House With Bold Reforms

When a new leader assumes a position, it is often necessary for him to undertake significant reforms. If he wishes to make lasting changes to the system, he should undertake to do so both quickly and boldly. To wait too long is to risk seeing one's foes united against you; and when embarking on a course of reform, it must be made clear that the old ways of doing things will no longer do. Bold adjustments are often more effective than half-hearted measures.

It was this principle of leadership that the late Roman emperor Julian the Apostate deployed upon first assuming the purple. His rule was a short one–lasting only from 361 to 363 A.D.–but during this time he was unafraid of steering the ship of state in bold new directions. Sometimes these new directions were accepted by the people; other times they were stoutly resisted. Julian was notable for being a passionate advocate of the old pagan religion of the ancient Greeks. He was also a respectable philosopher in his own right; no other emperor wrote with such erudition, not even Marcus Aurelius. Julian despised Christianity for a number of reasons (which are best left for a separate discussion) and was determined to see it phased out in favor of the old worship. One of his first acts as emperor was to order an ambitious program of repair and reconstruction of the old Hellenic temples in the eastern Mediterranean. One of his most ardent mouthpieces and advocates was the rhetorician Libanius, who says:

> If any city had temples still standing, he was delighted at the sight and thought them deserving of the greatest kindness, but if they had demolished all or the greater part of them, he called them polluted: he offered them a share in the benefits he dispensed, as being his subjects, but not without annoyance. In this activity, then, in setting the world under the guidance of the gods and effecting a reconciliation, he was like a shipwright who fits out a big ship with a new rudder after she has lost her old one, but the difference was that Julian restored to us our original protectors. [*Orations* XVIII.129; *trans. by A.F. Norman*]

Although Julian's anti-Christian campaign ultimately proved futile (for the people no longer felt as devoted to the old gods as they did to the new religion), his restoration program preserved for posterity many monuments and temples that might otherwise have vanished from neglect or malice. More effective was Julian's efforts to "clean house" when it came to administrative and bureaucratic matters. He was a man of austere tastes and very ascetic habits. The imperial court in Constantinople at that time was filled with bureaucratic functionaries, cooks, barbers, priests, secretaries, guards, and various other parasites of all types. Most of these people had little to do but stay on the government payroll and occupy their time with scheming and plotting. Here again Libanius paints us a picture:

> He next turned his attention to the state of the imperial court, where he found a useless horde of people maintained to no purpose. There were a thousand cooks, as many barbers, and even more butlers. There were swarms of waiters, eunuchs more in number than flies around the flocks in spring, and a multitude of drones of every sort and kind. There was one refuge for such idle gluttons, to have the name and title of being one of the emperor's household, and in very quick time a piece of gold would ensure their enrollment. All these, maintained to no purpose by the imperial purse, he regarded not as servants but as nuisances, and so he expelled them forthwith. [XVIII.130]

This purge of the imperial court is also confirmed by Ammianus Marcellinus (XXII.4), who goes into great detail about how the parasites hovering around the halls of power in the capital sapped the vitality of civic life. But the corruption did not end there. Ammianus also assures us that military discipline had seriously declined before Julian became emperor. Soldiers preferred to spent their time in effeminate plotting and scheming, instead of focusing on mastery of their trade. Instead of sleeping on beds of stone or wood, they preferred to sleep on "beds of feathers and folding couches." Julian was also careful to prune away the numerous "imperial agents" (*agentes in rebus*) that had multiplied before he took office. His predecessor, the emperor Constantius, was a schemer himself who apparently did not mind being surrounded by a horde of useless bureaucrats. These secretaries and mid-level functionaries were dangerous in that they could serve as focal points for conspiracies and intrigues against the emperor; at the very least most of them had do-nothing jobs, and enjoyed fattening themselves at public expense.

But Julian was no mindless autocrat, fixated on setting himself up as an infallible ruler. He understood the necessity of a government of checks and balances, working in harmony to advance the public good. He took steps to restore the old senate of Constantinople, which had long since languished in authority and prestige. In an edict that he issued in February, 362, he sought to protect senators from unfounded accusations and imperial intimidation.

Remarkable is the language of the edict; in it, Julian specifically considers himself a member of the senatorial class, rather than above it. He genuinely believed that the healthy functioning of government required the existence of an independent legislative and advisory body. He also encouraged the formation of local assemblies and councils in the various departments of the eastern empire.

To make bold changes, bold steps are sometimes necessary. When the machinery of government has become so clogged with special interest groups, lobbyists, functionaries, bureaucrats, hangers-on, schemers, and useless personalities looking for opportunities for graft, then a leader will need to take muscular steps to reform the system, despite all the screaming and shouting that will naturally result. The presence of such people does nothing but impede the rightful work of government. Political paralysis gives way to factionalism, and the people begin to lose hope that meaningful reforms will ever come. Modern leaders and governments in general have forgotten–if they ever knew it in the first place–that they were put there to *solve* problems, not to perpetuate them or the parasitic classes which they too often serve.

9. Dealing With Treachery And Treason

Betrayal, treachery, and treason are among the most hated of crimes. From antiquity until our own time, commanders have devised numerous ways to prevent or limit them. Some examples are presented here. The reader will discover that all of them involve either incentives or punishments; sometimes a mixture of the two is employed. The Roman commander Frontinus, in his *Stratagems* (III.16), provides us with several examples. When Hannibal invaded Italy during the Second Punic War, he was counting on the various municipalities in Italy to rise up against Rome and rally to his side. This plan was not delusional. Roman domination of Italy was resented by many of the regional Italic peoples; then, as now, Italy was diverse in culture and habits. After the Battle of Cannae, Hannibal sought the support of the people from a municipality named Nola. One of his captives was a man named Lucius Bantius, who was from Nola. In 216 B.C., Hannibal released him, sending him back to Nola and asking him to convince his people there to throw in their lot with Hannibal.

The Roman commander in the area, Claudius Marcellus, heard of Bantius's mission and sought to intercept him. Knowing that killing him would rouse the people of Nola against Rome, he sought to buy his support with bribery and flattery. He spoke to Bantius in person and called him an excellent soldier, and tried to persuade him not to defect to Hannibal. To further sweeten his words, he gave Bantius the gift of a horse (a very valuable item in those days). In this way was Bantius's loyalty secured: instead of using threats or terror, the Roman commander used flattery and payoffs. In our own time, we see this kind of tactic used by the United States in Afghanistan and Iraq, where the support of local communities is won by spreading around money and gifts. Bribery is often an effective inoculation against treachery.

The subtle Hannibal once dealt with treachery with a brilliant bluff. After he had crossed the Alps and had arrived in Italy, he was faced with some mutinous soldiers. He tried to persuade them to stay with him, but was unsuccessful; one night, a large group of them slipped way and melted into the countryside. Hannibal did not want the word to get out that some units had deserted, because he feared that might trigger more defections. So he told his army (falsely) that he had "dismissed" the deserters and sent them away because they were no longer needed. His army not only believed the story, but actually marveled at the confidence of their commander, who was so sure of victory that he could afford to dismiss surplus military forces. In this way Hannibal, that master of guile, solved his problem with the deserters.

During the First Punic War, the Carthaginian general Hamilcar (a common Carthaginian name and not to be confused with Hannibal's father) used a different method to prevent treachery. Hamilcar had attached to him many men from Gaul who were in the habit of defecting to the Romans. He realized that he needed to put an end to this immediately, and chose a ruthless and effective method of doing so. He had some of his best troops pretend to defect to the enemy; and when the Romans came out to welcome them, these "defectors" pulled out weapons and attacked the Romans.

Thus the Romans learned quickly not to trust Gallic defectors from that point forward. Potential defectors in Hamilcar's ranks began to think twice before betraying their commander. In modern times, we have seen variations of this tactic in America's wars in Korea (1950-1953) and Vietnam. There were many instances of "civilians" approaching American lines who suddenly pulled out weapons and started firing. With this tactic the enemy was able to drive psychological wedges between the American military and local civilians, a fact that helped further their cause.

Along these same lines, the Carthaginian general Hanno used an even more ruthless tactic to deal with betrayal in his army while campaigning in Sicily. Hanno learned that about four thousand Gauls were planning to desert to the Romans, for the reason that they had not received any pay for a long time. Hanno knew he was in a delicate situation: he dared not punish the Gauls for fear of triggering a general mutiny of his entire army. Instead, he destroyed them by stealth. To the disgruntled Gauls, he was all smiles, promising them that he would increase their pay substantially and give them other privileges. He also promised to allow them to leave camp and forage for food on a certain date.

At the same time, however, he secretly sent a trusted emissary, posing as a deserter, to the Roman commander Otacilius. The emissary pretended he was a fugitive from Hanno's army after having been indicted by Hanno for embezzlement. The "deserter" told Otacilius that at a certain day and time, he would be able to find a contingent of Gauls foraging for food in the countryside. Of course, these were the same four thousand disgruntled Gauls whom Hanno had allowed to leave camp. Otacilius had several units of his men lie in ambush for the Gauls at the given day and time, and they fell upon the Gauls, massacring many of them. The Gauls also killed many Romans during the melee. Through this devious ruse was Hanno able to solve two problems in one stroke: he disposed of the mutinous Gauls who were causing him problems, and at the same time he was able to weaken the Romans by inflicting casualties on them.

10. The Brutal Siege Of Amida

The Persian king Shapur II (A.D. 309–379) decided early in his reign to recover by force several of the Roman Empire's eastern provinces, especially the rich lands of Mesopotamia and Armenia. In the year 359 he focused his attention on capturing the city of Amida; the city was located in the spot currently occupied by Diyarbakir in Turkey. Its extended siege and dramatic fall are recounted in detail by Ammianus Marcellinus, whose account (*Res Gestae* XVIII.9) forms the primary source for the present article. The historian was personally present during the siege and took part in its defense, and his account of the battle forms one of the most dramatic episodes of his book. Ammianus tells us that the city's south side rested against the banks of the river Tigris. From its location, it looked down on the Mesopotamian plan; and within its thick walls was a fresh spring and a large garrison of troops. Its primary detachment was the Fifth Legion ("Parthica"), augmented by some native troops. Six additional legions had arrived to Amida to assist in the defense of the citadel. Within its walls was also a squadron of mounted archers (*comes sagittarii*) who were well-known for their capability and endurance.

When Shapur approached the city, Ammianus says that mail-clad cavalry and "shining weapons" were visible to the defenders as far as the eye could see. He rode up to the city gates and sent emissaries to demand the city's surrender; he was refused and personally attacked by the defenders. In a fury, he resolved not to rest until the city was stormed by force. The Persians surrounded the entire walls of the city and put it to unrelenting siege. "Looking out on so many people whose goal it was to destroy us and set fire to the Roman world, we gave up any hope of rescue; from this point our goal was to leave this life with glory. This was the goal of all of us." (XIX.2). Ammianus goes on to give a detailed account of the battle that raged back and forth between the attackers and the defenders. Profusions of arrows darkened the air; fixed defensive weapons called "scorpions" (*scorpio*) fired day and night at the attackers; and clouds of dust blotted out the sky during the day.

After the fifth day of battle, both sides agreed to a temporary truce. Ammianus says that the cries of the wounded were terrible, since not much could be done for them; and within the cramped walls of Amida were huddled a total of 120,000 people (both civilians and soldiers). The wounded tried to help themselves as best they could. Many expired gradually from loss of blood, or died quickly when they tried to remove arrows themselves from their bodies. Bodies began to pile up in the streets and inside dwellings. As if things could get any worse, a plague epidemic broke out after the tenth day of the siege; yet for some reason the disease dissipated, according to the historian, by the falling of "a light rain."

But by this time Shapur had constructed siege-towers and mantlets all around Amida's walls. Tunneling activity also began to take place; the idea was not so much to burrow into the city, but to undermine the walls' foundations and thereby cause them to collapse. A detachment of Gauls happened to be located at Amida; Gauls came from a long warrior tradition and demanded to be allowed to engage with the Persians outside the city walls. When they were denied, they "gnashed their teeth like wild animals" in frustration. But treachery, which so often plays a part in ancient battles, was present in the air. A deserter from the city allowed a small band of Persians to gain access to the city through a subterranean passage near the Tigris. Once this band was let in, their comrades outside the walls attacked again in force. Ballistae, scorpions, and archers rained projectiles on the attackers; and somehow the defenders managed to hold their position, forcing the Persians to back away from the walls. As the historian says (XIX.6):

> So fortune breathed on us some feeling of safety. [*Adspiravit auram quandam salutis fortuna*]

This feeling would prove to be short-lived. The decision was finally made to unleash the Gauls on the enemy. They were by this time literally hacking the walls of the city with their swords, behaving more like caged animals wishing to fling themselves on a tormentor. They burst out of the gates and attacked the Persians who were building siege-mounds, as well as other units stationed a greater distance away. These attacks caused the enemy great damage, and the Gauls returned to the city in triumph. A three-day truce was then declared. But in the long-term, there was little hope that the bottled-up defenders could long last against Shapur's army. He was patient and methodical: he ordered mounds and siege-towers to ring Amida's walls once again. The mounds were especially dangerous, because once built, the attackers could mount assaults directly over the city's walls. To his credit, the Persian king himself (according to Ammianus) entered the battle like a common infantryman; in those days, kings did not die in their beds. For a long time, we are told, the battle was undecided. And then, says Ammianus (XIX.8),

> The battle reached a point where the fate of the combatants was governed by some preordained event… [*Eoque producta contentione, cum sors partium eventu regeretur indeclinabili…*]

In other words, Fortune began to take control of events. The precipitated the final destruction of the city was the collapse of one of the mounds that had been built for the city's defense. It fell forward as if leveled "by an earthquake" and opened up a huge gap in the city's defenses. Defenders and attackers both poured into the gap to join in hand-to-hand battle, and terrible carnage ensued. But nothing could hold back the tide of the enraged attackers, and they burst into Amida. After participating in the defense for a short time, Ammianus himself apparently realized that all was lost, and resolved to make his own escape with a few of his comrades. In one night, he says, he was able to make ten miles on foot, primarily because of his "acquaintance with the area." But it was not easy, worn down as he was by thirst and lack of food. He would eventually find his way back to Roman Syria and to safety.

Thus was Amida taken in a dramatic siege, an event vividly described by a capable historian. Two final incidents have remained in my mind from reading his account. A day or so after making his escape from the city, he happened to see a ghastly and surreal sight. He saw a horse wandering alone in the countryside, without saddle or bit. One of its reins dragged the shattered fragments of a corpse. What had happened was that a rider, inexperienced in horsemanship, had tied his hand to one of the horse's reins. When he was thrown off the saddle, he could not extricate himself, and so was dragged to his death over the rocks of the mountainous deserts. Most of his body had been torn away, but the arm and torso were still attached to the horse's rein. The sight was disturbing enough for Ammianus to comment on it vividly.

The final sight that he records is also somehow unforgettable. He tells us that the corpses of Romans lying in the countryside quickly rotted in the open air, to an extent that they were not recognizable after five days or so. Yet the bodies of the Persians, he says, shriveled up like desiccated trees, without completely decomposing. Ammianus attributes this difference to the more simple diet and lifestyle of the Persians. It is difficult to know what to make of this comment, but it is a memorable one regardless.

11. Paulus Catena: The Psychology Of An Accuser

Witch-hunts and persecutions thrive in environments where certain conditions are met. There must be some driving motivation, such as greed, envy, ideology, or hate; there must be willing accomplices who spread accusations and create new ones; and there must exist some tolerance of the persecution, whether from the leadership at the top or from the affected group at large. When these conditions are met, witch-hunts can seize hold of a group and spread as quickly as a wildfire. They are sustained by fear and hysteria; the affected group is made to feel as if hidden enemies are lurking around every corner and hiding behind every curtain.

To better explore the anatomy of the witch-hunt, we will consider one such persecution that took place during the reign of Roman emperor Constantius II. Constantius employed in his service an evil and brutal hatchet-man named Paulus. The historian Ammianus Marcellinus (*Res Gestae* XIX.11) tells us that his nickname was Tartareus ("The Diabolical"); another of his monikers was Catena ("The Chain"). Had he lived in the twentieth century, he is the type of person who would have found productive employment as the head of the secret police in some authoritarian state. He first gained his sinister reputation for his "work" in Britain, rounding up suspected supporters of a usurper to the throne named Magnentius. These events took place after Magnentius's fall in 353 A.D. Paulus's fondness for chains as an instrument of torture and humiliation was what earned him the name Catena.

But as often happens in these situations, once accusations and persecutions begin, even their initiators lose control over them. Cruel and vindictive people are not driven by altruistic motives; they enjoy their power for the feeling it gives them. And when there are no targets for their witch-hunts, they invent targets. The fires need to be fed. Paulus's reign of terror became so out of control that one of the emperor's officials in Britain, a man named Flavius Martinus, tried to put an end to them. Martinus had become horrified at Paulus's kangaroo courts, spurious accusations, and vindictive lies. Unsurprisingly, Paulus then leveled accusations against Martinus himself; he would eventually be forced to end his own life.

Paulus's career did not end there. The historian Ammianus reports (XIX.11) that Catena delighted in putting innocent people under a cloud; his resolution to do evil was "fixed and unshakeable" (*obstinatum fixumque*). In Roman Egypt there was a province (called a "nome") called Thebais. In this province was a town called Abydum, where an old local god named Besa was worshipped. In those days, just as happens now in many parts of the world, people would visit holy sites and write prayers or requests on small slips of paper and deposit them at shrines of worship. Some of the emperor's spies were in the habit of reading such private notes, and maliciously passed them on to the imperial authorities. Apparently some of these little notes contained offensive sentiments. Constantius was a weak and narrow-minded man, the kind of insecure leader who cannot tolerate even the thought of dissent or disagreement. His entourage at court was filled with useless people who did little else but fan the flames of conspiracy and paranoia. Because he was "suspicious and mean-spirited" (*suspicax et minutus*), he resolved to purge the imaginary traitors that he believed existed in Thebais. This is how these things start. Constantius sent his chief inquisitor, his major hatchet-man, to do the dirty work; and this man was of course Paulus Catena. Ammianus tells us that Paulus took to his job with a salivating glee.

Such people live for opportunities to vent their sadistic impulses on the innocent or harmless. Paulus used the opportunity to conduct a reign of terror on an extensive scale. He based himself in Scythopolis, a city in Palestine, so chosen because it was "midway between Antioch [in Syria] and Alexandria." Paulus pulled a great number of important officials and learned men into his accusatory dragnet. Most of the accused were put to the torture; many were sent into exile and had their possessions seized. Those who were able to save themselves from the false charges were the ones who stood up to Paulus's lies and responded vigorously to them. Paulus liked to use deception and obfuscation to trick people into confessing things they had never done. Things got to the point where even someone's appearance and demeanor could set off an accusation:

> If someone was wearing on his neck a remedy [i.e., charm or medal] against the quartan fever or some other sickness, or was alleged to have passed by a funerary monument at night as supposed evidence of engaging in sorcery, or of collecting the sickening relics of tombs and communing with the spirits that inhabit such places, he was pronounced guilty and put to death. [*Res Gestae* XIX.13]

This is how bad things were: almost anything could trigger an accusation. Even trumped-up "evidence" of witchcraft and sorcery was used to malign and destroy innocent people. Yet there does seem to be a measure of justice in the world that falls on those who encourage and perpetrate such outrages. Accusers are often consumed by the lies and frauds that they themselves set in motion; and so are the wicked entrapped by the evil schemes they intend for others. So it was with Paulus Catena. When Constantius died, he was replaced by one of the most remarkable men ever to occupy the throne of Caesar: Julian, also known as Julian the Apostate. Julian was aware of Paulus's murderous record as a persecutor and a maligner of innocent people. He had Paulus arrested, put on trial, and burned alive in 361 or 362.

The lessons are obvious for us today. If someone is lying about someone else, or trying to demean another's accomplishments, or smear another with innuendo, it is important for the aggrieved party to correct the record with vigor and persistence. Lies, if repeated long enough without rebuttal, can sadly take on the patina of truth; and we live in a world where people too often believe the first thing that reaches their ears or eyes. Achievement will attract the malicious envy of detractors. Take heart, fight your corner, and keep working diligently towards your goals.

12. The Fragility Of Historical Knowledge: Lorenzo Boturini In Mexico

In the modern era we like to think of knowledge as something indelibly fixed and permanent. We take it for granted that it will always be here, like the Great Pyramid, and are apt to overlook the bitter struggles that our ancestors may have endured to acquire such knowledge. Information has not always been as easy to obtain as it is now. As we read about the adventures of scholars of the past, we get the distinct impression that the learned men who came before us had a hardiness and tenacity that is lacking in the modern era. I will let the reader judge for himself.

Lorenzo Boturini Benaducci was born of aristocratic lineage in Como, Italy, in 1702. He could supposedly trace his noble ancestry back over 900 years. After receiving an education in Milan and later in Vienna, he moved to Madrid to escape the political instability that plagued Austria at the time. In Madrid his natural charm and good graces endeared him to a female descendant of the last Aztec emperor, Moctezuma. This lady, whose name was Doña Manuela de Oca Silva y Moctezuma, asked Boturini to go to Mexico and assist in efforts to educate the native population. To fund this educational project, she would use the pension she received from the Spanish crown as a direct descendant of the Aztec royal family. She must have recognized the spark of genius in the idealistic young Italian. Behind many successful adventurers is often a shrewd woman.

So off went Boturnini to New Spain (Mexico) in 1736. He must have been a man of considerable religious sentiment also, for he allowed himself to become sidetracked by a desire to research the spiritual phenomenon of the Virgin of Guadalupe. Yet this apparent derailment had a hidden blessing: while he traveled all over the Mexican countryside, he would have frequent contact with native Nahuatl chiefs and notables. Everywhere around him, Boturini saw evidence of Mexico's fascinating and strange pre-Columbian art, writing, and inscriptions. In those days Mexican antiquarianism was vastly underappreciated; so the headstrong Italian took it upon himself to collect every scrap of Aztec art and writing he could obtain by purchase or otherwise.

Unfortunately, learned men are not always wise in the ways of worldly power. Boturini's efforts soon attracted the attention–or envy–of the local authorities, who did not appreciate an Italian nobleman sent by a descendant of Moctezuma to poke around in Spanish colonial territory. The so-called "Council of the Indies" had administrative authority over New Spain at the time, and word of Boturini's researches soon reached them. Word also reached the viceroy of New Spain, the Count of Fuenclara. With these political realities in the air, it was only a matter of time before some suitable pretext was found to take Boturini into custody and confiscate his extensive collection of Aztec artifacts and writings. In February, 1743, he was arrested and tossed in jail on the pretext of failing to obtain the necessary permits from the Council of the Indies to conduct his researches in Mexico.

As often happened in those days, he languished in jail for months. In August 1743, viceroy Fuenclara ordered Boturini to assist Spanish authorities in conducting an inventory of his Aztec antiquities. But the Italian, proud to the point of suicide, refused the order, demanding that he be permitted a suit of clothing (and a sword!) worthy of his rank and station. This of course turned out to be the wrong thing to do; he was immediately lodged in even worse accommodations–essentially thrown into a dungeon with common criminals. Boturini wrote a stream of letters to any official who would listen, complaining that he was:

> [S]tripped of his archives and his Historical Museum of the Indies, without there existing any indebtedness or criminal act to justify such seizure and...regarding the inventory, it is futile for His Excellency the Viceroy to bother requesting it, because he, Lorenzo Boturini, knows far better than anyone its value for the Catholic monarchy, and for a long time has intended to dedicate it to his majesty, may God protect him...

Boturini eventually relented and accepted the demand of the authorities to help with the inventory. He was then ordered to board the ship *La Concordia*, bound for Spain, and summarily expelled from Mexico. It was a bitter pill for the proud scholar to swallow, having spent a huge amount of money and labor in collecting his historical treasures. But Fate was not yet through with Boturini. On the way back to Spain, his ship was seized by English pirates, who promptly stole what little Boturini still had left to his name. They even took his clothes; he was forced to don the garb of the common sailor. His only possession was a manuscript draft of a history of New Spain he planned to write. But Boturini was more in his element back in the halls of power in Europe. He was able to vindicate himself and his activities. He petitioned the board of the Council of the Indies in Spain, and it graciously ordered that he be compensated for all damages incurred in his ordeal. The Council even gave him permission to found an academy in Mexico to conduct research on the country and its history. His collections were ordered to be restored to him on his return to Mexico. King Philip V even awarded him an annual stipend of 1000 pesetas.

Yet for some reason, Boturini never returned to New Spain. It is not clear why. Perhaps his experience had been so traumatic that he did not wish to risk a repetition of it. His collection of Aztec artifacts, art, and writings lay neglected in the hands of uncomprehending government bureaucrats, who did little or nothing to maintain it. Bit by bit, the collection began to waste away. According to one writer, one precious illuminated Mexican manuscript suffered a loss of 242 pages out of an original total of 330. Other original documents–maps, drawings, and pictographic books–were similarly neglected. With every inventory that was taken (1743, 1745, 1804, and 1823), the size of the collection diminished. The materials simply were not appreciated or properly understood. So Mexican history suffered a grievous injury to its written record. Some of the collection was scattered back to Europe; some of it was ruined through neglect; and some was undoubtedly stolen for the amusement of its custodians. We do not know.

What we do know is that knowledge is highly perishable, and that it takes scholars of courage, diligence, and wiliness to preserve it. At every step of the way, their efforts may be impeded by venomous bureaucrats, ignorant peers, ideological revisionists, jealous colleagues, an uninterested public, or any number of other tricks of Fortune. Humanistic knowledge is fragile and must be fought for again and again. Once won, knowledge does not remain won; every generation must do its part to prevent the historical record and artistic treasures from slipping into oblivion. We must give the utmost respect to those who labor–often in unrecognized and unappreciated silence–to preserve the legacy of mankind from the twin ravages of Ignorance and Neglect.

13. The Remarkable Memoirs Of Madame Roland

When a writer composes his or her memoirs while in prison awaiting execution, we owe it to ourselves to consider what they have to say. It may be a cliché that the prospect of death focuses the memory and concentration, but it is a cliché that is powerfully true. In Chapter 5 of *Thirty-Seven*, I discussed the fate of Boethius, who wrote his *Consolation of Philosophy* while languishing in a dungeon (and awaiting execution) for a crime he did not commit. I recently heard of another last testament written during captivity: the poignant memoirs of Jeanne Manon Roland (1754–1793), known to history simply as Madame Roland.

It is not a name that most readers are likely to be familiar with. She was a political figure who, together with her husband Jean-Marie Roland de la Platiere, played a minor role in the turbulent factional politics of the French Revolution. She was a supporter of the Revolution, but also a moderate and in some ways a traditionalist. But as the fires of fanaticism consumed Paris in the early 1790s, moderates often found themselves on the receiving end of suspicions, calumnies, and hostility. As she so aptly said later,

> On the throne today; tomorrow in irons. That is the common lot of the virtuous in time of revolution. When the people first rise up against oppression, wise men who have shown them the way and helped them to recover their rights come to power. But they do not stay there long. More ambitious characters soon emerge, flatter and delude the people and turn them against their true defenders.

She was born Marie-Jeanne Phlipon in Paris to a family of sufficient resources to provide for her education, something that was not common for women in those days. She showed an early aptitude for history and philosophy, consuming volumes by Plutarch, Voltaire, Montesquieu, and a number of authors from the classical canon. These gave her a humanistic outlook on life and an appreciation for the role of character and moral duties in history. In 1780 she married Jean-Marie Roland de la Platiere; he was twenty years older than she, but the match was apparently a successful one. When the revolution burst forth in 1789, she and her husband first joined the radical Jacobin faction, but then, displeased with its excesses, moved to the more moderate Girondist party.

Her outspokenness and influence over her husband did not endear her to the radicals. As the terror mounted, and arrests and executions became the order of the day, she along with many other would be swept away by the tides of hysteria. In June 1793 she was arrested for "treason" and thrown in jail; and there, writing on seven hundred small sheets of paper, she penned her biography for posterity. We must not expect a perfectly polished literary production here. Rarely has a book been composed under more unfavorable circumstances. But it remains a fascinating window into a mind of a soul that was at once vain, proud, combative, idealistic, generous, and brave. Only Rousseau exceeds her in honesty and blunt revelation; her account of her early life will surprise readers even today by its startling unwillingness to hold anything back. An early anecdote gives us an idea of her character:

> One day I was a little unwell, and there was talk of medicine. They brought the mixture and I put it to my lips, but the smell disgusted me and I pushed it away. My mother tried to overcome my repugnance and I wanted to obey her; I really tried, but every time the stuff was put under my nose my sense revolted and I turned away my head...At this point my father came in. He became angry and whipped me, attributing my refusal to obstinacy...All of a sudden–and I can feel it as I write, all these years later–a change of attitude took place inside me, a new strength flowed through my veins. My tears stopped abruptly and in a sudden calm all my senses seemed to coalesce into a single resolution...He could have killed me, I would not have uttered a sound.

As a youth, her imagination was fired by the great deeds and personalities of the past. She tells us:

> In refutation of [the philosopher Helvetius's] bleak doctrine I recalled the great sweep of history and the virtues of all the heroes who have adorned it. Whenever I read of some noble action I would say to myself "That is what I would have done!" I was passionate for the republics of the ancient world, adorned by men and deeds I could admire, and I persuaded myself that this was the only acceptable type of regime. I felt fully up to the level of these men and lamented that I had not been born among them.

Her views on morality and ethics could have been taken directly from the pages of Cicero:

> I had little difficulty in perceiving that personal well-being depends on being able to preserve what I might call the unity of one's nature; that is to say,

> the greatest possible consistency between one's beliefs and one's actions. The first thing is to decide what is right; after that one must act rigorously in accordance with the decision. One has a duty to oneself, quite independently of anyone else in the world, to control one's affections and one's habits so as not to become the slave of any of them...Moral health, by the same token, entails disciplining the passions and harmonizing the desires, and only self-control can ensure this...But virtue in the true sense of the word comes into effect only in a man's relations with his fellow men. One can be wise for one's own sake, but one is virtuous for the sake of others.

As for her views on life, character, and history, we can get a taste from the following quotes:

> The greatest fault of all in a man who seeks to govern is weakness, especially in times of factional strife. Men...who as ordinary individuals might very well be considered intelligent and worthy, are quite unfitted to govern any state. Their half measures are fatal. They are so keen to be conciliatory that they approach any challenge sideways on, so to speak, and land themselves inevitably in confusion and catastrophe. Conciliatoriness in a statesman ought to be confined to the way he conduct his business; I mean he should treat the people he employs with respect and should know how to take advantage of the enthusiasms and even the faults of those with whom he works. But when it comes to his principles and his actions they should be rigorous, ruthless and swift.

With regard to the habits of the mob, she noted the following truth, something with which Ibn Munir would have agreed:

> The animals in the fable habitually tremble before the lion of the forest, but when he is sick they creep up one after the other to insult him. Just so, when a

> man of virtue has been laid by the heels or his reputation undermined by his enemies, a rout of second-rate people, fired by ignorance and malice, will turn upon him.

She was wise in the ways that men and women differed, and made no attempt to berate Nature for the ways it assured the continuity of the species:

> As soon as a girl reaches adolescence, a crowd of pretenders follow her about like bees around a newly opened flower…They presented themselves in large numbers, and since it was not too easy to gain access to our apartment, most of them wrote to my parents. My father always showed me their letters. Quite independently of what the writer said about his state and fortune, I was influenced in the first place by the way he expressed himself…Reason and nature conspire so effectively to persuade a wise, modest young woman that she must get married that the only point left for deliberation is who should it be…

With regard to those who like to waste time, she said:

> One always has leisure if one is busy; it is the idle people who have no time for anything. Women who constantly exchange useless visits with one another and who think themselves ill-dressed unless they have spent hours in front of the mirror naturally find their days boringly long and too short for their duties. On the other hand, I have also seen so-called good housewives who are quite unbearable in company, and even to their husbands, because of their preoccupation with domestic trifles. I know of nothing more tiresome than this or better calculated to make a man look elsewhere for his pleasures.

These quotes, and many others like them, show Madame Roland to be an energetic and idealistic personality, a mixture of both traditional and forward-thinking sentiments, a woman tragically caught up in the irrational furor of her times. Her final words to the world are unforgettable in their poignancy and pathos:

> Farewell my child, my husband, my maid, my friends! Farewell glorious sun that ever filled my heart with contentment as it filled the skies with light...Farewell my peaceful study, where I ever strove after truth and beauty and learned to control my senses and to despise vanity. Farewell, dear —-; no, I am no saying farewell to you. Leaving this world brings me nearer to you.

Soon after these words were written, she was led to the scaffold and beheaded. She was only thirty-nine years old.

14. Great Deeds Of Valor From The Fourth Crusade

Geoffrey of Villehardouin (1160–1212?) is known as one of the first important names in French historiography. Unlike his predecessors, he was not a dry chronicler; he was a historian who participated directly in the events he described, and was reasonably objective by the standards of his day. His book, *The Conquest of Constantinople*, is a moving and pious account of his involvement in the Fourth Crusade. He was not born a nobleman; he earned his spurs as a knight through loyal service as a soldier and organizer of military campaigns. After his withdrawal from public life, he set out to record the great events he had been a part of, much in the same way that Bernal Diaz (one of Hernando Cortes's soldiers) and Usama Ibn Munqidh (an Arab knight of the Crusades) would do. Great deeds of valor are rightly celebrated in every culture and in every age, because (as Sallust tells us):

> Glory derived from riches and appearances is transitory and brittle, but masculine virtue is pure and eternal. [*Cat. 1*]

Like other men of his era, Villehardouin took it for granted that a man must display courage and fortitude in every aspect of his life.

For him, it could not be otherwise. Nothing useful or productive could be accomplished without it, and leaders who could not live up to this standard should in his view be speedily replaced. But he was not a fanatic or a reckless dolt; good judgment and caution played an essential role in forming the personality of a commander, and those lacking these qualities were rightfully deserving of scorn. This is a man who has earned his titles, rather than had them bestowed on him by virtue of birth or wealth. His philosophy and value system come through on every page of his history. And yet his account is also bursting with sincere passion; by reading him, we realize just how much manly spiritual idealism in the West has been lost or suppressed. Reading his account made me sorely regret that I cannot read Old French.

To get a taste of the flavor and intensity of Villehardouin's prose, consider the following passages. In one of his chapters, he describes the first siege of Constantinople, which took place from July 5 to July 17, 1203. Without going into too much detail on its origins and purposes, the Fourth Crusade (1202–1204) was a military campaign undertaken by a coalition of Western European forces ostensibly against Egypt and Palestine; in reality it was turned into an assault on the capital of the Byzantine Empire. Yet armies on the march do not ask political questions; the foot-soldier sees only the pack of the man in front of him, and does not concern himself with political machinations happening in board-rooms and conference-tables. Villehardouin does not dwell on these issues, nor should he be have been expected to. He was a fighting man with a mission and a purpose, and that was enough. His army finally arrived before the gates of Constantinople, that fabled and wondrous city, the sight of which must have awed the Crusaders. With his pulse racing, he tells us:

> The French planted two scaling ladders against a barbican [i.e., a fortified tower] close to the sea. The wall here was strongly manned by Englishmen and Danes, and the struggle that ensued was stiff and hard and fierce. By dint of strenuous efforts two knight sand two sergeants managed to scale the ladders and make themselves masters of the wall. A good fifteen of our men got up on top, and were quickly engaged in a hand-to-and contest of battle-

> axes against swords. The Greeks inside the barbican plucked up courage and fought back so savagely that they drove our men out, while retaining two as prisoners. These captives were led before the Emperor Alexius [the Greek emperor], who was overjoyed to see them…Many were wounded and many were left with broken limbs. [*Trans. by Margaret Shaw*]

We can almost feel the crash of stones hurled from mangonels, the screech of steel against steel, and the shouts of the belligerents. Villehardouin then relates:

> Let me tell you here of an outstanding deed of valor. The Doge of Venice, although an old man and completely blind, stood at the bow of his galley, with the banner of Saint Mark unfurled before him. He cried out to his men to put him on shore, or else he himself would deal with them as they deserved. They obeyed him promptly, for the galley touched ground and the men in it leaped ashore, bearing the banner of Saint Mark to shore before the Doge. As soon as the other Venetians saw this banner on land, and their lord's galley touching ground before them, every man of them felt deeply ashamed, and all made for the shore. The men in the transports leaped out and waded, while those in the bigger ships got into boats, and every one of them, each vying with the other to get there quickest, hastened to reach land. Then began a grand and marvelous assault on the city. Geoffrey de Villehardouin, author of this chronicle, here affirms that more than forty people solemnly assured him that they had seen the banner of Saint Mark flying from the top of one of the towers…

See here how different the ethic of that era was from our own! *See how the courage and tenacity of one old man can inspire others!* This is how these things are: courage, like cowardice, is infectious. But think about this: would a blind old man today put himself in harm's way, like the old Doge of Venice did when he insisted on going ashore into the thick of the fight? How do our own politicians of today compare with these men? Today's generals and politicians have no skin in the games they play. Never for a moment do they risk anything of their own: nothing, not their pensions, possessions, benefits, or comforts. And this is the problem. But let him continue his account:

> Now let me tell you of an event so marvelous that it might be called a miracle. The people within the city fled, abandoning the walls to the Venetians. These all rushed in through the gates, each trying to outstrip the others and took possession of twenty-five towers, which they manned with their own people. The Doge called for a boat to take messengers as quickly as possible to tell the barons that twenty-five towers had been seized, and to assure them that these could never be retaken…The Emperor Alexius now brought his men so far forward that either side could shoot at the other. On hearing of this the Doge of Venice sent orders to his men to come down from the towers they had taken, and declared he would live or die in the company of the pilgrims [his men]…I can assure you that God never delivered any people from greater peril than that from which He saved our troops that day…The people of Constantinople were utterly astounded. They went to the prison in which the Emperor Isaac, whose eyes had been put out, was confined. They clothed him in his imperial robes, and carried him to the great palace of Blachernae, where they set him on a high throne, and swore allegiance to him as their lord. Then…messengers were sent to tell…the barons that the usurper [Alexius] had fled, and the people of Constantinople had re-established his brother as their rightful emperor.

And then, finally, Villehardouin ends with these stirring words:

> As soon as the young prince heard the news he sent for the Marquis de Montferrat, who immediately

> summoned all the barons throughout the camp… Their joy on hearing it was such as cannot well be described, for no greater joy was ever felt by anyone in this world. The whole company joined in the most devout and reverent praises of Our Lord, for having within so short a time delivered them and exalted them so high from such a low estate. And therefore one may rightly say: *"The man whom God desires to help, no other man can harm."*

Of the truth of this last sentence, there can be no doubt. The actions of a single man can play a decisive role in the outcome of events, and we must strive to be counted among such men.

15. Edward King: Sacrificing Life And Fortune For Scholarship

Of some scholars, or patrons of the arts, it can be said that they sacrificed everything for their work. Of others, this cannot be said. Edward King, Viscount of Kingsborough, belongs to the former category. His name is almost entirely unknown today, but he occupies a significant place in the pantheon of heroes who helped bring the treasures of Mexican antiquity to the attention of modern scholarship. The least we can do here is honor his name. We are somewhat hampered by the fact that his life is known only in broad outline. He was apparently born in Ireland in 1795 to a noble family; he would later serve as a Whig member of Parliament from 1818 to 1826. He might have lived out his days in idleness and indolence, as so many of his station did, were it not for a chance encounter with an ancient Mexican manuscript in London in 1834. We must remember that in those days (as we have discussed already in these pages), Aztec and Mayan antiquities were barely known outside of New Spain (i.e., Mexico). His imagination was fired by the strange pictographs, weird symbols, and arcane symbolism of the codex, and he resolved to probe deeper into the subject.

He was hampered at the outset by his amateurish fixation on the ridiculous theory that the Mexican Indians were somehow connected to the fabled "lost tribes" of biblical Israel. Fortunately, this handicap ended up mattering very little, for we do not remember

Edward King today for his theories. We remember him because he undertook to reproduce–painstakingly and with great precision–the Mexican codices in pictorial form. No one had attempted to do this. In an age before photography and electronic scanning, the only way pictorial information could be reproduced was by hand. This took time, and a great deal of money. King had the money, of course; he was able to hire an artist named Agostino Aglio to make faithful reproductions of every codex he could lay his hands on. This work took Aglio five long years; he traveled personally to various locations in Europe to inspect manuscripts and make his drawings. King's plan was to publish a ten-volume study of Mexican codices, with each volume containing precise illustrations of manuscripts found in libraries and private collections all over Europe. In 1831, the first volume of his *Antiquities of Mexico* was published. It included not only information about the Mayans and Aztecs, but the Mixtec culture as well. Nine volumes would eventually be released, with the last two not seeing the light of day until after King had died in debtor's prison.

Soon after the publication of the first few volumes, King encountered serious financial difficulties. Like many enthusiastic patrons of the arts, he had underestimated the expense that his books would require, and overestimated the interest that the general public might have for such an undertaking. In those days before color printing became cheap and efficient, many of the illustrations in the books had to be actually completed by hand. This kind of system obviously did not lend itself to mass production. We have seen this sort of thing before: readers of my book *Thirty-Seven* will recall the story of American Civil War photographer Alexander Gardner, whose brilliant photographic sketch-book of the war was illustrated with photographic positives that had to be actually pasted by hand in each book. The venture was a brilliant idea, but it was not appreciated at the time, and the publication costs nearly overwhelmed Gardner. King's situation, by contrast, was far more serious.

With these difficulties, it was not long before King's creditors came calling. He had borrowed heavily to finance his project, and now he was unable to repay them. These were the days before grants and endowments were common; unless an artist or scholar could get direct support from a wealthy patron (which was rare), he was on his own. This was also the era before bankruptcy protections became easily available to distressed debtors. So he was taken into custody and clapped into debtor's prison in Dublin in 1837. The cause of death was apparently typhus, a foul disease no doubt contracted as a result of his fetid and miserable accommodations. He was only forty-two. So can a man's passions lead him to oblivion. Yet in some way there is something quietly heroic about King's quest. He followed his passions, and he left behind him a worthy monument to posterity. He did what no one before him had done, which was to reproduce in pictorial form all that could be learned about the codices of ancient Mexico. It was his toil, and it was his labor, that would inspire later generations of scholars and ethnographers. Those who take knowledge for granted today should remind themselves that what we now have at our fingertips often required untold sacrifices by visionary men to bring to the printed page. He gave his life for scholarship.

16. The Painted Books Of The Maya: Surviving By A Hair

Sometimes the precious things of this world survive by just a hair. *Just a hair*. The difference between victory and defeat, between survival and ruin, between conquest and destruction, between glory and despair: these are not differences of tremendous magnitude. They are fine-line distinctions; and when I say fine-line, I mean very fine. Fortune loves to play games with us, and when she casts her dice to predict our fate, the outcome often hangs by a hair. By such threads does the fate of man so perilously hang.

Consider the case of the ancient codices of the Maya. The books of the Maya suffered an even more tragic fate than the painted books of the Aztec or Mixtec peoples. Fire, neglect, apathy, and deliberate destruction were their fate; even after the 1500s, they were not considered important enough for serious study, and thus were scattered to various libraries or private collections in Europe, where they sat untouched for generations. Today there are only three known original Mayan manuscripts. They are named the *Codex Dresden*, the *Codex Tro-Cortesianus*, and the *Codex Paris*. This is all that remains of a literate civilization that recorded its astronomical observations, prophecies, calendar lore, and lineages of kings.

To show just how fragile the literary heritage of man is, let us consider the fate of one of these codices, the *Codex Paris*. This incalculably rare book was fished out of a wastebasket in the National

Library of Paris in 1859 by a scholar named Leon de Rosny. De Rosny was a botanist by trade; he knew nothing about Mexico and its rich history. But we do know that he accomplished something that could be called a miracle: he saved a Mayan codex from oblivion just by happening to notice something odd lying in a wastebasket. Who put it there, we do not know. The *Codex Paris* is small–it contains just eleven pages, and measures 1.45 meters by 22 centimeters wide. But it was found, and it survived.

Consider also the career of the *Codex Dresden.* The name "Dresden" is affixed to this codex because it came into the possession of the King of Saxony, whose library was located in the German city of Dresden. But we do not know how it got there. We have no record of how it was removed from the Yucatan Peninsula in Mexico, how it found its way to Europe, and exactly how the royal family of Saxony acquired it. Perhaps it was smuggled out of New Spain by an enterprising priest, who knew that a fair price could be had for such antiquities in Europe. This may be so; but we do not know with certainty. We do know that an unknown collector sold it to the rector of the king's library, Johann Christian Goetze, in 1739.

Goetze knew what he had. He had spent his life around rare books and manuscripts, and knew gold when he saw it. When he recorded the codex in the royal archives, under book no. 300, he wrote, "An extremely valuable Mexican books with hieroglyphic figures." Goetze was so impressed with the manuscript that in 1774, when he published his *Peculiarities of the Library of Dresden*, he gave the codex honorary mention:

> [It is] a Mexican book with unknown characters and hieroglyphic figures written on both sides and painted in various colors…Our Royal Library has an advantage over others: that of possessing such a treasure…which was found some years ago in a private library in Vienna; it was acquired easily and without cost because it was something unknown…

The book, a painted manuscript of 39 pages, was publicly displayed in 1834. According to the estimates of modern scholarship, the codex was composed sometime between the twelfth and fourteenth centuries A.D. Its subject matter is religious: it contains astronomical observations, describes various ceremonies, and illustrates scenes from the mythology of the god Itzamna. The first serious study of the codex was undertaken by the librarian Ernest Forstemann (1822-1906). Forstemann was a true scholar. Remarkably, he was a specialist in the German language, and had no background in Mexican antiquities. Yet his enthusiasm, diligence, and creative thinking enabled him to make insights into the codex that made his lack of formal training irrelevant. He published the first copy of the codex in 1880, although the Italian engraver Agostino Aglio had been the first to produce a hand-drawn facsimile in 1826. Forstemann knew how languages worked, and he brought his knowledge of German to bear on his task. Using deductive logic, he was able to decipher many of the numeric signs appearing in the codex (1, 20, 360, 7200, etc.).

Anyone who thinks that amateur scholars cannot make significant contributions to a field need only look at this history of the Maya codices. About 50 years after Forstemann made his discoveries, another amateur named John Teeple (a chemical engineer by trade) began to study the Codex Dresden in his spare time. His work resulted in more contributions to the field. After him came other amateur scholars, Martin Meinshausen and Paul Schellhaus, who did additional work.

The *Codex Dresden* again escaped oblivion by the skin of its teeth during the Second World War. During the war it had been housed in the wine cellar of the Japanese Palace in Dresden, along with other artistic treasures. When the city of Dresden was targeted by Allied firebombing in 1945, countless objects of historical value were lost forever. By some miracle of fate–similar to the *Codex Paris*'s discovery in a wastebasket–the book survived the firestorm intact. But it was nearly ruined when water seeped into the wine cellar in the recovery efforts after the attack. The codex was saved by diligent rescuers, and was secreted away for safe-keeping during the occupation period. It is now kept by the Dresden Museum. There it lies in repose to this day, having cheated both time and Fate.

17. What Were A Medieval Serf's Feudal Obligations?

Sometimes I think historians have exaggerated the misery of the medieval serf in Europe. I would not want to exchange my lot for his, of course, but it is a useful exercise to examine in detail just what his feudal obligations were. There is no strict definition of "feudalism," as it varied in time and place; but it found its fullest expression in medieval France. To understand why it developed, we must appreciate the profound insecurity and chaos that most of Europe was plunged into after the fall of the western Roman Empire. At that time, security and peace mattered more to the common man than his freedom; and the system worked well considering the environment of the times.

A serf had the right to work the lands of his lord, and in return he was given protection and tenancy. According to historian Will Durant's *The Age of Faith*, these were the basic feudal obligations:

1. Three annual monetary taxes: (a) a small head tax payable through the baron; (b) a nominal rent; and (c) an additional nominal tax imposed by the owner of the land on the serf on an annual basis.
2. A 1/10 share of the serf's crops or livestock, payable to the lord or baron.
3. A period of conscription for unpaid labor (called the *corvee* in French) that would be used to conduct public works projects.
4. The serf had to prepare his food on his lord's mill, press, oven, or house, and pay a small fee for such use.
5. The serf had to pay a small fee for the right to hunt or fish on the lord's lands.
6. Any legal actions the serf undertook had to take place in the "baronial court," or the courts controlled by the baron.
7. If war was declared, the serf had to serve alongside his lord.
8. If the baron was captured in war, the serf was expected to help raise the ransom for his release (ransoming of noble prisoners was a common occurrence in the medieval period).
9. If the baron's son was knighted, the serf had to contribute to a collective gift to the son.
10. Any goods that the serf sold at a market were taxable, with the small sales tax being paid to the baron.
11. The serf could not sell his own beer or wine until his lord had exercised his own right of first refusal.
12. The serf was usually expected to buy a certain amount of the lord's products (usually wine) each year.
13. If a serf's son entered the Church or left the manor, the serf had to pay a fine as compensation for the loss of one of the lord's men.

14. The serf would also have to pay a tax to the lord if one of his family married someone outside the manor.

15. On paper at least, there is evidence of a *ius primae noctis*, or the right of the first night, whereby the lord had the right to deflower a serf's new bride on the event of their wedding. We do not know how often this custom was actually enforced; in practice, a serf could "purchase" the right from the lord by paying a small fee, and this is probably how such things were handled in practice.

16. If the serf died childless, his property rights passed back to the lord, rather than to any other family members. Sometimes the lord was entitled, as a form of inheritance tax, to take one of the serf's domesticated animals as payment.

These were the basic feudal obligations owed by a serf to his baron, according to Durant. If the financial burden seems crushing, we must remember that in practice, each of the fees described were small. People still had to work, to eat, and to live their lives. Feudalism would not have lasted as long as it did had it been unreasonably burdensome. We should remember that one person, or one family, never paid all of these dues. In addition, inflation was not a problem in those days; these dues remained the same for a very long time, sometimes for centuries. Lords were also known to waive or overlook many fees that they were due, simply to preserve manorial tranquility. As Durant says:

> Thc [fcudal] ducs cxactcd of [thc scrf] wcrc largcly in lieu of a money rent to the owner, and taxes to the community, to maintain public services and public works; probably they bore a smaller proportion to his income than our federal, state, county, and school taxes bear to our income today. The average peasant of the twelfth century was as least as well off as some sharecroppers in modern states, and better off than a Roman *proletaire* in Augustus's reign.

This has the ring of truth. We like to think, in our modern era, that our lives are light-years ahead in improvement on the lives of our forefathers in past centuries. And in general this is so: no serious person can argue that the lot of the medieval serf is to be preferred to the lot of the average man in the United States of the

21st century. My purpose here is not to argue that the medieval serf's life was an ideal one. And yet there is still some lesson to be learned here. Does it not often seem true that the more "labor-saving" devices we invent, the harder we work? Does it not seem true that technology and gadgets look more like trade-offs, rather than panaceas?

The reader will have to reflect on these matters for himself. It may be disconcerting for readers to discover, when he adds up all his federal, state, and local taxes, that they may actually be paying more (on a percentage basis) than the serf of medieval times. Or he may be startled to find out that, when the hours are tallied up, he actually works longer and harder than any of his predecessors in recorded history. This knowledge, of course, might prompt uncomfortable questions. Perhaps the most we can say is that we should cultivate a healthy respect for the past. We should learn to be wary of simple answers, stereotypes, and easy solutions. Ancient and medieval man was not a fool; his social structures developed for specific reasons, and they served him well considering the challenges he was facing. One of the first lessons of history is that we should check our arrogance at the door; a healthy dose of humility does wonders for our understanding of the past.

18. How Benito Mussolini Took Power

Stalin biographer Stephen Kotkin spends several pages of his book discussing the lessons to be learned from Mussolini's seizure of power in Italy in the early 1920s. It was something that happened gradually, in stages, when institutions that should have been able to bring him to heel did nothing, either due to their own lack of resolution or tacit support of his power grab. Italy after the First World War was, like many European countries, rife with instability and factionalism. Mussolini's "fascist" party in 1922 had collected only 35 out of 500 seats in Italy's Chamber of Deputies; despite this apparent lack of popular support he was still asking to be appointed prime minister. He threatened to march on Rome himself with his private militia (*squadristi*) and take power with or without official permission. He had some support from the established institutions of the day: the monarchy, the army, the church, and big business.

In the wake of the Bolshevist radicalism that was threatening Europe, the establishment was looking for a charismatic figure who might be able to restore order and bring the county some measure of stability.

In the end, these temptations proved too attractive to resist. King Vittorio Emanuele III asked Mussolini to become prime minister. He thought that by making him part of a coalition, he would be able to restrain the worst of Mussolini's excesses. The so-called "March on Rome" took place only *after* he had been appointed prime minister. Arriving in Rome by train–not marching along with his men–Mussolini then had his 20,000 blackshirts parade around the city like conquerors. This was the origin of the myth of his "seizure" of power: but there was no seizure. The myth was another of *Il Duce*'s shabby lies, designed to glorify himself and his movement; in fact, he was appointed by the existing powers, who thought they could use him for their own ends. In this they were only partially correct.

Besides being favored by the powerful institutions of the country, Mussolini was also aided at critical junctures by the ineptitude of his political opponents. In the elections of April 1924, Mussolini's party won 374 seats out of 535; this amounted to 66.3% of the popular vote. There then occurred an event that proved to be of great advantage to him. Giacomo Matteotti, a law professor at Bologna and the son of wealthy family from the Veneto, publicly denounced the fascists in strident terms, calling the vote a fraud and the result of intimidation and *squadristi* violence. With this step, he had signed his death warrant. He was abducted eleven days later, bundled into the boot of a car, and stabbed repeatedly; his body was found two months later, dumped on the outskirts of Rome.

It was never established whether Mussolini was involved or knew anything about the plot beforehand. He was certainly not above using violence, or encouraging its use, against political opponents; but such a reckless step probably was taken without his knowledge or approval. Despite this, he was able to use the crisis that the murder generated to consolidate his hold on power. Antifascist demonstrations escalated in the streets, general strikes were declared, and it seems that Mussolini would have to resign. But the king did not call for him to step down. His political opponents then committed a grievous error: they left the field of political conflict and walked out of the Chamber of Deputies. Trying to imitate the ancient Roman plebian practice of going to the Aventine Hill to protest measures taken by the nobility, the anti-fascist deputies probably thought that by walking out of the chamber they could pressure Mussolini to resign. In this they were sorely mistaken. The situation was getting more and more dangerous by the hour, until finally Mussolini (on January 3, 1925) threw down the gauntlet. In a dramatic speech, he "assumed responsibility" (whatever that meant) for the crisis and dared those present to remove him or indict him.

Yet nothing happened. By exposing his opponents as all talk and no action, he successfully called their bluff. He also refused to permit the deputies who had boycotted the session to return to the Chamber. By the middle of January, it was clear he had won; all political parties except the fascists were outlawed and Italy was on its way to becoming a dictatorship. This was how he consolidated his hold on power. In retrospect we can see how this happened: (1) the established institutions of the country (monarchy, church, army, and big business) more or less supported Mussolini and thought he was preferable to the communist alternatives; and (2) at the critical moment, his opponents failed to muster the requisite will to call his bluff. The institutions that should have acted as checks and balances on his power failed. And failed miserably.

Readers will draw their own conclusions and lessons from this narrative of events. We may note also that this same "walking out" mistake was made by the Soviet Union in the early 1950s, when they thought that by boycotting the United Nations sessions on Korea, they could somehow prevent US military intervention in that country. This also turned out to be a delusion; for what the Americans did was simply to take advantage of the Soviet absence to vote for intervention in Korea under the flag of the United Nations. On the political scene today, it is clear that some power elites believe that they can use unscrupulous, amoral demagogues for their own ends. They know very well that such demagogues are venal, lacking in restraint, and totally unsuited for office. Yet they do not care; they believe they can use the arrogance and stupidity of the demagogue for their own selfish ends, and for the ends of those who support them. In this they are mistaken. By putting partisan, factional considerations ahead of the national interest, they reveal themselves to be men without moral courage. They will find out, all too soon, just how serious was the mistake they have made. Institutions in a democratic republic cannot long survive a coordinated attack from those who inhabit them. When long periods of wealth, affluence, and ease condition a population for moral corruption, the citizenry is unable to see what is right before its eyes. It is unable or unwilling to call corruption and evil by their true names. It mistakes stupidity and arrogance for strength and tenacity; it more wishes to be entertained than to be informed and provided for; and it uses the nascent dictator as the secret mouthpiece of its dreams and malicious fantasies.

And it is the public that will suffer, just as it was the Italian people of the 1940s who suffered for the venality and crimes of their leaders. Mussolini was a con artist, a fraud, and a liar, but he would never have taken power had not the powerful elites in Italy looked the other way and collaborated with him for their own selfish purposes. Political factionalism and its associated moral cowardice, plutocratic control of economic life, the concentration of wealth in the hands of too few, and public ignorance combine to produce one outcome: the slide into authoritarianism. When in doubt, one should never leave the playing field until the last hand has been dealt, and the final card played.

19. The Tripod's Prophecy, And The Death Of The Emperor Valens

On the subject of prophecies, men are accustomed to take differing viewpoints. Some say that the predictions of oracles and diviners mean nothing at all, and should be counted as so much nonsense: any "true" predictions they make are solely the result of blind coincidence. Others say that they have independent value as evidence of our imaginative capacity; and that prophecies are, more or less, records of our psychological projections and subconscious desires. Still others believe that they should be seen more as predictions of what *might* happen, rather than statements of what *will* happen. As in so many other things, it will be the responsibility of each reader to decide for himself. But it seems to me that we should at least acknowledge that such practices have been around for millennia, and that they are found across the globe within nearly every society and culture.

The following story is found in the pages of the late Roman historian Ammianus Marcellinus, who is generally seen as a reliable and sober guide. In the year 371 A.D. the emperor Valens found himself the object of plots and assassination attempts. A notary (*notarius*) named Theodorus enlisted a band of conspirators to try to depose the mercurial Valens. The plan was not successful. Theodorus and his associates were denounced in the city of Antioch, convicted of treason, and executed.

Valens was a "crude man" (*subrusticus homo*), but he knew how to hold on to power. He used the conspiracy as an excuse to round up as many imagined enemies as possible, and then try them on the flimsiest pretexts. In this he was aided by many sycophants, of the usual type that hover around men of power and influence. According to the historian, Valens had two major faults that made him especially susceptible to the manipulations of people around him: first, he was hot-headed and prone to unrestrained anger; second, he was not interested in making an effort to distinguish someone who was truly guilty from someone who was innocent. The inevitable result of these faults was that many innocent people were sent to the executioner for no other reason than falling afoul of Valens's temporary mood. And once this happened, it was nearly impossible for him to change his mind.

To make himself look good, he would sometimes make a big show of exercising "clemency," but this usually was itself a terrible punishment. He would drive a man into exile and confiscate his property, as if he was doing him a favor by not putting him to death. And as Ammianus says (XXIX.1.22), "Here we must take notice of the old adage, that no sentence is more cruel than that one which, while appearing to be lenient, is more severe." (*Unde animadversum est recte hoc definitum, nullam esse crudeliorem sententiam ea, quae est–cum parcere videtur–asperior*).

So this was the state of affairs. At last hearings were held to determine the guilt of Theodorus himself. Two witnesses, named Patricius and Hilarius, were summoned to provide testimony before the court. They said that they had learned information about the conspiracy through the use of a "Delphic tripod," a device for the making and interpretations of prophecies. The two men described (XXIX.1.29) how they made the tripod and then consecrated it according to ancient rituals. It had a large metal disc attached to its apex, and around its outer rim were inscribed the twenty-four letters of the Greek alphabet.

The device was placed on a metallic table, a linen thread was attached to the tripod, and to this thread was tied a ring as a weight.

Apparently certain incantations were recited, the ring would sway this way and that, and would at some point identify certain letters on the disc.

They then posed the question, "Who will succeed the emperor Valens?" The pendulum was then set to do its work. Eventually, the suspended ring indicated these four Greek letters: Θ E O Δ. Transcribed in the Roman alphabet, they stand for the sound *Theod.* Someone present said that the result proved that the conspirator Theodorus was guilty (in fact Theodorus had known nothing about this prophecy). When Hilarius had explained all of this to the judges present, they asked him what other information he had gleaned during the casting of the tripod's oracle. Hilarius nervously recited several verses to the judges, the last line of which ran thus:

While Ares, god of war, rages on the plain of Minas.

What was the meaning of these lines? Ares, the reader will recall, is the name of the Greek god of war, the Hellenic counterpart to the Mars of the Romans. But what was the *plain of Minas*? The soothsayers told the judges that the tripod had in fact foretold the death of the emperor Valens. On hearing this, the judges ordered the two soothsayers to be led off to the torture chamber. This chapter of the story would end here, as Valens was successful in wiping out those who had conspired against him. Or so it seemed. Some years later, in August 378, Valens was involved in one of the most catastrophic defeats the Romans ever suffered on the field of battle. Near the city of Adrianople, Valens ignored the advice of his generals who counseled him not to give battle to the Goths. But Valens insisted, confident of an easy victory that he wanted to have to his credit; and the Goths, making expert use of terrain and maneuver, surrounded and cut to pieces the Roman infantry. According to Ammianus, Valens's body was never recovered from the field; he died with his troops and may have been stripped of his identifying armor or clothing by the victorious Goths.

Now at this point we should recall the prophecy given seven years before by the hapless duo Patricius and Hilarius. Valens had been told of it, and had lived in fear of what it might mean. He thought that the "Minas" in the prophecy referred to a city in Ionia, near the city of Erythrae, since the word *Minas* is found in Homer (*Odyssey* III.172). For this reason, Ammianus says, Valens always "trembled" at the thought of getting into a conflict on the Asiatic mainland (XXXI.14.8). But the prophecy was not to be avoided. Valens was succeeded by Theodosius I, instead of the conspirator Theodorus; but both of them had names whose first four letters were as the prophecy foretold.

But this was not all. After the battle of Adrianople, which took place on a plain, survivors walked the terrain to bury the dead and salvage what they could. The historian tells us that, near the place where Valens was thought to have been slain with his troops, a small stone marker or monument was found. On this marker was attached a stone tablet inscribed in Greek. *The inscription stated that beneath the monument was buried a man named Minas.* This discovery was seen by some as fulfilling the last verse produced by the prophecy of the tripod, quoted above, and given seven years earlier before the judges.

20. How Venice Solved Its Political Corruption Problem

Corruption is like a virus, or a noxious weed. If you turn your back on it for even an instant, you will find it has found creative ways to grow and spread. Like any human activity, it can never be completely eradicated; but it can certainly be tamed and curbed, and prevented from interfering with the purposes of government. But it takes leadership and determination, and a willingness to take certain risks. And if anyone thinks that one man can make no difference in such matters, he need only study the example of Antonio Tron.

Let us go back to the Republic of Venice in 1491. According to historian Pietro Bembo in his *History of Venice*, electoral corruption had forced politics in the city to a crisis point. The procedure for electing magistrates (which in those days had civil as well as judicial responsibilities) had become thoroughly compromised. The reason for this was that the system for electing them did not provide electors with the privacy they needed to be truly neutral. To understand why this was so, we must explain the Venetian election process at that time. The electors (citizens of the republic) were brought into a hall and made to sit on wooden benches. Two separate wooden boxes, each a foot high, were then brought in; one box was green, and the other was white. The boxes were so constructed that they were wide at the top and narrow in the middle; this allowed someone to put his hand in the box, but only permitted one ballot to get to the bottom of the box. The bottom of each box was removable when the time came for counting votes. Each voter could cast his ballot as he pleased, by dropping the ballot in one box or another.

But these "ballots" were not papers at all; they were small cloth balls about the size of a walnut. The cloth balls were made to be loose and soft, so that people could not clearly hear it drop into one box or another, in order to preserve the voter's confidentiality. According to Venetian voting laws, each voter had to insert both of his hands into a box, and have in one of his closed fists the cloth ball. Then he would drop the ball into one box or another, and those around him would not be able to tell which box received the ballot. Balls that fell in the white box were "for" a candidate, and those in the green box were "against."

The system may sound secure and foolproof, but this was not the case. As always happens, the instincts of man found a way to express themselves in corrupt practices. Instead of implementing the system as it was designed, some powerful or influential electors would make a big show of openly casting a ball into the white box, and would then ask their friends to do the same. Peer pressure took hold, and no one would want to look bad in front of his colleagues. So they would fall in line and vote for someone or something that they did not believe in, just to avoid the condemnation of their peers. This was one of the reasons why the upper tiers of Venetian leadership became filled with mediocrities. The good men were afraid to run for office, and the bad ones flocked to politics. We see the same phenomenon today in our own political system.

Antonio Tron–about whom Pietro Bembo says disappointingly little–produced an innovation that helped solve this problem. His system was so successful, we are told, that it remained in use in Venice until the 1780s. Tron decided to invent a consolidated and improved voting machine; he also reformed the method by which voting took place. Instead of two separate boxes, he had them attached to each other, side-by-side, in one apparatus. Only one opening was made for the urns, and it was hidden behind a tube about the width of half a palm (*tubum prominentem circumduxit semi palmae spatio,* described in I.60). The idea was that a voter could put his hand into this tube and then direct hand towards either box, without anyone knowing which box he was aiming for.

Another of Tron's innovations was to make it easier to vote "no" for a candidate. The "no" box was made close to the tube of entry, so that someone who wanted to vote against someone could secretly drop his ball in the close cavity as his hand moved down into the tube. He could pretend to be extending his arm inside to reach the "yes" box, while actually he might have already dropped his ball in the "no" cavity. The idea was that voters could not pretend to do one thing (i.e., vote "yes" for a candidate), and secretly do another (i.e., reject him) without any fear of being detected.

This was the sophisticated innovation in voting procedure that Tron developed for use in Venice's Great Council, the Senate, and in the Council of Ten. According to Bembo, things began to improve immediately upon adoption of this new system, as voters could now feel free to cast their ballots without running afoul of partisan hacks or bigwigs. For especially serious matters, such as capital cases and important trials, a third voting urn was used in addition to the device just described. This was to be used if someone was undecided; this urn was kept separate from the other two urns.

This was not all. The Venetian Council of Ten did not just make improvements in voting machines and procedures. They sent a very clear message to the public that corruption, demagoguery, and insider dealings would not be tolerated. How this happened, we will now relate. An influential office-holder (one of the *Quarantia* for capital crimes) named Gabriel Bon, together with a man named Francesco Falier, proposed a new law whereby every citizen over forty years of age in dire financial condition would receive a public gift of one pound of gold. Citizens between twenty-five and forty who were facing financial hardship would receive, they proposed, a half of a pound of gold. The supposed purpose of the law was to take care of citizens who were in need.

So Bon and Falier proposed their law to the Senate and to the Great Council. But the Venetian senators were not fools. They could see that this law was little more than a disguised attempt by two ambitious politicians to curry favor with the masses by passing out public money. Bon and Falier thought that they might be able to win higher offices in the future if they could buy the love of the citizenry with gold from the treasury. The Senate sent the two politicians to see the Venetian doge, who warned them sternly to drop the proposal. The two men pretended to agree, but secretly made efforts to put certain provisions of the law into effect.

Now when the Council of Ten found out about this, they had Bon and Falier arrested and jailed. They were then banished to the island of Cyprus (a Venetian commercial possession), and were told that they would face the death penalty should they ever attempt to leave the city of Nicosia on the island. Some of Bon and Falier's associates were also sent into exile in Crete, and not permitted to leave the town of Rethymno. This severe sentence was meant to send a message: demagoguery, insider dealings, and corruption would no longer be tolerated. Determined and vigorous leadership, new procedures, and new ways of thinking can be very effective in limiting political corruption. But unless the will to solve the problem exists, little or nothing can be achieved.

21. The Roman Ceremony Of Deification

We read about how certain Roman emperors were "deified" after their deaths. Unfortunately it is not easy to learn the details about how this process was actually undertaken. I was fortunate to come across a rare description of how the deification (*deificatio*) ceremony took place in the humanist Biondo Flavio's *Roma Triumphans* (*Rome in Triumph*). This Renaissance Latin work, published in 1459, contains a wealth of information on Roman religion and ceremonies, compiled from a painstaking review of the Latin sources available to him.

The use of the word *deification* perhaps is the source of some confusion. The Romans, of course, did not literally believe that their departed leaders were made into gods. Rather, deification was a formal ceremony reserved as a mark of the highest respect that the religious and civil authorities could confer on an emperor; in practice, it was very much like the modern Roman Catholic Church's canonization of saints as a way to honor those who have rendered distinguished services. The Roman Church inherited many of the old imperial traditions before putting its own distinctive stamp on them. I do not mean that the specific procedure for deification and canonization was similar; I mean that the *purpose and significance* of deification was *roughly analogous* to the Church's honor of canonization. Flavio tells us:

> I do not doubt that it is commonly known–so that I do not particularly need to write about it–and generally understood that most of the Roman emperors

> were deified. But how this was actually done, and the specific procedure employed, I have not yet discovered in the extant Latin authors [*Sed quo id fieret modo, quis adhiberetur in re ordo, apud Latinos nondum invenimus*]. Recently, Marcus Barbo (the distinguished bishop of Treviso and a Venetian of patrician family) delivered to me a gift from my colleague Ognibene (from Brendola, near Vicenza), a man learned in Greek and Latin letters; this gift was an appropriate one for men nourished on the fine literary arts, and was provided to *Rome in Triumph* as it was being prepared. This was a written description–translated from the Greek historian Herodian–of the deification of the Roman emperor Severus. [II.42]

We should note that the emperor Severus (i.e., Septimius Severus) died in February 211. Flavio was able to acquire a description of how deification actually took place, but he had to rely on account of a Greek author. This kind of information in his day was not generally available, since many Greek works had not yet been translated into Latin or other European languages. What were the specifics of the process? First, there was a period of public mourning and celebration. The dead emperor's body was laid to rest in the manner befitting a monarch. A waxen image of the deceased was then crafted. This image was put on display in the palace, atop a large ivory couch that was draped with golden coverings. Mourning senators would sit on one side of the couch dressed in black, and on the other side sat distinguished or notable women dressed simply in white. The mourners engaged in the usual contemplations and paying of respects that one would expect to see at a state funeral. This stage of the proceedings lasted for about seven days. During this time, doctors would approach the couch and pretend to "inspect" the wax figure, and ceremoniously state that the emperor's end was near.

After the waxen image was pronounced "dead," a selected group of youths (prominent men in the senatorial and equestrian orders) would pick up the bier and carry it through the Via Sacra (Sacred Way) and then display it on the Roman Forum. The bier was laid down at a spot where there were stairs on both sides of it:

on one side was a chorus of children, and on the other side a chorus of women. Songs and eulogies were sung in honor of the deceased.

The bier was then transported to the Field of Mars to a wooden structure specifically built to house the bier. Its outside was decorated with richly adorned tapestries, cloths, and paintings; inside it was filled with firewood. This small hut had several levels to it, and on its peak was placed an eagle, apparently in some sort of cage or secured at the apex. Herodian describes the shape of this "funeral pyre" as very much like a lighthouse (*phari*). The emperor's bier was carried up to the second story of the structure, and placed there along with all sorts of spices, fruits, and aromatic plants. Most of these offerings were sent as marks of tribute or respect from different parts of the empire. At this point, the equestrian order staged a large cavalry display outside the structure, while chanting various hymns and songs. Chariots also circumambulated the structure, driven by men dressed in red garments and wearing masks of famous generals and emperors of Roman history.

Once these ceremonies have been completed, the emperor's successor would be given the honor of lighting the structure on fire. Once the fire begins to blaze, the eagle perched at the apex is released (probably by a rope connected to a cage). The flight of the eagle away from the burning funeral pyre was meant to convey the journey of the dead emperor's soul to heaven, where it would reside permanently with the pantheon of heroes. This is how the rite of deification is described by Biondo Flavio, who took it from the Greek historian Herodian. Ceremonies such as this perform vital functions: they affirm the community's faith in the continuity of leadership; they honor the deeds of those who rendered service to the state; and they help soothe the distress of a community stricken with grief at the loss of a capable leader.

22. The Fall Of Singapore: The Price Of Inept Leadership

It is a pleasant thing to recall our victories. Far less pleasant is to be reminded of our defeats. And yet there is something sublime in the recounting of a disaster; provided, of course, one does not have to be on the spot at the time of its unfolding. Catastrophes provide more fertile material for instruction than do successes; and the conscientious historian should make a strenuous effort to discover why they unfolded as they did. The capture of Singapore in

February 1942 by the Japanese Army remains the most terrible defeat of British arms in history. In that month around 130,000 British Commonwealth soldiers were surrendered to a Japanese force of about 35,000 commanded by Gen. Tomoyuki Yamashita. The outlines of the story are familiar to students of military history. Is there anything to be gained from recounting the tale yet another time? I believe the answer is yes. As historical memory slips further and further from the consciousness of the modern Westerner, it is absolutely essential for us to be reminded of the dear cost of complacency, unpreparedness, and ineptitude. For if any man is ever in need of a reminder of the price of complacency, he need only look at what happened in Singapore between December 1941 and February 1942.

By the fall of 1941, it had become clear that something was going to happen in East Asia. No one on the Allied side really knew precisely, of course; but it was clear that the Japanese Empire was gearing up for something big. The island of Singapore, situated at the foot of the Malay peninsula, was the most heavily fortified outpost of the British Empire in East Asia. Much has been made of the fact that Singapore's guns were directed out to sea and not back towards the peninsula; yet this was only one of many problems with the island's planned defense. Once the clouds of war began to gather, British military planners focused on defending the peninsula on the northern border with Thailand. Nominally neutral, Thailand was actually sympathetic to Japan and hosted some of its air bases.

It is very easy for an observer, writing many decades after the fact, to second-guess the decisions of others. More instructive is it for us to try to understand why such planners thought the way they did. Before December 1941, the British and the Americans entirely discounted the fighting capabilities of the Japanese Army. Although the evidence of Japanese competence was present before their eyes–from its long campaigns in China–the lesson did not take. No one in the West wanted to hear it, and no one was willing to listen. But there were other problems with the British position in Singapore, problems that went even deeper. This was a garrison army, an army that had little field experience and was led by mediocre commanders at best.

Commonwealth forces were composed of British, Indian, and Australian troops; these were good men, but they lacked a commander with the kind of aggressiveness and resourcefulness that the situation called for. They were not ready for the cyclone that was about to hit them; and when it did, they were not psychologically prepared to adapt to the situation. Worse still, the Singapore garrison could count on little direct help from London; Churchill had all he could do just to cope with Germany. Thus the stage was set for a calamity of unprecedented magnitude. On December 6, 1941, a Japanese convoy carrying Yamashita's 25th Army was identified in the Gulf of Siam. Once the Japanese hit the Americans at Pearl Harbor in Hawaii, all pretenses were dropped, and the gloves finally came off for all concerned. On December 8, Japanese infantry landed in northern Malaya. The British expected that they would be able to keep the Japanese bottled up in northern Malaya, but this did not happen. The speed and ferocity of Yamashita's advance threw the British into disarray; the general assumption had been that an Asian army would not be capable of outfighting a Western force. And in all fairness, it was an assumption held not just by the British, but by the Dutch, the Americans (who failed miserably in defending the Philippines), and the French (who ceded Indochina with barely a shot). The truth was that no one really knew how good the Japanese were. Within days after Pearl Harbor, they were all over East Asia. They were tough, they were ruthless, and they played for keeps.

Within days, Yamashita had an army of over 26,000 men ashore in Malaya, a feat that no Western army could have matched at the time. He had some artillery and tanks, and some planes based in Thailand, but it was not as much as Allied apologists would have liked to believe. In short order, the British ships *Prince of Wales* and *Repulse* were sent to the bottom by the Japanese. British aviation in Singapore proved to be just as outmatched as the infantry: the Japanese made short work of the Royal Air Force, and soon enjoyed uncontested control of the skies.

Yamashita steadily worked his way down the peninsula to the prize. Using night fighting infiltration tactics, the Japanese infantry hammered and sliced through its enemy; they were undersupplied and underequipped by Western standards, but they smelled victory and were filled with an iron determination to see the campaign through to the end. On the small unit level, the British were not fighting effectively; communications were bad, unit cohesion was even worse, and morale was approaching rock bottom. Here we must acknowledge a complete lack of imagination on the part of the British commander, Lt. Gen. Arthur Percival. He possessed vast numerical superiority, but was entirely ignorant of this fact; he was also unaware that Yamashita's army was stretched very thin, and was running short on all kinds of logistics and ammunition.

Had he ordered a breakout from Singapore to land behind the Japanese lines in Malaya, he might have changed the entire dynamic of the battle. Perhaps an innovative landing similar to the one made at Inchon in the Korean War in 1950 might have changed the outcome, or at least made it less humiliating. Although resources were scarce, an imaginative commander can always find ways of making things happen. But this did not happen. Instead, Percival ordered a withdrawal from the Malay Peninsula in late January 1942 to Singapore itself. In less than two months, Yamashita's men had moved over 500 miles on land, fighting all the way. The end was approaching fast. On the night of February 8, the Japanese came for Singapore itself. Something like a panic began to take hold of the Commonwealth forces; in the face of poor leadership, the man in the foxhole had all he could do to stay alive and keep fighting. The Australians (especially the 27th Brigade) put up a stout resistance in the face of relentless Japanese attacks, but were unable to hold the line; they were flung back by forces commanded by Lt. Gen. Takumo Nishimura and tried to regroup near the River Jurong in the middle of the island.

The men were bitter, frustrated, and uncomprehending as to why no one was coming up with creative solutions to the crisis. In retrospect, we must point out the utter failure of leadership on the part of Percival. He was too quick to cede ground to his enemy, he failed to deploy his forces effectively, and–it must be said–he lacked that killer instinct required to bring out the kind of elemental savagery needed to win battles.

In London, Churchill watched the situation unfold with mounting despair. It is difficult not to feel a measure of sympathy for him, forced to watch from the other side of the globe as the keystone of his position in Asia evaporated in the heat of the rising sun. But Churchill could be ruthless, too, and he made his intentions very clear to Percival: there would be no surrender. Officers and men were to fight to the last bullet. For some reason, these orders were not obeyed. As the Japanese began to bombard the city from the air, Percival chose to throw in the towel, and it was all over. On February 15, he met with Yamashita to parley for a surrender. The Japanese asked for unconditional surrender, and they got it; thus did the Singapore command condemn nearly 130,000 men to three years of brutal, degrading captivity in Japanese hell-holes, where many of them would be starved or worked to death. They would have been better off dying in a stand-up fight to the death, as Churchill had ordered.

It was the single greatest defeat of British arms in history. In London, Churchill was thrown into a deep depression. The old man tried to put a resolute face on the battle, but its reality could not be concealed. Privately, he was justifiably angered that his commanders had let him down. "They gave up too easily," he confided to an associate at the time. "They should have done a better job." This was an understatement, to say the least. But what had gone wrong? There were many things. The Commonwealth commanders had been insufficiently supported and supplied. They had completely underestimated their enemy. They had grown lax from staying in garrison for too long. And, quite simply, they had been outclassed and outfought by the Japanese.

The fall of Singapore in 1942 stands for the proposition that leadership in a crisis is everything; and Percival had simply not been up to the task. He might have gone down in defeat while fighting to break out, but he might just as well have succeeded. The Japanese were stretched very thin, and the right hammer-blow could have turned the battle into a long siege. If this had happened, they might have been able to hold out until the Americans could bring their full economic might to bear in the war. Or maybe not; we will never know.

Despite the magnitude of the disaster, the British were able to redeem their honor a few years later during General William Slim's brilliant campaigns in Burma. Meeting the Japanese on equal terms, Slim ground them down in an adroit series of interconnected campaigns that have not received the attention they deserved from military historians. Slim proved that there was nothing inherently superior about the Japanese, and nothing inherently inferior about the Commonwealth forces; it was simply a matter of vigorous leadership, confidence, and training. When all is said and done, the responsibility for the fall of Singapore in 1942 is to be found in the dismal failure of Commonwealth military leadership.

The lesson of Singapore is one that should be–indeed, must be–reflected on today. The West has enjoyed a long period of comfortable military superiority over its adversaries. It is used to control of the skies, control of the seas, and shaping the course of conflicts in ways that suit its purposes. Those advantages will not be enjoyed in future conflicts. A long period of relative peace has caused many to neglect, or forget entirely, the imperatives of preparedness, leadership, and the masculine virtues. We will pay a high price in the future if this forgetfulness and neglect is allowed to become a permanent fixture of our consciousness.

23. Military Adventurism Brings Disaster

In the year 1260, Tuscany was engulfed in war. The cities of Florence and Siena were engaged in mutual hostilities. About twenty-five miles from Siena was located the small town of Montalcino, which happened to be a friend and ally of Florence. The Sienese hoped that by staging an attack on Montalcino they might be able to compel the Florentines to send an expedition for its relief–an expedition that, they hoped, they could lure into a trap. To this end, the Sienese government publicly announced their intention to move against Montalcino, and watched to see what the Florentine response would be. The municipal government of Florence was not of one mind on how to deal with the crisis. There were some who advocated for prompt action to relieve their ally; others, men with military experience, counseled against a rash intervention and pointed out that Florentine forces would be drawn through the countryside at the whim of their enemy. They said that it would be imprudent and dangerous to be compelled to fight at a time and place that was not of their own choosing. But as often happens in such situations, the voices of rashness and ignorance were loudest. They berated the Florentine magistrates for their supposed inaction and excessive caution. The humanist Leonardo Bruni, in his Latin *History of the Florentine People*, explains further:

> The Florentine magistrates were, conversely, leaning towards sending an expedition. They were of such a mind due to their lust for glory and false hopes of [the enemy's] betrayal. Exiles had secretly sent some men under false pretenses during the deliberations; these men came to Florence in the greatest secrecy. [II.36].

These agents told the Florentines that the people of Siena were sick of war, and had no appetite for it, but that they were being led by strongman named Provinciano di Salvano who insisted on continuing the fighting. However, the agents dropped hints that if the Florentines were to send an expedition to Montalcino, an uprising would take place in Siena, di Salvano would be deposed, and the war could be concluded. Everything would turn out well; the outcomes could indeed be managed and controlled. This is what they told the magistrates of Florence. Leonardo Bruni tells us that some of the inexperienced magistrates, men who knew nothing of war, were enthusiastic to hear these kinds of statements. These men Bruni scornfully describes as

> Homines plebeios ac bellicarum artium ignaros, quales plerumque in magistratu esse solent.

In other words, "plebian types, and ignorant of the arts of war, the types that tend to proliferate in civil councils." They would not listen to the voices that advocated caution and restraint, but instead pushed for an immediate expedition to help their supposedly beleaguered allies in Montalcino. But there were some men in the city with military experience, and sensed that Florence was being baited into a trap. A man named Tegghiaio d'Aldobrando Adimari, who Bruni describes as a *vir disertus et magnae per id tempus auctoritatis* ("a well-spoken man of considerable authority at the time"), was chosen to make a direct appeal for caution to the Florentine magistrates. Tegghiaio began his speech with an invocation to patriotism seasoned by realism and restraint. Experts, he said, were unreliable because they saw everything except the larger picture:

> No one was ever so knowledgeable about something, such that what he did know exceeded what he did not know. [*Nemo autem usque adeo gnarus rerum umquam fuit, quin eidem longe plura ignota quam cognita essent.*] Thus if something must be built, we speak with builders and architects; if we must go to sea, we find captains to guide us. In war we must be even more careful in seeking sound counsel, since the dangers in waging it are that much greater. In other types of enterprises, the damage can

> be more easily tolerated, so to speak, since the bad outcomes can be contained and repaired. But besides everlasting disgrace, military mistakes produce death, wounds, and general ruin. Catastrophic missteps of this type can never be wiped away or corrected; so you must be guided in a mature fashion, and must listen to those who have had long experience in such matters. [II.39]

This was the warning that Tegghiaio conveyed to the magistrates of Florence. He continued by saying that even though the planned expedition might be derived from good intentions, it nevertheless was "more audacious than prudent" *(plus audaciae quam prudentiae)*. All things considered, he told them, it was simply not a risk that Florence could take. Its forces would be exposed to attacks on all sides, and it seemed that the Sienese would bring their German allies into the fight. He continued:

> To downplay the power of one's adversary when forming plans is to delude oneself. The harsh realities of war apply equally to all; and the luck of combat can go either way. The military capability of the enemy is such that no one should reject them out of hand…[*Verum communis mars et omnis fortuna pugnae anceps; copiae hostium tales, quas nemo sobrius aspernetur*.]

A sounder policy was the protection of Florence's own borders, where the city could be surer of victory; an expedition far away carried extreme dangers. "To prefer peril to victory," he said, "is sheer insanity." Bruni tells us that the magistrates did not receive Tegghiaio's speech well, knowing as they did that it exposed their own stupidity and rashness. There was even an arrogant upstart present named Expeditus, "the kind of man that excessive civil liberty can often produce." In typical fashion, Expeditus accused Tegghiaio of being a timid defeatist, a coward, and a subversive whose real goal was to shirk military service. He poured derision on the sound advice that he had just been given, and had Tegghiaio and his delegation dismissed without any further discussion. Bruni concludes that the magistrates chose to undertake the expedition very much out of a desire not to appear to be afraid of Siena. Thus they sacrificed the safety of their people in order to appease their own vanity.

So the expedition went ahead, and all opposition was shouted down in a chorus of accusation. A military force pitched camp near the river Arbia, which was about four miles from Siena. Soon after this the Florentine force was hit by a surprise attack of Sienese with their German allies. A disaster then unfolded; the Florentine line broke, and the expeditionary force was routed, despite much bravery on the Florentine side. According to Bruni, about three thousand men died in the battle, with about four thousand taken prisoner; all of the equipment was captured. When news of the disaster reached Florence, there was a wave of grief and anger that swept through the community.

There was no way to conceal the scale of the disaster from the public, and resentment ran high against those who had pushed for the expedition in the first place. As often happens, those who were most vocal in promoting the attack were nowhere to be found; or, if they could be found, they took refuge in platitudes about doing their best in the circumstances. It is a pattern that is not unfamiliar. It is very easy to launch expeditions; bringing them to successful conclusions is another matter entirely. There are many who believe that they can manage all possible outcomes of such enterprises; but this view ignores the lessons of history. It remains nothing but a comfortable delusion that the hard reality of events will dissipate in due course.

24. Even Trivial Incidents Can Spark Disaster When Wise Leadership Is Absent

The astute observer of affairs will keep his finger on the pulse of unfolding events. He will make his observations, draw his own conclusions, and adjust his behavior accordingly. It is of no use to pretend that something is not what it clearly is; to live in denial is to live with a suspended sentence hovering over one's head. For when the conditions are right for a fire, any spark can be the cause of a conflagration. The city of Florence was rent by factionalism in the year 1216. Then, as now, powerful noble families vied for control of the city's mercantile and political life, and this jockeying was the source of much civil tension. The citizens had been living under this tension for a long time and had grown weary of it. Their preference, in the words of historian Leonardo Bruni, were these:

> But the people, taking thought not only for the present but for the future tranquility of the city, wanted to put to rest entirely, if possible, the quarrels and enmities of the nobility. So they arranged numerous marriages between the leaders of the factions with a view to linking them in bonds of mutual obligation. Thus Foresi de'Adimari became the son-in-law of Count Guido Novello; the Donati intermarried with the Umberti; and many further bonds of this nature were sanctioned between the other families so as permanently to put to rest their quarrels. [*History of the Florentine People*; trans. by J. Hankins]

These were worthy sentiments. But it was not to be. As it turned out, tension and discord still simmered below the surface, and all that was needed was some incident to turn the city into an inferno of civil strife. The following story relates the source of the trouble. A youth named Buondelmonte was, in Bruni's words, "among the most wonderful knights of his time." Yet for some reason he carried a grudge against another noble named Oddo di Arrigi de'Fifanti. Each of these men had the support and backing of other powerful clans: Buondelmonte had his own resources, and the support of some families, while Oddo had the backing of the Uberti and the Lamberti families. Savvy observers could see that this rivalry would eventually lead to conflict unless some step were taken to assuage the pride of all concerned. A tie of marriage, it seemed, was the best option in pursuit of this goal.

So Buondelmonte was to be married to one of Oddo's relatives (a descendant of Oddo's sister). A formal announcement was made, wedding preparations were made, and all indications were that harmony would be preserved. But human nature is a fickle and intemperate thing; and nothing is so certain but that some people will do their best to sabotage stability if the drama thus created serves their own selfish interests. Some nobles, both men and women, whispered their disapproval of the planned wedding match.

A campaign of gossip and subversion was conducted by some people to undermine the chances for peace.

A "certain lady of the house of Donati," Bruni tells us, began to spread rumors that Buondelmonte had disgraced himself by agreeing to be married to a girl of inferior social status and beauty. She even told the young man directly that her own daughter, a great beauty, would have been a better match for him. In so many words, she told him that she would be saving her daughter for him. Of course, this statement was presented as a gentle admonition, but in reality it was a deliberate subversion of a carefully planned enterprise. By making this statement to the impressionable and hot-blooded youth, she planted the seeds of desire in his mind, a desire that would have momentous consequences.

Buondelmonte began to think about the lady of Donati's daughter all the time. According to Bruni, he ceaselessly compared his intended pride with the daughter of the Donati in appearance, bearing, and suitability. It is a feature of human nature never to be satisfied with what one has; and in the matters of beauty, lust, money, and power, it is nearly impossible for the undisciplined to be restrained their desires for constant betterment. Desire follows upon desire, and acquisition begets more acquisition, until some intervening force or personal ruin breaks the chain of cause and effect. After thinking the matter over, Buondelmonte went back to the lady and told her that he still had "time to correct his mistake" and that he would break off his engagement with Oddo's relative.

So he broke off the engagement. To add insult to injury, he decided to arrange the new wedding ceremony at the same day and time for which the old one had been scheduled. Of course, this sequence of events was deeply offensive to Oddo and his relatives, and they set about plotting some kind of revenge. Blame for the incident was affixed entirely on him. As news of the story spread to the relations and Oddo, the sentiments for a harsh revenge began to grow. All the repressed anger that had accumulated for many years was given full vent. Bruni says that one noble named Mosca Lamberti wanted Buondelmonte to die, and repeated a colloquial Italian saying:

> Cosa fatta, capo ha.

This conveys the meaning, "What has been done, has a mind of its own." By this he meant that the situation would take its own course. So he and a few other men set out to ambush Buondelmonte and kill him. We should note that even though the youth's action had been impetuous and rude, it was hardly a capital offense; the proper remedy in those days would have been for him to pay a monetary settlement as redress to the girl's family. But when passions are ignited, it is not easy to find voices of moderation and reason. So on Easter morning, as Buondelmonte was riding a horse in the city, he was pulled down and bludgeoned to death; Bruni says that although members of various families were there, Oddo himself had the primary hand in the killing.

As news of the murder spread throughout the city, both commoners and nobles took sides on the matter. Once passions were aroused, it was too late for voices of moderation to make themselves heard. The deeds of the conspirators were condemned as excessive, and soon open conflict broke out "with knives and blows, [in] a fever of death and destruction." Thus the republic was plunged into a conflagration of violence and destruction. The conditions for such strife had already existed, but it was the rash, intemperate behavior of the ruling classes that had condemned the citizenry to instability and danger. The elites had no respect for, or understanding of, their role in promoting civil stability and justice; blinded by selfishness and arrogance, and animated by the thought of additional spoils, they thought only of their own ends and goals. From this example, and many others like it, we can see that the responsibilities of leadership should fall only on the shoulders of those who can wield them with temperance, maturity, and wisdom.

25. Giano Della Bella Confronts The Nobility And Institutes Reforms

The city-state of Florence in the late 13th century was suffering from an imbalance of political and economic power. In its hands, the nobility had concentrated vast powers to the exclusion of the common citizens, who were either ignored or deliberately disenfranchised. Political leaders functioned as the hand-puppets of powerful families–the medieval equivalent of the modern corporate conglomerate or "special interest" group–who pulled the strings from behind the scenes. Demagogues, ever-ready to prey on the innocence or gullibility of the masses, promised what they never intended to deliver; and when they could not deliver, contented themselves with distracting the populace with frights, scares, amusements, or foreign military adventures. The good of the state, and the needs of the citizenry, were the farthest things from the minds of the nobility; what mattered to them was enriching themselves at the expense of the common good, and extracting an ever-greater share of the food from the common trough. The picture is one that will not be unfamiliar to the informed observer of the modern political scene. Into this picture stepped the figure of Giano Della Bella (1240–1305). Like many great reformers in history, he himself was a noble who grew disgusted with the avarice and lack of virtue displayed by his class.

The historian Leonardo Bruni called him *claris quidem maioribus ortus, sed ipse modicus civis et apprime popularis*, which means "born of illustrious ancestors, but a citizen both moderate and very much popular in his inclinations." Some men are born with an innate sense of justice, a feeling that overrides other considerations in their backgrounds; they recoil at the greed and corruption they see around them, and are willing to take steps to change things. Giano was outraged by both the arrogance of the nobility, as well as the blind inertia of the people, who were willing to sit in silence in the face of shameful servitude. He took to warning the people of Florence that their fates were all linked together, and that if the nobility were successful in pitting one group or faction against another, it would be successful in denying the people their rights:

> He thought it was extremely foolish to believe that violence would not eventually come to each man personally. When the first opponents were successfully subdued [by the nobility], such violence would then leap to each man's roof, spreading like a conflagration. Something had to be done now, so the growth of the evil was not simply allowed in silence. The evil had spread somewhat, to be sure; but it had not yet become so strong that it could not be remedied. But if they [the citizens] neglected their responsibilities any longer, and watched for one man or another to do something, they would in vain be looking for help against a debilitating pestilence (*frustra tandem auxilium contra inveteratam pestem optaturos*). [Bruni, *Hist. of the Florentine People* IV.27]

Eventually people began to listen to him and appreciate the content of his message. During one famous speech, he told the crowd:

> My fellow citizens, I have always been consistent in my thoughts. The more I think about the fate of our republic, the more I become firmer in my belief that it is essential to limit the unrelenting arrogance of the powerful families, or else lose our freedom altogether. I can tell we have reached the point where your patience and your liberty can no longer co-exist (*Eo quidem res deductas cerno, ut patientia vestra et libertas stare simul non possint*). I believe that no one with a sound mind would doubt which of these two things you should retain...to me it seems that the liberty of people is contained in two things: its laws and its courts....But when it happens that some are allowed to skirt the laws with impunity, one must conclude that liberty has disappeared...I believe it is absolutely necessary to increase the severity of punishment for powerful wrongdoers. If you want to shackle a giant and a midget, you do not use, I believe, the same kind of restraints. For the giant, one must use chains and heavy ropes; for the midget, one can use light ropes or thongs. [Id., IV.28—29]

The people of Florence were aroused by Giano's uncompromising talk, the like of which they had never heard before. Eventually a body of laws called the Ordinances of Justice were passed. The historian Bruni tells us that these ordinances targeted about thirty-eight powerful families who controlled the industry and economic life in Florence; the nobility were hit hard by the laws, and the good of the public began to replace what had previously been the good of a small minority. Giano himself was elevated to political power.

But the power of the arrogant oppressor is not so easily deterred; it has a way of lying low, licking its wounds like a beaten cur, and looking for the right opportunity to snatch back what it once lost. Reforms do not remain valid in perpetuity; each generation, if it wishes to preserve its rights, must take care to cultivate and nurture them, so that they do not wither and die from neglect.

This was the mistake of the American political system in the decades following the 1950s; as economic prosperity grew to unheard of heights in the 1960s, 1970s, and 1980s, the financiers and plutocrats whose greed had plunged the nation into depression in the 1930s were allowed to regain their hold over commercial and political life.

Political leaders shirked their duty to the people in order to be invited to the parties of the rich. Regulations that had been put in place for good reasons began to seem outmoded or irrelevant; greed and arrogance began to be conflated with strength and character; and the public, distracted with endless amusements and license that camouflaged itself as liberty, was paid to look the other way. The result was the catastrophic economic collapse of the early 2000s; and the reforms that have been so desperately needed are still missing. Thus wealth continues to aggregate in the hands of the few, reaching levels never before seen in the nation's history. Demagogues and charlatans distract the people with slogans and feel-good puffery that do little or nothing to address the root causes of the problems, and the courts and legislatures look for reasons to carry out the designs of the rich. The price for all this will eventually be paid; hubris, as Sallust tells us, ultimately turns inward on itself, and consumes its host.

But let us return to Florence. Giano's reforms naturally aroused extreme anger with the nobility, who screamed, as they do now, about "confiscation" and "unfairness." He was not helped by the short memory of the people, who are inclined to forget that hard-won reforms can vanish as quickly as the morning mist if money and power are allowed to concentrate too much in the hands of a few. Giano began to be blamed for riots he had not instigated. The poor wanted him to go farther than he did; the rich, less than he had. The result was that he began to be criticized by both extremes of society; factionalism gathered strength and bided its time.

But here again Giano proved he was the greater man. Not wishing to be blamed as the spark that touched off a civil war, he agreed to go into exile. "I cede to the slanders of my enemies, and permit a place for their jealousies." (*Cedamus potius inimicorum calumniis, et locum invidiae permittamus*). It was a cruel ending a man who had done so much for his republic. But it was the choice he made, and in some ways it was a very wise one. Giano had done his duty and had served with distinction, and that had been enough. For he knew that the heart of man is ungrateful, and possessed of a short memory; unless he is confronted with the immediacy of discomfort, he forgets the amplitude and duration of true pain. The reminders are never long in coming, of course.

26. The Recruit In The Soviet Army

In 1982 a former Soviet officer using the pen name Viktor Suvorov published a book entitled *Inside the Soviet Army*. The book discussed the doctrines, tactics, and organization of the Soviet Army. Reading it today feels like opening a time capsule; we even begin to feel in its pages a trace of nostalgia for the old empire. The author includes a section on the lot of the common soldier, describing in detail how he was called up, what he had to do, and what his training was like. These details we will summarize here. In the 1970s and 1980s, all Soviet men between the ages of 17 and 50 were subject to military conscription. Women were nominally exempt, but they too could be called up if they possessed special skills needed by the state. All of these candidates were kept on a master register, and could be ordered to report for duty if mobilization occurred. When a man reached the age of 18, he was required to do two years of military service on active duty; for those selected for the navy, the active service requirement was three years. The entire system was a vast bureaucracy, with huge volumes of men moving in and out of the armed forces every month of the year.

There were no volunteers–or very few, at any rate–in the Soviet Army. The system was too rigid, too inflexible, and too regimented to contemplate the wants or needs of the individual. Suvorov tells us that the typical 18-year-old who was called up for duty did three things before reporting: (1) he would get his friends together and beat up his enemies, or help them beat up their enemies; (2) tell his girlfriend that she had better write to him regularly, or he would beat her senseless; and (3) get roaring drunk the night before showing up at his recruit depot. When teenage recruits showed up at recruit depots, they were usually severely hung over and dressed in rags. Good clothing or personal possessions would be immediately requisitioned by older soldiers.

Recruits were separated into categories based on health and national origin. They had no say whatsoever in what branch of the military they would join; personal desires or requests counted for nothing, even less than nothing. One cardinal rule in forming units was to mix each unit so that it did not contain a majority of one nationality. Latvians, Ukrainians, Russians, etc., were not allowed to form a majority in any one unit; the obvious purpose for this precaution was to ensure that any possible civil disturbance could be suppressed with a minimum of fuss about offending the local population.

Corporal punishment was routine and expected; from the first moments, a recruit understood the consequence of disobedience was the weight of a sergeant's fist. The recruits would have their heads shaven, their filthy rags burned, and were then issued uniforms that usually did not fit well. Most of these new bodies had already been assessed in one way or another, based on political reliability, possible criminal record, family history, physical and mental development, and other factors. Based on the results of these screenings, he was assigned a category number. Category 1 soldiers, for example, were sent to divisional rocket or reconnaissance battalions; category 2 men were sent to artillery regiments, anti-aircraft regiments, or other units that demanded technical proficiency. "But nothing can be done about that," says Suvorov, "[for] the army is enormous and bright soldiers are in demand everywhere. Everyone is after the strong, brave, healthy ones. Not everyone can be lucky."

Soviet Army recruits were subject to rigorous physical hazing and discipline. Besides all the usual harassments expected of military life, recruits could expect to be slotted into a sharply defined caste system. Physical punishment, sleep deprivation, and endless hours of "busy work" were heaped on his narrow shoulders, with the expectation that the new recruit would learn the value of unquestioning obedience. Soldiers were housed in huge barracks rooms designed to hold five hundred men. The sergeants in charge would quickly make sure the new arrivals understood that there were four classes of men: those who would be leaving the army in 6 months, those who will leave after a year, those who will leave after a year and a half, and everyone else who had more than 18 months to serve. This latter class, the bottom, were called "scum." The new recruits had to do menial chores for the soldiers in the upper classes; it was just the way things were. But at least it was temporary. The "scum" could take refuge in the knowledge that in some months' time, they themselves would be able to dictate terms to a new batch of recruits.

For the Soviet soldier, every minute of every day was rationed. He quickly learned that each day contained 1,441 minutes. His day would be divided into segments of so many minutes each. Nothing was left to chance; and no room was permitted for one's personal wishes. In theory, he was allowed 480 minutes of sleep; but the scum, of course, got much less than this in practice. Reveille was normally at 0600 hours, but this could naturally be moved forward as required. Even food was rationed. In theory, a soldier was allowed 20 grams of butter per day; but since 10 of these were used in cooking, he only saw 10 grams in front of him every day. Breakfast was spartan: he received two slices of black bread, one of white bread, a bowl of kasha (buckwheat), and a mug of tea with a lump of sugar. Butter and sugar were used as a form of alternative currency for soldiers; everyone's goal was to hoard it. Suvorov tells one story of how a group of soldiers tried to make their butter last as long as possible by spreading it thinly on every slice they got. They were only able to distinguish the buttered slices from the unbuttered ones by holding them up to the light, and seeing which surfaces looked shiny. A typical day of drill consisted of the following subjects: political training, tactics, weapons training, drill, technical training, and physical defense. The amount of time devoted to each of these subjects varied greatly depending on which branch of the service a soldier was in. In words that soldiers the world over will instantly relate to, Suvorov says:

> Exceptional physical strain is put upon Soviet soldiers. During his first days in the army a young recruit loses weight; then, despite the revolting food, he begins to put it on, not as fat, but as muscle. He starts to walk differently, with his shoulders back, a mischievous twinkle appears in his eye and he begins to acquire self-confidence. After six months, he begins to develop considerable aggression, and to dominate the scum. In his battles with the latter, he wins not only because of tradition, or the support of his seniors, his NCOs and officers–he is also physically stronger than they are…Within a year he has become a real fighting man.

To some Westerners, with their refined, delicate sensibilities, all of this may seem brutal and dehumanizing. But they would be very wrong. Men are not transformed by fighters by benedictions or debates; they must be forged in fire and tempered with hammer and anvil. This is the way it always has been, and the way it must be. Suvorov notes that in the Soviet Army of the 1970s and 1980s, most foot soldiers did not know how to read or interpret a map. The reason for this was quite simple: it was not necessary. The function of the individual infantryman was to keep himself and his weapon in good working order, and be ready to attack in the direction he was told to attack. There was no need for him to obsess about map-reading. There were plenty of NCOs and officers who could do this when needed. Suvorov brings his worldly wisdom to bear when he reminds us:

> Those who build the Great Pyramids were probably not particularly well-educated and often they probably did not even understand each other, since slaves had been driven from distant areas to build the huge structures. But the pyramids turned out none the worse for that. The slaves were not expected to carry out intricate calculations or to make precise measurements. All that was required from them was obedience and diligence, submission to the lash and willingness to sacrifice themselves in order that some unknown but desirable aim should be achieved. Soviet generals adopt a similar position–surely it is not necessary to involve every slave in plans of enormous complexity.

Perhaps this is no longer the way things are done in the world's militaries in 2018. A premium is now placed on individual initiative and decentralized planning and execution. And yet it may be that we often neglect the lessons that can be learned from older systems. Have we erred too far in promoting choice and personal judgment, to the detriment of iron discipline and brute toughness? Time will tell. There are times when obedience, brute force, and tenacity are far more valuable than the dashing individualism we so much love to celebrate. We in the West seem to be constitutionally incapable of understanding that our current levels of comfort and opulence are but a temporary condition, which, in the right circumstances, may be replaced by conditions of the most raw and elemental type. When this happens, there will be little patience for the individualist ethic.

27. The Corrupt Rule Of Walter VI Of Brienne, The "Duke Of Athens"

The citizens of a free republic should always be alert to threats to their liberty. Such threats may come in a variety of forms; one of the most dangerous is that posed by a fraud or con artist who appears in the guise of a "people's champion." Skilled at manipulation and demagoguery, such men know how to take the measure of a crowd, or the tenor of the times; they know how to cast their voices so as to appear sympathetic to the legitimate aspirations of their people; and they are practiced at dangling before their gullible audiences the enticements that could be theirs, if only they agree to throw in their lot with him. It is a game as ancient as the advent of the tyrant Dionysius I of Syracuse. One particularly instructive example is found in the pages of Leonardo Bruni's *History of the Florentine People*. In the 1340s there came to power an ignorant, corrupt, and venal ruler in Florence known to history as Walter VI of Brienne. He liked to call himself "The Duke of Athens," not because he had earned this title meritoriously, but because of his noble family's interests in Greece. He thought that cloaking himself with the ancient glory of the city would somehow confer honor on himself; Bruni scornfully refers to Walter in the following way:

> Walter was a Frenchman, born of aristocratic background, whom people were in the habit of calling by the empty and maudlin title of "Duke of Athens." [*Gaulterius erat gallus, claro natus genere, quem nudo inanique titulo Athenarum Ducem vocitabant.* (Bruni, VI.111)].

He had an undistinguished background, notable only for his talent at constantly presenting himself as a success, even though the actual record of his achievements was meager. The Florentine nobility brought him into Florence in 1342 to rule the city, thinking that he would prove a useful front man whom they could control. Like all frauds and con artists, he had an innate belief in his own abilities, and this assurance often passed as genuine to those who came into contact with him. He had little respect for others; what mattered to him was his own infantile desires and those of his family. But he was aided by certain circumstances in Florence that made his path to power easier: first, the factionalism and discord that existed in the city at the time; second, the stupidity and avarice of the ruling elite, who thought they would be able to control him. He made a special effort to appeal to the poor and the dispossessed:

> He believed that it would involve little effort on his part to convert to his side the poor, the common laborers, and the entire mass of the citizenry; he understood that they cared little for concepts like dignity or liberty. [VI.112]

In this, of course, his instinct proved to be correct. For the masses are generally immune to the lessons of history; their attentions are fixed only on entertainments and on how they can profit from any given circumstance. The nobility of Florence should have known better; on their shoulders must fall most of the responsibility for what was about to happen. Bruni considers it a matter of first importance to describe how the despot insinuated himself into control of the republic. He believed the subject was "something worth recording, either as an admonition to citizens, or as a reprimand to those who would rule." (VI.117). Citizens, the historian believed, should fear nothing more than a loss of freedom; and the nobility should realize that nothing "tends to ruin more than unrestrained and irresponsible arrogance." As soon as he was elevated to power, Walter took steps to consolidate his rule. He made the security forces loyal to himself personally. An overbearing mountebank, he denigrated or attacked men of integrity and honor to excite the laughter of the crowd; but his secret goal was always to wear down the sanctity of institutions, so that he could ride roughshod over them more easily. So there was a purpose behind his behavior. He concluded a peace treaty with the city of Pisa on mediocre terms; but this did not trouble him, because the responsibilities of office did not trouble him. He acted more out of a desire to consolidate his own power than to advance the interests of Florence. He brought in French knights who would be loyal to himself personally, men who could be counted on the carry out his corrupt designs. He took steps to disarm the people; abolished civil offices he could not control; and he felt unrestrained to help himself to the public treasury.

What mattered to him was self-enrichment. His duties as leader were seen by him as a way to advance the cause of what would today be called his "brand." People who attempted to criticize him were exiled, tortured, or ridiculed into silence. As might be expected, the citizens of Florence were not so blind or unconscious as to accept this kind of treatment for long. Fear eventually evolved into hatred, and hatred into plans for action. But Walter was suspicious, and had his contingent of foreigners to protect his person. He got wind of one of the conspiracies against him, but when he tried to punish the plotters, a public revolt was triggered. Walter belatedly tried to make concessions to pacify popular anger at his conduct, but the virus of revolt was already abroad. People who had had relatives jailed or killed by Walter and his henchmen now saw their chance to expel the despot, and he was eventually forced to step down and flee the city amid a cacophony of popular rage. He had been in power for less than a year.

So ended the brief career of the "Duke of Athens." No matter the age, no matter the epoch, such personality types litter the pages of history. They are consummate seducers, always promising what they had no intention of delivering. They tend to make their appearance during times of factionalism, strife, and public apathy or exhaustion; and, backed by the ruling elites, such frauds even seem successful for a time. They now have the ability to harness resources that the tyrants of old could never have dreamed of: social media, the surveillance state, and militaries of unimaginable might. For a time, they strut the world stage, basking in their own munificence and fueled by their on arrogance and greed; that their edifice might be built on a foundation of sand never occurs to them until the very moment their world of illusion evaporates like the morning mist.

Yet the thoughtful student of history will remember that moral corruption can never be harnessed to good uses; nothing good can result from lies, corruption, and greed. Wicked actions remain wicked, regardless of the filter they might be passed through. The pursuit of unchecked power, contempt for established institutions, scorn for the rights of others, and a willingness to put his own interests before those of the republic he is tasked to serve: these are the hallmarks of the aspiring tyrant. And those who enable and praise such leaders must count themselves just as morally bankrupt as the venal frauds they seek to serve.

28. One Should Avoid Dangerous Places: The Rescue Of Euthymios

When considering tales from the lives of the great saints, we should be more mindful of the moral imparted by the story than strictly attentive to the accuracy of its details. We must take into account the perspective of the writer, his proximity to the events he describes, and his moral purposes. To do anything less would defeat the purpose of the anecdote. Yet I am confident that many of the stories related by the biographer of Euthymios the Younger (823 A.D.?–898 A.D.) are based on actual events, and are not the idle speculations of the cloister. One of these stories we will now relate.

Soon after he had arrived at Mount Athos in Greece, Euthymios the Younger acquired a reputation for his piety, courage, and special gifts. He was the kind of man that attracted others to him by virtue of his right actions and virtuous deeds. He eventually would ask several brothers of Athos to be his advisors; their names were John Kolobos and Symeon. These holy men were as devoted to spiritual progress as was their teacher Euthymios. In time these three monks, seeking a place even more isolated than Athos, formed the idea of moving to a remote island called Neoi, which in those days was uninhabited. This they did. And yet the universe has a way of imposing challenges upon the virtuous; and try as we might, we cannot escape trouble completely. It always has a way of finding us. According to his anonymous biographer, the sanctified activities of Euthymios and his brothers attracted the jealousy and anger of Satan, who sought to bring harm to them, and deflect them from their purposes.

Now we must remember that in those days, the Byzantine Empire and the caliphate of Baghdad were engaged in constant military struggle for control of the eastern Mediterranean world. The two superpowers would often raid each other, carry off each other's people as slaves, and encroach on one another's territory. It was simply the way things were. Rival ships roamed the seas, looking for plunder and spoils. One day, the brothers on Neoi saw that two Saracen (i.e., Arab) ships were approaching their island from over the horizon, and feared the worst. They knew that, in their exposed and indefensible position, they could offer no resistance. When the Arabs landed, they took the three holy men prisoner and deprived them of their meager possessions. The reader will recall that, in Western Europe at this very same time, Viking marauders were known to plunder monasteries remorselessly and show no mercy to holy men.

So Euthymios and his brothers were held captive on one Arab vessel, and their possessions were kept on the other ship. And here is where Euthymios's biographer tells us that a miracle occurred. The ship that was carrying the holy men came to a halt in the sea, and was unable to progress any further, while the other ship carrying their possessions was able to continue sailing. The Arab sailors were dumbfounded at this bizarre situation; but they were also deeply religious men, and soon began to draw their own conclusions. "By God," cried the Saracen captain who held the three Greek brothers in chains. "We are being punished by Allah for daring to harm these Men of God, even though they be deluded in their beliefs!" When the Arab crew heard this, they became deeply distraught, and wished to atone for their sin in holding the monks hostage. They asked the monks to forgive them for their conduct. Euthymios's biographer tells us how this happened:

> [T]hey prostrated themselves before the holy men and prayed to receive forgiveness for their rash deeds against them. And as soon as the [Greek] holy men with their customary compassion pardoned the Arabs, the ship was immediately seen to proceed on its voyage without any obstacle. Thus when the Arabs returned to the island [of Neoi] once more, they set about restoring the monks to their own cells. [*Trans. by Alice-Mary Talbot*]

It was a startling reversal. The monks then asked for their possessions to be returned to them. But the Arabs honestly told them that the possessions were on the other ship, and that they themselves did not have them. One of the monks then said, "If God wishes us to recover our possessions, surely that which pleases Him will be accomplished for us." And after he said this, surely enough, the other ship appeared in the distance and came to the island with their possessions. We are told that the Arabs "marveled at the extraordinary nature of this episode" and knew that they were in the presence of true holy men. However, more strange things were to come. Euthymios was able to use his powers of prophecy to reveal an unpleasant future for the sailors. During these happenings, one of the Arab sailors foolishly struck John Kolobos. Euthymios intervened to stop it, and said to them all, "If you had returned us to our cells without any abuse, you would have been allowed to return to your own homes without incident. But since you have angered God by laying hands on this brother [John Kolobos], you will soon learn how bitter the wrath of God truly can be." After saying this, the monks left them, and the sailors boarded their ships.

But it was only a short time before Euthymios's prophecy proved to be true. The two Arab ships crossed paths with a squadron of Byzantine biremes; and the ship carrying the sailor who had hit John Kolobos was seized. The other Arab vessel was not seized, and continued on its way back to Syria. Our pious biographer of Euthymios reminds us, "This was the work of the God of marvels and the One who glorifies those who glorify Him and delivers unto the day of destruction the impious and the foolish. The [Greek] fathers were thus unexpectedly delivered from captivity, and God was glorified and the monks were joyful, and only the Devil who stirred up jealousy against them was disgraced for having committed a transgression to no purpose." All the same, the biographer tells us, the monks soon moved back to Athos. For all men have a duty "to avoid dangerous places, and not tempt the Lord God even in places where He is able to save them, lest, by being captured again, they be judged by the pious to have brought it on themselves." This is without doubt wise counsel. One must not rely on good fortune alone to save oneself.

29. Dr. Johnson Makes An Eloquent Petition For Clemency

It is a noble thing to intercede on behalf of another's worthy cause. But the cause should be a worthy one; we must work to manage expectations; and, when every effort has been exerted, we must know when to let matters take their own course. Advocating on behalf of another in this way could almost be viewed as a form of public service. One of the law's fundamental rules is the principle of *proportionality*: a punishment should be reasonably proportional to the crime committed. The reader examining the following anecdote should ask himself whether the punishment was, in fact, proportional to the committed offense.

In the spring and summer of 1777, Dr. Samuel Johnson was involved in an application for clemency on behalf of an unfortunate clergyman named Dr. William Dodd. Reverend Dodd was a well-known preacher, writer, and manager of charitable institutions; he was, according to writer James Boswell, a former "Prebendary of Brecon, and a chaplain in ordinary to his Majesty [George III]." Dodd got himself into serious trouble by his extravagant spending habits; he soon ran up tremendous debts, and this led him to be tempted by conduct that he might never have indulged in otherwise. He forged "a bond of which he attempted to avail himself to support his credit"; that is, he forged documents in order to obtain a loan. Unfortunately for him, the person whose name he used to perpetrate the fraud was a man of standing and influence, the Earl of Chesterfield, a man Dodd had once tutored. Like most financial criminals, Dodd believed he would be able to make good on the loan before his artifice was detected. Of course, things did not turn out this way, and he was exposed and vigorously prosecuted.

In those days forgery was considered a serious crime. Boswell calls it "the most dangerous crime in a commercial country"; and once the Earl of Chesterfield testified against Dodd, the unlucky clergyman was sentenced to be hanged. Dodd's friends approached Samuel Johnson, who as a man of letters was seen as a neutral party who might be well-placed to intervene on Dodd's behalf. Johnson wrote him several speeches, little literary pieces that might today be called press-releases; Dodd was moved by these efforts on his behalf, and sent Johnson this note from Newgate Prison in May 1777:

> I am so penetrated, my ever dear Sir, with a sense of your extreme benevolence towards me, that I cannot find words equal to the sentiments of my heart... You are too conversant in the world to need the slightest hint from me, of what infinite utility the

> Speech on the aweful day has been to me. I experience, every hour, some good effect from it. I am sure that effects still more salutary and important must follow from your kind and intended favour. I will labour—God being my helper–to do justice to it from the pulpit...May God Almighty bless and reward, with his choicest comforts, your philanthropick actions, and enable me at all times to express what I felt of the high and uncommon obligations which I owe to the *first man* of our times.

In June, Dodd was even more direct, sending Johnson this message:

> If his Majesty [George III] could be moved of his royal clemency to spare me and my family the horrours and ignominy of a *publick death*, which the publick itself is solicitous to waive, and to grant me in some silent and distant corner of the globe, to pass the remainder of my days in penitence and prayer, I would bless his clemency and be humbled.

Johnson then wrote a formal petition for clemency, addressed to the king. The letter was made to appear as having come from Dr. Dodd himself; Johnson apparently thought that it would have a better chance of success if the appeal came directly from the convicted. The letter read as follows:

> May it not offend your Majesty, that the most miserable of men applies himself to your clemency, as his last hope and his last refuge; that your mercy is most earnestly and humbly implored by a clergyman, whom your Laws and Judges have condemned to the horrour and ignominy of a publick execution. I confess the crime, and own the enormity of its consequences, and the danger of its example. Nor have I the confidence to petition for impunity; but humbly hope, that publick security may be established, without the spectacle of a clergyman dragged through the streets, to a death of infamy, amidst the derision

> of the profligate and profane; and that justice may be satisfied with irrevocable exile, perpetual disgrace, and hopeless penury. My life, Sir, has been useless to mankind. I have benefitted many. But my offenses against God are numberless, and I have had little time for repentance. Preserve me, Sir, by your prerogative of mercy, from the necessity of appearing unprepared at that tribunal, before which Kings and Subjects must stand at last together. Permit me to hide my guilt in some obscure corner of a foreign country, where, if I can ever attain confidence to hope that my prayers will be heard, they shall be poured with all the fervour of gratitude for the life and happiness of your Majesty.

It was an eloquent plea, but Johnson was careful to manage his client's expectations. He wrote to Dodd, "I most seriously enjoin you not to let it be at all known that I have written this letter, and to return the copy to Mr. Allen in a cover to me. I hope I need not tell you, that I wish it success. But do not indulge hope. Tell nobody." Soon after this, Johnson also wrote a plea to the influential Charles Jenkinson, the First Earl of Liverpool:

> Sir, since the conviction and condemnation of Dr. Dodd, I have had, by the intervention of a friend, some intercourse with him, and I am sure I shall lose nothing in your opinion by tenderness and commiseration. Whatever be the crime, it is not easy to have any knowledge of the delinquent, without a wish that his life may be spared; at least when no life has been taken away by him. I will, therefore, take the liberty of suggestion some reasons for which I wish this unhappy being to escape the utmost rigour of his sentence. He is, so far as I can recollect, the first clergyman of our church who has suffered publick execution for immorality; and I know not whether it would not be more for the interest of religion to bury such an offender in the obscurity of perpetual exile, than to expose him in a cart, and on the gallows, to all who for any reason are enemies to the clergy. The

> supreme power has, in all ages, paid some attention to the voice of the people; and that voice does not least deserve to be heard, when it calls out for mercy. There is now a very general desire that Dodd's life should be spared. More is not wished; and, perhaps, this is not too much to be granted. If you, Sir, have any opportunity of enforcing these reasons, you may, perhaps think them worthy of consideration: but whatever you determine, I most respectfully intreat that you will be pleased to pardon this intrusion.

Unfortunately, however, the application for clemency failed. Either George III was not convinced of its merit, or he was preoccupied with the conflict then raging in the American colonies; we do not know. His appeals having been exhausted, Dodd prepared himself to face the executioner. He wrote this final poignant letter to Johnson:

> Accept, thou great and good heart, my earnest and fervent thanks and prayers for all thy benevolent and kind efforts in my behalf. O! Dr. Johnson! As I sought your knowledge at an early hour in life, would to heaven I had cultivated the love and acquaintance of so excellent a man! I pray God most sincerely to bless you with the highest transports–the infelt satisfaction of humane and benevolent exertions!...I shall hail your arrival there with transport, and rejoice to acknowledge that you were my Comforter, my Advocate, and my *Friend*! God be *ever with you.*

To this Johnson responded with this final letter. It is a brilliant piece of writing, capturing that fine balance between Stoic courage and tender sympathy:

> That which is appointed to all men is now coming upon you. Outward circumstances, the eyes and the thoughts of men, are below the notice of an immortal being about to stand the trial for eternity, before

> the Supreme Judge of heaven and earth. Be comforted: your crime, morally or religiously considered, has no very deep dye of turpitude. It corrupted no man's principles; it attacked no man's life. It involved only a temporary and reparable injury. Of this, and of all other sins, you are earnestly to repent; and may God, who knoweth our frailty, and desireth not our death, accept your repentance…In requital of those well-intentioned offices which you are pleased so emphatically to acknowledge, let me beg that you make in your devotions one petition for my eternal welfare.
>
> I am, dear Sir, your affectionate servant,
> Sam. Johnson

The execution was carried out soon after this letter was written. Johnson would later say of Dr. Dodd, "He was at first what he endeavored to make others; but the world broke down his resolution, and he in time ceased to exemplify his own instructions."

30. Washington Crosses The Delaware And Attacks

Anyone who thinks the American Revolutionary War was a gentleman's affair has been seriously misinformed. We are sometimes given the impression that genteel types in powdered wigs maneuvered this way and that, and at the end of the day, everything was neatly wrapped up as almost a foregone conclusion. This, however, was not the case, as D.H. Fischer's *Washington's Crossing* makes very clear. War is war, and there is no way to sugar-coat its effects and costs. Fischer reminds us just how desperate and uncertain "the cause" of the revolution was in the dark days of 1776. In some ways the war had started on a positive note. The early battles in Massachusetts had not been disasters for the rebels; they had held their own, even getting the better of the British Army now and then. But then things began to go sour. New York became an occupied city, as did most of the main transportation and urban hubs on the eastern seaboard. Washington's army–scraggly and undisciplined in the best of times–began to melt away under the effects of disease, poor supplies, and collapsing morale. Washington was getting routed in one battle after another, yet somehow managed to keep some level of discipline and cohesion to his men. It looked as if present trends continued, the war would be as good as lost in another year's time.

The posture and strategy of the British Army in the Revolutionary War has been a much-neglected subject in the United States, and Fischer does his readers a service by spending many fascinating pages on it. London was faced with a formidable problem: how to restore control over a vast area over three thousand miles away, and how to keep control once it was won. In the first place, manpower was a problem. The British Army was a highly disciplined and professional force, and at the height of the rebellion, about one-half of the entire British Army was engaged or garrisoned in the American colonies. But it was not enough. London knew from the start that it would have to rely on mercenaries; overtures were made to Russia and the German state of Hesse. Catherine the Great wanted nothing to do with sending Russian troops to the Americas, and politely declined. There was even talk of hiring Moroccan troops from the Barbary Coast, but these ideas came to nothing. In the end, it would be Hesse that would help fill the manpower needs of the British Empire.

Hesse, like many central German states, had a long tradition of military service. In the 1770s, soldiering was a highly respected profession in Hesse, and the British were offering generous payment terms. Discipline in the German military, however, was severe by modern standards. Corporal punishment meant nothing, and was doled out for even minor infractions. In the era before modern logistical and supply systems, militaries in Europe often relied on plunder and booty to sustain themselves in the field. This practice had been common in Germany during the Thirty Years War of the seventeenth century, and the tradition stayed alive and well during the American Revolutionary War.

In theory, plunder was supposed to be limited, and should have left something for the victimized civilians to live on; in practice, however, plunder could easily turn into pillage, and pillage into devastation. Readers of Fischer's book may be surprised to know how often captured rebels were summarily executed during the rebellion; rapes, robberies, and other crimes associated with counterinsurgency warfare were also alarmingly prevalent. This was no gentleman's war. The Hessians quickly developed a reputation for ruthlessness that did much to turn public sentiment in favor of the rebels, especially in New York and New Jersey. If you were a rebel or someone who supplied a rebel, you absolutely did not want to cross paths with a squad of Hessian jaegers.

But Washington still needed to win victories in the field. He could not rely on the mistakes of his enemies to win the war for him. Modern logic might assume that the best strategy for Washington would be to melt into the hills and pursue a purely guerrilla campaign. There were, in fact, some American generals who favored just this idea. But Washington thought that it would take too much time, and also believed that his army needed to be visible to the American people. The public, he reasoned, needed to see him moving around and doing things. The generals who opposed him–the Howe brothers and Cornwallis–were intelligent, competent, and sophisticated men. Cornwallis actually believed that a conciliatory policy should have been pursued with the Americans, but he of course kept these opinions to himself. But any neutral observer in 1776 would have concluded that the rebellion was either on its last legs, or was getting to that point very rapidly.

The electrifying publication of Thomas Paine's pamphlet *The American Crisis* was a significant boost to rebel morale. Paine was a dyed-in-the-wool radical, and knew how to write propaganda. In modern terms, his little pamphlet "went viral" all over the colonies. Printers were encouraged to churn it for free and distribute it as widely as possible. It was read in camp, in homes, in taverns, and in city halls. And its message was unambiguous: keep fighting, stay strong, and remain optimistic. Words do matter, and in this case they mattered a great deal. But Washington knew he had to have something positive happen on the ground. He emerges in Fischer's book as a truly great man, a leader who deserves every bit of the veneration that has been heaped on him over the centuries. He was emotional, and could weep without shame as he watched his men get mauled and bayoneted by Hessians, and he was not above making simple military mistakes that experience and prudence might have avoided. But he had a Stoic calm to his personality, and carried with him an aura of dogged determination. His physical bravery was extreme: he could walk the battlefield during a fight without flinching an eyebrow, calmly receiving messages and issuing orders.

When Washington heard that a force of Hessians was within his reach, he prepared to cross the Delaware River on Christmas 1776 and hit them in Trenton with everything he had. This was not an easy operation: the river was choked with ice, his men did not have proper boats, and supplies were running desperately low. And yet it succeeded. The Hessians were caught completely by surprise and put up little resistance; the rebels also captured a good deal of supplies. The operation showed a great deal of planning and operational competence, and signaled to the British that a long war lay ahead. This battle signaled the start of a month-long series of engagements in which the Americans outfought the British in the field. This, in the end, was what mattered.

The simple fact was that it was nearly impossible for the British to crush an insurgency spread over the entire eastern seaboard. They did not have the manpower, or the political will, to continue prosecuting the war indefinitely. One gets the impression, from reading the diaries and letters of the British officers of the time, that the Empire's heart was just not in the fight after 1777. And once the intervention of the French became a reality later in the war, it made no sense for London to continue the fight. The colonies were just too big, and the manpower needs of an occupying army too extraordinary, for the rebellion to be suppressed.

31. The Wisdom And Character Of Athanasios Of Athos

Of all the great and sanctified names of Mount Athos, few inspire more veneration than that of Athanasios. He lived from about A.D. 925 to 1001, and occupies a central place in the development of the monasticism there. As a young man he was a teacher and scholar in Constantinople, and mixed with the upper classes of that great city; he knew personally the Byzantine emperor Nicephoras II Phocas and served as his spiritual advisor. But at some point he underwent some kind of conversion experience, and abandoned his old life to pursue the road of religion. This pattern is not unknown among great holy men; we find it often repeated in the histories of the world's great faiths.

He moved to Mount Athos around 957 and worked long and hard to build the community there. In reading the account of his life that has come down to us, I was struck by how much he behaved like a good military commander. Perhaps monks and soldiers are two sides of the same coin. Athanasios never gave any orders that he himself did not carry out personally with his men. When he punished his brothers for some transgression, he would himself suffer the same punishment. As for physical labor, he was always the first to lift the heavy stones or logs. He nearly crippled himself when a heavy log fell on his leg, crushing the bones of his femur and foot; that accident kept him off his feet for over a year. He would eventually be killed in a construction accident in 1001 when the scaffolding inside the monastery's main church gave way while he was using it for restoration work. What leader today, we should ask, would be so selfless and tireless in his service to an ideal?

But it is his wisdom and knowledge of human nature that most impresses us. He combined pragmatic leadership techniques with a deep sense of compassion; and he was so persuasive, and so endowed with charismatic gifts, that he could win over almost anyone he dealt with. His biographer tells us:

> For he always used to say that this is the goal for every person who can do so: to take care of the body, recall the soul from the depths of despair, and bring forth the precious from the worthless. For in the knowledge that idleness stirs up many passions in the soul, he did not let them merely eat and relax, but like a wise physician he assigned some of them to the kitchen to cut up vegetables, and he sent some of them to the refectory to slice the bread, and some to the smithy to hold the bellows and assist the workers, so that, by being forced to focus their attention there, they would be delivered from wicked thoughts and come to repentance. [*Trans. by Alice-Mary Talbot*]

Occupied minds have little time for mischief, he knew. This is a principle that is much deeper than it appears. The turbulent soul needs to feel like it is taking action in some way; it needs to feel like it is advancing forward towards some positive purpose. Father Athanasios knew how to use just the right balance of kindness and firmness to get the best out of his brethren. One moving passage in the anonymous account of his life tells how, when one of his brethren died, he would stand before the body and shed tears into a metal vessel; then he would prostrate himself on the ground and offer prayers to God. "Then, rising to his feet, he would stretch out his arms, offer many thanks to God, give [the deceased] the final kiss and entrust him to the grave."

Many stories are told of his wise methods of handling his community. His way revolved around certain fixed principles: he would rebuke and exhort his men, bear their burdens with them, and adapt his style to each man he dealt with. It was gratifying to learn that in this period Athos was often visited by Catholic clerics from Italy; political or theological differences were not important to men of sincere mind and expansive outlook. When a novice was in need of being corrected, Athanasios knew that sometimes it was not a good idea to rebuke him directly. Sometimes the soft touch worked better. Instead, he would pretend to reproach one of the enlightened elders at Athos, a man whom he knew would be able to take criticism without hurt. In front of others, he would say something like, "Aren't you ashamed as an elder to be making the same mistakes as a novice would make?" The novice would hear this, and would get the message in an indirect but effective way. Usually the novice would then approach Athanasios and apologize to him, and beg his forgiveness. "In this way," says his biographer, "he achieved two very fine results: for the novices were corrected through the patient endurance of the perfected ones, and the perfected ones bore the burden of the weak and thus fulfilled the law of Christ."

Here is a story about Athanasios's wise but forceful way of thinking. Once some "Amalfitan elders" (presumably monks from the Amalfi region of Italy) paid a visit to Athos, and brought him a gift of the seasoning known in Latin as *garum*. I was surprised to learn that this Roman condiment was still being made in the Middle Ages; it is kind of fermented fish sauce to which various spices have been added. When the gift was received, Athanasios ordered his people to store it and bring it out at the next meal, when the guests would be eating with them. But the cooks did not do this, and used a different garum that they themselves had prepared, instead of the garum from the Amalfi monks. When someone complimented what he thought was the Amalfi garum, one of the Athos cooks said that he himself had made it. When Athanasios heard this, he was very angry, for he had told the Athos cooks to use the gift that the Amalfi monks had brought. He ordered that all the garum of this Athos monk to be poured out on the ground and destroyed; and "in this way he corrected his own disciple's disobedience and chased away the sin of arrogance."

Another story reveals the same qualities. When one of his cooks took it upon himself to prepare a batch of honey cakes, Athanasios considered it too self-indulgent. He was even more angered to see monks hoarding the cakes and fighting over them; he had a disgust for gluttony and thought it was a gateway to further moral corruptions. He told his brethren:

> How on earth have you gone so crazy that you disregard our ancestral traditions and bring disgrace on our communal way of life by impulsively seeking to eat these sweets? Don't you know that our forefather Adam was condemned to a life of toil on account of his impulsive eating from the tree?

Perhaps to us, the uninitiated, these rules seem unduly severe. But we must remember that they were part of the monastic way of life, and we should not be too quick to judge by our own measures. We must record one final trait of Athanasios that his biographer makes a point of recording. This was the trait of clairvoyance. Now I know that there are those who will scoff at such things; but here again, we should take care before passing judgment on the authenticity of such stories. It may be that a life of contemplation and ascetic denial has the effect of sharpening the senses to a high state of acuteness, to the extent that such a man acquires powers that cannot be readily explained. Here is the story. One winter, Father Athanasios called one of his brethren to his cell; but he did not tell him why he had called him. Athanasios was deep in contemplation, and nearly in a trance. He spoke to this other monk, a man named John, and said, "Call Theodore the Hunter for me." When this was done, Athanasios told Theodore:

> Go and have your midday meal; then take some food and run as fast as you can to Kerasea. When you are opposite Chalasmata, head toward the sea and you will find three men sick with cold and hunger, one of whom is a monk. So hurry now and reach them

> while they are still alive. Help them recover, and bring them here with you.

Theodore did as he was asked, and found everything to be just as Athanasios had said it would be. There was no way he could have known about this emergency, everyone believed, since he had been shut up in his cell for several days, and no one had spoken to him about it. But he knew nonetheless. I remember once when I was in Bosnia, I knew a Greek army officer who told me that he used to visit Athos on a regular basis, because he knew one of the monks there. At times, the monk would be able to tell him things about his life that he could not possibly have known through conventional means. The officer had no explanation for this; he believed it was evidence of divinely-inspired clairvoyance.

32. Age Of Spectacle: Chariots Races, The Hippodrome, And The Four Factions

To understand fully the social environment in which the eastern Roman empire operated, we must have some grasp of the unique culture surrounding Constantinople's Hippodrome in the centuries that followed the disappearance of the Roman empire in the west. In Byzantium, sport and politics achieved a strange admixture that has no exact historical parallel anywhere else; sport influenced politics, and politics guided sport. It was a peculiar world, but one that makes sense once we understand the conditions that existed at the time. We begin with the arena itself.

The Hippodrome was located at the site of the modern Atmeidan in Istanbul. Its construction dates to the reign of Septimius Severus (around 203 A.D.), but it was substantially enlarged by Constantine I after he made Constantinople his capital in 324. In shape it was a long racetrack, and the markers of its axis still stand today. The inspiration for this vast arena was almost certainly Rome's Circus Maximus, but its dimensions seem to have been smaller. Its main entrances were located on its western side, and the entire structure was laid out on an orientation of northeast to southwest. At the Hippodrome's northern end could be found stables and storage rooms (*carceres*) for horses and chariots. Above this was erected a distinctive building called the Kathisma, a sort of special imperial housing from which the emperor and his retinue could watch the games. It was apparently connected to the imperial palace itself. The Kathisma got its name from the special chair upon which the emperor would sit as he observed the proceedings; above this could be found the emperor's guards, who occupied a perch called the Stama.

The Hippodrome was a vast racetrack. A long, decorated "spine" (*spina*) in the form of a short wall was built down the center of the track, and at each end of the spine were goals. We are told that the emperor Theodosius the Great erected an Egyptian obelisk from the reign of Thutmosis III at the center of the spine. Chariot drivers had to complete seven circuits around the spine, and there was an artful mechanism for letting the crowds know how many circuits had been completed. Metallic casts of seven dolphins were placed at one end of the spine, and seven eggs at the other end; these symbols were respectively intended to represent the god Neptune and the legendary figures Castor and Pollux. As the drivers completed a circuit, the Hippodrome workers would remove an egg or a dolphin, thereby letting the crowd know how many circuits remained to be completed. We should note that the Hippodrome's interior was filled with exotic emblems and works of art, a fact that doubtless contributed to the sense of awe and grandeur imparted by the entire spectacle.

How many spectators did the arena seat? We do not know with certainty, but the figure must have been at least 100,000. The stadium's main entrance (the "Great Gate") was probably close to the Kathisma. We are also told that there was another gate, called the "Dead Gate," that was used for carrying out the corpses of participants who had been slain in the games. This is a sobering reminder of the seriousness with which games in the Hippodrome were treated. But the populace wanted entertainment; and in the era before mass media, television, or radio, the masses hungered for exciting diversions. No amount of cautionary speeches from ecclesiastical figures could satiate the lust for the games; indeed, such clerical fulminations may even have increased their allure.

Yet perhaps the most bizarre feature of Constantinople's chariot-racing culture was the rise of color-coded political factions that supported different chariot racers. These bore no resemblance to our modern football hooligans or drunken stadium rowdies; they were serious organizations that saw the Hippodrome as a forum in which they could flex political muscle. Byzantium had four factions, each identified with a particular color: the Blues, the Reds, the Greens, and the Whites. To understand how these groups congealed, we must remember that the empire at Constantinople was in no way a representative democracy. It was an absolutist monarchy. Allegiance to one of the factions was one of the few ways that the average denizen of Constantinople could make himself heard by the emperor. In some ways, the Hippodrome can be said to have been a kind of "popular assembly" for those who had no other way to petition the sovereign.

In any case, the factions were serious organizations. They had delineated hierarchies and command structures. They sponsored drivers and their equipment, and their leaders commanded allegiance from those who followed them. Even the emperor would have been allied with one group or another. Hence we hear that Theodosius II was aligned with the Greens, Justinian and Marcian with the Blues, and Zeno with the Greens. It is not clear if the factions represented competing political or religious ideologies, but it is hard to imagine that it was not so. Membership may have been based on what part of the city a person was from, or it may have been hereditary; we do not know with certainty. These color-coded factions even spread to other cities of the east. As noted earlier, the factions were far more than sporting clubs. They could be mobilized as armed militias, and even at time participated in military activities, or were used for construction projects. The leaders of the factions were headed by "demarchs," who in turn answered to Constantinople's Prefect. For centuries, the Hippodrome was one of the main centers of political and social affairs in the Eastern Empire.

It was regularly the scene of riots and revolts; the most serious of these, the so-called "Nika Revolt" of 532 A.D., was a horrific affair that began as a demonstration but quickly changed into an attempt to overthrow the emperor Justinian and his wife, Theodora. Justinian called in the army, headed by his favorite general Belisarius, and put down the revolt with brute force; the number of the dead is estimated to have been around 30,000. This, however, is a story to be told at another time. The Hippodrome and the culture that surrounded it are a stark testament to the ability of entertainment to influence political and social affairs. Such influence on a state is never beneficial or positive. For the mob is not guided by considerate rationality or purposeful vision; it is led only by the dictates of tumescent emotion, and the most unreasoning savagery.

33. Edgar Allen Poe's Sinister Inspiration For *The Cask Of Amontillado*

Most readers will be familiar with Edgar Allan Poe's macabre tale *The Cask of Amontillado*. It is a dark tale of revenge, in which one man deliberately intoxicates a hated enemy and then walls him up alive in a crypt. Like most writers, Poe took his inspiration from his life experiences, and then mixed those with the creative power of his imagination. Was *The Cask of Amontillado* based on an actual incident? The answer appears to be yes, at least in part. Poe was born in Boston but had spent his early years in Virginia. As a young man, he had made a reputation for himself as a hell-raiser, and was a source of constant anguish for his father. He gambled, drank, got into fights, and generally lived a dissolute life. By 1827 he had racked up large gambling debts, had dropped out of the University of Virginia, and literally had nowhere to go. So, after giving a false name and age to recruiters (probably to dodge creditors who might try to find him), he joined the army in May of that year under a five-year enlistment. He was stationed at Fort Independence on Castle Island in Boston Harbor. Military life actually agreed with Poe, as it often does to young men of ability who are looking for discipline and structure in their lives.

It was while he was at Castle Island that Poe, after reading some of the burial plaques and markers at the fort, learned of a violent episode that had occurred there many years before. A duel had taken place between two lieutenants, Robert Massie and Gustavus Drane, on the grounds of the fort on Christmas day in 1817. According to the story, Drane was a bragging, hateful bully who had already killed several men in duels based on trumped-up pretexts. Drane had focused on Massie as a victim, and had accused him of cheating at cards; based on this false accusation, he "demanded immediate satisfaction." Massie unfortunately complied, not wanting to look like he was backing down from a fight. Swords were named as the weapon.

Attempts at last-minute reconciliation failed. So within the inner walls of the fort, the duel actually took place. Massie was not able to hold his own against Drane, and was killed. Massie had been a popular officer and his brethren mourned his loss bitterly; he was buried him on the grounds with ceremony, and a marker was erected to his memory. According to legend, Drane vanished soon after this and was never seen again; his fellow officers had supposedly abducted him and walled him up alive in the fort. But is this story true? No, not entirely. Gustavus Drane did not die in 1817: he was promoted to captain and later died in 1846. Massie's grave was moved several times in the many decades following his death. For many years the Massie-Drane duel on Castle Island was considered just another tall tale of Boston Harbor that may have had some grains of truth, but had been wildly exaggerated by the unfortunate credulity of the locals.

But a new twist to the old tale came to light in 1905, eighty-five years after the duel had taken place. When Boston workmen were repairing parts of the old fort, they came across a section of the old cellar that their original diagrams showed was a small dungeon, but in reality was entirely walled off. The blueprints of the fort simply did not match what actually existed. Why had the dungeon been sealed up? No one seemed to know. The workers secured permission to explore the area further, and the wall was broken down. It was thick with layers of brick and mortar. Shining a light within the dank and fetid recess, the workmen made a strange discovery. Within was a skeleton shackled to the floor of the dungeon, with ragged scraps of an ancient US army uniform still draped over its bones.

Who this was, no one could tell. But if it was not Drane, then who was it? Some speculated that it may have been a convict or prisoner, since the fort had once been used as a prison. But if so, why had the person been chained to the floor and left there? Why had not the body been removed? And why would the dungeon cavity have been sealed up so completely? The more one thought about it, the more it seemed that only one conclusion could be possible: the occupant had been deliberately left there to die, with all evidence of his existence obliterated by sealing up the tomb. There must have been some truth to the old stories Poe had been told, after all; but after all this time, it is unlikely we will ever learn the details of how this sinister killing took place. The skeleton was buried in the Castle Island cemetery in an unmarked grave.

34. The Dream Of Maxen: A Celtic Myth Of *The Mabinogion*

Mabinogion is the name given to a collection of medieval Welsh tales drawn from the rich mythology of Celtic Britain. The earliest manuscripts date from around 1325, but it is certain that the tales on which they were based have roots that go back centuries before this time to an age in which Welsh and Roman elements blended to form a unique oral tradition. I have recently begun reading these tales, and it has been a refreshing experience in the literal sense of the word: they are unlike any other myths I have encountered. They conjure up a strange, almost hallucinatory dreamworld, where heroism and great deeds exist alongside magic and surreal alternative realities. Consider this strange yet transfixing passage from a tale called *Peredur Son of Evrawg*:

Peredur rode on towards a river valley whose edges were forested, with level meadows on both sides of the river; on the one bank there was a flock of white sheep, and on the other a flock of black sheep. When a white sheep bleated a black sheep would cross the river and turn white, and when a black sheep bleated a white sheep would cross the river and turn black. On the bank of the river he saw a tall tree: from roots to crown one half was aflame and the other green with leaves. Beyond that a young lord sat on a mound with two white-breasted brindled greyhounds on leashes lying alongside, and Peredur was certain he had never seen such a royal-looking lad.

The imagery and narrative style are quite unlike anything we might find in the literary traditions of Greece, Rome, or the Middle East. They are more surreal and hypnotic than even the Scandinavian myths. We will relate one of the tales here, a story called *The Dream of Maxen*. The protagonist of this story, Maxen, takes his modified name from a Roman emperor of late antiquity (Maxentius, who ruled from 306 to 312), and must have been inspired by the continuous contact of the Roman and Celtic cultures in Britain during that period. A version of the tale is also found in the *Historiae* of Geoffrey of Monmouth, and early English chronicler. This is the story as it is told in *The Mabigonion*.

Maxen was emperor of Rome and was better-suited to that job than any other leader of his time. One day he told his men that he wanted to go hunting. So the next day he and some of his retinue did just that; he was with thirty-two other nobles, and it gave him great pleasure that he was lord and master over all of them. As the day became hotter, the emperor decided to sleep for a bit; so his men made a makeshift shade for him by planting their spears in the ground and setting their shields over these. Underneath the emperor lay down and drifted off into sleep. He experienced a strange dream during this sleep. In the dream he traveled through a long valley and then ascended to reach the highest mountain in the world. After this he crossed a long and flat plateau; in this region were sparkling rivers and beautiful flora. He finally reached the mouth of a large river and then a great walled fortress. There was an open gate to this fortress, and Maxen entered this gate to see what was inside. He then entered a massive hall, adorned with gold and marble; he saw two young boys playing a game of *gwyddbwyll* (a Celtic board game in which one side tries to capture the other side's king). The hall was filled with rich couches and silver tables; everything was covered with "luminous stones" and precious metals.

Maxen saw other strange sights in the hall: there was a white-haired man sitting in a chair of ivory, decorated with strange and wonderful embellishments. Then he saw a beautiful girl sitting on a chair of red gold, dressed in all sorts of exotic and fine jewelry and accessories. She wore "shifts of white silk with red gold fastenings across the breast, and a gold brocade surcoat and mantle, the latter fastened by a brooch of red gold, a hairband with rubies and gems and pearls and imperial stones in alternation, and a belt of red gold." She rose to greet the emperor and he embraced her with desire. At this point, he awakened from his dream. But he could not remove the image from his mind that he had seen in the great hall: he desired this girl passionately, and was convinced that she must exist. Soon he could not think of anything else. So he sent messengers and scouts to various parts of the world to see if, in fact, the images he had seen were based on some reality.

And eventually his men were able to locate the place of his dream: they found out that the place was located in Britain. His messengers entered the same weird hall, saw the two lads playing *gwyddbwyll*, the mysterious woman seated in the red chair, and the other strange scenes in this place. They told the woman that they had been sent by the emperor of Rome to fetch her and bring her to Rome to be his empress. But she responded by saying that if Maxen wanted her, he would have to come in person himself and claim her.

So the messengers returned the Rome and told Maxen what they had found. They offered to take him to the location of the great hall. "Lord," they said, "we will guide you by land and sea to the woman you love; we know her name and her relatives and her birth." And so they did this, and the group returned to Britain after many adventures and obstacles. He entered the great hall, found the girl, and that night slept with her. Then as gifts she asked for the island of

Britain for her father, and various other territories for other members of her family. The emperor spent seven years away from Rome with her; and it was a custom that after spending a long amount of time away from Rome, the emperor could not return to the city. A new emperor was elected, and he sent Maxen a letter that he should not dare return to the city.

This Maxen refused to do. He resolved to retake the city by conquest and re-establish himself there. He made his way back to Italy with a small band of great fighters led by the brothers of Elen of the Hosts. These men were fighters better than any alive. Among these men were Kynan and Avaon, brothers of Elen of the Hosts. Maxen's efforts to retake Rome had reached stalemate; the two emperors were evenly matched and no progress was being made. The two brothers began to plan some stratagems that would enable Maxen to retake the city by force. They did this by scaling the walls of Rome at an unexpected time and place. So Maxen was restored to his throne, and this was accomplished by the valor and cunning of the men of Britain. The two brothers then set off on their own expeditions of conquest, subduing many peoples and cities. Eventually one of the brothers, Avaon, decided to go back to Britain with some of his men. The strange final words of The Dream of Maxen are these:

> Avaon and many of his men decided to go home, but Kynan and another group stayed, and they determined to cut out the tongues of the women, lest their own British language be contaminated. Because the women were silent and the men could speak, the men of Brittany were called Bryttanyeid, and there have often come and still do come men of that language from Brittany. This tale is called the Dream of the Ruler Maxen, and this is its end. [*Trans. by J. Gantz*]

This grisly ending is apparently meant to provide a mythological basis for the Welsh name for Brittany (Llydaw), which is taken to come from Lled-taw, or "half-silent."

35. Forensic Linguistics: The Footprint Of Language

There is a very good miniseries available on Netflix called *Manhunt*. It is a drama about the pursuit and capture of Theodore Kaczynski, the so-called "Unabomber" who confounded law enforcement for decades until he was finally captured in 1996. His case had been the longest and costliest in American law enforcement history. The drama closely tracks real events; the producers of the series (which stars Sam Worthington) made a conscious effort to reproduce the facts of the case with fidelity. The Unabomber case was buried under the media attention of even more dramatic terrorist cases in the years that would follow, of course. Most people have a passing acquaintance with it, and are vaguely aware that Kaczynski penned a document the media dubbed a "manifesto" in which he argued that industrial society and the technological revolution had been an unmitigated disaster for modern man. Notice here that I put the word manifesto in quotations. I did this because I do not think it appropriate to use this word for Kaczynski's tract. "Manifesto" carries connotations of a ranting tirade, and allows us to dismiss a writing so named as a manic screed.

But the Unabomber's tract was anything but this: he was deadly serious, and this former professor of mathematics lays out his case within a logical framework that follows from one point to the next with Euclidean inevitability. We can agree with his arguments, or not agree with them, but it is a serious mistake to dismiss such writings out of hand. When a criminal, a terrorist, or a zealot speaks his mind, investigators and law enforcement officers should listen, and listen very carefully. What is incredible about the Unabomber case was the absolute commitment of Kaczynski to his criminal purposes. The case and patience with which he constructed his bombs was amazing. He removed the labels from batteries so that they could not be identified; the bombs were encased in wooden boxes that he patiently carved himself; even the glue he used was made by his boiling of deer hooves. To mail his packages he would drive for hours on public buses. This was a man who was about as "off the grid" as one could get in modern society: he lived in a shack in wilds of Montana, with no electricity or running water, surviving on little more than $400 per year. He had only a few acquaintances and no contact with family. And if he had not given law enforcement the rope with which to hang himself (i.e., by publishing his tract), it is likely that he would never have been caught.

But how was he caught? He was identified primarily through the use of what has become known as "forensic linguistics." It is the systematic analysis of words and language. FBI profiler James R. Fitzgerald, as portrayed by the *Manhunt* miniseries, believed that language was the key to unlocking the Unabomber's secrets. By their choice of words, phrases, diction, idioms, and arrangement of ideas, Fitzgerald believed, people betray their background, parts of their lives, and the ways they think (e.g., the Unabomber's idiosyncratic use of the expression "eat your cake and have it too").

With enough data, a profiler could construct a reasonably accurate picture of a writer. Yet for some reason, Fitzgerald's superiors in the FBI were slow to credit this method. Trapped by traditional law enforcement thinking, they could not see forensic linguistics as the powerful tool that it is. They scoffed at what they thought was pointless word-play. But Fitzgerald was able to construct a working profile of the tract's author, so that when Kaczynski's brother recognized the tract for what it was, the FBI was able to proceed immediately to request a search warrant.

One of my favorite examples of the power of forensic linguistics is the Renaissance humanist Lorenzo Valla's (1407-1457) unmasking of the so-called "Donation of Constantine" as a forgery. The document, whose actual name is *Constitutum Constantini*, was purported to have been a written grant by the Roman emperor Constantine the Great to Pope Sylvester, shortly before the death of the former in 337 A.D. Constantine was alleged to have gifted title to the entire western empire to the pope before his death; and it was partially on this document that the medieval Church based its temporal claims of sovereignty over European rulers. The document's authenticity had been called into question by Nicolas of Cusa, who repudiated it; but it would not be until the brilliant Valla subjected it to devastating scrutiny that it was proven beyond all doubt to be a forgery.

Valla was among the most gifted of all the Renaissance humanists. From an early age he mastered nearly the entire corpus of classical Latin literature. He knew most of the *Aeneid* by heart, and seems to have been able to recall at will passages from Livy, Macrobius, Valerius Maximus, and many others. He was also proficient in Greek and Hebrew, giving him the rare ability to access Biblical texts in the original, without having to rely on the Latin Vulgate. Beyond all this, Valla was a master of the Latin language. He could read, write, and speak it fluently, composing works of great analytical depth and literary elegance. He was also a man of strong opinions who nursed a passionate sense of justice; when he set his sights on the Donation, he knew he had found a target worthy of demolition.

How did Valla go about proving the fraudulence of the Donation? He carefully scrutinized the language of the document, and pointed out its anachronisms, stylistic irregularities, historical mistakes, and impossibilities to show that it could not have been written by Constantine or anyone else in the fourth century. (We now know that the anonymous forger wrote it in the eighth century). Valla's "little work" (*opusculum*) is not written in the style of a modern forensic document; it is very rhetorical, sounding like an oration or declamation. But this does not detract in any way from his achievement. Writing his refutation in 1440, he called it *De falso credita et ementita Constantini donatione* (*On the Forged And Deceitful Donation of Constantine*). Only someone with an encyclopedic knowledge of Latin and ecclesiastical history could have done what Valla accomplished. Here are some examples of how he exposed the document's falsity (the quotes below are from G.W. Bowersock's 2007 translation).

Valla first points out the absurdity of an emperor giving away title to half of his empire to an ecclesiastical figure. Rulers do not act this way, Valla, pointed out. Kings and emperors do not just give away their holdings; everything they do is designed to enlarge their power, not to diminish it. Having pointed out this reality of power, Valla then proceeds to focus on the linguistic evidence:

> But it is now time, lest I go on too long, to administer a mortal blow to my opponent's case, already battered and mangled, and to slice its throat with a single stroke.

He can barely conceal his scorn as he picks apart the *Donation* page by page:

> Everything is stuffed with these words–*we decree, we adorn, imperial, imperatorial, power, glory*; and he has put *exists* in place of "is" since existing implies prominence or superiority, and *indeed* for *of*

> *course*, and *bed-mates* for "companions." Bed-mates are those who sleep together and have intercourse, and must naturally be understood to be whores.

Valla notes that the text of the document is filled with "barbarisms," or bad Latin prose that could only have been written by someone with an imperfect knowledge of the language. Specifically he notes the following:

(1) The use of the word "satraps" (*satrapes*), a word that has no antecedent in imperial decrees. Valla says, speaking to the long-dead forger, "You blockhead, you dolt! Do emperors talk that way? Are Roman decrees normally drafted like that? Who ever heard of satraps being named in the deliberations of the Romans?"

(2) The forger's bad Latin that comes across in numerous grammatical errors, such as the use of the phrase "leader to the priests" instead of the more correct "leader of the priests." The forger wrote *princeps sacerdotibus* instead of the more correct *princeps sacerdotum*.

(3) The use of the phrase "imperial sceptres" (*imperialia sceptra*) when there was only one (not more than one) imperial sceptre.

(4) The clumsy, overwrought wording of the document, which abounded in tautologies and unnecessary repetition:

> At this juncture it is pertinent to remark that no one would have acted to include all nations in a single phrase of donation, and that no one that had previously plodded through the most minute details such as *strap, shoes, and linen horsecloths* would not explicitly name provinces which today have one or more kings of their own or rulers equal to kings. Obviously this forger had no idea which provinces were under Constantine and which were not, for certainly they were not all under him. [*Sed ignoravit videlicet hic falsator, quae provinciae sub Constantino erant, quae non erant, nam certe cuncte sub eo non erant.*]

Through methods like these, Valla was able to prove beyond the slightest doubt that the Donation was a forgery from a much later century. Only someone who has painstakingly gone through a text in a foreign language word by word, sentence by sentence, and paragraph by paragraph, can truly appreciate the magnitude of Valla's achievement. The modern translator would we well-served by remembering this milestone of forensic linguistics. For my part, it reminded me of the translator's obligation to remain faithful to the original text as much as possible, while also selecting the precise word or phrase conveying the meaning and spirit of the original. For this lesson, I have Valla to thank.

There is another good example of textual analysis confirming authorship of an ancient work. Due to a copyist error, Cornelius Nepos's *Lives of the Great Commanders* (*De Excellentibus Ducibus Externarum Gentium*) was for centuries believed to have been written by one Aemilius Probus, who lived during the reign of the emperor Theodosius I (A.D. 379—395). In 1569, however, the Renaissance scholar Dionysius Lambinus demonstrated that the *Lives* could not have been written during the period of the later Roman Empire; its language and syntax marked it as a product of a much earlier era. The lesson here is that language matters. Words matter. Words and language have objective significance, and are meant to convey meaning. Yet we live in an age where, far too often, language is used to fortify ignorance and conceal objective truths. We are not just what we eat: we are what we say, and what we write.

36. The Genius Of The *Iliad*

About a year and a half ago, I listened to an audio book translation of the *Iliad*. I like listening to audio books in my car as I drive around during the day; I can control the content of what I hear, and can avoid listening to the news. It had been a long time since I had had any extended exposure to the poem, and was wondering if it might mean more to me than it did many years ago. The full appreciation of works of literature, we all know, is often time-specific. At one point in a man's life, a book may seem like a tiresome bore; then, with a refreshing interval of years, the same work can hit you like a bolt of lightning, activating previously dormant or attenuated perceptions.

What matters is to be exposed to greatness, even if it is not fully appreciated. The mind will find ways of appreciating it in time.

Sometimes we have to be ready when the good things come knocking; we need to be open to what they have to offer. What struck me about the *Iliad* was how fresh, intense, profound, and bursting with violent action it was. Anyone who is tempted to think that this old poem is a Milton-esque slumber party is in for a real surprise. The action is violent, and continuous: spears smash into faces, cleave through palates, shatter jaws and sinew, and spew blood over sun-baked helmets. Combatants taunt each other with the crudest insults; animals and weapons of war kick up clouds of dust; salt sweat stings the eyes, and controlled chaos seems to have the upper hand throughout most of the narrative. This is a heroic poem in every sense of the word: it generates an atmosphere of action, intensity, moral purpose, and unadulterated vigor.

But at the same time, Homer is capable of expressing the tenderest emotions, the most heart-felt impulses, and the most unrestrained surges of rage. Perhaps only Shakespeare was capable of such a range of dramatic intensity. He is a supreme genius, of course. But who was he, and from what environment did he emerge? His poems are, first of all, the oldest literary works of the Greek-speaking world. They are probably the earliest productions of European literature as well, for we know of no coherent narratives more ancient that are west of Babylon. For his origins we have only traditions. He was probably Ionian, and sprang from a rich tradition of oral storytelling, probably accompanied by musical instruments; "rhapsodist" actually means "ode-stitcher."

As for the century in which he flourished, we cannot be precisely certain. Most authorities date him somewhere between 900 and 700 B.C. Smyrna seems to have the strongest claim to being his city of origin, although there are six or seven other respectable contenders. Of course he had a great poetic tradition behind him to draw on; no great man springs up from nothing. But this does not detract from his awe-inspiring originality and creative genius. There are, of course, many fables and traditions that have sprung up around him. One story tells us that, in his old age, he was warned by an oracle to beware of the "young men's riddle." One day, when the old poet was walking around the island of Ios, he saw some boys fishing. He asked them how their catch was that day, and they gave the following strange reply:

> What we caught we left, and what we could not catch, we carried with us.

Homer, we are told, was unable to figure out the meaning of this riddle, and died of consternation. He was buried, supposedly, on Ios. According to one dubious tradition, he was buried near seashore, and inscribed on his gravestone were these verses:

> Here Homer the Divine, in earthly bed,
> Poet of heroes, rests his sacred head.

There are some who say that the name "Homer" was nothing but a convenient fiction, a name provided by history to lump together the work of many ancient poets. They say that Homer never existed. For my part I believe this is untrue. Those who take this position remind me of the people who argue that Shakespeare could not have written the plays ascribed to him, since he was only a "lowly actor" with a second-rate education. Whenever I hear talk like this, I can only shake my head. It is difficult for many people to believe that genius has a way of cropping up in the most unlikely places, and that a bright, inquisitive mind can perform miracles given the right circumstances. These critics, unable to work wonders themselves, refuse to credit them to anyone else. I have no doubt that there was a historical Homer; perhaps he had assistants to wrote down the vast quantity of verse he had memorized, and he then edited the final product.

Anyone who has been exposed to the *Iliad* will notice that it has a unified plot and subject, consistency of characterization, and narrative cohesion. It is, to me at least, undoubtedly the work of one creative mind, and not a collage of work done by different hands. His characters are men like ourselves, who feel pain, joy, rage, and resentment. Homer's style is simple and direct, but fond of arresting simile and metaphors, imagery from nature, and even technical details about warfare and seafaring. He can talk with authority on every detail of a ship at sea, a priest sacrificing an animal, or the residence of a king. Household implements like drinking cups and helmets were described by him in great detail; and archaeologists have excavated items that have been found to match his descriptions precisely. We have no doubt, when we read Homer, that we are in the presence of a true master. He is concerned with the Trojan War, an event that to him was hundreds of years in the past. We may be comforted to know that Homer believes the men of his era were poor imitations of the great warriors of old. The actual Trojan

War, we now believe, probably took place between 1194 B.C.–1184 B.C. We are already expected to know that a coalition of Greek warlords set sail to the Hellespont to attack the city of Troy. The events of the *Iliad* take place at the very end of the war, over a very short period of time. Homer is not concerned with tracing the genesis of the war: what matters to him is the rage of Achilles and its consequences.

Achilles feels slighted by his countrymen; he sulks in his tent, and stews with rage. He is finally roused to action by the death of one of his close comrades, and he wreaks a terrible revenge on the Trojan champion, Hector. The moral conflict between these two men–Achilles and Hector–is one of the fascinating threads that runs through the poem. Achilles is pure masculine energy, youth, and passion, barely seasoned with judgment and restraint; Hector is more of the reliable, domesticated father and devoted husband. But Homer's range of emotion never fails to astound us. Alongside battle scenes of blood-soaked ferocity, he composed scenes that show a great appreciation for the charms of women. In this passage, for example, he describes the parting of Hector and his consort Andromache (VI.400-455):

> Hector left in haste the mansion, and retraced his way between
> The rows of stately dwellings, traversing
> The mighty city. When at length he reached
> The Scaean gates, that issue on the field,
> His spouse, the nobly dowered Andromache,
> Came forth to meet him.
>
> Then answered Hector, great in war: "All this
> I bear in mind, dear wife; but I should stand
> Ashamed before the men and long-robed dames
> Of troy, were I to keep aloof and shun
> The conflict, coward-like. Not thus my heart
> Prompts me, for greatly have I learned to dare
> And strike among the foremost sons of Troy,
> Upholding my great father's fame and mine;
> Yet well in my undoubting mind I know
> The day shall come in which our sacred Troy,
> And Priam, and the people over whom
> Spear-bearing Priam rules, shall perish all."

Thus speaking, mighty Hector took again
His helmet, shadowed with the horse-hair plume,
While homeward his beloved consort went,
Oft looking back and shedding many tears.
Soon was she in the spacious palace-halls
Of the man-queller Hector. There she found
A troop of maidens–with them all she shared
Her grief; and all in his own house bewailed
The living Hector whom they thought no more
To see returning from the battle-field,
Safe from the rage and weapons of the Greeks.
[*Trans. by Wm. C. Bryant*]

This parting scene is one of the most famous in poem. Once we have drunk from Homer's well, we can understand why these epic poems functioned almost as Bibles for Greek civilization for many centuries. Every Greek was taught them; their stories and anecdotes were further sources of mythology and moral instruction. As a practical matter, someone who is at least generally aware of the plots of the *Iliad* and the *Odyssey* will be able to understand ten thousand references by other authors to an assortment of characters and stories. The influence of the Homeric poems down the centuries has been immense; they are one of the pillars of the Western tradition.

I suppose the reader at this point has some practical questions about diving into the *Iliad.* Should I buy a verse translation, or a prose translation? Well, why not buy both! Experiment with both of them, and see what speaks to you best. I have verse translations by Bryant and Lattimore, and a prose edition by B.V. Rieu. Each has its place. If I can offer any suggestion, it would be this: before attempting to read the Iliad, listen to it on audio book. Your mind will absorb much of it, and you will get a good sense of Homer's stately rhythms. You can then, at your leisure, read him in print.

37. The Mystery Of Cicero's Lost Work *On Glory*

Of the literary works of classical antiquity, only a fraction has survived to the present day. What fraction this is, we do not know with precision; some estimates place it at one-fourth, but the true figure will never be known. The reader may wonder how it can be that literary masterpieces could have been permitted to fade into obscurity, and then oblivion; but, on further reflection, he will marvel more at the fact that anything at all survived from antiquity than rue the losses we have suffered. Printing and the mass production of books are relatively new inventions. For most of history (in Europe at least) books could only be reproduced as fast as a copyist could transcribe them. Multiplicity was the only insurance against destruction: the more copies in existence, the better the book's chance of survival.

The easy availability of papyrus during Roman times was cut off during the generations of chaos and poverty that accompanied the transformation of the Western Empire into a patchwork of barbarian kingdoms. The vellum codex replaced papyrus, but it was far more expensive and scarce. Books could only be afforded by the very wealthy or by the Church. Even more fatal to the great works of antiquity was disinterest and neglect. Theology began to displace the pagan concern with philosophical questions; faith, for a time, pushed reason and philosophy firmly to the side. There was less and less interest in copying, reading, or studying the great pagan works on a wide scale. Precious manuscripts were overwritten or expunged to make room for missals, religious works, or ledgers. This picture was not uniform, of course, but it does summarize the general spirit of the era. We must not condemn the Church too much in this regard, for without its stewardship and protection of the works of Greece and Rome, we would today have nothing left at all.

When the Renaissance dawned during the life of Petrarch, this dismal picture began to improve. The spirit of the times was changing; new vibrations were in the air, and thoughtful men were seeking new ways of looking at the world. The age of the manuscript hunters had begun. The first true humanists–men like Petrach, Poggio Bracciolini, Leonardo Bruni, Lorenzo Valla, and many others–combed the ecclesiastical libraries of Germany, France, and Italy to see just what had been collecting dust on the cold shelves for so long. Petrarch himself was personally responsible for recovering many new writings of Cicero, as well as hundreds of examples of his personal correspondence to friends and associates. In one of Petrarch's letters, written to a papal secretary named Luca da Penne around 1374, the scholar describes his early love for Cicero and his works. He mentions that one of his early teachers,

Raimondo Subirani, had kindly lent him many books from his personal collection. Books were expensive rarities in the fourteenth century, and were often jealously guarded.

Petrarch tantalizingly mentions that among the books he was exposed to was a copy of Cicero's now lost treatise *De Gloria* (*On Glory*). It was apparently a short work, comprising only two books. By way of comparison, *De Officiis* (*On Duties*) is three books, and *De Finibus* (*On Moral Ends*) is composed of five. He was aware of its extraordinary rarity, for he describes it as *singulares libri duo De gloria*, meaning "two books of the precious *De Gloria*." But *On Glory*, if Petrarch indeed ever did have it, slipped through his fingers. Petrarch tells us that after his father died, he felt obligated to help one of his teachers who had fallen on hard economic times. At one point, we are told, this teacher was in such dire straits that he either absconded with, or was given, the manuscript of *On Glory*; the teacher claimed he needed the book for his own research.

Once lent, the book never came back; every time Petrarch would ask for it, he was put off by one excuse or another. He would eventually find out that the priceless manuscript had been pawned; and when he pressed the man to reveal who had bought it, the teacher tearfully protested that he could not reveal the secret for shame. The teacher eventually moved to Tuscany, and there died without ever revealing what had happened to the book. Petrarch bitterly lamented,

> And so in the end I was unable to discover, with any due diligence, the faintest clue about this lost work of Cicero; I could not have cared about anything else. Thus, at the same time, I lost both my instructor and my books.

No scholar or man of letters can read these words without feeling the acutest pain. For if Petrarch's story is true, then we must accept that a priceless work by one of the most famous of all Latin authors survived the Middle Ages, only to be lost in the fourteenth century through the callous stupidity of some private tutor. It is a bitter pill to swallow. If this teacher actually pawned the unique manuscript, it would have been an unforgivable crime. But is the story accurate? Is it possible that Petrarch was mistaken, and that his account (written just before his death) confused *De Gloria* with fragments of another Ciceronian treatise?

Cicero himself stated (*On Duties* II.9) that he had written a treatise called *De Gloria* in two books. So we know that such a work did exist. An 1893 article by Robinson Ellis that appeared in *The Classical Review* (Vol. VII) entitled "De Nolhac on Petrarch and the Humanists" discusses competing theories about the book's fate. Traces of *De Gloria* may have appeared here and there in the following two centuries after Petrarch's death. According to this theory, two Renaissance scholars (Philelfus and Pietro Alcionio) used it in their own writings. Several of Alcionio's contemporaries went even further, accusing him of plagiarizing whole sections of the only extant copy of *De Gloria*, and then destroying the sole original manuscript to cover his tracks. This accusation has not stood the test of time; it is beyond belief that any scholar, no matter how malevolent, would ever do such a thing; and in fact the 18th century humanist Girolamo Tiraboschi demonstrated that the accusation was spurious. Historian Pierre de Nolhac believes that neither Alcionio nor Philelfus actually had the book: for if they did have it, they would certainly have made such a momentous discovery known. This view is certainly a rational one, but gnawing doubts remain. In a 1908 article in *The Athenaeum Journal* (No. 4197, April 4, 1908) the question of the lost *De Gloria* again was raised. The editors had this to say about De Nolhac's findings:

> Petrarch claimed to have possessed in his youth the lost *De Gloria* of Cicero, which disappeared through the dishonesty of his tutor; but M. de Nolhac (in our opinion, on insufficient grounds) disallows the claim. In an age when the frontiers of the remains of Roman literature were still unmapped, it is likely enough that a young scholar might meet with a unique MS, the value of which he would only subsequently discover.

This to me seems logical and reasonable. Why should we question Petrarch's claim to have once had *De Gloria*? He had an unrivaled knowledge of Cicero in his day, and there is no evidence that he lost his faculties in his later years. As I see it, it is just as easy to believe that the manuscript is still out there, possibly buried among the vast holding of, say, the Vatican Library, some private collection, or some national museum. It is not unknown for such things to happen. Readers of my *Stoic Paradoxes* will recall that we noted (in the introduction to the *Dream of Scipio*) the full text of

Cicero's *De Re Publica* was finally located on a palimpsest in the Vatican Library in the eighteenth century, long after it had been thought to be irretrievably lost. Some classical authors have survived on the basis of a single manuscript. The work of Velleius Paterculus, who authored a Roman history in two books, was considered lost until its text was unearthed in 1515 by Beatus Rhenanus in the monastery of Murbach in Alsace. This manuscript was described by Beatus as almost hopelessly corrupt, but diligent work by him and others restored it to a condition of reasonable legibility. Copies were made, but the originally discovered manuscript somehow disappeared again.

New manuscripts, or fragments of manuscripts, of writers both ancient and modern are constantly being unearthed in out-of-the-way places around the globe. It is a sobering fact to remember that the converse is true as well: precious manuscripts and other works of art are being constantly misplaced. Knowledge is highly perishable. Its survival must be constantly fought for and safeguarded, and must never be taken for granted. For now the mystery of *De Gloria* remains unsolved, but we should not rule out the possibility that one day it may be found. Until that time, we must console ourselves with the musings of other writers on the topics of fame and glory. I like the following thoughts on the subject of earthly fame, taken from the writings of Dr. Samuel Johnson. The comments display his usual blend of wit and wisdom:

> Those who are oppressed by their own reputation will, perhaps, not be comforted by hearing that their cares are unnecessary. But the truth is that no man is much regarded by the rest of the world. He that considers how little he dwells upon the condition of others will learn how little the attention of others is attracted by himself. While we see multitudes passing before us, of whom, perhaps, not one appears to deserve our notice or excite our sympathy, we should remember that we likewise are lost in the same throng; that the eye which appears to glance upon us is turned in a moment on him that follows us, and that the utmost which we can reasonably hope or fear is, to fill a vacant hour with prattle and be forgotten.[25]

---

[25] *Macaulay's Essay on Johnson*, Boston: Allyn & Bacon, 1924, p. 128.

38. The Rose Of The Alhambra

We will tell the tale of the Rose of the Alhambra. For many years after the city of Grenada came under the control of the Spanish kings, it remained a quiet and secluded place. Mute and desolate were its haunting spires; and, while every stone bore a secret, they contented themselves with accommodating the restless spirits of an Almoravid past. But this changed with the accession of Philip V. After his marriage to Isabella, he desired to visit Granada with his retinue. The clatter of horses' hooves, the blaring of courtly trumpets, and the cries of heralds and pages again resounded through the walls of the ancient city.

One of the young members of the king's court was Ruiz de Alarcón. He was one of the queen's favorites, we are told; and his popularity was shared among the other ladies of the court. Although he was only eighteen years old, he had learned to appreciate the charms of women; they in turn rewarded him accordingly, making him wise beyond his years. One day, he went out for a walk among the groves of the Generalife, and had taken with him one of his favorite gyrfalcons. The sport of falconry had been brought to Europe through its contact with Arabic civilization. The young man unhooded his hawk, and let it roam the skies; but soon it got away from him, and seemed to settle in the distance upon some lonely Moorish tower. This tower was, according to legend, the Tower of the Princesses. In Spanish its name is the *Torre de las Infantas*; and it was once graced by the presence of three Arabic girls named Zayda, Zorayda, and Zorahayda.

Ruiz de Alarcón approached the front door of the tower, intending to retrieve his gyrfalcon. As he came closer, he could see it was decorated in splendid Moorish style, ornate and precisely geometric. He moved past a large fountain surrounded by flowers. Beyond this was a bird in a cage, a tortoise-shell cat, reels of silk fabric, and various other odds and ends. The young man was surprised to find these badges of feminine presence in so deserted and lonely a building. He came to the door and knocked on it; it was opened a crack, and he could see the face of a beautiful girl within.

"I must not open the door and allow you in, *señor*," she said bashfully.

"I am looking for my falcon, which is one of the favorites of the queen," he replied gently. "I cannot go back to court without it, for things will go very badly for me."

"So you are one of the men of the king's court?" said she.

"Yes," was the response.

"*Santa Maria*!" she cried. "I have been warned specifically about men like you, sir. My aunt has given me specific instruction on this point."

"I am only a harmless paige, and I am only wanting to enter to look for my falcon. I promise that I will do what I came to do, and then leave."

Ruiz de Alarcón could sense that the girl liked him, despite her protestations. His imagination was set afire at the sight of her *basquiña*, and he felt compelled to press the issue. She was surpassingly beautiful, with hair neatly arranged and garnished with a fresh rose. She had an olive complexion that hinted at her Moorish origins. The youth was enchanted, and felt as if he were under a spell. She eventually allowed him to enter the building, and he retrieved his bird. The girl sat down by the fountain and continued what she was doing, which was winding silk. She once dropped the spool, and the youth picked it up; when he gave it back to her, he tried to kiss her hand.

"Ave Maria, señor!," she exclaimed in confusion. And yet although she tried to express shock, the youth could see that, deep in her heart, she was feeling the stirrings of attraction.

"Sir, you should go now, for my aunt will soon be returning from mass," she told him.

"Not until you give me that rose in your hair," was the paige's reply.

"Take it, then, and go," she said breathlessly. And she removed the flower from her dark, silky hair, and presented it to him. As she did so, he kissed her hand. Her name was Jacinta. When the old aunt returned from mass, she could see that Jacinta was in an emotional state. Jacinta explained what had happened to her aunt, whose name was Fredegonda. As often happens in such situations, the aunt had taken it upon herself to be the guardian of the Jacinta's virtue, and viewed the whole incident with suspicion. As to the background of Jacinta, she was the orphan of an army officer who had died in battle; she had been educated in a convent, as women often were in those days, and had been placed under the guardianship of her aunt. But beauty has a way of making itself known, no matter how hard some may wish to suppress it; and Jacinta was locally known by the nickname of *Rose of the Alhambra*.

Eventually Philip V left Granada, and with him went Ruiz de Alarcón. Jacinta was thrown into a depression at this, for she had been attracted to him. "*Ay de mí*!" she cried. "He is gone, gone forever." But the aunt was secretly relieved at this, for she had no sympathy for the drama of young lovers. The weeks and months went by, and Jacinta became more and more disconsolate. Of course, Fredegonda did nothing to help the situation. "What do you expect?" she said. "Didn't I warn you how men behave?" Yet Jacinta had the good sense not to allow old Fredegonda's bitterness and cynicism to corrupt her innocence.

It happened that something strange and mystical occurred one night. Jacinta awakened after midnight and walked near the alabaster fountain, where she had first given Ruiz de Alarcón the rose in her hair. She began to think of her predicament, and tears fell from her face into the waters of the Arabesque fountain. The water then began to bubble, then froth; and then a ghostly female image appeared before her eyes, bedecked in rich Moorish robes. Jacinta, terrified, fled from the fountain, and later told her aunt what had happened. To her surprise, the aunt did not dismiss the story out of hand.

"You must have been thinking about the three Moorish princesses who once lived here. Their names were Zayda, Zorayda, and Zorahayda. The first two of these left this place; but Zorahayda died here in this tower, near the fountain. And I must tell you something else. Zorahayda's lover was your ancestor. He loved her dearly, but eventually he deserted her for a Spanish lady. So what you have seen is the spirit of the unfortunate Zorahayda."

And so now Jacinta, the Rose of the Alhambra, knew she was the fusion of these two cultures, the Spanish and the Arabic. She decided to see if she could see the ghost one more time. So in the early morning hours, she appeared beside the fountain. Soon the ghostly image of Zorahayda appeared; she was stately and beautiful in a dignified way, and her garments were inlaid with costly materials. In her hand was a silver lute. The spirit asked Jacinta why she was filled with sorrow.

"I lament my current situation," she told the apparition.

"I was once like you," said Zorahayda. "I was in love with a Christian, who left me for another. I must remain a spirit in this place until you, a girl whom I once resembled, anoint me with this fountain's waters. So come here, girl, and do so."

Jacinta dipped her hands in the fountain and sprinkled it over the countenance of the ghost. The spirit soon faded away, seemingly happy. The next morning, the silver lute–the same one given by the ghost–was there. Soon Jacinta began to play this lute which such extraordinary power and brilliance that she became known all over Grenada. Her skills were unsurpassed. The Tower of the Princesses had come to life once again, with some of the most hauntingly beautiful music that the area had ever heard. Soon her fame spread to Malaga, Seville, and Cordova.

Now Philip V was known for his distemper and occasional hypochondria. He had recently fallen into one of his bouts of depression. His assistants had heard about Jacinta's consummate skill with the lute, and decided that she might be able to restore the king to his former self. So Isabella herself asked for Jacinta to play the lute for the sick king. She agreed to do it, and was led down a great hall of one of Philip's palaces. The queen told her to take a seat beside his bed and start to play.

Jacinta started slowly, and then gathered force and power. Note danced from her lute like magic; her voice penetrated the halls of castle with clarity and force. She sang, almost as if under the spell of her ancestors, of the glories of the warriors and kings of the Umayyads, the Fatimids, the Almoravids, and the Almohads. Old ballads were given new life, and a new voice. The king was not only enchanted, but he was nearly ready to leap out of his bed and take up the sword. The king's misery was permanently banished, and in its place was confidence and dignity; for he knew what he was, and what his nation's glorious history had been. Faith and knowledge had redeemed all. And when Jacinta had finished, she laid eyes on Ruiz de Alarcón, who was also present in the palace. For the silver lute possessed special powers, and could make many things possible. The two of them would eventually be united in happiness. This, then, is the tale of the Rose of the Alhambra, as I have adapted it from the version told by Washington Irving.

39. The Bricklayer Of Granada

I was lucky enough today to find an old copy of Washington Irving's *Tales of the Alhambra*; the volume is lavishly illustrated and was actually published in Granada in the late 1940s. The following tale is found in this Andalusian collection; it reminds us of the influence of Fortune in the lives of mortals, a theme that we have explored frequently in these pages. There was once a poor bricklayer and stone mason in Granada who, despite all his religious observances and almsgiving, remained poor. He kept the days of the saints; he attended mass scrupulously; and he performed good works. Yet his station never seemed to improve. Despite this situation, he never abandoned himself to cynicism or despair; he was perpetually optimistic, an indication of his strength of character. One dark night, he was roused from his sleep by a heavy knock on his front door. The bricklayer heard a voice call to him from outside the door.

"O my brother in religion! I have heard you are a decent Christian and a man who can be trusted. I need your help tonight."

The mason opened the door and saw that before him stood a thin, hungry-looking priest. He said, "I am indeed willing to help you, *senhor padre*, provided I am paid, for you can see that I am not a wealthy man and cannot be running around working for free."

The priest promised to pay the mason, provided he was first blindfolded. The request was strange, but the mason agreed to do it, perhaps more out of morbid curiosity than anything else. The priest led the mason through a series of winding, labyrinthine lanes in the Alhambra, until they eventually came to a large house. They opened the huge door, designed in the ornate Arabic style, and then entered a capacious courtyard. At this point the blindfold was removed. The place was dimly lit, but the mason could make out a fountain in the old Moorish style. The fountain was not in use; and the priest asked the mason to make a special cavity under the base of the fountain. He provided the mason with tools, bricks, and other implements to accomplish this job. So the mason worked diligently on this project all night, but was unable to finish the job.

In the morning, the priest pressed a gold coin in the mason's hand. "Are you willing to come back and finish the job?" he asked.

"Absolutely, *senhor padre*, I am willing to do this, as long as I can be paid. For you know my circumstances," was the response. And so the mason returned the next night and finished the construction of the vault under the fountain. It was at this point that the priest gave the startling reason for the work.

"And now, brother, seeing how you have done such a good job with this vault, you must help me place the bodies that are supposed to be buried in it."

The mason was both dumbfounded and disturbed by these words, but there was something about the priest's demeanor or method that made it impossible for him to refuse. He had already expended much effort on the vault, of course; he thought that it could hardly matter now for what purpose the vault was to be used. So the priest conducted the mason to a secluded room of the estate, and showed him a series of jars. The poor mason was expecting to see embalmed cadavers, or something of the sort; yet before him were arrayed a series of ceramic jars. It soon became clear to him that the jars were filled with coins, and were very heavy. He and the priest stashed the jars in the newly excavated vault, and then sealed up the space. Once this was done, the area was made to look as if it had not been disturbed at all.

The priest then blindfolded the mason once again, and then led him through a confusing series of narrow alleys and streets, so that he could never know for certain where in the Alhambra the work had been done. The priest then gave him two more gold coins, and told him to wait there until he heard the cathedral bell toll for matins. He told the mason that if he removed the blindfold before then, he would be stricken by evil; then he left. When the mason heard the bell toll, he removed the blindfold, and saw that he was along the banks of the River Xenil. He then went promptly home.

The mason enjoyed the earnings he had made from constructing the priest's vault, but, when all was said and done, he still remained as poor as he was before. Yet, he still kept his religious observances, noting the days of the saints and the other appropriate holy days. It was in his nature. So things remained for a few years. Then something new happened.

One day, as the mason was sitting outside the front door of his house, a wealthy landlord approached him. This landlord had a reputation for being a greedy miser, and many people in Granada knew him by sight. The landlord said to him, "I hear, friend, that you are poor." The mason replied in the affirmative.

"I have a good job I can offer you," said the landlord. "I have a house here in Alhambra that costs me much to maintain. No one wants to live in it. But I have heard that you are good with masonry and bricklaying, and I would like you to do some jobs for me." The poor mason accepted this offer, more intrigued than anything else. The landlord conducted him to a vast, old Arabic house that was falling into serious disrepair. Yet, there was something very familiar about the house; he knew, he sensed, deep in his bones, that he had been there before some years earlier. He eventually realized that this was the very estate that the strange old priest had conducted him so many years earlier, and where he had helped him secret his treasure. He asked the landlord who had owned the house previously.

"It used to be owned by a strange old priest, whom no one much liked. He was a man of no consequence who now matters nothing at all. There were rumors that he had amassed a large amount of wealth. He died suddenly, and a horde of priests and friars scoured his property to see if they could find his money. No one ever found anything. All the same, there are rumors that the place is haunted with the ghost of the old priest, so no one will rent it. So I am burdened with the expense of maintaining this beautiful, but decaying, old building."

This is what the rich landlord told the mason. By now, the mason knew what to do, and he acted quickly. He told the landlord, "If you let me live here rent-free, I will do all that is necessary to repair and maintain the grounds. I will restore it as it needs to be restored." The landlord immediately agreed to this proposition, happy to find someone so willing to work so hard for nothing–or so it seemed to him. He said to himself, "By God! What a fool this poor old mason is! He is willing to stay in this place and restore it completely, and asks for nothing in return except free rent! What a naive fool!"

These were the thoughts that went through the landlord's head. So he agreed to the deal, and the mason moved in with his family. Soon, as the months passed by, the old house was restored. And something else very strange happened, too. People around Granada began to notice that the poor old mason's situation steadily improved. Slowly, steadily, he seemed to shed his old ways of poverty and take on the aspect of a gentleman. His clothing, food, and circumstances improved dramatically. No one could account for the source of this new good fortune; no one suspected where the money for this new transformation had come from. And yet it happened nonetheless.

Over time, the once impoverished mason revealed himself to be one of the richest men in Granada. He was observed to contribute frequently to the Church, and never revealed the secret of his wealth during his lifetime, except on his death-bed to his son. We cannot know where, or when, in life our fortunes will change. Riches are hidden behind the illusory facades of many things in this world. Yet we must be ready to seize upon the opportunities that present themselves, and be willing to submit to the judgments of Fortune.

40. Legends Related To The Conquest Of Spain

Musa Ibn Nusair (موسى بن نصير) lived from 640 to 716 A.D. and served as the Umayyad governor-general of the province of Afriqiyya (North Africa). It was he who planned and directed the Arab conquest of the Gothic kingdom of Spain. The biographer Ibn Khallikan, writing in Baghdad in 1274, sketched the outline of his career and notable deeds. Ibn Nusair's full name was Abd al-Rahman Musa Ibn Nusair, and he was noted throughout his life, we are told, "for prudence, generosity, bravery, and piety." No army under his command was ever defeated.

His ancestry has come down to us in garbled form. Ibn Khallikan says that his father was a commander of the bodyguard of one Muawia Ibn Abi Sofyan, and later entered the service of the governor of Egypt, Abd al-Aziz Ibn Marwan. His father may have been an Arab Christian or Persian slave who was freed through manumission; the specific details are not clear. In any case, his son Ibn Nusair was a man of great diplomatic acumen and military capability. He was given command of military forces in North Africa and ordered to continue the Islamic conquest of that region; through a combination of carrots and sticks he was able to subjugate the various Berber nations there and move towards Spain with a minimum of casualties. The Visigoths in Spain (who themselves had displaced the Romans) naturally looked upon these developments with great trepidation. They became even more alarmed when it became clear that the Arab armies intended to launch an all-out invasion of the peninsula.

Spain was seen as a rich prize. Ibn Khallikan relates this saying about Spain: "If the West form the tail of the bird which is represented by the inhabited portion of the earth, that bird must be a peacock; for its beauty lies in its tail [i.e., Spain]." Meaning that, since the Iberian peninsula was the end of the peacock's "tail," its plumage was the most desirable. It is said that one of Musa Ibn Nusair's commanders, Tariq Ibn Ziyad, gave the following speech to his men before they set out to attack the Goth king of Toledo, Roderic (known to the Arabs as Lodrik). It is a superlative example of military oratory, worthy of Alexander himself:

> My men! Whither can you fly? The sea is behind you and the enemy before you; nothing can save you but the help of God, your bravery and your steadiness. Be it known to you that you are here as badly off as orphans at a miser's table. The foe is coming against you with his troops, his arms and all his forces; you have nothing to rely on but your swords, no food to eat except what you may snatch from the hands of your enemies. If you remain some days longer in your present state of privation, without succeeding in any attempt, you will lose your energy; self-confidence will then replace the fear which fills the hearts of your adversaries and embolden them against you.
>
> Defend yourselves like men who have no assistance to expect; the inevitable result of your present state is that you must contend with this *taghia* [tyrant, i.e., Lodrik] who now comes against you from his strongly fortified city. But, to triumph over him is for you quite possible, if you are willing to expose yourselves to death...You know what this island [*jazeera*, i.e., the Spanish peninsula] produces; large-eyed maidens, daughters of the Greeks [Tariq mistakenly believed the Goths were related to the Greeks], graceful in their bearing, covered with pearls, coral and robes interwoven with pure gold–maidens carefully guarded in the palaces of crowned kings...
>
> May the Almighty aid such heroes as you are, so that you may gain renown in this world and in the next. Know also that I shall be the first in doing that to which I invite you: at the joining of the two armies in battle, I shall myself charge upon the *taghia* of the people of Lodrik and slay him, if God permit. Charge at the same time as I; if I die after killing him, I shall at least have delivered you from the

> harm he might do you, and you will have no difficulty in finding a brave and intelligent chief to be a commander over you. If I perish before reaching Lodrik., follow up what I commenced; charge you also upon him and, by taking his life, effect what is most important for the conquest of this island. Your adversaries will lose all hopes in losing him.[26]

"Wisdom," says Ibn Khallikan, "descended from heaven upon three different members of the human body: upon the brains of the Greeks, the hands of the Chinese and the tongues of the Arabs." The Spaniards, who inherited the blood and culture of the Arabs, learned their lessons well from this speech and others like it: over eight hundred years later, Spanish conqueror Hernando Cortes would give one very much like it to his own men in Mexico before setting out to overthrow the Aztec kingdom. History is not without a sly sense of irony. We will now relate two legends related to the conquest of Spain. They are both related by Ibn Khallikan in his biography of Musa Ibn Nusair, but remain almost unknown in the West.

The Tasks Of The Two Suitors. Before the Arab conquest, there was a king living near Cadiz who had a beautiful daughter. The reputation of this girl was carried far and wide among the many sovereigns in Spain. This fact, however, presented her father with an acute problem. If he offered her to any of the other sovereigns, he then risked offending the remainder. Uncertain how to proceed, he spoke to his daughter and the two of them agreed on a course of action. The daughter's idea was to impose two conditions. The first was that she would ask her suitors to be not just a king, but also a sage. The second was that she would require her suitors to accomplish some difficult task. So she and her father wrote to all the other kings and told them these conditions. Most of them were deterred by these conditions, and were never heard from again. However, two kings did respond, and stated they were willing to participate in the contest. The girl told both kings that she would assign them each a task, and would marry whomever accomplished his task soonest. This is what she said:

---

[26] Trans. by McGucken de Slane, *Biog. Dict.*, III.478.

> In our land [Spain] we need stone mills to grind our grain. I will ask that one king discover a way to power the mills using water that has flowed from that land lying across the strait [i.e., North Africa]. To the other king, I will ask that he construct a talisman to protect our country against the peoples of North Africa.

Each king accepted the task that was imposed on him, and set about their jobs quickly. The first king set out to build an aqueduct across the Strait of Ceuta that would be able to bring in water from what is now Morocco. Along the canal which was thus created, he constructed mills to grind grain. The second king–the one tasked with making a talisman–did not see his work proceed so smoothly. He experienced delays and work stoppages. His idea was to build a huge bronze statue of a Berber tribesman that was around seventy cubits in height. In the statue's left arm was a cloak; and in its right arm, the extended hand contained a key. The statue's gestures were such that it said to any ship sailing by, "You cannot enter here." We are told that whenever a foreign ship passed by the statue, the key would fall from its hand, thereby preventing any entry.

Now the king who was tasked with building the aqueduct actually finished his job before the other king. But he kept this fact a secret. The reason he did this was that he did not want his competitor to destroy the talisman upon finding out he had lost the contest. The winner wanted to have both the young girl and the talisman for himself. But the talisman-building king eventually did find out he had lost, of course. When he did, he happened to be at the apex of his statue, polishing its bronze face. When he was told that the aqueduct-building king had beaten him, he fell from the top of his statue and was killed. Thus the king who had built the aqueduct came into possession of the talisman and the girl. What is the meaning of this fable? Ibn Khallikan unfortunately does not provide any comment; but my view is that it encapsulates two messages. One message may be that much can be gained by stealth, secrecy, and daring; another message may in fact be a prophecy, that the conquest of Spain from North Africa was inevitable. Each reader, of course, will have to find his or her own interpretation.

The Chest Of Talismans. We now tell a second tale from Ibn Khallikan. He relates that, before the Arab conquest, the Gothic kings of Spain were much in fear of encroachment and conquest from North Africa, and would seek various types of talismans as divine protection. These kings collected all their talismans and placed them in a large marble chest in the city of Toledo. This marble chest they then placed inside a secure building with an immense locked door. The kings decided among themselves that, upon the death of each of their predecessors, they would add a lock to the door. Thus each generation was tasked with adding a lock to the immense doors of the building that housed the protective talismans. And so it was: for many generations (twenty-six, in fact), the Spanish kings kept this custom, and added locks to the doors.

All this changed with the accession of Lodrik, the king who was crushed by the Arab incursion into Spain, as we observed in the preceding paragraph. When Lodrik (Roderic) was elevated to the throne, he disregarded the customs of those who came before him. He was invested with impatience and foolishness. He told his ministers, "I can't stand not knowing what is inside that old building that houses the old marble chest of talismans. What could be in it? Surely this must be some useless old superstition that our ancestors erected for no good purpose. It has twenty-six locks on it. I wish to cut them all off." But his ministers were horrified when they heard this. They tried to dissuade him. "Sire," they said, "Even if this happens to be a superstition, it is not wise to tamper with it. All your ancestors respected this custom. For you to break it, would bring a curse down on your head from God."

But some men will not listen to such talk, especially when they think that they can gain treasure. For Lodrik thought that the marble chest contained gold and jewels. So he decided to cut the locks off the doors, and violate the marble chest. His men did so, and found inside the chamber they found a beautiful tablet of gold encrusted with jewels. Inscribed on the tablet were the words, "Table of Solomon, the Son of David, May God Place His Blessing on Both of Them." They then proceeded to open the marble chest itself. Inside the chest was a piece of very old parchment, upon which was drawn figures of Arab horsemen in military regalia. In their hands were long lances and swords. And on the parchment were written these words:

> This chamber and this chest were locked through prudence. When they are opened, the people whose

> images are on the chest will enter into the island of Spain, the empire will escape from the hands of the Greeks and their wisdom shall be obliterated.

And when Lodrik was brought this parchment by his men, he knew he was doomed. Soon after this, his kingdom was swept away. These are the follies of empires and kings.

41. How Were Ancient Books Made?

There has been surprisingly little information published on how books were made, edited, distributed, and stored in ancient times. Yet the subject holds real interest for many of us today. My goal in this short essay will be to summarize how books were made and stored during the Greco-Roman period. I am confident that readers will quickly appreciate just how much more convenient our access to written information is in comparison to what our remote ancestors had to contend with. What we today call "books" were in ancient times rolled sheets of pressed papyrus. The papyrus plant grew principally in Egypt; its reeds were harvested, split open, dried, and glued into long sheets that could then be written on or illustrated. According to Prof. G.W. Houston, whose essential *Inside Roman Libraries* forms the principal modern word on the topic, individual papyrus sheets were generally between 25 and 33 cm high. Writing was done on one side of the papyrus only, and it was done in columns perpendicular to the length of the roll. The written side was called in Latin the *recto* (from *rectum*, "right"), and the blank reverse side the *verso* (*versus*, "turning"). Written columns were normally about 5 to 7 cm wide in prose texts, but could be wider in the case of poetry. Sumptuously illustrated texts do not appear to have been very common; then as now, the goal of book dealers was to make book production commercially profitable.

The writers of papyrus texts generally had at least some training in the art of copying and interpretation. This could–and did–vary greatly from place to place. Better trained scribes knew how to write texts in such a way that the reader's eyes were not inordinately fatigued; some even made use of an optical effect known as "Maas's Law" that was used to compensate for the distortion effects of reading wound scrolls. Amazingly, ancient scribes never paid much attention to punctuation or even spacing between words; examples of ancient books that have survived often show a continuous line of letters. Readers were apparently expected to be able to supply their own mental word spacing and punctuation. Once book "volumes" were completed, they would be rolled up, either with a wooden dowel attached or without one. Sizes of books varied greatly, of course, depending on the type of work. A long work–such as a historical or geographical work–could fill a roll nearly 20 meters long. Short works of poetry were much smaller. If a papyrus book was damaged or defaced, it could be repaired by cutting out the affected part, recopying the text, and then gluing the new section directly back into the scroll.

Once a scroll was rolled up, the name of the author and the title of the work would be written on a strip of papyrus (3 cm x 8 cm in dimension) and glued to the outside of the roll. This title tag was called the *sillybon*. In practice it was easy for a reader to acquire a copy of a book. The simplest method was to buy a copy from a dealer; the Roman writer Aulus Gellius mentions his trips to booksellers in Athens to pick up volumes for leisurely reading. Another method was to copy a manuscript yourself; copyright laws did not exist in the ancient world, and no author expected to be able to make a living solely by writing. But transcribing a long piece of writing is tedious and dreary work, and it is difficult to imagine anyone but the most enthusiastic bibliophile attempting it. More likely would it have been for a reader to secure the services of a scribe or slave to do the work for him. For the wealthy this would not have presented any problem. Cicero seems to have had scribes (*librarii*) or skilled slaves living with him at certain periods of his life; the fact that so many of his works and letters have survived attests to the care with which he took in publishing his works.

Under such loose conditions, it was only natural that the quality of texts varied greatly. In theory, anyone could "publish" a book if he could hire enough scribes to release a batch of copies for sale. Untrained copyists could multiply errors in texts; omissions or deletions by careless copyists could significantly corrupt a text. The modern scholar often wonders–with not a little unease–just how far the texts that have come down to us may have deviated from the original words of the authors. But perhaps in practice corruption of texts presented little problem; it is likely that dealers and librarians knew where the best texts were, and sent scribes there to acquire the best copies.

Wealthy Greeks and Romans maintained their own extensive private collections before the advent of public libraries in the imperial period; Pliny the Elder and Varro were known to have vast collections, as did the physician Galen. If we may believe the testimony of his nephew, the elder Pliny was surrounded by books at all times; he even had books read to him while he ate and bathed. Prof. Houston notes that Cicero often complained of the difficulty of finding good texts. In one of his letters to his brother Quintus in 54 B.C., he notes that hunting for decent volumes was "a time-consuming task, and it takes a very careful man. I know this myself: after a lot of effort, I have accomplished nothing. I really don't know where to turn...copies that are on sale are full of errors."

Ancient books could not, like the modern codex book, be stacked on shelves. Collectors and librarians undoubtedly had sophisticated systems of cataloging and storage, and these probably relied on a combination of author and subject referencing. They could be stored in wall-niches (*armaria*), cabinets, bins, or even earthen jars. Insect larvae were a constant problem; there is evidence that cedar wood and oil from Phoenicia was sometimes used to ward off insect pests. The scribe's ink was generally made from soot (lampblack) mixed with water and gum arabic. Pens (*calamus*) were made from sharpened reeds split at the writing end to hold the ink; bronze pens were occasionally used, but the quill pen from bird feathers does not seem to have been used.

All in all, the realities of the production and dissemination of ancient books should give us a greater appreciation of the difficulties that scholars faced in classical times. Books took a considerable effort to produce, were not disseminated evenly, and could be filled with errors. One can only marvel at the effort it must have taken Roman writers like Varro, Cicero, Pliny, and Livy to collate, read, and use manuscripts in the days before mass printing or even properly indexed texts. On the other hand, ancient man adapted to the situation. Without the modern media as a distraction, he was able to develop his memory to a degree that would make us moderns blush in shame. By modern standards, the book business in ancient times was primitive; but we must remember that the situation was far better than it was in Europe during most of the medieval period, when books were even rarer. With the slow disappearance of the Western Empire after 450 A.D., the commercial market for papyrus in Egypt was cut off. Once this happened, books could only be produced in vellum or parchment, and these materials were extremely expensive. Only with the appearance of paper and moveable type in the fifteenth century did things truly improve. We should be grateful for our books, and respect the tremendous efforts that our ancestors made to put them in our modern hands.

42. The Villa Of The Papyri: A Glimpse At A Roman Book Collection

Sometimes an accident of history can preserve records of great value. As is well-known, Mount Vesuvius in Italy erupted in 79 A.D. entombing the towns of Pompeii and Herculaneum in ash and ejecta. In the eighteenth century, these sites began to be explored in a random and haphazard manner; one of the villas so discovered turned out to be the residence of a dedicated scholar. Some have speculated that the villa's owner may have been Marcus Calpurnius Piso, who was consul in 58 B.C., but we cannot be sure without further evidence. There were hundreds of papyrus book rolls (i.e., "volumes") spread out over several rooms, arranged in cabinets and cases.

As might be expected, the books were in a very fragile state of preservation. The heat and ash of the eruption had carbonized most of the rolls, and centuries of water and mineral immersion had made them still more delicate. It was, in fact, a miracle that they even existed at all. Techniques for "unrolling" and reading these books was not advanced when they were first discovered, and early attempts to preserve them or cut them open did more harm than good. Yet despite all this, we at least have something. What books are in this treasure-trove? Most of the books deal with Epicurean philosophy, in all its branches: physics, rhetoric, ethics, aesthetics, etc. Many of the books are works of the philosopher Philodemus of Gadara, who flourished in the first century B.C. We even have eight books of Epicurus's own work *On Nature*, which is a rare find. Epicurus himself was an extremely fecund writer, but very little of his output has survived. G.W. Houston's wonderful *Inside Roman Libraries* compiled a list of the authors of the Greek and Latin volumes at the villa that have so far been identified. The following is a list of the Greek authors thus far identified:

Carneiscus (Epicurean, prob. 2nd century B.C.)
Chrysippus (Stoic philosopher)
Colotes of Lampsacus (prob. 2nd century B.C.)
Demetrius Laco (fl. 100 B.C.)
Epicurus
Metrodorus of Lampsacus (3rd cent. B.C.)
Philodemus of Gadara (1st cent. B.C.)
Polystratus (Epicurean, 2nd cent. B.C.)
Zeno of Sidon (1st cent. B.C.)

Surprisingly few Latin works were found. What has been recovered are mostly scattered fragments of uncertain authorship. A poem about the Battle of Actium has been recovered (*Carmen De Bello Actiaco*), as well as some possible fragments possibly from the antique poet Ennius. A 1979 inventory of the recovered papyri listed 1,826 distinct items; that figure now stands at 1,850. Not all of there are book rolls, however; many of them are fragments. Prof. Houston estimates that the actual number of book rolls was probably somewhere between 600 to 1,000. By any standard, this was a respectable collection of Epicurean writings. Yet it is still only a tiny fraction of what was once a large corpus of material. The biographer Diogenes Laertius, whose precious *Lives of the Philosophers* I have often relied on, tells us that there were about 17 main Epicurean philosophers; and many of these writers authored dozens of works. The discoveries at the Villa of the Papyri fill us with regret, in many ways, by reminding us just how much of ancient literature has been lost.

But what do these papyri look like? In one of Cicero's surviving letters, he mentions how difficult it was for him to find well-edited texts of philosophical works. Sloppy editing and copying could pose something of a problem for scholars; dedicated men often had to seek out a particular exemplar and have it copied locally. Since all books had to be reproduced by a scribe's labors, there were always going to be mistakes. Some copyists were better than others, and some were better able to correct errors as they found them. Knowledge had to be worked for; it was not just served up to anyone on a silver platter, as we see today. The idea of laboriously copying out a book is something inconceivable to us in the modern era; that fact that this was how books were copied until the invention of print in the fifteenth century is something that should make us pause in wonder. Most of the books at the villa are between 19 and 24 cm. in height; the columns of written text are between 15 and 18 cm. When the book rolls were rolled up, their diameter was between 4 and 9 cm. Fully unrolled books could be between 9 to 12 meters long. Another interesting thing that scholars have noticed about the book rolls is that many of them contain "line counts"; that is, a number indicating the total number of lines in each roll. What was the purpose of such stichometric counts? One practical reason may have been to determine the copyist's fee. Then, as now, people working on texts often calculated their fees by the word or line. Another curious fact is that the book rolls were already quite old when Vesuvius erupted. Prof. Houston has estimated that the papyri were between 120 and 160 years old at the time of the eruption. This is impressive: while papyrus rolls were laborious and sometimes costly to produce, they could last more than one lifetime.

The inevitable impression that all this leaves on the reader is that knowledge is fragile and perishable. We should try to imagine the effort and time that it would have taken the owner of the Villa of the Papyri to assemble his collection. We should try to imagine the thousands of hours that copyists would have had to spend to produce the hundreds of rolls in the villa. And all this knowledge, all this effort, was gone in the blink of an eye, the victim of geologic circumstance. We gradually become aware just how precious books really are, and how we must ensure that physical copies of books–not digital copies–are protected and safeguarded. Historical memory in our era is vanishing at an alarming rate; and when I say alarming, I mean truly alarming. Many people in our societies have only the dimmest awareness of even recent historical events, if they have any awareness of them at all. Digitization is not a solution to the problem: in many ways, it is part of the problem itself. It provides a false sense of security, and arguably promotes a cavalier attitude towards the preservation of knowledge. Despite their sorry state, the papyri at the villa survived a physical disaster and the passage of centuries; they were at least readable to some extent. Had the "books" been electronic data in some computer, nothing would have survived at all.

43. Georg Wilhelm Freytag's Latin Compendium Of Arabic Proverbs

About a year ago one of the readers here at *Fortress of the Mind* informed me of a work of scholarship that he thought might be of interest. The work was Georg Wilhelm Freytag's monumental Latin treatise *Arabum Proverbia* (literally *Proverbs of the Arabs*, but better rendered as *Arabic Proverbs*), a three-volume collection of classical Arabic proverbs drawn from the *Compendium of Proverbs* (مجمع الامثال) of the medieval philologist Ahmad Ibn Muhammad Al-Maydani (احمد ابن محمد الميداني). I was able to locate this impressive yet forgotten work, and have found much pleasure in poring over its pages.

Georg Wilhelm Freytag (1788-1861) was a German orientalist and philologist. Born in Lüneburg, he attended the University of Göttingen, trained in theology, and apparently intended to enter the ministry. After a brief stint as a chaplain in the Prussian army, he undertook the serious study of near Eastern languages (Arabic, Hebrew, Turkish, and Persian) in Paris. He was eventually appointed a full professor at the University of Bonn, remaining in that position until his death in 1861. He was a serious and dedicated scholar; among other works, he produced a two-volume work in Latin on Arabic songs, a reference work on Hebrew grammar, and a massive Arabic-Latin dictionary.

Let us say a bit more about the *Arabum Proverbia.* Published in 1838, it is written entirely in Latin and Arabic. It contains thousands of proverbs covering a wide variety of subjects; the proverbs are printed in Arabic, followed by Latin translations and explanations. The three-volume set seems never to have been printed in a second edition after 1838. Freytag imports his proverbs wholesale from his source, the medieval compendium of Al-Maydani, but it is not a direct translation of that older work. He culled out the proverbs, but added his own translation and commentary for each proverb. The proverbs are arranged alphabetically (according to the Arabic alphabet) with the first letter of the first word in the proverb used as the marker. Al-Maydani, whose name has been Latinized as Meidanius, was born in Nishapur and died there in 1124; his *Compendium of Proverbs* is an incredible achievement for one mind. I have not examined Al-Maydani's original Arabic work, but in Latin translation it fills several large volumes. It does not appear that either Al-Maydani's Arabic text or Freytag's Latin text have ever been translated into English.

Freytag's text has been scanned and is available in digital form; and what purports to be a printed facsimile of this is available for sale. However, the printed facsimile contains significant scanning errors that make some pages illegible. As a useable reference work, it is entirely inadequate, in that it omits the second volume of the set, and carelessly deletes the first twenty pages of the third volume. To obtain my own physical copy, I bought the reprints of the first and third volumes, inadequate as they are, and brought a digital copy of the second volume to a printer to have it bound in six thick spiral binders. It was expensive, but to me worth the price; pains-taking scholarship is nothing less than a treasure. Yet the entire work needs a thorough overhaul: it should be typeset in modern font, properly indexed, and outfitted with new Arabic quotations that can be easily read. The proper solution is for someone to locate an original copy of the 1838 edition, and work directly from this archetype. Here are the contents of each volume (*tomus*):

Volume I: Introduction to the work, description of sources, and proverbs from the letters *hamza* (ء) to zad (ص). Freytag provides the original Arabic proverb, followed by a Latin translation and brief commentary to explain its origin or meaning.

Volume II: Proverbs from the letters *dhad* (ض) to *ya* (ي)

Volume III: Assorted proverbial sentiments (*sententiae proverbiales*), days noted among the Arabs for conflicts (*dies inter Arabes pugnis celebres*), assorted humorous sayings (*facete ingenioseque dicta*), and indices. Freytag makes an effort to organize his mass of proverbs by subject matter; he shows great sensitivity to the importance of his subject matter. For him, proverbs are not just noteworthy sayings; they are repositories of a people's cultural wisdom, and ought to be studied with assiduous diligence. In the introduction, he explains:

> Among all things produced from the human mind, none are found so worthy of our attention so much as the proverbs of nations; for just as a tree may be understood from its fruit, so may the natural condition of a people's mind be known from its proverbs. Proverbs acquaint us with the thinking, feeling, and habits intimately coherent in a people's regular life.

> History teaches the external history of a people; proverbs display what the nature of their souls may be. History describes the reasons for the thinking and actions of individual men and the power that a people might possess; proverbs paint the rationale for the thought and action of the entire nation. Although proverbs are spoken by individual persons, nevertheless, because customs come to be enshrined in proverbs, an entire people has asserted itself, such that the thoughts and feelings of an entire people must be deemed to be in rational harmony. And since the footprints of each specific nation's thoughts and feelings are impressed with proverbs, they are for this reason more worthy of our attention. In this respect it must be seen why Arabic proverbs, for which we here devote our energetic attention, are more deserving than others.

Freytag was not the first scholar to undertake a collection of proverbs drawn from Al-Maydani. Henricus Albertus Schultens published his own edition in 1795, but his work is not as extensive or as complete as Freytag's. In its scope, attention to detail, and execution, Freytag's *Arabum Proverbia* is a masterpiece of laborious scholarship. This long-neglected work deserves the services of a proper editor and translator. Even for those comfortable with Latin, the text in its present form is in need of a thorough overhaul. The Arabic text needs to be set in modern font (preferably without voweling), and the indices need to be updated with modern conventions. An English edition would help ensure that this classic reaches the audience that it deserves.

44. Friedrich Schlegel And The Beginnings Of Comparative Philology

The great antiquity and depth of Indian civilization had been known to Europe and the Middle East for many centuries; yet the precise contours of Indian advances in mathematics, literature, and philosophy were hidden behind the veils of preconception and confusion. We know that the caliph Harun Al-Rashid, in Baghdad in the 9th century A.D., commissioned translations of some prominent works of Indian literature, but such knowledge remained in the hands of scholars and was not widely diffused. Things began to change gradually with the advancement in geographic, scientific, and commercial knowledge in the 17th and 18th centuries. All learning builds on the shoulders of successive visionaries. The Italian Jesuit Roberto de Nobili (1577-1656) is generally credited with being one of the first, if not the first, learned Europeans who gained an intimate acquaintance with Indian civilization. He took up residence in India as a missionary, learned several south Indian languages, and integrated himself into Indian society; but timing is everything when it comes to the propagation of knowledge, and the European public was not yet ready to hear of his discoveries. A tremendous leap forward was taken with the researches of the Englishman Sir William Jones (1746-1794). He was a linguist of staggering ability: he was fluent in sixteen languages and competent in about a dozen others; even more importantly, he knew how to perceive connections that existed below the surface of linguistic data. This is what separates a linguist from a true philologist.

In one of the papers he presented to the Royal Asiatic Society in 1786, he proposed that Sanskrit, India's major literary language, shared a common ancestor with the so-called Indo-European languages. At some time in the remote past, Jones postulated, there must have been some original root from which grew the majority of Europe's languages. He was not the first to suggest this idea; there were other scholars who had offered the same suggestion, but conditions at the time had not been favorable to its receipt. Jones was also one of the first Europeans to translate a major work of Sanskrit literature, the play *Shakuntala* (अभिज्ञानशाकुन्तलम्), authored by the revered dramatist Kalidasa. But it was the rise of the Romantic movement in Europe that catapulted Sanskrit to the forefront of intellectual circles. That this happened is principally due to the efforts of a passionate German Romantic philosopher and linguist named Karl Wilhelm Friedrich Schlegel (commonly cited as Friedrich Schlegel).

He was born in Hanover in 1772 and, like many great linguists, came from a clerical background. By 1799 he had become a fervent Romantic and was entirely devoted to literary activities; he was acquainted with Schiller and Goethe, but they seemed not quite to know what to make of this tumescent, artistic soul. But he was a dedicated scholar with a solid grasp of the major European and Near Eastern languages, and possessed an intuitive ability to find connections between things that many others before him had overlooked. His moment of glory came in 1808 with the publication of a tremendously influential booklet entitled *Über die Sprache und Weisheit der Indier* (*On the Language and Wisdom of India*). Here Schlegel made his case that Sanskrit and the European languages shared the same ancestor. As we have noted, he was not the first to make this observation; but he was able to articulate his points in a way that the public could understand, and this made all the difference. Sanskrit was no longer the exclusive provenance of specialists; it was presented to the European public almost as a fraternal language. Let us pause to examine the major points in this passionate admixture of scholarship and Romanticism.

Before we begin, I cannot resist here quoting a favorite passage of mine from his essay "On the Limits of the Beautiful." It is an idea that resonates in my own experience, and encapsulates the classical ideal of reasonable moderation:

> The soul needs a certain amount of intellectual enjoyment to give it strength adequate for the daily struggle in which it is involved. The energies of the mind are as completely shattered and destroyed by constant restraint, as they are relaxed and enfeebled by perpetual enjoyments. To make pleasure the sole object of life is to defeat our own intention; for man exists but in accordance with the decrees of nature, and her laws stand in constant opposition to his own desires. Life is a stern struggle between conflicting powers. Every inordinate indulgence involves a corresponding amount of suffering. Those who yield their souls captive to the brief intoxication of love, if no higher and holier feeling mingle with and consecrate their dream of bliss, will shrink trembling from the pangs that attend their waking. Others, on the contrary, who devote themselves to glorious deeds, and seek enjoyment only in the intervals of more serious exertion, will have their best reward in the pure, unchanging happiness purchased by such self-denial. [*Trans. by E.J. Millington*]

We now return to Sanskrit. Here Schlegel exhorts us to see Indian literature as a worthy companion to the writings of classical Greece and Rome:

> The study of Indian literature requires to be embraced by such students and patrons as in the fifteenth and sixteenth centuries suddenly kindled in Italy and Germany an ardent appreciation of the beauty of classical learning, and in so short a time invested it with such prevailing importance, that the form of all wisdom and science, and almost of the world itself, was changed and renovated by the influence of that re-awakened knowledge. I venture to predict that the Indian study, if embraced with equal energy, will prove no less grand and universal in its operation, and have no less influence on the sphere of European intelligence.

Schlegel separates his book into discussions on (1) the Indian language generally; (2) the affinity of its roots; (3) the grammatical structure of Sanskrit; (4) the classification of language groups; (5) the origins of language; and (6) the differences between languages. There are some flights of fancy here, and odd digressions into metaphysics and religion that need not concern us; but here, at long last, is a clear and cogent demonstration of the common origins of the speech of Europe and India. Consider the following passage, where he provides specific examples of connections between Sanskrit, German, Greek, and Latin:

> I shall select a few of the most remarkable words signifying mind, thought, science, as affording particularly clear evidence of their common Indian descent. *Momoh monoson*, in the Latin *mens*, the verb *monyote* [he thinks] is found in the German *meinet. Motih* is the Greek *métis*. Another form, closely connected with this and with the German *muth* [spirit, courage], is found in *amódoh* [pleasure], *anmuth*; the a in the Indian *amódo* (which probably is also allied with the Persian *oméd* [hope]) is used merely as a prefix; from the same root we

> shall then have *unmadoh*; *un* being the regular form adopted for the sake of euphony, instead of *ut*; *unmadoh* [desperate, furious], literally the same as *ermens*, may have been contracted into the English *mad*. *Atmoh*, which signifies *ipse* and *spiritus*, has already been noticed in the Greek and German, *atmé* and *athem* [breath]...The Latin *vox* may have been derived from *vocho*, or from *vakyon*; both forms are in use. The root re signifies speech or language, *rede* in German. *Ganon* becomes in Latin *cantus*, from the root *gi*, *giyote* [he sings]; in the Persian *khöndan* [to sing and read].
>
> The Indian pronouns generally coincide with the Latin. Certainly *tvon* [thou] is common to all the derived languages; *vhon* [I] is, on the contrary, traced only in the Celtic on; the dative *moya* [to me] is nearest to the Greek *moi*; the me, which is used instead of *man* [me], and also in the fourth and sixth cases, is common to both Greek and Latin; but the root *svo* (whence L. *suus*, -a, -um [his] are derived, and is often prefixed as a particle in order to express self-reliance, or self-confidence, has in its declension cases which are precisely similar to the Latin, as *svon*, L. *suum*, *svan*, L. *suam*, etc.

At long last, we finally have what was so desperately needed: a clear demonstration of the common origin of the Indo-European family of languages. That Schlegel was able to record these connections, and present them to the lay reader in a way that was both intelligible and engaging, was a skill of considerable importance. What was once exotic and inaccessible now became comprehensible and accessible. From 1808 until his death in 1829, Schlegel was occupied with both literary work and appointments to various governmental posts. Both he and his brother August made significant contributions to German literature and philosophy. But it is for his work on Sanskrit that Schlegel is primarily remembered today; he functioned as one of the catalysts and engines of the budding study of comparative philology. Those that came after him would build on what he had begun. More than any other man of his era, he cut away the tangled overgrowths of linguistic speculation and ignorance to see what truly lay beneath.

45. Al-Minara: The Pharos Lighthouse Of Alexandria

One of the more fascinating of the seven wonders of the ancient world was the Pharos Lighthouse in Alexandria, Egypt. I have lately been reading the history of the Arab conquest of Egypt in the seventh century, and have become more acquainted with some of the monument's unique characteristics, and the legends that have surrounded it.

The structure itself was an immense, multi-storied tower that rose hundreds of feet into the air. Construction began during the reign of Ptolemy I Soter after 305 B.C., and ended during the tenure of his son Ptolemy II Philadelphus. Designed by Sostratus of Cnidus, it took twelve years of meticulous effort to complete. It seems that some of the Arab historians confused the construction legends associated with the lighthouse with those stories connected with Alexandria's largest obelisks. The Arabic name for the Pharos lighthouse was, with that beautiful simplicity associated with Arabic place names, simply "Al-Minara (المنارة)." The historian Ibn Al-Fakih, writing in the early 10th century, tells us that "The *minara* of Alexandria stands on a crab of glass in the sea…it has two pillars standing on two images, one of brass and one of glass, the brazen image in the form of a scorpion and the glass image in the form of a crab." Ibn Rustah, at about the same time, noted that "two monuments [were] standing on two figures of scorpions, mae of copper or brass, on which are inscriptions. It is also reported that the figure of the scorpion was melted by a fire kindled beneath it, and that the monuments fell." This legend solidified over time; so the historian Mas'udi later wrote:

> The *minara* was built on a foundation of glass in the form of a crab, on a tongue of land projecting into the sea. On the top of the lighthouse were images of brass. One figure pointed with its right hand to the sun, wherever it might be in the heavens, and lowered its hand as the sun sank; another pointed to the

> sea in the direction from which an enemy was approaching, and as the enemy drew near, it cried out in a terrible voice, which could be heard two or three miles away, and so alarmed the inhabitants.

How to account for these fabulous stories? It turns out that, as often happens in history, the legends have some basis in fact. We now know that two large granite obelisks in Alexandria, which were standing in front of a church called the Caesarion at the time of the Arab movement into Egypt, were in fact resting on four huge metal "crab" sculptures. According to the historian A.J. Butler, when one of the obelisks (the so-called "Cleopatra's Needle") was removed and sent to New York in the modern era, evidence of the metallic crabs could plainly be seen. Archaeologists were even able to make out inscriptions in Latin and Greek on them. The second obelisk could very well have been resting on crab sculptures made of black obsidian, which has a glass-like appearance. We may reasonably conclude, as does historian A.J. Butler, that the two large obelisks standing before the Caesarion rested on bases made of metallic crabs and obsidian scorpions.

One can easily see how the Arab historians might have confused the base constructions of the obelisks with that of the lighthouse itself. Not all of them made this mistake, however. The writer Istakhri notes, "The minara, founded on a rock in the sea, contains more than 300 rooms, among which the visitor cannot find his way without a guide." The historian Ibn Haukal says that the minara was "built of hewn stones fitted together and fastened [i.e., jointed] with lead; there is nothing like it on earth." The chronicler Idrisi says:

> [The *minara*] is unmatched in all the world for its architecture and strength of structure. It is built of the hardest Tiburtine stone, bedded in molten lead, and so firmly set that the joints cannot be loosened. On the north side the sea washes against it. Its height is 300 cubits, taking three palms to the cubit, and so its length is 100 statures of man. From the ground to the middle story are 70 statures, from the middle to the top 26, and the lantern on the top is 4 statures.

Even more intriguing is Istakhri's comment on the number of rooms in the lighthouse. What purpose would these rooms have served? The historian Makrizi makes this fantastical comment about the labyrinthine nature of the monument:

> It is said that whoever entered this lighthouse became distracted and lost his way, by reason of the number of chambers and stories and corridors which it contained...So it is reported that when the [Arabs] arrived at Alexandria in the caliphate of Al-Muqtadir with an army, a body of them entered the lighthouse on horseback and lost their way, till they came upon a crevice in the crab of glass upon which the structure was founded; and many of them fell through it and perished.

The mirror at the apex of the lighthouse was also a focus of amazement. Some writers say that a huge mirror of gilt metal was perched atop the structure, and had a diameter of "five spans." But the historian Mas'udi says the mirror was actually made of some kind of transparent stone. Yet another writer claims the mirror was constructed from glass. We cannot know for certain, but it seems metal would have been the easiest and most practical choice. The purpose of the mirror was undoubtedly to signal ships at sea; it could never have served as a weapon to focus the rays of the sun, as this would have required a mirror of immense proportions. It appears that during the daylight hours the mirror was used for signaling, and during the night a fire was kept burning to serve as a beacon. As for the comment by Mas'udi about the siren atop the lighthouse, I have been unable to find any additional details. It may be that some kind of siren was installed there that could be sounded by a human-powered machine; or perhaps there was some wind-powered apparatus that was activated by air blowing through it. We do not know.

The lighthouse must have been a wonder of engineering to last as long as it did. We know that Ahmad Ibn Tulun built a wooden cupola at its apex around 875 A.D.; for him to do this, the structure must still have been substantially intact over a thousand years after being raised. When this cupola was degraded, a small mosque was built by Al-Malik al-Kamil to replace it. But all buildings eventually degrade if they are not maintained; and in 955 A.D. a major earthquake serious damage to the lighthouse's superstructure. This lowered the building's height; for we know that in 1182 the writer Ibn Jubair records the minara's height as "over 150 cubits," which is much less than its original height. The end would come soon enough. In 1375 another earthquake brought down the entire structure except for the lowest tier.

So perished one of the noblest monuments of antiquity. Yet its legacy may live on, according to historian A.J. Butler, in the design of the medieval Egyptian minarets. According to Butler, "Though the medieval minarets of Cairo vary in combination of design, in many of them one may see an exact reproduction of the design of Sostratus [of Cnidus, the designer of the Alexandrian lighthouse], which was a tower springing four-square from the ground, then changing to a smaller octagonal and from the octagonal and from the octagonal to a still smaller circular shaft, and crowned at the top with a lantern." I must leave this this theory for the historians of architecture to debate. For me it suffices to know that all great deeds in history, and all the magnificent monuments created by the genius of man, impress their indelible stamp on the centuries that follow them. It remains for us only to honor them.

46. How Pompey Cleared The Mediterranean Of Pirates

The Mediterranean became infested with pirates as a direct consequence of Rome's Mithridatic Wars. Around 88 B.C. Mithridates VI of Pontus went to war against the Romans and moved into the province of Asia Minor. He took what plunder he could, and apparently decided that an effective way to wage irregular warfare against the Romans would be to encourage pirates to attack Roman shipping lanes.

But as often happens, it proved to be impossible to stop check this virus of robbery and murder once it had been let loose. Even after the Romans defeated Mithridates, the pirates did not pack up and go home; having had a taste of freedom and adventure, they found it was more profitable to steal than to go back to their old occupations. Soon they were sailing in squadrons of ships, even choosing "fleet" captains among themselves, and raiding small towns all over the eastern Mediterranean. The historian Appian says (XII.14) that they even recruited artisans expert in the use of iron, timber, and brass. They chose as their lair the province of Cilicia on the southern coast of Asia Minor, a place they called *Tracheia* ("craggy"). Soon their numbers had increased from a few thousand to tens of thousands, according to Appian, and their reach extended all the way to the Pillars of Hercules (i.e., the Straits of Gibraltar). "No sea could be navigated in safety," says Appian, "and land remained untilled for want of commercial intercourse."

To the Romans this situation soon became intolerable. Commercial shipping could not function properly, and prices for foodstuffs and other commodities began their predictable rise. But what to do? This was an enemy unlike any the Romans had encountered before. It was in many ways like the modern scourge of terrorism: the pirates had no ideology except profit, of course, but they were diffuse, difficult to find, and highly decentralized. But when the coast of Italy itself began to be raided–especially the coasts near Etruria and Brundisium–action could no longer be postponed. The Romans assigned the distinguished general Gnaeus Pompey in 67 B.C. the task of solving the problem once and for all. He was given power over the entire Mediterranean Sea, as well as inland a distance of 400 stadia from the coast. Soon Pompey had raised an army of 120,000 men with 4000 cavalry, along with 270 ships.

Pompey's "counter-insurgency" technique involved dividing the sea into sectors and making each of the 25 *legati* (assistants given the rank of praetor) assigned to him responsible for a specific area. He instituted coordination among the different sectors. One of the ways the pirates had been allowed to thrive was that, once driven out of one area, they could easily slip into another unpatrolled area. According to Appian, Pompey divided up the western Mediterranean as follows: Tiberius Nero and Manlius Torquatus were given Spain; Marcus Pomponius was given the waters of Gaul and Liguria; Lentulus Marcellinus and Publius Atilius were given the regions near Africa, Sardinia, and Corsica; and the coast of Italy was given to Lucius Gellius and Gnaeus Lentulus. The eastern Mediterranean was similarly divided into various regions commanded by Pompey's *legati,* in the following way:

Sicily and the Adriatic: Assigned to Plotius Varus and Terentius Varro
Peloponnesus, Attica, Euboea, Thessaly, Macedonia and Boeotia: Assigned to Lucius Sisenna
Greek island and the Aegean Sea: Assigned to Lucius Lollius
Bithynia, Thrace, the Propontis and the mouth of the Euxine: Assigned to Publius Piso
Lycia, Pamphylia, Cyprus and Phoenicia: Assigned to Metellus Nepos

The advantage of this "sector" method was that if a pirate force were driven out of one area, they would immediately be hammered by a force from another area. They were unable to rest and recuperate. Pompey himself made a tour of the entire region to make sure each man knew his responsibility. He inspected the western region in forty days, and took about the same amount of time to tour the eastern regions. The pirates had observed these preparations and originally thought they might be able to attack Pompey and demoralize him; but it soon became evident that the pirates were being squeezed in a vice-like grip. They could not leave their lairs without running a high risk of being captured and executed. He then moved against their main bases in Cilicia.

Many of the strongholds there surrendered without a fight; pirate supplies were burned or confiscated, and those caught were told to go back home. He seems to have chosen a policy of leniency: "Pompey…sent the pirates back to their respective countries. Many of them there found their own cenotaphs, for they were supposed to be dead. Those pirates who had evidently fallen into this way of life not through wickedness, but from poverty consequent upon the war, Pompey settled in Mallus, Adana, and Epiphaneia, or any other uninhabited or thinly peopled town in Cilicia Tracheia." (XII.14).

Thus the war against the pirates was concluded. Pompey had captured seventy-one ships and had had 306 turned over to him by surrender; and about 10,000 pirates had been killed in various engagements with the Romans. Every victory seems easy in retrospect, of course. But the campaign against the pirates was successful for very specific reasons. They are as follows: (1) deployment of sufficient forces to deal with the threat; (2) assignment of specific sectors of operation to local commanders, with each one made responsible for what happened in his area; (3) relentless pursuit of fleeing pirates so that they could not rest or hide; (4) a policy of "paroling" captured pirates and allowing them to return to their homes provided that they swore to abandon crime; (5) execution of the worst offenders; and (6) the capture of the main pirate strongholds in Cilicia. All of these factors implemented simultaneously meant that the campaign was successful. Counter-insurgency campaigns today employ precisely the same tactics, with emphases on different factors as the situation dictates.

47. The Alexandrian Library: Dissipation Through Neglect And Apathy

Nearly every scholar of classical antiquity seems to have an opinion about the destruction of the Great Library of the Ptolemies at Alexandria in Egypt. It has become something of a symbol of the triumph of ignorance and superstition over knowledge. There is much merit to this view; but the picture is a complex one, and it deserves serious consideration. The ruin of the library–and of others like it in the ancient and medieval worlds–was not a discrete, single event. It was the gradual outcome of a process that took place over generations. And when I say "process," I am referring to neglect, apathy, and negligence.

Myth and history must be kept firmly separated. We should first remember that the library was not like a modern "lending library;" nor was it similar to the public libraries of Rome during the imperial period. It was a royal research facility, and one was only granted access with special permission. The average person could not just walk into the library and start unwinding scrolls. The library was meant to serve as a symbol of the Ptolemaic dynasty's prestige and civilized dignity. As the scholar Michael Handis has shown, the mythologizing of the Alexandrian library started early and was continued during the Roman period. But we do not even know if the library was a separate building or a part of the research facility known as the Mouseion. We do not know precisely where the collection was, nor how many volumes it held; but this has not prevented speculation of the wildest kind.

A Byzantine writer of the twelfth century, John Tzetzes, gave the number of books at around 490,000; the Roman historian Ammianus Marcellinus (XXII.16.13) put the figure at 700,000, as did the writer Aulus Gellius (VII.17.3). We do not know the exact number; it probably fluctuated over time. There is no record of any collaboration or cooperation between the Alexandrian library and its other competitor of antiquity, the royal library of Pergamum. The crux of the matter is that we do not know exactly how the collection came to be destroyed. But we can make very informed guesses that tell us things we may not care to hear.

Let us summarize the available evidence. We know that Julius Caesar's troops accidentally caused a good portion of the collection to be damaged or destroyed in 48 B.C. When his men set fire to Pompey's ships in Alexandria, the fire spread through the docks and into part of the city, and the library building was one of the casualties. We also know that the Roman emperor Caracalla looted part of Alexandria and damaged some property in A.D. 215. Aurelian recaptured the city from Queen Zenobia of Palmyra, and there is clear evidence that much of the royal district was destroyed. Earthquakes shook Alexandria in A.D. 320 and 365, and these events may have caused further damage. And, finally, we know that Christian mobs attacked pagan temples and buildings around 391 in an attempt to carry out a decree of Theodosius II that mandated the closure of all pagan temples. Any one of these events–or all combined–could have dealt the library a fatal blow. We just cannot be certain.

That great popularizer of science, Carl Sagan, liked to present the ruin of the library as a specific event, a catastrophic triumph of ignorant mobs over rational, patient scholars like himself. Sagan may be forgiven for this; he was trying to make a point, even though his history was incorrect. I say "incorrect," because it is clear that the library and its holdings had already been dispersed or dissipated through neglect long before the fanatical mobs of Theodosius II. We can infer this, I think, from a careful examination of the sources. Both Aulus Gellius and Ammianus speak of the library in the *past tense*, as if it were a relic of the past: Gellius was writing around 160 A.D., and Ammianus around 360 A.D. The library was already a memory by their time. The historian Edward Gibbon also believed the collection had come to ruin long before A.D. 391: "[I]f we gradually descend from the age of the Antonines to that of Theodosius, we shall learn from a chain of contemporary witnesses that the royal palace and temple of Serapis no longer contained the four, or the seven, hundred thousand volumes which had been assembled by the curiosity and magnificence of the Ptolemies." (*Decline*, Ch. LI). Gibbon's editor and distinguished historian in his own right, J.B. Bury, writing in the early 1900s, agreed with him.

For a time before the modern period it was even fashionable to switch the blame for the library's destruction from Christian mobs to Arab armies. According to this now-discredited theory, the library was intact upon the arrival of Arab military forces in the early decades of Islam, but was maliciously torched. Paradoxically, this lie can be traced to the Arab historian Abu Al-Faraj, who apparently valued Oriental hyperbole and high drama over fact. The fantasy was demolished by historian A.J. Butler's masterful 1901 work *The Arab Conquest of Egypt*, which remains the most detailed authority on the subject. Butler notes that every contemporary source, both Greek and Arab, says nothing about any "library" at Alexandria that was destroyed during the conquest. Al-Tabari does not mention it; neither does Abd Al-Hakim. The Greek chronicler John of Nikiu, "who gives a very full account of the conquest of Egypt," (as J.B. Bury says), says absolutely nothing; had a library been burned, he would have recorded it. We must conclude from the weight of the evidence that the library had essentially ceased to exist at some point during the early imperial Roman period.

But how, we ask in dismay, could this have happened? Wasn't the collection valued? Did not anyone raise a voice in protest? To these questions, the philosopher can only shake his head and remind his interrogator of human nature. Knowledge is highly perishable, by its very nature. Unless it is constantly maintained and refurbished, it is in peril of being dissipated. We should be reminded that no library from antiquity survived. No Byzantine library escaped the centuries, and neither did any of the Islamic libraries. One scholar even reached this rather depressing conclusion:

> This is a sobering thought, which must ultimately call into question the wisdom of large concentrations of books, in ancient or modern times...Human efforts to bring all literature together may ultimately be doomed to frustration, but there is no doubt that large libraries contribute enormously to the advancement of knowledge *while they exist and are maintained.*[27]

[27] König et. al., *Ancient Libraries*, p. 374. Italics mine.

The point is that libraries, like all institutions of culture, must be maintained and refurbished by every generation. As I see it, the evidence points to a stark truth that tells us much about human nature. *The primary destroyer of the library, and perhaps of most cultural artifacts, was apathy.* How does this happen, in practice? It is very simple. It happens the same way official neglect happens today. A new king or government minister would have said to himself, "I don't think we need to allocate funds to the Alexandrian Library right now. I have other priorities. I would rather spend the money on ships, the army, or my new summer retreat." And this is how it starts.

Then, maybe 20 years later, another worthless ruler will come along and say, "I don't think we need to allocate funds to rehabilitate the Library, which is falling apart. I would rather spend the money on my boats, women, luxurious meals, and other things." So library staffs would be cut. Research funds would dry up. Scholars would get the clear message that they are not welcome. Then, one day, some crony or flunky of the king would say something like, "Your majesty, I would like to borrow some of the books from the library collection. I promise to return them." And the corrupt king or corrupt government ministers, being ignorant and dissolute fools, would permit it. They would not care if or when the books ever come back: which, of course, they never do.

This is how it happens. This is how neglect, negligence, and apathy combine to ruin a civilization's crown jewels. Remember that the temples and buildings of the ancient world that we still see around us got that way because there was no one left to maintain them. Allowed to fall into disrepair, they crumbled. It is the same with knowledge. The same process, I would argue, is happening all around us right now. But it is a stealthy, sneaky, incremental form of neglect. Our modern negligents and incompetents like to present their destructive tendencies as virtues. "We don't need physical books any more!," they shout. "We have everything in digital forms!" Or we hear voices telling us that it is "not important" to allocate funds for education, research, or inquiry. *Look at all the money we can save*, they proudly crow. How quickly they forget the lessons of the past. For learning and knowledge perish not though violence, but through apathy and neglect.

48. What Did A Roman Triumph Look Like?

Like the ceremony of deification, the Roman triumph (*triumphus*) is one of those rituals about which few readers may have a clear picture. This is unfortunate, for the ceremonial triumph provides a very revealing window on certain aspects of Roman society. Ancient writers mention it frequently, but almost always in passing; we are seldom offered a description of the event itself. Fortunately, the Greek historian Appian has done just this in his writings (VIII.9.66), and it will be useful for us to relate the specifics here.

The triumph was a ritual procession that had both religious (originally, at least) and secular significance. Like many Roman practices, it evolved over time; what was a relatively modest affair during the republican period would eventually become an elaborate, expensive celebration during the late imperial period. Appian lived from about 95 to 165 A.D. While we cannot be certain that he personally witnessed a triumph, or simply based his account on earlier written sources, his choice of words when describing the singing and dancing of the marchers and the jocular behavior of the soldiers gives a strong impression–to this reader at least–that he was writing from first-hand experience.

In either case, he is generally reliable and there is no reason to call him into question. The purposes of the triumph were, in my view, these: to honor a military commander of exceptional ability; to provide the public with an example of ideal Roman *virtus*; to unite the community around the military purposes of the state; and, most importantly, to drive home the point to the defeated that they were truly crushed. There may once have been overt religious elements to the triumph, perhaps inherited from the Etruscans, but it is often difficult to draw a clear line between the secular and the religious in such cases. The Roman religion was, after all, a state religion.

Only the senate could decree a triumph, and it was considered a supreme honor, given only to a general of exceptional achievement. Appian tells us that everyone in the procession wore crowns. Like a modern parade, there were various groups that followed one after the other:

1. Trumpeters came first, along with wagons laden with plunder taken from the military campaign.

2. Models of towers then followed. Perhaps these were constructed of wood, reeds, or other light materials. These were carried

by hand, and were meant to be representations of captured or destroyed cities. Pictures showing scenes of war would be displayed to the crowd along with the models of towers.

3. Gold and silver coin and bullion, and any other valuable articles of war followed.

4. After this came marchers bearing crowns that had been given to the triumphal general (*vir triumphalis*) during the campaign.

5. After this came white oxen, along with the captive enemy leaders. Appian mentions them as Carthaginian or Numidian chiefs, but in other campaigns we might imagine them as enemy leaders from different parts of the world. The significance of the white oxen must have had some religious origin, perhaps something originally related to sacrificial purity, or fertility.

6. Then came the Roman lictors wearing purple tunics. A lictor was something like a civil servant who attended a magistrate, bearing the bound rods and symbols of authority known as *fasces*. With the lictors was "chorus of harpists and pipers, in imitation of an Etruscan procession." These marched in regular order, keeping step with the music while dancing and singing. Appian says that these are called Lydi, "because, I think, the Etruscans were a Lydian colony." He mentions a memorable personage: "One of these [dancers], in the middle of the procession, wearing a purple cloak reaching to the feet and golden bracelets and necklace, caused laughter by making various gesticulations, as though he were dancing in triumph over an enemy."

7. Then came various incense-bearers.

8. After them came the victorious general himself. He rode in a chariot decorated with various designs, and wore a crown of gold and jewels. His toga was purple and "interwoven with golden stars." In his hand he carried a sceptre of ivory, as well as a laurel branch (a symbol of victory inherited from the Greeks). Boys and girls would even ride in the chariot with the victorious general. Mounted on horses to either side of the chariot would be young men from the general's family.

9. After this came the general's retinue of secretaries, aides, and weapons-bearers. These were attendants and trusted assistants who had been with him on campaign.

10. After this came the army itself, arranged by cohorts. All of the men were crowned with laurels, and the most honored, decorated fighters would be carrying prizes of war. This was one of the

rare occasions when Roman military discipline was relaxed; Appian says that "in a triumph everybody is free, and is allowed to say what he pleases." Thus during the procession the soldiers were free to praise or criticize officers as they saw fit: "they praised some of their captains, derided others, and reproached others."

This was the entire procession, according to Appian. It came to an end at the Capitol: "When Scipio arrived at the Capitol the procession came to an end, and he entertained his friends at a banquet in the temple, according to custom." All in all, the impression given is that of a festive atmosphere. But behind this, we should remember that triumphs were a deadly serious business. They were meant to celebrate conquest. Defeated captives could expect, like Jugurtha, to be put to death or sold into slavery unless some extenuating circumstance intervened.

49. Scipio Puts Down A Mutiny In His Army

There are times in life for calm reflection, and there are also times for ruthless and decisive action. When a man is faced with external danger and is being pressed by a crisis, he must act with speed and decision. The following anecdote, described in Appian's *Spanish Wars* (VI.7), demonstrates why Scipio Africanus is eminently deserving of the accolades that historians have accorded him. For he was not only a commander of prudence and wise judgment; he knew how to draw the sword when the situation called for it.

Military mutinies in the pre-modern era were serious affairs. Armies or naval vessels did not have the advantages enjoyed by contemporary communications and transport; isolated in remote parts of the world, they were dependent on iron discipline and vigorous leadership to maintain their cohesion. A commander who tolerated insubordination could very well be putting his mission in jeopardy, to say nothing of his own life. Scipio was in Spain to evict the Carthaginians and bring the region under Roman rule. Around 206 B.C., he became sick and temporarily assigned his command responsibilities to a colleague named Marcius. As sometimes happens in armies, troublemakers in the ranks saw this as an opportunity to revolt. Scipio's men had not been paid in some months; grumbling had increased, and there was a sense that things were approaching a crisis point. Many expected Scipio to die soon, and this no doubt stoked the fires of rebellion; for traitors love nothing more than to take advantage of opportunities. Some of the men seceded from Marcius and went off on their own; they were soon joined by other units of Scipio's army. A full-fledged mutiny was now underway. These events took place near a fort called Sucro along the Spanish coast; its most likely location is the modern town of Alzira.

Word of these happenings reached the Carthaginian commander, Mago. Anxious to exploit this situation, he sent the mutineers money and gifts, and asked them to join him. The rebels elected their own generals and centurions, and began to act as independent units. Scipio, still sick, got word of these events and resolved to take speedy action to deal with the crisis. But he knew he had to tread cautiously and proceed with stealth. His first move was to conciliate the rebels; he issued an apology to his men, acknowledging that he had been unable to pay them due to logistical difficulties. He asked his loyal unit commanders to try to win back the secessionists. He then issued a proclamation to the entire army, telling everything that he would now be able to pay them; they had only to come to come to the city of New Carthage on the Spanish coast.

The rebels were surprised at this sudden good fortune. Some believed that Scipio was playing for time; some thought he had a trick up his sleeve; others decided he was dealing in good faith. In any case, the rebels decided to go as a group to New Carthage and collect from Scipio what was owed to them. Scipio had senators who were in his army fighting with him. For in those days, legislators did not just sit in conference halls and talk, as they do now; they took to the field to match deeds with words. Scipio told his senators that when the rebel leaders arrived at the appointed meeting-hall in New Carthage, they should try to get close to the secessionists, remain alongside them, and try to befriend them. He instructed his military tribunes, his most trusted men, to position themselves at various points in the meeting-hall with their weapons at the ready; their instructions were to kill anyone who made a disturbance.

On the appointed day in New Carthage, Scipio arose early and sent messengers to the rebels that he was ready to meet them. This was at an earlier time than expected, so many were caught off-guard; and Appian says that many of them arrived at the forum marketplace dressed in a haphazard way without their weapons, as if they had just thrown on their clothing. Their understanding was that they were there to collect their money, and there were about eight thousand mutineers present. They were about to receive a rude awakening. Scipio began to chastise them for their disloyalty and insubordination, but promised that he would only hold the ringleaders responsible for what had happened. He then ordered his lictors to separate the crowd into two parts; his senators then hauled the rebel leaders to the center of the assembly hall.

When these rebel leaders began to shout out to their friends to help them, Scipio's men immediately killed anyone who responded. The crowd fell silent. He then had the secessionist leaders stripped and beaten with canes. When this was completed, he ordered their necks to be pressed to the ground, and then had them decapitated. The bodies of the traitors were dragged off, and all present were forced to witness this spectacle. The rest of the secessionists he pardoned, with strict admonitions that they were not to misbehave again. "In this way," says Appian, "was the mutiny in Scipio's camp put down." He continued with his campaign, and went on to conquer Spain.

50. Erasmus Loses All His Money, And Still Triumphs

We have observed many times before in these pages that disaster can often serve as an impetus to growth and eventual victory. This point was reinforced in an interesting story that I recently came across in a biography of the famous humanist Erasmus of Rotterdam. The reader should here be reminded that the life of the itinerant scholar and writer has never been an easy one. Desiderius Erasmus, who lived from 1466 to 1536, is considered by many to have been the greatest humanist of his or any other era; and he was one of the first writers of the modern era to try to make a living exclusively with his writing. Time and time again he turned down permanent academic and secretarial positions out of fear that employment would restrict his freedom of the pen. He wanted to be able to say and write as he wished. The price of this independence, of course, was a perpetual financial insecurity; he had to save his earnings carefully, as there was no way to predict when feast or famine might greet him on life's road. For him the price was worth it; but there were times that the price was very, very high. For most of his life he would find himself constantly seeking the patronage of the wealthy to support his scholarly pursuits.

Disaster struck him in January 1500 as he was leaving England at the conclusion of his first visit to that country. It had been a pleasant sojourn for him, and he had made a number of stimulating contacts, especially with Sir Thomas More and William Blount, the 4th Baron Mountjoy. Erasmus of course desired to take his monetary savings with him when he left England for France; this amount ran to about twenty pounds, which in those days was a significant sum. An old edict of Edward III (reaffirmed by Henry VII) prohibited the export of gold and silver from the country unless a valid exemption applied; and Erasmus had been assured by both Mountjoy and More that he would be exempt from the law, since his funds were not in foreign currency. To his anguish, he discovered that the customs officers in Dover interpreted the law to mean any currency, regardless of origin. He was permitted to retain a nominal sum but almost all of his precious savings was confiscated. It seems he was unable to reverse their ruling; or perhaps he made some effort to do so, but eventually gave it up as futile.

This event was a serious blow. Sensitive by nature, the incident darkened his views of England for many years after this; but to his credit he never lashed out at More or Mountjoy, the people on whose advice he had so mistakenly relied. He absorbed the bitterness of the event and channeled his energies into writing as if he were possessed by a demon. In a way, this is exactly how it was. He knew now that his back was up against a wall, and that he was writing for survival. There was no alternate plan. He would later say, "Things are with me as they are wont to be in such cases; the wound received in England begins to smart only now that it has become inveterate, and that the more as I cannot have my revenge in any way." Some months later he wrote, "I shall swallow it. An occasion may offer itself, no doubt, to be even with them."

So Erasmus had returned to Paris nearly penniless. What was his next move? What should he do now? With the need to earn an income now his entire focus, he hit upon an idea that can only be described as a stroke of genius. He found a way to turn his strengths into financial benefit. He knew that his knowledge of classical Latin literature had given him an armory of quotes, sayings, and adages.

Why not take this knowledge and create a compendium of such quotes, as a resource that could be used by students and writers? We should be reminded that this was a novel idea at the time. It was also an idea that happened to come along at just the right moment: this was the dawn of the age of printing, and good books might enable an author to earn something from his works. In classical and medieval times, it was understood that writing was not a profitable enterprise. It was the exclusive domain of the rich or the Church, and neither of these had to worry about earning a living.

Thus was born the idea of Erasmus's most-used work, the *Adagia.* The proverbs were drawn from both Latin and Greek sources, and Erasmus followed them with short explanations or illustrations. The first edition was published in Paris in 1500 and contained roughly 800 entries. As it went through edition after edition, the work would expand significantly, eventually comprising 3,000 entries. Erasmus organized and indexed the work in such a way that it could be used by speakers or writers needing just the right adage to flavor their efforts. He would continue to expand the work right up until his death in 1536, at which time it contained over 4,000 entries.

This is a particularly striking example of how disaster and tragedy can serve as the focus for future triumph. On the one hand, we could say that the confiscation of Erasmus's savings in England was a setback; and on the other, we may reasonably wonder if the *Adagia* would ever have been published but for this tragedy. There are valid arguments both ways. My own opinion is that serious setbacks can, indeed, be turned to our advantage, provided we do not allow them permanently to darken our vision. We must never allow ourselves to descend into bitterness or despair; for these are wells that have no bottom to them. Erasmus had the tenacity and strength of character to seize the moment, swallow his anguish, and continue to move forward.

NON COMEDETIS FRVGES MENDACII.

INDEX

A

B

C

D

E

F

N

O

P

Q

R

S

T

U

V

W

X

Y

Z

QVINTVS CVRTIVS
FORTRESS OF THE MIND

www.ingramcontent.com/pod-product-compliance
Lightning Source LLC
Chambersburg PA
CBHW070834020826
48982CB00019B/1098/J

* 9 7 8 0 5 7 8 6 4 5 8 7 2 *